Ba

C000182316

Japan

www.baedeker.com

Verlag Karl Baedeker

SIGHTSEEING HIGHLIGHTS ✶ ✶

Japan is a distant country, seemingly full of mystery to Westerners, with a wealth of old temples, shrines and cultural treasures. On top of that it has historic towns and a scenic diversity from bizarre volcanic mountains to wide plains full of cherry trees and archipelagos with tranquil bays.

Sacred places

To this day Nara has remained one of the country's most significant cultural sites and the location of numerous temples. Todaiji is the most imposing of them all.

1 Akan National Park

2 Daisetsuzan National Park

3 Towada-Hachimantai National Park

4 Hiraizumi

5 Matsushima

6 Chubu-Sangaku National Park/ Japanese Alps

© Baedeker

7 Nikko

8 Takayama

10 Tokyo

9 Fuji-san

11 Kamakura

12 Matsue

13 Kyoto

14 Himeji

15 Nara

17 Kurashiki

16 Hiroshima

18 Inland Sea

19 Kotohira, Kompira-san

20 Yoshino-Kumano National Park

21 Koya-san

22 Aso-Kuju National Park

23 Beppu

24 Nagasaki

25 Okinawa

1 ✳✳ Akan National Park
Sub-arctic virgin forests extend around three lakes, which have particularly vibrant colours in the autumn.

2 ✳✳ Daisetsuzan National Park
Japan's biggest national park boasts 2000m/6500 ft mountains, which have earned it the name »Roof of Hokkaido«

3 ✳✳ Towada-Hachimantai National Park
A crystal-clear, huge crater lake, surrounded by thick forests, hot springs and lava domes.

Skyscrapers
With the Tokyo Metropolitan Government Building the Japanese star architect Tange Kenzo has given the city a modern landmark.

Festivity
During the annual festival of the city's founding, Kyoto's inhabitants dress up in historic costumes from every period.

4 ✳✳ Hiraizumi
The one-time »Kyoto of the north« is now a quiet village with a famous temple.

5 ✳✳ Matsushima
The magical bay with hundreds of rocky islands covered in pine trees is one of Japan's three most famous landscapes.

6 ✳✳ Chubu-Sangaku National Park · Japanese Alps
In the summer these mountains are popular amongst hikers, in the winter large amounts of snow ensure fun on the ski slopes.

7 ✳✳ Nikko
Nikko attracts visitors with magnificent mausoleums in a sea of cedars, the national park west of the town with scenic beauty.

8 ✳✳ Takayama
This attractive small town in the Japanese Alps is an arts and crafts centre with a long tradition.

9 ✳✳ Fuji-san
The country's highest mountain is a sacred place and Japan's hallmark, commanding awe in those who see it.

Hot springs
The famous spa of Beppu is just the right place for a Japanese bath done in style

BAEDEKER'S BEST TIPS

This is a compilation of the most interesting Baedeker tips mentioned in this book! Experience and enjoy Japan from its best side.

🔳 How to get there
These tips will help you find even the most complicated Japanese addresses. ▶ **page 111**

🔳 Take an icebreaker through the pack ice
Every day in winter the *Aurora* sets off on a trip through the drift ice off the coast of Abashiri. ▶ **page 187**

🔳 Underwater world
Discover the beauty of Ashizuri Marine Park from a boat with a glass floor. ▶ **page 199**

🔳 Outdoor bathing
The spa of Kurokawa Onsen is known for its open-air baths. Why not give them a try, or, even better, spend the night here, too! ▶ **page 202**

Dream in white
The magic of the drift ice off the coast of Abashiri attracts large numbers of visitors every winter

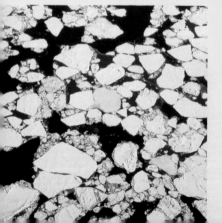

🔳 Japanese paper
In the small town of Ogawa with its workshops for hand-made paper, tourists are allowed to try their own hands at the art of paper making. ▶ **page 219**

🔳 Mount Fuji at sunrise
Anyone willing to climb Mount Fuji at night time will be rewarded with a magnificent sunrise. ▶ **page 237**

🔳 Experiencing Zen
To dive deeper into Zen Buddhism, spend the night in the Eiheiji temple and experience the daily lives of the monks. ▶ **page 242**

🔳 Thirst quencher
After visiting Hakodate's sights, why not stop for a refreshing, home-made beer at Hakodate Beer? ▶ **page 253**

🔳 Tea in the garden
In a garden west of Himeji Castle visitors have the chance to experience the tea ceremony. ▶ **page 261**

🔳 A taxi ride on the water
Hiroshima is a city on the water, so why not explore the city from the water, too? Gangitaxi makes it possible! ▶ **page 270**

🔳 Potatoes done differently
Kagoshima is known for its liquor made of sweet potatoes. More than 100 varieties and many other products made from potatoes can be found in the shopping quarter. ▶ **page 293**

◼ No on Sundays
Kanazawa is a centre of No stagecraft and it has its own theatre specially for No performances. ► page 309

◼ Market day
East of Kochi Castle a market rich in tradition is held every Sunday.
► page 326

◼ Take a boat through the rapids
A boat trip through the Kuma rapids, among the most famous in Japan, is highly recommendable. ► page 333

◼ Ivy Square
An old textiles factory in Kurashiki was transformed and now houses studios, cultural facilities and even a hotel.
► page 334

◼ A rewarding walk
A stroll along the Philosophers' Walk in Kyoto is particularly lovely during the cherry blossom in the spring and when the leaves change colour in the autumn.
► page 354

◼ Cycling on Shikoku
Shikoku is wonderfully suited to cycling. It is a great way to explore some of the 88 temples of pilgrimage around Matsuyama. ► page 386

◼ Kettles and kokeshi
Morioka's best-known products are iron-ware and wooden dolls known as kokeshi. ► page 395

◼ »Moving Forward«
Those who book on time can visit the Toyota factory in the town of Toyota near Nagoya. ► page 408

◼ Colourful spring festival
Every year in May a lively spring festival is celebrated at Toshogu shrine.
► page 444

Wooden dolls
The traditional wooden kokeshi dolls can be bought in Morioka

◼ Underwater paradise
Okinawa is an attractive destination for divers and snorkellers. The island of Ishigaki is considered one of Japan's best places to go diving. ► page 454

◼ Lively all-female opera
Anyone spending some time in Takarazuka near Osaka should not miss the famous Revue Theatre. ► page 470

◼ Drum roll
Sado is home to the internationally famous taiko drum group Kodo, which puts on a world music festival every year in August. ► page 475

◼ Dining on the water
A pleasure with hundreds of years of tradition is a meal in a yakata-bune, a narrow, covered boat, while it drifts in leisurely fashion across Tokyo Bay.
► page 517

◼ Multimedia in the evening
Even after darkness falls it is well worth visiting the huge electronics quarter of Tokyo with its flickering neon advertise-ments and newest range of goods from the world of entertainment. ► page 536

Delicious presentation
Speciality restaurants not only serve tasty food, they also take great care in the presentation of what they sell
▶ page 122

BACKGROUND

PRACTICAL INFORMATION FROM A to Z

Price categories

▶ **Hotels**
Luxury: more than ¥ 20,000
Mid-range: up to ¥ 20,000
Budget: up to ¥ 8000

For an overnight stay
in a double room

▶ **Restaurants**
Expensive: more than ¥ 3000
Moderate: up to ¥ 3000
Inexpensive: up to ¥ 1500

for an entrée without drinks

Wellness, the Japanese way
Those who want to can have themselves buried in the hot sand on Ibusuki beach
► page 274

TOURS

SIGHTS FROM A to Z

Garden design
*The lovely Golden Pavilion in Kyoto is
surrounded by an extensive, beautifully
designed pond garden*
► **page 368**

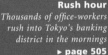

Rush hour
*Thousands of office-workers
rush into Tokyo's banking
district in the mornings*
► **page 505**

Background

ALL ABOUT JAPAN'S GEOGRAPHY
AND POPULATION, ABOUT EMPERORS,
SHOGUNS AND THE SAMURAI, ABOUT
WHAT DEFINES SHINTO AND
ZEN BUDDHISM, AND WHO SHAPED
THE COUNTRY'S DESTINY.

MYSTERIOUS REALM

What do other countries have that Japan lacks? Old temples, festivals, imposing castles, attractive landscapes, gardens, elegant shops, top restaurants … it's all there! And there many more things that only Japan has to offer, such as its Shinto shrines, hot springs, traditional No drama and the sophisticated tea ceremony. However, few people know about these gems.

Japanese cars and hi-fi equipment, cameras, mobile phones and computer games have long found their way to the most remote corners of the earth. Children go crazy about anything the Japanese toy industry comes up with, be it Tamagotchis, Pokémon or Yu-Gi-Oh. Teenagers read mangas, adults swear by shiatsu and reiki, feast on sushi or keep fit with Japanese martial arts. On the other hand, who

has ever been to Japan? In comparison with other far-away destinations the number of foreign tourists who go to Japan is minuscule. This is just one of the reasons Japan has a mysterious and exotic aura.

Lonely Island

Presumably this feeling of strangeness also has something to do with Japanese history: after all, the country was isolated from the rest of the world for more than 250 years. During this period of isolation the military rulers kept a watchful eye on their subjects, making sure they did not leave Japan and li-

Landmark
Torii of the famous Itsukushima shrine in front of Mount Fuji

mited contacts to foreign countries to the Chinese quarter in Nagasaki and a Dutch trading post on an island in that city's harbour. After many troubled years marked by civil war there was permanent peace in the country. This allowed a middle-class culture to develop in the towns and cities, and the typically Japanese arts such as kabuki theatre, woodblock prints and geisha entertainment to flourish. The forced opening of the country and the subsequent restoration of imperial rule in 1868 was the beginning of a new era marked by a thirst for knowledge and great curiosity. Western know-how was introduced, foreign fashions copied and industrialization proceeded at a great pace. This caused Japan to take on many Euro-American traits on the outside, but behind the façade the Japanese self-image shaped by centuries-long traditions continues almost unbroken.

← *At the Gion Matsuri festival in Kyoto*

Strongholds
Countless castles and forts once covered the land. The surviving or reconstructed ones, such as Nagoya Castle, are testimony to Japan's powerful rulers, great warriors and of the art of Japanese military architecture.

Wonderland of technology
Mobile phones, tamagochis, hybrid engines or robots: in Japan the newest inventions quickly become standard parts of everyday life.

Gardens of contemplation
Japanese gardens are aesthetic works of art, representing the totality of nature in a small space and often even incorporating the surrounding landscape into the overall picture. As places full of harmony and tranquillity they also serve inner contemplation.

Typically Japanese

One of the special experiences of a trip to Japan, besides visiting an onsen, is staying in a ryokan. These Japanese guesthouses provide traditional accommodation with sliding doors made of paper, low tables and tatami mats.

Lively festivals

The entire country carefully maintains its customs and traditions: regardless of whether it is a religious festival, an event from a city's history or simply the cherry blossom celebration, there are numerous occasions for grand processions, firework displays, dancing and other entertainment.

In touch with the gods

Most Japanese people perform religious rites as a matter of course, without calling themselves religious. Temples and shrines shape the appearance of every place and their faith permeates everyday life here in very subtle ways.

Opposites Attract

It is the contrast between age-old traditions and a modern lifestyle that makes a trip through the country so fascinating. Visitors to Tokyo are overwhelmed by the sea of skyscrapers, the huge department stores and the fast pulse of the metropolis. In rural Japan there are paddy farmers, small fishing boats and wooden shrines. Pilgrims climb holy mountains just as they always have, while drivers go to shrines to subject their new vehicle to ritual cleansing in order to protect it from accidents. The shinkansen, a comfortable high-speed railway, rushes from city to city, while slow trains filled with uniformed school children, dozing employees and chatty pensioners cosily trundle from one small town to another. Old customs such as a bath in an onsen, the cherry-blossom viewing, or lively festivals around portable shrines have survived to this day, while Japan develops robotic dogs and hybrid engines. Irrespective of the country's geographical diversity – it reaches from temperate Hokkaido in the north to subtropical Okinawa in the south – the great sense of tradition and a simultaneous love of all things new is characteristic of the entire island realm.

See It for Yourself

Anyone wanting to understand the Japanese nature and way of life has to get on a plane and see the country with their own eyes. Those who take a closer look will discover the Japanese sense of beauty in the midst of all the kitsch and commerce: it manifests itself in an object's appealing packaging, for example, or in the artistic arrangement of a traditional meal. Visitors who take the time to get to know Japanese people will learn to appreciate their unobtrusiveness, their ability to adapt and their politeness and maybe discover the secret of communication without many words. Not every mystery will be solved during the trip, but the odd cliché will definitely start to falter.

For the eyes
When it comes to preparing a meal, beauty and harmony are important

Facts

How many volcanoes does the country have? What minorities call Japan home? What does the new generation in the Japanese imperial family have to do with the constitution? And what structures determine the economy?

Natural Environment

The island country of Japan, situated in an arc off the east coast of   **An island country**
the Eurasian continent, stretches over an area of 2790km/1730mi
from the northeast to the southwest, with a maximum breadth of
400km/250mi (on average 230km/140mi). The main land mass
(97%) is formed by the islands of Hokkaido, Honshu, Shikoku and
Kyushu, which faces the Korean peninsula. The remaining land area
is made up of 3918 smaller, sometimes tiny and often uninhabited islands, islets and rocks.

This landmass is deeply indented, hence the country's incredibly   **Sea**
long coastline of 29,700km/18,450mi and close interplay with the
surrounding sea: in the north, between the Russian island of Sakhalin and the Kuril Islands (Russian; the southern part is claimed by Japan), the Sea of Okhotsk stretches to the northern coast of Hokkaido; the Sea of Japan is located between Honshu and the Asian mainland (Russia, China, Korea); the Japanese islands of Kyushu and
Shikoku are separated from Honshu by the Inland Sea. To the east
and the south the Pacific Ocean surrounds the island arc. Two chains
of smaller islets stretch out into the Pacific: south of Tokyo the Nan-
po Islands, southwest of Kyushu the Ryukyu Islands (Nansei Islands)
with the island of Okinawa, which was occupied by the United States
until 1972. This arc runs from the Chinese island of Taiwan and separates the East China Sea from the Pacific.

Natural Regions

The Japanese archipelago consists of the peaks of a mountain range   **Geology**
that rises up steeply from the Japan Trench (8412m/27,600ft) and
the Izu-Bonin Trench (10,340m/34,000ft) out of the Pacific Ocean.
This mountain range is folded several times and reaches altitudes of
more than 3000m/10,000ft. It is separated from the Asian mainland
by the 3000m/10,000ft depression of the Sea of Japan. The northern
arc off the island of Sakhalin is crossed by the volcano-ridden Fossa
Magna, which shapes the natural scenery of central Japan and its pe-
ripheral regions. The island chain was originally connected to the
mainland; its separation took place in the lower Miocene (Aquita-
nian, 20–23 million years ago) through the gradual lowering of the
Sea of Japan. The country's former connection to the mainland,
which influenced its development in many ways, can still be recognized today: Hokkaido is only 45km/28mi away from Sakhalin and
from Kyushu to the Korean peninsula it is no more than 200km/
125mi as the crow flies.

← *Since Japan is in a tectonically active region, hot springs bubble up from
the ground all over the country; this one is a mineral spring in Beppu.*

Mountains (-yama, -sen, -san, -zan, -dake, -take, -mine)

Topographically, Japan is a very mountainous country, as around 70% of its total area is taken up by densely forested mountains. Around 7% of the country is considered inaccessible. Despite some relatively extensive lowlands, only around 18% of the land can sustain permanent agricultural activity. 11% consists of grassland and pasture, and the actual settlement area makes up only around 3%. The central area of Honshu, which is divided by the rift of the Fossa Magna, has the highest and steepest peaks (including the 3776m/12,388ft Mount Fuji, the country's highest mountain and hallmark); more gentle hills and slopes are primarily found on Hokkaido, which was less affected by the movements of the earth's crust.

Volcanoes ▸

Japan is located in the Pacific Ring of Fire **Pacific Ring of Fire** and, being a relatively young land mass, displays continuing activity. Of Japan's total of 285 volcanoes, 36 are still considered active today, although since 1900 only 20 have erupted. New volcano formations have also been observed, such as the Showa-Shinzan volcano on Hokkaido, which formed between 1944 and 1945. The largest and best-known volcano is Mount Fuji, which is no longer active and erupted for the last time in 1707. The volcanoes considered particularly active are Mount Asama (central Honshu), Mount Aso (central Kyushu), Sakurajima (southern Kyushu) and Mount Mihara on Izu

Landscape with design – a tea plantation in Kochi Prefecture on Shikoku

Oshima. Two particularly beautiful volcanoes are Mount Fuji with is classic cone shape (many cone-shaped volcanoes in other parts of the country are named after Mount Fuji, such as Satsuma-Fuji) and Mount Aso, considered the world's largest volcano: plains and villages lie in its ancient caldera. Thick forests, crater lakes and countless hot springs (onsen), around which some enchanting settlements have formed, shape the appearance of the extensive mountain landscape.

Japan's enormous mountain ranges leave little room for any lowland such as the Kanto and Nobi plains (Honshu), the Tsukushi Plain (Kyushu) as well as the plains of Ishikari and Konsen (Hokkaido); the coastal lowland is usually only **a narrow strip** between the foothills of the central mountain range and the sea. Fertile plains can be found along the lower river courses, which are put to agricultural use, especially rice cultivation. The country's largest basins are the Yamagata Basin (northern Honshu) with the town of the same name, the Kofu Basin (central Honshu) with the town of Kofu, and the Kyoto Basin, which surrounds the city of Kyoto.
The great expanse of mountainous country covering all of the islands is matched by the number of plateaus, which, between early summer and autumn, are amongst Japan's most attractive recreational areas.

Plains (heiya), basins (bonchi), plateaus (daichi)

Because of the small distance from coast to coast (230km/140mi on average) and its mountainous character of the terrain, rivers are **relatively short and have steep gradients**. Differences in altitude, massive debris deposition and seasonal fluctuations in water volume (snow melt in spring, typhoons in autumn), particularly in the rivers flowing from Honshu's main mountain range (the »Japanese Alps«) into the Pacific, make them unnavigable over long distances. On the other hand they offer numerous opportunities for white water rafting as well as boat trips through gorges covered by wonderful, deep forests and bizarre rock formations. The rapids on the Kiso (near Nagoya), Hozu (Kyoto), Tenryu (Shizuoka Prefecture) and Kuma (Kumamoto Prefecture) rivers are the best-known; the gorges (-kyo) of Kurobe-kyo, Tenryu-kyo (central Honshu), Soun-kyo (Hokkaido) and Takachiho-kyo (Kyushu) are amongst the most beautiful. Of the three largest rivers, Shinano, Tone (both central Honshu) and Ishikari (Hokkaido), the last-named forms the widest plain.

Rivers (-kawa, -gawa)

Many of the lakes, most of which are in national parks and were mainly formed as a result of volcanic activity, stand out through their incredible beauty. The natural dams of Inawashiro (northern Honshu), Chuzenji (Nikko) as well as the five Fuji lakes were formed, like many others, through lava flows which blocked their river channels. Thanks to the mountain location, most of the lakes, some of which boast an **unusual intensity of colour**, remain almost completely unspoiled. The lakes of Hokkaido, for example: Lake Mashu, claimed to be the world's clearest lake, Lake Akan and Lake Shikotsu. In addi-

Lakes (-ko, -numa, -ike)

tion to the northern crater lakes of Tazawa, **Japan's deepest lake** (425m/1395ft), Towada and the dams already mentioned, the country's most remarkable inland waters include Lake Ashi (Hakone), not far from Tokyo and one of the most beautiful holiday spots, and Lake Biwa (near Kyoto), Japan's largest lake, They are also noteworthy for their rich fish stocks.

Coast

A vast number of small islands, some of them with enough space for several towns, others consisting of nothing more than some tree-covered rocks, surround the four main islands or are part of the archipelago that pushes hundreds of kilometres into Pacific waters.

Large minor islands ▶

Amongst Japan's largest minor islands are Sado in the Sea of Japan, Awaji and Shodo-jima in the Inland Sea, the Tsushima Islands between southern Japan and Korea, the Amakusa Islands west of Kyushu, the Tanegashima Islands and Yaku-shima as well as Okinawa. In addition several enchanting archipelagos such as the Goto Islands west of Kyushu belong to Japan. The **islands in the bay of Matsushima** (Honshu) are considered to have some of Japan's most beautiful scenery. Most of these islands have beautiful white beaches suitable for swimming, interspersed by ragged rock formations and steep rocks here and there.

Coastal regions ▶

There are around a thousand islands scattered across the **Inland Sea** (Setonaikai), the narrow waterway between the main islands of Honshu, Shikoku and Kyushu. Some of mainland Japan's most beautiful strips of coastline, with impressive changes in landscape between crescent-shaped bays and bizarre rias, are those around Sanriku (Iwate Prefecture), Kumano (Kii Peninsula) as well as the capes of Muroto and Ashizuri (Shikoku) and the coasts of Shima Peninsula (Mie Prefecture). Contrasting with these are the large beaches of Uchiura Bay (Hokkaido), Miho no Matsubara (Shizuoka Prefecture) and many more. Wonderful stretches of coastline can also be found along the Oga Peninsula (Akita Prefecture), the Noto Peninsula (Ishikawa Peninsula) and the Sotomo Peninsula (Fukui Prefecture) in the west of Honshu on the Sea of Japan, the island group of Oki (Daisen-Oki National Park, Sea of Japan) and the Kujukushima Islands (Saikai National Park, Kyushu).

Climate

Climate factors

The climatic differences within Japan result from the country's great north-south extent (20° to almost 46° north) as well as from the long mountain ranges that run along its vertical axis. Facing the Sea of Japan and the continent is Ura-Japan (inner Japan), facing the Pacific is Omote-Japan (outer Japan).

There are four clearly defined seasons comparable to those of Europe, with fairly constant weather conditions during the summer and winter months as well as greater weather fluctuations during the transitional periods of spring and autumn.

Rugged Japan at the rocky coast near Jodogahama on Honshu

Winter

Winter begins around mid-December almost at the same time in the entire country, when cold Siberian air masses sweep over from the northwest. The duration and intensity diminish from north to south. Between northern Japan (Hokkaido) with its biting cold and southwest Japan (Okinawa), where temperatures are above freezing all year round, there is a significant difference in temperature.

Spring

Starting in mid-February temperatures all over the country begin to rise. In southern Kyushu and Shikoku spring already begins in March with the annual cherry blossom, while the weather remains cold and changeable in Hokkaido and Ura-Japan. By the end of April the cherry blossom has also reached the north of the main Japanese island of Honshu. Further warming makes May a pleasant month with temperatures resembling those in much of Europe in summer.

Summer

From the end of May the main summertime rainy season begins with the **plum rain** (bai-u). It is linked to the front of maritime tropical air masses coming up from the south, pushing the polar air masses away to the north and west. For that reason these rains start earlier in the south, last longer there and are also more plentiful (Okinawa: second half of May; southern Kyushu: first half of June; Tokyo: ten days later; Hokkaido: July). During this time it is oppressively clammy, with almost no wind, cloudy skies and high humidity, and the rain is fine and penetrating; leather, paper and other organic materials quickly start to get mouldy.

Around mid-July the rains stop, and stable tropical air masses dominate all of Japan. The prevalent weather is sunny and hot, only occasionally interrupted by thunderstorms and typhoon rainfalls. During this time of year the north of the country is warm, too, so that rice can even be cultivated in Hokkaido. From the second half of July until August the weather is often considered oppressively hot. These are the dog days of summer with high temperatures (max. approx. 35°C/95°F) and relatively high humidity, when everyone who can flees to the cooler, fresher resorts and spas of central Japan's mountainous region. The summer comes to an end around mid-September. Colder air masses from the continent push the maritime tropical air masses back southwards. Precipitation falls along the front between the two air masses, resulting in the autumnal rainy season (shu-u), the counterpart to the early summertime »plum rain«.

Typhoons ▶ From the end of August to mid-September the probability of typhoons hitting Japan is greatest. They reach Okinawa from the southeast, where they then change direction to the northeast. Most of the approx. 30 cyclones forming over the northwestern Pacific every year do not, however, reach Japan directly. A typhoon causes around 300mm/12in precipitation in southwest Japan, 150mm/6in in central Japan and even less in the north; these are significant proportions of the country's total annual precipitation. Storm surges, breached levees and floods in the wake of typhoons are real dangers in light of the many low-lying, densely populated areas (such as Tokyo).

Autumn October is a month frequently characterized by clear weather, colourful leaves and occasional night frosts. In the mountainous country of central Japan this is the time of year when the first snow falls. Winter begins in mid-December.

Flora and Fauna

Biodiversity The fact that the country extends across 25 degrees of latitude and thus across several climate zones, its moist oceanic climate, and the different altitudes of the mountain ranges are the reasons why Japan has such an unusual wealth of plant and animal species. Of course human beings have caused great changes through intensive use of the land, so that the endemic flora can now only be found in inaccessible areas and those locations that are economically uninteresting.

Flora Around **two-thirds of Japan's landmass is forested**. The largest part
Coastal regions ▶ of the coastal regions is evergreen broad-leaved forest of the temperate zone with laurel trees (teriha-boku), different species of oak (kashi), Japanese chinquapin (shii) and camellias. Towards the south they become more and more interspersed with palm trees, tree ferns, camphor trees (kusunoki, yabunikkei) and in the riparian lowlands

with light green bamboo groves (on Honshu, Shikoku and parts of Kyushu, amongst other places). The southern Ryukyu Islands to Okinawa are dominated by evergreen castanopsis forest. The coasts are lined by mangrove swamps, which are bordered on the landward side by a thicket of pandanus (adan), wild fig (gajumaru) and sago palm (sotetsu) trees.

Deciduous broad-leaved and mixed forests dominate the climatic transitional zones of northern Honshu, between the warm-temperate and subtropical zones. They reach higher and higher altitudes towards the south and on Kyushu can even be found at altitudes of 1000m/3300ft and 1500m/5000ft. They mainly consists of oaks, Japanese chinquapin and pine trees (matsu), which can be found in every region of the country regardless of the climate zone as a result of their undemanding nature. In the forests of the temperate zone cryptomeria japonica (sugi), Japan's most significant timber wood, is overabundantly represented thanks to afforestation measures; other species include the maple (akagi) with its beautifully coloured foliage

◄ Transitional zone

In the colder regions Japanese macaques have learned to bathe in the hot springs

during the autumn, the Japanese cypress (hinoki), birch trees, beeches and paulownias (kiri). In the north, on Hokkaido, the forests covering the land are made up of subarctic conifers, particularly mountain pines (haimatsu) and other pine species.

Alpine flora ▶ Above 2500m/8200ft in central Honshu there is also a species-rich alpine flora in alternation with thick mountain pine forests. The alpine meadows that exist in Europe are however absent here. Towards the north the vegetation line drops and on Hokkaido it reaches an altitude of only 1500m/5000ft.

Amongst the other commonly represented wild and cultivated plants around 50% are thought to have been introduced from the Asian mainland. They still frequently carry the sobriquet »Japanese«, »japonica« or »nipponica« (such as the Japanese almond, quince and cherry).

Fauna Japan's fauna also displays great biodiversity and like the flora can be distinguished by region and altitude; the diversity of habitats, the immense forested areas and the meeting of warm and cold ocean currents provide the perfect conditions to allow this diversity to thrive. Another factor of fundamental significance for Japan's biodiversity was that the Ice Age only had a small impact, resulting in the conservation of some ancient animal species. At the same time the discovery of bones and the evident similarities to the bones found on the mainland was evidence for the land connection that existed between Japan and the continent in prehistoric times. **Separation lines** between the habitats of individual animal genera were recognized by zoologists Shozaburo Watase and Thomas Blakiston.

Watase's Line ▶ The division known as Watase's Line runs between the islands of Yakushima and Amami Oshima (latitude 30° N.) south of Kyushu and marks the **boundary of the fauna of the southern Pacific tropical islands**; amongst the animals living south of this line, the protected Ryukyu rabbit and the Amami spiny mouse are particularly noteworthy.

Blakiston's Line ▶ The **northern distribution boundary** for different animal species, called Blakiston's Line, is located in the Tsugaru Straight between Honshu and Hokkaido. Hokkaido's fauna, which shows a clear relationship to that of Siberia, includes brown bears, red deer, sables, xerinae, mouse and rabbit species as well a number of northern bird species (including the large-billed crow and Blakiston's fish owl).

Between the lines ▶ Between these two separation lines of animal geography, the genera most commonly at home are those related to the fauna of the northern Chinese mainland, whose predecessors got here over the former land bridge between the continent and Japan. These species include foxes, Japanese macaques, chamois, wild boars, Asiatic black bears, edible dormice. Amongst the bird species are the Japanese green woodpecker, the green pheasant, the copper pheasant, the thrush and others. Species under special protection are the Japanese crested ibis (toki), as there are only a few specimens left on the island of Sado; the oriental stork, of which there are also only very few specimens left in Hyogo Prefecture; and the giant salamander, which goes back to the tertiary period and can be found in the mountain streams of western Honshu and northern Kyushu.

The marine fauna also displays great diversity and surprising beauty, as in the immense richness of forms and colours in southern Japanese waters with their coral-fringed islands; species deserving particular mention are sea snakes (hydrophiidae), relatively small elapidae that occur exclusively along the coasts of the Pacific and Indian Oceans where the water temperatures are quite high.   ◀ Marine fauna

Japanese carp (koi), which can live up to 60 years, enjoy great popularity as ornamental fish in garden ponds.

Population · Politics · Economy

Population

According to figures from 2007 the average population density in Japan was 338 people per sq km/876 per sq mi. This is of course purely a statistical average that says nothing about the actual, regionally   **Population distribution**

Many Japanese young people like to dress up to look like characters from mangas and computer games

Facts and Figures *Japan*

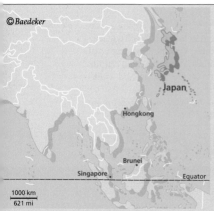

© Baedeker

Japan
Hongkong
Brunei
Singapore
Equator

1000 km
621 mi

Location and area
► fourth-largest island state in the world
► latitude from 45°33'–20°25' north
► longitude from 123°–149° (disputed) east
► length from northeast–southwest 2790 km/1730 mi
► max. width 400km/250mi; average width 230km/140mi
► land area: 377,682 sq km/145,824 sq mi
► main islands' landmass (97 %): Hokkaido (77,900 sq km/30,080 sq mi), Honshu (230,832 sq km/89,125 sq mi), Shikoku (18,799 sq km/7258 sq mi) and Kyushu (44,380 sq km/17,135 sq mi)
► additional 3918 small islands

Population
► approx. 127.7 million inhabitants
► population density: on average 338 inhabitants per sq km/876 per sq mi
► largest cities: Tokyo (8.13 million inhabitants), Yokohama (3.59 million), Osaka (2.6 million), Nagoya (2.2 million), Sapporo (1.82 million), Kobe (1.5 million), Kyoto (1.47 million)

Religion
► approx. 85 % Buddhists (see p.58)
► approx. 90 % Shinto adherents (see p.58)
► less than 1 % Christians
► numerous so-called new religions

State
► name: »Nihon« (»ni« = day, sun, »hon« = root)
► parliamentary monarchy
► head of state: Emperor (Tenno) Akihito (since 1989)
► prime minister: Taro Aso (since 2008)
► parliament: legislative lower house (Shugi-in, 480 seats) and advisory upper house (Sangi-in, 242 seats)
► administrative structure: 47 prefectures

Economy
► GNP: US$ 5614 billion (2007)
► annual per capita income: US$ 34,252 (2007)
► unemployment rate: 3.8 % (2007)
► employment structure: 6% agriculture, 21 % industry, 73 % services (2007)

300 km
186 mi
© Baedeker

RUSSIA
Sea of Okhotsk
CHINA
Hokkaido
Sea of Japan
NORTH KOREA
Sado
SOUTH KOREA
Oki
Honshu
Tokyo
Fuji
JAPAN
Tsushima
Goto Islands
Seven Izu Islands
Shikoku
Kyushu
Tanegashima
East China Sea
Yakushima
Pacific Ocean
Ryukyu Islands
Okinawa
*Disputed betwe
Japan and Russ

highly differentiated population densities. While only the valleys are inhabited and cultivated in the mountain regions, the people in the industrial conurbations in the few plains and basins live in very crowded conditions. Hokkaido has the lowest population density with only 72 inhabitants per sq km/194 per sq mi; while the population density in Tokyo has now even reached 5748 per sq km/14,900 per sq mi. Migration into the cities and urbanization of the rural areas as a result of a severe wage gap intensify this imbalance. More than 80% of all Japanese people now live in towns and around 20% in cities of more than 500,000 inhabitants. In all of this the urban fringe areas, home to the masses of part-time and second-income farmers, the rural way of life has largely remained extant.

An estimated 15,000 **Ainu**, mostly fully assimilated, live on Hokkaido. They are most likely the descendants of the country's original inhabitants; they display physical traits different from those of Japanese people, being tall with fair skin and a strong beard growth, and until the beginning of the 19th century they made up the majority of the population in northern Japan, living from hunting and fishing. Today only a few thousand of them identify fully with their archaic cultural heritage. Amongst the approx. 1.31 million **foreigners** in Japan, Koreans represent the largest minority, constituting 40% of all non-Japanese, followed by Chinese (19.3%), Brazilians (14.4%), including many ethnic Japanese whose ancestors once emigrated to Brazil, and Filipinos (7.1%). These ethnic groups are mainly concentrated in Tokyo and Osaka. **Minorities**

The approx. 2 million **Burakumin** form a minority which is not ethnic, but social in nature. This is a group that has remained underprivileged to this day because their activities, usually in connection with the killing of animals or the processing of animal products, are impure according to Buddhist teachings.

State and Constitution

Replacing the Meiji constitution of the year 1889, the current constitution (Nihon Koku Kempo; proclaimed on 3 November 1946) came into effect on 3 May 1947 in the Empire of Japan (Nippon or Nihon: »land of the rising sun«), and became the basis for a democratic society. After that the **emperor** (tenno; since 1989 Akihito, born 1933), previously the absolute ruler, became but a symbol of the state and the unity of the nation. The Japanese people is the sovereign entity. Further important points of the constitution are the separation of powers, the guarantee of human rights and the renunciation of wars of aggression. **Democratic parliamentary monarchy**

The state's highest organ is the Diet (kokkai), which is voted for in general and secret elections and which appoints the prime minister. It consists of the House of Representatives (shugi-in), which is responsible for the country's legislation, and the House of Councillors ◀ Parliament or Diet

Japan *Political Structure*

Nippon • Nihon

日本

— Regional borders
— Prefectural borders

Sea of Okhotsk

Kuril Islands

Hokkaido HOKKAIDO

Asahikawa 1 Kushiro

Sapporo

Hakodate

Aomori 2

TOHOKU

3

Akita 4

5

6

Sendai

Sea of Japan

Sado Niigata

15 *Honshu*

7

Toyama 8

16 9 Nikko

Kanazawa Utsunomiya 10

17 19 20 11 TOKYO KANTO

Oki 18 13 12

KINKI Gifu CHUBU 21 14 Yokohama

Matsue 31 27 26 Kyoto Nagoya 22

Tsushima CHUGOKU 34 32 25 23 Hamamatsu

Hiroshima Okayama 33 Himeji Nara 24

Shimonoseki 35 Kobe 28 29 Ise

Kitakyushu Takamatsu Osaka

Goto 40 39 Wakayama

Islands 44 Matsuyama 30 *Seven Izu Islands*

Fukuoka 38 36

45 41 SHIKO- 37

Naga- Kumamoto KU

saki 43 42 *Shikoku*

Kyushu Kagoshima KYUSHU

46

East *Tanegashima*

China

Sea *Yakushima*

Ryu-kyu Islands

Naha 47

Okinawa

Pacific

Ocean

REGION
  Prefecture

HOKKAIDO
  1 Hokkaido

TOHOKU
  2 Aomori
  3 Akita
  4 Iwate
  5 Yamagata
  6 Miyagi
  7 Fukushima

KANTO
  8 Tochigi
  9 Gumma
10 Ibaraki
11 Saitama
12 Chiba
13 Tokyo
14 Kanagawa

CHUBU
15 Niigata
16 Toyama
17 Ishikawa
18 Fukui
19 Gifu
20 Nagano
21 Yamanashi
22 Shizuoka
23 Aichi

KINKI
24 Mie
25 Shiga
26 Kyoto
27 Hyogo
28 Osaka
29 Nara
30 Wakayama

CHUGOKU
31 Tottori
32 Okayama
33 Hiroshima
34 Shimane
35 Yamaguchi

SHIKOKU
36 Kagawa
37 Tokushima
38 Kochi
39 Ehime

KYUSHU
40 Fukuoka
41 Oita
42 Mayazaki
43 Kumamoto
44 Saga
45 Nagasaki
46 Kagoshima
47 Okinawa

(sangi-in), which has an advisory function. The prime minister appoints the ministers in his cabinet, which forms the executive power; this cabinet is answerable to the Diet (not to the emperor) and can be forced to resign by a vote of no confidence.

Even though the tenno, who is also the high priest of the Shinto religion, merely carries out official representational duties, he enjoys the highest respect. The public are very interested in the ups and downs of the imperial family, particularly in Naruhito and Masako, the couple that will succeed to the throne. When they had a daughter in December 2001 after eight years of marriage, a discussion about the succession broke out, because only a man through the male line can succeed to the throne. Since, according to opinion polls, a large majority of the population were in favour of recognizing a female head of state, it did not seem unlikely that there would be a change to the constitution; there was even a corresponding recommendation by a specially formed expert council. Then the brother of the heir to the throne, Prince Akishino, became the father of a son in September 2006, which has removed the issue of constitutional reform from the agenda.
A further point in the constitution, much debated again in recent times, is **Japan's renun-**

Constitutional debates

◄ Succession to the throne

◄ Defence policy

ciation of warfare and the threat of military violence. The decision
to deploy Japanese troops to Iraq in 2004, the army's first foreign
mission since World War II, was thus highly controversial, even
though the soldiers were only allowed to provide humanitarian relief.

Strictly speaking, according to its
constitution Japan is even forbidden
to have an army, which is why the
Japanese army, a professional force
with the world's fourth-largest military budget (!), is officially called
»Self-Defence Forces« (jieitai). A
considerable part of the population regards the **pacifist article 9** of
the Japanese constitution as inviolable. The government under Shinzo Abe however pursued a different direction and in January 2007
pushed through the Diet the transformation of the »Japan Defence
Agency« into a Ministry of Defence, with greater powers. This was
justified by, amongst other things, the North Korean nuclear tests
and China's arms build-up.

Political parties After all the political parties were disbanded during World War II
and their subsequent re-admission post-1945, the country's two lar-
gest parties, the liberals and the democrats, merged to become the
conservatively oriented Liberal Democratic Party (Jiyu Minshuto) in
1955, which since then has ruled the country almost without inter-
ruption. Together with its small coalition partner, the New Komeito
Party for clean politics (Shin Komeito), it now has more than two-
thirds of the representatives in the lower house. The largest opposi-
tion party is the Democratic Party of Japan (Nihon Minshuto); subordinate roles are played by the Social Democratic Part of Japan (Nihon Shakai Minshuto) and the Communist Party (Nihon Kyosanto)
as well as some splinter groups of the right and the left.

Administration Japan is a centrally governed unitary state, which is divided into 47
prefectures for administrative purposes. They are the 43 rural prefectures (ken), two urban prefectures (fu; Kyoto and Osaka), the capital
Tokyo (to) and the island territory Hokkaido (do). The prefectures
are in turn divided into cities (shi), towns (cho) and villages (son).
Each prefecture is governed by a directly elected prefect, who also represents the interests of the prefecture at central government level.

Economy

Modern industrial nation In 2007, Japan, with a gross national product of 5,164 billion US dol-
lars, lay in second place worldwide, behind the United States of
America. The achievement behind this figure becomes clear when it
is considered that Japan's development into a modern industrial
country only began after the Meiji emperor ascended the throne in
1868. World War II not only caused Japan to lose its overseas posses-

Toyota's modern engine factory in Fukuoka Prefecture

sions, but also inflicted incredibly severe damage on the country's industrial facilities. Only in 1951, in the wake of the Korean War, was Japan's economy able once again to reach its pre-war production level and manage without economic help from the US. During the mid-1950s active investment was effectively promoted by governmental measures.

Growth

The main emphasis lay on the iron and steel industry and coal mining. Soon new industrial sectors were added, in particular the manufacture of consumer goods such as cars and televisions. The rapid double-digit economic growth only slowed down again in the early 1970s through the strengthening of the yen and the oil crisis. Although growth has since remained moderate, Japan gradually rose to become a **leading economic power** and the largest net creditor in the world. At the end of the 1980s, the time of the bubble economy, share and real-estate prices shot up to dizzying heights as a result of speculative trading. When the government and national bank took counter-measures, the »bubble« burst and Japan slipped into a recession. Unemployment rose to more than 5.0%, exorbitantly high for Japan, (now 3.8%). The old employment structures are beginning to weaken. Some companies are faced with the problem of having too large a workforce. Reducing this surplus of employees is not easy because Japan largely practises what is called lifetime employment. Once a year school-leavers and/or university graduates are taken on, and so far they have been able to assume they will stay in the company until they retire, usually at the age of 60. A wage and promotion system based on the **seniority principle** means there is generally a close, loyal bond between Japanese employees and their employers. This powerful identification with the company is most likely the reason for the unusually effective quality control and very low absenteeism. The extremely high life expectancy of the Japanese population, the still inadequate social security system and the gradual decrease in population are causing problems for the traditional employment pattern. Lower labour costs mean that more and more Japanese companies are investing in China and South East Asia. Many young Japanese people are no longer able to find employment and have to keep afloat by taking odd jobs.

Agriculture Only 13.3% of Japan's total land area is used for agricultural production, and there are wide regional differences; the island of Hokkaido is very strongly agricultural. Before World War II around 50% of all those gainfully employed were still working in the primary sector. The rapid industrial development of the past decades has reduced this figure to just 5%. The most important crop is **rice**, which is cultivated on an area of around 2.5 million ha/6.2 million acres, close to half of the entire area used for agriculture, and yields around 7.8 million tons annually; the large rice monocultures can be found on the main island of Honshu. Other crops include wheat, barley, sugarbeet, horseradish, cabbage, citrus fruits, pulses, potatoes and not least **tea** in quite large amounts. Rearing livestock is of lesser significance; while the number of sheep and goats has been decreasing, poultry has been steadily increasing. The **breeding of silk worms**, bound to mulberry growing, is not to be underestimated; its main centre is central Honshu.

Fishing Fishing has always played a prominent role in Japan. The country accounts for around 15% of global earnings from fishing. Since the 1986 moratorium on commercial whaling Japan has repeatedly tried to circumvent regulations by participating in whaling for »scientific purposes«. The once famous pearl culture is declining.

Natural resources Japan has many, though not very productive, natural resources. The country's mining only makes up 1% of global output and Japan is almost entirely dependent on imports from other countries. Japan has a near-to-complete import dependence on bauxite, iron ore and crude oil; 92% of the country's copper needs are imported, as are 85% of its coke requirements. Japan has become the main buyer of these raw materials on the global market.

Industry

The country's main economic activity is the production of industrial goods. Here Japan is in second place in the world behind the United States. The **most important areas of production** are steel (Japan is the leading crude steel producer in the developed world), automobiles (passenger vehicles: global leader, with predominantly automated production; motorbikes) and ship building, pharmaceuticals (world leader), paper, optical equipment and toys, home electronics as well as electrical engineering and computer technology. Industry is focused on the coastal areas, particularly in the old Pacific port towns and their surroundings. These locations have significant advantages with regard to minimizing transport costs.

Energy industry

In the area of energy supply, and here specially of crude oil, Japan is highly dependent on imports. The country has to import nearly 99.7% of its petroleum requirements. In order to reduce this great dependence, the country has increasingly banked on the development of **nuclear energy**. By 1980 more than 20 nuclear power stations were in operation; by 2007 this number had increased to 56. Twelve more are in the planning stage. Thus a turning away from nuclear energy is not in sight, even though accidents regularly take place, as in Tokaimura in 1999.

Playing with the future – Japan is the world leader when it comes to developing robots. This one here, called »Seisaku Murata«, can cross a three-metre/4ft beam accident-free.

History

What is so special about the burial mounds of the kofun period? During which era did the shoguns seize power? Why did the country seal itself off completely from the outside world for centuries?

Early History

approx. 7000 to 250 BC	Jomon period: pottery culture with typical cord patterns
250 BC	Yayoi culture; first contacts with China and Korea

Stone Age

It is not known when humans settled in Japan, but researchers (such as John Hall) have dated the beginning of the pre-ceramic cultural phase to around 150,000 BC. Even though numerous primitive **stone tools**, mainly made of agate, slate and obsidian, have been found, scientists hesitate to use the word »Palaeolithic« because of the uncertainty about their dates.

The discoveries from the Neolithic age (New Stone Age), on the other hand, can be classified better. A discovery in the kanto layer, where the geological strata allow it to be dated with sufficient certainty, is assumed to date back to 8000 BC. It consists of axes and stone knives; the shape of the axes resembles those from comparable periods on the south Asian mainland, while that of the knives resembles those in Siberia and northern China. Thus it seems evident that the spheres of influence of northern and southern cultures merged in Japan around this time, but it is by no means proven that Japan has been continuously occupied since the early pre-ceramic phase.

Jomon culture

From around 700 to around 250 BC the **cord pottery culture** (Jomon culture) developed. Important discoveries from this culture of hunters and gatherers come from northern Honshu and the Kanto Plain. Initially these people inhabited pits with tent-like roofs. In the middle of the Jomon period there were already houses without central support posts. Dogs appeared as the companions of the hunting clans. Soon pottery vessels of colossal dimensions were being made; jug-like ceramic stoves sometimes replaced the fire pit. As can be concluded from weapons (wooden swords, bows, arrowheads) and tools (fish-hooks, harpoons, axes, hammers), this period can be seen as a belated Neolithic period, which soon merged with a Bronze Age culture.

Yayoi culture

From around 250 BC to the third century AD the Yayoi culture made its way to the Japanese islands from the south. The **potter's wheel** and **farming techniques**, particularly irrigated rice cultivation, were introduced. Bronze objects of Japanese origin made their first appearance. Since bronze mirrors and weapons from China, which previously experienced the flowering of the Han period (202 BC to AD 220), were also found in the tombs of the middle Yayoi period (nor-

← Fragment of a picture scroll from the early 14th century with a depiction of the Battle of Rokuhara

thern Kyushu), it is unlikely that the new techniques that appeared significantly earlier on the mainland were the products of independent development in Japan. In addition Korean and Chinese historians are agreed in their opinion that Japanese people had settled in Mimana on Korea's south coast around the time of the conquest of Korea by the Han dynasty. The Yayoi pottery of thin reddish clay displays less diversity in shape compared with the late Jomon period; instead of the cord impression, patterns were painted, carved or drawn into the moist surface with a comb.

Korean influences ► Almost identical pottery wares were found in the vicinity of Seoul (Karakuri on the Han River, South Korea); linguistic comparisons of the expressions for simple cultural techniques in Korean and Japanese, as were done by Ohno Susumu for example, confirm the theory of Korean influence. The horses of the Yayoi period, of medium size, resemble those of the Korean Stone Age; the Jomon horses, of which there are only a few traces, were smaller.

Grave finds ► The characteristic finds from graves are **imported bronze mirrors**, which were later seen as symbols of the solar disc and divine origin in Japan; bronze weapons and their stone replicas; and bell-shaped ritual objects (dotaku), which were possibly buried as sacrificial gifts, in the late period with beautiful figure ornaments. Funerary jars and stone box tombs were the main form of burial at the time, but dolmens were also erected.

Reconstructed building from a settlement dating back to the late Yayoi period in Toro, Shizuoka

Japanese Antiquity

3rd century	Empire is unified under the Yamato rulers
594	Buddhism is declared the state religion
604	First Japanese »constitution«; concentration of the power in hands of the imperial family
645	Taika Reform based on the Chinese model
710	Nara is founded as the first permanent capital; the Kojiki annals are written
720	The country's first chronicle, Nihon shoki, is written
794	The seat of government is transferred to Heiankyo (Kyoto). The Hiragana and Katakana syllabaries are developed
1156–59	Heiji Rebellion between the Taira and the Minamoto

During the **period of the burial mounds** (Kofun period) from the end of the 3rd to the 6th century AD the population, which had greatly increased in numbers as a result of the new farming methods, was organized into ever-larger domains and finally unified into one large realm under the Yamato rulers. During this process the peaceful village communities under the control of a religious leader were transformed into small kingdoms tightly run on military lines, with fortified centres or powerful troops. Such kingdoms are described in the Chinese Wajin-den chronicle, although the names and dates belong in the realm of legend.

Kofun period (3rd–6th centuries)

In Japan written annals throw light on this period through anecdotal accounts. They were however still written in Chinese characters used phonetically, the two main ones being the Kojiki and the Nihon shoki, of which many aspects are more literary than historical. These annals mention **Empress Jingu** who is said to have ruled from 201 to 269 BC. She is described as a shamanistic prophetess, who gave birth to the later emperor Ojin after a successful military campaign against Korea. The power relationship between Japan and Korea was the opposite of today's situation; Japanese military expeditions to Korean are well documented only from the second half of the fourth century. The legend probably stems from the fact that the Japanese chroniclers patriotically placed a military undertaking by the Empress Saimei (mid-7th century), which can be regarded as historical, back in the Kofun period. What is clear however is that soon after these legendary events (Ojin is in many cases considered the founder of the Yamato dynasty) the unification of the majority of the Japanese islands was achieved.

◀ Written records

The archaeological evidence of this developmental stage is provided by the famous Kofun burial mounds. The first appear at the end of

◀ Kofun burial mounds

Kofun Burial Mound

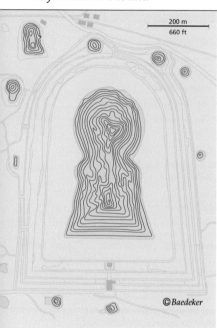

200 m
660 ft

©Baedeker

the 3rd or the beginning of the 4th century AD in the Kansai area. They most likely go back to Korean models and were built by the Yamato rulers, who were able to raise the necessary manpower, on a larger scale as a symbol of their power. The time of the giant burial mounds is the 5th century AD; the mausoleums of emperors Nintoku and Richu date back to this period; their existence as historical figures is highly probable. The late phases in the development of burial mounds reach into the 6th and 7th century and thus overlap with the introduction of Buddhism.

The **floor plans** of the Kofun burial mounds vary: there are round and square burial mounds; however, the characteristic outline in Japan is a round mound with a rectangular or trapezoidal front building, which resembles a keyhole from above. Many tombs are surrounded by moats. During the early period the dead were laid to rest in hollowed-out tree trunks, later in stone sarcophagi, whose round shape still resembled that of the tree trunks, and finally cubic or house-shaped sarcophagi made of stone slabs were used. Initially burial objects included simple metal tools and arrowheads. There was a strange custom of replacing iron, bronze or wood objects with accurate stone replicas, whose manufacture must certainly have been more of an effort than producing the originals. Objects that testify to the warlike times when the realm was unified under the Yamato rulers are weapons, particularly suits of armour, shields and swords.

Burial objects ▶ The most common burial objects, and also the most instructive for historical research, are the clay figures that have become famous under the name »**haniwa**«; often the entire period is named after them in art history. Their style is simple and realistic; there are modelled buildings ranging from peasant storehouses to stately reception halls, replicas of utility objects, animal figures and numerous depictions of humans, whose clothes give away their profession and social rank. Together with the occasional wall paintings and reliefs on metal objects, particularly on mirrors, the haniwa figures are a good source for that period's living conditions, about which there are otherwise only legendary accounts recorded in hindsight.

Buddhism, like Confucianism, made its way to Japan via Korea and set in train a significant intellectual and cultural development, but was also the cause of conflict between secular and priestly interests on numerous occasions. The power struggles associated with the adoption of Buddhism between the Mononobe, who held fast to the national Shinto religion, and the Soga, who defended Buddhism, ended in 587 with the victory of the Soga and with the coming to power of Prince Shotuko-taishi, the strongest proponent of the new faith. He commissioned the construction of the Shitennoji temple (in Osaka) and in 594 declared **Buddhism to be the state religion**. Shotoku-taishi also took over the Chinese system of a centralized bureaucratic state as well as the Chinese calendar, and in the time that followed he also promoted the cultural influence of China on the Japanese mainland.

Asuka period and Hakuho period (552–710)

The Taika Reform by Prince Nakano-oe (626–671, posthumously Emperor Tenchi) and his confidant Nakatomi no Kamatari (614–669, first ancestor of the Fujiwara) completed the reforms of Shotoku-taishi. The code, which also followed the Chinese example, included a land reform, the introduction of an education system and the affirmation of imperial central power.

◄ Taika Reform

The city of Nara, which lends its name to an entire era, developed into a centre of cultural blossoming. Based on the Chinese town planning model, it was the beginning of a permanent capital; previously the seat of government had been changed after the death of a ruler, since it had thereby become impure.

Nara period (710–784)

The 8th century saw the creation of the first significant works of Japanese literature: legends and historical events of Japan are compiled in the Kojiki; the Nihon-shoki (also Nihongi) make up the most important source of the country's early history; of course this history is infused with myths and legends. The Manyoshu (»collection of ten thousand leaves«), Japan's first anthology, begun in the 5th century, was completed in 759.

◄ Origin of literature

During the government of Shomu-tenno (724–749) Buddhism enjoyed a golden age and the construction of provincial temples strengthened the clergy. The »seven great temples of Nara« in particular threatened the imperial dynasty. Ganjin and other Chinese priests taught Buddhism in Japan. Empress Shotoku-tenno (during an earlier incumbency Empress Koken) was under the influence of the priest Dokyo, who in 765 had been appointed Grand Minister and who as »monk-emperor« (from 762) was the exponent of a striving for power on the part of the Buddhist clergy; but in 770 after the empress's death he was exiled.

◄ Heyday of Buddhism

In the year 794 the **permanent capital of Heiankyo** (Kyoto) was founded. The clergy's power was broken; what followed was a phase of national reflection with the development of independent cultural forms and syllabic scripts (katakana and hiragana) peculiar to Japan.

Heian period (794–1192)

After the fall of the T'ang dynasty Japan's contacts with China weakened.

Shadow emperors ► The emperors' attempts to gain independence were prevented by the **Fujiwara** clan, who bound the imperial family to them by marriage and brought about its political insignificance; from 859 they ruled as »shadow emperors« (guardians of emperors not yet of age). The Taika Reform that began in 645 failed once and for all; governors, officials and monasteries acquired fiefs; the armed nobility ordered to protect them became more influential.

By 805 the priest Saicho (Dengyo-dashi, 776–822) had returned from China and founded the **Tendai school** in Japan. A year later the priest Kukai (Kobo-daishi, 774–835), who had also returned from China, founded the **Shingon school**. Both schools created significant centres of esoteric Buddhism.

War between the Taira and the Minamoto ► The decentralization of power led to unrest; the military gained strength, especially the Minamoto family (also Genji) in the east of the country and the Taira family (also Heike) in the west. The power of the Fujiwara was gradually taken over by the Taira. During the time that followed the two families feuded severely with each other; after battles in the Tohoku region (1083–87) the Minamoto were victorious. Around 70 years later the tide turned: in the **Heiji War** Taira no Kiyomori beat the Minamoto and, after he was appointed Minister (»dajo daijin«), brought about heyday of the Taira family. A short while later the fortune of war changed again in the **Gempei War**. The Minamoto, who became strong again under Minamoto Yoritomo (1147–99), destroyed the Taira in the decisive battle of Dannoura, where the child emperor Antoku was also killed.

Medieval Japan

1192	Emperor Go-Shirakawa appoints Minamoto Yorimoto to be the first shogun in Japan's history.
1274 and 1281	Failed Mongolian invasions on Kyushu
1401	Start of diplomatic contacts with Ming-dynasty China
1534	Portuguese land in Tanegashima.
1568	Oda Nobunaga brings peace to the realm after a long period of civil war.
1592–93	Campaigns to conquer Korea

This era is characterized by the complete disempowerment of the emperor and the **usurpation of state power by the shoguns** (military rulers), who governed the country according to the strict ethical principles of their class. In 1192 Minamoto Yoritomo transferred the seat of government to Kamakura in order to escape the luxurious life at court and founded the eponymous shogunate. He created a firm government and secured the country's borders by stationing troops. His policies, later continued by the Hojo, were based on the **ethics of the »bushido«** (»way of the warrior«: loyalty, courage, defiance of death; ▶ Special p.54), which also influenced society as a whole. After his death his widow Hojo Masako and her father Hojo Tokimasa assumed power. In 1205 Tokimasa's son Yoshitoki became the first regent for the shogun (shikken); this office continued to remain in the Hojo family.

(margin) **Kamakura period and Yoshino period (1185–1392)**

The priests Honen and Shinran, whose Jodo and Jodo-shin-shu schools found widespread acceptance amongst the people, were exiled in 1207. The murder of Minamoto Sanetomo, Yoritomo's son, marked the end of the Minamoto line; in the wake of this event civil war erupted; the imperial family's attempt to win back power failed however. Around 1250 the story of the house of Taiga founds its literary echo in the *Heike-monogatari*.

Kyushu saw Mongol invasions in 1274 and 1281. Both times a typhoon (»kamikaze«, i.e. »divine wind«) suddenly arose and destroyed the Mongol fleet. National cohesion was strengthened, but the samurai showed growing dissatisfaction.

(margin) ◀ Mongol invasions

In 1333 Go-Daigo-tenno exploited the weakness of the Kamakura shogunate to overthrow the Hojo clan. He sent his commander Ashikaga Takauji into battle against the Kamakura shogunate, which fell after ten years of fighting. Initially the emperor took over the power of government again, but he was banished by Takauji, who appointed Komyo-tenno as rival emperor in 1336. Komyo-tenno then founded the northern court and proclaimed Takauji shogun. Go-Daigo fled with the imperial regalia to Yoshino, where he founded the southern court. The Namboku-cho period (»period of the northern and southern courts«) was named after this configuration.

During this time the power of the shoguns diminished. The country became involved in decades of civil war caused by regional rulers and monasteries striving for power as well as the confrontations between supporters of the two imperial courts. Nevertheless these years saw the development of **significant new arts** (such as the »No« form of Japanese theatre and the tea ceremony). After the abdication of Go-Kameyama, the third descendant of Go-Daigo, the entire empire, including the regalia, went to the northern emperor, but the peace thus obtained only lasted for a short while. Yoshimitsu, the third Ashikaga shogun, transferred his official residence to Muromachi (Kyoto) and brought about a period of cultural blossoming.

(margin) **Muromachi period and Azuchi-Momoyama period (1338–1600)**

The subsequent dispute amongst the Ashikaga led to the outbreak of the **Onin Wars**. The growing decentralization of power strengthened

the daimiates (the regional fiefdoms), who were aspiring to independence as autonomous states. Artists and scholars fled to remote provinces where new cultural centres were formed. Oda Nobunaga's entry into Kyoto in 1568 allowed him to break the power of the monasteries and daimiates and bring peace the country. The first contacts with Europe had begun 25 years earlier when the Portuguese landed in Tanegashima; one result was the influx and widespread distribution of firearms. In addition the missionary **Francisco de Javier** (Francis Xavier) brought Christianity into the country. He was supported by several daimyo, who saw the new religion as a means to develop their power. European learning, particularly medicine and the natural sciences, began to spread, as did the first trade contacts with more distant countries; Nagasaki opened up to foreign trade in 1571. Oda Nobunaga permitted the activity of Christian missionaries as a counterweight to the Buddhist monasteries.

In 1573 the last Ashikaga was deposed, marking the end of the Ashikaga shogunate. Nobunaga cemented his power and in 1576 he transferred his official residence to Azuchi Castle in Omi. Some ten years later he was murdered by his vassal Akechi Mitsukide. **Toyotomi Hideyoshi** continued the work of unifying the realm. He had the administration reorganized and provided the foundation for the feudal age. As minister he expelled the Christian missionaries. After his victory over the Hojo in Odawara (1590) the country's unification was complete.

At this point military campaigns in Korea began; both in 1593 and in 1598 they ended in ceasefire. Around the same time the first persecutions of Christians began.

Early Modern Period

1600	Battle of Sekigahara Beginning of the Tokugawa shogunate
1603	Transfer of the seat of government to Edo (Tokyo)
From 1616	Japan sealed off against foreign countries: prohibition of foreign travel
1853–54	The US Commodore Matthew Perry uses his fleet to force Japan to open.

At the Battle of Sekigahara **Tokugawa Ieyasu** was victorious over Hideyoshi's son Hideyori in 1600 and laid the foundation for the Tokugawa shogunate, which was to control the destiny of the country until 1867.

Edo period (1600–1867)

← *Tokugawa Ieyasu's armour in Okazaki Castle*

During the Edo period Japan completely sealed itself off from the outside world after a temporary opening to the West. In the **period of peace lasting more than 250 years** a web of control was set up by the shogunate that influenced practically all areas of life; this prevented any stronger concentration of political and economic power. Ieyasu, appointed shogun by the emperor, transferred his seat of government to Edo (Tokyo) and supported Buddhism and Confucianism. After his abdication in favour of his son Hidetada, trade and the economy were developed; a Dutch trading post was set up on Hirado off the northwest coast of Kyushu. Nevertheless there were renewed persecutions of Christians.

Battle of Osaka ▸ In the Battle of Osaka (1614–15) Ieyasu beat Hideyori, the last of the Toyotomi dynasty, who subsequently committed suicide. In the period that followed Japan entirely cut off contacts to other countries; relations with England and Spain were terminated and foreign travel was prohibited. The Shimabara Rebellion, in which the subjects of the Christian daimyo fought back against the oppressive taxation imposed on them, resulted in the final prohibition of Christianity. The only foreigners that were still tolerated were the Portuguese and the Dutch, but they were not permitted to leave their trading post. From a domestic point of view the following 200 years were characterized by peace and a great blossoming of urban bourgeois culture.

Forced opening It was only in 1853 that Japan opened up to the outside world again, although this opening was not voluntary: the Unites States commodore **Matthew Perry** anchored in Uraga Bay with his »Black Ships« in order to set up a trading post. In 1854 the Convention of Kangagawa was signed by Japan and the United States, opening the

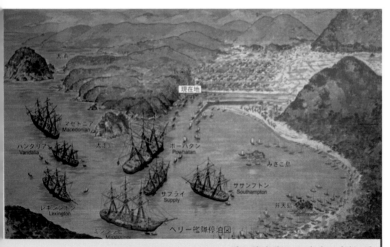

The »Black Ships« in the bay of Shimoda

ports of Shimoda and Hakodate to foreign trade. Treaties with Russia and England followed; the Treaty of Shimoda with Russia fixed the Russo-Japanese border in the Kuril Islands between the islands of Uruppu and Etoforu. Sakhalin (Karafuto in Japanese) was considered the joint property of both states. The abdication of the shogun and the transfer of power to Emperor Meiji ended the period of the shoguns.

Modern Times

1867	The Meiji period brings far-reaching reforms and a further opening of Japan to the west.
1894–95	First Sino-Japanese War
1904–05	Russo-Japanese War
1914–18	World War I: Japan on the side of the allies
1939–45	World War II: Japan on the side of the axis powers
14 August 1945	Japan capitulates after atomic bombs are dropped
1952	End of occupation of Japan
1956	Japan becomes a member of the United Nations.
1995	Disastrous earthquake in the greater Kobe area; poison gas attack on the Tokyo underground by the Aum cult
2005	Expo in Aichi (near Nagoya)

Meiji period (1867–1912)

The Meiji period was marked by comprehensive reforms and a subsequent opening of Japan to the rest of the world. The country took great pains to catch up with the West in the industrialization process. The state system was reorganized by a constitution. The focal point of the Meiji Reform was to have Japan's standard of knowledge catch up with that of other countries. Emperor Meiji transferred the seat of government to Edo and called it Tokyo (»eastern capital«).

◄ **Abolition of the class system**

From 1870 the class system so far in place was abolished, surnames were introduced and public primary schools were set up; the traditional lunar calendar was also replaced by the solar calendar. In exchange for Sakhalin Japan was given the entire Kuril chain by Russia. In 1889 a national constitution based on the Prussian model with a bicameral system was introduced; Japan became a constitutional monarchy. Victory in the Sino-Japanese War made the country a major Eastern power that had to be taken seriously.

◄ **Russo-Japanese War**

Japan was also the winner of the Russo-Japanese War (1904–05). In the Treaty of Portsmouth (USA), Japan was awarded the southern half of Sakhalin Island (Karafuto) and the protectorate over Korea.

Five years later Korea was annexed by Japan. Emperor Meiji died in 1912; his son Yoshihito (posthumously Taisho) became his successor.

Taisho period (1912–26)

From 1912 onwards Japan increasingly pursued a policy of expansion in East Asia and chose the side of the allies in World War I; the arms build-up promoted the development of heavy industry. Japan conquered the German possessions in China (Qingdao) and in the Pacific. The period following the First World War brought growing social tensions and a serious economic crisis. In 1923 the **Kanto earthquake** devastated the Tokyo-Yokohama region. The death of Emperor Taisho (1926) ended the Taisho era named after him.

Showa period (1926–89)

Taisho's successor was **Emperor Hirohito**. The Great Depression temporarily provided Japan with an export boom in cheap goods. In 1931 Manchuria was occupied and made into a Japanese protectorate under the name of Manchukuo. As a result of international criticism of this behaviour Japan left the League of Nations, of which it had been a member since 1920. During the second Sino-Japanese War (1937) Japan advanced into China's interior and also blockaded the entire Chinese coast. In December 1937 Japanese soldiers occupied the Chinese city of Nanking and committed a massacre in which up to 300,000 people were killed.

World War II ▶

During World War II Japan was on the side of the axis powers and extended its domination over all of southeast Asia. The Japanese attack on the US naval base of **Pearl Harbor** (1941) ignited the war in the Pacific. With the intention of creating a »Greater East Asia Coprosperity Sphere« through a Pax Japonica, the Japanese advanced to the coast of the Asian mainland and took Hong Kong, Singapore and Rangoon; at the same time they attacked the Philippines, the Dutch East Indies and also occupied the island of Guam. Air-raids on northern Australia and the landing on the Aleutian Islands as well as New Guinea meant that at its peak Japanese power extended over an area containing more than 450 million inhabitants.

Hiroshima and Nagasaki ▶

After bitter retreats on all the fronts costing many lives, Japan was finally forced to **capitulate unconditionally** when the first atomic bombs in the history of humankind were dropped on Hiroshima and Nagasaki in 1945. The emperor announced surrender over the radio on 14 August 1945; Japan had to give back all conquered territories and was occupied for the first time in its history. In the wake of these events Hirohito abandoned the traditional »divinity« of the emperor; under the new constitution he merely assumed a representational function as a symbol of the state and the unity of the nation. Under the **Treaty of San Francisco** in 1951 Japan lost possession of Korea, Taiwan, the Pescadores Islands, the Kuril Islands and south Sakhalin; its relationship with the USSR and China was not settled.

Democracy and rise to a global economic power ▶

At the end of the war the victorious powers insisted Japan become a democracy. After its devastating defeat the country not only recovered relatively quickly: within a few decades it had become a leading global economic power, during which time ties to the Western world were greatly intensified. In 1956 Japan became a member of the United Nations.

In 1965, as a result of this enormous economic growth, the yen became a fully convertible currency. Okinawa, which served the United States as a supply base during the Vietnam War, fell under Japanese suzerainty again in 1972. During the 1970s the global energy crisis brought Japan, which was almost entirely dependent on petroleum imports, into serious economic difficulties. Negotiations with the Soviet Union about a peace treaty and a return of the Kuril Islands ended without a result.

The world economic summit that was held in Tokyo in 1986 attested to the significance that Japan had attained in the global economy.

On 7 January 1989 Emperor Hirohoto died; his son Akihito became the new emperor. He chose the name »heisei« (»creating peace«). In January 1995 the highly industrialized conurbation of Kobe was devastated in a disastrous earthquake in which more than 5000 people lost their lives; hundreds of thousands became homeless and the economy suffered serious damage. The decades-long debate about the transfer of Japan's capital gained new momentum as a result of bigger and bigger infrastructure problems in the Tokyo area.

Heisei period (since 1989)

The Japanese public are very interested in events concerned with the imperial family.

Under Koizumi Junichiro, one of the most popular prime ministers of post-war Japan, the country displayed greater self-confidence: in January 2004 it deployed soldiers to an area of international conflict, Iraq, for the first time since World War II. Koizumi also effected the return of several Japanese who, during the 1970s and 1980s, had been abducted by North Korea in order to teach Japanese to spies. From a domestic political standpoint Koizumi's successor Abe Shinzo also had reforms on his agenda, including the privatization of the postal service, the combating of corruption and measures to contain the country's enormous debt. He also pushed through the creation of a ministry of defence. Present prime minister Aso Taro has to face the global financial crisis.

Religion

What defines Buddhism and what characteristics does it have? What is meant by »bushido«? How did Shinto develop? And what role does religion play in the everyday lives of the Japanese people?

Religious beliefs during Japan's early history until the beginning of
the classical period (i.e. the time of the burial mounds) were akin to
animism. Shamans invoked the »kami«, the embodiments of **natural
forces**, in order to bring success in hunting and fishing or good harvests later on.

It was only under the influence of Chinese civilization that the Japanese natural religion obtained a spiritual background, a ritual, religious architecture in a real sense of the term and visual representations of natural spirits, which were now personified but previously
(and to some extent again today) had been worshipped in the form
of fetishes. Initially the cult later named Shinto (»way of the Gods«)
took over from the social and state philosophy of Confucius (Latin-
ized from the Chinese Kung fu-tse or Master Kung, actually Kung
Chin; c. 550 to c. 479 BC) the teaching of ancestor worship and the
idea of the son of heaven, i.e. the divine origin of the ruling family,
which was developed during the Chou dynasty in China. Both concepts were greatly welcomed by the Yamato emperors, who were
bent on ideological justification of their entitlement to rule over all
of Japan.

Afterwards, from the late nature doctrine of Taoism (named after
the original mystical aphorisms *Tao-te-ching* by Lao-tse; 4th–3rd centuries BC), and particularly from the *I Ching* (*Book of Changes*), the
dualistic principle of **yin and yang**, i.e. of passive female and active
male opposites, became amalgamated with archaic natural rites and
the art of soothsaying. Finally the sun god Amaterasu, taken over
from earlier cults, was declared first ancestor of the imperial line and
placed at the top of a multifaceted hierarchy of natural and ancestral
gods.

Buddhism

Buddha (Sanskrit: »the awakened one« or »the enlightened one«) is
the honorary title of the religion's founder; he is also named Gautama or Gotama after a clan of seers from his home in northern India
or, after his own family (Shakya), Shakyamuni, i.e. the ascetic from
the house of the Shakya. Coming from an old ruling family, he was
born around 560 BC in the foothills of the Nepalese Himalayas.
When he was 29 years old he renounced wealth, power and his nobility in order to study the teachings of asceticism as a pilgrim. Disap-
pointed by his teachers, he gathered his own disciples around him
and dedicated himself to ascetic life far removed from all bookish
wisdom. While meditating under a fig tree (bodhi) he had an enligh-

← *A monk calls to prayer*

tenment, which he taught from then on as the »four truths«: all existence is continuous suffering; its cause is craving; ceasing to crave will bring release from suffering; and the way leading to this cessation of suffering is the »noble eightfold path«. The eight paths to this cessation are: right awareness and right thinking; right speech, right actions and right livelihood; right effort, right understanding and meditation.

Buddha's teachings ► After initial resistance by the proponents of the traditional nature worship, Buddhism was accepted by the Japanese upper class and in 594 was declared the **state religion** by Crown Prince Shotoku and was subsequently definitive for Japan's cultural life for several centuries. What came to Japan was no longer the pure teaching of Gautama. His teachings mention neither God nor the afterlife and their path to salvation required every believer to show absolute self-discipline and self-denial. Since such properties could only be expected from a small elite, alongside the demanding **»low vehicle«** (Hinayana), whose followers did not permit any deviations from the demands of the Buddha, there arose the **»great vehicle«** (Mahayana) which was widespread amongst lay people, who, since they believed that strict adherence to the »eightfold path« was impossible because of their entanglement in the shackles of daily life, the Bodhisattvas (Sanskrit: »those whose being is enlightenment«; Japanese »bosatsu«) were created as auxiliary constructs, comparable to the Christian helper saints. They are ascetics who have reached the degree of perfection allowing them salvation and entry into Nirvana, but who, out of pity for imperfect believers, have chosen to remain in a kind of intermediate world where they take on the role of mediators.

Development of schools ► Even though the origin and nature of Buddhism were completely undogmatic, and even though Buddhism has always responded to all other religions and world views with serene tolerance, schools (Japanese »shu«) had already formed in India and China that wanted to soften or circumvent the founder's world-negating demands in order to make the teachings more accessible to the people. They were joined in this by a few Japanese schools. Of the six schools of the Nara period, the Hosso, Ritsu and Kegon schools still have a following, albeit a small one.

Tendai The Tendai school, founded in 805 by Saicho (767–822; posthumously Dengyo-daishi) later turned the inner torments of entanglement in the world's confusion into real daemons, whose evil influence had to be banished with incantations and ritual sacrifices.

Jodo The Tendai priest Genshin (942–1017) reified the abstract Buddhist terms even more by adding a paradisiacal afterlife to the daemonic underworld. In this he was the forerunner of the Jodo school founded by Shinran (1173–1262), which soon had many followers because it denied the existence of hell. It bases itself on the »Pure Land doctrine«, which was developed in India in the first century BC and later, probably through a misunderstanding about the idea of salvation in Christianity, found many adherents because of its simplicity. Jodo revolves around the summoning of strangely sexless representations of a Bodhisattva by the name of Amida. The worship of the Amida image is said to wash away all sins and impurities of the believer and secure passage into the Pure Land.

The teachings of Nichiren (1222–82) are even more popular. He reduced the religious requirement to such an extent that he merely considered one of the sentences from the Lotus Sutra (in Japanese »Hokke-kyo«, which is why the school is also called Hokke-shu), one of the countless Buddhist texts, to be sufficient in order to achieve salvation. If a believer merely prayed: »Worshipped be the sutra of the lotus of the wonderful law«, the believer's soul achieved the level of perfection! Despite or rather because of this incredible simplification, the school has remained very popular amongst some Japanese people to this day.

Nichiren

Procession at Shinshoji temple in Narita

ZEN AND THE WAY OF THE SAMURAI

The introduction of Zen Buddhism in Japan occurred during the war-torn Kamakura period (1185–1333). In this era, also termed the beginning of the Japanese feudal period, the shoguns' power was consolidated after the disturbances of the Gempei War. They relied on an aspiring warrior caste, whose members called themselves samurai.

These rough warriors were lacking in the literary education of the courtly nobility, whose effete life-styles they despised. This explains the samurai's great interest in the new teaching that considered all bookish wisdom as a mere hindrance on the path to the final truth. The Rinzai sect in particular, with its ascetic way of life and spontaneous, sudden moment of enlightenment, attracted many members of the new knighthood.

After defeat in the **first Mongolian invasion** in 1274 had only been prevented by a sudden storm, since the Japanese defences proved to be insufficient, the Hojo regents placed the training of their warriors in the hands of Zen monks. This proved successful when the Mongols tried to attack a second time in 1281. The samurai were able to withstand the Mongols' superior forces for seven weeks until again a typhoon, later called »kamikaze« (»divine wind«),

destroyed the enemy fleet. The Zen training consisted above all of swordsmanship and archery in addition to general exercises in intellectual discipline.

Swordsmanship

A sword fighter who had achieved a state of »mushin«, which could be translated as »non-thinking« or »no consciousness«, through Za-zen meditation and practicing Koan (p.56f.), acted **intuitively**. His mind was free from all emotions, from fear and even from a longing for victory. The fighter's body and his sword merged into a single instrument of the unconscious. He was thereby superior to an opponent who had to plan his actions rationally before putting the plan into operation.

For a samurai a sword was not just a weapon; it was also considered a symbol of the code of honour known as **»bushido«** (Way of the Warrior). It

Archery is one of Zen's traditional, meditative disciplines.

Bushido: the »Way of the Warrior« determined a nation's ethos.

required fearlessness in the face of death, fealty, contempt for money and possessions, and unconditional defence of his own honour and that of his family. If this honour was infringed, a samurai had to be willing to restore it through committing ritual suicide (the term »harakiri« is not much used in Japan) at any time, to which end he always carried a second, shorter sword on his belt.

The **swords** were made using a method that had been handed down unchanged for centuries. The smith and his workshop underwent a ritual cleansing before he started his work. A piece of steel of varying degrees of hardness was hammered into a blade of countless layers by constant reheating and folding of the metal. The blade's core thereby remained soft and ductile, while to the outside the hardness of the layer increased towards the edge.

Archery

A Japanese bow, made of several bamboo slats and the wood of the carissa tree, is asymmetrical. It has its grip in the lower third. The Zen technique of archery, like that of Zazen meditation, was mainly based on **proper breathing**. Accompanied by exactly measured breaths the bow was drawn. The release of the bowstring from the thumb, like the attack

of a sword fighter, took place intuitively, independent of the will. If the marksman was fully proficient at the sequence of events, he no longer had to make an effort to hit his target consciously: that would happen by itself. Seemingly unintentionally the hand would release the arrow in exactly the moment when its tip was aiming at the target.

! Baedeker TIP

Book recommendation

The famous samurai Miyamoto Musahi explains the spirit of martial arts in his book »The Book of Five Rings« (►Literature, p.136).

A Means to Self-Awareness

The martial arts of medieval Zen have been kept alive to this day. Kyudo, archery, is still practised in the same form as it was in the heyday of the Zen samurai.

The former fighting techniques serve not just to strengthen the body, but are also understood as means to achieve self-awareness and change in consciousness. Practiced in the spirit of Zen the techniques lead to »kensho«, which means »seeing one's nature«, i.e. an insight about the true self.

Soka Gakkai Nichiren was the forerunner of what is called the »value creation society« of today. Thanks to generous donations from industrial circles the controversial Soka Gakkai is able to build huge temples, whose overblown style contradicts the simple aesthetic principles of Japanese architecture, however. The political arm of this school is the conservative **Kemeito Party** founded in 1964, which as the coalition partner of the LDP has a significant influence on government policy.

Zen Buddhism

Japanese origin Zen Buddhism developed as an independently Japanese contribution to meditative Buddhism. It has not just permeated the country's entire spiritual life, but has also had a lasting influence on Western thinkers.

The Japanese word »zen« is a short form of »zenna« (later »zazen«) and means **»meditative exercise«**, particularly an immersion exercise in a seated position (»Dhyana« in Sanskrit) that first came to China from India with Buddhism in its original form. There it was called »channa«, but because of the great influence of the eclectic Mahayana schools and the rational Chinese position of the new faith's official administrators, it was initially pushed into the background.

Like Taoism, Chan and later Zen is **not a religion in the true sense of the word**. It has no theological concept of God, no rites, no dogmas and no holy scriptures. It does not require analysis and rational understanding, but rather a direct, intuitive way of perception. The world of things is treated as Western people often treat the world of faith and spirits: a conventional way of seeing that stands for something that is not real.

? **DID YOU KNOW ...?**

■ The roots of Zen lie in Buddhism, but many Zen masters do not feel bound to a particular religion. The core of Zen lies not in philosophical systems, but rather in mystical experiences.

Transcendental wisdom ▶ Novices have to free themselves from all rationally justified distinctions of logical, discursive thinking by means of strict self-discipline. The goal is to achieve transcendental wisdom, which removes all of the polarity between the individual self and the universe. This central concept of Buddhism, **becoming one with all creation**, was called »prajnag« in India. It names the same state of enlightenment that Gautama once achieved under the bodhi tree and is thus to be equated with the achievement of buddhahood that rests deep within every human being.

Satori ▶ The Japanese later coined the expression »satori« for this state. This state of consciousness and the path that leads there cannot be described by words and logical terms, since they are beyond the limits of what is rational. A Zen master who has already reached satori thus has the problem of how to bring his students closer to enlightenment other than through instruction in the technique of »sitting immersed« (zazen). The solution consisted in non-rational riddles called »koan« in Japan. In one of the best-known riddles the master claps his hands and says: »This is the sound of two hands. What is the sound of just one hand?« The student is then invited to find an answer that spontaneously and intuitively corresponds to the illogical nature of the riddle without getting lost in rational explanations. At times the student and teacher play long **question-and-answer games** called »mondo« by the Japanese. These techniques shake the trust of the novice in discursive ways of thinking and are meant to free him of the shackles of the rather simple logic of the syllogism. Initially, when the number of monks was still smaller, the Chan masters would have given every one of the students an individually tailored koan. Later, when the monasteries had greater numbers of followers, the time-tested riddles of the T'ang period were used, which had been recorded in writing at the time. A suitable koan was chosen from these traditional collections, which was then given to a whole number of adepts. The collections of sayings, now very extensive, are not, however, considered to be dogmatic holy texts, since the only Zen dogma is that there are no dogmas.

The famous Chinese Chan masters founded their own schools,   ◀ Rinzai whose teachings later also made their way to Japan. That of Lin-chi (died 867) is called Rinzai in Japan; it favours the »sudden« path to satori via the koan technique. The school of Tung-shan (807–869) and of Tsao-shan (840–901), whose Japanese name is Soto, a merger of Tsao and Tung, relies more on the »gradual« path through the practice of sitting immersed.

The first Zen master in Japan was the former **Tendai monk Eisai** (1141–1215), who studied the Chan techniques on two trips to China until he believed he had achieved enlightenment and on his return in 1191 founded a Rinzai monastery on Kyushu. In Japan the founder of the Soto school is considered to be Dogen (1200–53), who also came from a Tendai monastery and travelled to China in order to learn about the new teachings. Once returned to Japan, he spent several years as an itinerant monk until he was able to found his own monastery in 1236.

Great Buddha of Kamakura

Shinto

The syncretistic evolution of Shinto from archaic natural religions and Chinese rites has already been described. Only in the 18th century was it presented to Japanese people, who by their nature are un-dogmatic, as particularly »Japanese«.

History

Archaeological relics from the Jomon culture (from around the 5th century BC) indicate totemism, nature worship and the cult of a fertility and mother goddess; elements of a matriarchal society have survived in the role of the female shamans and shrine dancing-girls of later Shinto. There is evidence of **sun worship** for the Yayoi period (until AD 300). Chinese annals of the 4th century report about clans and their deities (clan gods or ujigami), naturalistic and animistic cults, shamanism and the worship of divine forces that provide food. In the centuries before the start of historically meaningful written traditions (*Kojiki* 712, *Nihon-shoki* 720) **ancestor worship developed**. It was presumably influenced by Confucian writings from early on; the cult of the clan deities was reinforced by the **Ise shrine** in the national sanctuary dedicated to the sun goddess Amaterasu. Only when Buddhism was introduced did the native cult of the »800 myriad kami« receive the distinctive name Shinto (**»way of the gods«**).

In the following centuries the Shinto cult was closely connected to state representation and government dealings in the imperial palace. A kind of symbiosis with Buddhism was achieved in Ryobu-Shinto (»the way of the gods of two kinds«): the kami were seen as reincarnations of Buddha and Bodhisattva, the sun deity equated with the Dainichi Nyorai (Great Sun Buddha). Since the 14th century there have been attempts to re-establish the archaic Yuiitsu-Shinto and purge it of its Confucian ingredients.

State religion ▶

As part of the Meiji restoration, patriotic intellectuals made it their goal to turn the thesis of a »national teaching« (»kokugaku«), developed by **Motoori Norinaga** (1730–1801) and based on the mythological passages in the *Kojiki*, into the official mentality or »yamato gokoro« (»Japanese spirit«) and later into the national religion. As a result of chauvinist zeal, during this process the Chinese elements, which are also to be found everywhere in the Shinto religion, were either negated or dismissed as »superficial Chinese ways of thinking«. When such characteristics could no longer be kept secret by apocryphal historical misrepresentation, which was a not uncommon thing

A woman in the traditional dress of the Heian period (8th–12th centuries) walks through the Shinto shrine of Hongu in Wakayama Prefecture on Honshu

to do, they were ignored as un-Japanese. After Japan's total defeat in World War II the emperor had to renounce his divinity, and state Shinto was abolished; the shrines and priests are now dependent on the support of the faithful. Nonetheless many politicians still never miss the opportunity to pay their respects to a Shinto shrine on important public holidays even if privately they have quite different spiritual ideas; because even though Shinto was officially put on par with other religions after 1945, the former state religion is still very popular amongst large parts of the population.

The Shinto cult is very simple for its adherents: it involves cleaning the hands and mouth, pulling on the hemp rope and clapping the hands, which is meant to call the deity's attention, monetary donations and the purchase of a charm. During the **festivals** (matsuri) the actions of the shrine priests (kannushi) and followers are more extensive: the god's incantation is followed by the exorcist cleansing (ha-rai) or the more popular washing off (misogi) of moral and ri-

Rituals

tual impurities; after food and sake have been sacrificed, an originally shamanic trance dance (kagura) and court dances (bugaku) are performed for the gods' entertainment. Performances with a well-developed local flavour can be part of the semi-sacred acts, the most spectacular of which is the procession with a portable shrine (mikoshi). In this shrine, as well as in the main hall of the actual shrine, a symbol representing the god (shintai, divine body) can be found, hidden from the eyes of the believers. A noticeable characteristic of the shrine is the generally red gate (torii) made of vertical and usually of two horizontal beams.

Other Religions

Christianity Catholicism was brought to Kyushu in 1549 by the Spanish Jesuit missionary **Francisco de Javier** (Francis Xavier). This marked the beginning of the »Christian century« during which southern and western Japan learned about the Christian faith and liturgies, but also about Western culture, way of life and technology; Christian literature and painting developed and Western musical instruments were popular for a short time. The feudal rulers in the southwest of Japan, however, mainly promoted Christianity for economic reasons as well as for political power, which moved the shogunate authorities to prohibit it in 1614; bloody persecutions led to the virtual extinction of Christianity by 1638. It was merely in remote areas that laypeople known as hidden Christians (kakure kirishitan) could orally pass on doctrines and customs in secret. The prohibition was not lifted until 1873; but even after **religious freedom** became anchored in the Japanese constitution of 1889 the Christian mission still had difficulty in asserting itself against native religions and traditional prejudices. Only during the course of the democratization that was ordered after World War II did Christian influence become noticeable again. Today around 400,000 Japanese people acknowledge their Catholic faith, while there are around 750,000 Protestant and approximately 25,000 Orthodox Christians.

New religions Since the mid-19th century numerous new religions, some of them outside the traditional doctrines, have developed in Japan. They are mostly based on the teachings of charismatic founders and often represent syncretistic and sometimes also monotheistic standpoints. The following are some of the more than 300 new religions, to which a total of 4.8% of the population adhere.

Tenrikyo ▶ Tenrikyo (»teaching of divine reason«; founder: Nakayama Miki, 1798–1887); emerged from Shinto, messianic, monotheistic.

Mukyokai ▶ Mukyokai (»without a church«), founded by the Protestant Uchimura Kanzo (1861–1930); represents a form of non-institutionalized Japanese Christianity based solely on the Bible.

Groups basing themselves on Nichiren include Nichiren Shoshu (»true school of the Nichiren«), founded in 1913, which pursues a belief system based on Nichiren as the Buddha of the present-day end-of-the-world (»Mappo«). A number of movements have split off from it, including the lay organization Soka Gakkai, which is active worldwide with 12 million members. The Omu Shinrikyo movement founded by Asahara Shoku is apocalyptic and esoteric. It is notorious as the Aum cult which unleashed a poison-gas attack on the Tokyo underground in 1995. It once had 40,000 members in Japan and Russia, but this figure has sunk to 2,000. The movement is now called »Aleph«.

◄ Nichiren Shoshu

◄ Aleph

The above-listed denominations, with the exception of Christianity, do not exclude each other in Japan. Of course there were battles about prestige and privileges, about economic and political power with and amongst the major Buddhist temples during the Middle Ages and early modern age, fought by huge armies of warrior monks. These battles did not, however, stem from arguments about doctrine; they were generally justified by moral reasons. The terrible persecution of Christians at the beginning of the Edo period also had political causes; for the Tokugawa, the Christians were terrorists threatening the peace of the realm and the power of the shogunate. Japanese thinking and feeling was and to a certain degree still is **harmonizing and non-discriminating**. This attitude led to syncretism in Japanese religious life, which allows individuals to be a part of several faith communities at once. Japan owes to Shinto the integration of people into family and state, dogmatized and elevated into the political sphere by Confucianism. The spiritual and speculative dimensions, a hint of transcendence and individual realization was added by Buddhism. The impulse to develop a social awareness crossing the traditional limits was finally provided by Christianity.

Syncretism and religiosity

◄ Harmonization as a principle of faith

The Japanese have chosen those elements from the obviously polymorphic teaching and faith tradition of the Buddhism of the Great Vehicle that fit their religious attitudes well. These elements include the cult of the auxiliary deities, the conception of the redeemer Buddha and Bodhisattva, magical and esoteric practices (consecration of building sites, exorcisms), the nature of devotional objects, and burial and commemoration rituals. Buddhist philosophy or concepts, such as the state of »detachment« (»muga«) achievable through meditation, regardless of how great their significance was for art and intellectual life, never determined the everyday life of any layers of society as lastingly as the system of incantations, burial rites, charms, taboos and fortune telling (palm reading) did.

◄ Pragmatic treatment of religion

Arts and Culture

How is the typical lacquer ware made? What is a netsuke? What special features characterize Japanese gardens? How is the classical tea ceremony performed? And which traditional forms of theatre have survived in Japan?

In Europe the concept of Japanese art is usually associated with works from the 17th and 18th centuries and is often seen as just a variant of Chinese art. Chinese influences did play an important role, but stimuli from the Indian cultural sphere can also be observed: they are testimony to the transnational force of Far Eastern religions, which are closely connected to the creation of art and also led to the development of individual artistic styles in Japan.

Overview of Japanese Art History

Jomon

The archaic period lasted until the historical founding of the Japanese empire in the first century AD. The Jomon period (7th millennium to 3rd century BC) saw the development of pottery whose wealth of forms proves the high level of Japanese craftsmanship. The fact that this art, which is called »Jomon pottery« because of its **rope pattern**, has been found at more than 70,000 sites shows its wide distribution. The containers were still made without the use of a potter's wheel; in addition there were also some terra cotta products that emphasized gender-specific traits, and masks in the shape of animal heads.

Yayoi

As a result of Japan's geographical isolation, knowledge of bronze production reached the country relatively late, probably via China, around the 3rd century BC. Those spreading this culture pushed the Jomon people away to the north. The technique of producing pottery became more refined and the **potter's wheel** came into use. Yayoi pottery was fired red, sometimes painted or adorned with rope or comb patterns. Bronze was used to make mirrors and weapons, amongst other things, as well as cylindrical bells surrounded by a metal band (»dotaku«). The dead were buried in stone slab graves or clay funerary jars.

Kofun

The Kofun period began around AD 300. Its most eye-catching remains are the **huge burial mounds** on a keyhole-shaped floor plan (particularly in the Kinki region). An increasing social differentiation can be seen in them; during the later period the rich burial objects also include Chinese jade jewellery in addition to weapons and suits of armour. As a protective measure against erosion the sarcophagus is surrounded by **»haniwa«**, originally simple clay cylinders, which later developed into representations of houses, animals and finally humans. The climax of this culture is marked by the graves of the

← *The torii is a characteristic feature of every shrine complex, including Shiga shrine*

emperors Ojin and Nintoku. On the basis of stylistic examinations of the burial objects it seems likely that these artefacts were left by an equestrian people that had come via Korea. In the mid-4th century there was an increase in contacts with Korea, where the new techniques originated (iron casting, weaving, hard-fired Sue pottery). Architecture also became more elaborate during this time.

Asuka The spread of Buddhism marked the onset of the Asuka period (552–645), which, besides Shinto nature worship, also saw the beginning of the cult of anthropomorphic deities. Japanese masters picked up elements from Greek, Persian and Indian civilizations via China and developed them into a high art. Temple architecture started to develop independently and a large number of cult images were created. A particularly noteworthy example is the **bronze Shaka Triad** (623) in the Horyuji near Nara by Tori Busshi, Japan's first visual artist known by name. It still clearly shows the Chinese influence, while the gilt wooden statue of the Guze Kannon is more strongly individualized and already displays the beginning of a specific Japanese style. The Miroku statues in the Chuguji monastery and the Koryuji temple, representations of Buddha lost in meditation, have overcome the material laws resulting from the wood and display a physicality that has seemingly come to life. A new method that emerged was the dry lacquer technique on a wooden core. Around the middle of the 7th century the tamamushi-no-zushi domestic altar was built. It is the earliest example of Japanese art painting. The **lacquer technique** developed.

Terra cotta figures called »Haniwa« were the burial gifts of the Kofun period

The Hakuho period was also under the influence of Buddhism. The Japanese delegations at the Chinese court (Sui and T'ang dynasties), the cultural centre of eastern Asia at the time, became transmitters of style elements. Sculpture displayed great vitality; an Indian influence also manifested itself in the flowing, smooth body shapes. One example is the bronze Buddha head (685) in the Kofukuji temple in Nara. A noteworthy degree of perfection was achieved in the **murals** of the hall in the Horyuji temple, which was destroyed by fire in 1949. Here too there were similarities to Indian models, but the Japanese style remained dominant. During this period artistic work also spread to remote parts of the country for the first time and led to locally specific variations, notably in religious art.

Hakuho

During the Nara period (710–79) the bronze statue of Daibutsu, the **Great Buddha**, was made. The best examples of the balanced aesthetic and accuracy of the art of the time, which increasingly displayed individual traits, are the statues of the Nikko-bosatsu and Gakko-bosatsu (Bodhisattva) in the Todaiji temple (Nara), as well as the representation of Buddha's six disciples and the guardian deity in the Kofukuji temple (Nara), which were made in the same dry lacquer technique as the Fukukensaku Kannon in the Todaiji temple. The seated statue of the blind priest Ganjin, who founded the Toshodaiji temple after 753, stands, with its inward orientation, in stark contrast to the works of the Hakuho period. Gigaku masks, which were probably already used for theatrical representations, display caricature exaggerations of physiognomic features. As human representation became individualized, one art forms that appeared was portrait painting.
The **collection of Emperor Shomu**, which allegedly contains 100,000 pieces, dates back to the Nara period. It is kept in the treasury of the Todaiji temple, which holds artworks from the entire eastern cultural area of that period, a small proportion of which are exhibited in the national museum in Nara.

Nara

The arts and culture of the early Heian period (794 to c. 900) were largely determined by two schools of esoteric Buddhism that were becoming increasingly more widespread, namely Tendai and Shingon. Religious mystification resulted in entirely new forms of the visual arts that let go of the realism of the previous period and pushed artistic creativity into the background in favour of an almost schematic symbolism. Thus the »**mandara**« (mandala, mystic diagram) became very widely distributed. This representation of the esoteric-Buddhist world-view is grouped in numerous compartments and sub-compartments around a Buddha (the enlightened one) or Bodhisattva (those on the path towards enlightenment) in order to help decipher in pictorial terms the complicated religious doctrines.
The preferred material for sculptures was wood. First they were carved out of a block. The limits posed by the language of symbols was overcome by, for example, the expressiveness of the fearsome

Heian

◄ Wooden sculpture

faces of the gods of light. In general the statues are surrounded by an aura of spirituality that can only be appreciated through meditation. Good examples are the Yakushi-nyorai of the Jingoji temple in Kyoto and the Nyoirin-Kannon in the Kanshinji temple of Osaka.

Departures in Shinto ▶ Shinto also began to turn towards anthropomorphic representations of its deities. Less restricted by iconographic rules than Buddhism, such works still showed the realism and accurate representation of the Nara period.

National reflection ▶ During the late Heian period (around 900 to 1184) the newly built capital Heiankyo (Kyoto) became the country's cultural centre as a result of the relocation of the imperial court. The break with China at the end of the 9th century initiated the period of national reflection, which pushed specifically Japanese aspects of the arts into the foreground and let them flourish. At the imperial court significant literary works were written in the **newly introduced »kana« scripts**. The emperor, robbed of his political power by the Fujiwara clan, devoted himself to the refined cultural and artistic life at court. Palace buildings increased in size (Shinden-zukuri) and became the new symbolic form for representing the Buddhist belief system presented in the mandala images. The basis of this change is the replacement of the esoteric Buddhism of this world by the teaching of the Pure Land (»Jodo«), a generally comprehensible proclamation of salvation in another world that is based in the belief in Amida and the invoca-

Development of sculpture in wood ▶ tion of his name. The **Amida statue by Jocho** (died 1057) is testimony to the high level that the art of sculpture had achieved. The new method of assembling wooden sculptures from several components made them more dynamic. At the same time the terrifying faces of earlier sculptures softened into the peaceful expression of the Amida representations. Artists withdrew from monastic seclusion and founded workshops and schools, thereby confronting the changing cultural trends of their time. The religious symbolism was overlaid with aesthetic realism, expressed in softer, almost feminine forms. Examples of the subtle expression of these sculptures are the **Kannon statues**, particularly those of the Kichijo-ten in the Joruri temple of Nara, as well as the representations of the seven-year-old Shotoku-tashi in the Horyuji temple in the Nara Basin.

Painting ▶ The gold leaf much used on sculptures and incredibly detailed painting found their counterpart in the national **Yamato-e** paintings, very different in style from Chinese painting, which culminated in the emaki, picture scrolls mostly modelled on literary specimens with a religious or historical content. One of the best-known scrolls, the »Genji-monogatari«, narrates life at the court during the 12th century; a characteristic feature is the parallel perspective used, in which absent roofs allow viewers to see the interior of a room; another is the stylized representation of human beings.

Under the influence of Jodo teachings, scenes about believers being accepted into paradise or about the return of the Amida Buddha dominate in religious painting. Lacquer art, which had attained a sub-

Detail of a picture scroll from the Kamakura period with scenes from the Heiji Rebellion

stantial degree of autonomy, also reached a peak. Through the **makie technique** (decoration by applying gold or silver powder onto fresh lacquer) outstanding works were created.

The Kamakura period (1192–1333), shaped politically by the strengthening of the military in the provinces, followed in the footsteps of the art of the Nara period in its simplicity and powerful expression and brought sculpture to a zenith that it never reached again. Unkei (died 1223), Kukei (late 12th century) and Jokei (c. 1200) spread the new style. Unkei's turning away from the Heian period can already be seen in his early works, such as the Dainichi-nyorai in the Enjoji temple (1178) in Nara. On the basis of naturalism individual, secular portraits appeared. The new style is represented in Nara by the Nio statues of the Nandaimon Gate of the Todaiji temple as well as the statues of the priests Muchaku and Seshin (both in the Kofukiji temple), which are considered some of the most significant works.

Resumed contacts with China (Sung dynasty) resulted in the introduction to Japan of Zen Buddhism, which largely corresponds to the spirit of the Kamakura period. It rejects all external means to achieve salvation, which instead must be obtained by looking within. In art this attitude resulted in a drastic limitation of the means of expression, which on the one hand caused stagnation, but on the other

Kamakura

◄ Influence of Zen Buddhism

hand brought the expressive power of **calligraphy and wash painting** to a pinnacle of perfection. Picture scrolls and portraits enjoyed growing popularity; feudal society discovered itself, as it were. Creating accurate likenesses became the artistic goal; one noteworthy example is the portrait by Minamoto Yoritomo of Fujiwara Takanobu (1142–1205). **Picture scrolls, which attained a length of up to 25m/27yd**, were popular and had wide distribution. The subjects expanded to include biographies, stories of the origin of temples and shrines and heroic self-portrayals of the ruling military class (*Heiji-monogatari*); satirical works such as the animal sketch scroll *chojugiga* (in the Kozanji temple near Kyoto), which satirized life at court, were also produced.

Arts and crafts ► Arts and crafts flourished particularly. Damascus blades of outstanding quality were made; the tradition of lacquer work and textile art was carried on. Toshiro, who returned from China, produced significant pottery around 1230 and thus laid the foundation in Seto for the opening of around 200 kilns.

During the **Muromachi period** (1338–1600) the rediscovered courtly elegance of the Heian period combined with the influences of Zen Buddhism. The Zen aspect had

Muromachi a greatly reductive effect on design techniques and replaced the colourful Yamato-e with **monochrome ink and wash painting** in which beautifully sketched suggestions triumphed over fully detailed designs: the object was no longer the representation of the motif on hand, but its quintessence, which came to the artist in spontaneous enlightenment. Ink and wash paintings are limited to a few emphatic brushstrokes, whose vitality is underlined by shading. Two significant 14th-century painters are Mokuan and Kao. The imaginary portraits of the two Chinese monks Kanzan and Jittoku (T'ang dynasty, 618–907) area a popular motif. Resting in their enlightenment, they stand in contrast to the intellectual demands of other schools.

Landscape Landscape painting also flourished and achieved great mastery during the 14th and 15th centuries. The most noteworthy artists include Josetsu, one of the greatest teachers of the 14th century, Mincho (1352–1431) and Shubun (early 15th century). The paintings of the Chinese Sung and early Ming dynasties (10th–15th centuries) were the models that had the greatest influence on works by Noami (1397–1471), his son Geiami (1431–95) and his grandson Soami (1472–1525). The unequivocally most significant landscape painter of his time was **Sesshu Toyo** (1420–1506), who was able to draw on far richer sources during his stay in China in 1468–69. As no other he combined Chinese technique with a clearly Japanese choice of motifs and captured the timelessness of Japanese landscape; some examples are »ama-no-hashidate«, the »haboku« landscape now in the National Museum of Tokyo and not least the »Long Landscape Scroll«, which is reminiscent of the Sung dynasty models, but forms a contrast to the picture scrolls of the Heian and Kamakura periods. The tea ceremony (►p.95) became ever more popular; its complex refinement also had a fertilizing effect on Japanese pottery, painting and garden design. Zen's closeness to nature allowed a number of priests to become the best garden architects of the time.

◄ Tea ceremony and garden design

During the late Muromachi period there was a counter-trend to the art shaped by Zen Buddhism, which preferred the decorative element. The **Kano school**, founded by Kano Masanobu (1435–1530) and strengthened in its tradition by Kano Motonobu (1476–1559), was at the centre of the new trend. Art had become separated from its religious ties and was wholly permeated by secular subject matter. During the course of its existence, more than 300 years, the school was entrusted with the interior decoration of most of the newly built palaces and temples, whose landscape and animal pictures can still be seen today in many places, for example Kyoto. In the 15th century a renewed revival of Yamato-e took place outside of Kyoto.

◄ Counter-movement to Zen

During the second half of the 16th century the country was pacified by the shoguns Nobunaga, Hideyoshi and Ieyasu. This political renewal also brought about a reorientation of the culture, which had lost its courtly accent during the Momoyama period (1573–1603) and turned towards the bourgeoisie. The Kano school devoted itself to decorating the interiors of the massive castles being built at that time. It combined the linearity prevalent in ink and wash painting with the colourfulness of Yamato-e into an exuberant, magnificent form in which figures stand out from the gold-leaf background. Towards the end of the 16th century the stylistic merging of the Kano schools with the **Tosa school** in the tradition of Yamato-e was achieved. Kano Eitoku (1543–90) created the screen and sliding-doors décor of Azuchi Castle.

Momoyama

Nanban art narrates the arrival of Europeans in Japan. This genre marked a greater orientation towards the individual; gatherings of people diminished to smaller groups, and in the subsequent period were even further reduced to individual representations, which was an absolute innovation of this artistic genre.

◄ Nanban art

Crafts developed even further: lacquerwork and metalwork decorated the rooms and became symbols of wealth of the emerging bourgeoisie, particularly the merchants. Contacts with foreign countries broke through the isolation of the Japanese island realm and brought the technique of oil painting and new aspects of art and reflection on art into the country. Pottery received new impulses from the masters who came into the country as a result of the military campaigns in Korea; in Kyoto **Chojiro** (1515–92) made the first raku tea bowls in the preferred colours of black and red; new factories were set up (Seto-yaki, Oribe-yaki and Shinto-yaki).

◄ Crafts

Edo

During the Edo period (Tokugawa period; 1603–1868) bourgeois culture fully asserted itself. Cut off from all contacts to the outside world and hemmed in everywhere by the constraints of the strict class system, the bourgeoisie turned towards enjoyment of the arts and an elaborate, elegant lifestyle.

Painting ▶

From the end of the Momoyama period the Kano school was already displaying signs of stagnation, even of a waning of creative powers as a result of routine, and was undermined by the appearance of new styles and artistic techniques. Groupings such as the Korin (Rimpa) school, founded by Honami Koetsu (1558–1637) developed. One of its members was **Ogata Korin** (1658–1716), who brought a demanding, decorative style of painting with typically Japanese motifs to a zenith. His best-known works are the *Red and White Plum Trees* and *Irises* folding screens, to name but two. Another member of this group, which was located north of Kyoto, was the painter Tawaraya Sotatsu (c. 1600 to 1640), whose painting style also developed from the Yamato-e and the Tosa school, and from whom folding screens on the theme of the Tale of Genji and a Bugaku scene are still extant. Honami Koetsu created the most significant pottery and lacquer works; another master potter of this group was Ogata Kenzan (1663–1743). These artists' diversity gave new stimuli to the entire Japanese art world. In addition to Chinese influences, European elements also increasingly appeared; a change from the traditional parallel perspective to the use of the central perspective took place.

Nihon-bashi Bridge and Fuji-san: colour woodblock print by Ando Hiroshige (1830)

At the beginning of the 17th century the Bunjinga style developed, in which intellectuals and calligraphers created illustrations to literary works; their brilliance, not bound to any artistic tradition, was an outstanding achievement.

◄ Bunjinga

The technique of making woodblock prints, which up until this point had only been used for illustrations in books, became independent under the name of **ukiyo-e** (»pictures of the floating world«), which quickly became very widespread, and after the introduction of colour printing from several woodblocks (from 1765) developed further into **nishiki-e**. Motifs include the worlds of eroticism, theatre and places of entertainment as well as women. During the late period of ukiyo-e numerous landscape pictures of outstanding quality were produced by **Hokusai** (1760–1849) and Hiroshige (1797–1858).

◄ Woodblock prints

In the field of pottery glazed goods painted with enamel colours were developed. The discovery of kaolinite deposits around 1600 caused the production of porcelain to grow rapidly. Nabeshima porcelain was reserved for use by the aristocrats; cruder export goods, destined for Europe and elsewhere, were produced in Imari.

◄ Pottery

The Meiji period was Japan's first big step into modernity. The rapidly progress of opening to the West also affected artistic developments. Painting split into two directions: **Nipponga** represented traditional Japanese painting, while the painters of **Yoga** adopted western techniques and forms of expression, particularly oil painting. Members of the latter group, which particularly oriented itself to Parisian models, were Kuroda Kiyoteru (1866–1924), Ishida Ayusai (1891–1926) and Yasui Sotaro (1880–1935).

Meiji

Arts and Craftsmanship

The oldest free-formed pottery in Japan dates from the Neolithic Jomon period (7th millennium to 3rd century BC). It was characterized by the multifaceted rope patterns (Jomon) and was dark in colour. Between 300 BC and AD 300 the light Yayoi pottery wares of simple décor evolved. They were already made on potter's wheels and were followed by Sue pottery taken over from Korea. The thin-walled containers were dark and fired at high temperatures, they had a bare, linear style and remained in production until the Heian period (8th–12th centuries). The clay cylinders known as »haniwa«, which were later also shaped into figures and added to graves as funerary objects, are also from the time of Sue pottery. Chinese pottery was already appreciated during the Nara period (8th century), being imported or copied in the form of glazed pieces (such as the roof tiles of temples). This influence increased during the Kamakura period (12th–14th centuries). The kilns in Seto near Nagoya, with

Pottery

their glazed goods in yellowish and darker colours, were particularly popular with tea masters; in addition pots and vases were produced in olive-coloured and brown glazes (celadon). In this way the **Six Ancient Kilns** became the best-known: Echizen (Fukui Prefecture), Shigaraki (Shinga Prefecture), Tamba (Hyogo Prefecture), Bizen (Okayama Prefecture), Koseto and Tokoname (both Aichi Prefecture), where predominantly unglazed, robust utility objects were produced, which became very popular with the tea masters of later times. Only the light to dark brown and yellowish-green Koseto goods (»ko« means old, to distinguish them from newer seto goods) were glazed and were also given transparent ash glazes. The influence of Korean masters, which can already be seen in these wares, was a

Japanese pottery is a craft of long-standing tradition

defining factor towards the end of the 16th century. Kyushu was the first big centre of their work; the Karatsu-yaki and Satsuma-yaki wares with their simplicity and calm colours were typical. Hagi (Yamaguchi Prefecture) also gained increasingly in significance. The tea masters saw Zen Buddhist aesthetic characteristics in the shapes of the freely designed tea bowls made of rough clay. The spontaneous aspects of colour and shape, chance features, even mistakes that occurred during the firing process, were considered to be the highest degree of artistic design because these goods displayed naturalness. The **Raku tea bowls**, which derive from Chojiro (1515–92), were greatly valued with their thick glazes of black, brown and red-brown to red with lighter areas. They take their name from a seal with the inscription »raku« (joy) which Toyotomi Hideyoshi awarded Chojiro's son Jokei. Well-known raku masters were Ninsei (died 1678 or 1695) and Kenzan (1664–1743), the latter a member of an artists'

circle founded by Koetsu (1558–1637) which produced goods north of Kyoto in Takagamine. Koetsu himself created magnificent tea bowls; Ninsei, Kenzan's teacher, reached creative mastery with works using enamel paint on a glazed body, a method that became known in the 17th century. At the time pottery primarily stood in the service of the tea ceremony. In combination with the aesthetic of Zen

Buddhism, Japanese pottery attained the greatest significance, and is still equally worthy of this status today as a result of the efforts of such famous artists as Kawai Kanjiro (1890–1966), who worked in Kyoto, and Hamada Shoji (1884–1978), who made Mashiko into one of Japan's most popular pottery towns.

Some of the most important Japanese kilns (in alphabetical order) are:

Classical kilns

Bizen (Okayama Prefecture): unglazed goods in dark grey to reddish colours, which were given natural glazes through falling ash; wrapping the goods in rice straw produce irregular glaze strips. Initially manufactured as utility ware, Bizen-yaki was later discovered for the tea ceremony. One of the Six Ancient Kilns (12th–16th centuries).

Echizen (Fukui Prefecture): large, thick-walled stone containers in grey-brown to reddish-brown colours with greenish ash glazes. One of the Six Ancient Kilns (12th–17th centuries).

Hagi (Yamaguchi Prefecture): wares that have been in production continuously since the 17th century with thick craquelure glazes in milky to grey-yellow colours begun by the Korean Li Kyong.

Mino (Aichi Prefecture): the kilns of Mino have been used since the end of the Muromachi period (16th century) to fire white Shinto wares, Seto-yaki and green Oribe goods.

Seto (Aichi Prefecture): Japan's oldest pottery centre, which began producing glazed goods in the Kamakura period (12th–14th centuries). Dark brown to black glazes were produced from the 16th century, craquelured yellowish glazes (Ki Seto) and a number of other varieties were added later. Today Seto is Japan's largest pottery centre and the name Seto-mono (Seto ware) became synonymous for ceramic goods in general. One of the Six Ancient Kilns.

Shigaraki (Shiga Prefecture): transparent yellowish-grey to grey-green ash glaze with grey-brown to dark brown colour with light graining, in production since the Kamakura period (12th–14th century), one of the Six Ancient Kilns, the preferred pottery of the tea masters during the 16th century.

Shinto (Aichi Prefecture): pottery in production since the 16th century for the tea ceremony, yellowish to light red colours with grey-white glazes; produced to this day in continuing tradition. The name goes back to the great tea master Shinto Soshui (16th–17th century).

Takatori (Fukuoka Prefecture): grey-brown body with a sprinkled glaze in brown to red-brown colours. This pottery was largely influenced by the tea master Kobori Enshu (1579–1647).

Tamba (Hyogo Prefecture): long firing times produced dark brown to red-brown colours with a thick ash glaze. Since the 16th century one of the Six Ancient Kilns; now in production in Tachikui near Sasayama.

Tokoname (Aichi Prefecture): brown body with green natural glazes. After the end of the 16th century only a small production output, from the 19th century architectural ceramics. Also one of the Six Ancient Kilns.

Metal-working

Bronze casting and metal craft ▶

The earliest evidence of metal-working in Japan dates back to the Yayoi period (around 300 BC to AD 300). These are longish bells (dotaku), jewellery and cult objects made of bronze or iron. With Buddhism, new and finer techniques made their way to Japan from the mainland during the 8th century, which led to the very highest standards, particularly in bronze casting. Jewellery, cult objects, metal fittings, containers and sculptures were produced by different methods under the constant influence of Chinese and Korean teachers. The most outstanding example of bronze casting during that period is the Shaka triad by Tori-busshi in the Horyu-ji (from 623). The Nara period (8th century), under the influence of the Chinese T'ang dynasty, produced large-scale realistic cast bronze sculptures, of which the Great Buddha in the Todai-ji (752) is particularly noteworthy. It was only after 800 that metal-working was able to break loose from mainland models and find its own forms. With the flourishing of wood sculpture, the technique of bronze casting faded into the background. Metal craft concentrated more and more on the production of utility objects, jewellery and ornaments made of more precious metals, which already bore the typical natural décor of Japanese embossing.

Swords ▶

During the turbulent Kamakura period (12th–14th centuries) the craft of producing swords and weapons gained paramount importance. Its finest achievements date from the early 14th century. While the single or double-edged sword with a straight blade (tsurugi) used on the mainland was still in general use in Japan up until the 9th century, the beginning of the 10th century saw the introduction of a single-edged sword with a slightly curved blade (nihonto), which was used just in Japan. Production followed the Damascus principle, meaning that different layers of metal were welded one on top of the other, then folded or twisted and hammered. As in other cultures, the armourers also enjoyed extremely high prestige in Japan; their work was accompanied by cult rituals. Swords can be seen in a number of Japanese historical museums, and the **Sword Museum in Tokyo** probably contains the best collection in the world.

Textile working

The use of the loom is already documented in the Yayoi period (3rd century BC to 3rd century AD). It is probably also during this period that Japan saw the beginning of **silkworm breeding**. Other weaving materials besides silk included hemp, nettle and different bast fibres. A large number of well-developed weaving techniques already existed during the Nara period (8th century), which had all been adopted from China and Korea: the most widespread textiles were twill, damask, simple brocade and gauze. The economic growth that came with the shogunate in the 13th century brought more refined weaving techniques to Japan from the mainland, such as silver and gold brocades, as well as satin. Cotton only began to be processed in the 15th century.

In addition to weaving, dyeing was also always of great significance. Since the cut of the traditional dress hardly changed at all over the centuries, developments in fashion and style mainly expressed themselves through colour and patterns. Three basic dyeing procedures which are still used in the textile industry today were already well-developed in the 8th century. They are batik, dyeing folded fabrics with templates, and tie-dying, which creates attractive, random patterns. Since the 13th century the combination of different dyeing techniques and embroidery, particularly with gold and silver thread or application of gold and silver leaf, has produced magnificent effects.

◄ Dyeing

Japan's opening during the Meiji era (19th century) brought in industrial methods which quickly displaced the old techniques. However, they still have their place in crafts and are also used in the manufacture of highly precious cloths for ladies' silk kimonos, which are still sought after and popular for festive occasions, although they are very expensive.

At the centre of the weaving industry is the **Nishijin weaving district in Kyoto**, which has a distinguished tradition. Today both natural and synthetic fibres are processed, new weaving techniques developed and old, lost methods revived here. The leading dye centres are Kyoto and Kanazawa, as well as the Miyagi and Yamagata prefectures and Tokyo. Northern Japan, particularly Aomori, is known for its geometric embroidery on dark backgrounds. On Hokkaido, particularly around Sapporo and in the Ainu villages of Chikabumi and Shiraoi, cloths are still produced with traditional Ainu appliqués.

◄ Textile centres

A good overview of the craft of cloth-making in Japan is given by the **Yokohama Silk Museum** and the **Nishijin textile centre in Kyoto**.

Lacquerware, which was originally produced on the Asian mainland, found its way to the Japanese islands in its simplest form even in prehistoric times. The sap of the **lacquer tree** (Rhus verniciflua), which is resistant to acids, heat and moisture when dried, was used to coat utility objects to protect them, and it was recognized very early on that the addition of natural pigments produced a simple pattern.

Lacquerware

Highly developed lacquer techniques came to Japan from China during the 6th century with Buddhism, which were subsequently improved upon. Soon Japanese lacquer masters were producing exquisite works, superior to the Chinese goods in craftsmanship and artistry. Tins, boxes, small pieces of furniture, plates and dishes, cult objects, jewellery, sculptures and other things made of wood, bamboo, leather, metal, ceramic, cloth and even paper were coated with lacquer for both decoration and protection. Lacquer art achieved its zenith at the end of the 15th century. Japan's opening during the mid-19th century allowed Japanese lacquerware to become world famous; young lacquer artists were soon working in Europe and America, where they taught their skills. Today the most outstanding masters, who have the honorary title of »Living Human Treasure« (literally »Bearer of Intangible Cultural Heritage«) teach and work at art academies and specialist workshops.

Processing techniques ▶ Japanese lacquer art uses three different processing techniques, all of which are utilized in several variations: the two-dimensional technique, inlaid lacquer and carved lacquers.

The **makie gold lacquer techniques** (»makie« means »sprinkle painting«), which are among the two-dimensional techniques, are the most significant developed independently in Japan; by the Heian period (8th–12th century) they had already matured to the highest perfection in terms of craftsmanship and artistry. The patterns of the **togidashi** are created by sprinkling gold and silver powder on a wet lacquer surface, which is then covered by several more black lacquer coats after drying. The subsequent burnishing of the surface with charcoal gradually allows the gold powder pattern to appear in unsurpassed delicacy. The **hiramakie** technique involves sprinkling the decoration directly onto the lacquer surface. **Takamakie** is a sprinkle picture technique with a raised image, while the **okibirame** technique replaces the metal powder with metal flakes.

Lacquer painting ▶ Lacquer painting was particularly widespread during the 7th century. Negoro-nuri is a two-dimensional technique in which a red surface layer is burnished to such an extent that the black lacquer base appears in places. It was already in use during the Muromachi period and is still highly popular today.

Inlay technique ▶ The first evidence of inlaid lacquers dates back to the Nara period (8th century). In Japan they are often associated with makie techniques. Initially mother-of-pearl inlays were preferred, later also gold and silver foils, corals, ivory and various semi-precious stones.

Carved lacquer ▶ Carved lacquer works (tsui-shu) only started being produced in the 15th century in imitation of Chinese lacquerwares and could hardly be distinguished from them. An independent Japanese carved lacquer style only developed during the 17th century. Besides the very elaborately worked real carved lacquers, where thick layers of lacquer are sculpted, the simpler kamakura-bori technique developed early on; here wood that had already been carved was covered with lacquer.

All lacquerware gets its shine from having its surface polished, which is an elaborate and time-consuming process. This production method, which requires so much effort and care, is the reason why lacquerware has been precious in all ages, even surpassing porcelain in value. Today lacquer art is still important in the old production centres of Tokyo, Kyoto and Kanazawa; further traditional workshops can be found in Takamatsu and Nagoya. Simpler goods for household use are primarily produced in the prefectures of Fukushima, Ishikawa, Toyama and Wakayama.

◀ Centres of lacquer art

Netsuke (»ne« means »root«; »tsuke« means »to attach«), which appeared during the 15th century and became extremely popular in the 17th century, are **fasteners** that are artistically formed into figures, animals, plants and different objects for pouches and bags in which all sorts of everyday objects such as money, medicine or tobacco were carried. The knobs have one or two holes for the pouch cords and when pushed through under the belt they prevent the pouches from slipping. On the one hand the shape of a netsuke has to be able to fulfil this function. On the other it must also fit well in the hand and may not have points or sharp edges. Originally the miniature sculptures were carved from roots, but later ivory, horn, bamboo, nutshells, lacquer, ceramics, porcelain, semi-precious gems and metal were also used more and more. The choice of motifs was completely unrestricted and drew upon all the practical areas of life, mythology, religion, legend and poetry or came from the artist's imagination. Today netsuke are popular collector's items.

Netsuke

Netsuke from the Edo period in the shape of a wasps' nest

Paper and its various manufacturing techniques presumably first came to Japan from China via Korea in the 7th century AD. Here paper was produced in great variety and had very different uses, from delicate paper dolls, to colourful boxes, printed wallets, paper-covered dividing walls and sliding doors, artistic calligraphy and origami, those little marvels of the art of paper folding. Initially reserved for courtly circles, paper and paper art finally also found widespread distribution amongst the bourgeoisie during the Edo period (from the mid-17th century).

Paper

Japanese paper is a firm paper with long fibres made from the bast of the paper-mulberry plant (Broussonetia papyrifera); rice paper, a very delicate, but surprisingly firm and durable material, is produced

◀ Japanese paper

from the white pith of the rice-paper plant (Tetrapanax papyrifera) of the aralia family. The fine mitsumata paper on the other hand is obtained from the rind of the thymelaeaceae plant Edgeworthia chrysantha.

The **Paper Museum in Tokyo**, well worth a visit, presents not just all the different papers and prints, but also the tools and equipment used in their production.

Packaging One Japanese craft deserving attention is the art of packaging (**psutsumi**), which pays homage to the need for harmony. The idea, which has a long tradition, is based on the notion that »pure« things should not be openly presented, but rather be attractively enveloped. Originally packaging was mainly used for the transport and storage of food. The sense of beauty as an aesthetic demand joined with this practical aspect, and over time a real art form emerged. It still lives on today, particularly when presents are being given.

Materials ▶ The preferred natural materials used for packaging since time immemorial are rice straw, bamboo and cedar wood. Since rice is one of Japan's staple foods, rice straw is in plentiful supply; at the same time it is robust and elastic and is a good material for basketry and lacing. Rice straw is used to bind breathable containers for eggs or rice balls; rice-wine containers are wrapped in rice-straw mats. The fast-growing bamboo plant, which symbolizes strength and fertility, provides useful covers and jackets for many different foods; bamboo grass is an important raw material for basket-making. Little wooden boxes of many different shapes are used, for example, to conserve fish or rice under artistically bound lids.

The packaging serves not only conservation purposes; it can also give food flavour: rice cakes are wrapped in cherry leaves in spring, in oak leaves in early summer and in camellia leaves in winter; bamboo, reed and wild-rice leaves in turn provide completely different nuances of taste.

Garden design Japanese gardens, with their atmosphere of calm, their harmony and their complexity in spite of their small size, exert an extraordinary appeal on the beholder. Unlike Western gardens and parks, Japanese parks and gardens leave the gardener's hand hidden; the degree of perfection lies in the **apparent fortuitousness**, in the natural manner with which the totality of nature is expressed.

Gardens of the Nara period ▶ Shaped by the Chinese example, wonderful gardens were already being planted during the Nara period (8th century), when pond islands were connected with the banks and with each other through small arched bridges. During the subsequent Heian period (8th–12th centuries) gardens developed as an extension to the generous, elegant shinden-zukuri architectural style. The court nobility set up colourful pleasure gardens with lakes, waterfalls, artificial islands and Chinese-style pavilions. These extended private parks were popular for walks and boat trips and were created without religious and symbolic

Please read from back to front!

PICTURE STORIES

Japanese comics, manga, have long had a large following in Europe. However, these comics have a much higher standing in Japan than they do here: manga represent 38% of Japanese printed matter!

Statistically speaking every Japanese person buys 15 manga a year. There are manga **for every taste** and every demographic: manga for boys, girls, women, men, senior citizens, homosexuals, history fans, fantasy, horror or sci-fi enthusiasts and many more. There are even manga written by fans, unofficial sequels to popular series called Dojinshi, and non-fictional mangas with an educational intent, for example about the economy or religion.

A distinction is made between comic magazines (mangazasshi), published weekly or monthly, and paperbacks, in which several chapters of a popular series appear as an omnibus edition (tanko-bon). Japan's biggest **manga magazines** are Shonen Sunday (since 1959) and Shonen Jump (since 1968), which target an adolescent readership.

From Brush to Print

The beginnings of these »spontaneous images«, a title the woodblock-print artist Hokusai was the first to use for one of his sketch books, go far back. Precursors could already be seen in **caricatures** in temples dating from the 7th century. In the 12th century Abbot Toba Sojo drew funny images about life in a monastery. His way of representing amusing scenes in a single long picture scroll became popular during the Edo period and was thus called Toba-e (Toba image). The same period also saw the development of kibyoshi, which already narrated a continuous story consisting of individual images and text, and which had a satirical content.

With Japan's opening to the west the first humorous depictions in the form of a comic strip addressing politics and certain customs started appearing in newspapers and magazines at the end of the 19th century. Brushes were soon replaced by pencils, speech bubbles as used by the Americans, who were the authoritative voice on comics, were adopted, and simpler printing techniques were developed. All of these facts led to the mass

distribution of comics, for which the name manga asserted itself at the beginning of the 20th century.

Modern Manga

Tezuka Osamu (1928–89) is considered the founding father of the modern manga; he created the basis for the current manga style, such as the extremely large, round children's eyes or the enlarged details so characteristic of mangas. Some of the series he wrote include *Kimba the White Lion* (1950) and *Astro Boy* (1952), a story about a small robot boy called Tetsuwan Atomu. The latter was the first comic series aired on Japanese television. Tezuka also created the first manga for girls: *Ribon no kishi* (1953; *Princess Knight*) about a princess, who, disguised as a knight, has to defend her claim to the throne. His Japanese fans gave Tezuka the honorary title of »god of manga« for his achievements.

One manga character from the 1960s is as famous in Japan as Micky Mouse and Donald Duck: the blue robotic cat **Doraemon**, who travels into the past in order to save a child from the financial ruin awaiting it in the future. It was conceived in 1969 by Fujiko Fujio, the pen name of a duo consisting of Motoo Abiko and Fujimoto Hiroshi.

Moving Images

Many manga are made into animated films (**anime**) and often the artists creating the manga and anime films are the same. Airing a manga as a television series causes the characters to become better known and thus leads to the production of related paraphernalia such as toys, Gameboys and video games, manga cards and such like. Manga fans sometimes even go so far as to style themselves like their favourite characters and go to »**Cosplays**« (from costume plays) in these outfits, where a colourful parade of manga and anime characters takes place.

Fantasy Realms

The **subjects** addressed by manga are many and the differences in quality can be immense. Those series that have a heroine or hero with magical powers who is fighting for the good are highly popular amongst young people. The *Sailor Moon* series by

Very popular amongst the young people of Japan: manga lookalike contests

Takeuchi Naoko, for example, fits this pattern. It was broadcast in an English version and has been highly popular in the West. The cases of *Dragon Ball* by Toriyama Akria or *Angel Sanctuary* by Yuki Kaori are similar. They deal with the impending apocalypse or earth ruled by androids; the heroes set of on a quest in search of magic balls or wondrous crystals; extra terrestrials or angels contact them... there are no limits in these fantasy worlds. When creating manga, the artists (manga-ka) often make use of **old myths** from Japan or other places around the world and avail themselves of Japanese symbols, whose meaning quite often escapes Western readers. A lot of it is pure entertainment, some of it fine art.

One manga, *Vagabond* by Inoue Takehiko, was awarded the Tezuka Osuma Cultural Prize in 2002 and also appeals to adults. It is based on the story of Miyamoto Musashi, the legendary 17th-century sword fighter. Those who prefer a more humorous tone can try the pirate story *One Piece* by Oda Eiichiro (from 1997) which is filled with gags. Anyone enjoying a bit of a mystery will like *Case Closed*, a story about detective Conan who was transformed into a little boy when his enemies poisoned him. One of the most influential manga series in Western countries is *Akira* by Otomo Katsuhiro (film 1988, original 1982–1990), a science fiction drama set in neo-Tokyo in 2019.

Japanese manga are read from top to bottom and from right to left, but in the West some publications »flip« the order of scenes to give readers the more familiar left-to-right direction.

In Search of Manga

Japanese manga have become so successful that some people even travel to Japan as manga tourists: there are already several **manga museums** in various cities (including one dedicated to Tezuka Osamu in his birth town Takarazuka and another one that opened in Kyoto in 2007). The Tokyo district of Nerima is not just home to many studios, but also to many manga-ka, and in the district of Akihabara an Anime Center was opened in 2006 (www.animecenter.jp). There are countless manga cafés, where visitors can meet like-minded people, read manga and surf the internet.

One place that almost enjoys cult status is the comic shop **Mandaroke** in Tokyo (Shibuya, Utagawa-cho 31-2, Beam Building, BF 2, tel. 03/3477-0777, www.mandaroke.co.jp, open daily noon–8pm), with branches in other districts of Tokyo as well as Nagoya, Osaka and Fukuoka.

meaning. In the 11th century garden design reached another perfection, which can still be seen in outlines in the garden of the Byodoin temple in Uji near Kyoto; other examples from this period are the gardens of the Motsuji temple (Iwate Prefecture) as well as the garden of the Joruri-ji temple in Kyoto.

Zen gardens ▶ Zen Buddhism put its emphasis elsewhere. Its strong influence on the life of the Kamakura period (12th–14th centuries) soon spilled over into garden architecture and replaced courtly elegance with **austerity and simplicity**. A garden had so far been used mainly for walks, games and edification. Now it became an artistic arrangement, whose the most important principle was symbolism, and as a result was no longer designed to be accessed, but to be viewed from the veranda. Its formal principles predominantly came from the monochrome landscape painting of the Chinese Sung dynasty. The main goal of Zen landscape gardeners was to create the appearance of infinite space in a limited area. In order to produce this appearance of infinity they used optical illusions that suggested larger distances. The natural perspective was amplified by using large rocks with austere forms and plants with big, light leaves in the foreground, while the background was often fitted with small, smooth stones and small-leaved, dark and often miniature trees. Paths and watercourses became narrower further away, their meandering course giving the illusion of greater length and their end disappearing behind rocks and bushes so that they appeared to continue. The outer walls were made of dark, natural material or covered by bushes; every trace of human intervention was carefully disguised. This created the impression of untouched nature; on the other hand the gardens were composed in such a way that they appeared to beholders like a painting made of natural components.

The **most famous landscape gardens in the Zen style** are to be found in Kyoto: they are the gardens of the Saiho-ji (around 1339) and the Tenruy-ji (around 1343), designed by the Zen master Muso during the rule of Takauji; the Golden Pavilion Temple Garden (1397), planted by shogun Yoshimitsu; and the garden of the Silver Pavilion (1484), which was created under the aegis of Yoshimasa.

Stone gardens ▶ While reality and abstract design come together in a positively confusing way in landscape gardens, **pure abstraction** was achieved in the stone gardens (kare sansui). These are dry gardens without water and vegetation, their compositions consisting solely of sand and stone. Nevertheless these gardens can depict landscapes in very small spaces, where the carefully raked sand represents the surface of rivers or seas with stones appearing to be rocky islands. Their bare simplicity means they are closest to the Zen teachings in their artistic expression; at the same time many of them can be seen as the most perfect spatial representation of ink and wash landscapes from the Sung dynasty, which so lastingly influenced the Zen arts. The best examples of this type of garden can also be found in Kyoto (e.g. Ryoanji).

Garden of Enkakuji temple in Kamakura

The classical simplicity of the stone garden was carried into the tea gardens (roji) of the Momoyama period (16th century), where a bare appearance was however abandoned and nature seemed to live in unaltered, though compressed into a small space. The deliberate naturalness of plants left to grow unhindered was expressed in a different way by the tea houses that are part of the roji. Still, the Momoyama period revelled in realistic joie de vivre, which displaced the mystical Zen gardens, preferring the grandeur and diversity of expansive promenade gardens. A good example of such a garden is that of Nijo Palace in Kyoto.

◄ Tea gardens

The dawn of the Edo period at the beginning of the 17th century brought hardly any new stylistic elements; nevertheless some wonderful gardens were created at the beginning of this era, such as those belonging to the Katsura Imperial Villa and the Nanzenji temple in Kyoto. An increase in size, such as in the gardens of Korakuen (Okayama) and Rikugien of Tokyo, led, on the one hand, to the creation of attractive promenade gardens, but in some ways also foreshadowed the fading of this typically Japanese art form, which reached the end of its development even before the beginning of the modern age.

◄ Gardens of the Edo period

The art of flower arranging has struck deep roots in Japanese cultural life as a means of aesthetic expression. Originally introduced

Ikebana

Flower arranging as an art form – ikebana arrangement in a fitting setting

from China as floral decoration to be placed in front of Buddhist statues, flower arranging evolved into an independent art form as a result of dissociation from its religious purpose.

Courtly circles already enjoyed flower arranging competitions (hana-awase) during the Heian period (8th–12th centuries); during the Muromachi period (14th–16th centuries) larger sectors of the population began to enjoy this art, which, with the later inclusion of a vase and a bowl into the overall picture, gained even greater expressiveness.

The linear structure of an arrangement, which philosophically symbolizes the trinity of heaven, humanity and the earth, attested from early on to the typically Japanese orientation towards naturalism. This can be seen in the way the branches and flowers used are left in their natural state. Ikebana complemented the tea ceremony, which was particularly popular during the 15th and 16th centuries; leading masters of later periods, however, largely separated it from this function and developed it further. It reached its peak of popularity during the Edo period (17th–19th centuries) and – paving the way for today's schools – new techniques emerged. The effect of the arrangements placed in the decorative alcoves (tokonoma) were varied and increased by the use of new materials and receptacles. Today different schools continue to cultivate old traditions and also developing new create ideas. Amongst the best-known are the Ohara, Sogetsu, Ikenobo, Misho and Keikei schools.

The art of the bonsai, the »potted tree«, now famous and appreciated throughout the world, was **probably of Chinese origin**, but there is evidence that this art existed in Japan from the 11th century onwards. Zen Buddhism had a fundamental impact on it. The seeds or shoots of particularly suitable plants such as junipers, pines, spruces, cryptomerias and several species of maple, to name a few, are raised into miniature trees with a height of between 20cm/8in and 60cm/24in by pruning shoots and roots, by forming the branches with wires and by adding small, carefully judged doses of nutrients to just a small amount of soil. Cut areas have to be arranged in such a way that scars heal completely and remain wholly invisible. Wires are removed after a year to prevent them from cutting into the bark. Under the gentle hand of a grower,

Bonsai

> **?** **DID YOU KNOW ...?**
>
> ■ »Bonsai« is the art of depicting three elements in miniature form: living nature is represented by a tree; a stone, and fine gravel as a symbol for water, typify the natural elements; and human beings are represented in the form of their work, a bowl. Only the harmony between these three elements can make a successful bonsai.

the bonsai, planted in a shallow bowl, on a piece of bark or on a stone slab, is made into an artwork that recreates a natural situation in perfect harmony with its surroundings. Over decades the trees develop into windblown, gnarled and deformed structures as well as into light copses and delicate miniature bushes bearing flowers and fruit, changing their appearance from season to season just like their fully-grown counterparts. Bonsai trees can become several hundred years old. They are grown by many Japanese families and handed down through the generations. The **main growing centres** are Omiya (near Tokyo), Kurume, Nagoya and Takamatsu (Kinashi). Bonsai trees are traded like antiques; but in addition to their age the overall aesthetic appearance also contributes to the high price.

Architecture

Japanese architecture is characterized in its basic elements by simplicity, functionality and harmony with the surrounding environment. Its consistent observance of proportions related to the use of the building is a feature not found in the West until the early 20th century. Aside from the city architecture of recent times, single-storey ground-level homes, often combined with a clear division into the individual living areas, constitute by far the most prevalent type of buildings. The use of screens and movable walls makes rooms very variable, and the **openness of the architecture** results in an interplay between the exterior and the interior in a way unimaginable in more solid styles of construction. Wood has always been the preferred

Simple, functional, harmonious

building material in this forested country; its structure as an aesthetic component is an essential part of the overall impression. Practical considerations favour this material because the country is located in a very active earthquake zone where a building made of wood, which has elasticity, provides significantly greater protection than a rigid stone building. As with the visual arts, Japanese architecture also shows signs of Chinese influence, which became a determining element during the 7th and 8th centuries and provided new impulses in the 13th century that were later completely assimilated, leading to the independent development of future architectural styles.

Kofun period The oldest examples of native architecture come from the haniwa of the Kofun period (3rd–7th centuries), terra cotta burial objects depicting single-storey and two-storey houses with the characteristic gable roofs. Archaic building styles, influenced by the stilt houses of the south Pacific, had almost no differences between the architecture of homes, shrines and palaces. Thus **Japan's oldest architectural style**, taisha-zukuri, which can still be seen in the Shinto shrines of Izumo-taisha (Izumo) and Sumiyoshi (Osaka), can also be regarded as the style used for other structures of this period. Its main characteristics are a projecting pitched roof, an entrance opening at the gable wall, four corner pillars, a square floor plan and one central pillar.

taisha-zukuri ►

Shimmei-zukuri ► This style continued to develop and became the shimmei-zukuri style, still extant in the Naiku and Geku buildings of the Ise shrine (both originally erected in different places). The entrance was moved to the side with the eaves, while the crossed gable rafters (chigi) and the log-shaped crossbars on the gables to secure the thatched roofs became prominent features. Simplicity and consistently straight lines have remained characteristic of Shinto architecture to this day; the very old element known as torii, the entrance gate to the shrine, is also part of this architectural style, but its origin and function are still not known for certain.

Asuka period At the beginning of the Asuka period (6th–7th centuries) Buddhism came to Japan during the rule of Empress Suiko; it confronted the country with an unfamiliarly complex architecture developed in an advanced culture and civilization. The rigid form was replaced by soft lines and for the first time decorative elements were used. At the centre of Buddhist religious structures, which are fundamentally different from the profane buildings and the Shinto shrines which closely resemble the latter, is the pagoda (to), actually a reliquary. One such was integrated into the Shintennoji temple in Osaka as a central part of the structure in 588. Its architecture is determined by **strict symbolism**: the central pillar represents the world's axis, the five storeys the Chinese elements (fire, water, air, earth and empty space), the summit (sorinto) the nine heavenly spheres. The Horyuji temple near Nara has the traditional floor plan: the pagoda is at the

Artistic roof construction at Ise shrine

centre, next to it the Golden Hall (kondo), both enclosed by a gallery surrounding the interior courtyard into which the lecture hall (kodo), flanked by the library (kyozo) and the bell tower (shoro), is integrated. The priests' homes, the temple office and treasury are all located outside the central courtyard.

The new architectural style brought with it a change from thatched ◀ Characteristics
roofs to shingle roofs; the beams became more differentiated and the wood constructions were given decorative elements. The walls were plastered with clay and painted red. The great emphasis on symmetry is expressed in the introduction of a second pagoda, seen in its original form in the Yakushiji temple (only one pagoda still survives), which was built in Asuka in 680 and later moved to Nara. This three-storey pagoda has the appearance of being a six-storey building as a result of decorative mezzanine storeys (mokoshi), making it unique. The pagodas best exemplifying the 8th century, such as those in the Taimadera temple, are simple three-storey constructions.

During the Nara period (8th century) temple complexes increased in **Nara period**
size; the buildings were elevated on stone pedestals. Chinese influence caused the roofs to become more curved; hipped roofs were preferred, often fitted with a single-pitch roof below that had decorative elements (shibi) at the ends. The most significant temple complexes of the capital of this time are the Kofukuji temple (710) and the **Todaiji temple** (745–752). The latter is a classic example of that

period: here the Daibutsuden, the largest temple hall ever built in Japan, despite the smaller reconstruction of 1708 is still **the most extensive wooden structure in the world**.

◀ Chinese influence ▶ During this period the influences of the early Chinese T'ang dynasty can be seen; they are particularly clear in a golden hall supported by classical rows of columns in the Toshodaiji temple. In the lecture hall of the same temple, once a part of the imperial palace, is the only example of 8th-century feudal architecture with the typical hipped roof (irimoya) of the Todaiji temple, as well as the octagonal Yumedono Hall of the Horyuji temple, a unique construction in the style of a Chinese pavilion.

Heian period During the Heian period (8th–12th centuries) the symmetrical form of the temple complexes was lost. The emerging Buddhist Tendai and Shingon schools preferred **mountain sites**; religious buildings had to adapt to the specific topographic conditions. The only surviving buildings of the esoteric Buddhism of that time are the five-storey pagoda built in 824 and the Golden Hall of the Muroji temple in Yamato. Both schools introduced a spatial separation between monks and laity, which made an additional veranda necessary; this veranda became important in its own right in the 11th century as a worship hall (raido).

Shinto shrines ▶ Even Shinto shrine architecture took on Buddhist elements, for example in the loosening of the previously strict linearity and the painting of the wooden structure. Corridors and two-storey torii are doubtless of Buddhist origin, for example at the Kasuga shrine in Nara and the Usa shrine on Kyushu.

Residential buildings ▶ Far less shaped by Chinese influences, residential buildings remained largely stuck in the simplicity of the national Shinden-zukuri style. Halls of different sizes built on stilts were connected by galleries; the markedly austere exterior line was broken by shifting the parts of the building, which gave the architecture its characteristic lightness. Artistic finery and pleasure in the decor come out in the interior architecture.

Kamakura period The Kamakura period (12th–14th centuries) brought **three new styles** of military strictness and vehemence. On the one hand the native wa-yo building style was introduced, on the other the protruding tenjihu-yo style, which is of Indian origin according to its name but actually came from southern China. It is represented in the southern gate (nandaimon) built in 1195 of the Todaiji temple. This style, with its gravity, stands in stark contrast to the elegant, light buildings of the Heinan period and did not manage to establish itself. The equally vehement kara-yo style (Chinese style), which came to Japan with Zen Buddhism, determined the architecture of this persuasion from that time on. It can be seen in the Kenchoji temple (Kamakura) built in 1253, the Nanzenji temple of 1293 and the Daitokuji temple of 1319 (both in Kyoto), as well as in the relic hall of the Engakuji temple (Kamakura; 1285).

The Chinese influence on Heian-period architecture can be seen here at Byodo-in temple

Palace and residential architecture during the Heian period were defined by the shinden-zukuri style, which hardly changed during the Kamakura period but, under pressure of defence requirements, became the buke-zukuri style (»warrior dwelling«) on a tighter floor plan.

Until the early Muromachi period (from the 14th century) Zen Buddhism acted as the source of a new aesthetic and promoted the further development of the kara-yo style, which increasingly began to make use of Japanese style elements and culminated in a perfect synthesis between the majestic style of Chinese origin and the light grace of the national Japanese style in the **Kinkakuji temple** in Kyoto, built

Muromachi period

in 1397. Zen architecture also had an impact on Shinto, whose shrine complexes were extended to several buildings.

The secular buke-zukuri architecture, in style of the abbots' houses, transformed into shoin-zukuri, which gets its name from the window bay of the study (shoin). The floor of these buildings is covered in straw mats (**tatami**); the tokonoma alcove for the scroll painting had a purely decorative purpose. This style was the basis of classical residential architecture, whose main characteristics included wood as a building material, movable walls (fusama) and sliding doors leading out to the garden (shoji). A forerunner of this building style that was influenced by great tea masters and intent on simplicity is the Togu-do hall in the Ginkakuji temple built by Shoku in 1483, which despite later changes provides a comprehensive impression of that style.

Momoyama period

During the Momoyama period (16th–17th centuries) shoin-zukuri reached perfection and found its climax in the Katsura Imperial Villa (early 17th century) near Kyoto, in the Kohoan of the Daitokuji temple and in the Hiankaku of the Nishi-honganji temple (both in Kyoto), which are distinguished by their **harmonious austerity**. This simplicity was taken to extremes in the tea houses (Chashitsu, Sukiya), which turned towards ancient Japanese forms and building materials. At the same time the indigenous Japanese style gained a **rich interior décor**; functionality was ornamentally enriched, walls and doors were magnificently painted and metal joints formed into decorative fittings.

Castles and shrines ▶

At the centre of the building activity stood the impressive castles, which were gradually losing their military character and becoming prestigious princely buildings with high main towers (tenshukaku) and numerous curved decorative gables. The best examples are **Himeji Castle** (late 16th century), Kumamoto Castle (around 1600) and Nagoya Castle (1610). Nijo Palace, built in 1603 with lavish architectural ornamentation, is a real highlight. The Gongen style shrines of the Momoyama period are similarly magnificent. They took over the architectural canon of Chinese Buddhism, which divided the shrine into a worship hall, an intermediate building and a sanctum. This style is also represented by the **Toshogu shrine**, built by the Tokugawa shoguns as a mausoleum during the Edo period (from the 17th century); it is lavishly decorated with carvings, gold decor and colourful paintings.

Modern times

From 1868 Japanese architecture experienced a change with the dawn of the modern times, during which the country opened up to western influences. English Gothic brick architecture was imitated for example. Only later was there a re-orientation towards the country's traditional forms. Industrial architecture and civil engineering followed international customs and patterns in their utilitarianism. During the 1920s modern architecture developed in Japan, too, in clear relation to contemporary modernization efforts in Europe by the Bauhaus, Le Corbusier and others. Architects worth mentioning are Horiguchi Sutemi; Yoshida Tetsuro, who successfully connected to international architecture; Bauhaus-educated Maekawa Kunio; and Sakakura Junzo, who worked sporadically in Le Corbusier's studio and whose designs included the Japanese pavilion of the Paris World Fair of 1937. Best-known in the West are **Tange Kenzo and Ando Tadao**, who have designed excellent works not just in Japan (Tange Kenzo: Hiroshima Peace Memorial Museum, 1946–56; Tokyo Metropolitan Government Building, 1988–91; Ando Tadao: Naoshima Contemporary Art Museum, 1989–92, 1997) but also around the world (Tange Kenzo: reconstruction of Skopje, Yugoslavia, 1965; Ando Tadao: Benetton factory in Treviso, 1991–93). From 1960 onwards the Metabolist movement primarily devoted itself to town planning and tended towards futuristic and utopian designs. **Isozaki Arata** built a huge, self-supporting sports arena for the Olympic games in Barcelona in 1992. For EXPO 2000 in Hanover a self-supporting hall made of paper material was built. This tendency towards futurism has continued with the huge new main station in Kyoto and the Umeda Sky Building in Osaka by Hiroshi Hara.

The Catholic St Mary's Cathedral in Tokyo was designed by the famous architect Tange Kenzo

Theatre

Japan's traditional forms of theatre that still survive today have their roots in the **ritual dances of prehistory**; they developed in close connection with people's lives and their needs. The invocation of hunting success, obeisance to the sun goddess Amaterasu, who gives light and life, sacrifices and glorification of the stag, both in its role as hunters' prey and as the gods' messenger, and thanksgiving for rich catch of fish are all contents of the dances performed by priests and shamans, all with their own characters in different parts of the country; these dances still exist in fragmentary form in a number of folk dances and courtly dances as well as in classical theatre.

Kagura   The historical works *Kojiki* (712) and *Nihon-shoki* (*Nihongi*, 720) give accounts of expression through dance, which originated in mythology. According to them the storm god Susanoo-no-mikoto became so angry with his sister Amaterasu-omikami that she withdrew to a cave, causing light to disappear from the world. It was only the goddess Ama No Uzume who managed to entice the sun goddess back out by dancing in front of the cave, thus bringing sunlight back to the world of man. While this legend of the cave is the origin of kagura, the oldest Japanese ritual dance, mime dances (sato-kagura) were developed to be performed in Shinto shrines: the sequence comprises summoning the gods (kami-oroshi) and entertaining the gods through dance (kami-asobi), the conveyance of requests and towards the end of the dance the sending-back of the gods (kami-oku-ri). These dances also formed the basis for later forms of theatre and other performing arts, which appeared in Japan from China (gigaku) as early as the 7th century and increasingly during the 8th; together with the introduction of musical instruments and Buddhist spirituality they developed early forms of popular dance and music theatre (sarugaku).

No   The Sarugaku players Kan'ami (1333–84) and his son Zeami Motokiyo (1363–1443) developed the Sarugaku plays into the lyrical, melodramatic No theatre, whose stylized sophistication utilizes dance as a dramatic highlight, while appearing to give up realistic expression in favour of greater symbolism. There are 240 No dramas existing today, around half of which are attributed to the aforesaid artists. Zeami in particular was the author of significant publications on art theory in which the aesthetic principles of No are fixed.

Origin ▶   The No plays, which are as popular as ever, have seen few changes to their performances in 600 years. They have their roots in **sangaku** (»music for distraction«), which became **sarugaku** (»monkey music«) during the Heian period. This popular form of entertainment was a kind of mockery with artistic feats and dances in which Buddhist and Shinto priests were often ridiculed in a burlesque or even

The setup of a No stage follows strict rules

obscene manner. **Dengaku** (»field music«), which had developed from rural harvest dances, also influenced No theatre. In the 13th century these ribald spectacles were given more serious content and a more organized structure; professional actors started to perform them. The plays thus created were called sarugaku-no-No (»art sarugaku«) and dengaku-no-No. Later the name was simply abbreviated to »No«. In its function No theatre already resembled European mystery plays, but in its character it was still a people's theatre.

No theatre today is performed by Kanze (the largest school), Komparu, Hosho, Kongo and Kita, which go back to the 14th century as a family tradition (though Kita was only founded in the 17th century). In emulation of the fact that No performances were originally staged outdoors, the 5.4m/18ft square roofed stage made of plain cypress wood is moved, open to the sides, into the auditorium. **The backdrop is always a picture of a pine tree** in front of which the musicians (the lead instrument is a flute accompanied by three drums) are seated; they accompany the recitations of the chorus seated on the right-hand side of the stage. The walkway leading from downstage left, which is lined by three pines arranged to give a sense of perspective, is the stage access for the main actor (shite), his companion (tsure) and the supporting actor (waki), all always played by male actors. The supporting actors, who are sometimes in a masks and sometimes not, are there to promote understanding; the story is

◄ Five schools

◄ No stage

acted out by the shite in a stereotypical mask; he meditatively immerses himself in his role of deity, spirit, dead warrior or beautiful woman in the mirror room (kagami-no-ma). The waki's introductory explanations are followed by the performance of the elegant and magnificently dressed shite; his actions, rich in symbolic movements, are almost abstracted. The fundamental aesthetic principle is not violated in any way by the dramatic events and not undermined by any realism.

Kyogen Kyogen performances, **humorous interludes of the No dramas**, which developed an independent form parallel to No theatre but are still closely connected to it, use the popular speech of the 16th century to caricature society and often approach the tragicomic. It is different from No theatre in the dialogue between the two actors or groups, the very rare use of masks as well as the very realistic portrayals given.

Bunraku Bunraku puppet theatre goes back to the 16th century, when blind musicians' recitations from the great war narratives such as the Heike-monogatari accompanied by biwa music enjoyed great popularity. In the second half of the 16th century their popularity increased because of the adoption of the Joruri-junidan-zoshi love story. At the same time the biwa was replaced by the shamisen from Okinawa; towards the end of the century primitive puppets were introduced. The subjects focused on historical models and current events; by entirely avoiding subjects taken from legends and fairytales, the puppets shook off the unreality they were associated with, and thereby achieved a flowering that lasted until the 18th century, almost displacing the Kabuki theatre. The »Japanese Shakespeare« **Chikamatsu Monzaemon** (1653–1724) wrote around 100 pieces just for the Bunraku. This form of theatre began to deteriorate in 1780, a process that was only stopped when Uemura Bunrakuken set up a puppet theatre in Osaka at the beginning of the 19th century.

Kabuki The bourgeois Kabuki theatre (»ka« means »song«, »bu« is »dance«, »ki« means »performing arts«) has its origin in the Edo period (17th–19th centuries). It makes use of several elements from the different theatrical styles, which are combined into an independent art form that flourished until not too long ago. Consisting of acting, dance and music and also limited to only male actors, Kabuki is very vivid and diverse in its performances and for that reason addresses a wider audience than the classical, formal No theatre.
Kabuki theatre derives from a **religious folk dance** (nembutsu-odori) that was performed by Okuni, a dancer of the Izumo shrine in Kyoto and from which the onna-kabuki, popular song and dance plays mostly with erotic content developed; in 1632, around 30 years after it had come into existence, it was condemned as immoral by the shogunate and forbidden for women. Boys under the age of 15 took

over the Kabuki roles (wakashu-kabuki) but in the opinion of the shogunate they were no less morally suspect. As a result only men were allowed to be actors, the contents were limited to realistic events and thus the basis of the dramatic form of theatre was created. As a result, actresses were banned from Japan's stages for some 260 years; until 1891 the stages were entirely dominated by male actors, a trend that still continues.

Today there are around 300 classical Kabuki plays, categorized as jidai-mono (historical dramas mostly with tragic contents), sewa-mono (stories of bourgeois life) and buyo-ge-ki (dance plays). The dramas with a realistic character often make use of alienating elements such as exaggerated recitation.

Doll representing a kabuki actor

Tea Ceremony

Chanoyu, the tea ceremony (also known as sado, chado) is, on the surface, the traditional method of preparing and serving macha, powdered green tea. However, although the function of the tea ceremony is often not seen as anything more than a traditional relic in the training of marriageable Japanese women. it has its roots in the Japanese people's aesthetic and religious sense. In order to gain any understanding of the actions and meaning of the tea ceremony, it is necessary to consider the cultural historical and religious developments that have led to it as it is practised today.

Centuries-old ritual

Important criteria in the execution of a tea ceremony are the observance of inner and outer purity (sei), awe for all life (kei), harmony (wa) and silence (jaku). These prerequisites are guaranteed by detailed, fixed rules that may differ depending on the school, but whose quintessence is the same.

◄ Important criteria

The actual cornerstone for the rules of the tea ceremony as practised today was laid by Noami (1397–1471) and Murata Shuko (1423–1502). Shuko founded one trend in Nara characterized by simplicity and a strong connection to the things of everyday life. The orientation towards tranquillity and acquiescence led Shuko to the fundamental beliefs of Zen Buddhism, whose teachings say that the soul finds contentment through the performance of everyday activities. Chado, the »way of tea«, seemed to Shuko to be a suitable way to obtain this goal. Noami, formerly Shuko's teacher, picked up his idea. The final form of the tea ceremony that has survived unaltered

Basic rules of the ceremony

The tea ceremony is one of Japan's well-maintained traditions

to this day goes back to Sen no Rikyu (1522–91). He brought the schools and practices existing at his time together into a formally consolidated art form.

Historic tea houses Surviving examples of historic tea houses are the tea house of the Ginkakuji temple in Kyoto (1482), which Shuko designed, as well as the tea room of the Shokintei house belonging to the Katsura Imperial Villa built in Kyoto in 1624, which is attributed to the tea master Kobori Enshu (1579–1647). Enshu is also thought to be the creator of the Shunjuan and Kohoan tea houses that are part of the Daitokuji temple (1324) in Kyoto. A number of artworks by both Sen no Rikyu and Kobori Enshu have survived for posterity in this temple; it also contains the grave of both the tea masters. Sen no Rikyu was the builder of the tea house belonging to the 15th-century Myokian temple in Yamazaki near Osaka, which is now considered a national treasure. Another significant tea house, Rokusan, is in the National Museum of Tokyo.

Tea ceremony Every tea ceremony begins with the assembly of the participants (rarely more than five) in the yoritsuki, a waiting room. The role of the shokyaku, the **guest of honour** falls to a participant chosen by the host and tea master; the participant will keep that role until the end of the ceremony.

The guests' path leads from the waiting room through the front part of the tea garden (soto-roji) to a covered bench (koshikake), which is located at the entrance to the inner part of the garden (uchi-roji). This is where the host welcomes the participants wordlessly, just as he issues the request to walk along the path to the tea house by bowing in silence. The garden represents a complex picture of nature in a very small space; its artistic design gives the impression of naturalness and its perfectly designed beauty puts the guests in the right mood for the tea ceremony. The path leads past trees, bushes and stone lanterns (ishi-doro), and over stepping stones set in the moss-covered ground to a »chozubachi«, a stone water-basin, where the guests cleanse their hands and mouth, led by the guest of honour.

The tea house (sukiya) located at the back of the inner garden conveys an inconspicuous, rustic impression; it has a thatched roof, and the structure and building materials are very simple. Stones, bushes and moss shimmer with drops of water just recently sprinkled, giving the scene a fresh and cool appearance. The guest of honour is the first to enter the tea room (chashitsu), whose deliberately low entrance forces him and the following guests to move on their knees: this gesture symbolizes the equal standing of everyone and the humility of the individual. The customary size of the tea room is 2.7m/9ft square; the floor is covered by four and a half straw mats (tatami). The simplicity of the building materials is also noticeable here.

◀ In the tea house

One after the other the guests first admire the scroll picture (kakemoto) hanging in an alcove (tokonoma), which can either be an ink and wash painting or calligraphy. At the centre of the room a hearth is set into the floor; next to it is the tea equipment, consisting of chawan, a tea bowl; chaire, the tea caddy; chasen, a small bamboo brush to stir the powdered tea; and hisaku, a bamboo ladle. Every single piece is of marked simplicity and chosen by the tea master with great care. After the participants have appreciated the room, decor and equipment, the tea master enters the tea room from the preparation room (mizuya) in order to welcome with a bow the participants sitting in a row. During the following events the tea room remains closed off from any disturbances from the outside. The tea master himself serves **kaiseki, the typical dish** of the tea ceremony, which is laboriously prepared and whose individual foods, as is the custom, have to be eaten completely. After the end of the meal sweets are served; this marks the end of the first part of the tea ceremony.

◀ First part of the ceremony

The guests are asked to step into the garden for a break, where they take a seat on a bench until the sound of a gong calls them back into the tea room, which they enter after a renewed cleansing of their mouth and hands. In the meantime the scroll picture in the alcove has been replaced by a vase with flowers. Now the main part of the tea ceremony can begin: **gozairi**. The tea master takes a container with cake from the preparation room, which he sets before the guest

◀ Main part of the tea ceremony

of honour, after which he begins to **prepare the thick tea** (koicha). To do this he fills two to three spoonfuls of powdered green tea into the tea bowl after cleaning the tea equipment with a specially designed cloth (fukusa). Then he takes the ladle to pour hot water on to the tea and whisks it with a bamboo brush until it is frothy. Koicha is usually prepared from young leaves from tea plants that are at least 20 and often even more than 50 years old. Once the tea is prepared the tea bowl is placed on a certain point next to the stove, from where the guest of honour, who has previously eaten his cake, picks it up with a bow to the other guests. This is done in a set manner, by placing the bowl into the left hand, while cupping it from the side with the right hand. The first taste of the tea is followed by a compliment for the tea master. After two further sips and an admiring remark about the tea bowl's appearance it is passed on to the next participant, but not before carefully cleaning the part that touched the mouth with a paper towel (kaishi). After the last participant has sampled the tea, the bowl goes back to the guest of honour, who in turn hands it over to the tea master. The gozairi comes to an end after everyone in order has praised the artistic design of the tea equipment.

End of the ceremony ▶ The end of the tea ceremony is called **usucha**. It mainly distinguishes itself from the gozairi by its less formal nature. To prepare the more watery tea (macha), leaves from 3 to 15-year-old tea plants are used. Two spoonfuls of this tea are prepared separately for each guest in a smaller tea bowl; and the tea bowl is completely emptied every time. When the last guest has handed back the bowl, the tea master and host takes away the equipment and with a low bow indicates the end of the tea ceremony. The parting guests also bid their farewells with a bow and will make sure to thank the host in person or in writing for this invitation.

Geishas

Not a high-class prostitute! Japanese geishas are not high-class prostitutes. **Geisha** means »person of the arts«. She is an artist who spends years learning the skills of playing music, dancing, ikebana and cultivated conversation. She must also be able to perform the tea-ceremony perfectly. The task of geishas is to create a relaxed, pleasant atmosphere in the reserved, male-oriented Japanese society, for example in traditional restaurants and tea-houses. Only then do they wear their full »professional uniform« of precious kimono, wooden sandals (geta), and beautifully arranged hair, with faces covered in white make-up, with red lips and discreetly tinted nape of neck. Kyoto is the stronghold of geisha culture in modern Japan.

Geishas are trained from the age of 16, mostly in geisha houses (okiya), and the trainees are known as »maiko«. To start with they

learn the art of the »minarai« or »os-haku«: wine servers, who also serve the food, sing and dance, but are not permitted to participate in conversations. After their training they either work for an agency (kenban) that places them with companies, or freelance. Geisha parties are expensive and exclusive, but still an important part of Japanese lifestyle. To be invited by a Japanese person to such a party is a great honour, but foreigners unable to speak Japanese will only understand a fraction of the appeal of the invitation.

It takes years of training to become a geisha

Famous People

Who invented the cultured pearl? Which film director became the stylistic role model for Westerns? What did the 47 Ronin do? In Japan the surname usually precedes the given name. This book also follows this practice.

Ganjin (688–763)

Ganjin (Chien Chen in Chinese) was a high priest during the T'ang **Chinese priest**
Dynasty in China. Shomu-tenno invited him to Japan, where his task
was to spread Buddhism. In the year 742 Ganjin left for Japan for
the first time, but was forced to abort this trip and four further ones
because of pirate raids, storms and because he was shipwrecked. During one of these luckless sea voyages he lost his eyesight. Only in
754, at the age of 66, did he reach **Nara**, where he taught in the Todaiji temple and ordained priests. After the Toshodaiji temple was
built he moved there and subsequently died there on 6 May 763.

Hirohito – Showa Tenno (1901–89)

No other Japanese emperor ruled as long as he did. However, even **Japanese**
though he ascended the throne in 1926, the Japanese people heard **emperor**
his voice for the first time on 15 August 1945, the day he had to an-
nounce **Japan's surrender** on the radio. He himself lost his divine
status as the direct descendant of the sun goddess, but he did not lose the throne, even though his share of responsibility for the war is
contentious to this day. However, General Douglas MacArthur, to
whom the emperor offered his resignation, did not prosecute him at
the War Crimes Tribunal, because he believed he was necessary for
peace in the country. The Japanese constitution designed by the
Americans also sees him as the »symbol of unity of the Japanese people«. And thus his post-war role was limited to a representational
function. From that time the shy emperor travelled the country to
get closer to his people, wrote books about his passion, marine bio-
logy, and led a private life with his family free from debauchery and
scandals. When he died of cancer on 7 January 1989 an entire era
came to an end, namely the era of **»enlightened peace«** (showa),
which not only encompassed the period of nationalism and war, but
also Japan's rise to become a global economic power.

Hiroshige Ando (1797–1858)

Hiroshige Ando, born in Tokyo, is considered one of the main artists **Woodblock print**
of coloured woodblock prints. In Europe he became famous above **artist**
all for his landscape pictures, which influenced painters such as the
Impressionists and Vincent van Gogh.

Hokusai Katsushika (1760–1849)

Hokusai Katsushika, probably the most famous painter and wood- **Painter**
block printmaker of modern Japan, was also born in Tokyo. He got

← *The Japanese Emperor Hirohito and Empress Nagako in the garden*
  of the imperial palace in Tokyo; photograph taken in March 1924

the inspiration for his work not least from European art. Hokusai's work consists of individual images, series of landscapes and figures, book illustrations and caricatures. In the late 19th century his art also attained considerable renown in Europe. Around 1830 he created what is probably the most famous Japanese work of art: **The Great Wave off Kanagawa** from his *36 Views of Mount Fuji*.

Kitano Takeshi (born 1947)

Entertainer and film maker

Kitano Takeshi (»Beat Takeshi«) is one of the most colourful figures of modern-day Japan: his career began as a stand-up comedian in a Tokyo strip joint. During the 1970s he enjoyed success with a partner as »The Two Beats« (hence his nickname) and later, on his own. He subsequently hosted a radio show in which he chatted about many different subjects without any taboos. In 1983 he got his first role as an actor (in *Merry Christmas, Mr Lawrence*, by Oshima Nagisa), and six years later directed his first film (*Violent Cop*; Japanese title *Sono otoko kyobi ni tsuki*). His all-round talent made him so popular that he sometimes had nine television appearances in one week. When he was taken to hospital as a result of a serious accident with a scooter, he discovered his artistic vein while in rehab and started to paint. He achieved his international breakthrough in 1997 with his film **Hana-Bi**, for which he received the Golden Lion in Venice. He not only starred in the lead role, but was also the scriptwriter, editor and director. He had similarly great success in Europe with his film *Zatoichi* (Silver Lion 2003).

? DID YOU KNOW ...?

- If you are not a fan of Kitano Takeshi as an antihero in movies, you may enjoy watching him as an entertainer in game shows such as *Takeshi's Castle*, which has been shown outside Japan.

Kurosawa Akira (1910–98)

Director

If Japanese film is on the European and American radar at all, it is thanks to one man: Akira Kurosawa, born into an old samurai family in Omori, a district of Tokyo. The first time he received international attention was in 1950 with **Rashomon**, in which the murder of a samurai and the rape of his wife are narrated from different perspectives. It won an academy award in 1952 and is now a cult movie. He had a lasting influence on Hollywood with **The Seven Samurai** (1953): through his remake by John Sturges as the Western *The Magnificent Seven*, and stylistically through slow-motion recordings of the action scenes with several cameras, as they were used later by Sturges and also Sergio Leone. However, Kurosawa was anything but an »Eastern« director. Although his main subject was the Japan of the samurai, the proud warriors in his films had to recognize that their time was coming to an end. Thus for example in *Kagemusha*

Scene from »The Seven Samurai«

(1979), in which the traditional ruling system of the Samurai was drowning in the onslaught of new firearms, and in *Ran* (1985), reminiscent of Shakespeare's *King Lear*, in which Prince Hidetora goes mad because his sons have allied against him. It was films like this that made Kurosawa known in the West; other works, such as *Rhapsody in August* (1991) with Richard Gere, which attempts to handle the trauma of Hiroshima and Nagasaki, are hardly known.

Mikimoto Kokichi (1858–1954)

He was Japan's »pearl king«: Mikimoto Kokichi, who came from a modest background, is considered the inventor of the method to produce cultured pearls. Towards the beginning of the 20th century he successfully managed to stimulate the production of pearls by introducing small foreign bodies into the shells of oysters. There is still a cultured pearl facility in Toba near Ise (southern Honshu).

Inventor of the cultured pearl

Miyamoto Shigeru (born 1952)

Hardly anyone knows his name, but his **Super Mario** invention is famous amongst computer game enthusiasts around the world. After studying industrial design he created a classic video-game figure for Nintendo: the lovable, somewhat chubby, moustached Mario (origi-

Game developer for Nintendo

nally only called Jumpman), who jumps and runs around to save his girlfriend from the clutches of the monkey Donkey Kong. Further variations of this game followed, as did entirely new games into which Miyamoto often incorporated his own childhood experiences. He apparently enjoys designing computer games so much that he would even do it for free. At the same time he is something of a critic of his own industry, since he says the purpose of his games is to get people together, not to isolate them from each other in front of monitors.

Momofuko Ando (1910–2007)

Food manufacturer

55,000 people came to his funeral in the Osaka baseball stadium, and quite certainly every one of them had his invention at home: Momofuko Ando, born in Taiwan, who became a Japanese national at the age of 23, dreamed up the **dry noodle**. He wanted to meet the great demand for food in starving postwar Japan – not with Western-style bread as the government wished, but with traditional Japanese noodles. But they had to be convenience noodles. In 1958 he introduced the first pre-cooked instant noodles (in Japanese »chikin ramen« because of the »chicken« taste), and in 1972 marketed the invention for the first time in combination with instant chicken broth in a styrofoam beaker: the »hot cup« was born. His Nissin corporation has since sold almost 100 billion of these.

Mori Ogai (1862–1922)

Doctor and translator

Mori Ogai, born in Tsuwano, completed his medical studies in Germany. Later he served as a doctor in the Japanese army. He achieved international significance, however, as a writer and translator; he was the first to provide the full translation of **Goethe's *Faust*** into Japanese. He also significantly contributed to the distribution of European philosophical thought in Japan.

Forty-Seven Ronin (17th–18th century)

Legendary samurai

The 47 Ronin, glorified as heroes in Japan, are historical characters. These samurai were followers of the daimyo Asano, who had been summoned to the court of the shogun. During an audience in 1701 the courtier Yoshinaka Kira insulted him. In order to defend his honour, Asano immediately attacked the courtier with a sword, but only caused minor injuries. It was, however, a severe offence to draw a weapon at court, for which Asano was sentenced to commit suicide. His 47 samurai subsequently sought to revenge themselves on Yoshinaka Kira for their master. As a cover, they dissociated themselves from their dead master, whereby they became ronin, masterless warriors. In order to make Kira feel safe they threw all knightly virtues over board and led a debauched life. In the second year after Asano's suicide they attacked. After this act of revenge, which was also proof of their unconditional loyalty to Asano, all 47 of them committed ritual suicide.

Tange Kenzo (1913–2005)

Tange Kenzo, born in Imabari (on the main island of Shikoku) is one of Japan's best-known architects. Originally he was influenced by European New Objectivity, which he combined with Japanese architecture and then developed an independent style. He was offered a chair of urban planning at the University of Tokyo. In addition to numerous prestigious individual buildings, primarily in Japan, including **Tokyo's City Hall** (►p.532), he also developed town planning concepts such as for the reconstruction of the Macedonian town of Skopje, which was destroyed in 1963 by an earthquake.

Architect

セットは
生ビール又は
潤（金）
枝豆冷奴付

なす田楽
420

ビール
1000

Practicalities

WHICH TRAVEL DOCUMENTS DO YOU NEED FOR THE TRIP? WHERE CAN THE BEST RYOKAN BE FOUND? HOW TO ORDER IN A JAPANESE RESTAURANT? WHERE CAN YOU BUY A KOKESHI DOLL AS A SOUVENIR?

Accommodation

Hotels During the peak season for Western visitors (April–May and September–November) as well as during the Japanese holiday season (July–August and December–January) demand for places to stay is great, making timely reservations necessary for all types of accommodation. Even remote holiday spots receive a very large number of visitors during these times. In addition to Western-style hotels Japan has a large number of its traditional inns (ryokan) and guesthouses (minshuku).

---

i Price categories

■ Luxury: more than ¥ 20,000
■ Mid-range: up to ¥ 20,000
■ Budget: up to ¥ 8000 a night for a double room, breakfast not included

■ Hotels and guesthouses ▶Sights from A to Z

Directories, including list of less expensive accommodation, are sent out by the Japanese tourist information centres (▶Information) as well as by the airlines JAL and ANA (▶Arrival). Further useful websites when searching for accommodation are: www.jpinn.com, www.yadoplaza.com/att_japan, www.japaneseguesthouses.com.

Categories ▶ Japanese-style accommodation usually charges per person, while Western-style hotels and guesthouses give their prices per double room. For that reason the price categories given here refer to a room for two people, using the cheapest rate available. In a ryokan the price usually includes two meals; these weren't considered in the calculation here, meaning that a room costing ¥ 13,000 per person, incl. two meals, still falls into the »mid-range« category. Another factor to be taken into account is that breakfast is not always included in the price. Some accommodation also only offers a Japanese breakfast (miso soup with rice and nori).

Western-style hotels All larger towns and important destinations have hotels of the upscale international standard. These hotels, in the context of their category, are very well equipped and are characterized by their first-class service. In most cases the hotel also has speciality restaurants and shopping arcades; they often even have a carefully landscaped garden. The rooms are fully air-conditioned and usually also have a television. The prices correspond to international standards.

Business hotels Comparatively cheap accommodation, especially for people travelling alone, is provided by the business hotels. They are generally located close to railway stations and have a much larger number of single and double rooms. The service is usually reduced (no room service), but almost all business hotels have a restaurant with Japanese and Western cuisine. Visitors should not expect the staff to speak another language, since the business hotels were originally meant for Japanese people travelling on business. Recommended chains: Toyoko

← Display in a restaurant

Inn (www.toyoko-inn.com), Washington Hotel (www.wh-rsv.com) and Hotel Sunroute (www.sunroute.jp).

One Japanese invention is the **pod hotel**, groups of pre-made containers of approx. 1.10m/4 ft 6 in in width, 2.20m/7ft in length and 1.20m/5ft in height (not for people who tend to claustrophobia!), which have nothing but a bed, air-conditioning and a television set. They are usually to be found close to railway stations and are often for men only.

Ryokan are Japanese-style hotels. There is far more of a family atmosphere than in Western hotels. The rooms are laid out with straw mats (tatami) and divided by folding screens. Meals are served in the room.

New Otani hotel in Osaka

Visitors should be aware of the following when staying in a ryokan: ◄ Code of conduct
upon entering, street shoes have to be exchanged for slippers that will be ready; these slippers in turn have to be taken off when entering a tatami room; there is a special pair of slippers for going to the toilet. The maid leads the guest to the room, serves the welcome tea and agrees a convenient time for the evening meal. The ryokan's comfortable yukata, a kind of house kimono, is the customary dress within the house and garden.

The bath (o-furo) is almost always a gender-segregated communal ◄ Bath
bath. The custom is to lather up in soap outside of the bath, rinse off thoroughly and then get into the very hot water. When leaving the bath do not let the hot water out!

The maid serves the guest during the meal after the bath and then ◄ Eating, sleeping,
leaves when asked. Towards the evening the room is transformed in- garden
to a bedroom with just a few changes; the beds laid out on the floor are very comfortable thanks to the soft mattresses. Guests should not forget to take a stroll in the ryokan's garden, which is often a work of landscape art in a very small space.

A lack of foreign languages and experiences with foreign guests ◄ Reservations
means some owners and employees of ryokan react very shyly to foreigners' reservation requests. For that reason it is recommended to have reservations done through a Japanese travel agency. More than
2000 ryokan are part of the Japan Ryokan Association, and they are trying more to adapt to foreigners' needs; sometimes this happens at the cost of the traditional Japanese style. The ryokan of the top categories can stand comparison with top-grade Western-style hotels regarding comfort (and price).

A ryokan is a traditional Japanese hotel

Minshuku The guesthouse-like family businesses called »minshuku« offer an acceptable and inexpensive alternative to hotels and ryokan. Such enterprises can be found in all parts of the country; booking agencies can usually be found at the central stations. Reservations are also placed by the Japan Travel Bureau (▶Information) and the central office of the minshuku. Visitors cannot always expect knowledge of foreign languages.

Kokumin Shukusha These people's lodges were created at the instance of the Japanese government. The approx. 340 hotels belonging to this group are located exclusively in spa towns and holiday areas, and are also open to foreign travellers. The rooms are largely kept in the Japanese style, but the communal facilities tend to correspond to Western standards.
The level of comfort is generally less, but not least because the natural setting the people's lodges are a good way to get some rest and relaxation. It is advisable to book through a Japanese travel agency.

Kokumin Kyuka Mura There are around 30 of these holiday villages (some of which have people's lodges) in Japanese national parks; besides inexpensive accommodation and an attractive setting they offer plenty of leisure facilities, such as sports fields, water sports, ski facilities, hiking trails and camp sites. They too are very popular during the peak season. Reservations are possible via the Japan Travel Bureau. Information available at www.qkamura.or.jp/index_e.php.

The Welcome Inns are not a closed hotel group; this is much rather Welcome Inns
a reservation system containing particularly inexpensive accommodation (Western-style hotels, business hotels, ryokan, guesthouses,
minshuku and others) and which is sponsored by the Japan National
Tourist Organization (JNTO). Reservation centres can be found at
the Tourist Information Centres (TIC; Information) in Tokyo (Narita International Airport and city centre) and Kyoto. It can also be
done online: www.itcj.jp.

Youth Accommodation

Japan is the country with the highest density of youth hostels outside
Europe. There are around 450 hostels, mostly situated in picturesque
areas; the vast majority are run pri-
vately. Reservations are essential;
there is a reservation centre in Tokyo, most Japanese youth hostels
are connected to its computer.
A requirement for the use of the
private youth hostels is an international hostelling membership card;
a stay in any one youth hostel is limited to three days.

i   Japan Youth Hostels, Inc.

▪ Kanda Amerex Building, 9th Floor
   3-1-16 Misaki-cho, Chiyoda-ku
   J-101-0006 Tokyo
   Tel. 03/32 88-14 17
   Fax 32 88-12 48
   www.jyh.or.jp

Addresses

The *Asahi Evening News* contained the following advertisement by a Address
hospital: »Use the west exit of Ikebukuro Station. Stay on the main structure
road for the next 500 metres, which is six minutes' walk. When you
get to a petrol station, turn right into the small road between the
grocer's and a letter box.«

!   *Baedeker* TIP

How to get there

Visitors should have the address they are looking for
written in Japanese characters in their hotel and take
along the address's telephone number: if the taxi driver
does not know how to get there he can phone for
directions. Often there are signs in the vicinity of a
block listing all families living in the surrounding area,
but they are written in Japanese characters. In big cities
police officers (▶personal safety) can also help.

This is often the way directions to friends, temples or shops are given, with a drawing if possible. Addresses in the European sense do not exist as such in Japan.

Example ▶ 12–18 A Shiroganedai 5-chome Minato-ku is a house or a flat in the administrative district of Minato in Tokyo. The district in turn is subdivided into a sub-district; Shiroganedai is one of them. Every sub-district is again divided into blocks (chome). And in such a block the property 12–18 will be located. There are no street numbers. Where numbers exist, they are not organized by location but by the year the building was constructed. There is not just one house standing on this property; house A has to be found. To do that the doors have to be checked to see if they contain the name of the acquaintance. This is difficult even for Japanese postmen and taxi drivers. However, taxi drivers do not usually have a problem finding famous sights, hotels and such like.

Arrival · Before the Journey

By air   Most visitors arrive in Japan by air. There are direct flights by major European and international airlines, e.g. British Airways from London. Various routes to Japan are possible from Europe: over Greenland and Alaska (Anchorage) to Tokyo; via Moscow and Siberia to Tokyo; as well as the southeast Asia route with stopovers.
A direct flight takes between eleven and twelve hours. Most international flights arrive at Tokyo's Narita Airport. There are however also connections to Kansai International Airport (near Osaka) and to Nagoya for the new Central Japan International Airport (Centrair).

By rail   An extravagant way of travelling to Japan is to take a train to Moscow and then change into the Trans-Siberian railway via Omsk and Irkutsk to Nakhodka; from there a ship goes to Yokohama. The journey takes ten days from Moscow.

Travel Documents

Documents   Travellers from the European Union only need a **valid passport** to enter Japan, as long as their stay is no longer than six months and the purpose of the visit is not job-related. In all other cases a visa is required. The permitted length of stay for tourists is 90 days; anyone wanting to stay longer will have to request an extension document from the municipal administration of the Japanese town before the 90 days are up; this document has to be handed over when leaving the country.
The conditions for being allowed into the country are a return or onward ticket as well as proof of sufficient funds for the stay in the country.

On entry, all those over 16 are photographed and have digital finger-prints taken. These data are then compared with a database »as a precautionary measure against acts of terrorism«.

Foreign nationals need a Japanese translation of their licence in order to be allowed to drive; this translation can be done by embassies in Tokyo and consulate generals in other Japanese cities. Further information is available form the Japan National Tourist Organization (► Information).

Vehicle documents

 AIRLINE CONTACT NUMBERS

JAPAN AIR LINES (JAL)

► **www.jal.com/en**
Toll-free number within Japan for international flights:
tel. 01 20/25-59 31
domestic flights:
tel. 01 20/25-59 71

► **JAL in Australia**
Tel. 01 300/52 52 87

► **JAL in Europe**
European Reservation Center in London
www.jal.com/en
Tel. 08 45/77 47 700

► **JAL in New Zealand**
Tel. 0800/52 57 47

► **JAL in North America**
www.ar.jal.com
Tel. 1 800/525 36 63

ANA ALL NIPPON AIRWAYS

► **www.anaskyweb.com**
Toll-free number within Japan for International flights:
tel. 0120/029-333
Domestic flights:
tel. 0120/029-222

► **European Sales Office in London**
Tel. 08 70/837 88 11

► **North American Sales Office**
Tel. (1) 800/235 92 62 837

AIRLINES IN JAPAN

► **Air Canada**
Toll-free number within Japan:
Tel. 0120/048 048
Within Tokyo:
Tel. 03/5405 8800

► **American Airlines**
Toll-free number within Japan:
Tel. 0120/000-860
In Tokyo:
Tel. 03 /3214-2111

► **British Airways**
In Tokyo:
Tel. 03 / 3570 8657

► **Air New Zealand**
Toll-free number within Japan:
Tel. 0120/300-747
Within Tokyo:
Tel. 03/5521-2727

► **Qantas**
Toll-free number within Japan:
Tel. 0120/207-020
Within Tokyo:
Tel. 03/3593-7000

► **United Airlines**
Toll-free number within Japan:
Tel. 0120/11-44-66

Health insurance All visitors are advised to find out what kinds of agreements they have with their health insurance company in the event that there are health problems. It is definitely worthwhile purchasing travel health insurance for foreign travel, with emergency return transport.

Vaccination regulations It is not normally necessary to get any vaccinations in order to enter Japan. However, anyone travelling to Japan with a stopover along the southeast Asia route should enquire with the health authority or the responsible travel agency about the regulations regarding the countries entered during the journey.

Customs Regulations

Entry Objects for personal use and part of the tourist equipment can temporarily be taken into Japan duty free. A written entry declaration is necessary if the amount brought in exceeds the duty free limit and if there is any unaccompanied luggage.

These are some of the items visitors may take into Japan duty free: 400 cigarettes, 100 cigarettes or tobacco products up to 500 g/17.6 oz; 3 bottles of alcoholic beverages at 0.76 l/3.2 fl. oz each; 75 ml/2.5 fl oz perfume; other goods up to a value of ¥ 200,000. It is illegal to bring drugs and pornography into the country; a permit is required to import certain plant species as well as pets.

Departure When re-entering the EU travellers are allowed to import 200 cigarettes or 100 cigarillos or 50 cigars or 250 g/8.8 oz of tobacco, as well as 1 l/0.26 US gal of spirits containing more than 22 % alcohol, or 2 l/0.53 oz containing less than 22 % alcohol or 2 l/0.53 oz of sparkling wines or fortified wines, 500 g/17.6 oz coffee or 200 g/7 oz coffee extract, 100 g/3.5 oz tea or 40 g/1.4 oz tea extract, 50 g/1.8 oz perfume or 0.25 l/8.5 fl oz toilet water. Tobacco and alcoholic beverages are only duty free for individuals over the age of 17 and coffee for travellers over 15. Goods that are **gifts** or meant for personal use are duty free up to a value of EUR 175.

Electricity

The mains provide 100–110 volt alternating current (60 Hertz in the west of Japan, 50 Hertz in the east).

Most of the larger hotels have outlets for both 110 volts and 220 volts. Western standard plugs cannot usually be used; special adapter plugs can be purchased from an electrical retailer. **Appliances with a voltage switch** have to be set to 220 volts before being connected back to the 220-volt mains because they could otherwise sustain irreparable damage.

Emergency

GENERAL EMERGENCY
▶ **Police**
Tel. 110

▶ **Fire brigade, ambulance**
Tel. 119

Etiquette and Customs

Even though lifestyles are becoming increasingly westernized, espe- **Etiquette**
cially in Japan's cities, the etiquette developed from the country's
centuries-old tradition is still given a lot of importance. The Japanese
are known for being **polite**; Japanese people would never directly
contradict the person they are talking to, they would rather try to
find a conciliatory circumlocution. Impatience and a display of anger
or disapproval are considered a loss of face; communication is characterized by smiles and outward calm.

It is not generally customary for two people to shake hands to greet **Welcoming**
each other; instead they bow to each other.

Great value is placed on the correct dress, even though Western in- **Clothes**
fluences are also constantly increasing here too. Men should not
wear shorts or brightly coloured shirts. In the world of business a
dark suit and tie are obligatory. Perfume and aftershave should only
be used sparingly, since Japanese people often find these fragrances
overpowering.

When entering a Japanese home or temple the street shoes must be **Shoes**
exchanged for slippers; rooms fitted with tatami (bamboo mats) are
only entered with socks. Bathrooms and toilets often have special
slippers ready.

It is definitely polite to slurp soup. On the other hand it is not done **Eating**
for people to blow their nose during a meal. In Japan blowing one's
nose is considered very crude; used handkerchiefs should not be put
into a pocket, but thrown away immediately. Chop sticks must not
be stuck into the rice, as this is reserved for a ritual sacrifice to the
dead. Rice wine (sake) is drunk warm.

Tips are not generally the norm in Japan. Exceptions are the **Western** **Tips**
hotels, where the bellmen who carry the suitcases up to the rooms
get approx. ¥ 200. In ryokan it is customary to give the maid a tip at

the beginning or end of the stay. It is definitely considered tactless in Japan to hand over money openly.

Sitting   Kneeling is strenuous for many Europeans. If this becomes uncomfortable, it is acceptable to sit more comfortably: men can sit with their legs crossed, while women can sit to the side instead of on their heels. When stretching out the legs it is important not to point your feet at anyone.

Sleeping   In a ryokan the kimono is tidily bound left over right; only for the dead is it tied right over left. Nor under any circumstances may the rice-filled pillow point to the life-threatening north.

Business cards   In Japan it is far more common to exchange business cards than it is in Europe; for that reason it is a good idea to stock up before leaving. They should be printed in Roman and Japanese script; there are printing shops that will do this. Business cards are presented with both hands while bowing, and they are treated carefully. Instead of a signature, most Japanese make a seal (inkan or hanko), which tourists can also have made by a seal-maker – a pretty souvenir.

Festivals, Holidays and Events

»Golden Week«   The days from the 29 April to 5 May are part of the »Golden Week«, since there are several holidays this week and a day falling between two national holidays is also a holiday. If an official holiday is on a Sunday, the next working day is also a holiday.

Festivals   Despite the growing influence of the modern West, when it comes to their customs the Japanese firmly hold to their age-old traditions. This becomes clear in the many religious festivals, where rich decor and precious gowns can be seen. Since many festivals follow the **lunar calendar**, only approximate dates can be given for these events.

▶ IMPORTANT HOLIDAYS AND FESTIVALS

HOLIDAYS

1 January: Shogatsu/Ganjitsu
(New Year)
2nd Mon in January:
Seijin no hi
(Coming-of-Age Day)
11 February: Kenkoku Kinen no hi
(National Foundation Day)
20 or 21 March: Shunbun no hi
(vernal equinox)
29 April: Midori no hi
(Greenery Day)
3 May: Kenpo kinenbi
(Constitution Day)
5 May: Kodomo no hi
(Children's Day)
3rd Mon in July: Umi no hi
(Marine Day)

Mount Wakakusa near Nara is lit up in the light of the grass fires

3rd Mon in September: Keiro no hi
(Respect-for-the-Aged Day)
23 or 24 September: Shubun no hi
(autumnal equinox)
2nd Mon in October: Taiiku no hi
(Health and Sports Day)
3 November: Bunka no hi
(Culture Day)
23 November: Kinro Kansha no hi
(Labour Day; in the country, Harvest
Festival)
23 December: Tenno Tanjobi
(The Emperor's Birthday)

JANUARY

▶ **Everywhere**
Shogatsu. First shrine visit in the
New Year; street decorations; im-
portant family celebration like
Christmas in the West (1 January).

▶ **Harumi, Tokyo**
Dezome-shiki. New Year's parade
of the fire brigade in traditional
uniforms; acrobatic performances
at the top of high bamboo ladders
(6 January).

▶ **Dazaifu (Fukuoka Prefecture)**
Usokae. Festival of the Dazifu-
Temmangu shrine (7 January).

▶ **Nara**
Wakakusa-yama-yaki. Grass fire
ceremony on Wakakusa Hill (on
the day of Coming-of-Age celebrations).

▶ **Osaka**
Toka Ebisu. Festival with a procession in the honour of Ebisu, the
patron god of business and luck
(middle of the month).

▶ **Akita**
Bonten-matsuri. Miyoshi shrine
festival, procession (middle of the
month), procession (middle of the
month).

FEBRUARY

▶ **Everywhere**
Setsubun-matsuri. Festival in
temples and shrines at the end of
winter with the call »Luck in, devil

out!« to drive out the devil (beginning of the month).

▶ **Nagasaki**
Lantern festival for the Chinese New Year with lion dances, a costume parade and thousands of Chinese lanterns (beginning of the month).

▶ **Sapporo**
Snow festival with large snow sculptures (beginning of the month, seven days long).

▶ **Kamakura**
Kamakura-matsuri in Kamakura (Yokote, Akita Prefecture). Children celebrate it in snow huts (middle of the month).

▶ **Okayama**
Hadaka-matsuri, Saidaiji temple. Hordes of men only dressed in loin cloths fight for two wooden lucky charms (3rd Sat).

▶ **Tokyo**
Plum blossom festival of the Yushima Tenjin shrine near Ueno (different events between 8 February and 8 March).

MARCH

▶ **Nara**
O-mizutori. Opening of the well at the Todaji temple in expectation of the longed-for spring.

▶ **Everywhere**
Hina-matsuri. Doll festival for girls, families with daughters set up dolls at home (3 March).

▶ **Takao (near Tokyo)**
Hi-watari. Priests of the mountain temples walk barefoot over the glimmering wood of a bonfire (fire

for the souls of the deceased; 2nd Sun) at Takao Mountain.

▶ **Nara**
Kasuga. Dance festival (middle of the month).

APRIL

▶ **Everywhere**
Hana-matsuri. In all Buddhist temples Buddha's birthday is celebrated (8 April).

▶ **Tokyo**
Cherry blossom festival of the Yasukuni shrine (beginning of the month).

▶ **Takayama**
Takayama-matsuri. Festival of the Hie shrine with a procession (middle of the month).

▶ **Nikko**
Yayoi-matsuri. Festival of the Futarasan shrine; procession with floats (middle of the month).

MAY

▶ **Fukuoka**
Hakata-dontaku. Festival procession with figures from the world of legend; floats, riders (beginning of the month).

▶ **Nikko**
Festival of the Toshogu shrine with a spectacular procession, more than 1000 people in the traditional dress of the early Tokugawa period accompany three portable shrines (17–18 May).

▶ **Kyoto**
Aoi-matsuri. Festival at the Shimogano and Kamigamo shrines in remembrance of an imperial procession. An ox cart is pulled

through the streets between the two shrines, accompanied by a large following; shrines and floats are decorated with mallow blossoms (middle of the month).
Mifune-matsuri. Festival on the Oi River with pretty old boats (3rd Sun).

► **Tokyo**
Kanda-matsuri. Festival of the Kanda-Myojin shrine; two huge litters are carried through the city; tea ceremony (middle of the month, every two years).
Sanja-matsuri. Festival of the Asa-kusa shrine; this festival is one of the most famous festivals in Tokyo and goes back to the Edo period; young men, women and children carry portable shrines on their shoulders; in addition lion dances and Binzasara dances are performed (3rd weekend, three days).

JUNE

► **Morioka**
Chagu-chagu Umakko. Mounted procession with magnificently adorned horses to the Hachiman shrine (2nd Sat).

► **Osaka**
Rice planting festival of the Su-miyoshi shrine. Young girls in traditional rural dress plant rice seedlings on the shrine's paddy field to ask for a good harvest (middle of the month).

► **Tokyo**
Sanno-matsuri. Festival of the Hie shrine: one of the biggest and most joyous festivals in Tokyo; procession with portable shrines through Akasaka (middle of the month).

JULY

► **Everywhere**
Tanabata. Star festival; according to Japanese legend the two stars Vega and Altair, which are separated and love each other, can only meet in the Milky Way once a year on this day; children attach to bamboo branches colourful paper streamers on which they have written poems (7 July).

► **Fukuoka**
Hakata Yamagasa. Festival with street processions from the beginning of the month to the middle of the month (highlight of the festival is on the 15 July).

► **Kyoto**
Gion-matsuri. Gion festival at the Yasaka shrine with wonderfully decorated floats (16–17 July).

► **Haramachi (Fukushima Prefecture)**
Soma no Maoi. Horse race with riders dressed in samurai armour (end of the month).

► **Nachi Katsuura (Wakayama)**
Nachi Himatsuri. Fire festival of the Nachi shrine; twelve giant torches are lit and carried by priests dressed in white (middle of the month).

► **Tokyo**
Fireworks in Asakusa at the Su-mida River (end of the month).

JULY/AUGUST

► **Everywhere**
Bon celebration. All Souls festival in remembrance of the dead, who come to visit the earth at this time, according to Buddhist belief; small lights are lit for their souls (de-

pending on the region in July or August, middle of the month).

► Miyajima
Kangensai music festival of the Itsukushima shrine. Classical court music and dances are performed on nicely decorated boats.

AUGUST

► Aomori and Hirosaki
Nebuta-matsuri in Aomori and Neputa-matsuri in Hirosaki. Large illuminated dummies made of papier-mâché representing people, animals and also birds are pulled through the streets on floats (beginning of the month).

► Akita
Kanto-matsuri. Divine help for a rich harvest is requested; young men balance 8m/25ft bamboo poles weighing 60kg/130lb each decorated with 96 lanterns through the streets (beginning of the month).

► Nikko
Waraku Odori. Folk dance festival (beginning of the month).

► Hiroshima
Peace festival. Remembrance day for the atomic bombs that were dropped on Japan (6 August).

► Sendai
Tanabata-matsuri. Star festival: the streets are decorated with colourful paper streamers and flags (beginning of the month).

During the Jidai-matsuri the participants dress up in historic costumes from every period for the procession to celebrate the founding of Kyoto

▶ **Yamagata**
Hanagasa-matsuri. More than 10,000 people dance through the city streets dressed in hanagasa, a low, round straw hat decorated with artificial flowers (beginning of the month).

▶ **Tokushima**
Awa-odori. Folk dance festival; guests are allowed to participate (middle of the month).

▶ **Kyoto**
Daimonji. Fire festival on the Nyoigatake (middle of the month).

SEPTEMBER

▶ **Kamakura**
Yabusame. Archery on horseback at the Tsurugaoka Hachimangu shrine (middle of the month).

OCTOBER

▶ **Nagasaki**
Okunchi festival at the Suwa shrine. Procession with dragon dance (beginning of the month).

▶ **Tokyo**
Furusato Tokyo Matsuri to celebrate the building of Edo castle with a colourful programme, harbour festival, beauty competition, floats and lantern procession (1st weekend).
Oeshiki-matsuri. Festival of the Homonji temple, procession with large lanterns decorated with flowers (middle of the month).

▶ **Himeji**
Kenka-matsuri. Festival of the Matsubara shrine; young people show their dexterity (middle of the month).

▶ **Nikko**
Autumn festival of the Toshogu shrine with a procession (middle of the month).

▶ **Kyoto**
Jidai-matsuri. City-founding festival (end of the month).

▶ **Kurama (Kyoto)**
Fire festival of the Yuki shrine. Torches are lit along the road leading to the shrine and children carry torches to the shrine (end of the month).

OCTOBER/NOVEMBER

▶ **Tokyo**
Chrysanthemum displays at the Asakusa Kannon temple, in the Yasukuni shrine, the Meiji shrine and in the Shinjuku Gyoen garden.

NOVEMBER

▶ **Hakone**
Daimyo-gyoretsu. Festival procession in Hakone Yumoto (beginning of the month).

▶ **Karatsu**
Okunchi-matsuri. Festival of the Karatsu shrine with a colourful procession (beginning of the month).

▶ **Tokyo**
Tori-no-ichi. Rooster markets at the Otori shrine in Asakusa on the day of the rooster; along the streets leading to the shrine stalls sell »bear paws«: bamboo rakes hung with jewellery (middle of the month).

▶ **Everywhere**
Shichi-go-san. 7, 5 and 3-year-old children dressed in kimonos visit a shrine (middle of the month).

DECEMBER

▶ **Nara**
On-matsuri. Procession with historical masquerades (middle of the month).

▶ **Tokyo**
Hagoita-ichi, Toshi-no-ichi. Market of the Asakusa Kannon temple towards the end of the year, amongst other things New Year's decorations are sold (middle of the month).

▶ **Oga (Akita-ken)**
Namahage. Men in devil masks go from house to house looking for naughty children (end of the month).

Food and drink

A feast for the eyes — Anyone going on a culinary journey of discovery in Japan will not be helped much by experiences with other foreign cuisines. When it comes to the traditional Japanese cuisine, comparisons really cannot be made, except for a few dishes that have foreign influences. The differences already start with the **attitude towards food**, which is understood as a unity of taste, appearance and tableware, where all three factors are of equal importance. Culinary treats are best discovered the Japanese way, by allowing the eyes to participate in the meal and by being willing to discover the characteristics of unfamiliar tastes. Since Japanese people are gourmets, do not hesitate to trust whatever their cuisine has to offer.

Basic ingredients ▶ The basic ingredients are rice, fish, eggs and vegetables; given that the land has so much coastline, fish is used much more than meat. Fish is available all year round; as there are many different varieties and prices to choose from, it is recommendable as a basic dish for foreigners.

Meals — The traditional Japanese **breakfast** (asa-gohan) consists of rice, raw egg, a bowl of bean paste soup (misoshiru), pickled vegetables (tsukemono) as well as dried seaweed (nori) and sometimes fish. The Japanese drink green tea for breakfast, as they do for all other meals, too. However, more and more Japanese people also eat toast with butter or jam and drink coffee.
Lunch is usually a light meal and often just a quick Western-style bite; where this is not the case the preferred meal consists of cold or hot noodles, sushi or a bowl of cooked rice and slices of fish or meat (donburi). Obento is a special lunch, where the food, consisting of fried fish or meat and pickled fruit, is packaged in a wooden box. These meals are primarily sold as on-the-go lunches for travellers at every Japanese railway station; often they are local specialities. The good quality and low cost make these lunches highly recommendable. The main meal of the day is the **evening meal** (ban-gohan); in

EATING WITH CHOPSTICKS

Chopsticks, called »o-hashi«, are the typical eating utensils used in Japan. They come in many different forms: from natural wood or bamboo chop sticks to artistically lacquered chop sticks, and even sticks made of ivory.

Chopsticks have been around since the Western Han Dynasty (206 BC–AD 220) in China. Since fuel was scarce the food was chopped up before cooking in order to reduce cooking times. The soups enriched with chopped-up ingredients so popular in the Far East are sipped, while bigger chunks are eaten with chop sticks. Even long noodles can be eaten with chop sticks if they are brought to the mouth, while holding the bowl underneath so that they can be bitten off and the remaining noodles fall back into the soup.

How is it Done?

Eating with chop sticks is much less complicated than it may initially appear. Hold them as follows: the lower chopstick is placed in the bend between the thumb and index finger as well as on the end of the ring finger, while the top chopstick is held by the thumb, index finger and middle finger, allowing it to be manoeuvred. Once the chopsticks are in place tap them on the table to ensure the tips come together.

Table Manners

Noisy slurping is not exactly aesthetic to European ears. However, our refined table manners were only adopted at the court of the Sun King Louis XIV. Before that people ate with their hands. In return, the Japanese consider it rude for anyone to blow their nose during a meal; necessary snuffling is allowed. It is also not permitted to stick the chopsticks in the rice at the table: that is only acceptable during ritual food sacrifices for the deceased.

Japan – pure heaven for those who like to try a bite of everything

Japanese households it is a combination of native and Chinese cuisine; rice and soup are indispensable components. Fish, meat and vegetables are also served in any combination and variation. Usually green tea and rice wine (sake) are also part of the meal; the latter is an ideal supplement to the meal, particularly when drunk hot. Japanese people also enjoy one of the excellent Japanese beers (biru) afterwards.

Manners! ▶ According to Japanese table manners it is impolite for diners to pour their own drinks, instead they pour them for each other; the individual dishes are not eaten one after the other, but side by side: the soup is not the starter, but is drunk throughout the meal.

Restaurants

There is hardly a country in the world whose cuisine is not represented in the cities of Japan. French, Italian, German, Chinese, Russian, Indian and Thai restaurants stand side by side, flanked by many Japanese speciality restaurants. They can be found on the street, in the upper storeys of the skyscrapers and in the underground levels. Hotel restaurants are more expensive.

Tableware   One pleasant custom is the oshibori: moist, hot cloths handed out to
Chopsticks ▶ refresh the face and clean the hands. Chopsticks (ohashi; ▶Baedeker Special p.123) can cause problems; here it is best to bring the bowl or plate close to the mouth (chop sticks can be used to push the

food), which is not considered impolite. Every meal is served on spe- ◀ Dishes
cial dishes: rice in a porcelain bowl, soup in a lacquer (or also plastic) bowl with a lid and fish and meat on porcelain or ceramic plates.
Water and tea are free with a meal.

In Western restaurants visitors will find a legible menu in English   Menu
and the usual cutlery; it is customary to pay at the exit, not at the
table. In fast-food restaurants and department store cafés visitors
should pay for their chosen food with coupons upon entering. A
special feature allows guests who do not speak the language to
choose their food: most of the restaurants have display cases with
plastic replicas of the different dishes. Pointing to the chosen meal
with the finger suffices to order.

It is **not customary** to give tips; better restaurants add a 10–15% ser-   Tips
vice charge to the bill. When the bill adds up to more than ¥ 7500
tax at 6% is added to the total.

In sushi restaurants it is customary to sit at a bar behind which the   Speciality-
ordered sushi is prepared; otherwise a selection of different kinds   restaurants
can be ordered. Kaiten-Zushi bars are popular. There the sushi is on ◀ Sushi
a moving belt that runs around the bar past the guests.
The tables of yaki (grill) restaurants have hotplates or hearths built ◀ Yaki
into them. They are used to cook dishes such as sukiyaki. Others
have charcoal grills next to the entrance on which yakitori are prepared, for example. Many of these unusually small restaurants are i-
ncredibly cosy and definitely worth experiencing, despite seating arrangements that are generally uncomfortable for Europeans.

In addition to the aforementioned options there are countless oppor-   Feeling peckish
tunities to pick up a noodle soup while on the go: on the streets, in
department stores or at stations. Those who are more thirsty than
hungry and only want a small, inexpensive snack should try either
the beer halls or the cafés. Japanese-style **pubs** (izakaya) serve more
than just beer, sake and whisky, namely roast chicken, fried fish or
smaller dishes depending on the season.

Japanese Menu

Eel, grilled over charcoal, basted in a special sauce and usually served   Kabayaki
on rice. Just as tasty as yakitori.

This **feast** is an exemplary demonstration of the three proverbial   Kaiseki
characteristics of Japanese cuisine: good taste, decorative presentation and exquisite tableware. Its preparation is very time-consuming,
and it is popularly served during the tea ceremony. Special care is given to preserving the natural flavour of all ingredients, such as fish,
vegetables, seaweed and mushrooms.

Mizutaki   Similarly to shabu-shabu, several ingredients such as chicken, pork and beef slices are cooked in a special broth and refined with a sour soy mixture.

Nabemono   This highly tasty dish, like fondue, is cooked while eating. The ingredients – meat, vegetables, fish, fruits de mer, and also chrysanthemum leaves – are cooked in a cast-iron pan in a mixture of soy sauce, sugar and sake, and before eating are dipped in a variety of sauces. A variation with noodles and tofu is the famous **sukiyaki**; as sauce there is also a dish with beaten raw egg.

Okonomiyaki   A type of pancake that diners usually prepare themselves at the table. Depending on personal preference meat, seafood and/or vegetables are added to the batter. The whole dish is coated with a thick brown sauce.

Ramen   A noodle soup originally from China. Sapporo, Wakayama and Hakata (Fukuoka) are particularly famous for ramen. The soup is served in special ramen restaurants, but also at snack bars and as ready-meals in supermarkets.

Sashimi   This dish made up of bite-sized chunks or slices of raw fish is a particular delicacy of the Japanese cuisine; it is definitely worthwhile throwing any reservations over board. The tender meat of the tuna is

Shabu-shabu – very thin slices of meat are cooked with vegetables in broth

a real joy. The fish is dunked in a soy sauce mixed with Japanese horseradish (wasabi, hot!).

Wafer-thin slices of meat, dunked with chop sticks into a boiling broth, which also contains vegetables. Meat and vegetables are dunked into sauces together. — **Shabu-shabu**

Buckwheat noodles with different ingredients, garnished with a broad range of ingredients. Similar to spaghetti and is also eaten cold (zaru-soba). — **Soba**

Different varieties of raw fish or squid and prawns, amongst other things, are served in small balls of vinegared rice and dunked in soy sauce before eating. This dish is best eaten with the hands. Sushi wrapped in seaweed (nori) is called maki-zushi. — **Sushi**

Prawns, slices of fish and different vegetables are coated in a batter of flour, egg and water and deep-fried in vegetable oil. The food is freshly prepared and before eating dunked in soy sauce mixed with ginger and wasabi. — **Tempura**

This dish is similar to sukiyaki; it is boiled fish with different vegetables, not prepared in a pan but on a steel plate. — **Teppan-yaki**

A breaded pork schnitzel, fried in a lot of oil and eaten with raw chopped cabbage. — **Tonkatsu**

»Udon« is the name of a Japanese noodle dish. The thick noodles are usually served in a large bowl with broth, which is sometimes enriched with meat, fish or vegetables. — **Udon**

Small pieces of chicken, liver and vegetables are lined up on a bamboo skewer. The skewer is grilled over an open fire. Perfectly suited as a snack. — **Yakitori**

Drinks

Green tea (o-cha) drunk without anything being added to it, may seem a bit bland in the beginning, but in combination with Japanese dishes is highly recommendable. — **Green tea**

Sake, which is brewed from rice (!), has an alcohol content of approx. 15% and is drunk both hot and cold. Sake is an ideal accompaniment to the taste of Japanese meals. — **Sake**

Beer has been brewed in Japan since the end of the 19th century; today it enjoys great popularity. The best-known brands (usually lightly hopped »lager«) are Kirin, Sapporo, Asahi and Suntory. — **Beer**

Wine | The northern foothills of Mount Fuji near Kofu (Yamanashi prefecture) are the only place where wine has been cultivated in Japan – in relatively small quantities and since the end of the 19th century. In addition to the expensive Japanese wines (white and red; dry) there are imported wines from European wine countries.

Spirits | Japanese people love whisky, because it gives them an exotic, i.e. American feeling. However, it is almost always drunk strongly diluted.
Shochu, which does not have a particularly pleasant taste, is a Japanese spirit obtained from the residues of sake production. Western palates and throats are better off trying awamori, which is prepared from sweet potatoes.
Ume-shu, plum schnapps, is also popular.

Tips | If alcoholic beverages are being consumed in a jolly group it is best to take care. Rice wine (sake) gives some drinkers a headache, mostly because it is being drunk in ever greater quantities. By the way, the Japanese consider those who hold their glass in their left hand to be boozers.

Health

Communication aids | The »Tourist's Language Handbook«, which is available in the Tourist Information Centres (▸Information) for free, contains a bilingual section with medical terms, questions and answers, which can be useful when trying to communicate with a doctor.

Pharmacies
Opening hours ▸ | In Japan a lot of medication is available without a prescription; English-language package inserts are generally obligatory. Pharmacies are usually open Mon–Fri 9am–6pm.

Information

Tourist information centres (TIC) | Tourist information centres (TICs) staffed with employees who speak foreign languages can be found in Tokyo and Kyoto as well as in Kansai International Airport and Narita International Airport.

Tourist Information System | The Tourist Information System created with the help of the Japan National Tourist Organization offers local and regional tourist information and also has English-language leaflets available. The offices can be recognized by their logo, a red question mark. Addresses ▸ Sights from A to Z.

USEFUL ADDRESSES

JNTO

► **Japan National Tourist Organization (JNTO)**
10th Floor, Tokyo Kotsu Kaikan Building 10-1, Yuraku-cho 2-chome, Chiyoda-ku J-100-0006 Tokyo
Tel. 03/32 01-3331, fax 32 14-76 80
daily 9am–5pm

JNTO OVERSEAS OFFICES

► **Japan National Tourist Organization Australia**
Self-service room only
Level 7, 36-38 Clarence Street
Sydney NSW 2000
travelinfo@jnto.org.au
Internet www.jnto.org.au

► **Japan National Tourist Organization Canada**
481 University Avenue, Suite 306
Toronto, ON M5G 2E9
Tel. 416/366 71 40
Internet www.jnto.go.jp/canada/

► **Japan National Tourist Organization UK**
5th Floor, 12 Nicholas Lane
London, EC4N 7BN
Tel. 020/73 98 56 78
Internet www. seejapan.co.uk

► **Japan National Tourist Organization USA East Coast**
One Rockefeller Plaza, Suite 1250
New York, NY 10020
Tel. 212/757 56 40
www. japantravelinfo.com

► **Japan National Tourist Organization USA West Coast**
515 South Figueroa St., Suite 1470
Los Angeles, CA 90071
Tel. 213/623 19 52
www.japantravelinfo.com

IN THE INTERNET

Useful information about Japan can be found on these websites amongst others:
www.japan-guide.com
www.japanvisitors.com
www.gojapan.about.com
www.att-japan.net
www.jref.com

DIPLOMATIC REPRESENTATION IN JAPAN

► **Australian Embassy**
2-1-14 Mita, Minato-ku
Tokyo
Tel. 03/52 32-41 11
www.australia.or.jp/englisch

► **Canadian Embassy**
7-3-38 Akasaka, Minato-ku
Tokyo
Tel. 03/54 12-62 00
www.canadanet.or.jp/
english.shtml

► **Embassy of the Republic of Ireland**
2-10-7 Koji-amchi, Chiyoda-ku
Tokyo
Tel. 03/34 32 63-06 95
www.embassy-avenue.jp/ireland/
index_eng.html.

► **New Zealand Embassy**
20-40 Kamiyama-cho,
Shibuya-ku
Tokyo
Tel. 03/34 67-22 71
www.nzembassy.com/
home.cfm?c=17

► **Embassy of the United Kingdom**
2-10-7 Koji-amchi,
Chiyoda-ku
Tokyo

Tel. 03/52 11-11 00
www.ukknow.or.jp/index_e.htm

▸ **Embassy of the United States**
1-10-5 Akasaka, Minato-ku
Tokyo
Tel. 03/32 24-50 00
http://japan.usembassy.gov/
t-main.html

JAPANESE EMBASSIES

▸ **In Australia**
112 Empire Circuit, Yarralumla
Canberra, ACT 2600
Tel. 02/62 73 32 44
www.japan.org.au

▸ **In Canada**
255 Sussex Drive
Ottawa, Ontario, K1N 9E6
Tel. 613 241 8541
www.ca.emb-japan.go.jp

▸ **In Ireland**
Nutley Building, Merrion Centre
Nutley Lane, Dublin 4
Tel. 01/202 83 00
www.ie.emb-japan.go.jp

▸ **In New Zealand**
The Majestic Centre
100 Willis St.
PO Box 6340, Wellington
Tel. 04/473 15 40
www.nz.emb-japan.go.jp

▸ **In United Kingdom**
101-104 Piccadilly
London W1V 9FN
Tel. 020/74 65 65 00
www.botschaft-japan.de

▸ **In USA**
2520 Massachusetts Ave, NW
Washington DC 20008
Tel. 202/238 67 00
www.us.emb-japan.go.jp

Language

Communication
Knowledge of Western languages is not yet very widespread in Japan; in addition the completely different writing system is a barrier to Europeans that should not be underestimated. Guides and employees of larger hotels at least generally speak English; there is also often the opportunity to get students with a knowledge of foreign languages to act as guides. Anyone relying on their knowledge of English should make sure to use simple sentences and clear pronunciation; the English spoken by Japanese people can be hard to understand. The average Japanese, and particularly the older generation, generally do not have much knowledge regarding other languages; this is also true of taxi drivers and the staff working for the public transportation system.

Transcription
The phonetic structure of the Japanese language does not cause much of a problem when transcribing Japanese symbols into Roman ones, as it is done in the »50-sound table«. It is based on the »hebonshiki romaji« (named after the American philologist James Curtis

Hepburn), which was set up by an academic commission in 1885 and which is also used for the transcriptions in this guide. In addition there is also the »kunreishiki romaji«, recommended for official use in Japan.

The pronunciation of the syllables transcribed according to the hebonshiki system follows the English language for the consonants and Italian for the vowels. There is one special feature that needs to be taken into account:

Vowels are always short, as long as they are not marked by a length sign (a line above the vowel). (Length-signs are not used in this book.) A double consonant does not lead to a shortening of the previous vowel (as it often does in English for example); instead the sound is spoken twice with a slight gap (as in book-case).

The e is never silent; a short i and u are often almost inaudible at the end of a word (»miruku« has a similar pronunciation to the English word »milk«). The s is always voiceless (as in »hiss«); the w is like the English w, and the case is similar for the letter f (the bottom lip and top incisors do not touch); the sound of the letter r is somewhere between an r and an l; ng are spoken as two sounds (as in »ungodly«).

Knowledge of some elementary words and phrases is very useful and is gratefully welcomed by the Japanese people. It is thus a good idea to learn at least a few rudimentary expressions. A helpful brochure when out and about is the **Tourist's Language Handbook«**, published by the JNTO.

JAPANESE

At a glance

Thank you	arigato gozaimasu
You're welcome	do itashi mashite
Excuse me	sumimasen
Yes/no	hai/iie
I don't understand	wakarimasen
Yesterday	kino
Today	kyo
This morning	kesa
This evening/tonight	komban
Tomorrow	ashita

Greetings

Good morning	ohayo gozaimasu

»jin«, »ki«, »ame« – three examples of kanji characters

THE WORLD'S HARDEST LANGUAGE AND WRITING SYSTEM?

»Nihongo wo hanashi masu ka?« A blank look and a shrug of the shoulders is probably the most common answer when this question is asked by a Japanese person, but all it means in English is »Do you speak Japanese?« After all, how many non-Japanese people are able to speak this language?

However, maybe the Japanese language is not so difficult after all. Many grammatical difficulties that we have when we are learning other European languages are not an issue with Japanese. First of all there are no differences in stress: every syllable is emphasized the same. Verbs are not inflected, there is no gender, no plural and often not even the person is indicated. The meaning of a sentence only becomes clear from the sequence of words, as is the case with many agglutinative languages with added syllables. What is difficult, but socially significant, are the words used to express politeness that are always adapted to fit a given situation. However, if a foreigner leaves these forms out, every Japanese person will show sympathetic understanding. When foreigners then learn that Japanese sentence structure follows the pattern subject–object–verb (e.g. I rice eat), making sentences is no longer so difficult: »yes, I eat rice – hai, (watashi wa) gohan wo tabe masu«. Here the syllables »wa« and »wo« label the subject and object respectively, »masu« with a silent »u« is the polite form of performing an action. The only difficulty is in remembering vocabulary that is so rich in vowels.

Logographs and Phonograms

The language thus seems learnable. However, what about its written characters? Here too there are learnable classifications. The first thing to know for anyone wanting to learn Japanese is that the Japanese writing system was originally adopted from the Chinese characters in the 6th century. These Chinese kanji characters have been modified somewhat in Japan. This first occurred in their pronunciation. This means there are two different ways to read any given kanji; »kun« is the Japanese way, »on« the Chinese way. Since the polysyllabic Japanese language is not linguistically related to the monosyllabic Chinese language, a number of Chi-

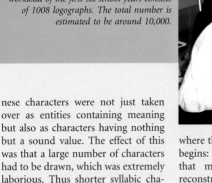

The dual Japanese writing system consists of logographs (kanji) and phonograms (kana) and requires a lot of effort to learn. The workload of the first six school years consists of 1008 logographs. The total number is estimated to be around 10,000.

nese characters were not just taken over as entities containing meaning but also as characters having nothing but a sound value. The effect of this was that a large number of characters had to be drawn, which was extremely laborious. Thus shorter syllabic characters were made that allowed all of the sounds of the Japanese language to be represented in writing.

The syllabary later termed hiragana goes back to the court ladies of the Heian period, who were not able to speak Chinese, but who wanted to write things down in Japanese. The other syllabary used in Japan, katakana, was developed by students of Buddhism in order to make notes to Chinese texts. Both syllabaries consist of 46 characters: the rounded symbols of hiragana are mainly used for endings and prepositions, while the angular characters of katakana are used for words of foreign origin and foreign proper names.

Highly Complex Writing System

It is not the language, but the writing system that causes visitors familiar with Western languages to despair. Is it really impossible to get to grips with Japanese? Since the Japanese writing system is a mixture of kanji and kana characters, it is absolutely necessary to have experience with kanji. This is

where the satisfying mental adventure begins: it is truly exciting to discover that many brush strokes can be reconstructed with some imagination to an original picture character. Isn't it fascinating, for example, that the character for »person« (jin) still has something recognizable as a head, a torso and two legs? The symbol (ki) meaning »tree« also still has something resembling a trunk, a treetop and branches. Even more complicated characters such as the one for »rain« (ame) can still be identified, with its cloud hanging in the sky and rain drops falling to the ground. To look for a word in a kanji dictionary, it is necessary to count the number of brush strokes a character contains.

These days Japanese children go to primary school for six years, during which time they will learn 1008 kanji characters. Official publications make use of only 1945 basic characters known as joyokanji. However, anyone wanting to read pre-war literature will need to know thousands more kanji, including ones that have up to 23 brush strokes. The characters are read from top to bottom; the text is read from right to left: Japanese newspapers and books are read »from back to front«.

Good day	konnichiwa
Good evening	kombanwa
Good night	oyasuminasai
I am English	watashiwa igirisu-jin desu
I am American	watashiwa amerika-jin desu
Pleased to meet you	hajime mashite
What's your name?	onamae wa?
My name ...	... to moshimasu
Goodbye	sayonara

On the go

Left / Right	hidari / migi
North / East / South / West	kita / higashi / minami / nishi
Where is ...?	... wa dokodesuka?
Where is the post office?	yubinkyoku wa dokodesuka?
Where is the bank?	ginko wa dokodesuka?
Where is the railway station?	eki wa dokodesuka?
Where is the department store?	depato wa dokodesuka?
Where is the taxi stand?	takushi noriba wa dokodesuka?
Where is the luggage room?	nimotsu azukarijo wa dokodesuka?
Where is the youth hostel?	yusu hosuteru wa dokodesuka?
Where is the toilet?	toire wa dokodesuka?
Hairdresser (for women)	bi-yoin
Hairdresser (for men)	tokoya
Tourist information centre	kanko annaijo
Hotel	hoteru
Reservation	yoyaku
Bill	kanjo
Doctor	isha
Airport	hikojo, kuko
Underground	chikatetsu
Luggage porter	akabo
Ticket machine	kippu-uriba
Block (houses)	-cho, chome
City quarter	machi
City district	-ku
Town/city	-shi
Village	mura
County	-gun
Prefecture	-ken

Shopping

| Please show me this | kore o misete kudasai |
| How much does it cost? | ikura desuka? |

That's too expensive	takasugimasu
Please show me something cheaper	mo sukoshi yasui no wo misete itadakemasenka?
I will take this	kore wo kudasai
Colour film	purinto yo kara firumu
Colour film for slides	suraido yo kara firumu
Camera	kamera
Watch	tokei
Craft products	mingeihin
Souvenir	miyagehin
Doll	ningyo
Toy	omocha
Cigarettes	tabako

Food

Restaurant	resutoran
Clear soup	konsome
Thick soup	potaju
Table salt	shio
Pepper	kosho
Cake	keki
Coffee	kohi
Black tea	kocha
Beer	biru
Milk	miruku
Bread	pan
Menu	menyu

In the doctor's surgery

Hospital	byoin
Doctor	isha
Dentist	shi-ka, ha-isha
I am sick	byo-ki desu
Please come quickly	hayaku kite kudasai
I can only speak English	eigo shika hanashimasen

Numbers

0	zero
1	ichi
2	ni
3	san

4	shi, yon
5	go
6	roku
7	nana, shichi
8	hachi
9	kyu
10	ju
100	hyaku
1000	sen
10,000	ichi-man
32,520	san-man ni-sen go-hyaku ni-ju

Literature

Non-fiction books **Alan Booth**: *The Roads to Sata*: A 2000-mile Walk Through Japan, Kodansha America, 1997. Well-written account of a journey from the far north to the far south of Japan, full of insights about the country.

i **The best films**

- *Spirited Away* by Miyazaki Hayao
- *Hana-Bi* by Kitano Takeshi
- *Rashomon* by Kurosawa Akira
- *The Twilight Samurai* by Yamada Yoji
- *Tokyo Story – Tokyo Monogatari* by Ozu Yasujiro
- *Minbo - or the Gentle Art of Japanese Extortion* von Itami Juzo

Alan Booth: *Looking for the Lost – Journeys Through a Vanishing Japan*, Kodansha America, 1996. The last travelogue by this connoisseur of Japan.

Ian Buruma: The Wages of Guilt: Memories of War in Germany and Japan, Vintage, 1995. An analysis of how Germany and Japan have coped very differently with their past.

Peter Carey: *Wrong about Japan: A Father's Journey with his Son*, Vintage Books USA, 2007. Novelist Peter Carey and his 12-year-old son discover Japan by tracking down the world of manga comics.

Alex Kerr: Dogs and Demons: The Fall of Modern Japan, Penguin Books, 2002. A sobering account of the effects of economic growth on Japanese culture and the environment.

Musashi Miyamoto: *The Book of Five Rings: A Classic Text on the Japanese Way of the Sword*, Shambala Publications 1993. In this book the famous Samurai and master of the sword (1584-1645) writes about the spirit of martial arts.

Robb Satterwhite: *What's What in Japanese Restaurants*, Kodansha International, 1996. A really useful travel companion that explains the different kinds of Japanese food.

Abe Kobo: *The Woman in the Dunes*, Penguin Classics 2006. A major work by one of Japan's most talented 20th-century authors, who is often compared to Kafka.

Fiction

Arthur Golden: *Memoirs of a Geisha*, Vintage 1998. Bestseller about the fate of a young geisha. Those wanting to discover the true story of the geisha on whose life Golden's novel is based, should also read the autobiography *Geisha of Gion* by **Iwasaki Mineko** (Simon & Schuster, 2003).

Mori Ogai: *Not a Song Like Any Other: An Anthology of Writings by Mori Ogai*, University of Hawaii Press, 2004. Mori Ogai (1862-1922), who wrote essays, short stories and novels in addition to his interest in art and the theatre, was one of the leading artistic and intellectual figures of the Meiji period.

Haruki: *A Wild Sheep Case*, Random House 2002. Murakami, well-known contemporary Japanese author, almost enjoys cult status. He writes fantastic stories with sci-fi elements and nameless »heroes«.

Nagai Kafu: *A Strange Tale from East of the River*, Tuttle 1972. Tender love story set in Tokyo's brothel district in the 1930s.

Natsume Soseki: *I am a Cat*, Tuttle, 2002. Besides Ogai the other great author from the Meiji period. Critical, satirical novel from the point of view of a tomcat.

Oe Kenzaburo: *A Personal Matter*, Grove 2000. Autobiographical novel: The author learns to accept his mentally disabled son.

The Pillow Book **Sei Shonagon**. Penguin Classics, 2006. Classic story of Japanese literature, written by a court lady of the Heian period. Amusing and poetic scenes, observations from her everyday life, insights and aphorisms.

Uno Chiyo: *The Story of a Single Woman*, Owen, 1992. Autobiographical novel about the life of an unconventional Japanese woman. Uno founded the first Japanese fashion magazine (1936), sometimes worked as a waitress, a shop assistant and as a reporter and associated with well-known Japanese authors.

Yoshikawa Eiji: *Musashi*, Corgi, 1990. Extensive historical novel about the master of the sword Musashi; made into a film several times and also performed on stage.

Yoshimoto Banana: K*itchen*, Faber and Faber, 1997. Popular with young people: stories about loss, dreams, unconventional families, unlikely events. Here about a young orphaned woman who finds a friend whose mother was once a man…

Media

Radio   BBC World Service can be received on shortwave and via USEN cable, channel E-17; Voice of America on various frequencies (see www.voanews.com for details).

Television   The national Japanese television service broadcasts two programmes, one of which is of a generally entertaining character, while the other is more educational and informative. In addition there are private broadcasters with different programmes. In hotels with cable or satellite television English-language programmes can be watched.

Newspapers   The biggest daily newspapers in Japan are *Yomiuri Shimbun*, *Asahi Shimbun*, *Mainichi Shimbun* and *Chunichi Shimbun*. The most important business paper is *Nikkei Shimbun*. Newspaper stands at railway stations also carry various English-language newspapers from Japan such as *The Japan Times*, *Daily Yomiuri* and *Asahi Evening News* for example.

Money

Currency   The currency of Japan is the yen. There are 500, 1,000, 2,000, 5,000 and 10,000 yen bank notes as well as 1, 5, 10, 50, 100 and 500 yen coins.

Foreign currency regulations   There are no restrictions on bringing yen and foreign currencies into Japan; however, it is a good idea to declare any larger sums of money. There is no upper limit to the amount of foreign currency that can be taken out of Japan, while exports of ¥ are limited to ¥ 5 million.

How to pay?   A surprising fact: although Japan has a lot of highly modern technology, paying with a credit card is still not very widespread, except in large hotels and shops: **cash** is still the main way to pay. Visitors wanting to take out money with the main credit or debit cards should use the **ATMs (cash machines)** in the Japanese post offices, which are linked to the Cirrus and Maestro systems.

i | Exchange rates

- ¥ 100 = GBP 0.72; GBP 1.00 = ¥ 137
- ¥ 100 = USD 1.06; USD 1 = ¥ 93
- ¥ 100 = EUR 0.79; EUR 1 = ¥ 126

Banks open Mon–Fri 9am–3pm. **Warning:** Foreign currency and traveller's cheques are not accepted by every bank. Anyone needing money outside the banks' opening hours is dependent on large hotels; occasionally large department stores also exchange foreign currency. Banks have a **receptionist** who will take customers to the right counter and issue a number. Visitors should come with plenty of time and have their passport and hotel address ready.

National Parks

In March 1934 Japan's first three national parks were set up: Setonai-kai, Unzen-Amakusa and Kirishima-Yaku. Currently Japan has 28 national parks, which are spread all across the country. They were set up in areas where the landscape displays special characteristics and often include cultural monuments such as temple and shrine complexes. Coastal waters may also be included in the protected areas and the majority of the Inland Sea was also declared a national park. Since Japan's landscapes are not as open and extensive as those of Europe or North America, many national parks consist of a number of non-contiguous protected areas.

Far-flung

Japan's national parks (▶ map p.140), with more than 2 million ha/ 5 million acres, cover 5.4% of the country's total area. Another 3.6% of the area are taken up by the 55 quasi-national parks.

Total area

Opening Hours

Small shops open daily (including the weekend) from 10am–8pm, department stores Mon–Sun from 10am to at least 7pm, but they usually close on one weekday. Over New Year almost everywhere is closed. However, every Japanese town has convenience stores open 24 hours. They are called **Combini** in Japan.

Shops

Most museums close on Mondays and are generally open Tue–Sun 9am–5pm.

◀ Museums

Pachinko

Those who enjoy playing on slot machines at home should have a go in one of Japan's Pachinko halls. Steel balls, if they fall properly,

National Parks in Japan *Map*

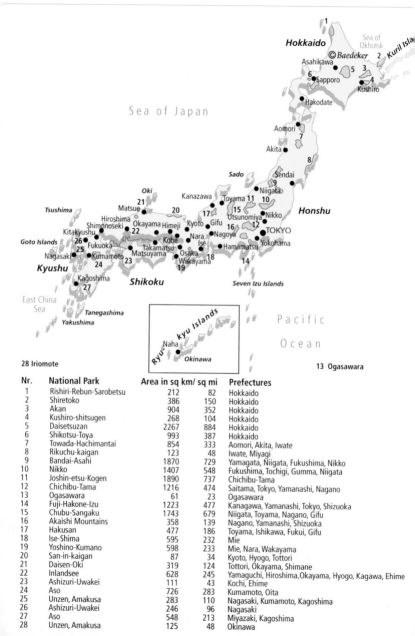

28 Iriomote

13 Ogasawara

Nr.	National Park	Area in sq km/	sq mi	Prefectures
1	Rishiri-Rebun-Sarobetsu	212	82	Hokkaido
2	Shiretoko	386	150	Hokkaido
3	Akan	904	352	Hokkaido
4	Kushiro-shitsugen	268	104	Hokkaido
5	Daisetsuzan	2267	884	Hokkaido
6	Shikotsu-Toya	993	387	Hokkaido
7	Towada-Hachimantai	854	333	Aomori, Akita, Iwate
8	Rikuchu-kaigan	123	48	Iwate, Miyagi
9	Bandai-Asahi	1870	729	Yamagata, Niigata, Fukushima, Nikko
10	Nikko	1407	548	Fukushima, Tochigi, Gumma, Niigata
11	Joshin-etsu-Kogen	1890	737	Chichibu-Tama
12	Chichibu-Tama	1216	474	Saitama, Tokyo, Yamanashi, Nagano
13	Ogasawara	61	23	Ogasawara
14	Fuji-Hakone-Izu	1223	477	Kanagawa, Yamanashi, Tokyo, Shizuoka
15	Chubu-Sangaku	1743	679	Niigata, Toyama, Nagano, Gifu
16	Akaishi Mountains	358	139	Nagano, Yamanashi, Shizuoka
17	Hakusan	477	186	Toyama, Ishikawa, Fukui, Gifu
18	Ise-Shima	595	232	Mie
19	Yoshino-Kumano	598	233	Mie, Nara, Wakayama
20	San-in-kaigan	87	34	Kyoto, Hyogo, Tottori
21	Daisen-Oki	319	124	Tottori, Okayama, Shimane
22	Inlandsee	628	245	Yamaguchi, Hiroshima,Okayama, Hyogo, Kagawa, Ehime
23	Ashizuri-Uwakei	111	43	Kochi, Ehime
24	Aso	726	283	Kumamoto, Oita
25	Unzen, Amakusa	283	110	Nagasaki, Kumamoto, Kagoshima
26	Ashizuri-Uwakei	246	96	Nagasaki
27	Aso	548	213	Miyazaki, Kagoshima
28	Unzen, Amakusa	125	48	Okinawa

bring a prize announced by ringing and flickering lights: new balls. One Japanese in three spends several hours a week on this **popular game of luck and skill**; at the end the balls won can be exchanged for olive oil, cigarettes, ladies' stockings or similar items. On closer observation of the winners it becomes clear that the material prizes are often exchanged for cash in a side street, unofficially of course.

Personal Safety

Japan is a country in which foreigners can move about freely alone both during the day and at night. The crime rate is lower than in the West.

A safe country

A noticeable feature of Japan's towns and cities are the small huts, called »koban«, to be found at every larger intersection: a guard house for police officers equipped with a telephone, beds and a place to cook and from which the officers look after their area. They go on patrol from here, usually in groups of two. Since they usually work in the same area for years they know every family and every address in their area. This facility is also very helpful for tourists. Anyone who has lost their way, for example, can approach the closest koban without hesitation to ask a police officer for advice. If the officer does not speak any English, he will phone the police headquarters, where there is an interpreter available.

Police koban

Japan is located in a tectonically active zone, which frequently experiences **earthquakes**, which is why special safety standards have to be adhered to in construction. Major cities have disaster protection rooms as well as an earthquake early warning system. Submarine quakes and volcanic eruptions cause »**tsunamis**«, gigantic flood waves reaching a height of 35m/115ft near the coast and capable of causing a vast amount of damage. In the event of an earthquake it is important to stay away from windows and not rush outside, but to find shelter under something solid, such as a table.

◄ Correct behaviour

Post · Telecommunications

Post offices are generally open Mon–Fri 9am–5pm; some main post offices are open daily and for longer hours.
The red letter boxes have two slots: the right-hand one is for express mail and international post, while the left-hand slot is for domestic post.

Post

◄ Letter boxes

Postage ▶ Letters (up to 25g) within Japan ¥ 80, to Europe ¥ 110, international aerograms ¥ 90, postcards within Japan ¥ 50, to Europe ¥ 70.

Telephone The green and grey public telephones in Japan can be operated with both coins (¥ 10, ¥ 100) and phone cards. The latter can be bought from one of the numerous Combini (convenience stores) open 24/7 such as Lawson or Seven Eleven, at kiosks or right next to the telephone from vending machines. A local calls costs ¥ 10 per minute. International calls are very expensive by comparison. In addition not every public telephone can be used to make international calls; only grey and green-golden NTT telephones can be used if they are marked as such (»International & Domestic Card/Coin Telephone«) as well as IC telephones. Warning: the latter telephones only work if a corner of the phone card is removed and the card is then placed into the »card holder« (not a slot).

Before entering the international dialling code the **dialling code of the telephone company** has to be dialled. There are currently three telephone companies offering international direct-dial calls: KDD (001), IDC (0061) and Nippon Telecom (0041). First the number of the telephone company has to be dialled, then 010 and then the country's dialling code. A call from Japan to London could thus have the following number: 001-010-44-208-... If all that is too complicated it is possible to dial 0051 to get the help of an English-speaking **operator**. The charges are lower at the weekends, at night time and on public holidays.

> **! Baedeker TIP**
>
> **Calling cards**
>
> There are also calling cards that have a code, with which phone calls can be made from a mobile phone or a private landline. The special international calling cards usually have less expensive rates.

> **i International dialling codes**
>
> - to UK: 0044
> - to Australia: 353
> - to Switzerland: 1
> - to USA and Canada: 61

Mobile phone It is best visitors enquire before their trip whether their mobile phone can be used in Japan or not. This is not generally the case. It is possible to rent a mobile phone in Japan for the duration of the trip, such as from Rentafone, www.rentafonejapan.com, tel. 080/32 40 91 83, or Japan Handy Phone, www.japanphone.com, tel. 03/52 25 21 25.

Prices · Discounts

An expensive country Japan, being an industrialized country, has a high price level. Tokyo in particular is definitely not a cheap destination, but there are ways

WHAT DOES IT COST?

**O-bento
(snack box)**
from ¥ 650

**Lunch
menu**
from ¥ 800

**Cup of
coffee**
¥ 350–400

**Glass of beer
in pub**
¥ 650–700

Night in a youth hostel
approx.
¥ 3000 per person

Night in business hotel
from ¥ 5500 per person

Night in a ryokan
from ¥ 12,000 per
person

to save some money. Udon in one of the many noodle bars is filling and can be bought for as little as ¥ 500. Water and Japanese tea are served everywhere free with a meal. Anyone feeling thirsty during the day can purchase a drink from a vending machine, which are available at every street corner and have a wide selection of refreshments on offer. Youth hostels, which are also open to older people, can be found in every town worth visiting. Those who insist on a private bathroom are best off booking a room in a business hotel. Travellers with a limited budget would do well to spend not too much time in Tokyo and visit more rural regions instead, where everything is less expensive. Those who have the time can get to their destination with a comparatively cheap slow train or a bus instead of the shinkansen. Depending on how long and how far the trip is going to be, a JP Rail Pass (►p.156) could also be worthwhile. It can also be used to get a 10% discount for rooms in hotels belonging to the JP Group (www.jrhotelgroup.com).

Welcome Cards give different discounts to entry fees, tickets for local transport, accommodation and restaurants. They are available free from the tourist information centres in various cities.   ◄ Welcome Card

Big cities often have inexpensive day passes for public transport. It is best to ask for a »ichinichi-joshaken«.   ◄ Local transport

Students holding a valid international student identity card will get a reduced entry fee to most of the sights and museums. The Japanese Tourist Centre (► Information) publishes a brochure called **Affordable Japan** with tips and addresses. Further information can be obtained from **www.jnto.go.jp/affordable**.   ◄ Student Identity Cards
◄ Further information

Shopping

After traditional arts and crafts threatened to disappear as a result of industrialization around 1900, efforts were made shortly after the   Traditional art turn of the century to revive old techniques. Yanagi Soetsu (1889–1961) made an outstanding contribution. He assembled a folk craft collection of inestimable value from all parts of Japan. In 1931 he and the potters Kawai Kanjiro and Hamada Shoji founded an association for Japanese folk craft (Nihon Mingei-kyokei) and five years later the Japan Folk Crafts Museum (Nihon Mingeikan) in Tokyo.

Despite a flood of industrial souvenirs and an overlap between art and kitsch, there are still a lot of goods from traditional artistic, high-quality production distinguished by their characteristic style, love of detail and good quality.

Duty-free shopping

Japan has a rich selection of industrial products as well as arts and crafts. Foreign visitors can buy a lot tax free; shops carrying such goods will have a sign at the entrance reading »**tax free**«. In order to take tax-free goods out of the country a form called the Record of Purchase of Commodities Taxfree is needed, which the vendor will add to the customer's passport. The amount saved is 5%. Excluded from tax-free purchases are food, medication, cosmetics, alcohol, tobacco and batteries.

The **purchase of electronic goods** is only a good idea if they are guaranteed to work in Europe. Visitors should make sure the items can be set to the necessary voltage (the Japanese mains only use 100 V alternating current!). Otherwise an adapter (hen'atsuki) will also have to be bought. Another thing that should not be forgotten is that the maximum free luggage allowance in the aeroplane as well as the home country's customs regulations set limits to any shopping spree.

> ## ! Baedeker TIP
>
> ### Where to find...
>
> A good overview of traditional arts and crafts is available in the hall of the Japan Traditional Craft Center amongst other things, which hosts permanent and changing exhibitions and has a well-organized video corner (near Ikebukuro station, 1st & 2nd Floor, Metropolitan Plaza, 1-11-1 Nishi-Ikebukuro, Toshima-ku, Tokyo, www.kougei.or.jp/english, open daily 11am–7pm).

Popular Souvenirs

Pottery

Japanese pottery (yaki), famous from an early date and decisively influenced and developed further by Korean masters since the time of Toyotomi Hideyoshi's military campaigns (1592–98) is, despite all its variety, characterized by simple forms and low-key aesthetic decor. The numerous factories located all around the country have sales rooms and exhibition rooms, offer tours of the works and also maintain hobby workshops. The most significant pottery towns are Mashiko (Toshigi Prefecture), Seto and Tokoname (Aichi Prefecture), Tajimi and Toki (Gifu Prefecture), Kanazawa (Ishikawa Prefecture), Shigaraki (Shiga Prefecture), Kyoto (Kyoto Prefecture), Imbe (Okaya-

A pretty souvenir – traditional Japanese wooden sandals

ma Prefecture), Hagi (Yamaguchi Prefecture), Arita and Karatsu (Saga Prefecture) as well as Sarayama (Oita Prefecture).

The lacquerware tradition is carried on in the old production centres **Lacquerware** of Tokyo, Kyoto and Kanazawa; further workshops can be found in Takamatsu and Nagoya. More basic goods for everyday use are produced in the prefectures of Fukushima, Ishikawa, Toyama and Wakayama. More information about the various production techniques: ►Arts and Culture, p. 71)

There are also different options when it comes to dyeing textiles. The **Textiles** three methods of tie-dye (kokechi), batik (rokechi) and the stencil technique for folded fabrics (kyokechi) have been used since early on. Patterned **kokechi fabrics** are mainly produced in Okinawa as well as in the prefectures of Kumamoto, Kagoshima, Ehime, Shimane and Niigata. Leaders in dyeing technique are Kyoto and Kanazawa as well as Tokyo and the prefectures of Miyagi and Yamagata. Indigo-blue fabrics are very popular. In the past this colour was used to dye farmers' clothes because it is said to repel insects. Aomori in northern Japan is known for **geometric embroidery** on a dark background; on Hokkaido**appliqué products** as they were once made by the Ainu can still be found.
Real kimonos cost a fortune, but they can be got for less money on flea markets or in second hand shops. Another nice souvenir is the cotton yukata (nemaki) worn in Japan after taking a bath and for sleeping.

Paper   Japanese paper has a large variety of applications: for the production of dolls, colourful boxes, to cover folding screens and sliding doors as well as for the artistic art of paper folding (origami).
The art of paper making probably came to Japan from China in the early 7th century. Today the most important paper mills are located in the Iwate (Higashiyama, Yanagifu), Niigata (Oguni), Nagano (Matsumoto), Saitama, Gifu, Fukui, Kanazawa prefectures, as well as in the cities of Tokyo and Kyoto.

Netsuke   The small sculptures known as netsuke that appeared in the 15th century originally served as fasteners for cords pulled through under the belt to hold wallets, writing utensils and such like (► Arts and Culture, p.77). Netsuke sculptures, which are pleasant to handle because of their smooth surface, are mainly made of bamboo, wood, ivory, lacquer, porcelain or semi-precious stones and have been collectors' items for some time now. Old ones are hard to find these days, and even new netsuke go for handsome sums.

Metal wares   In the category of metal wares the bronze vases made in Kyoto and Tokyo deserve mention, as do the cast-iron tea pots and water containers from Morioka and Kyoto. Some of the best metal works are the swords, mainly produced during the 14th century, which can cost several tens of thousands of euros.

A Tokyo institution – Mitsukoshi department store has a long tradition

Fans are decorative and also practical on hot summer days in Japan. *Fans*
They can be bought in any price range and in very diverse designs.
The best-known ones are folding fans (sensu) from Kyoto and round
fans (uchiwa) from Marugame and Shikoku.

European feet will need to get used to the traditional Japanese wood *Geta/Zori*
sandals (geta), but they are definitely more comely than the flip-flops
used in Europe. Sandals that are not elevated are easier to walk in.
They are called zori. Both are said to be good for the feet in that the
straps apparently stimulate acupuncture points between the toes.

Japanese dolls are less toys than decorative objects. **Kokeshi**, simple *Dolls*
wooden dolls from northern Japan with a cylindrical body, a large
head and red and black paint, are both affordable and popular. The
dolls known as **kimokomi-ningyo**, named after their manufacturing
technique are more elaborate: the torso has narrow ridges into which
different bits of fabric are stuck; the clothes are stuck to the doll's
body and cannot be removed.

Japanese sweets are not everybody's taste. However, they are definite- *Sweets and*
ly pretty to look at. Every place has its own specialities. Since it is *snacks*
customary to bring something from a trip for friends and colleagues
every station has many stands selling boxes filled with the local
sweets.
Japanese sweets (wagashi) are divided into »dry« and »moist«. The
former group includes sweets such as salty senbei (rice cakes) and
colourful higashi made from rice powder, which somewhat resemble
glucose in their appearance and which are made in the shape of sea-
sonally fitting flowers and leaves. The latter group includes yokan, a
gel-like block made of bean paste.

Bamboo can be used in a large number of applications: it is used for *Bamboo*
the manufacture of chopsticks, Japanese recorders (shakuhachi), baskets and a lot more. The bamboo goods from Okayama Prefecture
and from Beppu, for example, are well-known.

Japanese whisky is of course is far cheaper here than at home, and is *Whisky*
something for connoisseurs.

Where to Shop?

Tokyo's International Narita Airport is particularly good for shop- *At airports*
ping: it has around 40 shops, including souvenir and book shops, camera, cosmetics, pearl, and toy shops as well as a duty-free shop;
Osaka's International Kansai Airport also has numerous shops, including shops carrying women's wear and men's wear, children's clothes, leather goods, kimonos, watches, jewellery, pearls and traditional Japanese arts and crafts.

Department
stores

Department stores (depatos) provide outstanding quality in Japan. The department store chains Daimaru, Sogo, Seibu, Isetan and Matsuzakaya are represented not just in Tokyo but also in other cities. The Tokyo department store **Mitsukoshi** has a tradition going back more than 300 years; **Matsuya** is the largest store in the well-known Ginza shopping street in the district of Chuo-ku. Another recommendable department store chain is **Tokyu Hands**. The necessary equipment for every hobby can be bought here, as well as camping equipment, household goods, stationery, even Western sweets: in short, there is almost nothing this store does not sell.

Muji shops

It is well worth visiting a Muji shop: they sell all sorts of goods from office material to objects for the home and food to furniture and clothes. This brand, which does not really want to be one (»muji« means »no logo«), is characterized by a very simple, functional design and clear colours such as dark blue, brown, black and white.

Spas

Springs steeped
in legend

The hot springs, whose existence Japan owes to its volcanoes, are a blessing. There are thousands of these **onsen** all around the country. Spas have sprung up around many of them. Almost every old-established onsen has a story about the spring's discovery. Maybe a wounded mountain god put down his bow and lo and behold! A spring bubbled up from the ground. Or a young poet of the Heian period, who fell ill when she was searching for her father, saw the healing Buddha, who sent her to a spring. Regardless of whether these stories are from the realm of legend, it is clear that the roots of the Japanese bathing tradition reach far back into the past.

Onsen

Company trips with overnight stays in a nearby hot spring resort are especially popular towards the end of the year. After the bath the employees relax in a yukata (a light cotton kimono) to have some food (and drink!) together and generally to have a good time. Families also like to take short trips to an onsen. The **rotemburo** are particularly attractive. These are open-air onsen, high up in the mountains or with a view of the sea. They are especially soothing during the winter, a fact Japanese monkeys also appreciate. The baths made of cypress wood are extremely stylish. Not only does the wood have a pleasant scent, it is also said to contain antibacterial properties. Officially only the springs with a water temperature of at least 25 °C/ 77 °F and a certain **mineral content** are considered onsen. Depending

i Further reading

■ The Japanese Spa: A Guide to Japan's Finest Ryokan and Onsen, Akihiko Seki, Elizabeth Heilman Brooke, Tuttle Publishing 2005.

Baths play an important role in Japanese culture

on its composition the onsen water can help with rheumatic complaints, muscle pain, skin diseases and neuralgias; some baths are even said to help with diabetes and haemorrhoids. In some onsen visitors can be buried in sand (sunaburo) or bathe in mud (doroyu). But even those who are completely healthy will feel the soothing, relaxing effect of the water.

Visiting an onsen is surely one of the most attractive aspects of a trip to Japan. However, the large number of onsen makes it impossible to issue recommendations: every region has its own famous or hidden onsen. In any case visitors should visit an onsen at least once while in Japan. The tourist information centres can help with choosing one.

Those who do not make it to an onsen but who still want to breathe in a bit of the Japanese spa atmosphere should visit a sento. These **public baths** are becoming rarer and rarer since the vast majority of Japanese homes now have their own bathrooms, but some very atmospheric bath houses have still managed to survive even in the big cities of Tokyo and Osaka. In addition the 1990s saw the development of what are called super sento, huge facilities with up to 20 baths, saunas and other extras, most of which are not however fed by natural springs. An upmarket

Sento

! **Baedeker** TIP

Best time to go

A good time to visit an onsen is after 6pm because most guests then go and have dinner in the ryokan.

version is Kenko Land (»health land«), which in addition to providing bathing facilities also offers food, karaoke, massage chairs and other pleasures.

Etiquette   Given such an old bathing culture, it is not surprising that the Japanese people generally prefer an evening bath to a morning shower. The Japanese consider it to be almost a crime to get into a bubble bath without having washed in advance. The same rules that apply at home apply in the onsen and the sento.

Today almost all baths have gender-segregated areas; mixed bathing was prohibited by the American occupying forces after the war. Shoes are taken off in the entrance area and exchanged for slippers. There are baskets or shelves in the bath's anteroom, where visitors can put their clothes and a towel. The actual bathing room is entered naked. Japanese visitors usually bring a narrow, thin towel with which they cover their genitals and which they also use as a flannel (but which they never take into the water). These cloths can usually be bought at the bath. Visitors sit on a small stool in front of a tap and cover themselves in soap. Soap and shampoo is usually provided for this purpose. After having washed and showered visitors can enter the bath. Since the water is often **very hot** it is best to take care when getting in. Onsen are not for swimming, they are for sitting and relaxing. A minshuku may only have one bath available. In that case visitors should ask when the bath is free, but do not pull the plug after the bath!

And do not wash afterwards as that would cause the effect of the minerals to be lost. To prevent too much strain on the circulation it is recommended that visitors also take a short break afterwards.

Sports

The way of war   Visitors to Japan who want to experience sports will do so as spectators above all. Japan's **traditional sports** (with the exception of sumo) are grouped under the heading of »budo« (»the way of war«). All martial arts belonging to this category are based on the Zen philosophy that strives for perfect harmony between body and mind, which is at least as important to the athlete as the purely physical aspect.

Since World War II Western, and especially American, sports have also found their way to Japan.

Japanese Sports

Aikido   Aikido, a method of self-defence that emerged during the 12th century, was given its modern form by Ueshiba Morihei (1883–1917). Weapons are only used when the opponent is also armed; complete bodily control is crucial for the outcome of a fight.

Kendo, a martial art, derives from sword fighting

Judo

Judo, which has also become ever more popular in Western countries, evolved from jujutsu, as practised by the samurai. The goal of this martial art is for a fighter to use the opponent's strength to his personal advantage; only holds and throws are permitted. The level achieved by a judoka is shown by the colour of the belt. In the international sport there are seven weight classes.

Karate

Anyone who identifies karate with spectacularly shattering a brick with the hand is on the wrong track. The legendary karateka Oyama Masutatsu has described the »empty hand« fighting technique (since karate does not make use of any weapons) thus: »Karate is not a game. It is not a sport. It is not even a technique of self-defence. Karate is a discipline which is half physical, half spiritual. The karateka with the necessary years of practice and meditation behind him, is a cheerful and peaceful person. He has no fear. He remains calm in a burning house«.

Kendo

Kendo, which developed from the former art of fencing with swords is now practised with bamboo staves. The fighters wear protection for their heads and faces as well as a breastplate made of leather and bamboo. Kendo is part of the Japanese police training programme; spectators are allowed to attend the training sessions.

Kyudo

Kyudo, the ancient art of archery, still has a large number of followers today. An asymmetrical bow with a length of around 2.25m/7.5ft is used. The purely athletic aspect greatly fades into the background in favour of the meditative component. Schools and training halls are often attached to temples; over the centuries several different teachings have evolved.

BATTLE OF THE GIANTS

Sumo wrestling is Japan's oldest sport. Fattened up with chanko-nabe, a protein-rich stew, the sumotori, who can weigh up to 200kg/440lb, have become ideal athletes and national heroes in Japan. However, is all of this really Japanese and most of all, is it athletic?

Sumo as a Religion

Sumo is both. Wrestling is more of a religion than a sport, since according to legend this wrestling match is a symbolic, historic fight between two gods about the ownership of a province. It is more likely, however, that the first sumo contests took place at shrines and represented rituals for the gods to ask for a good harvest. One fact reminiscent of this relationship is the roof in the style of a Shinto shrine hanging over the ring (diameter: 4.5m/15ft).

Rules and Ranks

The rules of sumo wrestling are more complicated than they may appear at first: there are more than 80 techniques, ten different ranks and very specific rituals but, surprisingly, no weight classes. The highest rank in sumo wrestling is yokozuna, which the Japan Sumo Association awards to a sumo wrestler under certain conditions. In the past 300 years only 69 wrestlers have reached this rank. In contrast to all other ranks, a yokozuna cannot be demoted; the wrestler will keep this title until he leaves the sport to make way for someone better. Even the referees (gyoji) have different ranks, which can be seen by the colour of the tassel on the fan with which they give the starting signal.

Heya

Sumo wrestlers belong to certain »stables« (heya), which they never change during their career. They also live in these training camps (of which there are currently 55) until they withdraw from the sport. They give themselves fine-sounding stage names, such as »Young Flower«, »Rich Sea« or »Little Brocade«, have magnificent loin cloths made and wear their hair in a bun as was the style during the Edo period.

Tournaments

There are six large Sumo tournaments (Hon-Basho) a year, all of which last 15 days: in Tokyo in January, May and September, in Osaka in March, in Nagoya in July and in Fukuoka in November. No-one staying in Japan during one of the tournaments should

Sumo wrestler wearing a »tsuna«, a rope wrapped around the hips with specially folded paper strips marking the wearer as yokozuna

wrestler except those of the lowest ranks fights every day, i.e. a total of 15 times. The wrestler who has the most victories by the end of the tournament wins the Emperor's Cup.

miss the opportunity to attend one of these very Japanese spectacles. The entrance of the Sumo wrestlers into the arena (Do-hyo-iri) is in itself an impressive sight. No less imposing is the conclusion of the event, consisting of a dance with a bow performed by one of the sumo wrestlers.

Two sumo wrestlers dressed in loin-cloths compete in a match. At the beginning cleansing salt to ward off evil spirits is thrown; the bodies loosen up and drive away more evil spirits by stomping sideways from foot to foot. Before the actual, very short and entertaining fight the wrestlers stare at each other for some time. In the past this mental test of strength, which also increases the tension, could last forever; these days a maximum of four minutes is permitted. The colossi suddenly collide with each other. The decision is usually made within seconds: either the opponent has been knocked out of the ring or he is lying on the ground. During a sumo tournament the lowest ranks are the first to compete, while the yokozuna fight last. Every sumo

? DID YOU KNOW ...?

■ that the the yokozuna's hair knot is cut off in a final ceremony at the end of his career?

Sumo and the Rest of the World

For some time now Sumo has enjoyed increasing popularity outside Japan. More and more foreigners can now be found in the Heya, particularly from Mongolia and eastern Europe. Many Japanese consider this a threat to the Japanese tradition, which is why it has been determined that there may only be one foreigner per heya, unless that stable had already accepted more than one foreigner. The first foreigner to reach the highest rank in sumo was Akebono from Hawaii, who was a yokozuna from 1993 to 2001. The two current yokozuna, Asashoryu and Hakuho, are not Japanese either; they are from Mongolia. To find out more about sumo and the heroes of this sport, take a look at the official website of the Japan Sumo Association: http://sumo.goo.ne.jp.

Sumo | Sumo is considered to be Japan's national sport. In this type of wrestling the aim is to get the opponent out of the fighting ring (diameter 4.50m/15ft) or to get him to touch the floor with a body part other than the soles of his feet (▶Baedeker Special p.152).

Western Sports

Baseball | Baseball is as popular in Japan as soccer in Europe. It was introduced at the end of the 19th century by the Americans. Almost every school has a baseball team and the university team play-offs in August have almost the entire country on the edge of its seat. On a national level there are two professional leagues, each of them containing six teams, which are usually sponsored by big businesses such as the newspaper giant Yomiuri (Yomiuri Giants) or the chocolate manufacturer Lotte (Chiba Lotte Marines). The season lasts from the end of March to the end of September. After that the top teams of the two leagues compete against each other seven times in the Japan Series.

Soccer | Japan had a growing interest in soccer long before it hosted the World Cup in 2002 together with Korea. Japan has had a professional league since 1993, called the J-League (Japan League), which consists of 18 teams. The biggest successes of Japan's national team were reaching the knock-out stage in the 2002 World Cup and winning the title in the 2004 Asia Cup. Today some of Japan's top footballers play in Europe.

Time

Japan has Japan Standard Time all year round. It is nine hours ahead of Greenwich Mean Time, and eight hours ahead of British Summer Time.

Toilets

In this respect visitors have to adapt to the country's customs, as they will often find not a place to sit, but a basin in the floor or sometimes a high-tech toilet with every imaginable electronic gimmick. When necessary visitors can ask the waiter for the »o-te-arai« or the »toire«.

Public toilets can be found at all of the sights and in every underground station, but not always with toilet paper. Another alternative is to seek out one of the toilets in the numerous department stores.

Transport

Rail

The punctuality, speed and comfort of the trains make them Japan's most-used means of public transport. The Japanese national railway (Japan Rail, JR, www.japanrail.com) has a route network of a good 21,000 km/13,000 mi, which reaches to the country's most remote regions.

Route network

Part of this route network consists of shinkansen routes, travelled by one of the world's fastest trains. The shinkansen (literally »new trunk line«) can travel the 1177km/731mi distance from Tokyo to Fukuoka (Hakata) in just under five hours at speeds of up to 220kmh/ 135mph; the average speed of the newer Nozomi Shinkansen is no

◄ *Shinkansen*

Japan *Main Rail Connections*

— Main lines
— Shinkansen

less than 245kmh/150mph. A journey on the shinkansen from Tokyo to Kyoto past Mount Fuji is one of the really special experiences of a trip to Japan.

Hikari, Kodama, Nozomi ▶ The Tokyo-Fukuoka route is travelled by the »Hikari« (»light«) and »Kodame« (»echo«) trains in regular intervals. The Hikari stops at fewer stations than the Kodama and thus gets to its destination faster. The »Nozomi« (»hope«) departs every hour and only stops in Yokohama, Nagoya, Kyoto, Shin-Osaka, Shin-Kobe, Kokura and Hakata as well as sometimes in Shin-Yamaguchi. In addition to these particularly fast trains there are also express trains (»Tokkyu«), fast trains (»Kyuko«), high-speed trains (»kaisoku«) and regional trains (»futsu«).

Seat reservations ▶ Seat reservations are necessary on the shinkansen routes and are still possible a short time before departure. Reserved seats, couchette coach tickets and premium tickets for first class (»green car«) are available from the ticket windows in the railway stations and the green ticket windows of the Japan Travel Bureau (JTB).

A special feature of Japanese stations is that the markings of the train doors and carriage numbers are on the station. The trains stop exactly where their markings say they will.

Private trains ▶ Around cities and nearby recreational areas private companies also operate trains. The tickets are often significantly cheaper than those of JR. During the peak season it is necessary to book in time.

Japan Rail Pass Not valid on private trains! ▶ Foreign visitors can purchase the Japan Rail Pass, which can be used on all JR lines (trains, buses, ferry, but not for the »Nozomi«) and is valid for 7, 14 or 21 days. The prices are between ¥ 37,800 and ¥ 79,600 for first class and between ¥ 28,300 and ¥ 57,700 for second class. Children between the ages of 6 and 11 travel half-price.

In addition to the rail pass good for the entire route network there are also regional passes valid for shorter amounts of time: the JR Hokkaido Rail pass is good for all of Hokkaido (3 or 5 days), the JR East Rail Pass for northern Honshu north of the greater Tokyo metropolitan area (5 or 10 days or any 4 days in one month), the JR West Rail Pass for south-western Honshu (either the San'yo region, 4 or 8 days; or the Kansai region, 1–4 days) and the JR Kyushu Rail Pass for all of Kyushu and its neighbouring islands (3 or 5 days).

Vouchers for the Japan Rail Pass can be obtained on presenting a passport in one of the overseas offices of the Japan Travel Bureau and its co-operation partners (▶ Information), as well as from overseas offices or agencies of Japan Air Lines and All Nippon Airways (▶ Arrival) when bought in conjunction with a plane ticket. These vouchers are exchanged for the relevant Japan Rail Pass after arrival at the respective JR Travel Service Centre or at the ticket office. More information at www.japanrailpass.net as well as in the brochure that is supplied with the pass.

Buses

Buses are a cheaper alternative to travelling by rail, particularly for those travelling at night and not in possession of a rail pass. They are safe and comfortable, but journey times are longer than in the fast trains. Most of the bus companies depart from close to railway stations.

By Boat

Numerous ferries, some of which also transport vehicles, connect the main Japanese islands with each other and with the large number of smaller islands. Hydrofoils and motorboats go back and forth on the shorter distances; longer routes across the Inland Sea as well as to Okinawa are travelled by luxury ships. The route of the Inland Sea ferries is as follows: Osaka-Kobe-Sakate-Takamatsu-Imabari-Matsuyama-Beppu.

Public Local Transport

The number of tram lines has been greatly reduced in recent times. The signs are usually entirely in Japanese. This is also true of buses. Passengers enter city buses at the back and take a number; it gives information about the ticket price announced by a panel at the front of the bus. The money is dropped into a small container next to the driver. Passengers who do not have the exact money can change coins and ¥ 1000 bills in the small money changer also next to the driver.

Trams
Buses

The cities of Tokyo, Osaka, Nagoya, Yokohama, Fukuoka and Sapporo all have underground railways. English-language underground maps make orientation easy, especially since the stops are marked in both Japanese and Roman script. Next to the name of a stop is also the name of the adjacent stops. Passengers stamp tickets at the ticket machines before crossing the barrier; the fare depends on the distance and is announced on the ticket machine (usually only in Japanese). If there is any uncertainty about the correct ticket price it is best to get the

Underground railway

! *Baedeker* TIP

Saving money on local public transport

It is worthwhile enquiring about cheaper day passes, which allow an unlimited number of trips in a day.

cheapest ticket and then pay the difference at the barrier at the destination or at the »Fare Adjustment Counter«. Tickets have to be handed over upon leaving the station: do not throw them away!

After the mountain regions were made accessible, and particularly following the introduction of winter sports to Japan, numerous cableways were built.

Cableways

Taxi Taxi stands can generally be found at stations, airports and major hotels. The prices are shown on the taximeter; it is not customary to give tips. In the hours between 11pm and 5am the fare is 30% higher; it could be, however, that the driver will demand a much higher price during these hours or in bad weather, even from Japanese people. In that case it is customary to signal acceptance of paying twice or three times the normal amount by lifting two or three fingers.

It is a good idea to write down the name of the desired destination in Japanese writing on a piece of paper, which can then be shown to the taxi driver (most drivers only speak Japanese). Given the Japanese system of naming streets and houses it is not unusual for taxi drivers to have to ask the way themselves. Do not expect the driver to help with loading or unloading any luggage, even if there are many bags; in addition passengers should pay attention to the automatic opening and closing of the rear nearside door.

During rush hour it is not advisable to take a taxi, particularly in Tokyo, because of the many traffic jams.

Some tourist towns like Nara or Kamakura run **bicycle rickshaws** during the holiday season. They are quite expensive.

By Car

Japan has a well-developed motorway network (subject to tolls) of around 2200 km/1400 mi and a major road network of around 40,000km/25,000mi. Cities and their surrounding areas have signs in both Japanese and English, but in rural areas European drivers will have a harder time getting their bearings given that the signs are often only in Japanese.

Driving regulations ▶ In Japan cars **drive on the left!** Traffic signs largely correspond to international norms. It is generally cheaper to do without private vehicles and use public transport or to join organized tours.

When to Go

Spring The best times to go to Japan are spring (end of March to the middle
Autumn of May) and autumn (mid-October to the beginning of December). As a result of the great length of the country in a north-south direction it can still be quite cool in the north in March, while the cherry blossom is already starting in the south.

Summer The summers in the plains are hot and sometimes humid. At this time of year the coasts and mountain regions are more pleasant. The amount of precipitation during the wet season (tsuyu, baiu; June–July) is less in the northeast than it is in the south. September (and in the south already July) marks the start of typhoon season.

Japan Five Region-typical Climate Stations

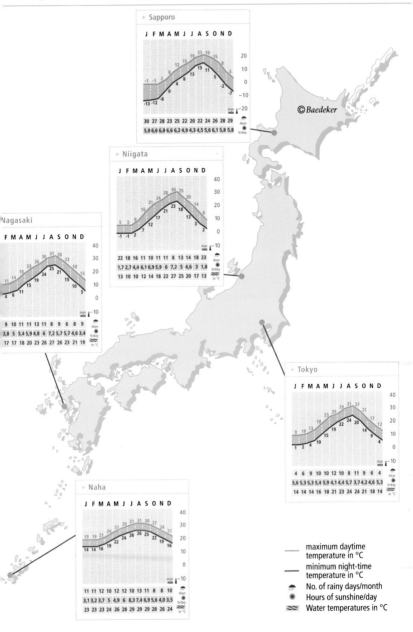

▶ Sapporo

J F M A M J J A S O N D

20
10
0
−10
−20

-1 -1 4 12 15 19 21 19 15 8 3
-13 -12 -6 13 2 -2 -7

30 27 28 23 25 22 22 24 26 28 29 *days*
5,8 6,6 6,6 6,8 6,6 6,2 4,9 4,3 4,5 5,6 6,1 5,8 5,8 *h/day*

▶ Niigata

J F M A M J J A S O N D

40
30
20
10
0
−10

5 5 9 16 22 28 30 25 20 14
-1 -1 2 7 12 17 23 18 12 7 2

22 18 16 11 10 11 11 8 13 14 18 23 *days*
1,7 2,7 4,4 6,1 6,9 5,9 6 7,2 5 4,6 3 1,8 *h/day*
13 10 10 12 14 18 22 27 25 20 17 13 *in °C*

Nagasaki

F M A M J J A S O N D

40
30
20
10
0
−10

11 19 23 26 31 28 23 18 13
4 6 11 15 19 24 21 15 10 5

9 10 11 11 13 11 8 9 8 9 *days*
3,8 5 5,4 5,9 4,6 6 7,2 5,7 5,7 4,6 3,4 *h/day*
17 17 18 20 23 26 27 26 23 21 19 *in °C*

▶ Tokyo

J F M A M J J A S O N D

40
30
20
10
0
−10

9 10 15 19 23 25 29 31 27 22 17 14
1 2 4 10 15 19 22 24 20 9 4

4 6 9 10 10 12 10 8 11 9 6 *days*
5,6 5,3 5,3 5,4 5,9 4,1 4,4 5,7 3,7 4,2 4,6 5,3 *h/day*
14 14 14 16 18 21 23 24 24 21 18 14 *in °C*

▶ Naha

J F M A M J J A S O N D

40
30
20
10
0
−10

19 19 21 24 27 29 31 31 30 29 24
14 14 16 19 22 26 26 25 24 16

11 11 12 10 12 12 10 13 11 8 8 10 *days*
3,1 3,2 3,7 5 4,9 6 8,3 7,4 6,9 5,6 4,0 3,5 *h/day*
23 23 23 24 26 28 29 29 29 28 26 24 *in °C*

─── maximum daytime
temperature in °C
─── minimum night-time
temperature in °C
No. of rainy days/month
Hours of sunshine/day
Water temperatures in °C

© Baedeker

During the wintertime central and northern Japan are covered by a
thick blanket of snow, allowing winter sports to continue in some
places up until May. The western coast of Honshu is particularly cold
and snowy, while the temperature on the east coast and in the lowlands only rarely drops below freezing. The **Okinawa Islands**, in Japan's far southwestern corner, have their own climate with an average annual temperature of 23°C/73 °F.

Since Japanese people are keen travellers it is generally necessary to
book early. This is particularly true of the time during which the Japanese holidays take place (21 December to 5 January) and during
the winter sports season, where it is advisable to book several
months in advance. The peak times for domestic Japanese travel activity are the Golden Week at the beginning of May, the Bon festival
(13–15 August, in some regions in mid-July) and the summer holidays (mid-July to the end of August).

The cherry blossom and the autumn leaves are part of the country's
special attractions and it is thanks to them that many places owe
their fame. During those times the Japanese come in great numbers
to their parks and landscape protection regions in order to enjoy this
natural spectacle under the trees.

Travel clothes should be adapted to the seasons. During the rain and
typhoon season (June and September) rain gear is needed. Sun protection is needed during the summertime. Fans and a face-cloth are
also a good idea.
It is definitely advisable to bring shoes that can be put on and taken
off easily, i.e. without laces or buckles if possible!

← *Cherry blossom is part of Japan's special attractions*

Tours

TO THE HIGHLIGHTS IN
THE LAND OF THE RISING SUN:
THE MOST FAMOUS TEMPLES
AND SHRINES, VOLCANOES AND
TRANQUIL LAKES, LIVELY CITIES
AND HIDDEN MONASTERIES.

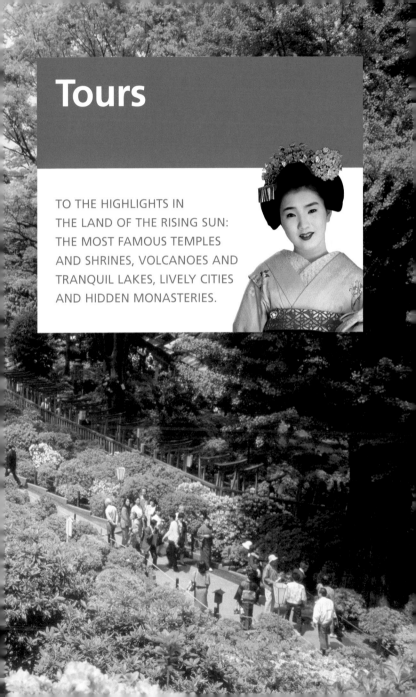

← *Going for a walk in garden of Nezu*

TOURS THROUGH JAPAN

The traditional Japan tour, which is also the typical tour of most study trips, takes all the main highlights into account, but is entirely on the beaten track. That's why we make some suggestions here that also lead to more remote areas and to hidden natural and cultural treasures.

▬ TOUR 1 **Japan Done Differently**
This tour across northern Honshu and Hokkaido will allow visitors to enjoy glorious natural landscapes, experience a lot of original atmosphere and, with the right timing, lavish festivals.   ▸ **page 174**

▬ TOUR 2 **The Call of the Mountains**
This tour explores the mountainous world of the Japanese Alps, makes a detour to the Sea of Japan and saves one of the best features till last: a view of Mount Fuji.   ▸ **page 176**

▬ TOUR 3 **On Pilgrimage**
This classic tour leads southwards to the Kinki region to the country's most significant temples and shrines, and is rounded off with a relaxing short stay on the largest island of the Inland Sea.   ▸ **page 178**

▬ TOUR 4 **Around the Inland Sea**
This tour runs along the Inland Sea through western Honshu and then to the quiet, rural island of Shikoku.   ▸ **page 180**

▬ TOUR 5 **Southern Charm**
A round trip through Kyushu will let visitors enjoy the relaxed atmosphere of southern Japan. This can be followed up with a swimming and diving trip to Okinawa.   ▸ **page 182**

A view of Mount Fuji is one of the undisputed highlights of any trip to Japan

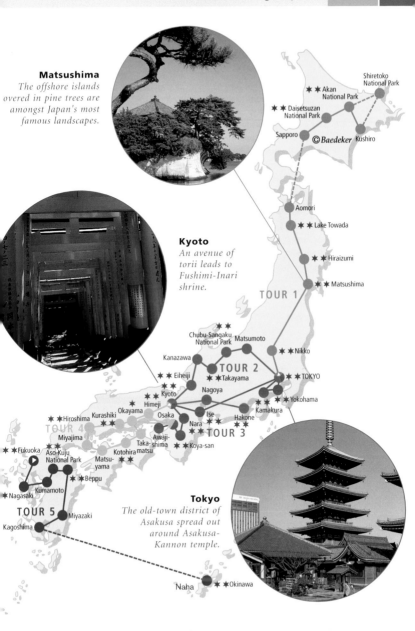

Matsushima
The offshore islands covered in pine trees are amongst Japan's most famous landscapes.

Kyoto
An avenue of torii leads to Fushimi-Inari shrine.

Shiretoko National Park

✱ ✱ Akan National Park

✱ ✱ Daisetsuzan National Park

Sapporo   © *Baedeker*   Kushiro

Aomori

✱ Lake Towada

✱ Hiraizumi

✱ ✱ Matsushima

TOUR 1

✱ ✱
Chubu-Sangaku National Park   Matsumoto

Kanazawa   TOUR 2   ✱ Nikko

✱ ✱ Eiheiji   ✱ Takayama   ✱ ✱ TOKYO

✱ ✱ Kyoto   Nagoya   ✱ Yokohama

Himeji   ✱ Kamakura

✱ ✱ Hiroshima   Kurashiki   Okayama   Osaka   Ise   Hakone

TOUR 4   ✱ ✱   ✱ Nara   ✱ ✱ TOUR 3

Miyajima   Awaji-shima   ✱ ✱ Koya-san

✱ Fukuoka   Aso-Kuju   Taka-   Kotohira ✱ ✱
National Park   Matsu-   matsu
    yama

Kumamoto   ✱ Beppu

✱ Nagasaki

TOUR 5   Miyazaki

Kagoshima

Tokyo
The old-town district of Asakusa spread out around Asakusa-Kannon temple.

Naha   ✱ ✱ Okinawa

Travelling in Japan

Culture in the Western sense

Anyone planning a trip to Japan is probably not thinking of a beach holiday. Although Japan, being an island, also has some nice beaches, particularly in the south, the country's appeal lies more in its **impressive places of cultural interest**, which provide many contrasts and insights into the customs and everyday life of Japanese people. Since the media here prefer to portray Japan by its most curious exports, visitors coming to see the country often find themselves confronted with many a surprise: even the city of Tokyo, which is popularly depicted from the point of view of its overcrowded transport, its sea of skyscrapers and bright neon advertising, has places of relaxation, alleyways of an almost rural character and idyllic gardens.

It is hardly possible to get to know all of Japan in a single trip, if only because of its vast north-south extent. In order to travel from Hokkaido to Okinawa it would take around two months for visitors wanting to experience all the country has to offer. Only rarely do visitors have so much time available, let alone the money such a holiday would cost. The average visitor to Japan has three weeks at the most. For that reason it is a good idea for visitors to combine two of the above-mentioned tours or to pick out those places they find the most interesting. The times given are only approximate guidelines: some can complete a tour in fewer days but those prefer not to rush from place to place should allow for some extra time.

DON'T MISS

- Tokyo, one of the world's largest cities
- Kyoto, the ancient imperial residence
- Nara, rich in temples and shrines
- Nikko with its splendid mausoleums
- Kamakura, the town of the Great Buddha
- and Mount Fuji (at least from a distance). These places are without a doubt some of the country's greatest attractions.

Where to go?

Generally it can be said that both the north and the south have a little bit of everything: beautiful landscape, traditional customs, typical Japanese architecture, interesting museums and a diverse cuisine, but visitors who prefer a rustic atmosphere and cooler temperatures and who enjoy hiking and biking are better off in the **north**. Those with a special interest in the world of Buddhism and Shinto should focus on **central Honshu**, while visitors who also want some rest and relaxation on the beach in addition to Japan's cultural attractions will find what they are looking for in the **south**. Some places are must-sees for all visitors to Japan. However, travellers who just focus on the highlights will miss a lot of what Japan has to offer, namely wonderful mountain landscapes, remote sites of pilgrimage, rugged coasts, restorative hot springs, historical towns and modern leisure facilities.

The easiest and most comfortable way to travel in Japan is by rail. **How to travel?**
The network is extensive and, apart from a few minor stretches, is
run by Japan Railways (JR). Although train tickets are not cheap, es- ◀ by rail
pecially for the super-high-speed »bullet« trains (shinkansen), foreign tourists have to opportunity to buy a **Japan Rail Pass** before
their trip, which will definitely be worthwhile if visitors travel a lot
and over long distances (▶p. 156). The shinkansen trains are excellent: clean, comfortable, punctual and fast; the slower trains are also
all very acceptable. The only disadvantage is that it is difficult to stow
away larger items of luggage.

It is not a good idea to drive around Japan by car. While British and ◀ by car
Irish visitors may not find **driving on the left** a problem, they still
have to organize the translation of their driving license into Japanese
and face high costs: parking is limited and as a result expensive, and
the motorways are subject to tolls.

Domestic flights are worthwhile for visitors who have little time. ◀ by air
One disadvantage is that this does not allow visitors to experience
much of Japan's countryside.

It is enjoyable to ride a bike through Japan's rural regions, but is a ◀ by bicycle
lot more laborious in the towns and cities and requires a lot of skill,
since cycle paths are not generally available, and cyclists have to use
the pavement.

Japan's Regions

The Neglected North

There is much to be explored in the predominantly agricultural
north of Japan. Tourists interested in festivals and other traditions
can have a lot of fun if they are in the right place at the right time.

The scenic highlights of Tohoku (northern Honshu) are the east **Northern Honshu**
coast near **Matsushima** with its numerous pine-covered islands and
further north around Miyako the **Rikuchu-kaigan National Park**, as
well as the west coat near **Oga**. The **Bandai-Asahi National Park** in the
interior protects several regions: the three holy mountains Dewa
Sanzan, the Azuma Mountains and Lake Inawashiro. Further beautiful lakes are **Tazawa-ko** and the larger **Towada-ko**. The cities of the
north are merely starting points for these scenic attractions, unless
visitors have come for one of the big **festivals**, such as the Nebuta-
matsuri in Aomori, the Tanabata-matsuri in Sendai or the Kanto-
matsuri in Akita (all three in August). These festivals are very jolly
and the participants loudly process through the towns. Northern
Honshu's architectural treats are the castle of **Hirosaki**, which is particularly pretty during the cherry blossom, and the temples of **Hirai-**

zumi, which once rivalled Kyoto with their splendour. Towns such as **Aizu-Wakamatsu** and **Kakunodate** still have picturesque samurai houses.

Hokkaido

Those who make it up the Strait of Tsugaru to Hokkaido will be rewarded with even more secluded landscapes (at least outside the tourist season). This island, formerly the territory of the Ainu, who are now largely assimilated, was not settled by Japanese people until the mid-19th century. The densely populated, highly industrialized Japan feels worlds away. A feeling of open scenery and unspoiled local character is in the air.

The gateway to Hokkaido is the port town of **Hakodate**, which was one of the first to open up to trade with the West. **Sapporo**, the capital of the prefecture, is a young town with not many traditional attractions apart from an impressive snow festival in February. The neighbouring city of **Otaru** is known for its glass and its romantic canal quarter.

The main reasons for a trip to Hokkaido, however, are its natural attractions: the volcanoes, crater lakes and hot springs in the national parks of **Shikotsu-Toya**, **Daisetsuzan** and **Akan** , the flora and fauna in the remote **Rishiri-Rebun National Park**, the waterfalls and steep cliffs in **Shiretoko National Park**, the drift ice off the coast near **Abashiri** (in the winter) and the marshland around **Kushiro**. The national parks are not just good places for hiking, but also for riding, fishing, rafting, biking and, in the wintertime, for skiing and snowboarding.

From Tokyo to the Sea of Japan

Kanto and Chubu

Most foreign tourists tread Japanese soil for the first time in **Tokyo**, which leaves them both fascinated and overwhelmed. The city is enormous and confusing, and anyone who really wants to explore it will need a lot of time: there are many interesting museums, quarters all with their different styles, shopping (best done at the end of a trip) and an unsurpassed range of entertainment from kabuki to karaoke. At some point everyone gets the desire to escape from this behemoth – an easy thing to do, as there are many highlights to be seen not far away: **Kamakura** with its Great Buddha, **Nikko** with its splendid mausoleums and Lake Chuzenji nearby, the garden of **Mito**, Chinatown and the port of **Yokohama**, the seaside towns on the **Izu peninsula**, the mountains of **Chichibu-Tama National Park** and last but not least **Mount Fuji** with the Fuji lakes and the holiday town of **Hakone**. Good bases for trips to Chubu (central Honshu) and the Japanese Alps are the arts and crafts centre **Takayama**, the Olympic town of **Nagano** or the castle town of **Matsumoto**. **Kamikochi**, **Karuizawa** and **Omachi** are attractive small mountain towns that all make for good starting locations for a number of hikes.

A trip to the Alps to the old postal stations of Tsumago and Magome in the **Kiso Valley** can also be organized from the industrial centre

Nicely restored historical village – Tsumago in Kiso Valley

Nagoya, Japan's fourth-largest city and home to the significant Atsuta Shrine as well as several interesting museums.

Beyond the mountains on Honshu's west coast are **Kanazawa** with one of Japan's three most famous gardens, the Kenroku-en and the **Noto peninsula**, which still has a very traditional Japanese atmosphere and a ragged coastline with wild, romantic scenery. Even further north off the coast of Niigata is the island of **Sado**, which has held on to its very own customs and traditions as a result of its relative isolation.

Cradle of Japanese Culture

The heart of the Kinki region, which stretches westwards from Lake Biwa over Himeji and southwards all the way to Wakayama, is of course the old imperial city of **Kyoto** with its countless temples and shrines, gardens and old imperial buildings, entertainment districts, shopping and a lot more. Further highlights await in the surrounding area: above all **Nara**, the seat of the imperial family before it was moved to Kyoto. Japan's largest freshwater lake, **Biwako**, is also in the

Kinki

vicinity of Kyoto. One of its main attractions is Hikone Castle on its eastern shore. Leaving the lake it is possible to take a cableway up **Mount Hiei**. Perched on its peak is the Enryakuji Temple, one of the most influential in the country. A scenic highlight on the shore of the Sea of Japan is the **Ama-no-hashidate** spit, one of the classical »three most beautiful landscapes of Japan«.

The most important Shinto shrine, the **Ise Shrine** is also in the Kinki region. It is a prime example of the simple, natural building method typical of Shinto architecture. **Himeji Castle**, probably the country's most beautiful castle and one of the few surviving originals, is equally characteristic of indigenous Japanese architecture.

The monasteries on **Koya-san** are a special kind of spiritual experience; visitors can stay overnight in temple lodgings and participate in the early-morning meditations. Koya-san is very close to the **Yoshino-Kumano National Park**, famous for its magnificent cherry blossom, its waterfalls and its gorges. Both places seem far away from the hubbub of the Greater **Osaka-Kobe** area. These industrial and port towns do not have any stunning sights, but they are good places for entertainment, eating out and shopping.

The Tranquil West

Chugoku Western Honshu (Chugoku) is traditionally sub-divided into two parts: the San'in coast, which faces the Sea of Japan and is relatively sparsely populated, and the San'yo coast, which faces the Inland Sea and is livelier, congested and highly industrialized. The San'yo coast has a number of attractions, including the landscape garden of **Okayama**, one of the classical three most beautiful gardens of Japan, the picturesque city of **Kurashiki** with canals and old warehouses, the city of **Hiroshima**, which is worth a visit not just because of its historical monuments, and the nearby shrine of **Miyajima** with its much-photographed Torii (at least during high tide), which stands in the water, and not least the picturesque backdrop of the **Inland Sea** with its island labyrinth; the largest islands are **Awajishima** and **Shodoshima**, but there are countless smaller ones. Towards Kyushu the sights become more sparse and less significant: the prefectural capital of **Yamaguchi** was once a famous artistic centre, and the garden created by Sesshu behind the Joeiji Temple is still testament to this era. Nearby are the **Akiyoshi Cave** and, at Honshu's western tip, the historically significant **Shimonoseki**, which has a nice view across the Kanmon Straits to Kyushu.

The **San'in coast** is even more tranquil and quite remote: public transportation is slow here. The attractions include the pottery centre of **Hagi**, the idyllic castle town of **Matsue** and the significant shrine of **Izumo**, where all of the country's Shinto gods (kami) gather once a year. One of this region's scenic curiosities are the dunes of **Tottori**, which are really only worth a visit for visitors who are passing through anyway.

However, the San'in coast is ignored by most tourists, just like Japan's fourth-largest island Shikoku, which can be reached from Honshu via three bridges or by ferry. There are no architectural masterpieces here, apart from maybe the castles in **Kochi** and **Matsuyama**. The appeal here derives from the natural scenery, the village-like character and the many temples visited by ambitious pilgrims on the 88-temple pilgrimage. However these days few undertake this pilgrimage on foot; most opt for a comfortable coach. Pilgrims dressed in white with a straw hat, bell and walking stick are a common sight on Shikoku. Their starting point tends to be **Tokushima**. Mount Bizan has a fine view of the Inland Sea.

Shikoku

The coastal landscapes are most impressive near **Uwajima**, in the **Ashizuri-Uwakai National Park** and at **Cape Muroto**. Although created by human hand, Ritsurin Garden in **Takamatsu** is a highlight of the area's natural beauty. Nearby is the shrine of **Kotohira**, which is dedicated to seafarers and all travellers in general, and thus ought to be a must-see for all overseas tourists.

Southern Flair

In the past foreign influence came into the country via Kyushu, the southernmost of Japan's four main islands. Ceramic art came to Kyushu from Korea for example, a tradition that has been carried on for centuries in **Arita**. The first Europeans to come here also landed in the south of Japan: in 1543 the Portuguese arrived at the island of Tanegashima, which is part of the **Satsunan Islands**. In their wake Christian missionaries came to Japan, including Francis Xavier. During the Edo period, when Japan closed itself off to the outside, **Nagasaki** was the window to the world, because it was the only place to maintain trading contacts with the Chinese, Dutch and the Portuguese, to which the beautifully situated city owes its unique mix of East and West.

Kyushu

The modern entry to the island is **Fukuoka**, Kyushu's largest city, because this is also the final terminal of the shinkansen from Honshu. The city does all it can to be a worthy cultural centre and to build a bridge to mainland Asia.

The island's volcanic landscapes are protected in various national parks: the **Unzen-Amakusa National Park** near Nagasaki, the **Aso-Kuju National Park** in the centre of the island and the **Kirishima-Yaku National Park** in southern Kyushu. Part of the latter is the island of Yakushima, which has 32 volcanoes and ancient cedars; it has been included in the UNESCO list of World Heritage sites. The area around **Miyazaki** is also quite picturesque: the small island of Aoshima has washboard-like sedimentary rocks, and the **Takachiho Gorge** is deeply rooted in Japanese mythology.

There are not many important temples and shrines on Kyushu, and the only noteworthy castle is **Kumamoto Castle**. The emphasis here is on relaxation: in addition to the famous town of **Beppu** with its bubbling ponds and hot springs, there are plenty of other hot springs where visitors can relax. One special attraction is the sand baths of **Ibusuki**, where visitors are buried head to toe in hot sand.

Okinawa

The largest city in the south of the island is **Kagoshima**, the gateway to the south-western islands and to **Okinawa**. This archipelago is a world apart: from the language to music and architecture, the culture here is very different from that of the rest of Japan, a consequence of the fact that the archipelago was only conquered from Kyushu in the 17th century. Before that it had long been an independent kingdom (Ryukyu) with strong links to China. During World War II fighting was heavy here, and at the end there were gruesome mass suicides. The islands were given back to Japan by the Americans in 1972, but to this day house many American military bases, which cause controversy amongst the population. As a result of the tropical climate, it is best to travel here in the winter between November and April. The main attractions are the beaches, many of which are good for diving. The beaches on **Miyako** and **Ishigaki** are particularly nice. **Iriomote** on the other hand is famous for its unique flora and fauna. The main island of Okinawa, in addition to its seaside entertainments, also has some cultural attractions in store in its capital of **Naha**, where visitors can admire the reconstructed palace complex of the Ryukyu kingdom.

Suggested Tours

Tokyo

Almost all of the suggested routes start in Tokyo and include **at least two days in this city**. It is best not to plan too much on the first day, since jetlag will still most likely be an issue. One idea would be to visit Asakusa, the old town district around the Asakusa-Kannon temple, followed by a boat trip on the Sumidagawa all the way to the Hama-Rikyu garden or even further to Odaiba, reclaimed from the sea.

After that a trip to Shinjuku is pleasant. There is a good view of the city from the modern city hall. Visitors who are not yet tired can spend the evening here or in the entertainment district of Roppongi. On day two early risers can visit the Tsukiji fish market and then stroll across Ginza, which is lined with exclusive and very traditional shops. It is not far from there to the imperial palace, which is not, however, open to the public. A good idea for the afternoon is a trip to Harajuku to the Omotesando, »Tokyo's Champs-Élysées«. Not far away is Meiji Park, where the city's most significant shrine is dedicated to Emperor Meiji. Visitors interested in museums are better off going to Ueno Park, where they will find the famous National Museum amongst others. Depending on the preferred option visitors can, in the early evening, admire the sea of neon advertising in Shibuya (one stop from Harajuku) or from Akihabara (two stops form Ueno) and enjoy a spot of shopping.

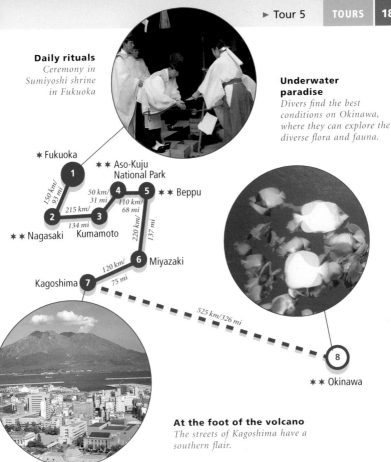

Daily rituals
*Ceremony in
Sumiyoshi shrine
in Fukuoka*

**Underwater
paradise**
*Divers find the best
conditions on Okinawa,
where they can explore the
diverse flora and fauna.*

* Fukuoka

** Aso-Kuju
National Park

1

2   3

** Nagasaki   Kumamoto

4   5   ** Beppu

150 km/ 93 mi
50 km/ 31 mi
215 km/ 134 mi
110 km/ 68 mi
220 km/ 137 mi

6   Miyazaki

Kagoshima   7

120 km/ 75 mi

525 km/326 mi

8

** Okinawa

At the foot of the volcano
*The streets of Kagoshima have a
southern flair.*

Travel onwards by rail to **❼Kagoshima** (two hours), the »Naples of   The Naples of
Japan«. The town on the extremely active Sakurajima volcano was   Japan
once home to a powerful ruling family, a reminder of which is the
Shoko-Shuseikan Museum. Otherwise the attractive Iso landscape
garden is a good place to relax and take a trip by ferry to **Sakurajima**
(15 minutes), in order to gaze at the lava fields from viewing platforms and walk to a buried shrine, of which nothing is now visible
but the torii.

Anyone wanting even more relaxation in the south can fly to **❽**** ****   Okinawa
Okinawa** (1¼ hours to Naha). Plan at least two days for a trip
around the island and lazing on the beach of the main island, longer
to include other islands in the excursion. Otherwise take the train
from Kagoshima back to Hakata (2½ hours) or fly to Tokyo (1 hour
50 minutes).

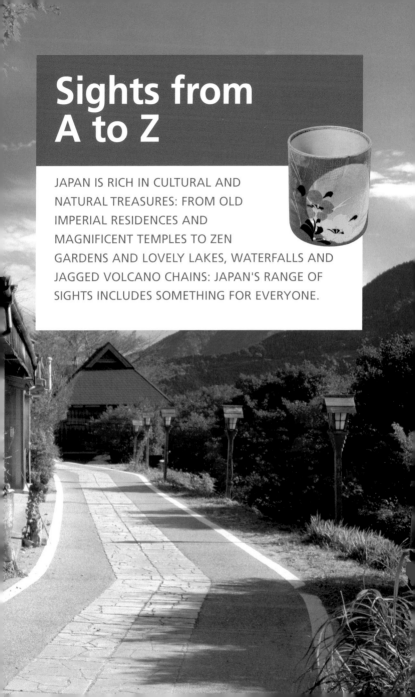

Sights from
A to Z

JAPAN IS RICH IN CULTURAL AND NATURAL TREASURES: FROM OLD IMPERIAL RESIDENCES AND MAGNIFICENT TEMPLES TO ZEN GARDENS AND LOVELY LAKES, WATERFALLS AND JAGGED VOLCANO CHAINS: JAPAN'S RANGE OF SIGHTS INCLUDES SOMETHING FOR EVERYONE.

Abashiri

Main island: Hokkaido	**Prefecture:** Hokkaido
Population: 41,000	

網走

Many Japanese people associate Abashiri with its high security prison, but tourists are generally more interested in the drift ice, the »dream in white« off Japan's coast.

Port city

← *Tea houses in Wakayama Prefecture*

The city of Abashiri is located in the northeast of the Japanese main island of Hokkaido on the Sea of Okhotsk at the centre of the Abashiri Quasi-National Park, which extends along the coast in a north-south direction. The Ainu and Moyoro settled here as much as 2000 years ago; today Abashiri is a transhipment centre for the agricultural products of the Abashiri Plain, a fishing port and the centre of the fish-processing industry. During the winter (January to March) the port of Abashiri is closed because it is frozen over.

What to See in Abashiri

Tentozan

There is a nice view of the city, the surrounding lake district and the sea from Mount Tentozan to the south of the railway station (207m/679ft).

Okhotsk Ryuhyo-kan ►

The Okhotsk Drift Ice Museum is sited on the top of the mountain. Visitors can experience the **magic of the drift ice** in the summer in a cold room that is kept at -15°C/5°F (open April–Oct daily 8am–6pm, Nov–March daily 9am–4.30pm, ¥ 520).

Hoppo Minzoku Hakubutsukan ►

There are two more interesting museums around the mountain: the Museum of Northern Peoples portrays the way of life of peoples living in sub-arctic zones around the world, from the Inuit to the Sami (open Tue–Sun 9.30am–4.30pm, July and Aug daily 9.30am–4.30pm, ¥ 450).

Abashiri Kangoku ►

The notorious prison from the Meiji period, which was still in use up until 1984, is now a museum documenting the everyday lives of its inmates (open April–Oct daily 8am–6pm, Nov–March daily 9am–5pm, ¥ 1050, 4km/2.5mi from the station, www.kangoku.jp/world). All three museums can be reached by bus on the Tentozan line in 10–15 minutes.

▶ VISITING ABASHIRI

GETTING THERE

By rail: from Sapporo JR Hakodate main line and JR Sekihoku main line (5½ hours); from Asahikawa JR Sekihoku main line (3¾ hours); from Kushiro JR Semmo main line (3 hours).

EVENTS

Ryuhyo-matsuri (drift ice festival; mid-February); Orochon fire festival (end of July), in Chuo Park.

1.5km/1mi northeast of the station is the shell mound of **Moyoro-kaizuka** with excavation sites containing numerous vestiges of the Moyoro, the Ainu's predecessors, who settled here.

Around Abashiri

Southwest of the town is Lake Abashiri with a circumference of 44km/27mi, which is part of Abashiri Quasi-National Park (bus 10 minutes from Abashiri station). Enjoy some rest and relaxation in the Memambetsu onsen and Abashiri-Kotan onsen on the lake's southern shore.

Lake Abashiri

Southeast of Abashiri (bus 30 minutes from Abashiri station) lies the Koshimizu Gensei Koen garden on the shore of Lake Tofutsu. The best time to visit is from May to September for the **wild flower display**; in the wintertime visitors can watch around 2000 Siberian swans here.

Lake Tofutsu

10km/6mi northwest of Abashiri, in the coastal region, is the Notoro Lagoon (bus to Ubaranai); even further north is the Saroma Lagoon, at 150.4 sq km/58 sq mi Japan's third-largest lake. More than **300 species of flowers** bloom around the lake from mid-May to September. During the winter, pack ice drifting down from the north gives the region a special appeal.

Notoro Lagoon
Saroma Lagoon

Aizu-Wakamatsu

K 6

Main island: Honshu
Population: 120,000

Prefecture: Fukushima

The castle town of Aizu-Wakamatsu, the prefecture's second-largest town, is known for its production of lacquerware (Aizu nuri), which is based on a tradition of more than 300 years. A further product famous since ancient times are hand-painted candles, a luxury only the aristocracy could afford in the past.

会津若松

What to See in Aizu-Wakamatsu

Tsuruga Castle located 3km/2mi south of the railway station was built in 1384 by Ashina Naomori; when it was destroyed by imperial troops all that was left were ditches and walls. The five-storey main tower is a 1965 reconstruction. Later the tea house as well as two fur-

Castle
🕐
Opening hours:
Daily
8.30am–4.30pm

ther buildings, Hoshii Yagura (a former warehouse) and Minami Nagaya (gatehouse wing) were rebuilt.

Museums

The Fukushima Museum east of the castle is worth a visit. It has, amongst other things, archaeological finds (open Tue–Sun 9.30am–5pm). Not far north of the castle is the Aizu Sake History Museum (Aizu Shuzo Rekishikan) in an old brewery, where visitors can witness the traditional brewing method for **sake** (rice wine). Open: 17 March – 30 Nov daily 8.30am–5pm, 1 Dec – 16 March daily 9am–4.30pm, ¥ 300.

Aizu buke-yashiki

Take the bus (15 minutes) to get to the Aizu buke-yashiki complex east of the town, which includes old samurai houses and museums, such as the **Karo-Yashiki**, a residence which belonged to a military leader and has been reconstructed true to the original; it has 38 rooms, including a richly decorated entrance hall (modelled on Nijo Castle in ►Kyoto) and a garden (open daily 8.30am–5pm, ¥ 850).

Higashiyama onsen

Around 5km/3mi southeast of Aizu-Wakamatsu (bus, 20 minutes) is the Higashiyama onsen hot spring (hot springs with temperatures of 45°C/113°F and 68°C/154°F) in a valley surrounded by hills, but open to the west. This popular spa town extends to both sides of the Yugawa River.

Seaburi

Southeast of the Higashiyama onsen is Mount Seaburi (871m/ 2858ft); visitors have a choice of two cableways, one of which offers a fine panoramic view of the mountains.

Monument and arched bridge in the park of Aizu-Wakamatsu

ⓞ VISITING AIZU-WAKAMATSU

INFORMATION
Tourist information
In the station: tel. 02 42/32 08 66
Daily 9am–5.30pm
In the castle complex:
tel. 02 42/29 11 51
Daily 8.30am–5pm
www.city.aizuwakamatsu.
fukushima.jp/e

GETTING THERE
By rail: from Tokyo (Ueno station)
Tohoku shinkansen line and JR Banetsu-saisen line via Koriyama (2½
hours).

EVENTS
Aizen autumn festival, 22–24 September, with a samurai parade.

Kitakata north of Aizu-Wakamatsu has many surviving old ware-   **Kitakata**
houses, which now house galleries and arts and crafts shops. Try the
Kitakata ramen in one of the numerous noodle restaurants. They
are famous in all of Japan.

❮ ✸ Akan National Park

N 3

Main island: Hokkaido   **Prefecture:** Hokkaido
Area: 904 sq km/349 sq mi

Akan National Park in the east of Hokkaido Island in- 阿寒国立公園
cludes the area around Lake Kussharo, Lake Akan and
Lake Mashu. Large parts of the park are covered by
sub-arctic primeval forest. Autumn is a wonderful time to go, as
the park's splendid colours give the landscape a special appeal.

What to See in Akan National Park

Lake Akan (419m/1375ft above sea level) in the western part of the   ✸ ✸
national park has a circumference of 26km/16mi and a depth of   **Lake Akan**
36m/120ft; it is known for its rich fish stocks (trout, salmon) and especially for the globular **Marimo algae**, or lake ball, which reaches a
diameter of up to 30cm/12in only here. The algae, which usually live
on the bottom of the lake, drift up to its surface when the sun is
shining, giving the lake a shimmering green colour. This species,
which also occurs in Lake Yamanaka (Yamanashi Prefecture) and
Lake Sakyo (Aomori Prefecture) is protected. Take a round trip on a
boat to get to the Marimo Exhibition Center on Churui-jima island
in the lake; it is dedicated to this unusual plant. Two volcanoes tower
over the lake: to the south Me-Akan (1499m/4918ft), to the east O-
Akan (1371m/4498ft). They make a wonderful backdrop to the lake
and its many small islands.

Akan-kohan onsen

On the lake's southern shore is the spa town of Akan-kohan-onsen, which is also a junction for many bus lines that go through the park. In the Ainu Kotan, the largest Ainu settlement on Hokkaido, the Ainu culture has been mercilessly marketed until not much authenticity is left. It is definitely worth climbing the still active **Me-Akan** (11.5km/7mi to the peak; from Me-Akan-onsen 2.5km/1.5 mi). The view from the peak includes the Sea of Okhotsk, the Pacific and the plains of Tokachi and Nemuro. Since the volcano is still active, it is sometimes closed to climbers.

✳

View ▶

Lake Mashu

✳ ✳

Around 20km/12.5mi north of Teshikaga (bus, 35 minutes) lies the unique Lake Mashu (351m/1152ft above sea level). Steep cliffs of up to 200m/660ft and thick forests make it almost impossible to access the crater lake, which has a circumference of 20km/12.5mi and a depth of 212m/696ft; the view from one of the two high viewing platforms on the western shore is all the more beautiful.

Kawayu-onsen

The best starting point for a detour to the foot of the active Io-zan volcano (512m/1680ft) is the romantically situated spa town of Kawayu-onsen (with a railway station); its hot springs have temperatures of 40°C/104°F to 60°C/140°F.

▶ VISITING AKAN NATIONAL PARK

INFORMATION
Tourist information centres
Akan-kohan and Kawayu-onsen

GETTING THERE
By rail: from Abashiri or Kushiro JR Semmo main line to Kawayu and Teshikaga (Mashu).

By bus: from Abashiri to Akan-kohan (5 hours); from Kushiro to Akan-kohan (2 hours) or via Teshikaga to Kawayu-onsen (2 hours).
By boat: round trips on Lake Akan; boat trips from Akan-kohan.

Steaming fumaroles at Me-Akan

From here it is 1.5km/1mi south to the foot of the volcano, where visitors can experience sulphurous vapours that emerge numerous openings in the ground, colouring the rocks a yellowish-green with their precipitation.

Not far from Kawayu-onsen to the northwest is the largest lake in Akan National Park: Lake Kussharo (121m/397ft above sea level, circumference: 79.5km/49mi, depth: 120m/394ft). Tomoshiri Island lies in the middle of this lake; on its southern shore is the spa town of Wakoto-onsen and in the surrounding area underground hot springs warm up the lake's beaches and water.

Lake Kussharo Wakoto-onsen

It is possible to get a particularly nice view of the lake from the Bihoro Pass (525m/1722ft; bus from Wakoto-onsen or from Bihoro); the road crossing it leads from Teshikaga on to Bihoro and further to ▶Abashiri.

Bihoro Pass

Akita

L 5

Main island: Honshu   **Prefecture:** Akita
Population: 335,000

The town of Akita is famous in all of Japan for its spectacular Kanto festival, where artistic performances are intended to invoke divine help for a good harvest. The beauty of the girls from Akita (Akita-obako) is legendary nationwide.

秋田

The prefectural capital of Akita lies on Honshu's northwestern coast on a plain surrounded on three sides by mountain ranges and bordered to the west by the Sea of Japan. It is the centre of the surrounding area in matters of agriculture and education policy.

Centre of the surrounding area

What to See in Akita

Senshu Park, 1.2km/0.7mi northwest of the station, contains the remains of a former castle as well as the Akita-Hachiman shrine. The prefectural art museum (Kenri-tsubijutsukan) and the art museum (Hirano Masakichi-bijutsukan; with works by Fujita Tsuguharu, van Gogh and Cézanne amongst others) are also part of the park. The folk art museum Akarenga Kyodokan (not far from the station) in a red and white brick building of 1910 has regional arts and crafts and more on display.

Senshu Park

◀ Museums

The Kanto Festival Center (Neburinagashi-ken, open daily 9.30am–4.30pm, ¥ 100, 10 minutes' walk from the station, in Omachi) is dedicated to the famous Kanto-matsuri as well as the town's other festivals.

Kanto Festival Center

▶ VISITING AKITA

INFORMATION
Tourist information
In the railway station
Tel. 0 18/8 32 79 41, daily 9am–7pm

GETTING THERE
By air: from Tokyo (Haneda Airport; 1 hour); from Osaka (1½ hours).
By rail: from Tokyo (Ueno Station) with the Akita shinkansen (4 hours); from Aomori with the Ou main line (2½ hours).

EVENTS
In *Akita*: Kanto-matsuri (beginning of August), Akita-Hachiman shrine; young men carry long bamboo poles with up to 50 lanterns.
In *Yokote*: Bonten-matsuri (mid-January): procession with colourfully decorated poles to the Asahi shrine; Kamakura festival (mid-February), children build igloos, in which wall altars are set up.

Around Akita

Kakunodate Southeast of Akita go via Omagari and further with the JR Kakunodate line to Kakunodate. This small, dreamy town surrounded by mountains was once the castle of the Tozawa family and later of the Satake family. The old samurai houses are worth visiting; furthermore Kakunodate is one of the best-known **cherry blossom sites in northern Japan** (end of April). Also well-known are boxes and other objects made of polished cherry tree bark (Kaba-zaiku). Further north lies Lake Tazawa (▶Towada-Hachimantai National Park).

Shirakami Sanchi Across the border to Aomori Prefecture runs the Shirakami Sanchi mountain range, which has been awarded **UNESCO World Heritage** status. The birch forests here are home to Japanese serow (a chamois species) and the kumagera or black woodpecker. The Anmon-no-taki waterfall with its crystal clear water is particularly beautiful (from Akita Ou mainline to Higashinoshiro, from there the Gono line to Shirakami; approx. 1 hour).

✴ Ama-no-hashidate

H7•h2

Main island: Honshu   **Prefecture:** Kyoto

天橋立 **Ama-no-hashidate, a spit in the western part of Wakasa Bay in the Sea of Japan, is one of the three coastal landscapes of Japan that have been praised for their beauty since ancient times (▶Baedeker Special p.380). Pine trees with bizarre formations increase the appeal of the area.**

A headland 3.6km/2.2mi long and between 37m/40yd and 110m/ 120yd wide separates the Aso-no-umi lagoon from Miyazu Bay, a part of Wakasa Bay (western Honshu). The name stems from Ama-no-ukihashi (»floating bridge of the heavens«) and relates to a legend according to which the gods Izanagi and Izanami stood here when Japan was created.

»Bridge of the heavens«

What to See in Ama-no-hashidate

Monju, located close to Ama-no-hashidate station, is the most suitable starting-point for a walk over the spit. The town is home to the Chionji temple; to the south a cable car makes its way up Mount Monju. Don't miss out on a swim in the crystal clear water of the lagoon.

! *Baedeker* TIP

A worthwhile excursion

A boat trip from Ama-no-hashidate through the lagoon to Ichinomiya is a great idea; from here take a trip to the Kasamatsu Park, then return on foot over the spit to Ama-no-hashidate.

The southern part of the spit, not far north of Monju, has the Hashidate-Myojin shrine; at its northern end is the town of Ichinomiya at the foot of Mount Nariai. From Kasamatsu Park, which is half way up and can be reached via a cableway, visitors have a magnificent view of the lagoon and spit.

Ichinomiya

◄ Kasamatsu Park

View of »bridge of the heavens« Ama-no-hashidate

▶ VISITING AMA-NO-HASHIDATE

GETTING THERE

By rail: from Kyoto JR San-in line (2 hours; from Miyazu private-line fare must be paid); from Osaka JR Fukuchiyama line and Mayzuru line (2¼ hours).

By bus: from Ama-no-hashidate and Miyazu to Ichinomiya (15 or 30 minutes).
By boat: ferry from Ama-no-hashidate to Ichinomiya (15 minutes).

Nairaiji

There is a bus connection (3km/2mi) from the Kasamatsu terminal to Nariaiji, a temple belonging to the Shingon sect founded in the 8th century; it is the 28th of the 33 Kannon temples of pilgrimage in the western region of Kansai. There is a good view from Ochi Park near Iwataki (bus from Ama-no-hashidate station).

✳
View ▶

Aomori

L 4

Main island: Honshu
Population: 299,000

Prefecture: Aomori

青森

Aomori, whose roots reach back to the Jomon period, is situated in the far northeast of the main Japanese island of Honshu on Aomori Bay, the western part of Mutsu Bay. The town is known for its spectacular Nebuta festival.

Economy

In 1906 Aomori, the capital of the prefecture with the same name, was opened up to foreign trading. Today forestry and fruit-growing are important economic activities in the surrounding area. Aomori is also significant from a traffic standpoint as the starting point of the undersea Seikan Tunnel, which connects the two main islands of Honshu and Hokkaido.

What to See in Aomori

Sannai
Maruyama Iseki

Southwest of the station (bus, 20 minutes) are the remains of a settlement from the **Jomon period**. The tombs, ruins and ditches, which were only discovered in 1992, are 4000–5500 years old. The museum exhibits bones, pottery and other discoveries (open April–Oct 9am–6pm, Nov–March 9am–4.30pm, free admission).

Munakata-
Shiko Museum

The Munakata Shiko Memorial Museum east of the station is well worth a visit (bus, 10 minutes; open Tue–Sun 9.30am–5pm, ¥ 300). The Azekura-style building displays works by the famous woodblock-print artist Munakata Shiko (1903–75).

Around Aomori

Asamushi-onsen

20km/12mi to the northeast (bus, 45 minutes; JR Tohoku main line, 25 minutes) are the Asamushi-onsen hot springs (springs from 58°C/136°F to 79°C/174°F); the **Asamushi Aquarium** has around 4500 species of marine animals on show (Ken-ei Asamushi Suizoku-kan; open daily 9am–5pm, in the summer until 6pm, ¥ 1000). Further north is the Natsudomari Peninsula; swans from colder regions come to its coasts to overwinter; in the spring camellia japonica flower everywhere.

Shimokita Peninsula

In the east and north Mutsu Bay, the western part of which is Aomori Bay, is framed by the Shimokita Peninsula, which rises out of the Tsugaru Strait in the shape of an axe. To get here from Aomori take the Noheji JR Tohoku mainline, then JR Ominato line to Ominato.

▶ VISITING AOMORI

INFORMATION

Tourist information
Town of Aomori: 1st floor, JR Bus Building, 1-3-29 Yasukata
Tel. 0 17/7 23 46 70
Daily 8.30am–5.30pm
Aomori Prefecture: 2nd floor, ASPM, 1-1-40 Yasukata
Tel. 0 17/7 34 25 00
Daily 9am–6pm
At the airport: tel. 0 17/7 39 45 61
Daily 9am–6.30pm

GETTING THERE

By air: from Tokyo (Haneda Airport, 1¼ hours).
By rail: from Tokyo (Ueno station) JR Tohoku shinkansen line to Hachinohe (3 hours), further to Aomori (1 hour) with the JR Tohoku line.

EVENTS

The *Nebuta-matsuri* procession is one of the prefecture's largest festivals. After dark huge illuminated papier-mâché figures (nebuta) are carried through the streets. The custom goes back to a ruse attributed to Sakanoue no Tamuramaro (758–811); he wanted to trick the hostile Emishi about the size and position of his troops, so to confuse them he had such figures moved through the town. Ten huge nebuta figures are on display in the Nebuta no Sato (bus from the station, 35 minutes).

Colourful float at Nebuta-matsuri

Mutsu ▶ The peninsula's largest town with a population of 46,000 is Mutsu, a fishing and agricultural centre (Ominato line to Shimokita, then Shimokita-Kotsu line to Tanabu). Towering 828m/2717ft above the

Osorezan ▶ town to the northeast is the no longer active **volcano** Osorezan (also Usorisan; May–Oct bus from Tanabu station). The mountain has been considered holy since the 9th century and on the northern shore of its crater lake, which is covered in solfataras, stands Entsuji temple, presumably founded by the priest Ennin (also Jikaku-daishi, 794–864); its big annual festival takes place from 20 to 24 July. Osorezan is considered the **entrance to the world of the dead**. For that reason many pilgrims choose this place to make contact with their ancestors with the help of blind female mediums (itako).

Arita

E 8 • b 4

Main island: Kyushu   **Prefecture:** Saga
Population: 15,000

有田 **Around 300 porcelain workshops are located in and around Arita, some of which have been in operation for centuries; they are the town's most important economic activity; Arita enjoyed a worldwide reputation for its ceramic goods as early as the 17th century. Ceramic wares here are still often fired according to traditional methods; the area around Arita provides the best raw materials.**

Porcelain town with a global reputation Arita, in the far northwest of the main Japanese island of Kyushu, is situated in a long, narrow valley surrounded by densely forested mountains at the foot of Mount Kurokami. The townscape is dominated by numerous porcelain shops and the high chimneys of the potteries. In addition to tableware Arita now also produces tiles and industrial porcelain.

Initially all the ceramics were painted blue on a white background (sometsuke), but from 1644 onwards **Sakaide Kakiemon** (1595–1666) replaced this method by multi-coloured firing techniques with enamel; Kakiemon's rich red tones are characteristic. This style was soon copied, but the individual potteries developed their own designs over time. All of the Arita-yaki became known overseas under the name of Ko-Imari (»ko« means »old«). The porcelain was shipped from the port of Imari, 12km/7mi north of Arita. There are three different types of porcelain.

Traditional Arita porcelain

Kakiemon, whose main colours are red, blue and yellow, flourished in the second half of the 17th century (1659–91) under the 5th and 6th Kakiemon generations.

Iro-Nabeshima (»Iro« means »colourful«), which uses the enamel colours of red, yellow, light green and cobalt blue, flourished between 1688 and 1735 under the Imayzumi family (porcelain painters).

Ko-Imari is characterized by sometimes lavish decoration, and uses blue as an underglaze as well as the colours red and gold. Ko-Imari reached its peak during the Genroku period (1688–1704), which was the pinnacle of Japan's bourgeois culture.

Kakiemon and Nabeshima are now amongst the greatest treasures of ancient porcelain ware.

 ARITA

INFORMATION
Tourist information
In the station, tel. 09 55/42 40 52
Daily 9am–5pm

GETTING THERE
By rail: from Fukuoka (Hakata station) JR Sasebo line (1½ hour).

EVENTS
Porcelain market (end of April/beginning of May).

> **! Baedeker TIP**
>
> **Visiting a workshop**
> Witness the production of the famous Arita-yaki ceramics in the manufactures of Arita Bussan Co. Ltd.; Korasha Co. Ltd. Fukagawa; Kakiemon; Gen-emon Iwao Taizan and Imaemon.

What to See in and Around Arita

The Kyushu Ceramic Museum south of the station and the Arita Ceramic Museum (Arita Toji-bijutsukan; east of the station) have excellent works of early and contemporary pottery masters on display (both open Tue–Sun 9am–4.30pm).

✳ Pottery museums

Not far south of the museum in the Arita park is the tomb of the Korean ceramics master Ri-Sampei and the Tozan shrine, which has the largest torii made of ceramics in Japan.

Tozan shrine

Around 5km/3mi north is Mount Kurokami and the nature reserve of the same name.

Kurokami

12km/7mi north of Arita is the port town of Imari (from Arita JR Matsuura line); the worthwhile sights here are the **ceramic village** of Okawachiyama (bus from the station, 15 minutes) as well as the nearby Imari-Arita ceramic hall and the Imari hall (some shops; ceramic markets in April and November). The attractive Iroha Islands are dotted around the bay.

Imari

15km/9mi east of Arita (JR Sasebo line) is the spa town of Takeo-onsen with its old gate tower. Toyotomi Hideyoshi, the unifier of Japan,

Takeo-onsen

is said to have stayed in the historic post station. The **plum garden** Mifunegaoka blossoms at the beginning of March.

Ureshino   14km/9mi south (bus from Arita, 40 minutes) visitors can enjoy the beautiful landscape along the Ureshino River, a forested, hilly area with big tea plantations. The spa town of Ureshino-onsen has hot springs (36°C/97°F to 98°C/208°F), a number of good hotels and ryokan. A bus route (Sonogi line) goes to Sonogi, and from there onwards to ▶ Nagasaki as well as to the ▶ Unzen-Amakusa National Park.

★ Ashizuri-Uwakai National Park

e–f 4–5

Main island: Shikoku   **Prefectures:** Kochi and Ehime
Area : 111 sq km/43 sq mi

足摺宇和海国立公園 **The largely pristine landscape of the Ashizuri-Uwakai National Park is distinguished by its crystal-clear sea water and long white sandy beaches, which are great for swimming. The coastal landscape, one of the most beautiful in Japan, is dotted with enchanting fishing villages.**

Location   The Ashizuri-Uwakai National Park, founded in 1972, incorporates the coastal regions in the south of the main Japanese island of Shikoku. It includes the towns of Tatsukushi and Minokoshi and extends all the way to Cape Ashizuri, the southern tip of the island; in addition the highly indented southwest coast of Shikoku with its offshore islands is also part of the park. The most convenient starting points for excursions to the park are the towns of Tosa-Shimizu and ▶Uwajima.

What to See in the Ashizuri-Uwakai National Park

Tosa-Shimizu   Tosa-Shimizu (population 23,000) at the park's eastern fringe is a port with significant deep-sea fishing. From here the 13km/8mi **Ashizuri Skyline** road leads to Cape Ashizuri, which has good views and a lighthouse (bus connections).

The buses to **Cape Ashizuri** take two different routes: one goes along the west coast, the other through the middle of the headland; there is also a road

▶ ASHIZURI-UWAKAI N.P.

GETTING THERE
By rail: from Kochi JR Dosan line and Tosa-Kuroshio line to Nakamura (2 hours).
By bus: from Nakamura to Tosa-Shimizu (1¼ hours) and to Cape Ashizuri (2 hours).

along the east coast (travel time between 30 and 50 minutes). The bays north of the headland with their 80m/260ft cliffs are battered by high waves. Many people who were tired of life have leapt from these cliffs, which is why signs warn those contemplating suicide to think of their families.

> ! **Baedeker TIP**
>
> **Underwater world**
> A half-hour tour with a glass-bottom boat reveals the beauty of Ashizuri Ocean Park (Ashizuri Kaichu Koen) with its long coral banks and colourful fauna.

Near the white lighthouse of 1914 stands the Kongofukuji temple, built in 822 byKobo-daishi. The current buildings date back to 1662. The temple is dedicated to the thousand-handed Kannon and is the 38th of the 88 pilgrimage temples on Shikoku. There is a statue of John Manjiro (Japanese name: Nakahama Manjiro), who was shipwrecked and rescued by an American ship in 1841 and returned to Japan after spending several years in the United States.

Kongofukuji

13km/8mi west of Tosa-Shimizu are the towns of Tatsukushi and Minokoshi (bus 40 minutes). The bay of Tatsukushi has a nice white sandy beach. West of Tatsukushi in **Nagashima** is the 25m/82ft-tall building of the Kaiteikan underwater observatory, whose observation chamber is 7m/23ft below the surface. A short walk away (footpath, 10 minutes) the Kaiyokan Aquarium has numerous rare species of fish.

Tatsukushi and around

★ ★ Aso-Kuju National Park

c–d 4–5

Main island: Kyushu
Area: 726 sq km/280 sq mi

Prefectures: Kumamoto and Oita

The scenery in the Aso-Kuji National Park alternates between the green of gentle fields and thick forests and the black-brown of bare, solidified lava fields and bizarre mountain massifs. The park encompasses the Aso volcano and the Kuju mountains, as well as Mount Tsurumi, Mount Yufu and Mount Takasakiyama, all located west of the spa town of ►Beppu.

阿蘇くじゅう国立公園

Aso National Park is mainly known for the crater of Mount Aso, one of the world's largest calderas (from 18km/11mi to 24km/15mi diameter). In recent times five volcanic peaks have developed within this caldera. One of them, Nakadake, is still active today. It is among the most active volcanoes in the world and spews greater or smaller amounts of ash almost every year.

Aso crater

▶ VISITING ASO-KUJU NATIONAL PARK

GETTING THERE

By rail: from Kumamoto or from Oita JR Hohi main line, stations in Tateno, Akamizu, Uchinomaki and Aso (Kumamoto–Aso 1¼ hours) and others.
By bus: from Beppu via Yufuin-onsen to Aso (further to Kumamoto).

ACCESS TO THE PARK

A good way of getting to Beppu (also by bus) is along the Trans-Kyushu road (Yamanami Highway), which goes to Nagasaki. At the spa town of Yufuin-onsen the road to Kuju turns south and crosses the 1320m/4330ft-high Mikinoto Park, before it reaches Mount Kuju and the Senomoto Plateau. A country road branches off here to the Kuju Plateau.

Starting point for excursions to this plateau and the Kuju mountains is the town of Kanno jigoku (bus from Beppu, 1¾ hours; in addition there are bus connections to Miyaji station, one hour).

The Kurokawa River flows past the crater region of Aso to the north, the Shirakawa River to the south. Both of them rise in the park and meet west of the mountain near Toshita.

What to See in the Aso National Park

Kuju Plateau
Kuju Mountains
The Kuju Plateau is a well-known recreation area. In summer it is covered by the red flowers of the large azalea fields. In winter it is visited by a large number of skiers. One of the inhabitants' main sources of income is rearing livestock. Some farms offer Japanese tourists, for whom grazing cows and horses are a rare sight, the opportunity to milk cows and ride ponies.

To the north are the Kuju Mountains, which are forested at lower altitudes and covered in a rich alpine flora higher up. The southernmost and highest peak, Kuju (1787m/5863ft), is also the **highest mountain on Kyushu**. Further conspicuous peaks are Daisen, Waita, Hossho, Ogihana and Mimata. The southern gateway to this region is the town of Miyaji, which has a railway station.

Kuju
There are different routes to choose from when **climbing Mount Kuju**; however, you need sturdy legs for this excursion. At the mountain's northern foot is Kuju-Tozanguchi (Kyudai train line from Oita to Bungo-Nakamura, then bus); from here the ascent of 6km/3.5mi takes two hours. Another path to the peak starts in Minami-Tozanguchi (JR Hohi main line to Bungo-Taketa, then bus).

The most popular ascent starts in Shuchikujo (bus from Bungo-Taketa) at the mountain's southern foot. The peak of Mount Kuju can be reached in four hours via the Tembodai lookout point, which has a lovely view of the Aso region and the bay of Beppu to the east.

✶✶ Aso

The Aso massif rises south of Kuju. The Aso volcano has five peaks **Japan's largest** inside a crater that is on average between 800m/2625ft and 900m/ **active volcano** 2950ft high. They are: Takadake (1592m/5223ft), the highest, Neko-dake (1408m/4619ft), Eboshidake (1337m/4386ft), Nakadake (1506m/4941ft), the only volcano that is still active, and Kishimadake (1321m/4334ft). Mount Aso's crater extends 23km/14mi in a north-south direction and 16km/10mi in an east-west direction. At 255 sq km/98 sq mi the Aso crater is one of the largest in the world. The area it encompasses, from the wide Asodani Valley in the north with the towns of Aso and Ichinomiya to the Nangodani Valley in the south with the town of Takamori, is now a densely populated place. The fertile volcanic soil is used for agriculture.

Two routes lead up Nakadake, whose crater has a diameter of 600m/ **Nakadake** 650yd and a depth of around 160m/525ft. From Aso station (JR Ho-hi main line) the Aso Kanko Toll Road (bus route, 50 minutes) makes its way over the Kusasenri Plateau to Asosan-Nishi, from

In the crater of Mount Nakadake solidified lava and rubble shape the landscape

Aso Volcano Museum ▶ where a cableway goes up the edge of the crater. On the way there is the Aso Volcano Museum (Aso Kazan Hakubutsukan), which has photographs from within Mount Naka, some of them taken by cameras positioned in the crater (open daily 9am–5pm, ¥ 840).

Asosan-Higashi From Miyaji station the Sensuikyo Gorge toll road (bus route, 15 minutes) makes its way to Asosan-Higashi, which is also a starting point for a cableway up to the rim of the crater. There is a bus connection between the lower stations of the two cableways, so that visitors can go up one cableway and come down the other. When the volcano threatens to erupt, the cableway stops operating; there are protective bunkers at various points along the way.

Aso shrine The beauty of the green land in the Aso caldera, with gentle hilltops, evergreen forests and small villages contrasts with the rough beauty of the bubbling volcano crater surrounded by solidified lava. The Aso shrine is located in the northern region, 1km/0.6mi north of Miyaji station; it is dedicated to the Takeiwatatsu-no-Mikoto deity. According to legend it was founded in AD 100, which would make it the oldest shrine of the historical province of Higo (modern-day Kumamoto Prefecture). The current buildings (main hall and gate) date back to 1842.

✴ Aso-onsen One of the most beautiful views of the Aso regions can be had from the attractive holiday town of Aso-onsen (Uchinomaki) northwest of Aso station. It also has hot springs. A bus route leaves from here to Daikambo (936m/3071ft) to the north (30 minutes). It is the northern peak of the old crater wall, from where visitors can enjoy a wide view of the crater region with its five peaks.

Yunotani-onsen Several **hot springs** have made the Aso region a lively recreation area. 6km/4mi southeast of Akamizu station and the Eboshidake's northwest hillside is Yunotani-onsen, which is the highest spa town in the crater region at 800m/2625ft. It has views of the plain of Kumamoto, the bay of Ariake and the area around Unzen.

The summer recreation area of Tarutama-onsen (bus from Aso-Shimoda station, 30 minutes) is located on the southwest slope of Mount Eboshi at an altitude of 667m/2188ft. The town is the starting point for an attractive walk to the **Kusasenri Plateau**. To the south the town of Jigoku-onsen lies at an altitude of 750m/2461ft.

! **Baedeker TIP**

Outdoor bathing

The town of Kurokawa Onsen, known for its open-air baths (rotemburo), is located 6km/4mi west of Yamanami Highway (one hour by bus from Aso). There is a choice between just enjoying a bath here (tickets at the ryokan reception) or combining it with an overnight stay, such as in the stylish Okunoyu, which has a nice rotemburo by the river (tel. 09 67/44 00 21, www.okunoyu.com, from ¥ 15,900 per person including two meals).

Awajishima

H 7 • g 3

Prefecture: Hyogo
Area: 593 sq km/229 sq mi

Population: 160,000

炎路島

The island of Awaji is considered the cradle of Japanese puppet theatre: it is said that centuries ago a banished courtier made some puppets to keep himself amused and to dispel the boredom of rural life. The island is also a lovely place to enjoy some relaxing hours on the beach.

The densely populated island of Awaji is in the east of the Inland Sea. Separated from Honshu in the north by the narrow Akashi Strait and from Shikoku in the south by the Naruto Strait, a stretch of water only 1400m/1500yd wide, Awaji is a link between the largest and the smallest of the Japanese main islands. Since 1985 the Naruto Strait has been spanned by the 1.6km/1mi-long Onaruto-kyo (bridge), which connects Awaji with Naruto on the main island Shikoku. Awaji was the epicentre of the severe 1995 earthquake, which delayed the completion of the Akashi-Kaikyo Bridge.

Bridge between the islands

▶ AWAJISHIMA

INFORMATION

Tourist information
In Iwaya, Awaji Interchange Service Area
Tel. 07 99/72 01 68
Daily 9am–5pm

GETTING THERE
By boat: ferry connection from Kansai Airport to Sumoto (1 hour).
By bus: JR bus from Shin-Kobe to Sumoto (1½ hours), from Osaka (2 hours). There are several lines on the island.

What to See on Awajishima

The main town on the island and also the most important tourist centre is Sumoto (population 44,000), located around half-way along the east coast. Bus routes to all parts of the island start from here; national expressway no. 28 goes north to Iwaya and southwest to Fukura. Sumoto's surroundings are a popular holiday area with white beaches, bizarre pine forests and various leisure activities.

Sumoto

Around 6km/4mi northwest of Sumoto (bus, 10 minutes) the 448m/1470ft Mount Senzan rises; on its summit is the **Senhoji temple** built by the Shingon sect. The temple dedicated to the thousand-handed Kannon contains a bell cast in 1283 and a gong presumably dating back to the Muromachi period (1338–1573). There is an impressive view of the mountain giants of Shikoku in the west and the Kitan Strait in the east from the summit of the mountain.

Senzan

✳

◀ View

! **Baedeker TIP**

Dance of the puppets

Performances of the Awaji Ningyo Jorurikan puppet theatre take place daily in the Onaruto-kyo Memorial Hall (tel. 07 99/52 02 60, open 9am–5pm, ¥ 1260).
There is a bus connection from Fukura (just under 30 minutes).

In the north of the island (bus from Iwaya, 15 minutes, then 15 minutes on foot) is the impressive **Honpukuji**, a unique example of modern Japanese temple architecture by Ando Tadao. The innermost sanctum below a pond is bathed in reddish light.

South of Sumoto there are remains of an old castle complex in **Mikuma Park**; even further south is Ohama beach, with white sand, deep blue water and green pine groves; it is one of the most beautiful swimming beaches in the entire Kansai region. Smaller, pretty bathing resorts can be found along the east coast, at Osaka Bay as well as on the west coast (Lake Harimanade).

Fukura   The port of Fukura (bus from Sumoto, 40 minutes), the western gateway to the island, is the home of the **Awaji puppet theatre**, which is based on a 400-year-old tradition. Higher up at Fukura visitors have a good view of the Naruto whirlpool (▶Inland Sea).

Goshikihama   One of the west coast's **most beautiful beaches** is Goshikihama (bus from Sumoto, 50 minutes), a 4km/2.5mi beach which got its name from its colourful pebbles (»Go-Shiki-hama« means »five-coloured beach«); Kei-no-Matsubara, a 3km/2mi white sandy beach, is also very beautiful.

★ Bandai-Asahi National Park

K–L 5

Main island: Honshu
Area: 1870 sq km/722 sq mi

Prefectures: Fukushima, Yamagata and Niigata

磐梯朝日国立公園   **Bandai-Asahi National Park, Japan's second largest, protects a picturesque landscape of mountains and lakes that is home to a large number of wild animals. The higher regions of the mountain chains are covered by snow for most of the year and winter sports are possible here until well into summer.**

Four regions   Bandai-Asahi National Park in the north of the Japanese main island of Honshu is divided into four non-contiguous regions. The southern part is made up of Lake Inawashiro with its immediate surroundings; the Bandai-Azuma Mountains to the east, Mount Iide to

This national park protects some wonderful landscape

the northwest of the lake; and finally the region with the largest area, the Asahi massif and the three holy Dewa-Sanzan mountains to the far north.

What to See in the Bandai-Asahi National Park

The area around Lake Inawashiro is best accessed from the town of Koriyama to the east. From here take the JR Banetsu-Saisen line via Bandai-Atami to Lake Inawashiro (altitude: 514m/1686ft, area: 104 sq km/40 sq mi), Japan's fourth-largest lake. It has been dammed by lava from the Bandai and Nekoma volcanoes and is now used to irrigate the area surrounding Koriyama as well for the production of electrical energy. The best view of the lake is from the Kohiragata-Tenjin shrine 1.5km/1mi from Sekito station.

Lake Inawashiro

The town of Inawashiro is located north of the lake; buses (30 minutes) leave there for Numajiri-onsen 19km/12mi to the northeast, which, together with the neighbouring Nakanozawa-onsen, is one of the region's most popular ski resorts. Numajiri-onsen is the starting point for an ascent of the 1700m/5577ft Mount Adatara (climb 10km/6mi, around 4 hours), which is already in the Bandai-Azuma Mountains.

Numajiri-onsen Nakanozawa-onsen

Noji-onsen is 13km/8mi further north near the Tsuchiyu Pass, the start of the **Bandai-Azuma Skyline Drive**, a mountain road around

Noji-onsen

⏵ BANDAI-ASAHI N.P.

GETTING THERE

By rail: from Tokyo JR Tohoku shinkansen line to Fukushima and Koriyama (1½ hours); light railways from Koriyama to Inawashiro (40 minutes) and Aizu-Wakamatsu.
By bus: from Fukushima, Inawashiro (40 minutes) and Yamato to different destinations in the national park. Excellent roads and a dense bus network make this national park very accessible.

30km/20mi long. The road runs at an average altitude of 1350m/4430ft and climbs to a maximum altitude of 1622m/5322ft; there are nice views along the way. The road comes to an end at **Azuma-Takayu-onsen** near Fukushima.

The 1819m/5968ft **Bandai massif** can also be reached from Inawashiro; its massif contains several peaks. A bus route runs to Omote Bandai Tozanguchi (20 minutes), where the drive up in the bus begins.

This route goes past the Hanitsu shrine and Umagaeshi to the summit of Akahani. There is a wonderful view here of the northern slope with its lakes and craters that were formed during the 1888 eruption.

✳
Akahani

Bandai-Kogen The Bandai-Kogen Plateau at an altitude of around 800m/2600ft at Bandai's northern foot is covered by **more than 100 lakes**, which were formed by the big eruption of 1888; a special features of these lakes is that they have water of different colours. The largest lakes are Hibara, Onogawa and Akimoto. This attractive area has hiking trails, camp sites and leisure facilities to offer (such as rowing boat rentals).

Azuma Mountains

Fukushima The Azuma Mountains northeast of the Bandai Massif are best reached via the university town of Fukushima on the JR Tohoku main line. The capital of the prefecture of the same name is around 30km/20mi east of the massif. The Azuma Mountains are divided by the Okura River into Higashi-Azuma (east-Azuma) and Nishi-Azuma (west-Azuma). The bus servicing this area uses the Bandai-Azuma-Skyline toll road (see above). The highest elevation of the eastern volcano region is Higashi-Azuma (1975m/6480ft); the neighbouring Azuma-Kofuji (1705m/5594ft), also called Azuma-Fuji because of its resemblance to Mount Fuji and the 1949m/6394ft Issaikyo, which last erupted in 1893.

Azuma-Kofuji
Issaikyo Jododaira, located on the Bandai-Azuma-Skyline (see above) between Azuma-Takayu and the Tsuchiyu Pass close to the peak of Azuma-Kofuji, is the base for climbing both this mountain and the Issaikyo. It takes around 30 minutes to climb to the peak of Azuma-Kofuji; the hike to the top of Issaikyo and back takes about an hour.

West of Fukushima is the hot springs town of Azuma-Takayu-onsen (altitude: 750m/2460ft; bus from Fukushima and from Jododaira, both 45 minutes), which has a view of the basin of Fukushima. Many souvenir shops in the town sell the famous **Kokeshi puppets**. Next to this town is the dreamy Nuruyu-onsen on the eastern slope of Azuma-Kofuji.

★
Azuma-Takayu-onsen

One of this region's most beautiful towns is Tsuchiyu-onsen (altitude: 435m/1427ft; bus from Fukushima, 30 minutes), traversed by a bubbling mountain stream. The Tsuchiyu Pass, which connects Fukushima with Inawashiro, offers some impressive views.

Tsuchiyu-onsen

The Tengendai Plateau on the northern slope of the 2024m/6640ft Nishi-Azuma makes up the northern part of the Azuma region. The plateau, with an altitude of around 1300m/4300ft can be reached via Shirabu-onsen (cableway, seven minutes), a popular summer and winter sports destination.

Bandai-Asahi National Park

Nishi-Azuma is flanked by Nishi-Daiten (1982m/6503ft) and Higashi-Daiten (1928m/6325ft). The pretty spa towns of Nuruyu-onsen, Azuma-Takayu-onsen and Goshiki-onsen are situated in the northeastern foothills of this group.

Nishi-Azuma

The northernmost section of the national park contains the Dewa-Sanzan (»Three Mountains of Dewa«) with the peaks Gassan, Yudono and Haguro; the best starting base is Tsuruoka (▶ Sakata, around).
All three of the mountains are considered holy in the ascetic, exorcist **Shugendo teachings**, which have also been influenced by Buddhism. Every year pilgrims dressed in the clothes of the Yamabushi (itinerant monks) go to the shrines, particularly to the Dewa shrine festival that takes place in mid-July. They worship En no Gyoja as their forerunner; however, the sect's founder was the priest Shobo (832–909) from the Shingon sect; he gave the teachings of this ascetic and magical faith an authoritative framework. An excursion to this mountain world, which is still quite remote despite the pilgrimages, is a real highlight of a trip through northern Japan.
The highest of the Dewa-Sanzan is the 1980m/6496ft **Gassan**. It is ascended from the southwest via the 1504m/4934ft Yudono, which can be reached by bus (1 ¾ hours) from Tsuruoka. Yudono is considered the seat of the mountain deity Oyamatsumi-no-mikoto, who is worshipped at a waterfall fed by a hot spring.

★
Dewa-Sanzan

◀ Pilgrimages

!   *Baedeker* TIP

Around the Azuma Mountains

A good bus route for a round trip is the one from Fukushima via Azuma-Takaru-onsen, Jododaira, the Tsuchiyu Pass and Iizaka-onsen to Bandai-Kogen (trip duration around 3 hours) and back.

✴
View ►

The peak of Gassan is the shrine of the same name dedicated to the moon deity Tsukiyomi-no-mikoto. From up here there is a wonderful view of the mountain landscape and the Sea of Japan.

Haguro

Travelling east from Tsuruoka (bus, 45 minutes) visitors will get to the 419m/1375ft Haguro with the Dewa shrine. The shrine dedicated to the Ideha-no-mikoto deity can be reached via a long set of stairs set between ancient trees; on the way visitors pass what is said to be the oldest pagoda in the Tohoku district (14th century).

✴ ✴ Beppu

F 8 • d 4

Main island: Kyushu
Population: 135,000

Prefecture: Oita

別府

Beppu, one of the best-known cultural and bathing towns in Japan, attracts millions of tourists from home and abroad every year with its hot springs and boiling hot »pond hells«.

Important spa

Beppu is situated on a narrow strip of flat land on the northern coast of Kyushu island. Mount Tsurumi (1375m/4511ft) and Mount Takasakiyama (625m/2051ft) are further inland; Beppu's urban area extends to their foothills. The port is situated in the innermost corner of Beppu Bay. The spa area also includes the towns Hamawaki-onsen, Kamegawa-onsen, Shabaseki-onsen, Kannawa-onsen, Myoban-onsen, Horita-onsen and Kankaiji-onsen in addition to Beppu.
The production of bamboo goods is also of economic significance (around 60% of Japan's total production).

More than 3000 hot springs

The area around Beppu, which is visited by several millions of visitors every year, owes its reputation to its more than 3000 hot springs containing alkali, sulphur, carbon or iron; they reach temperatures of up to 100°C/212°F and eject as much as 140,000 cu m/ 5 million cu ft every day, which are used to feed a large number of baths. Columns of steam shroud the townscape in a constant veil of fog. Most hotels have access to the hot springs. It is customary to stroll down the street in a yukata, a light cotton kimono, after taking a bath.

What to See in Beppu

Takegawara

The Takegawara spa dating back to the Meiji period is located in the town centre (10 minutes from the station). It is Beppu's best-known spa (open daily 6.30am–10.30pm, ¥ 100; sand bath daily 8am–9.30pm, closed 3rd Wed of the month, ¥ 1000).

▶ VISITING BEPPU

INFORMATION
Tourist information
In the railway station (town exit)
Tel. 09 77/24 28 38
Daily 8.30am–5pm
www.beppu-navi.jp
Here visitors can get the
bus pass »My Beppu Free«.

GETTING THERE
By air: from Tokyo (Haneda Airport)
to Oita (1½ hours; onwards by bus or
hovercraft).

By rail: from Tokyo (central station)
JR Sanyo shinkansen line to Kokura
(5¾ hours), then JR Nippo main line
(1¼ hours).
By bus: from Oita to Beppu (1 hour);
several local lines.
By boat: from Osaka/Kobe Kansai
Steamship across the Inland Sea (13
hours); further routes from Hiroshima
(8 hours).

WHERE TO STAY
▶ Mid-range
Miyukiya
6 Kumi Kannawa, Beppu-shi,
Oita-ken 874-0042
tel. 09 77/66 03 60, fax 66 03 88
info@miyukiya.net
Near the Oita Kotsu Bus Center. By
bus 10 or 20 from station or taxi (15
minutes)
Pleasant ryokan with a total of twelve
Japanese-style rooms, six in the old
house (kyukan), six in the new house
(honkan). Has a pretty little rotemburo and an inside bath (no mixed-sex
bathing). Very tasty food. Last drinks
at 11pm. Several »hells« can be
reached on foot from here.

▶ Budget
Minshuku Kokage
8-9 Ekimae-cho, Beppu-shi,
Oita-ken 874-0935
tel. 09 77/23 17 53, fax 23 38 95
Near the station
13 simple rooms, ten of them with
bathrooms. Breakfast and supper are
available on request. A member of the
Japanese Inn Group. The owner
speaks a bit of English. Coin-operated
washing machine and dryer available.

*Women in Yukata on their way
to the bath*

The steam rises over the spa's »Sea Hell«

Approximately the same distance from the station is the Beppu-Furusato-kann **museum** containing archaeological finds from the surrounding area and exhibits relating to the hot springs.

Kankaiji-onsen

West of Beppu Park (3.5km/2mi from the station) the spa town of Kankaiji-onsen lies half way up Mount Tsurumi in a particularly beautiful, idyllic region; it has a magnificent view of the bay. Not far north is the **modern bath complex** Suginoi Palace with several large swimming pools surrounded by plant arrangements.

Kannawa-onsen

Opening times of all the »hells«:
Daily 8am–5pm, general ticket ¥ 2000

Kannawa-onsen, around 7km/4.5mi northwest of Beppu (bus from Beppu station, 20 minutes) is known for its **boiling-hot springs**; they are called »jigoku« (»hells«) and supply the town's households with hot water, amongst other things. The largest of these springs is Umi-jigoku; it is an approximately 120m/390ft-deep, emerald-green pond with a water temperature of 94°C/201°F and yields 360 cu m/13,000 cu ft every day. Nearby is the Oniyama-jigoku hot spring with a few pitiful alligators. The healing steam can be inhaled in the Kinryu Jigoku. Access to the springs leads past booths, zoos or fuming dragons, before the natural spectacle can be enjoyed.

Chinoike-jigoku ▶

Further north is the blood-red mud pond Chinoike-jigoku (93°C/199°F, around 165m/540ft deep), which feeds the large mud baths nearby, and the Tatsumaki-jigoku geyser, which throws out a jet of hot water every 25 minutes.

Evening atmosphere at Lake Biwa

Sakamoto

The JR Kosei line leaves Hama-Otsu and runs along the southwest shore of Lake Biwa. The Saikyoji temple, also belonging to the Tendai sect, was founded in the 7th century by Shotoku-taishi; it is located 2km/1mi northeast of Sakamoto station (Keihan-Ishisaka private line) and is famous for its art treasures from the Momoyama period (1573–1600).

Ogoto-onsen

The JR Kosei line passes the spa town of Ogoto-onsen, a popular holiday destination for anglers, water sports enthusiasts and hikers. Behind the town is the 848m/2782ft **Mount Hiei**, which has a cable-way running up to its peak (►Kyoto, around).

Katata

Die JR Kosei line runs northwards to Katata, where the Ukimi-do temple (aka Magetsu-ji) of the Rinzai sect stands in the lake. It too is one of the classic views (omi-hakkei; »descending geese at Katata«). The 1350m/1475yd Biwako-Ohashi bridge spans the lake from Katata to the eastern shore and to Moriyama.

Horai

The 1174m/3852ft Mount Horai rises at Shiga station with a panoramic view of the lake. The mountain can also be reached by bus from Otsu station to the winter-sports resort of Biwako Valley. From here take a mountain railway up the 1103m/3619ft Uchimi, then a chairlift up to the peak of Mount Horai.

◄ **Hira**

North of the 1051m/3448 Mount Hira (chair lift to the top) is another of the famous omi-hakkei (»evening snow on Mount Hira«).

Chikubu

The island of Chikubu is located in the lake's northern area. It has steep cliffs and is covered by bamboo and cedar forests. Sights worth visiting here are the Tsukubusuma shrine, built in 1603 by Toyotomi Hideyoshi, presumably from parts of the famous Fushimi Castle, as well as the neighbouring Hogenji temple, dedicated to the goddess of mercy and luck. It was founded by the priest Gyoki (670–749) on the orders of Emperor Shomu.

✳
Ryozen

From Omi-Shiozu station at the lake's northern end the JR Hokuriku main line runs along the eastern shore. Mount Ryozen (1084m/3556ft) can be climbed from Maybara station 9km/5.5mi to the southeast. There is a lovely panorama from the top.

Hikone

Next is the old castle town of Hikone (population 94,000), once a station on the Tokaido (»eastern sea road«) and since the construction of the castle the seat of the Ii family, who, at the Battle of Sekigahara fought alongside the later shogun Tokugawa Ieyasu against the feudal lords.

✳ ✳
Castle ►

The castle, completed in 1622, is 1km/0.5mi west of the station and consists of the three-storey main tower as well as the Suanju and Tempin towers. The latter has a museum with pieces owned by the Ii. The »drum gate« (Taiko-mon) and the Sawaguchi-tamon tower are also part of the complex. The castle looks particularly beautiful in moonlight (biwako-hakkei). At the foot of the castle is the Ii residence (Rakuraku-en) built in 1677. It has an attractive garden (Genkyu-en) and the Konki Park with a bronze statue of Naosuke (castle and garden open daily 8.30am–5pm, ¥ 500).

Matsubara

Hikone Beach is at Matsubara; Ryotanji temple, brought here in 1614, is located by Mount Ohara. It has an attractive Zen garden. Seiryoji temple houses the graves of the Ii.

Taga shrine

Southeast of Hikone (Omi private train; change in Takamiya) is the Taga shrine, dedicated to the two gods Izanagi and Izanami. It is said to be of around the same age as the Ise shrines and is one of the most significant in the Kinki region.

Omi-Hachiman
Chomeiji temple ►

The JR Tokaido main line leaves Hikone and, staying close to the lake, makes its way south to Omi-Hachiman (population 63,000). Northwest of the town (25 minutes by bus, then 15 minutes on a footpath) the Chomeiji temple is set over the lake. It was probably founded by Shotoku-taishi (573–621) and renewed during the 16th century.

Azuchi

East of Omi-Hachiman is the town of Azuchi, the location of a once magnificent castle that belonged to Oda Nobunaga (only some wall fragments remain); the tomb of Nobunaga is also here, as is the Sokenji temple with its statue.

Kusatsu

In Kusatsu the interactive Biwako Hakubutsukan (bus from the station's west exit, 20 minutes) is dedicated to life around Lake Biwa (open Tue–Sun 9.30am–5pm, ¥ 500). The town was once at the junction of two important trading routes, the Tokaido and the Nakasendo. Reminding visitors of this past is the lovingly restored former Kusatsujuku Honjin guesthouse (from the station ten minutes to the south), which provided accommodation to feudal lords, shogunate officials and other high-ranking people from 1635 to 1870 (open Tue–Sun 9am–5pm, ¥ 200).

Located at the lake's southern end is Ishiyama; the Keihan private line (ten minutes) departs from here southbound to Ishiyama temple. It belongs to the Toji school of the Shingon sect and was founded in the 8th century by the priest Roben, then rebuilt twice, in the 12th and 16th centuries. It is **one of the 33 temples of pilgrimage of Kansai**. Amongst the temple's sights are the Todai-mon gate with Nio statues by the famous sculptor Unkei and his son Tankei, the Hondo main hall with a statue of the Nyorai-Kannon and the neighbouring Genji-no-ma room, in which, it is said, the court lady Murasaki Shikibu (975–1031) wrote the famous novel *Genji-monogatari* (*Tale of Genji*). The Tahoto pagoda, in its modern form, dates back to 1190. From Ishiyama JR station a Teisan line bus takes a little less than 50 minutes to reach Miho Museum in the mountain woods. In this building, designed by I.M.Pei, high-quality Asian and ancient (Egyptian, Mesopotamian) art is on display.

★ ★
Ishiyama
temple

Miho Museum

★ Chichibu-Tama National Park

K 7 • l–m 2

Main island: Honshu
Area: 1216 sq km/470 sq mi

Prefectures: Saitama, Yamanashi and Nagano

秩父多摩国立公園

This national park, rich in beautiful views, extends northwest of Tokyo over the Kanto Mountains. The mountain landscape, which has an average altitude of around 1000m/3250ft, is traversed by numerous rivers and gorges and has attractive forests. This recreation area is much appreciated by the inhabitants of Tokyo and Yokohama as it is easy to reach.

The most important gateways to the national park are the towns of Ome at the headwaters of the Tama River (Okutama) in the east as well as Chichibu in the north. The 2595m/8514ft Mount Kimpu and the 2592m/8504ft Mount Kokushi are the region's highest mountains; together with Mount Ryogami (1724m/5656 ft), Mount Mikuni (1828m/5997ft) and Mount Mizugaki (2230m/7316ft) they make a wonderful hiking area. Mount Daibosatsu (2057m/6749ft) rises to the south.

Mountains

What to See in the Chichibu-Tama National Park

Ome (population 110,000) at the southeast fringe of the national park is a centre of the textile industry. The Ome Railway Park, part

Ome

of the Nagayama Park, can be reached on foot from the station in 15 minutes and is worth a visit.

Yoshino Baigo
The next station to the east is Hinatawada; the plum groves of Yoshino Baigo, which blossom from the end of February to mid-March (round trips at this time), are 800m/0.5mi away and are accessible via the Jindaibashi Bridge spanning the Tama River. During the whole of March the **folkloristic plum festival** takes place here.
The Yoshino Gorge, Temma Park, the Taisei-in temple and the Atago shrine, all nearby, are worth visiting.

Mitake
Take the JR Ome line to get to the station at the foot of the densely forested Mount Mitake (930m/3051ft). The Tama River (to the north) and Yozawa River (to the south) have created some romantic gorges, the mountainsides contain picturesque hiking trails lined by cherry trees, azaleas and maples.

Takimoto Mitakesan Fujimine
There is a bus connection (ten minutes) from Mitake station to the cableway Takimoto lower terminus. The cableway takes six minutes to reach the Mitakesan mountain station (or take a footpath from Takimoto, 2½ hours); from here take the chair lift to Fujimine, where there is a viewing platform above Mitake-daira.

▶ VISITING CHICHIBU-TAMA NATIONAL PARK

GETTING THERE

By rail: from Tokyo (Shinjuku station) JR Chuo line to Tachikawa (40 minutes), then JR Ome line to Okutama (1¼ hours); from Tokyo (Ikebukuro station) Seibu-Ikebukuro line to Seibu-Chichibu (1½ hours), then Chichibu railway to Mitsumineguchi (20 minutes); from Tokyo (Ikebukuro station) Tobu-Toio line to Ogawamachi (1¼ hours).
By bus: several regional lines.

EVENTS

Mitake shrine: processions with portable shrines take place during the Hinode-matsuri festival (beginning of May), in which men in samurai armour also participate.
Chichibu shrine: Kawase-matsuri (July) with turbulent processions; Chichibu-Yo-matsuri (3rd Dec) with processions of fantastically illuminated floats and a big firework display.

ROUND TRIP

The following route is a great option for a round trip: from Mitsumineguchi take the bus to Owa, then the cableway to the peak of Mount Mitsumine; from here continue on foot to the shrine (20 minutes), further to Lake Chichibu (1½ hours) and back to Mitsumineguchi (40 minutes).

WHERE TO STAY

▶ **Budget**
Oku Chichibu Lake View Youth Hostel
Otakimura
Tel. 04 94/55 00 56
A youth hostel on the banks of Lake Chichibu.

The summit of Mount Mitake commands a wonderful view on clear days of the mountains of Nikko and Tsukuba to the northeast and east respectively. The **Mitake shrine**, founded around 800, is located close to the peak (foot path from Fujimine, 30 minutes). The building displays the Shimmei-zukuri style, but the main shrine was rebuilt during the Meiji period.

★
◀ View

Saiwai station is the starting point for an attractive walk through Mitake Gorge to Mitake station (approx. 45 minutes). Not far from the gorge is the **Gyokudo Art Museum**, with works by the painter Kawai Gyokudo (1873–1957) and a remarkable rock garden.

◀ Mitake Gorge

The JR Ome line ends in Okutama near Lake Okutama, which has rich fish stocks (bus from the station, 20 minutes); it has been dammed by the 149m/490ft-high Ogochi dam, which is 535m/585yd across. There are around 6000 cherry trees on the northern shore, which blossom in mid-April. Okutama is an inexpensive base for tours to the Tama Alps.

Okutama

Around 15km/9mi northwest of Okutama (bus, 40 minutes) is the town of Nippara, which is known for its **dripstone cave**, the largest in the Kanto region. The cave is 800m/2635ft deep; a 280m/305yd section is lit and accessible to the public (open April–Nov 8am–5pm, Dec–March 8.30am–4.30pm, ¥ 600).
The area around Nippara contains some bizarre rock formations; the foliage colours in October are very attractive.

Nippara

The national park's northeastern gateway is the town of Chichibu (population 61,000), known for its silk textiles (Chichibu-meisen). The Chichibu shrine is located in a grove of ancient trees; together with the Hodo shrine in Nagatoro and the Mitsumine shrine on the mountain of the same name it is the most significant in the region. The town's landmark is **Mount Bu-ko** (1336m/4383ft), which rises to the south; the Hashidate dripstone cave lies to the west (15 minutes on foot from Urayamaguchi station)

Chichibu

The final stop of the Chichibu Railway is **Mitsumineguchi**, which is the point of departure for buses to Owa at the foot of the 1101m/

! *Baedeker* TIP

Japanese paper

The small town of Ogawa is interesting (Tobu-Tojo line from Tokyo, Ikebukuro station). It has several production workshops for hand-made paper. The Kubo Kobo factory (tel. 04 93/ 72 04 36) is open to the public. Why not try making some paper in the Ogawa-washi Taiken-gakushu Center (tel. 04 93/72 72 62, daily except Tue)!

3612ft Mount Mitsumine; there is a 1900m/6250ft cableway to the peak. The **Mitsumine shrine** situated here is said to have been founded 2000 years ago, and during the Tokugawa period it was a centre for mountain ascetics who were part of the Tendai sect.

Lake Chichibu At the mountain's northwest foot is the artificial Lake Chichibu, which is crossed by two suspension bridges. The area is popular with anglers and hikers. The Mitsumine mountain road runs from the lake to the treasury of the Mitsumine shrine 6km/3.5mi away.

Nagatoro At the headwaters of the Arakawa (called Sumida further downriver) north of Chichibu is the town of Nagatoro (population 9000). The valley is known for its unusual rock formations. In spring the 1.5km/1mi cherry-tree avenue is very impressive; it connects the town to Kami-Nagatoro. In the summer the azalea blossom and in the autumn the leaves of the maple trees are also beautiful sights.

✷
Hodo ▶ Take the bus from Nagatoro to the foot of the 497m/1631ft Mount Hodo. A cableway leads up to the peak. There is a nice view of the surrounding mountains from up here, as well as of the Nagatoro Gorge and the Chichibu Basin. The Hodo shrine is situated on the mountain.

Riding the rapids ▶ The Oyabana-bashi bridge, 700m/765yd from Kami-Nagatoro station, is the starting point (both riverbanks) of the Arakawa boats that ride the rapids all the way to the Takasago-bashi bridge (around 50 minutes).

✷ Chiran

Main island: Kyushu
Population: 15,000

Prefecture: Kagoshima

知覧

Chiran is set in an enchanting landscape of hills, covered by vast tea plantations. The town is a real village idyll, known for its old gardens and the most excellent green tea.

History The town of Chiran is in the southwest of Kyushu Island, around 30km/20mi south of the prefectural capital of Kagoshima. During the Edo period Chiran was one of the 102 castle towns that were on the border to what was then Satsuma; in World War II it was the location of a flying school and an air force base. From here the »special attack forces«, the Kamikaze pilots, took off.

What to See in Chiran

✷
Samurai houses and gardens Around the mid-18th century Shimazu Hisamine, the lord of Chiran castle, visited Kyoto, the capital at the time; he was so impressed by the **landscaping of the gardens** there that he invited gardeners to his home town and create a number of extremely attractive dry gardens (karesansui). They were made on the land owned by the samurai, which was divided into lots. A total of seven gardens and samurai houses survive unchanged. They all lie on one of the roads built in a

chequer-board pattern south of the town hall. The properties are protected from onlookers on the street by stone walls and hedges. This emphasizes the town's medieval atmosphere. Traditional Japanese landscape gardening arranges trees, rocks and sand on an area of only 200–280 sq m (240–335 sq yd) in complex landscape images whose background is formed by the bright green hills.

The **garden of Saigo Ikkei** in the karesansiu style is a composition of moss, pebbles and raked sand, which symbolizes water. The **garden of Hirayama Soyo** was created between 1751 and 1772. Between 1781 and 1789 the **garden of Hirayama Ryoichi** was made in the shakkei style, which, following the principle of »borrowed landscape«, incorporates the background into the overall picture. Other noteworthy gardens are the gardens of Sata Minshi, Sata Naotada, Sata Mifune and the garden of the Mori family. The latter, in contrast to the others, is in the style of hill gardens (tsukiyama), including a small pond. This complex, created in 1741 extends to198 sq m/ 237 sq yd and also has a residential home and warehouse from the Edo period that are worth visiting (open daily 9am–5pm, ¥ 500).

▶ VISITING CHIRAN

GETTING THERE
By bus: from Kagoshima (Bus Center; 1¼ hours) and Ibusuki.

★★ Chubu-Sangaku National Park · Japanese Alps

J 6 • k 1

Main island: Honshu
Area: 1743 sq km/673 sq mi

Prefectures: Nagano, Gifu, Toyama and Niigata

The »Japanese Alps« is a much visited hiking and climbing area in the summer, while it attracts good numbers of skiers in the winter. A comparison with the European Alps is quite justified because of the character of its landscape and the large amount of snow that falls here during the winter.

中部山岳国立公園

Chubu-Sangaku National Park in the heart of the Japanese main island of Honshu contains the northern (Hida Mountains) and central regions of the high mountains known as the »Japanese Alps« as well as the country's highest peak after Mount Fuji.

The flora is diverse and varies according to altitude; at higher elevations there are ptarmigan and mountain antelopes.

The hot springs that well up all over the park have facilitated the development of spas and tourist towns, the best-known of which is Kamikochi at an altitude of 1500m/5000ft. The Kurobe River traverses

The high mountains

the mountains from the south to the north; a large lake created by the **Kurobe Dam** is an impressive scenic feature.

What to See in the Chubu-Sangaku National Park

Kamikochi Valley   The Kamikochi Valley surrounded by imposing mountains is fed by the headwaters of the Azusa River, which then makes its way through the Matsumoto Basin as the Sai after joining several other tributaries.

Kamikochi   The town of Kamikochi (1500m/4921ft), which is overrun in the summer, has the best tourist facilities and thanks to its location is an excellent base for climbing the surrounding mountains. The nearby Taisho pond was created in 1915 after the Yake volcano erupted and its volcanic emission dammed the Azusa River.

Snow-covered mountain ranges in the Japanese Alps near Kamikochi

from the time when the islands were the **imperial place of exile** for, amongst others, Go-daigo, who revolted against the military regime in 1331.

To get to the Shimane Peninsula, either take a boat from Sakaiminato or cross the 1714m/1874yd bridge across a natural channel connecting the lagoon with the sea. At its eastern tip is the fishing port of Mihonoseki, which is probably the national park's most attractive coastal town. The name means »Miho barrier« and refers to the former existence of a checkpoint. The **Miho shrine** consecrated to the Kotoshironushi deity and located in the eastern part of the town is one of the oldest shrines in the area.

Shimane

◀ Mihonoseki

West of Mihonoseki, along a picturesque strip of the northern coastline, is the Kaga-no-kukedo cave. It can be reached by bus from the town of Matsue. Tripper boats enter the cave via a narrow opening from the seaward side.

◀ Kaga-no-kukedo

The most suitable starting point to visit the section of the national park located in the west of the Shimane Peninsula is the town of Izumo, an important transport, trading and agricultural centre in the region. The Izumo Mingeikan folk art museum, housed in the historical residence of the Yanoto family, is worth a visit.

Izumo

◀ Museum

Above the entrance to Izumo shrine the traditional »shimenawa« ropes made of rice straw separate this world form the world of the gods

Tachikue-kyo ▶ 8km/5mi south of the station is the gorge Tachikue-kyo (Ichihata private line, 30 minutes) that formed as a result of erosion. The headwaters of the Kando River run through it. The gorge is particularly attractive during the autumn.

★ ★
Izumo-
Taisha shrine

🕐
Opening hours:
Daily 8am–6pm

To the northwest is the well-known Izumo-Taisha shrine (bus, seven minutes), Japan's oldest Shinto shrine. It is consecrated to Okuninushi-no-mikoto, the god of agriculture and medicine. According to legend he founded a state in the Izumo region and later retreated to the shrine specially built for him; it was originally meant to be a large palace. An unbroken line of his descendants subsequently worked as priests in this shrine. Okuninushi is also considered the protector of newlyweds, which is why couples come here to ask for a happy marriage. The shrine, alongside the Ise shrine and the Kompira shrine (Shikoku), is **the country's largest Shinto centre of pilgrimage**. It is particularly well visited during the time of the shrine festivals. On a total area of 16.4ha/40.5 acres, the shrine complex encompasses a large number of buildings representing the early Japanese architectural style Taishazukuri. The characteristic features of this style are a projecting pitched roof, cylindrical ridge-beams, crossed gable beams and the entrance located in the gable wall. The modern buildings largely date from the year 1874, the honden main hall from 1744.

The haiden prayer hall is adorned with a very heavy rope (Shimenawa) over the entrance, which separates the secular from the sacred area. The roofs are covered in cypress bark. Leading up to the shrine, which is enclosed by a double fence, is a cedar-lined avenue. In two elongated buildings on each side of the main shrine, according to Shinto teaching, all of the Shinto gods come together once a year in the 10th lunar month (October). For that reason all of Japan calls October the »godless month« (Kannazuki) and only Izumo calls it the »**month of the present deities**« (Kamiarizuki). To the left of the entrance is the **treasury** (museum) and behind it the hall for sa-

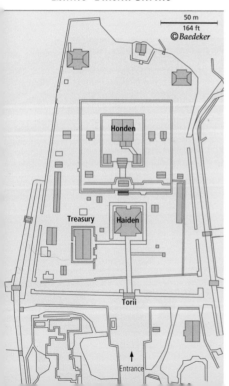

Izumo-Taisha Shrine

50 m
164 ft
© Baedeker

Honden

Treasury   Haiden

Torii

↑
Entrance

cred dances (kagura-den). The forested Yakumo and Tsuruyama hills form the backdrop to the shrine.

Around 700m/765yd west of the shrine is Inasanohama beach (2km/1mi south of Taisha station; bus). To the northwest Cape Hino-misaki, the western tip of the Shimane Peninsula, rises out of the Sea of Japan (bus from Taisha, 35 minutes). On the cape are the Hino-misaki shrine and Japan's allegedly tallest lighthouse (44m/144ft). ◀ Cape Hino-Misaki

The westernmost section of the Daisen-Oki National Park is the region surrounding the extinct Sambe volcano. At the mountain's southern foot is the spa town of Sambe-onsen with saline springs reaching temperatures of up to 43°C/110°F. Thanks to its attractive surroundings it is one of the most popular holiday towns in the San-in district. The 1126m/3694ft Sambe, also known as Iwami-Fuji, is can be reached by a mountain road (including buses). **Sambe** **Sambe-onsen**

✶ Daisetsuzan National Park

M 3

Main island: Hokkaido **Prefecture:** Hokkaido
Area: 2267 sq km/875 sq mi

The area of the Daisetsuzan National Park contains high mountains reaching altitudes of more than 2000m/6500ft, which is why the park also has the sobriquet »roof of Hokkaido«. At higher altitudes the park boasts an unusually rich mountain flora; small mountain towns are located at the foot of the mountains between pristine forests and crystal-clear rivers. 大雪山国立公園

The Daisetsuzan National Park lies at the centre of the northernmost of Japan's main islands. The park region contains three volcanic mountain ranges with the island's highest peaks: the 2290m/7513ft Asahi, the 2141m/7024ft Tomuraushi and the 2077m/6814ft Tokachi. The park's eastern section contains the 1962m/6437ft Ishikari as well as Lake Shikaribetsu and Lake Nukabira. The Tokachi, Ishikari and Chubetsu Rivers all have their source in the national park and form beautiful gorges. The best-known is Sounkyo, 50km/30mi east of the town of Asahikawa. **Mountain peaks and hot springs**

What to See in the Daisetsuzan National Park

The town of Asahikawa, separated into a northern and southern part by the Ishikari, Hokkaido's longest river, was a garrison of the Tonden-hei pioneers, who pushed back the Ainu, Hokkaido's original inhabitants, during the period of colonization in the 19th century. **Asahikawa**

Chikabumi ▶ 4km/2.5mi northwest of the station (bus, 20 minutes) is Chikabumi, home to the Kawamura-Ainu Museum, in which **Ainu dances** are performed and Ainu crafts are sold.

Kamui-kotan ▶ A particularly pleasant excursion leads to the Kamui-kotan gorge (bus, 30 minutes) 13km/8mi west of the town. It was carved into the Yubari Mountains by the Ishikari River. The narrow gorge, the legendary home of the Ainu, is particularly beautiful during the cherry-blossom season and in the autumn. In the rock walls 9km/5.5mi from Ino station around 200 prehistoric cave dwellings as well as stone, iron and pottery fragments have been discovered.

Kaguraoka Park ▶ 3km/2mi southeast of Asahigawa station (bus, 20 minutes) is the Kaguragaoka Park (around 45ha/17 acres), a nature reserve on the Chubetsu, one of Ishikari's tributaries. The Kamikawa shrine consecrated to the town's patron god is situated in the park. The hilly terrain provides a nice view of the town and the Kamikawa Basin.

✳
Sounkyo
gorge

In the north of the park, between the northern foothills of the Daisetsu and the southern Obako, the 24km/15mi Sounkyo gorge is a destination for sightseeing buses. The road winding through the gorge has the most picturesque view of the region's beautiful scenery. There are rock walls of up to 150m/490ft on both sides, over which here and there waterfalls plummet into the valley (Ryusei-no-taki, Ginga-no-taki). At the upper end of the gorge are the Kobako (»little box«) and Obako (»big box«) basins, so called because the vertical walls give visitors the impression they are standing on the bottom of a box.

Sounkyo-onsen ▶ In the middle of the gorge is the town of Sounkyo-onsen, one of Hokkaido's most popular holiday spots and the starting point of a cableway that runs up to 1300m/4265ft in several stages; to get even higher take the chairlift. From the top there is a wonderful panorama of the surrounding mountains and the forested landscape with its idyllic towns. At higher altitudes there is a diverse mountain flora.

Daisetsu
Highway

The Daisetsu Highway, the connection to the ▶Akan National Park runs from the gorge eastbound to the 1050m/3445ft Sekihoku Pass at the eastern edge of the national park.

Tenninkyo West of the pass, 40km/25mi southeast of Asahikawa, are the Tenninkyo hot springs, from where visitors can climb the 2141m/7024ft Mount Tomuraushi (to the south) and the 2290m/7513ft Mount Asahi (to the north, via Yokumambetsu). From Tenninkyo it is a five-minute walk to the 250m/820ft Hagoromo (»plumage«) waterfall surrounded by steep rock walls; the area immediately surrounding it is also called the Tenninkyo gorge. There are also hiking trails that lead from here into the mountains.

Sounkyo, a gorge with spectacular waterfalls, is particularly beautiful →
in the autumn when the leaves change colour

Yukomambetsu-onsen
East of this gorge, on the southern slope of Asahi, is the spa town of Yukomambetsu-onsen (1050m/3445ft), 43km/27mi southeast of Asahikawa. The town is a convenient base for **excursions into the mountains**, such as Asahi (ascent 4 hours), the 2246m/7369ft Hokuchin, the 1984m/6509ft Kuro (all to the north) or Mount Aka (to the east; 2078m/6818ft).

Tokachi
The national park's southwestern region can be reached from Asahikawa by rail via Shirogane-onsen. The Tokachi volcano attains a height of 2077m/6814ft just 8km/5mi away from the attractive town. The last time it erupted was in 1962; its slopes are considered amongst Hokkaido's four best **skiing areas**. In the volcano's immediate surroundings are Mount Biei (to the north, 2052m/6732ft) and Mount Kami-Horokamet-toku (to the south, 1887m/6191ft).

Nukabira Dam
To the east of this mountain range, beyond the Tokachi River, Nipesotsu (2013m/6604ft) and Upepesanke (1870m/6135ft) form a further mountain range. The lake formed by Nukabira Dam (600m/1970ft) is located on its eastern slope; it is fed by the Otofuke River and has a circumference of 33km/21mi as well as an area of 8.2 sq km/3.2 sq mi. The surrounding region is an attractive recreational area with pretty towns. Nukabira-onsen close to the lake has hot saline springs with temperatures up to 60°C/140°F.

Lake Shikari-betsu
After 23km/14mi the road leaving from here in a southwesterly direction leads to Lake Shikaribetsu (also by bus from Obihiro, 2 hours) on the western slope of Mount Tembo (1174m/3,852ft). The lake, at an altitude of 798m/2618ft, with a depth of up to 104m/341ft and a surface area of 3.7 sq km/1.4 sq mi, is situated in the middle of

▶ VISITING DAISETSUZAN NATIONAL PARK

GETTING THERE

By air: from Tokyo to Asahikawa (1 hour 40 minutes) and to Obihiro (1½ hours).

By rail: to Asahikawa from Abashiri (Sekihoku main line, 3¾ hours), Furano (Furano line, 1¼ hour) and Sapporo (Hakodate main line, 1½ hours). From Sapporo JR Nemuro main line to Obihiro (3 hours), then JR Shihoro line to Nukabira (1¾ hours). From Asahikawa JR Sekihoku line to Kamikawa (¾ hour). From Asahikawa JR Furano line to Biei (northwest of Shirogane-onsen).

By bus: from Asahikawa to Sounkyo-onsen (2 hours); as well as to Yukomambetsu-onsen (3 hours) and Tenninkyo-onsen (1½ hours); from Sounkyo-onsen to the Sekihoku Pass (1 hour).

ACCESS TO THE PARK

Asahikawa is a convenient starting point for a trip to the national park, which in this case is accessed from the northwest. The park's southern access point is the town of Obihiro.

Fuji-san – a sacred place and Japan's hallmark

a forest and is particularly beautiful during the autumn when all the leaves turn red. On the shores of the lake are the spa towns of Shikaribetsu Kohan-onsen (west) and Yamada-onsen (north).

Fuji-Hakone-Izu National Park

►Fuji-san, ►Fuji lakes, ►Hakone, ►Izu.

◄ ✶ Fuji-san

Main island: Honshu
Altitude: 3776m/12,388ft

Prefectures: Yamanashi and Shizuoka

Japan's highest and most beautiful mountain can be seen all the way from Tokyo on clear days. The correct Japanese name for it is Fuji-san (the name Fujiyama is not used in Japan). The volcano, which is worshipped as holy, was seen as the seat of the gods in earlier times.

富士山

Mount Fuji, the highest elevation of the central Japanese Fuji volcano range, was already exalted in ancient times in **poetry and paintings**, for example in the verses by Yamabe Akahito (8th century) and in the woodblock-print series *Views of Mount Fuji* by Hokusai (1760–1849). The area is part of the Fuji-Hakone-Izu National Park. Since the 12th century it has been considered the gateway to another world, according to Buddhist teaching. Until 1868 women were not

Japan's
holy mountain

permitted to set foot on it or any other natural places considered holy. Today Mount Fuji is climbed by around 300,000 people every year, who are thereby performing an almost religious act, whose climax is experiencing sunrise from the summit (goraiko).

Geology ▶ Mount Fuji was created during the quaternary period around 300,000 years ago and is a strato-volcano. Its almost circular base has a diameter of 35–40km (22–25mi). Its name is thought to come from the Ainu word for fire. 18 eruptions are historically confirmed, the most severe being those in the years 800, 864 and 1707. During the 1707 eruption Edo (Tokyo), 100km/60mi away, was covered in a thick layer of ash and the 2702m/8865ft Hoeizan lateral crater was formed. The volcano has not erupted since then. The five ▶Fuji lakes are located on the volcano's northern slope.

Mountain Routes

★★
Climbing to the edge of the crater
Five mountain routes lead to the top of Mount Fuji; each of them is subdivided into ten stages (gome) of unequal length (»ichi-gome« means »first stage«, »ni-gome« is »second stage« etc.). At the end of each stage climbers find stone orientation pointers and sometimes a protective cabin.

It is usual to start climbing in the early afternoon, so that the 7th or 8th station is reached by nightfall. After an overnight stay climbers set off for the peak early in the morning to walk around the crater. At around noon it is time to start the descent, reaching the base is again in late afternoon. In winter the mountain is closed because of the serious threat of avalanches. The **official mountaineering season** lasts from 1 July to 26 August. Of the five different mountain routes, Kawaguchiko, Fuji-Yoshida, Gotemba, Subashiri and Fujinomiya, the Kawaguchiko route is the best for those hikers arriving from Tokyo, while Subashiri is the best for the descent. For those coming from Osaka or Kyoto the Fujinomiya route is probably the best. **Don't be confused: there are four 5th stations**, depending on the route.

Kawaguchiko route
Leaving Kawaguchiko station (JR Fujikyuko line from Tokyo, 2 hours) there is a bus connection via the Fuji-Subaru mountain road to the 5th station (Go-gome). This route has nice views of the Fuji lakes. The 5th station (2305m/7562ft) is the starting point of the climb, which is often done on horseback up to 2700m/8900ft. Even bikers try to get this far. At the 6th station this route merges with the Yoshida route and the actual 6km/3.5mi climb to the peak begins (5 hours). Here the Mt Fuji Safety Guidance Center hands out leaflets with guidelines for climbers: »Pay attention to the official routes, the weather and falling rocks. Make sure to have the right equipment and take your rubbish home.«

Subashiri route
The Subashiri route is usually chosen for the descent. It leads to the new 5th station (Shin-gogome) east of the peak. From here there is a

Fuji-san Map

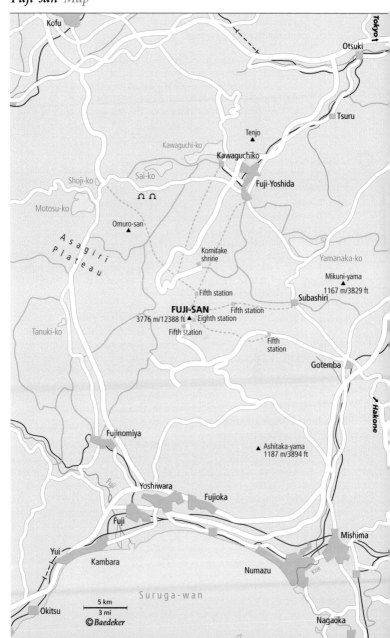

Kofu
Otsuki
Tsuru
Tenjo ▲
Kawaguchi-ko
Kawaguchiko
Fuji-Yoshida
Shoji-ko
Sai-ko
Ω Ω
Motosu-ko
Omuro-san ▲
Yamanaka-ko
A s a g i r i
P l a t e a u
Komitake shrine
Mikuni-yama ▲
1167 m/3829 ft
Subashiri
Fifth station
Tanuki-ko
FUJI-SAN
3776 m/12388 ft ▲
Fifth station
Eighth station
Fifth station
Fifth station
Gotemba
Fujinomiya
Ashitaka-yama ▲
1187 m/3894 ft
Hakone
Fuji
Yoshiwara
Fujioka
Mishima
Fuji
Yui
Kambara
Numazu
Kise
Okitsu
S u r u g a - w a n
Nagaoka
Tokyo
5 km
3 mi
© *Baedeker*

bus to Subashiri and further to Gotemba station, which has a train connection to Tokyo (1¾ hours). At the 8th station this route merges with the Fuji-Yoshida route.

Fuji-Yoshida Route There is a bus connection from Fuji-Yoshida station at the northern foot of the volcano to the Fuji-Sengen shrine; from here it is around 2½ hours on foot to Umageashi (as well as a road, approx. 30 minutes) and another 6½ hours to the peak. At the route's end-point is the Kusushi shrine. The descent to the 5th station takes around 2 hours.

▶ VISITING FUJI-SAN

INFORMATION

Fuji-Yoshida Tourist Information Service
Next to Fushiyoshida station
Tel. 05 55/22 70 00
Daily 9am–5.30pm

Fujikawaguchiko Tourist Service
In front of Kawaguchiko station
Tel. 05 55/72 67 00
Daily 9am–5pm

Internet
www.yamanashi-kankou.jp
(including a list of cabins with telephone numbers)

GETTING THERE

By rail: from Tokyo (Shinjuku station) JR Chuo main line via Fuji-Yoshida to Kawaguchiko (2 hours; change in Otsuki into the Fuji-Kyuko line); from Osaka JR Tokaido shinkansen line to Mishima (3¼ hours); from Kozu or Numazu JR Gotemba line to Gotemba.
By bus: from Tokyo (Hamamatsucho or Shinjuku Bus Terminal) to the 5th station of the Kawaguchiko route (2½–3 hours); from Mishima (Fujinomiya route) to the new 5th station (Shin-gogome; 2 hours); from Fuji-Yoshida (Fuji-Yoshida route) to the Fuji-Sengen shrine (5 minutes); from Gotemba (Gotemba route) to the 5th station (45 minutes).

EVENTS

The beginning and end of the climbing season are celebrated on 1 July and 31 August with a ceremonious festival.

RIGHT EQUIPMENT

Solid footwear, a torch, rainwear, food, drink, sunscreen and warm clothes and if possible hiking sticks are indispensable for climbing Mount Fuji; even in the middle of summer (July/August) the temperatures at the summit are on average only 5°C/41°F–6°C/43°F.

IMPORTANT TIP

Climbing Mount Fuji is not a walk in the park. Accidents are reported again and again, and climbers have lost their lives. For that reason it is important to be well prepared and careful!

WHERE TO STAY

During the climbing season all the cabins are open so that accommodation is available in one of the mountain stations (timely reservations required).

Climbers can reach the new 2nd station (Shin-nigome) in 45 minutes by bus from Gotemba station (JR Gotemba line from Tokyo). The 11km/7mi ascent takes around 6½ hours. This rocky route is better suited for the way back; descent to the 7th station approx. 1 hour; from here to the 2nd station there is the Suna-bashiri (»sand run«) short cut, where climbers can run down a 7km/4.5mi stretch of the slope covered in volcanic ash in around half an hour. Around 1km/0.6mi south of this route's 5th station is the Hoeizan lateral crater. Like the Subashiri route this ascent also has a nice view of sunrise above the 3rd station.

Gotemba Route

◄ Hoeizan Crater

This route's new 5th station (shin-gogome) can be reached in 1½ hours by bus from Fujinomiya (JR Minobu line) station. The edge of the crater is 5km/3mi away and can be reached in 4–5 hours on foot; the path above the 8th station (Munatsuki-hatcho) is quite steep and leads directly to the Okunoin (inner shrine of the Sengen shrine) on the summit. There is also a bus connection from Mishima to the 5th station (2 hours).

Fujinomiya Route

✳ ✳ Summit of Mount Fuji

Mount Fuji's summit region consists of the »Naijin« (holy place) crater with a diameter of 500m/550yd. **Eight peaks** form its rim: Kengamine, Hakusan (also Shaka), Kusushi, Dainichi (also Asahi), Izu, Jujo (also Seishigadake), Komagatake and Mishimadake. There are two possible round trips from the Kengamine peak (Ohachi-meguri). A route easier than the steep path leading directly over the ridges is that along the inner edge of the crater, which with a total length of 3.5km/2mi is the shorter choice. North of the Komagatake, at the end point of the Fujinomiya route, is the Sengen shrine and not far east on the outer crater slope the Gimmeisui (»silver shimmering water«) spring.
A few hundred metres further westwards is a weather observation station, where meteorologist Nonaka Itaru performed the first meas-

The summit region

urements in 1895. At the foot of the Hakusan, which rises above the crater in the north, is the freezing cold spring called Kimmeisui (»golden shimmering water«).

★ ★
Round view ▶

There is a far-reaching, magnificent panoramic view from the top of Mount Fuji, which encompasses the main Japanese islands almost in their entirety.

Half-Way Up: Walk around Mount Fuji

At the elevation of the 5th or 8th stations of the ascent routes (around 2500m/8200ft) the Ochu-do-meguri hiking trail makes its way around the mountain cone. Plan around 8–10 hours of walking for the 20km/12.5mi route. The starting point is optional; the difficult sections are the Hoeizan on the eastern slope and the Osawa gorge in the west, Fuji's largest gorge. This circular hiking trail is called the »border between heaven and earth«.

Baedeker TIP

Closing festival at Mount Fuji
To end the official Mount Fuji climbing season, the Yoshida no Hi-matsuri festival is held here on the 26 August: in the evening torches and beacons are lit along the Fuji-Yoshida Route and a procession with a 1125kg/2480 lb portable shrine is held.

★ Fuji Lakes (Fuji-goko)

K 7 • 12

Main island: Honshu   **Prefecture:** Yamanashi

富士五湖 At the Fuji's northern foot lies the scenically very attractive region of the five Fuji lakes (Fuji-goko), a popular recreational area for Tokyo's inhabitants and a destination appreciated by foreign visitors all year round.

Paradise for water sports enthusiasts

The climate of the lake district, which is at an elevation of more than 600m/2000ft, is pleasantly fresh; in springtime the cherry trees and azaleas are in bloom, and in autumn the forests turn vibrant colours. In summer large numbers of water-sports enthusiasts find good places to indulge in their hobbies, in winter skiers and ice-skaters come. The region is part of the Fuji-Hakone-Izu National Park.

Lake Yamanaka is in the far east of the lake district; further westwards are Lake Kawaguchi, Lake Saiko, Lake Shoji and Lake Motosu. For visitors coming from the direction of Tokyo, the town of Gotemba is the most convenient starting point, while those coming from around Osaka, Kyoto and Nagoya are better off choosing the town of Fujinomiya to the southwest of Mount Fuji as their base.

▶ VISITING FUJI LAKES

GETTING THERE

To Gotemba and Kawaguchiko
►Fuji-san.
By rail: from Tokyo JR Tokaido main
line to Fuji, then JR Minobu line to
Fujinomiya.

By bus: from Kawaguchiko via Koyodai, Fugaku Fugetsu, Lake Shoji and
Lake Motosu as well as via the
Fujinomiya Toll Road to Fujinomiya
(1 hour); from Kawaguchiko to
Gotemba (1¼ hours) and Mishima (2
hours).

From Gotemba to Fujinomiya

The route described below touches all five Fuji lakes as well as the
starting points of the footpaths up Fuji-san.

At an altitude of 982m/3222ft Lake Yamanaka is highest and with an **Lake Yamanaka**
area of 6.5 sq km/2.5 sq mi also the largest of the five. The area surrounding it is one of Japan's most-visited mountain health resorts.
The town of Asahigaoka, which can be reached by bus from Gotemba or also directly from Tokyo, is located on the lake's southern
shore. Visitors can enjoy a round trip on the lake; not far away are
the **Fuji golf course** as well as a number of camp sites.
The lake is home to the green Marimo lake balls, which also occur in
Lake Akan on Hokkaido and in Lake Sakyo on Honshu, as well as
eels, carp and fish of the salmon and trout families. Ice fishing for a
fish species called wakasagi is a popular sport in winter. The nearby
Katsura River is rich in trout.

North of Lake Yamanaka the town of Fuji-Yoshida (population **Fuji-Yoshida**
54,000; train and bus connections from Tokyo) is known for its silk
textiles (kaiki).

Northwest of Fuji-Yoshida (bus connection; train connection from **Lake Kawaguchi**
Tokyo) is the second-largest and most beautiful of the Fuji lakes, Kawaguchi-ko (822m/2697ft; 6.1 sq km/2.4 sq mi). A cableway leads up
from its eastern shore to **Mount Tenjo** (1084m/3556ft); there is a
wonderful view of the lake from the top with an impressive reflection
of Mount Fuji.
In the middle of Kawaguchi-ko on the densely forested **Unoshima Island** is a shrine consecrated to Benten, the goddess of luck, and numerous leisure and relaxation facilities. Around 1km/0.6mi northwest of Kawaguchiko station is the Fuji Museum (local history, collection of erotica), and near the tollgate of the Fuji-Subaru road
(► Fuji-san) the visitor centre of the Yamanashi Prefecture (previously Fuji National Park Museum) with a collection about the natural history of Fuji.

Kawaguchiko is the starting point of a route up ►Fuji-san as well as for boat round trips (1 hour) on the lake. It is spanned by the 1260m/1380yd Kawaguchiko O-hashi (toll fee) bridge in the east.

✱
Koyodai

There are worthwhile excursions to the region to the south of the lake, such as to the Koyodai (»Maple Hill«, bus and a 20-minute footpath from Kawaguchiko station), which has one of the best views of the surrounding forests.

Not far southwest from here is the Narisawa Hyoketsu ice cave and further west (footpath 20 minutes; also a bus from Kawaguchiko station) the Fugaku Fuketsu cave with lava and ice formations.

Jukai

Between Lake Saiko and Lake Shoji to the west is the area called Jukai (»sea of trees«), a pristine forest. This wilderness with a circumference of 16km/10mi is affected by **magnetic volcanic rock**, which impairs the accuracy of the compass needle, thus frequently causing hikers to get lost in it.

Lake Shoji

The idyllic Lake Shoji is surrounded on all sides except the south by forested mountain peaks. It has a size of 0.75 sq km/0.3 sq mi, making it the smallest of the five Fuji lakes (bus connections from Fuji-Yoshida, Kawaguchiko and Fujinomiya). In the wintertime wakasagi (a species of the salmon family) are caught here.

✱
Eboshi

Starting at the northern shore it is possible to climb to the top of Mount Eboshi (1257m/4124ft; also called Shoji-Panorama-dai) in 1½ hours; there is a wonderful view of the lake, Mount Fuji and the »sea of trees« from the peak.

Lake Motosu

The deep-blue Lake Motosu (bus connections from Fuji-Yoshida and Fujinomiya) completes the arc of the Fuji lakes in the west. With a depth of 126m/413ft it is the deepest of the lakes and does not freeze over in the winter.

✱
Fujinomiya Toll Road

The onward journey to Fujinomiya over the 22km/14mi Fujinomiya Toll Road (bus, 1¼ hours) is worthwhile because of its wonderful view of Mount Fuji. Around half way along the road are the **Shiraito Falls**, where the 130m/140yd-wide Shiba River plummets 26m/85ft down a steep rock face. On the other side of the road is the Oto-dome-no-taki waterfall.

Fujinomiya

Fujinomiya (population 112,000) is the site of the Sengen shrine (1km/0.6mi northwest of the station) built in 1604. It is the **main Sengen shrine** in the Fuji area. The shrine is consecrated to the goddess Konohana-Sakuyahime-no-mitoko. Taisekiji Temple is also worth seeing. It was founded in 1290 by a disciple of Nichiren. To get to ► Tokyo from Fujinomiya, take the JR Minobu line southbound to Fuji station, then change into the JR Tokaido main line.

Fukui

J 6 • j 1

Main island: Honshu   **Prefecture:** Fukui
Population: 251,000

Fukui, which was destroyed in World War II and in 1948 by a devastating earthquake, and does not itself have any historical sights, but is a good base for attractions in the surrounding area.

福井

The prefectural capital Fukui on the northern coast of central Honshu is one of the main centres of the Japanese textile industry. The manufacture of silk textiles goes back to the 10th century. Fukui gained historical significance in the 17th century when it was the seat of the Matsudaira, the first of whom was the daimyo Matsudaira Hideyasu.

Silk city

What to See in and around Fukui

Asuwayama Park (also Atagoyama Park), on a hill 1km/0.6mi southwest of the station, has a beautiful view of the city and Mount Hakusan. The park is home to the Fujishima shrine dedicated to Nitta Yoshisada (d. 1338), a supporter of Emperor Godaigo's southern court.

Asuwayama-Park

The main attraction near the city is the Eiheiji temple 16km/10mi to the east (train connection, Shosan-Eiheiji private line, 25 minutes, also a bus connection) in the village of Shi-bidani; it is one of the two main temples of the Soto sect as well as a working monastery. The complex contains more than 70 buildings, including the seven main buildings (Shichido-garan) belonging to a complete temple complex. The area on which it was built in 1243 is dotted with centuries-old cedars and was left to the Zen priest Dogen (posthumously Joyo-daishi) by the then steward Hatano Yoshishige.

The temple complex is accessed through the dragon gate (Ryumon); behind it a stone stairway leads to the Chokushi-mon gate; only imperial messengers may pass through it, and the doors bear

✶ ✶
Eiheiji temple
🕐
Opening hours:
8am–5pm, sometimes closed for several days in a row, ¥ 500

▶ VISITING FUKUI

INFORMATION
In the station, tel. 07 76/20 53 48
Daily 8.30am–7pm

GETTING THERE
By air: from Tokyo (Haneda Airport) to Komatsu (1 hour), then by bus to Komatsu station (10 minutes) and onwards by rail to Fukui (30 minutes).
By rail: from Tokyo (central station) JR Tokaido shinkansen line to Maybara (2¼ hours), then JR Hokuriku main line (1 hour); from Osaka JR Hokuriku main line (2 hours).

Eiheiji temple complex is situated under old cedars

the emperor's emblem. Here the tour turns to the left via the temple office to the Chushaku-mon gate between the two-storey sammon main gate (1749) and the Butsuden (Buddha hall) originally built in 1338. This hall at the centre of the main complex, which is made up of seven buildings, contains the statues of the **Buddhas of the Three Ages** (Sanzebutsu). It was restored in 1902 and is considered the temple's most beautiful building. Behind it is the Hatto Dharma hall. It can hold up to 1000 people and was rebuilt in 1843. Like the Butsuden it is a fine example of the architecture of the Sung period (10th–13th centuries). To the right of the Buddha hall are the kitchen and the refectory Ku-in, to the left of it is the Sodo meditation hall (also Zazen-do), built on the model of a Zen temple of the Sung period. It is only open to the public when no meditation exercises are going on. Diagonally behind it (turn left twice at the Hatto) is the Joyo-den founder's hall, a memorial for Dogen and other abbots of the temple as well as for its founder Hatano.

! | **Baedeker** TIP

Experiencing Zen
Those who want to delve a little deeper into Buddhism can spend the night in the temple and witness the monks' daily lives, which includes getting up at 3.30am (¥ 8000, advance booking required, tel. 07 76/63 36 40, fax 63 36 31)

Maruoka
Castle ▶

12km/7.5mi north of Fukui is the town of Maruoka (JR Hokuriku main line). Take the bus from here to get to Maruoka Castle (also Kasumiga-jo, »castle of fog«), situated a little outside the town. It was built in 1575 by Shibata Katsuie, a commander under Oda Nobunaga. It is one of the oldest castle complexes in all Japan.

Around 30km/20mi further northwest (Keifuku private line to Mikuni-Minato, then by bus) is the Tojimbo coast, which has basalt rock formations, some of which are up to 90m/295ft high. They are part of the Eichzen-Kaga-kaigan Quasi-National Park. Off the Tojimbo coast is the island of Ojima, which can be reached via a bridge. It is home to a small shrine.

Tojimbo
Ojima

✶ Fukuoka

F 8 • c 4

Main island: Kyushu
Population: 1,310,000

Prefecture: Fukuoka

Japan's eighth-largest city is the administrative and economic centre of the main island of Kyushu and is also one of the most progressive cities in the south of the country. In recent years it has developed into southern Japan's cultural centre.

福岡

Fukuoka, the prefectural capital on Hakata Bay, is also the northern gateway to Kyushu Island. The city districts constituting modern-day Fukuoka are separated by the **Naka River**. The older Hakata, the city's eastern district, used to be called Nanotsu and was both a port and a trading centre. In the 17th century the castle town of Fukuoka was built to the west of Hakata. In 1889 the two towns were merged, but Hakata continues to be a shopping centre first and foremost, while finance and administration are seated in the district of Fukuoka. The city's most important commodities are chemical products, electronics, tools, textiles (Hakata-ori silk) and food; another famous product is the Hakata-ningyo porcelain doll.

Economic centre

In the second half of the 13th century Fukuoka was the **scene of brutal battles against the Mongols** under Kublai Khan. The first invasion attempt was repelled in 1274, but the second already followed in 1281, at which point the Mongolian army was strengthened to 100,000 men. The attack came to a standstill at the 3m/10ft defence wall built at Hakata Bay between Hakozaki and Imazu and a sudden devastating typhoon (thus called »kamikaze«, meaning »wind of the gods«) destroyed the entire Mongolian fleet.

What to See in Fukuoka

Shofukuji temple is 1km/0.6mi to the northwest of Hakata station, the main station located to the southeast of the city centre. It is one of the oldest Zen Buddhist temples in Japan. It was most likely founded in 1195 by the priest Eisai (1141–1215) on the orders of Minamoto Yoritomo. Eisai brought Zen Buddhism and tea culture to Japan from the court of the Chinese Sung dynasty.

Shofukuji temple

Higashi Park Not far north of the temple is Higashi Park, which has a memorial in remembrance of the two Mongolian invasions as well as the statues of the Buddhist sect founder Nichiren (1222–82) and Emperor Kameyama (1249–1305).

✳ Hakozaki shrine Even further north is the Hakozaki shrine (also Hakozaki-Hachiman shrine; train connection from the station or Hakozaki underground line from Nakasu-Kawabata). It was founded in 923 and is one of the country's most famous Hachiman shrines. The prayer hall (haiden) and the main hall (honden) were built in 1546, the stone torii in 1609; the two-storey gate tower was built in 1594 of nothing but wood without the use of a single nail.

✳ Sumiyoshi shrine The Sumiyoshi shrine, one of Kyushu's oldest, is located around 800m/875yd southwest of the central station. Like the one in Osaka it is dedicated to the patron gods of seafarers. The main building constructed in the classical style and renewed in 1623 is particularly impressive. The shrine is surrounded by a wood of Japanese cedars and camphor trees and has a good view of the Naka River.

> ! **Baedeker TIP**
>
> **Quiet oasis**
> Not far from the Sumiyoshi shine is the Rakusui-en, a wonderful little garden on the property of an old villa that belonged to a merchant from the Meiji era (open daily except Tue 9am–5pm, ¥ 100).

A stroll through the city centre will bring visitors to a modern architectural shopping marvel south of Nakasu Island: **Canal City**. The aim of this trend-setting »city within a city« with its curved shapes is to amaze customers who shop in this multifunctional paradise containing cinemas, hotels and seven floors of shopping heaven.

Kushida Jinja This attractive shrine founded in the 8th century has held on to the atmosphere of old Hakata. The ginkgo tree in the forecourt is said to be more than 1000 years old. This is also the starting point of the famous Hakata Gion Yamakasa festival that takes place every July.

Asian Art Museum Further north on the 7th and 8th floors of the **Riverain Center Building** is the impressive Asian Art Museum, displaying modern art from more than 20 countries and regions in Asia (open daily except Wed 10am–8pm, ¥ 200).

Nakasu The district of Nakasu is located on an island formed by two arms of the Naka River. It is Fukuoka's entertainment district, with numerous cinemas, bars, restaurants and other entertainment options.

Hakata Harbour Further downstream is Hakata Harbour in Hakata Bay. The ferries that dock at Hakata pier service the islands of Iki, Tsushima, Hirado, the Goto archipelago as well as Yobuko and Shikanoshima.

▶ VISITING FUKUOKA

INFORMATION

Tourist information
In the station, tel. 0 92/4 31 30 03
Daily 8am–7pm
Tenjin, ACROS Building, 2nd floor
Tel. 0 92/7 25 91 00
Daily 11am–5pm

International Association
Tenjin, IMS Building, 8th floor
Tel. 0 92/7 33 22 20
Daily 10am–8pm

The *Welcome Card Fukuoka*, with
which a large number of concessions
are available, can be obtained from this
office.

GETTING THERE

By air: from Tokyo (Haneda Airport;
1¾ hours); from Osaka (1 hour).
By rail: from Tokyo (central station)
JR Tokaido and Sanyo shinkansen line
via Osaka (5 hours); local lines from
Fukuoka to the hinterland, to Nagasaki
(Nagasaki main line, 2 hours).
By bus: from Fukuoka station to the
city centre (15 minutes); from the
airport to the station (15 minutes).
By boat: ferry connections to Iki Island
(2¾ hours); to Izuhara (Tsushima
Islands; 5 hours).

GETTING THERE
FROM NEARBY

Fukuoka has three *underground lines*:
the Kuko line runs from the airport via
Hakata station and Tenjin, the city
centre, all the way to Meinohama in
the west of the city; the Hakozaki line
connects Nakasu-Kawabata station in
the centre with Kaizuka in the east; in
2005 the city's third underground line
was opened; the Nanakuam lines runs
from Tenjin-Minami southwest to
Hashimoto, but is of less significance

to tourists. A one-day pass (ichi-nichi-
ken) for the underground costs ¥ 600
and is also good for discounts for
various attractions.
The *ring bus* through Fukuoka's city
centre (from the station via Canal City
to Tenjin for example) is a service
useful for tourists; it costs ¥ 100 per
trip.

EVENTS

Tamaseseri (two teams battle to get a
ball said to bring good luck; beginning
of January), Hakozaki shrine; Hakata-
dontaku (festival procession; beginning of May); Hojo-ya (shrine festival;
mid-September), Hakozaki shrine.

SHOPPING

The city's main shopping street is
Watanabe-dori in Tenjin. There is an
underground shopping centre below
it. Tenjin has all of the big department
stores such as Daimaru and Mitsukoshi. Other great places to shop are
Canal City and Hawks Town.

GOING OUT

The city's number one entertainment
centre is *Nakasu*.
Musicals and kabuki performances are
staged in the Hakataza, a theatre in the
Riverain Building (Plan: Asian Art
Museum).

WHERE TO EAT
▶ Moderate
① *Kisuitei Waraku*
Chuo-ku, Tenjin 1-11-11,
Tenjin Koa 7th Floor
Tel. 0 92/7 16 74 01
Daily 11am–10.30pm
The owner personally goes to the
market every morning to buy the
ingredients for his Japanese dishes,
such as sashimi.

Shopping on seven floors in Fukuoka's Canal City

② *Marumiya*
Hakata-ku, Nakasu, 4 chome 1-19
Tel. 0 92/2 82 45 17
Mon–Sat 6.30pm–4am

Lively izakaya in the Nakasu entertainment district. Serves inventive pub food.

▶ **Inexpensive**
③ *Ramen Stadium*
Amusement Building, 5th floor,
Canal City; daily 11am–11pm
Fukuoka is famous for its ramen and the »Ramen Stadium« serves this noodle soup in every variation. If this is not enough, try some more at one of the city's numerous noodle stands.

WHERE TO STAY
▶ **Luxury**
① *Sea Hawk Hotel & Resort*
Hawks Town, 2-2-3 Jigyohama,
Chuo-ku, 810-8650 Fukuoka
Tel. 0 92/8 44 81 11
Fax 8 44 78 99
www.hawkstown.com/e_site
For fans of super-modern skyscraper architecture. All rooms have sea views and every possible amenity. Architecturally the building is based on a cruise ship.

② *Ever Green Marinoa Hotel*
Nishi-ku, Odo 2-12-43,
819-000 Fukuoka
Tel. 0 92/8 95 55 11
Fax 8 95 55 22
www.evergreenmarinoa.com
Quite far west in the city, with sea views. The all-white hotel exudes simple elegance. Nearby: the Sky Dream Fukuoka (Ferris wheel).

▶ **Budget**
③ *Kashima Honkan Ryokan*
Hakata-ku, Reisen-machi 3-11
Tel. 0 92/2 91 07 46
Classical, comfortable ryokan with a traditional Japanese garden. The rooms do not have their own bathrooms.

Around 2.5km/1.5mi southwest of the station the old Kikuya, Iseya and Edoya streets are lined by several old samurai homes, including that of Kido Koin, the first prime minister of the Meiji period.

samurai houses

Around Hagi

Around 5km/3mi north of the station is the Koshigahama Peninsula with its 112m/367ft-high extinct Kasayama volcano. Further eastwards the Myojin lagoon and the Myojin-ike pond are set in attractive landscape. This coastal area and that west of Hagi make up the Kita-Nagato-kaigan Quasi-National Park (80 sq km/30 sq mi), which also includes around 60 islands.

Koshigahama

The largest of them is Omishima (18 sq km/7 sq mi) west of Hagi, which can be reached via a bridge (from Hagi JR San-in line to Senzaki, onwards by bus to the island town of Odomari). The varied landscape is worth an excursion. At the centre of the island is the town of Ohibi with the Saienji temple (separate entrances for men and women). The Seigetsuan temple has a »grave of the whales«, set up in 1692; according to an old custom any embryos found inside captured whales were buried here until 1870.

◄ Omishima

The island round trips, which last around two hours, all leave from Senzaki.

◄ Trips around the islands

An excursion from Hagi southwest to the large Akiyoshi-do **limestone caves** (bus from Higashi-Hagi station, 1¼ hours), one of the numerous dripstone caves in the Akiyoshi Plateau, is also very picturesque. Of the approx. 10km/6mi cave system, 1km/0.6mi can be accessed by visitors (from Hagi by bus via Yuda-onsen).

Akiyoshi-do

Hakodate

L 4

Main island: Hokkaido
Population: 321,000

Prefecture: Hokkaido

Hakodate, which is dominated by the mountain of the same name in the south, is the southern gateway to Hokkaido and the island's third-largest city. The port town is located in the south of the Oshima Peninsula on the Tsugaru Strait, which separates Honshu from Hokkaido.

函館

The city name first appears in the 15th century in connection with the construction of a castle by the Kono family. This makes Hakodate older than the megacity Sapporo; it has been known as a fishing port since 1741. Commodore Perry, who forced Japan to open up to foreign trade, visited the city in 1854; just the following year its port was made the supply base for foreign ships as a result of the Treaty

Hokkaido's most important port

Tasty food from the sea is sold on this morning market

of Kanagawa. According to the peace treaty between Japan and the United States, Hakodate and four other ports were allowed to start trading with other countries in 1859. Since then the city has been Hokkaido's most important port. In 1930 it still had more inhabitants than the island capital of Sapporo, but in 1934 a large fire destroyed around two thirds of the city. Since 1988 Hakodate has been connected to ►Aomori (Honshu) by the 240m/260yd **Seikan railway tunnel**, which runs under the seabed.

What to See in Hakodate

Not far from the station the interesting **morning market** (Asa-ichi) takes place every day, except Sundays, starting at 5am. Around 600 stalls offer a large range of goods. It is best to go early in the morning!

Hakodate (Mount) Take the bus from the bus stop to Mount Hakodate (335m/1099ft) 3km/2mi to the southwest. From here the view of the harbour bay and the Tsugaru Strait is very attractive, particularly at night time. The mountain was formed when a volcano erupted under the sea; its highest point is Gotenyama, the northern peak. Between 1899 and the end of World War II the mountain was part of the fortification zone; after that it became a popular destination for leisure excursions.

View ► A cableway runs between the foot of the mountain and its peak. There is a viewpoint at the top from where visitors have a wide view of the Sea of Japan, the Pacific and the main island of Honshu. There is a bust of Ino Tadataka (1745–1818) in the wall; he produced the first reliable map of Japan.

There is also a monument in honour of **Thomas W. Blakiston** (1832–91) at the summit. He lived in Japan from 1861 to 1884, during which time he created a significant ornithological collection, now in Sapporo's botanical garden. Blakiston discovered that the Tsugaru Strait was the dividing line, now known as Blakiston's Line, of certain species' habitats.

Motomachi Motomachi, the **former foreigners' district**, lies at the foot of the mountain in the northwest of the city. Several buildings still bespeak the fact that Hakodate was one of the first Japanese cities to open up to foreign trade at the end of the Edo period. Hakodate's former district office (Kyo-Hakodateku-Kokaido), which was constructed of wood in 1910, is one of the most impressive examples of Western architecture (open April–Oct 9am–7pm, Nov–March 7am–5pm, May–Aug daily, otherwise closed on undetermined days, ¥ 300).

Hakodate Park, famous for its magnificent cherry and plum blossom, can be found at the mountain's eastern foothills (2.5km/1.5mi from the station; tram connection to the Aoyagi-cho stop). The park also contains the **Hakodate Museum** (Shiritsu Hakodate Hakubutsu-kan), which was opened in 1879 at the instigation of the American advisor Horace Capron (1804–85), who participated in the colonization of Hokkaido. It contains works by Japanese artists, prehistoric finds and objects from the Ainu culture (open Tue–Sun 9am–4.30pm, Nov–March until 4pm, ¥ 100).

> | **Baedeker** TIP
>
> **Thirst quencher**
> Anyone feeling a little parched after a busy day of sightseeing can try a home-brewed beer in Hakodate Beer (5 minutes west of the station towards Motomachi, red brick building with large stairs, open daily 11am–10pm).

Hakodate Park

Around Hakodate

Around 7km/4.5mi to the east (tram and bus connections from the station, 30 minutes) is the idyllic spa town of Yunokawa-onsen (hot springs with temperatures up 66°C/150°F). It was established in 1654, making it one of Hokkaido's oldest spas. 3km/2mi east of the town is a Trappist convent (buses from Yunokawa-onsen and Hakodate) founded in 1898. Its butter and cheese specialties are typical of Hokkaido (shop opening hours: 21 April to 31 Oct daily except Wed 8am–5pm, 1 Nov to 20 Apr Mon–Sat 8.20am–4.30pm).

Yunokawa-onsen

Esan (618m/2028ft) is an active volcano 50km/30mi east of Hakodate (bus, 2½ hours); it forms the southern tip of the Oshima Peninsula. There is a beautiful view of the surrounding area from the top; the **mountain flora** includes around 150 rare plant species. Cape

Esan

▶ VISITING HAKODATE

INFORMATION
In the station; tel. 01 38/23 54 40
April–Oct daily 9am–7pm,
Nov–March until 5pm
www.city.hakodate.hokkaido.jp/
kikaku/english

GETTING THERE
By air: from Tokyo (Haneda Airport; 1¼ hours); from Sapporo (Chitose Airport; 45 minutes).
By rail: from Tokyo JR Tohoku shinkansen line via Hachinohe (3½

hours) and JR Tohoku line (7¼ hours.); from Sapporo JR Hakodate main line (3½ hours), also night train (11¾ hours).
By boat: ferry connection from Aomori to Hakodate (3¼ hours).

EVENTS
Cherry blossom festival (beginning of May);
harbour festival (with a firework display and folk dances; beginning of August).

Esan with the spa towns of Esan-onsen and Ishida-onsen is located in the southeastern foothills of the volcano.

Onuma Quasi National Park

To get to the Onuma Quasi-National Park (95 sq km/37 sq mi) leave Hakodate northbound (JR Hakodate main line, 25 minutes); it contains Mount Koma and the three picturesque lakes Onuma, Konuma and Junsainuma. Scattered across the lake district are around a hundred small, forested islands; for the best view of the pretty landscape climb up Konuma Hill located between Lake Konuma and Lake Junsai.

Koma ►

The Quasi-National park's northernmost point is the active Koma volcano (also Komagatake), which has three peaks: Sahara (1115m/3658ft), Kengamine (1140m/3740ft) and Sumidamori (880m/2887ft). The slopes are covered by broad-leafed trees and conifers at lower altitudes, while alpine plants (such as mountain azaleas) are prevalent at elevations above 600m/2000ft. The cone-shaped silhouette (particularly obvious when looking at it from the north) has earned the mountain the sobriquet »Oshima-Fuji«.

Trappist monastery

There is a Trappist monastery (daily tours, for men only) 26km/16mi west of Hakodate (JR Esashi line to Oshima-Tobetsu, then a 30-minute walk); it was founded in 1895 by Okada Furie, who originally came from France but was then granted Japanese citizenship. This monastery together with the nunnery near Yunokawa-onsen is Japan's only Catholic monastery. It too produces dairy products.

Esashi

The fishing village of Esashi (population 14,000) is situated on the Oshima Peninsula's west coast (83km/52mi from Hakodate; JR Esashi line, 2½ hours). During the Edo period it was home to around 30,000 inhabitants. Some of the old homes have survived, such as those of the Nakamura and Yokoyama families (around 100 years old). The small local museum exhibits cannon from the warship *Kaiyomaru*, which sank in 1868 in a battle between the troops of the Tokugawa and those loyal to the emperor.

Okushiri

A ferry (2½ hours) connects Esashi with Okushiri Island 143km/89mi off the coast to the northwest. The scenically attractive, forested island was once a penal colony. Its inhabitants live mainly off fishing and agriculture; it has attractive opportunities for anglers and camping enthusiasts; the coast has impressive views of the sea. The best viewpoints are Nabetsuru-Iwa, Cape Inaho (northern tip) and Cape Aonae (southern tip).

Matsumae

The town of Matsumae is located 92km/57mi southwest of Hakodate; during the Edo period it was called Fukuyama. The current fishing port was Hokkaido's only castle town during that period and also its political centre (seat of the Matsumae family). The castle complex can be reached by bus from the station in 5 minutes.

✷ Hakone

K 7 • l–m 2

Main island: Honshu   **Prefectures:** Kanagawa and Shizuoka

The area around Hakone boasts volcanoes, numerous hot springs and a number of historical attractions. Lake Ashi is particularly attractive.

箱根

The Hakone region is bordered in the north by ▶Mount Fuji and in the south by the ▶Izu Peninsula. It is one of Japan's most popular holiday destinations and is visited in summer and winter alike. The landscape is part of the Fuji-Hakone-Izu National Park.

Holiday region

Hakone is situated in the crater (40km/25mi circumference) of the extinct Hakone volcano, whose centre subsided and became a caldera around 400,000 years ago. Later eruptions formed the Kamiyama volcano (the highest mountain in the Hakone region at 1438m/4718ft), the Komagatake volcano (1327m/4354ft) and the Futago

▶ VISITING HAKONE

INFORMATION

Tourist information
In Hakone-Yumoto,
Hakone-machi Kanko Bussankan,
diagonally across from the station
Tel. 04 60/5 89 11
Daily 9.30am–5.30pm
www.hakone.or.jp/english

GETTING THERE

By rail: from Tokyo (central station)
JR Tokaido shinkansen line or
JR Tokaido line to Odawara (40
minutes or 1½ hours); from Tokyo
(Shinjuku station) Odakyu private
train line to Hakone-Yumoto
(via Odawara; 1½ hours.).

Connections in the Hakone area:
Hakone-Tozan train line form Oda-
wara via Hakone-Yumoto, Tonosawa,
Miyanoshita and Kowakudani to Gora
(approx. 1 hour).
Hakone-Tozan bus route from Oda-
wara via Hakone-Yumoto, Tonosawa,
Miyanoshita, Sengoku and Sengoku-

kogen to Togendai (approx. 1 hour).
Izu-Hakone rail-bus line from Odawara via Hakone-Yumoto, Miyanoshita, Kowakudani, Sounzan, Owakudani and Ubako to Hakone-en
(approx. 1½ hours).
Izu-Hakone cableways from Hakone-
en up Mount Komagatake (8 minutes). In addition a cableway from
Gora via Mount Sounzan and Owakudani to Togendai.
Ferry connections on Lake Ashi from
Togendai via Hakonemachi to Moto-
Hakone (30 minutes); from Kojiri via
Hakone-en to Moto-Hakone (30 minutes).

ROUND TRIP

From Tokyo (Shinjuku station)
Odakyu line to Hakone-Yumoto;
Hakone-Tozan train line to Gora;
cableway to Togendai; ferry to Moto-
Hakone; on foot via the Hakone
Museum to Hakone-machi; bus to
Atami; JR train line to Tokyo (approx.
6 hours).

The kanji for »big« shines from the hillside

EVENTS

Ume-matsuri (plum blossom festival; beginning of February), in Odawara; Sakura-matsuri (cherry blossom festival; beginning of April), in Odawara; Oshiro-matsuri (festival procession with old costumes; beginning of May), in Odawara; Kintoki-matsuri (with a mountain climbing competition and »lion dance«; beginning of May), in Sengokuhara; Tsutsuji-matsuri (azalea festival; mid-May), in Kowakudani; Kojo-sai (sea festival; end of July), in

the Hakone shrine; Torii-matsuri and Ryuto-sai (light festival; beginning of August), on Lake Ashi; Daimonji-yaki (light festival, the Chinese symbol »dai« meaning »big« is created out of torches on the mountain's slope; mid-August); Daimyo-gyoretsu (festival procession in historical costumes; beginning of November), in Hakone-Yumoto.

WHERE TO STAY

► **Luxury**
Fujiya Hotel
359 Miyanoshita, Hakone-machi, 250-0404 Kanagawa-ken
Tel. 04 60/2 22 11
www.fujiyahotel.jp/english
Japan's oldest Western-style hotel. Nice, individually designed rooms spread over several buildings. French and Japanese restaurants.

volcano (1091m/3579ft). Lake Ashi was created from the former crater lake. Two rivers flow out from the lake: Hayakawa and Sukumo, both of which have formed romantic gorges. The pleasant climate and the excellent tourist facilities make this area very attractive, particularly as a nearby recreational area for the inhabitants of Tokyo, Yokohama, Kobe and Osaka. The copious hot springs were already attracting visitors in need of relaxation during the Heian period (8th to 12th century); many artists, Ando Hiroshige included, have painted this landscape.

A Drive through Hakone

The round trip described here can easily be done on public transport, since the region has good train, bus, cableway and ferry connections.

Odawara   The starting point of the round trip is Odawara (population 185,000), which can be reached from Tokyo on the shinkansen or the Odakyu Electric Railway. The old **castle town** of Hojo is situated on Sagami Bay at the eastern foot of the Hakone Mountains. During the Edo period it was considered a particularly difficult section of the Tokaido road. The reconstructed castle is 400m/450yd from the station (on foot 10 minutes); its five-storey main tower houses a museum exhibiting weapons and objects pertaining to the local history. The coast between Odawara and Kozu (second station towards Tokyo) has some good **swimming beaches**.

Yumoto, the region's oldest spa town at the confluence of the Hayakawa and the Sukumo, is located to the west of Odawara (train and bus connections). It has hot springs with temperatures ranging from 35°C/95°F to 74°C/165°F and is the starting point of the Daimyogyoretsu procession. To the south of the station is the Sounji temple founded by Hojo Soun (1432–1519), which belongs to the Rinzai sect. Few of its buildings are still extant. The portrait on silk of the temple founder is worth seeing; the Hojo tombs are also in the grounds.

Yumoto

The traffic junction Miyanoshita (12km/7.5mi west of Odawara), together with Sokokura and Dogashima, is one of the region's liveliest towns. The climate stays temperate during the summer; the numerous hot springs have temperatures ranging from 62°C/144°F to 78°C/172°F. There are good hotels and shops here; a dense road and hiking network means there are also good transport and facilities for walking. North of the station is the oldest Western-style hotel in Japan: the Fujiya Hotel, opened in 1878. South of the hotel is the 802m/2631ft Mount Sengen (ascent 1 hour; nice view of Hakone). The western descent route goes via the Chisuji-no-taki Falls towards Kowakudani.

Miyanoshita

Fujiya Hotel in Hakone is a real classic

Sengokuhara A bus route runs from Kowakudani northwest to Sengokuhara, situated on the plain of the same name in the middle of a thick forest. The plain is bordered to the north and west by the outer crater edge of Fuji with Mount Kintoki, Mount Nagao and Mount Maru: the ideal terrain for 20 golf courses.

Kowakien Garden Not far from the Kowakien-mae bus stop (2 minutes from Kowakudani) is the Kowakien Garden entertainment centre with a hotel, ryokan, outdoor swimming pools and a botanical garden as well as a children's village. The Mikawaya ryokan is nearby with its Horaien Garden, famous for its azalea blossom (azalea festival in May; other places to see azaleas are the garden of the Yamano hotel in Moto-Hakone and Gora Park in Gora).

Gora The route leaves Kowakudani northbound to Gora (altitude: 800m/ 2,625ft) on the eastern slope of Mount Sounzan. From here there is a nice view of the Hayakawa's headwaters. South of the town is the Hakone Open Air Museum (Chokoku-no-mori) with sculptures by modern artists (Moore, Rodin, Bourdelle etc.) and a Picasso pavilion (open March–Nov daily 9am–5pm, Dec–Feb until 4pm, ¥ 1600).

Hakone Open Air Museum ►

Hakone Art Museum ► The Hakone Art Museum is located to the southwest of Gora in Gora Park (which is also popular during the azalea blossom season). It exhibits Japanese and Chinese porcelain as well as old paintings (open April–Nov daily except Thu 9am–4.30pm, Dec–March until 4pm, ¥ 900).

Cableway to Lake Ashi There is a cableway connection from Gora eastbound to the northern shore of Lake Ashi. The journey can be broken at a number of stops along the way. The first stop along the way is Sounzan, where it is necessary to change into another cableway.

✳
Owakudani ► Owakudani station (»valley of the great steam«) has a viewing platform with a nice view of Mount Fuji. This region has plenty of solfataras, which can all be reached from this station in just a short time. The natural science museum provides insights into the local fauna, flora and geology.

Togendai ► The cableway ends in Togendai at the lake's northern shore. There are ferry connections departing from Togendai and Kojiri (somewhat further south) to Hakone-en (eastern shore) and Moto-Hakone as well as Hakone-machi (southern shore).

✳
Lake Ashi Lake Ashi (also Lake Hakone; circumference: 17.5km/11mi; area: 6.9 sq km/2.7 sq mi, depth: 42m/138ft) is situated at an altitude of 723m/2372ft. It is Hakone's main scenic attraction and known for its wonderful reflection of Mount Fuji. It also has good **fishing** (trout, perch) and **water sports activities**. The 12km/7.5mi Ashinoko Skyline Drive (toll road) runs along its western shore. It has some great views of Mount Fuji as well as of Sagami Bay and Suruga Bay.

The traffic junction at the northern shore consists of the towns of Togendai and Kojiri. Take the road along the eastern shore to get to Hakone-en, which is home to the big Hakone-en Park leisure centre. It has swimming pools, ice rinks, golf courses, camp sites as well as an »international village« with typical houses from 29 countries and a folk-art exhibition. The 1327m/4354ft Mount Komagatake rises in the northeast. There are two cableways leading to the peak, where there is an ice rink: one from the town and one from the mountain's southeastern foot. There is a great view of Mount Fuji and the Izu Peninsula from the top.

◄ Togendai, Kojiri

◄ Hakone-en

Moto-Hakone is located on the lake's southern shore; on a hill to the northwest of the town (footpath, 15 minutes) is the Hakone shrine (also Hakone-Gongen) in a thick forest. It was founded in 757 by the priest Mangan (its current form dates back to 1667) and is consecrated to the god Ninigi, his consort Konohana-Sakuya-hime and their son Hikohohodemi. The treasury next to the main hall contains a picture scroll depicting the shrine's foundation, a wooden statue of the shrine's founder and a sword belonging to Soga Goro, one of the Soga brothers who avenged the death of their father, dying in the process (12th century).

Moto-Hakone
◄ Hakone shrine

There is a 2km/1mi-long avenue lined with sugi trees from the old Moto-Hakone post station to Hakone-machi; it was once part of the Tokaido road from Kyoto to Tokyo and an important checkpoint for the processions of the daimyo, who had to appear in Edo before the

Hakone-machi

Fuji-san together with Lake Ashi is one of Japan's most famous landscapes

shogun every two years; the shogun would hold their wives hostage in the capital to guarantee their continued loyalty to the government. Somewhat outside the modern town (footpath, 5 minutes) is the reconstructed checkpoint with a guard house, originally built in 1618 by the Tokugawa to protect the capital Edo (Tokyo); it was left open in 1869. The Hakone palace garden next door was originally part of an imperial villa; the Historical Museum (Hakone-shiryokan) at the entrance exhibits objects pertaining to the history of the Tokaido road and the checkpoint. The Hakone Museum opposite the Hakone Hotel is similar, with old coins, seals, documents and maps.

◀ Museums

Leave Hakone-machi in the Hakone Bypass (bus), which makes its way through the beautiful valley of the Sukumo River back to Odawara.

★★ Himeji

Main island: Honshu   **Prefecture:** Hyogo
Population: 453,000

姫路

The lofty castle of Himeji is one of the few completely surviving complexes of this kind in Japan and is one of the country's cultural treasures. In spring the park surrounding the castle attracts many visitors, who come here to celebrate the cherry blossom.

The town of Himeji is located in the west of the Japanese main island of Honshu, northwest of Kobe. It is an industrial and trading centre on the Himeji plain as well as an important port in the Inland Sea.

What to See in Himeji

★★
Castle
▶3 D p.262/263

The castle, **Shirasagi-jo, »White Heron Castle«**, rises in the heart of the city on Himeyama Hill (north of the station; footpath 10 minutes). It is the climax of medieval Japanese fortification architecture and a Unesco World Heritage Site. The 46.4m/152ft main tower is connected to the outer towers via passages; overall the complex contains 38 buildings and 21 gates, which impress visitors with their contrast between the white exteriors and the grey natural stone walls. There is a fine view of the surrounding area from the top floor.

! *Baedeker* TIP

Tea in the garden
West of the castle is the Koko-en, a complex of nine gardens designed in the Edo style. Why not experience the tea ceremony in the tea garden (open daily 9am–5pm, July–Aug until 6pm, ¥ 300)?

Hiromine

3km/2mi north of the station (bus, 25 minutes) is Hiromine Hill with an attractive grove of plum trees at its foot; on its peak is the

storey building was destroyed in a fire in 1337. The central room has an altar with a statue of the Monju-bosatsu (god of wisdom).

The **treasury** Sankozo opposite the Golden Hall is much newer (1955). It houses the temple's valuables, such as the grave goods and sarcophagi of the Fujiwara, as well as sculptures and sacred items. The Hiraizumi Bunkashikan museum in front of the temple exhibits further antiquities.

The magnificent interior of Chusonji temple

Yoshitsune-do

Around 1.5km/1mi southeast of the Golden Hall (1km/0.6mi north of the station) is the small Yoshitsune-do hall on the site of the former residence of Yoshitsune, who was murdered here.

Motsuji temple

500m/550yd west of the station is the Motsuji temple, founded in 850; during the time of the Fujiwara it was the region's most significant temple. Today there are only a few surviving fragments. The Jodo-Teien temple garden is quite famous; it is in the style of the Heian period paradise pond gardens, one of the few examples of this type of garden (open April–Oct 8.30am–5pm, Nov–March until 4.30pm, ¥ 500).

Around Hiraizumi

Takkoku-no-Iwaya

A bus leaves the station (20 minutes) to the Takkoku-no-Iwaya cave to the southwest. In the cave Sankano-ue-no-Tamuramaro (758–811), who was sent here to fight rebellious tribes, had a temple built that was consecrated to the patron god of warriors, Bishamonten. The original building burned down in 1946; the current building is a reconstruction from 1961. A depiction of the Dainichi-nyorai, the elemental form of all the possible Buddhas and Bodhisattvas, was carved into a rocky outcrop near the cave, probably in 1087 (open daily 9am–4.30pm, ¥ 300).

Gembikei-, Geibikei gorge

Not far to the southwest is the wonderful Gembikei gorge (bus from Hiraizumi, 40 minutes), through which the Iwai River flows. The Geibikei gorge formed by the Satetsu River northeast of Ichinoseki (train, 35 minutes) is also worth visiting.

Kurikoma

To get to the extinct Kurikoma volcano (1627m/5338ft) take the bus from Hiraizumi southbound via Ichinoseki (bus from Ichinoseki 2¼ hours) to Sukawakogen-onsen at the mountain's northwestern foot (3 hours). The 5km/3mi ascent from Sukawa-onsen takes around 1½ hours. There is a lovely view of the surrounding area from the peak of this densely forested mountain.

Hirosaki

L 4

Main island: Honshu
Population: 174,000

Prefecture: Aomori

弘前

The former castle town of the Tsugaru family is now the third-largest city in the prefecture and the seat of a university. A lot of fruit is cultivated in the region around Hirosaki, particularly apples and cherries.

The town of Hirosaki is in the far north of the Japanese main island of Honshu, at the southernmost point of the Iwaki Basin, which extends northwards across the Tsugaru Peninsula; it is surrounded by mountains to the south and west.

What to See in and around Hirosaki

✳
Castle

The centre of the town is **Hirosaki Park** (also Oyo Park) 2km/1mi west of the station. It contains the remains of Tsugaru Castle: five gates, one old wooden bridge and the main tower of 1611. The tower houses a small exhibition of old weapons and armour. The park is one of the best known cherry-blossom sites in Japan (blossom time is end of April to mid-May; open 01Apr–23Nov daily 9am–5pm, ¥ 300, otherwise free). The Hachiman shrine is to the north of the castle and around 1.5km/1mi to the southwest is the 17th century Choshoji temple

Cherry blossom in the park in front of Hirosaki Castle

⏵ VISITING HIROSAKI

INFORMATION
In the station
Tel. 01 72/26 36 00
Daily 8.45am–6pm
At the southern entrance to
Hirosaki Park
Tel. 01 72/37 55 01
Daily 9am–6pm,
in the winter until 5pm

GETTING THERE
By rail: from Tokyo (Ueno station)

JR Tohoku main line to Aomori (3¾
hours.), from Aomori JR Ou main line
(30 minutes).

EVENTS
Neputa-matsuri (night-time procession; early August), with huge illuminated figures on floats; the festival goes
back to a cunning military ruse with
which Sakanaoue-no-Tamuramro
wanted to deceive his enemy about the
real strength of his troops.

1.5km/1mi west of the station (bus, 10 minutes) is Saishoin temple
with a lovely five-storey pagoda from 1672.

✱ ✱
Saishoin temple

13km/8mi further northwest (bus, 40 minutes) is are the hot springs
of Hyakuzawa-onsen. It is also the location of the magnificent Iwakisan shrine. Its original buildings were constructed between 770
and 781. The current buildings predominantly date back to the 17th
century. The shrine's rich interior has given it the sobriquet »Nikko
of the north«; the annual festival takes place at the beginning of August.

**Hyakuzawa-
onsen**

✱
◄ Iwakisan shrine

Mount Iwaki rises 1625m/5331ft next to the town. To get to its peak
take the panoramic toll road and then a cableway. The Iwakisan
shrine's innermost sanctum is in southern foothills; the mountain,
thought to be the seat of a deity, is visited by many believers between
25 July and 15 August.

◄ Iwaki

✱ ✱ Hiroshima

G 7 • e 3

Main island: Honshu   **Prefecture:** Hiroshima
Population : 1.14 million

**When visiting Hiroshima, it is hard to imagine that this modern,
friendly city was the scene of the world's first atomic bomb
attack.**

広島

The prefectural capital of Hiroshima is located in the west of the
main island of Honshu on the Inland Sea; six arms of the Ota River
flow through it. The city, whose outline resembles the shape of a
hand, is situated in the Bay of Hiroshima. The city suffered a tragic

Tragic history

Hiroshima Map

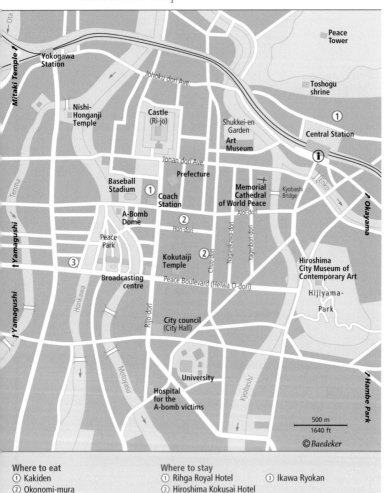

Peace Tower

Yokogawa Station

Mitaki Temple

Ota

Johoku dori Ave.

Toshogu shrine

Nishi-Honganji Temple

Castle (Ri-jo)

Shukkei-en Garden

Art Museum

① Central Station

ℹ

Enko

Jonan dori Ave.

Prefecture

Tenma

Baseball Stadium

① Coach Station

Memorial Cathedral of World Peace

Kyobashi Bridge

Okayama

Yamagushi

② A-Bomb Dome

Hon-dori

Aioi-dori

Nagarekawa-dori

Yagenbori-dori

Peace Park

③

② Kokutaiji Temple

Chuo-dori

Hiroshima City Museum of Contemporary Art

Broadcasting centre

Peace Boulevard (Helwa O-dori)

Hijiyama-Park

Yamagushi

Honkawa

Rijo-dori

City council (City Hall)

Motoyasu

University

Kyobashi

Hambe Park

Hospital for the A-bomb victims

500 m
1640 ft

© Baedeker

Where to eat
① Kakiden
② Okonomi-mura

Where to stay
① Rihga Royal Hotel
② Hiroshima Kokusai Hotel
③ Ikawa Ryokan

event in world history when it was completely destroyed by an atomic bomb in 1945. Reconstruction made it into the largest city in, and today it is its administrative and tourist centre of, the district of Chugoku. Large industrial complexes extend along the coast in the south of the city, particularly petrochemicals, metallurgy, ship-building and automobile production (including the headquarters of Mazda), as well as agricultural products and fish processing.

In 1593 Mori Terumoto (1553–1625) built a castle on the estuary of the Ota River, which he called Hiroshima-jo (»wide islands«). Soon this name was used for the entire settlement area. The town was the seat of the Mori and Fukushima families and later also of the Asano family, who laid the foundation for its later development. After the Asano were deprived of their power during the Meiji reform the harbour was extended under municipal supervision in 1889; further growth from 1894 came with the construction of the train line between Kobe and Shimonoseki, which touched on the city. As a result of its favourable location Hiroshima was the location of the imperial headquarters during the Sino-Japanese War from 1894 to 1895; several institutions and industrial enterprises settled here as a result of its being a garrison town on that as well as later occasions, so that in 1940 Hiroshima had 344,000 inhabitants, making it Japan's seventh-largest city. On **6 August 1945** at 8.15am local time the first atomic bomb to be used in anger was dropped by the US Air Force on Hiroshima; it completely destroyed the city and according to official estimates killed around 200,000 people. At the time it was thought that the area would remain uninhabitable for decades to come, but by 1949 it was possible to begin reconstruction. In 1974 the population was double what it had been before the war. However the atomic bomb still effects the population through increased cancer rates.

History

! **Baedeker TIP**

Black Rain

A classic book of what is known as A-bomb literature is the emotional novel *Black Rain* (Kuroi ame, 1965–66) by Ibuse Masuji (1898–1993). It describes the atomic bomb attack on Hiroshima and its consequences through the fate of young Yasuko, who kept a diary about her experiences.

What to See in Hiroshima

The wonderful Shukkei-en garden extends along the bank of the Ota (700m/765yd west of the station, 5 minutes by bus); it was created by Asano Nagaakira as a replica of the famous landscape garden at West Lake in the old southern Chinese capital of Hangchow (Sung Dynasty).

✶ ✶
Shukkei-en

2km/1mi west of the station (bus, 10 minutes) is the castle (also Rijo, »Carp Castle«), built in 1593 and made the residence of Fukushima Masanori; in 1619 it became the property of Asano Nagaakira. The five-storey main tower is a reconstruction of 1958; it houses a local museum. There is a nice view of the city, the harbour and Miyajima Island from the top floor.

Castle

Not far to the south of the castle is the Atomic Bomb Dome, the ruins of the former Hiroshima Prefectural Industrial Promotion

✶
Atomic Bomb Dome

▶ VISITING HIROSHIMA

INFORMATION

Tourist information
In the station (south exit):
Tel. 0 82/2 47 67 38
Daily 6am–midnight
In the rest house in the Hiroshima
Peace Memorial Park:
Tel. 0 82/2 61 18 77
April–Sept 9.30am–6pm
(01–15 Aug until 7pm),
Oct–March 8.30am–5pm
www.hiroshima-navi.or.jp
www.city.hiroshima.jp

! Baedeker TIP

A taxi ride on the water

Hiroshima is a city on the water, so why not explore it from the water too? Gangitaxi makes just this possible: the small motorboat taxis for 2–6 people go around the Peace Memorial Park or from there to the station. To get one, hail it and get in at the nearest »gangi«, the steps leading from the street to down to the water, which were once used to bring goods ashore (they operate in good weather 10am–5pm, 10 minutes ¥ 500, tel. 0 82/2 30 55 37).

GETTING THERE

By air: from Tokyo (Haneda Airport; 1½ hours).
By rail: from Tokyo (central station) JR Sanyo shinkansen line via Kyoto and Osaka (4½ hours).
By bus: from Hiroshima airport to the city centre (35 minutes).
Ferry connections: to Kure, Takamatsu, Beppu and Imabari (Shikoku).

LOCAL TRANSPORT

The city's most practical means of transport is the **tram**. It runs from the station (south exit) to the city centre and the harbour approx. every 10 minutes between 6am and 11pm. One ticket costs ¥ 150 (a day ticket may be worthwhile: ¥ 600). No. 2 and no. 6 go to the city centre and the Peace Memorial Park. No. 1 and no. 5 go to the harbour.

EVENTS

Peace festival (in remembrance of the atomic bomb attack, first held in 1947; 6 August).
Hiroshima harbour firework display (4th Sat in July).

The following website is helpful: **www.gethiroshima.com/en**; it has many tips, including restaurants and nightlife.

SHOPPING

The Tokyu Hands and Mitsukoshi department stores can be found in **Aioi-dori** (Tatemachi). Parallel (to the south) to this main road is the **Hondori** shopping street with many little shops and bars. The Motomachi CRED (Pacela) complex has a modern mall with a lot of shops and restaurants, south of the castle near the Rihga Royal Hotel

GOING OUT

Hiroshima's entertainment district is **Nagarekawa** east of the Chuo-dori. It has plenty of bars and night clubs. The Nagarekawa-dori and the Yagenbori-dori, which runs parallel to it, offer a great selection of entertainment venues.
In the summer it is nice to sit in one of the **outdoor cafés**, which are otherwise quite rare in Japan; they even come with a sea view. One such café is to the west of the station at the Kyubashiga-

wa near the Kyobashi Bridge between Aioi-dori and Jonan-dori.

WHERE TO EAT
► Moderate
① *Kakiden*
Higashi-ku, Hikari-machi 2-8-24
Tel. 0 82/2 64 59 68
Mon–Sat 11am–2pm and 5pm–10pm
5 minutes' walk from the station's shinkansen exit. Serves Hiroshima's speciality: oysters in all variations and other seafood.

► Inexpensive
② *Okonomi-mura*
Hiroshima is famous for its okono-miyaki. Okonomi-mura serves this speciality on three storeys, where several okonomiyaki outlets can be found next to each other. Don't be put off by the somewhat bare exterior. It is best to choose a fairly busy restaurant as that is a sign of good quality. Itsukushima (4th floor, straight to the left out of the lift) has an English menu. Okonomi-mura is not alto-gether easy to find: take the tram to Hatchobori, go down the Chuo-dori (southbound) and look for the build-ing on the right-hand side behind the Parco department store.

WHERE TO STAY
► Luxury
① *Rihga Royal Hotel*
Naka-ku, Motomachi 6-78
Tel. 0 82/5 02 11 21
www.rihga.com/hiroshi
Large, elegant high-rise hotel near the castle and architecturally modelled on it; with several restaurants (such as the Teppan-yaki) and bars, Sky Lounge on the 33rd floor.

► Mid-range
② *Hiroshima Kokusai Hotel*
Naka-ku, Tatemachi 3-13
Tel. 0 82/2 48 23 23, www.kokusai.gr.jp
The benefit of this hotel is its central location. Both Western and Japanese-style rooms.

Baedeker recommendation

► Budget
③ *Ikawa Ryokan*
Naka-ku, Dobashi-cho 5-11,
Tel. 0 82/2 31 50 58,
ikawa1961@go.enjoy.ne.jp
Comfortable accommodation not far from the Peace Memorial Park. Both Western and Japanese-style rooms, with or without bath-rooms. Tram towards the waterfront or Miyajima to the Dobashi stop.

Hall, which was at ground zero. Absolutely everything was destroyed within a 3km/2mi radius of here.

Two arms of the Ota River, the Honkawa and the Motoyasu flow around an island to the south, which can be reached by a bridge. It includes the Peace Memorial Park (bus and tram from station, 15 minutes). Here there are thousands of colourful paper cranes: the children's memorial, begun by the two-year-old Sadako Sasaki, who died of leukaemia in 1955. The park contains the **Peace Memorial Hall**, the atomic bomb museum (Peace Memorial Museum), open March–Nov 8.30am–6pm, August until 7pm, Dec–Feb until 5pm, ¥ 50) and the **memorial cenotaph** for the A-bomb victims, designed

Hiroshima Peace Memorial Park

Peace Park Map

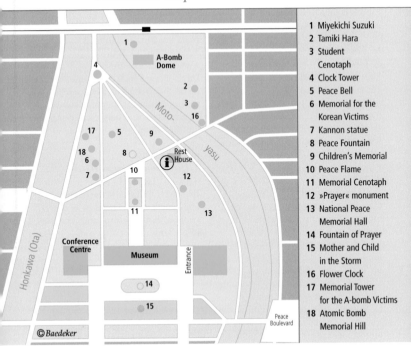

1 Miyekichi Suzuki
2 Tamiki Hara
3 Student Cenotaph
4 Clock Tower
5 Peace Bell
6 Memorial for the Korean Victims
7 Kannon statue
8 Peace Fountain
9 Children's Memorial
10 Peace Flame
11 Memorial Cenotaph
12 »Prayer« monument
13 National Peace Memorial Hall
14 Fountain of Prayer
15 Mother and Child in the Storm
16 Flower Clock
17 Memorial Tower for the A-bomb Victims
18 Atomic Bomb Memorial Hill

© Baedeker

by the famous architect Tange Kenzo. The cenotaph under the stone arch contains a list with all the names of the victims and it bears an inscription which may be translated: »Rest in peace, for the error must not be repeated«. The Atomic Bomb Dome can be seen through the concrete arch. Remembrance celebrations take place in front of this cenotaph on 6 August. The Atomic Bomb Memorial Mound contains the remains of more than 70,000 victims.

Hijiyama Park The 100m/110yd wide Peace Boulevard (Heiwa Odori) leaves the park in the south and heads east (1.5km/1mi south of the station; bus 10 minutes) to Hijiyama Park, which is situated on a hill covered in cherry trees and has a lovely view of the city. The park also contains the **Museum of Contemporary Art** exhibiting a collection of works by national as well as international artists (open Tue–Sun 10am–5pm, ¥ 320).

Memorial Cathedral of World Peace Northwest of the park (1km/0.6mi west of the station) is the Memorial Cathedral of World Peace, which was built in 1954 at the instigation of the German Jesuit priest Hugo Lassalle, who experienced the atomic bomb explosion. It is one of the biggest Catholic churches in

◂ Benesse House

bustle. For that reason the Benesse House art museum also has a luxury hotel with artworks in every room and a view of the sea (open daily 8am–9pm, ¥ 1000 for day visitors, double rooms from ¥ 30,000, tel. 0 87/8 92 20 30). Furthermore new artworks are constantly being created, and in the context of the **Art House Project** artists redesign old houses in the village (open Tue–Sun 10am–4.30pm, ¥ 500, www.naoshima-is.co.jp).

? DID YOU KNOW ...?

■ ... that Beethoven's 9th symphony, which is played all across the country at New Year, was performed for the first time in Japan by the inmates of the German POW camp in Bando?

Naruto

The 441m/1447ft Konaruto Bridge is the connection between the small harbour town of Naruto and the island of Oge to the northeast (bus from the station, 20 minutes), on which Naruto Park is located. From the island's northern tip there is an impressive view of the raging rapids in the strait as well as of Mount Naruto (cableway from

★ ★

Senjojiki). The **rapids** are formed by the different water levels of the

Strait ▸

Inland Sea and the open sea, which then try to balance out during high and low tide, causing strong currents of up to 20kph/12.5mph to form in the narrow strait. The whirlpools reach diameters of 20m/22yd. Boat tours to the rapids depart from the harbour. A bus runs between the station and a viewing platform (20 minutes).

Bando

A train line leads to the town of Bando 11km/7mi to the southwest. Bando was the location of a camp in which 953 German soldiers captured in Qingdao (China) were imprisoned from 1917 onwards. In 1972 the Doitsu-kan (German house) was built, a museum with German folk art and documents from the prison camp. Six years later the German Park was added and in 1993 a new home was built

🕐

for the Doitsu-kan (open Tue–Sun 9.30am–4.30pm, ¥ 300). There is also a life-size model of the prison orchestra playing Beethoven's Fifth Symphony. The museum maintains a lively cultural exchange program with its twin city of Lüneburg, Germany.

▶ VISITING INLAND SEA

INFORMATION

On internet at the following web address: www.anchorage.jp/setouchi.

GETTING THERE

By boat: from Hiroshima (directly or via Kure) to Matsuyama (1–2¾ hours); via Kure to Imabari (1½ hours). There are also numerous shorter lines.

WORTHWHILE DESTINATIONS

The most worthwhile destinations around the Inland Sea are Awaji, Himeji, Hiroshima, Kobe, Kurashiki, Matsuyama, Miyajima, Okayama, Osaka, Shodoshima, Takamatsu and Yamaguchi (▶see separate chapters).

✳ Ise-Shima National Park

Main island: Honshu   **Prefecture:** Mie
Area: 520 sq km/200 sq mi

Ise-Shima National Park is located on the 伊勢志摩国立公園
Shima Peninsula, which forms the south-
eastern park of Mie Prefecture on Honshu. Its main attractions are
the Ise shrines, venerated as national holy places. They are attrac-
tively situated between wonderful trees south of the town of Ise.

The attractive coast facing the Pacific is broken by numerous inlets, a
classic ria landscape. The look of the landscape is shaped by thick
forests, subtropical vegetation along the coast as well as many small
islands.

✳ Grand Ise shrines

The national park's northern gateway is the town of Ise (population   **Ise**
106,000), which was formed by merging the towns of Uji and Yamada. Ise contains the administration of the Ise shrines, as well as its library, which is rich in Shinto literature; it is also home to the Cho-
kokan Museum (antiques) and the Nogoyokan Museum (agriculture).

The two shrines, approx. 5km/3mi apart (exterior shrine, Geku; inte-   **History and**
rior shrine, Naiku) were originally built in other locations and later   **architecture**
brought to their current positions.
The Geku is said to have initially
been built in Manai (historical
province of Tamba, now Kyoto
Prefecture) and moved to Ise in
478 under Emperor Yuryaku
(457–479). The Naiku was once
part of the imperial palace, was

 Tip

■ Western visitors should behave with reserve
and also respect the ban on taking photographs.

then brought to Kasanui (Yamato province) during the reign of Emperor Sujin (3rd century) or later and finally transferred to its current location. Both shrines have the same priest; originally one of the
emperor's sisters was priestess.
The shrines, built of costly cedar and cypress wood, represent the
Shimmei-zukuri style, whose characteristics are the pitched roof, the
crossed gable bargeboards (chigi) and the cylindrical wooden beams
(katsuogi) on the ridge of the roof. The only ornamental elements
are the finely worked gold and copper platings on the beams and
doors. Apart from the Izumo-Taisha shrine, the Ise shrines are the
only Shinto places of worship in Japan that have remained unaffected
by the influences of Buddhist architecture.

In a cycle of 20 years the shrines are taken away and the wood distributed to all the shrines around the country, where it is then used as consecrated building material. The 65 buildings are rebuilt as precise replicas of the old ones, directly adjacent to where the previous buildings stood, and after their completion the deity is brought to the new shrine. This ceremony, called **»Sengu-shiki«**, last took place in October 1993.

The Ise shrines became greatly significant as a result of the efforts to return Shinto to its pristine form after it had been mixed with Buddhism for centuries. In connection with these efforts endeavours made in the 18th century then led to the reintroduction of the empire on a Shinto foundation in the 19th and elevated Shinto to the status of state religion. After World War II Shinto lost this official status again, but its place of worship in Ise remains the destination of countless pilgrims.

Outer shrine

The outer shrine (Geku) is not far from the Uji-Yamaha (Kinki-Nippon Railway) station to the southwest. A bridge leads to the 89ha/220-acre shrine complex. Pass through the first torii to see the buildings on the right-hand side in which the imperial family usually stay during their visits to Ise: Anzaisho, the house for the emperor, and Sanshujo, the house for the family members. Behind the second torii on the right is the **kagura-den hall for cult dances**. The kagura dance, which was widespread until 1868, was performed only in these shrines during the Meiji period. Here it is danced by young girls (who will accept donations). Since the abolition of state Shinto Ise, just like all the other shrines, is dependent on donations, which were used for example to finance the last reconstruction of the buildings. The shrine also sells souvenirs and charms. The next hall is the cult hall.

Somewhat further on is the **main shrine**, which has a four-fold fence. The outermost fence or itagaki is a wall of cedar wood. The main entrance is located along one of the short sides, smaller entrances can be found on the other three sides. Alternating short and long posts made of cedar wood form the sec-

Geku Outer Ise Shrine

50 m
164 ft
© Baedeker

Shoden
Koden-chi
Anzaisho (Saikan)
Kagura-den
Maga-tama

P
P
P

1 Main entrance
2 North entrance
3 First torii
4 Second torii
5 Itagaki
6 Treasuries
7 Mike-den
8 Kazenomiya Shrine
9 Takanomiya Shrine
10 Tsuchinomiya Shrine

Sacred   Park

Hordes of visitors at the entrance gate to the inner shrine

ond fence, soto-tamagaki. Only priests, the emperor and imperial envoys are allowed to pass through the second fence; all other visitors have to stop at the gate on the southern side, whose white curtain obscures the view of the interior of the shrine complex. Within the bounds of the second fence, uchi-tamagaki, and the fourth, mizu-gaki; both have a gate on the southern side. The main shrine, the shoden, made of naturally coloured cedar wood with sparse metal ornamentation and a thatched roof, stands in the innermost courtyard. To the right and left of the gate are the two ho-den treasuries, where the shrine's cult accessories and ceremonial gowns are kept. Between the first and second fence on the northern short side is the mike-den hall, where food sacrifices are made twice a day.

South of the main shrine is the 4.5ha/11-acre sacred park (Geku-Jin-en) with several smaller shrines such as the Kazenomiya shrine (consecrated to the wind god) and the Taganomiya shrine (dedicated to the god Toyouke).

◀ Sacred Park

The inner shrine (Naiku), 5km/3mi southeast of Geku, is **Japan's largest national holy place**. To get to it take the Uji Bridge, which crosses the Isuzu River. The bridge goes straight to the first torii. Beyond it steps lead down to the river, where the pilgrims wash their hands and mouth in ritual preparation for their prayers. Behind the second torii a path lined by ancient cedars begins, which leads to the temple office and the kagura-torii dance hall. A rice silo and several other smaller buildings are nearby, behind them the fenced-in sho-den main shrine, whose complex resembles that of the Geku and

★
Inner shrine

Naiku *Inner Ise Shrine*

50 m
164 ft
© Baedeker

Uji Bridge

Isuzu

Kyozensho

Rest House
for Pilgrims
(Sanshuden)

Aramatsuri-
no-Miya
Shrine

1

Saikan

2

Karuga-
den

3

4

6 6

Shoden Koden-
chi

5

Kazahinomi-
no-Miya shrine

Isuzu

1 First torii
2 Steps to the river
3 Second torii
4 Rice silo
   (Imibiyaden)

5 Minie Chosha
   (Hall for the ceremonial
   preparation of the
   sacred food offerings)
6 Treasuries

which is also surrounded by four wooden walls; again visitors are only allowed to pass through the outermost one.

The Naiku is said to house the Ya-ta-no-kagami mirror, which, along with the jewel and the sword is one of **Japan's three imperial regalia**. According to tradition the sun goddess Amaterasu gave it to her nephew Ninigi-no-mikoto to take to earth, where he then founded the imperial dynasty. The mirror, venerated as a symbol of the sun goddess, was originally kept in the imperial palace in the care of an imperial princess acting as high priestess, but the sacred site was moved from the palace during the reign of the legendary emperor Sujin, which completed the separation of temporal and spiritual power. However, even until 1339 the Ise priestess remained a member of the imperial family.

Ise-Shima Skyline

The 16km/10mi Ise-Shima Skyline (toll road) begins northeast of the Naiku. It runs eastbound over the Asama Mountains to Toba; along the way there are magnificent views of the bays around Toba and Ise as well as of the national park's mountains. The view from the top of Mount Asama (553m/1814ft) is also fantastic (north of the road, bus from Naiku-mae, 40 minutes).

★
Kongosho-ji

The Kongosho-ji temple, which belongs to the Rinzai sect, stands on the peak of Mount Asamo. The temple allegedly contains a statue of Kokuzo-bosatsu by Kobo-daishi (774–835) as well as sculptures of the Shinto deity Uho-Doji and a portrait of General Kuki Yoshitaka (1542–1600). The year of foundation of the main hall is unknown.

Toba

The town of Toba has a population of 30,000 and can also be reached directly from Ise, 14km/9mi to the west, on the Kinki-Nippon Railway in 15 minutes. Not far from the station is a 48m/157ft **look-out tower** with a nice view of the bay and its several small islands. 500m/550yd south of the station is the Toba Tourist Center, which also has plenty of views. Not far from the pier (boat trips around the bay) is the Toba Aquarium (diving demonstrations; open 21 Mar to 31 Oct 9am–5pm; 1 Nov to 20 Mar 9am–4.30pm; 20 July to 31 Aug 8.30am–5.30pm; admission ¥ 2400). The 51m/167ft Hiyori Hill is another good viewpoint.

Futamiga-ura

Northwest of Toba (bus connection) is Futamiga-ura on the bay of the same name. are The two rocks Meoto-Iwa, which according to Japanese mythology symbolize the island realm's creator deities Izanagi and Izanami, rise out of the sea. The rocks are connected via a long straw rope (shimenawa), which is ceremoniously renewed every year in early January. The torii on the 9m/30ft rock, the larger of the two, is particularly beautiful during sunrise.

Pearl Island

A 63m/69yd bridge leads from Toba to the pearl island of Mikimoto Shinju-shima, where Mikimoto Kokichi (1858–1954) set up the first facility for producing cultured pearls. In this procedure a foreign body is inserted into the pearl oysters. The cultured pearl then develops around it in approximately seven years. The vast majority of modern cultured pearl production comes from this region. There is a monument to Mikimoto on the island as well as a cultured pearl information facility with diving demonstrations. The **Mikimoto Pearl**

 ## VISITING ISE-SHIMA NATIONAL PARK

INFORMATION

Tourist information
In Kintetsu Ujiyamada station
tel. 05 96/23 96 55
Daily 9am–5.30pm

At the entrance to the exterior shrine
tel. 05 96/28 37 05
Daily 8.30am–5pm

www.isejingu.or.jp/english

GETTING THERE

By rail: from Nagoya or from Osaka and via Kyoto with the Kintetsu line to Uji-Yamada (1½ hours or 2 hours) or JR line from Nagoya to Ise-shi (1¾ hours), from here onwards via Toba to Kashikojima.
By boat: ferry connections from Irako (Atsumi Peninsula) to Toba (Isewan Ferry Line; 1 hour).

Connections within the national park: bus from Uji-Yamada on the Ise-Shima Skyline via Naiku and Toba to Kashikojima (2½ hours).
Ferries from Kashikojima to Wagu, Goza and Hamajima (all around 30 minutes); from Hamajima to Goza (15 minutes); from Toba to Irako (1 hour).
To the shrine: bus from Ise-shi or Uji-Yamada to Naiku-mae, to the Geku on foot from Uji-Yamada station or JR Ise-shi.

EVENTS

Toba
Around mid-June the Shirongo-matsuri festival is celebrated; more than 200 divers dressed in white collect abalone (marine snails). At the end of July the Toba Port Festival takes place with folk dances, a firework display and more.

Museum is definitely worth visiting. One of its exhibits is a 1.2m/ 3.9ft pagoda made of more than 10,000 pearls (open Jan–Nov 8.30am–5pm, Dec 9am–4.30pm, ¥ 1500, www.mikimoto-pearl-museum.co.jp).

Ise Toll Road Take the 25km/15mi Ise Toll Road in a southbound direction to **Kashikojima** (also Kinki-Nippon Railway or bus from Ise-shi via Toba). The town is situated on the northern coast of Ago Bay; its clear waters also house extensive banks of cultured pearl. Here too visitors can watch divers dressed in white (Ama) as they go about their work. Kashikojima is home to the National Pearl Research Laboratory; not far from the station is the Shima Marineland, a strange building in the shape of an ammonite that contains an aquarium (open daily 9am–5pm, July–Aug until 5.30pm, ¥ 1250).

Goza Take a boat across Ago Bay to the town of Goza (there is also a bus from Toba); it is situated in the far west of the peninsula of the same name; there is a nice view of the bay and the Pacific from the 99m/ 325ft Mount Kompira, which towers above the town in the south.

Cape Daido ▶ Further eastwards is Wagu. Beyond the town the road leads to Cape Daido with steep cliffs and big waves.

Matsusaka To the northwest outside of the national park is the town of Matsusaka (population 113,000; JR line and Kinki-Nippon Railway from Nagoya), which is known for its livestock farming. It is said that **the best beef in the country** comes from here. The animals are given beer to drink, and are also massaged with it. The Matsusaka Park 1km/0.6mi southwest of the station contains the remains of the old castle as well as the house of the scholar Motoori Norinaga (1730–1801), which was relocated here and contains personal items as well as some of his manuscripts.

★ Izu Peninsula

l–m 2–3

Main island: Honshu   **Prefecture:** Kanagawa

伊豆 半島   **Varied landscape, including a coastline dotted with bays, forested mountains, hot springs and romantically situated baths, makes the peninsula with its mild climate a popular destination all year round.**

Hot spring peninsula The Izu Peninsula south of Mount Fuji protrudes into the Pacific. It is bordered in the west by Suruga Bay, in the east by Sagami Bay. Large parts of it belong to the Fuji-Hakone-Izu National Park. The name Izu comes from the old term Yu-Izu (»Yu« means »hot water«, »Izu« means »spring«).

The Amagi Mountains, the peninsula's mountain ridge, are the continuation of the Hakone Mountains. The highest elevation is the 1407m/4616ft Amagi, source of the Kano River which makes its way northwards through the peninsula and flows into the sea in Suruga Bay.

The best starting points for trips into the surrounding area are the towns of Atami, Mishima and Numazu, all three of which can be reached from Tokyo. The most convenient road connection is the Tomei Express Highway, which runs close to Mishima and Numazu. The peninsula itself also has public transport, namely the Izu-Kyuko and Izu-Hakone trains as well as several bus routes.

East Coast of the Izu Peninsula

The spa town of Atami (population 49,000) is situated on a magnificent strip of coastline in the far north of the peninsula's east coast. It is one of the country's most modern spas. The apricot garden is worth a visit (Atami-baien; bus from the station, 15 minutes). Around 800 trees blossom from January to the end of March. **Atami**

The MOA Art Museum (MOA bijutsukan, bus from the station) exhibits colourful woodblock prints (ukiyo-e), ceramics, objects of precious metal and lacquerware, amongst other things. Many of the exhibits are classified as **»national treasures«** or »objects of significant cultural value«. The reconstructed Golden Tea Room of Toyotomi Hideyoshi is especially impressive (open daily except Thu 9.30am–4.30pm, ¥ 1600, www.moaart.or.jp). ★ ◄ MOA Art Museum

Open to modern things, too – a laser installation in MOA Art Museum

▶ VISITING IZU

INFORMATION

Atami
Shinsui Park, Chisaki
Nagisa-cho
Tel. 05 57/85 22 22
April–Sept 9.30am–6pm,
Oct–March 9.30am–5.30pm

Ito
In the station
Tel. 05 57/37 61 05
Daily 9am–5pm

www.shizuoka-guide.com

In light of the relatively high prices the
Mount Fuji Welcome Card is a worthwhile investment. It can be printed out
from the following website:
www.mtfuji-welcomecard.jp.

GETTING THERE

By air: from Tokyo (Haneda
Airport) to Oshima Island.
By rail: from Tokyo (central station)
JR Tokaido shinkansen line to Atami
(50 minutes) and Mishima (1 hour);
or to Shimoda (2¾ hours); JR Tokaido
main line to Atami 1¾ hours),
Mishima (2¼ hours) and
Numazu (2½ hours); from Tokyo
(central station) JR Ito line via Atami
to Ito, then Izu-Kyuko private train
line to Shimoda; from Mishima Izu-
Hakone private train line to Shuzenji.
By boat: from Tokyo (Takeshiba Pier)
to Okada (Oshima Island; 4–7 hours);
from Yokohama to Okada (Oshima; 6
hours); from Atami to Motomachi
(1–2 hours); from Ito to Motomachi
(1½ hours); from Shimoda to Motomachi (1½ hours) as well as to the
islands of Kozu, Shikine, Niijima and
Toshima.

EVENTS

Atami ume-matsuri (with geisha dances and tea ceremony; mid-January),
in Atami's apricot garden; Kurofune-
matsuri (celebration commemorating
the landing of Commodore Perry in
1853, mid-May), in Shimoda; Genji-
ayame-matsuri (procession with portable shrines, dances; beginning of
July), in Izu-Nagaoka-onsen; Tarai-
nori kyoso (race in wooden tubs on
the Matsukawa River; first Sunday in
July), in Ito-onsen; firework display
(July–August), in Atami; Ito Anjinsai
(commemoration of William Adams,
the English adviser and shipbuilder of
the Tokugawa, processions and a firework display; beginning of August), in
Ito; shrine festival (annual festival,
procession with floats; mid-August), at
the Mishima-Taisha shrine.

WHERE TO STAY / WHERE TO EAT

▶ **Luxury**

Baedeker recommendation

Seiryuso
2-2 Kochi, Shimoda-shi
415-0011 Shizuoka-ken
Tel. 05 58/22 13 61, fax 23 20 66
www.seiryuso.co.jp
A country guesthouse in the middle of a
wonderful garden with rooms furnished in
the style of days gone by; superb comfort
and Japanese specialities.

Asaba Ryokan
3450-1 Shuzenji, Shuzenji-cho
Tagata-gun
410-2416 Shizuoka-ken
Tel. 0 55/8 72 70 00
Fax 8 72 70 77

This attractive house from 1675 built in the traditional style with balconies, terraces and a pond offers comfort in pleasant surroundings. Occasionally No performances are given during banquets. The restaurant serves Japanese dishes.

▶ **Mid-range**
Shimoda View Hotel
633 Kakizaki, Shimoda-shi

415-0013 Shizuoka-ken
Tel. 05 58/22 66 00
The main hotel is situated atop a hill with a magnificent view of the sea and the Izu Islands. 5 minutes to the beach. Tatami and Western rooms, rotemburo with a panorama of the bay. On the menu: primarily typical onsen dishes, i.e. mainly seafood.

South of Atami the coastal road (parallel to the Ito train line) makes its way to Ito (population 71,000), the peninsula's second-largest town. There are around 700 hot springs here, which supply the households and baths, and some of them have already been in use for several centuries. 1.5km/1mi south of the station is the Jonoike pond and east of it the Butsugenji temple of the Nichiren sect, whose founder lived here in exile from 1261 to 1263.

◀ **Ito**

2 km/1mi southeast of the station is a monument to William Adams (1564–1620), who built the first Western ship in Japan here. The English merchant came to the Japanese main island in 1600 in a ship that was the only one of an entire merchant fleet to survive a storm. Here he gained the trust of Ieyasu, the first Tokugawa shogun, and instructed him in weapons technology, shipbuilding and navigation. He later married a Japanese woman and adopted the Japanese name Miura Anjin. A commemoration is still held at his tomb in Yokusuka every year for Adams and his wife.

◀ **Monument to William Adams**

There is a bus connection from Ito station (20 minutes) to the Omuroyama-shizenkoen nature park in the vicinity of a 321m/1053ft volcano with a pretty view of the Amagi Mountains and the island of Oshima to the east.

◀ **Omuroyama-shizenkoen**

The Ippeki crater lake (circumference: 4km/2.5 mi; bus from the station, 25 minutes), in which there is a lovely reflection of the Amagi Mountains, can be found to the southwest of the nature park. The area around its shoreline is famous for its cherry blossom. Jogasaki beach is to the east; it is a 10km/6mi ria coastline of volcanic origin. The Izu Ocean Park (Izu Kaiyo-Koen; bus from Izu-Kogen station, 10 minutes) is at the centre of this region; it has several rocky swimming pools and is a good place to go diving.

◀ **Ippeki**

The Ikeda Art Museum (Ikeda-nijusseiki-bijutsukan; bus from the station, 25 minutes) displays 20th century works by Picasso, Chagall, Matisse and others as well as colourful Japanese woodblock prints.

◀ **Ikeda Art Museum**

The Izu cactus garden (Izu-saboten-koen; bus from Ito, 40 minutes) is located at the foot of Mount Omuro (581m/1906ft) to the south of the crater lake; it has a peacock farm and a viewing platform (open daily 9am–5pm, Nov–Feb until 4pm, ¥ 1800).

◀ **Cactus garden**

Shimoda   Far in the south of the peninsula's east coast is the harbour town of Shimoda (population 32,000; Izu-Kyuko train line, from Ito 1 hour); it is the starting point for ferries to the seven Izu Islands. The **»Black Ships«** of the American Commodore Matthew Perry (1794–1858) anchored in Shimoda Bay in 1854; it was their presence that led to the signing of the Convention of Kanagawa (31 March 1854) and the opening of the ports of Shimoda and Hakodate to foreigners. The first diplomatic representative of the United States in Japan, Townsend Harris (1804–78) resided here from 1856 to 1857, but then moved his official residence to Yokohama, which opened up to the outside as the result of a trading agreement signed with the United States in 1858.

Kakisaki ▶   The Gyokusenji temple, formerly the official residence of Townsend Harris, is located 2km/1mi east of the town in the village of Kakisaki. Apart from a portrait and some souvenirs of Harris it contains the eight-volume diary of a village inhabitant about the life of the diplomat. The graves of American and Russian sailors are nearby. In mid-May the **three-day festival** Kurofune-matsuri takes place in Shimoda in honour of the landing of Commodore Perry. Opposite the temple

Bentenjima ▶   is the small island of Bentenjima, site of a temple consecrated to the Benten, the goddess of happiness. It was from here that Yoshida Shoin (1830–59) rowed out to the Black Ships to ask to be taken to America, but his undertaking failed and he was taken captive.

Shimoda Park ▶   Shimoda Park on a hill near the harbour has an excellent view of Cape Suzaki (east). The lower terminus of a cableway up Mount Nesugata is close to the railway station. There is a lovely view of the Izu Peninsula's southern tip. The observation post monitoring the Black Ships anchoring in the bay stood here.

Hofukuji temple ▶   The Hofukuji temple is not far from the station. It has a small museum, which is dedicated to Okichi Tojin, Harris's alleged mistress.

Ryosenji temple ▶   The Ryosenji temple is located south of the station; it was in this temple that the negotiations for the Japanese-American treaty took place. This treaty and that with Russia were then signed in the Chorakuji temple next door.

Aquarium ▶   The aquarium with several hundreds of species of the local marine fauna, built into a cave, is definitely worth a visit (open March–Oct daily 9am–4.30pm, otherwise until 4pm, ¥ 1700).

Shimoda Kaiko-Kinenkan ▶   Not far from Shirahama beach to the east is the Shimoda Kaiko-Kinenkan commemorative hall with memorabilia from the time of the Black Ships.

Yumigahama Beach ▶   With its white sand and numerous pine trees, Yumigahama Beach southwest of Shimoda (bus from the station, 20 minutes) is one of the island's most beautiful beaches.

✳
Cape Iro   From the southernmost point of the Izu Peninsula, Cape Iro (bus from Shimoda, 40 minutes), there is a picturesque view of the chain of the seven Izu islands. Not far from the cape visitors can admire more than 3000 plant species in the jungle park (Jungle-koen; opposite the lighthouse).

proselytized with the support of Shimazu Takahisa (1514–71). However, just ten years later the missionary fell out of favour and had to leave the city. Nevertheless more than 600 Japanese converted to Christianity during this short time. Nariakira, the 28th Shimazu (1809–58), introduced Western technologies, thereby laying the foundation for the city's industry; the first modern Japanese warship was built here, for example. It was used in the battle against units of the British fleet in 1863.

The city's most famous son was the **samurai Saigo Takamori** (1827–77), who returned here after differences of opinion with the Meiji government in Tokyo. On 15 February 1877 he went to the capital with 10,000 soldiers in order to negotiate with the government about the preservation of old laws. After suffering many losses in battles against overwhelmingly superior government troops, he returned to Kagoshima and made a last stand with a few loyal followers on Mount Shiroyama, where he committed suicide on 24 September 1877. This event marked the end of an uprising that went down in history as the Satsuma Rebellion. The posthumously rehabilitated Saigo is still considered the embodiment of Kagoshima's local identity.

◄ Satsuma Rebellion

What to See in Kagoshima

The 107m/351ft Shiroyama Hill rises to the southwest of Kagoshima station; steps lead up to the hilltop. The remains of Tsurumaru-jo Castle, destroyed by fire in 1874, can still be seen at the foot of the hill; there is also a bronze statue of Saigo, who committed suicide in the nearby cave, where there is a memorial. The top of Shiroyama commands a view of the bay and the Sakurajima volcano. The Terukuni shrine with a large stone torii can be found to the south of the hilltop. It is dedicated to Shimazu Nariakira.

Shiroyama

> ## ! Baedeker TIP
>
> ### Potatoes done differently
>
> Kagoshima is famous for its Imo-Shochu liquor, which is distilled from sweet potatoes. »Satsu-Maymo no Yakata« in the Tenmonkan shopping quarter behind the Tenmonkan Arcade in a side street of the Tenpark-dori (Tenmon-kandori tram stop, tel. 0 99/2 39 48 65, open daily 10am–7.30pm) has more than 100 varieties of liquor and many other products made of potatoes.

Not far to the south in the Francis Xavier Park a memorial with a bronze bust and the ruins of a Christian church, one of the first to be built on Japanese soil, commemorates the first missionary. In 1949 the Francis Xavier Memorial Church was built here in honour of the 400th anniversary of the saint's arrival.

Francis Xavier Park

The Nanshu shrine, dedicated to the patriot Saigo, lies 1km/0.6mi northwest of Kagoshima station; the cemetery of the nearby Joko-myoji temple contains the tombstones of Saigo and his followers.

Nanshu shrine

Shoko-Shuseikan Museum
2.5km/1.5mi north of the station is the Shoko-Shuseikan Museum, housed in a factory building of 1852 of a type unique in Japan. It produced glass, ceramics, ship components and threads. The museum displays objects from the 700-year Shimazu family history (open daily 8.30am–5.30pm).

Across the rail tracks is Ijin-kan, the former residence of the English engineers working in the Shuseikan.

★★ Iso Park
A little further north is Iso Park, also called Sengan-in; it was once a summer residence of the Shimazu family (17th century). It is one of Kyushu's most attractive landscape gardens and has the best view of Sakurajima (open daily 8.30am–5.30pm, ¥ 1000). A cableway leads up Mount Isoyama, where there is a small amusement park.

Kita-futo
The harbour's northern pier, not far from the station, has one of Japan's largest aquariums (Kagoshima Suizokukan, open daily 9.30am–6pm, ¥ 1500). The harbour boardwalk is very romantic during sunsets.

▶ VISITING KAGOSHIMA

INFORMATION
In Kagoshima-Chuo station
Tel. 0 99/2 53 25 00
Daily 8.30am–7pm
www.city.kagoshima.lg.jp

Prefecture Kagoshima
3rd floor
Kagoshimaken Sangyo
Kaikan, 9-1 Meizan-cho
near the Asahi-dori tram stop
Tel. 0 99/2 23 57 71
Mon–Fri 8.30am–5.15pm
www.pref.kagoshima.jp

GETTING THERE
By air: from Tokyo (Haneda Airport; 1¾ hours); from Osaka (1 hour); from Nagoya (1¼ hours).
By rail: from Tokyo (central station) JR shinkansen line via Nagoya, Kyoto, Osaka, Okayama and Hiroshima to Hakata (5 hours), then JR Kagoshima main line to Shin-Yatsushiro (1¾ hours) and onwards with the Kagoshima shinkansen (50 minutes); from Miyazaki JR Nippo main line (2 hours).

EVENTS
Soga-don no Kasayaki (ceremonial burning of paper parasols; end of July); Myoen-hi Mayri (procession of boys in Samurai armour; end of Sept); Ohara-matsuri (procession with singing; beginning of Nov).

WHERE TO STAY
▶ **Mid-range**
Nakazono Ryokan
1-18 Yasui-cho, Kagoshima-shi
Kagoshima-ken 892-0815
Tel. 0 99/2 26 51 25, fax 2 26 51 26
Twee little two-storey guesthouse in a favourable location close to Kagoshima station (seven minutes on foot). Japanese-style rooms, communal baths. The helpful owner, Mr Nakazono, speaks English.

Around Kagoshima

The active Sakurajima volcano can be found in the bay east of the city (ferry connection, 15 minutes); it has three summits: Kita-dake (1118m/3668ft), Naka-dake (1110m/3642ft) and Minami-dake (1060m/3478ft). Of the three craters only Minami-dake is still active today; a constant smoke column can be seen towering above it. Sakurajima is part of the ►Kirishima-Yaku National Park. Sakurajima's **eruptions** can be traced back to the year 708. A particularly famous eruption took place 1914, when the 400m/450yd-wide and 72m/235ft-deep strait, which until then separated the volcano from the Osumi Peninsula to the east, was filled up with lava, with the result that Sakurajima is now a peninsula that can be reached via a road from Osumi. One special feature here is the »Sakurajima-daikon«, a root vegetable growing in the volcanic soil; they can reach a weight of up to 45kg/100 lb. Harvest time is January and February.

★ ★
Sakurajima

There is a good road (bus round trip, 1¾ hours) from Hakamagoshi in the west of the peninsula through the lava fields; the small town of Kurokai lies to the south. It has a stone torii that was covered in lava up to the height of its cross-beam in 1914.

◄ ★ Kamakura

K 7 • m 2

Main island: Honshu
Population: 175,000

Prefecture: Kanagawa

鎌倉

Thanks to its numerous sights Kamakura is a much-visited tourist destination: the main attraction of this historic town is the Great Buddha, and there are plenty of picturesque temples and shrines to be explored.

Kamakura, Japan's former capital, is around 40km/25mi southwest of Tokyo on Sagami Bay. It is edged by forested hills; the Miura Peninsula extends into the Pacific in the southeast. The mild climate and the **beaches** attract visitors from the Tokyo-Yokohama area in the summer. Just 50 years ago Kamakura was a small seaside town; now it has become a residential suburb of Tokyo and Yokohama, and home to many intellectuals. Kamakura has 65 temples and 19 shrines as well as plenty of art treasures. The Wakamiya-oji, a road leading northwards from the coast, divides the town.

Temple town

After the Minamoto emerged victorious against the Taira in the final battle of the Genpai War at Dannoura (1185), Minamoto Yoritomo (1147–99) made the town of Kamakura the seat of his military gov-

History

Highlights Kamakura

Tsurugaoka-Hachiman shrine
The town's most important Shinto shrine houses numerous art treasures in its magnificent buildings.
► page 297

Great Buddha
Japan's second-largest statue is considered the finest of all the Buddha statues and is the main attraction for all the visitors to the town.
► page 300

Hase-dera
It contains a lovely Kannon statue.
► page 300

Engakuji temple
One of Buddha's teeth is kept here in a precious reliquary.
► page 302

Kenchoji temple
This magnificent Zen temple has an ancient bell that is well worth a visit.
► page 302

ernment (Kamakura-bakufu) in 1192 in order to escape the decadent life at court in Kyoto. He thereby also secured his power over the east of the country, which was entirely under his control. He founded a strict knightly cult and until 1333 Kamakura remained the centre of feudalism maintained by knightly families. After Yoritomo's death his sons Yoriie and Sanetomo initially took over the shogunate, but upon their assassination the Minamoto line came to an end. The Hojo clan grabbed power. The decline of the Hojo as the country's rulers was accompanied by fierce wars, in which the town was largely destroyed. During the subsequent Muromachi period (1338–1573) Kamakura blossomed again as the administrative seat of the eastern provinces under the rule of the Ashikaga shoguns, but with the relocation of the administration to Odawara it soon reverted to being a quiet fishing village.

North and Northwest

Jufukuji temple   Go 500m/550yd north from Kamakura station in the town centre to get to the Jufukuji temple; it belongs to the Rinzai sect and was founded by Masako, Yoritomo's wife, in 1200. It was once one of the five large Zen temples (Kamakura-gozan) situated on hills (the others are Kenchiji, Engakuji, Jochiji and Jomyoji). Of the temple complex only the reconstructed main hall with a wooden statue of Jizo, the patron god of children, still exists. The hill behind the temple complex contains the tombs of Masako and her son Minamoto Sanetomo (1192–1219).

Eishoji temple   The Eishoji temple with a nunnery is not far from here to the north. It belongs to the Jodo sect and was founded by Eisho, Tokugawa Ieyasu's wife, in 1636.

It is a 20-minute walk from Kamakura station (to the northwest) to the Zeniarai-Benten shrine, which is consecrated to Benten, the goddess of luck. There is also the option of taking a hiking trail here from the Jochiji temple. According to popular belief any money washed in the shrine's spring in the time of the snake (one of the animals of the Chinese zodiac) will double or triple. The torii leading to the consecrated cave were donated by thankful believers.

Zeniarai-Benten shrine

Northeast

The Tsurugaoka-Hachiman shrine lies northeast of the station (bus, 3 minutes). The Wakamiya-Oji road leading to the shrine is divided by three torii and becomes narrower towards the north. Between the second and third torii the road is lined by cherry trees and azaleas. The Tsurugaoka-Hachiman shrine was founded by Minamoto Yoriyoshi (998–1075) in 1063, but was only brought to its current location by Yoritomo in 1191. It is consecrated to Hachiman, the god of war, who was particularly worshipped during the Kamakura period; Hachiman is identified with the legendary emperor Ojin and was also the patron deity of the Minamoto clan. The current shrine buildings from 1828 represent the magnificent style of the Momoyama period (1573–1600). The shrine houses **valuable art treasures**, such as suits of armour, swords and masks. To the left of the stone steps leading to the shrine a 22m/72ft ginkgo tree with a circumference of 7m/23ft marks the spot where Sanetomo, the third Kamakura shogun, was murdered in 1219, presumably from jealousy of his position, by his nephew Kugyo, just eight years his junior.

★ ★

Tsurugaoka-Hachiman shrine

To the right of the steps is the lesser Wakamiya shrine (1624), dedicated to Nintoku-tenno, son of Ojin. A popular theme of Japanese literature is the dance that Shizuka, the mistress of Minamoto Yoshitsune (1159–89), had to perform in front of his brother Yoritomo when the shrine was complete. She is said to have been forced to reveal Yoshitsune's hiding place. The memorial for Yoritomo and Sanetomo, the **Shiraha-tasha**, is not far from the minor shrine. The shrine's name means »white banner« and derives from the banner of the Minamoto.

The **Kamakura Museum** (Kamakura Kokuhokan) built in 1928 in the style of the Shosoin of Nara, can be found to the right of the shrine; it contains art treasures from local temples and shrines as well as from private collections from the Kamakura and

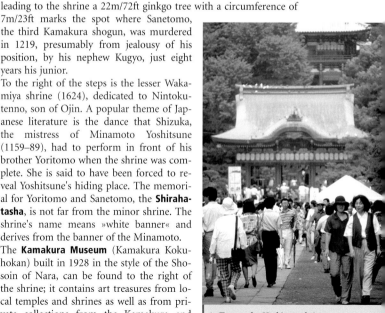
At Tsurugaoka-Hachiman shrine

Muromachi periods; it also has many ukiyo-e woodblock prints on display (open Tue–Sun 9am–4pm, ¥ 300). The museum for modern art is next door.

Yoritomo's tomb
Kamakura shrine ▶

A pagoda surrounded by a 1.6m/5ft stone wall marks the tomb of Yoritomo, founder of the Kamakura-bakufu, 500/550yd northeast of the shrine. Go east to get to the Kamakura shrine (Kamakura-gu, there is also a bus from Kamakura station, 10 minutes), built in 1869 in the middle of a grove and dedicated to Prince Morinaga (1308–35); it has a splendid treasury. Morinaga, son of Emperor Godaigo, was murdered in a nearby cave by the brother of the ruling shogun because he attempted to win back power for the imperial family. His tomb can be found 200m/220yd to the east on the Richi-kozan hill.

Kakuonji temple

700m/765yd north of the Kamakura shrine is the Kakuonji temple built in 1218 under Hojo Yoshitoki; it belongs to the Shingon sect (Sen-yuji school). The Aisendo Hall contains a wooden statue of the seated Yakushi-nyorai; next to him, amongst other statues, are two bosatsus and a representation of Jizo, the patron god of children. The **caves** (yagura) in the hill behind the temple are believed to be old burial sites because of bones found in them.

Zuisenji temple

1km/0.6mi east of the Kamakura shrine visitors will find the remote Zuisenji temple (Zen temple) belonging to the Engakuri school of the Rinzai sect after a longish walk. Its garden, created by **Muso-Ko-kushi** (also known as Soseki, 1275–1351), is a famous example of the landscape gardening shaped by Zen Buddhism at the end of the Ka-makura period. The temple was also founded by Muso-Kokushi, but was renewed in the 14th century. The 1m/3ft wooden statue of Mu-so-Kokushi that is kept in the founder's hall is one of the best art-works of the Muromachi period (open daily 9am–5pm, ¥ 100). There is a lovely view of the town from the hill behind the temple.

Samponji temple

The Samponji temple (also Sugimoto-dera, bus from Kamakura sta-tion, 7 minutes) to the south of the Kamakura shrine was presum-ably founded in 8th century; it contains three wooden statues of the eleven-headed Kannon (two of them probably date back to the Heian period). The temple is still known under the name »Sugimoto-Kan-non« as it was once the starting point of the **pilgrimages** to the 33 Kannon temples in the Kanto region.

Jomyoji temple

350m/380yd to the east (bus from Kamakura station, 8 minutes) an avenue lined by cherry trees leads to the Jomyoji temple founded by Ashikaga Yoshikane (d. 1199) in 1188; it is one of the five large Zen temples in Kamakura.

Great Buddha of Kamakura →

Southeast

Ankokuronji temple

Southeast of Kamakura station there are several temples belonging to the Nichiren sect, including the Ankokuronji temple, which was founded in 1274 on the site of Nichiren's hermitage. One of its most significant treasures is an old copy of the *Rissho-ankokuron*, a polemic directed against other sects, written by **Nichiren Shonin** (1222–82).

Nichiren, who came from Kominato on the Boso Peninsula, started spreading his teachings in his home town after spending three years living in a monastery in Kyoto. He was ousted from there because of his doctrines and in 1253 founded the Nichiren-Hokke sect, set up the hermitage and wrote the aforementioned polemic manuscript. His criticism of the government and attacks on other sects led to his banishment to the Izu Peninsula (1261–63). After his return he continued spreading his teachings. He only just escaped execution and was banished to Sado Island in 1271, where he continued to write further treatises, such as the *Kaimokusho* (1272). From 1274 until his death he lived in the remote Kuon-ji temple on the slope of Mount Minobu (west of Mount Fuji) and in the Hommonji temple in Ikegami (modern-day Tokyo), which he founded.

Komyoji temple

In the far southeast of the town (bus from Kamakura station, 10 minutes) the Komyoji temple, founded in 1243 and belonging to the Jodo sect, houses a number of valuable pictures and picture scrolls.

Southwest

★★ Great Buddha

Kamakura's best-known attraction, the Great Buddha (Daibutsu), can be found in the southwest of town (bus from Kamakura station, 10 minutes). It is part of the **Kotokuin temple**, which belongs to the Jodo sect. The bronze sitting sculpture of Amida is Japan's second-largest statue after the Daibutsu in the Todai-ji in Nara. It weighs 93t, is 11.4m/37ft tall and is considered the country's most beautiful and consummate Buddha statue. It was cast in 1252 by Ono Goroemon or Tanji Hisatomo and was surrounded by a large hall that was damaged by a storm in 1369 before being washed away completely by a tidal wave in 1495. The hand gesture (mudra) expresses firmness of faith (open April–Sept daily 7am–6pm, Oct–March until 5.30pm, ¥ 200; for a small additional fee it is possible to enter the statue).

★ Hase-dera

Not far from here to the southwest is the Hase-dera temple of the Jodo sect; its main hall contains the statue of the eleven-headed Kannon. The 9.3m/31ft gilded wooden statue is said to have been carved by the priest Tokodu from half of an old camphor tree (the other half was used to carve the Kannon statue of the Hase-dera in Nara).

Kamakura Map

Where to eat
① Kaikotei
②③ Hachinoki

Where to stay
① Kamakura Park Hotel

The temple also owns the town's third-oldest bell, cast in 1264. There is a nice view of the beaches in the south of Kamakura from the temple (open daily 8am–5pm, Oct–Feb until 4.30pm, ¥ 300).

Further to the southwest is the Gokurakuji temple (Enoden private line from Kamakura station). Apart from various temple treasures such as the Shakyamuni statue, not much has survived of the temple founded in 1259 by Hojo Shigetoki (1198–1281).

Gokurakuji temple

The beaches of Yumigahama (to the east) and Shichirigahama (to the west) lie to the south, beyond the rail lines. The latter has a nice view of Enoshima. The 2km/1mi-long **Yumigahama beach, one of the nicest in the Tokyo area**, is the scene of a lively town festival at the beginning of August.

Beaches

Around Kita-Kamakura

★★
Engakuji temple

Kita-Kamakura station to the north outside of the main urban area is the starting point for a trip to the Engakuji temple not far to the east. This temple, belonging to the Rinzai sect and centre of the Engakuji school, was founded in 1282 by Hojo Tokimune and run by a Chinese abbot. Despite sustaining severe damage in the earthquake of 1923, the reliquary hall (shariden) of 1285 survived as the best example of the powerful Kamakura-period architecture. It contains a precious quartz reliquary with one of Buddha's teeth (only accessible on 1–3 January).

Bell-tower ►

The bell-tower to the right of the two-storey gate contains a bell cast in 1301; with a height of 2.6m/9ft it is the town's largest. Behind the main building is the tomb of Tokumine; the tea house (Butsunichian) is prettily located with its tea room (ensoku-an) and an adjoining garden (open April–Oct daily 8am–5pm, Nov–March until 4pm, ¥ 200).

Tokeiji temple

Walk five minutes south from Kita-Kamakura station to get to the Tokeiji temple of the Rinzai sect (Engakuji school).
According to a law of Hojo Sadatoki (1271–1311) women abused by their husbands were considered divorced upon entering this convent. This led to the temple being given the sobriquet »Enkiridera« (divorce temple). The first abbess was also the temple founder and widow of Sadatoki. The main hall contains a wooden statue of the Sho-Kannon.

Jochiji temple

A footpath leads to the Jochiji temple (Rinzai sect), close by to the south in an old cypress copse. It was founded in 1283 by Hojo Morotoki and is another of the five large Zen temples of Kamakura. The wooden statue of Jizo (patron god of children) by the sculptor Unkei was the only temple treasure to survive the 1923 earthquake.

★
Kenchoji temple

Go southeast of Kita-Kamakura station to get to the Kenchoji temple (bus, 4 minutes; also a connection to the Tsurugaoka-Hachiman shrine, 6 minutes), which is surrounded by tall cedars. The founder of this temple, built in 1253 for the Chinese priest Tai Chiao (in Japanese Daigaku-zenji), was Hojo Tokiyori (1227–63). In 1415 the temple buildings burned down, but the Tokugawa commissioned them to be rebuilt in the 17th century. The gate and main hall represent the Chinese style of the Sung dynasty. Noteworthy **temple treasures** are Kamakura's second-oldest bell, cast in 1255, and the wooden statue of the temple founder, a masterpiece of the Kamakura period. The Chinese juniper trees in front of the Buddha Hall have been designated national treasures. The tomb of Tai Chiao, who was active as a political advisor and spiritual leader under the Hojo, is situated on a hill behind the temple (open daily 8.30am–4.30pm, ¥ 300).

▶ VISITING KAMAKURA

INFORMATION

At the station's east exit
Tel. 04 67/22 33 50
Daily April–Sept 9am–5.30pm,
Oct–March until 5pm
www.city.kamakura.kanagawa.jp

Extensive background information on
the many temples and shrines can be
found on this excellent website:
www.kamakuratoday.com/e

GETTING THERE

By rail: from Tokyo (central station)
JR Yokosuka line via Yokohama (1
hour).

EVENTS

First shrine visit (1–3 Jan), in the
Tsurugaoka-Hachiman and Kamakura
shrines amongst others; Setsubun
(driving out the winter; early Feb), in
the Tsurugaoka-Kamakura shrine and
the Kenchoji temple amongst others;
Kamakura-matsuri (town festival with
historical processions and a tea ceremony; early to mid-April); annual
festival of the Tsurugaoka-Hachiman
shrine (with Yabusame, equestrian
events and archery; mid-Sept); Men-
kake-gyoretsu (masked procession;
mid-September), at the Gongoro
shrine; Takigi-no (night time open-air
No performances; end of Sept), at the
Kamakura shrine.

WHERE TO EAT

▶ Moderate

① *Kaikotei*
3-7 Sakanoshita, Kamakura-shi
Tel. 04 67/25 44 94
Daily 11am–9pm
Take the Enoden line to Hase station,
from there around ten minutes' walk.
Kaiseki (lunchtime, from ¥ 5500) and
soba (from ¥ 800) in a 180-year-old

building which the owners rebuilt and
fitted with Japanese antiques in a quiet
residential area.

② *Hachinoki*
7 Yamanouchi, Kamakura-shi
Tel. 04 67/22 87 19
Tue–Fri 11.30am–2.30pm,
Sat, Sun, holidays 11am–4pm
③ *Branch* in Kita-Kamakura, near the
Tokeiji temple, tel. 23 37 22, daily
except Wed 11.30am–7pm, and right
next door another one, tel. 23 37 23,
which has the same opening hours.
Famous restaurant with shojin-ryori
(vegetarian monks' fare) and kaiseki.
Delicious! Reservations are absolutely
necessary!

WHERE TO STAY

▶ Luxury

① *Kamakura Park Hotel*
33-6 Sakanoshita, Kamakura
Kanagawa, 248-0021
Tel. 04 67/25 51 21, fax 25 37 78
www.kamakuraparkhotel.co.jp
Western-style hotel with some Japanese rooms, an open-air Japanese bath
on the roof and a Japanese restaurant.
All rooms have sea views.

▶ Mid-range

Kannonzaki Keikyu
On the Miura Peninsula
2 Hashirimizu, Yokosuka-shi
Kanagawa-ken 239-0811
Tel. 0 46/8 41 22 00
Fax 8 43 73 98
hotelinfo@kannon-kqh.co.jp
Thanks to its proximity to the beach,
this beautiful building, a member of
the Relais et Châteaux, with modern
rooms and terraces with a view over
the Tokyo Bay, is ideal for water-sports
enthusiasts and those in search of
some rest and relaxation.

Surroundings of Kamakura

Katase The west of town is the popular seaside town of Katase, on the mouth of the river of the same name. There private train lines from Fujisawa and Kamakura station. The aquarium (with dolphin shows) is located at the Shonan Park west of the river. There are numerous swimming pools and boat rentals along the river.

Ryukoji temple 100m/110yd to the northeast of Enoshima station is the Ryukoji temple. It was completed in 1288 in the place where **Nichiren** was intended to be executed and belongs to the Nichiren sect. The delegates of Kublai Khan were executed in the same spot in 1275. The Oeshiki-matsuri festival takes place here towards mid-September.

There is a wide beach in front of the 600m/660yd Benten-bashi bridge. Several warning signs explain what to do in the event

Enoshima of tsunami tidal waves. Cross the bridge to get to the forested Enoshima Island (bus from Kamakura station to Enoshima-kaigan, 20 minutes). More than 300 stone steps lead to the Enoshima shrine, which houses a famous statue of Benten, the goddess of luck.

Miura Peninsula

To the southeast of Kamakura the Miura Peninsula forms the dividing line between Tokyo Bay (to the east) and Sagami Bay (to the west). The mild climate has made this area a preferred residential area of Tokyo's affluent inhabitants, especially since it has lovely beaches that are good for swimming.

Zushi The town on the peninsula closest to Kamakura is Zushi (bus, 20 minutes; JR Yokosuka line, 5 minutes). Take the bus from here (15 minutes) to get to the seaside resort of Hayama with a wonderful view of Sagami Bay and Mount Fuji. Towards the south Hayama Park extends along the coastline.

Yokosuka The city of Yokosuka (population 427,000) is located along the peninsula's east coast; it is the largest city along this stretch of coastline. Until the end of the World War II it was also a naval port; today a US Navy base is located here. There are train connections to/from Tokyo and Yokohama. The city extends across several hills (Okosu, 242m/794ft, and Takatori, 139m/456ft). **Mikasa Park** 1km/0.6mi east of the station is worth a visit (bus from the station, 5 minutes). Off the coast lies the *Mikasa*, launched in 1900; later the flagship of Admiral Togo, it was used in the Russo-Japanese War (1904–05), decommissioned in 1923 as the result of the Washington Naval Treaty and set up as a museum ship in 1961 (open April–Sept 9am–5.30pm, March and Oct until 5pm, Jan, Feb, Nov and Dec until 4.30pm, ¥ 500). There is a ferry connection from the park to the small island of Sarushima (10 minutes), a former base of the shore batteries and today a popular water sports area.

To the west of Yokosuka visitors in Tsukayama Park are the tombs of William Adams (Miura Anjin in Japanese; 1564–1620, ►p. 287), a British maritime pilot who stranded in southern Japan, and his Japanese wife. Adams was an adviser and shipbuilder in the service of Tokugawa Ieyasu. The castle of Prince Miura was situated in Kinugasa Park, from where visitors have a pretty view of the peninsula; the cherry blossom starts at the beginning of April.

◄ Tsukuyama Park

The eastern port on Miura is Yokosuka's southeastern district of Uraga, from where ships entering Tokyo Bay were monitored during the Tokugawa shogunate (1603–1867). Commodore Biddle handed over a letter from the president of the United States in 1846, and seven years later Commodore Perry anchored outside the harbour to initiate the opening of Japan with the handover of a further letter from the US president.

Uraga

The deep-sea fishing port of Miura (bus from Kurihama, 40 minutes) can be found in the far south of the peninsula. The small island of Jogashima, which has a lighthouse and an attached museum, can be reached via a 575m/630yd bridge; there is view of Misaki harbour to the west. Numerous small bays to the north of it are good places to swim, e.g. near Aburatsubo (boat connection from Misaki, 15 minutes) with the marine park of the same name.

Miura

Kanazawa

Main island: Honshu   **Prefecture:** Ishikawa
Population: 450,000

Kanazawa is the largest and most attractive city of Hokuriku district and also its cultural centre. A fair bit has survived from the splendid days of old, such as Kenroku-en Park in the heart of the city, considered one of Japan's three most beautiful gardens.

金沢

Kanazawa, the capital of Ishikawa Prefecture, is situated on Honshu's northwestern coast, where the Noto Peninsula reaches far into the Sea of Japan, into which the Asano River flows. Today Kanazawa is a city with a university and industry as well as the seat of an art academy.

Seaport and university town

Kanazawa Map

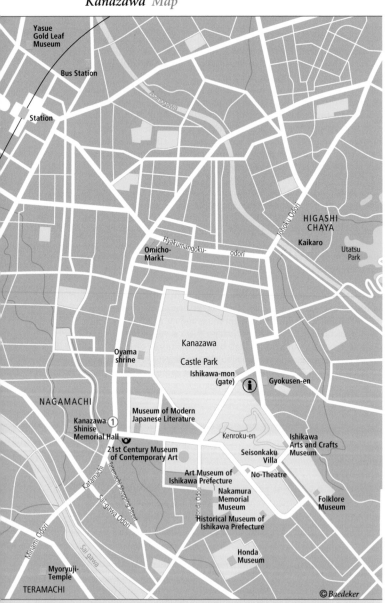

Yasue
Gold Leaf
Museum

Bus Station

Station

Asanogawa

HIGASHI
CHAYA

Johoku Odori

Kaikaro

Utatsu
Park

Hyakumangoku-
odori

Omicho-
Markt

Kanazawa

Castle Park

Oyama
shrine

Ishikawa-mon
(gate)

ⓘ

Gyokusen-en

NAGAMACHI

Kanazawa ①
Shinise
Memorial Hall

Museum of Modern
Japanese Literature

Kenroku-en

Ishikawa
Arts and Crafts
Museum

21st Century Museum
of Contemporary Art

Tatemachi Shopping Street

Katamachi

Sai-gawa Odori

Seisonkaku
Villa

No-Theatre

Art Museum of
Ishikawa Prefecture

Honda Odori

Nakamura
Memorial
Museum

Folklore
Museum

Historical Museum of
Ishikawa Prefecture

Minami Odori

Sai-gawa

Honda
Museum

Myoryuji-
Temple

TERAMACHI

© *Baedeker*

Where to stay
① Excel Tokyu Hotel

What to See in Kanazawa

In the centre of town (bus from the station, 15 minutes) are the re- **Castle**
mains of a castle destroyed in a fire in 1881; the Ishikawa-mon gate
and the 54m/60yd-long samurai residence (Sanjukken-nagaya) are
still extant.

Beyond the road is the wonderful Kenroku-en Park. With an area of ★★
10ha/25 acres it is the largest of the three famous gardens of Japan **Kenroku-en**
(the other are two in ►Mito and ►Okayama). The park, belonging
to the residence of the Maeda and completed in 1837, embodies, according to its name, the unification of the six qualities: honour, ceremony, expanse, artistic design, coolness and scenic harmony
(open March to 15 Oct 7am–6pm, 16 Oct to Feb 8am–4.30pm, ◷
¥ 300). The information office and parking spots can be found at the
park's northern end. The Hisagoike pond (to the right) and the Ka-
sumikgaike pond (to the left) can be reached from here. The Hia-
goike pond has a small waterfall at its eastern end; on the shore of
the Kasumigaike are the Kotoji-toto stone lantern and a bronze statue of the legendary hero Yamato-takeru (►Nagoya) further to the
east. The Seison-kaku house built in 1863 for the daimyo's mother is
in the southern part of the park, and the Kanazawa shrine is nearby.

*Kenroku-en is one of Japan's most famous gardens and
thus attracts large numbers of visitors*

21st Century Museum of Contemporary Art	Not far from Kenroku-en and the town hall is the circular complex of **Kanazawa 21**, opened in 2004; it is worth a visit for its futuristic architecture alone. It exhibits contemporary art, including some works that are quite hard to stomach (open Tue–Sun 10am–6pm, Fri and Sat until 8pm, www.kanazawa21.jp).
Oyama shrine	It is a ten-minute walk from the main shopping street Korinbo to the Oyama shrine (2km/1mi southeast of the station, Minami-cho bus stop), which is dedicated to Maeda Toshiie. It was initially built in 1599 in a different location and then brought to its current site in 1873; the three-storey gate built by a Dutch architect in 1875 is quite remarkable: it has elements of Eastern and Western building styles and is a nice example of Meiji architecture.
Ozaki shrine	Not far to the northeast of the Oyama shrine is the heavily ornamented Ozaki shrine (Musashi-ga-Tsuji bus stop), which is compared to the Toshogu shrine in Nikko.

▶ VISITING KANAZAWA

INFORMATION

Tourist information
In the station, tel. 0 76/2 32 62 00
www.city.kanazawa.ishikawa.jp
www.kanazawa-kankoukyoukai.gr.jp/
kanazawa_e

Ishikawa Prefecture
www.pref.ishikawa.jp

GETTING THERE

By air: from Tokyo (Haneda Airport) to Komatsu (1 hour).
By rail: from Tokyo (central station) JR Tokaido shinkansen line to Maybara (3 hours), then JR Hokuriku main line (2 hours);
from Tokyo (Ueno station) JR Joetsu shinkansen to Nagaoka and Hokuriku main line (4 hours).
By bus: from Komatsu Airport to Kanazawa (50 minutes).

EVENTS

Hyaku-mangoku-matsuri (procession with historical costumes; mid-June).

MADE IN KANAZAWA

Local commodities include hand-dyed silk fabrics (kagayuzen) and elegant porcelain goods (kutani-yaki) with colourful designs. They can be bought in Katamachi and Korinbo, the *main shopping streets*.
Almost 100% of the traditional Japanese *gold leaf* is produced in Kanazawa. The Yasue gold-leaf museum close to the station (west exit) shows how (open daily 9.30am–5pm, ¥ 300).

WHERE TO STAY

▶ **Luxury**
① *Excel Tokyu Hotel*
2-1-1 korinbo kanazawa,
Ishikawa 920-0961
Tel. 0 76/2 31 24 11, fax 2 63 01 54
www.tokyuhotels.co.jp
Modern hotel in walking distance of Kenrokuen Park. Ten rooms specially for women (with special accessories). The Kincharo restaurant serves regional specialities (kaga ryori). Cheaper with online reservations.

West of the Oyama shrine (5 minutes from the Korinbo bus stop) the Nagamachi quarter with old samurai houses from the Edo period is worth seeing.

Nagamachi

The old Higashi Chaya (also Higashi Geisha) quarter is particularly picturesque; it is to be found in the northeast of the city on the far side of the Asano River. Here visitors can stroll past the wooden façades of old geisha houses. One of them, the Shima-Chaya House, is accessible to the public (open daily 9am–6pm, ¥ 400).

✱ Higashi Chaya

The 141m/463ft Utatsu Hill rises to the east of this district; the area surrounding it is a nature park with an aquarium and a zoo. It also contains the Utatsu and Toyokuni shrines as well as monuments to the priests Nichiren and Rennyo and the authors Izumi Kyoka (1873–1939) and Tokuda Shusei (1871–1943), both born in Kanazawa.

Utatsu

In the southwest (bus from the station, 20 minutes) in the temple district of Teramachi is the Myoryuji temple of the Nichiren sect, which has also been given the nickname Ninja-dera because of its labyrinthine rooms and secret passages; it was also designed to be a refuge with an underground passage allegedly leading to the nearby riverbank. It can only be viewed in the context of a guided tour. Have your hotel book by phone in advance (tel. 0 76/2 41 08 88).

Myoryuji temple

> ## ! Baedeker TIP
>
> ### No on Sundays
>
> Kanazawa is a centre of No stagecraft; it has its own theatre for No performances, the Ishikawa-Kenritsu Nogaku-do (tel. 0 76/2 64 25 98). Tickets and a taxi for the No theatre should be booked through the hotel.

Around Kanazawa

The Yuwaku-onsen spa (Hokuriku Railway, bus, 50 minutes) can be found southeast of the town; it is the site of the Edo-Mura open-air museum. The 16ha/40-acre site contains a collection of samurai houses, old houses of the citizenry, a temple gate and a bell-tower from the Edo period.

Yuwaku-onsen

Leave Yuwaku-onsen southbound via Komatsu to reach the quiet spa town of Awazu-onsen (JR Hokuriku main line, 40 minutes; then bus, 10 minutes), the oldest spa town in the Hokuriku district, its hot springs with temperatures of 50–58°C (122–136°F).

Awazu-onsen

Further along the JR Hokuriku main line is Kaga; take the bus from there (10 minutes) to the more lively spa Yamashiro-onsen. The Kutani-yaki Hall with a nice collection of Kutani-yaki porcelain as well as some ceramics workshops is located half-way to Kanazawa (train, 40 minutes). In the mid-17th century kaolinite, which is necessary

Kutani-yaki Hall

for the **manufacture of porcelain**, was discovered in Kutani village south of Yamashiro. Artists trained in Arita soon became masters of overglaze painting, founding the reputation of Kutani-yaki, which is still sought after.

Hakusan Another bus route leaves Kanazawa station southbound for Haku-sanshita (1 hour 20 minutes), situated in the Hakusan National Park, which covers 473 sq km/183 sq mi. The 2702m/8865ft Mount Hakusan is one of Japan's three holy mountains. Of the five access routes (Iwama, Chugu, Itoshiro, Hirase, Ichinose), Ichinose is the most popular when coming from Kanazawa. It is a 40-minute bus ride from Haksusanshita to Ichinose and the neighbouring Haku-san-onsen, the starting point of two different ascent routes that come together at Midagahara at an elevation of 2450m/8040ft. There is a cabin nearby (Murodo) that is open during the summer. Mount Hakusan's five peaks (view of the Tateyama Mountains and the Norikura to the southeast) are reached through thick forests and a rich alpine flora. The highest of the five peaks is the 2702m/8865ft Gozenmine, followed by Tsurugigamine (2656m/8714ft) and Onanji (2646m/8681ft); the two southern peaks are Bessan and San-nomine.

Karatsu

E 8 • b 4

Main island: Kyushu **Prefecture:** Saga
Population: 79,000

唐津 **Karatsu is one of Kyushu's most popular seaside resorts; it is also the starting point for trips to the surrounding area, which is characterized by wooded hills and wide beaches.**

Gateway to China The port of Karatsu is situated on Kyushu's northern coast. Karatsu and the surrounding coastal area are part of the Genkai Quasi-National Park, which extends 90km/55mi; the town makes up the attractive southern part of the national park. Separated from mainland Korea by the Tsushima Strait, Karatsu, as one of the largest ports in northern Kyushu, gained significance early on as the gateway to the Asian continent, which is alluded to in the town's name (»kara« means »China«, »tsu« means »harbour«). Karatsu is one of the best-known production sites of Japanese ceramics. During the Japanese military campaigns in Korea, Korean ceramic masters settled here and had a great impact on the local Japanese artists. In the 16th century the rapidly increasing popularity of the tea ceremony put Kara-tsu next to the leading production sites of Mino and Kyoto as the place of origin of tea bowls (chawan); at the same time the town was an export harbour for ceramic goods from the surrounding area.

What to See in Karatsu

The town's **landmark** is its castle (bus, 10 minutes) 1.5km/1mi northeast of the station; it was built on a headland near the mouth of the river Matsuura in 1602. Today it is surrounded by the May-zuru Park. The five-storey main tower, now rebuilt after being demolished during the Meiji period houses a museum exhibiting an interesting collection of old ceramics amongst other things. There is a nice view of the town from the castle, as well as of the beaches Nishi-no-hama to the west and Higashi-no-hama to the east with the Higashi-no-hama Koen amusement park (open daily 9am–5pm, last entry 4.40pm, ¥ 400).

Castle

600m/650yd northwest of the station is the Kinshiji temple of the Rinzai sect. It was built in 1599 and is also named Chikamatsu temple after the famous playwright Chikamatsu Monzaemon (1653–1724), who spent his early days here.

Kinshoji temple

The **Karatsu shrine** is around 800m/0.5mi to the north of the station; it was founded during the Nara period (710–794). The **annual festival** (Karatsu okunchi-matsuri) celebrated for the first time in 1752 developed on the basis of the famous Gion-matsuri in Kyoto. The floats used during this festival are otherwise on display in the nearby Hikiyama cultural centre.

Around Karatsu

A 5km/3mi road leads southeast to the 284m/932ft Mount **Kagamiyama**; the **Einichi temple** of the Soto sect was founded at its foot in 1575. A switchback road leads up to the peak (a lovely view of the bay of Karatsu). The temple consecrated to Benten, the goddess of fortune, commemorates the legend associated with the mountain: in the 6th century the military leader Otomo-no-Sadehiko interrupted his journey to Korea in Matsuura (at the time Hizen province) and fell in love here with Sayohime, an aristo-

▶ VISITING KARATSU

GETTING THERE

By rail: from Fukuoka (Hakata) JR Chikuhi line (1 hour); from Saga JR Karatsu line (1¼ hours).

EVENTS

Castle festival (beginning of May); Okunchimatsuri (procession with floats; beginning of November).

Magnificent floats at Okunchi festival

cratic lady. When he departed she waved to the ships for a long time with a handkerchief and was turned to stone. The mountain owes its sobriquet of Hirefuruyama (»hire« means »cloth«, »furu« »to wave«, »yama« »mountain«) to this legend.

Seven caves 14km/9mi northwest of Karatsu, in Minato Yakatashi, the Nanatsu-gama, the seven caves, are definitely worth a visit. These basalt grottos created by erosion have a maximum height and width of 3m/10ft and a depth of 110m/120yd. When the sea is calm the insides can be viewed in boats from Karatsu and Yobuko.

! **Baedeker TIP**

Early-morning trip to the market
The colourful morning market held by the fishermen and farmers in Yobuko (from 7am to noon, but it is best to be there before 9am) is well worth a visit. One of the things sold on this market is squid (ika), for which this town is famous.

The small fishing harbour of **Yobuko**, 13km/8mi northwest of Karatsu (bus, 30 minutes) lies close to the northern tip of the Higashi-Matsuura Peninsula and is the starting point for ships going to the islands in the Genkai Sea.

Iki A ferry plies back and forth to and from Iki Island (Indoji;139 sq km/54 sq mi, population 43,000), which gained historical significance through the attempted Mongolian invasions under Kublai Khan (1274). The Shinjo shrine in Katsumoto was built to commemorate that time; it is consecrated to Iki's governor, Taira Kagetaka, who fell during the fighting. Not far from the **port of Gonoura** in the southwest of the island are the ruins of a castle built by Toyotomi Hideyoshi as a base for his troops during his military campaigns against Korea.
There is a ferry connection between Gonoura and ►Fukuoka.

Cape Hato The underwater observatory Genkai Kaichu Temboto is located at Cape Hato on a headland extending far into the sea (open daily 9am–6pm, Oct–March until 5pm, ¥ 550).

Karuizawa

K 6 • 11

Main island: Honshu **Prefecture:** Nagano
Population: 140,000

軽井沢 **At an altitude of 1000m/3300ft, Karuizawa is one of the most popular recreational areas all year round. During the summer many people from Tokyo come here to escape the hot and humid city and enjoy the green surroundings and fresh mountain air.**

Karuizawa is northwest of Tokyo in central Honshu, at the foot of
the active Asama volcano (2542m/8340ft). The average temperature
in August is 20.5°C/69°F, and the winters here are grim and cold.
There are many weekend and holiday homes, hotels and more in the
northern part of town. The newer southern part has been developed
into a recreational area.

Mountain resort

What to See in Karuizawa

2km/1mi north of Karuizawa station is Kyu-Karuizawa, Japan's oldest mountain resort and the centre of this region. During the summertime tourist onslaught (particularly from Greater Tokyo) several
shops from the capital and Yokoha-
ma open branches here. Not far
from the main road is St Paul's
Church, built by an American architect. Further north visitors can
see the former **Mikasa Hotel**, Japan's oldest hotel built of wood.
The eastern part of town the area
around the Kumoba-ike pond is a
nice place to go for walks.

Kyu-Karuizawa

KARUIZAWA

GETTING THERE

By rail: from Tokyo Asama shinkansen
(JR Hokuriku shinkansen line, 70
minutes).

It takes around one and a half hours to climb up to the Usui Pass
(995m/3264ft) from Kyu-Karuizawa station for a fine view of the
peaks of Mount Asama, Mount Haruna and Mount Yatsugatake. The
Kumano shrine is close to the Sunset Point viewing platform.

Usui Pass

Not far from the spa town of Hoshino-onsen is the wild-bird sanctuary of Yacho no Mori (bus from Naka-Karuizawa station to the Nish-
iku-Iriguchi bus stop, then 5 minutes on foot) with two bird
hides. Further north are the Sengataki Falls (bus from Naka-Karuizawa, 12 minutes) as well as the Karuizawa Skating Center, an ice rink
measuring 4ha/10 acres.

**Forest of wild
birds**

◄ Sengataki
Falls

Even further north are the Shiraito Falls (bus from Karuizawa station, 30 minutes; there is also a footpath), which are 70m/77yd wide
with a drop of 3m/10ft.

**Shiraito
Falls**

The Onioshidashi Highway runs east past Mount Asama (2560m/
8399ft) to the lava fields of Onioshidashi (bus from Karuizawa or
Naka-Karuizawa, 1 hour), which were formed in 1783 during a large
eruption of Mount Asawa, whose northern foot they covered. A trip
through the Onioshidashi rock garden takes around half an hour.

**Onioshidashi
Highway**

After Mount Aso on Kyushu, Mount Asama is Japan's most active
volcano; however, since 1753 no more major eruptions have been recorded. During increased activity, access to the mountain is pro-

★
Asama

hibited; the administration of Karuizawa and Komoro provides information. Good starting points to climb Mount Asawa are the stations of Karuizawa, Naka-Karuizawa, Shinano-Oiwake, Miyota and Komoro, all located on the JR Shin-etsu main line. The most recommendable route is the ascent from Karuizawa or Naka-Karuizawa with a subsequent descent to Komoro.

✳ Kirishima-Yaku National Park

F 9 • c–d 6

Main island: Kyushu **Prefectures:** Kagoshima und Miyazaki
Area: 456 sq km/176 sq mi

霧島屋久国立公園 Volcanic mountain ranges with lava fields and wonderful crater lakes as well as wide beaches and hot springs characterize the landscape of the national park, which consists of separate areas not adjacent to each other. The scenery is particularly beautiful during the summer blossom and in autumn when the leaves turn red.

Dimensions   The Kirishima-Yaku National Park in the south of the Japanese main island of Kyushu includes the Kirishima mountains, the island of Yakushima to the south, part of Kagoshima Bay with the Sakurajima volcano as well as the southernmost strips of coastline of the Satsuma and Osumi Peninsula, which make up Kyushu's southern tip.

What to See in the Kirishima-Yaku National Park

Kirishima mountains   The national park's northernmost part encompasses the region of the Kirishima mountain range, which extends along the border area between the Kagoshima and Miyazaki prefectures. The highest peaks are Karakuni (1700m/5577ft) in the north and Takachiho (1574m/5164ft) in the south. Between them are Shishito (1428m/4685ft), Shimmoe (1421m/4662ft) and Nakadake (1332m/4370ft). There are around ten crater lakes in this area including Onami, Fudo, Byakushi and Miike, which can be distinguished by the different colours of their water. The rich flora consists of dense primeval forest at lower elevations and at moderate elevations the forested zone silver firs (momi) and red spruces (aka-matsu), while at higher altitudes the flora consists of broad-leafed trees. Many places are known for their beautiful vegetation, such as Lake Onami surrounded by maple trees and conifers and Mount Shimmoe with its fields of azaleas.

Kirishima-onsen   Kirishima-onsen is an extensive spa region in the southwest foothills of Mount Karakuni. The best-known spas include Hayashida-onsen, Iodani-onsen and Myoban-onsen, all of which lie close together and can be reached by bus (50 minutes) from Kirishima-Nishiguchi.

18km/11mi east of Kirishima-Nishi-guchi is **Hayashida-onsen** (bus, 40 minutes) with its sulphur and siderite springs ranging in temperature from 40°C to 60°C (104–140°F).

To the southeast of Mount Kirishima, Mount Takachiho (Takachiho-no-mine), made famous by the myth, has a height of 1574m/5164ft. The base for a climb to the summit is the town of Takachihogawara (bus from Kirishima-Nishiguchi, 50 minutes) at the mountain's western foot. The 2.3km/1.4mi ascent takes around 1½ hours. Close to the peak a constant column of smoke emanates from an active crater, which is 86m/282ft deep with a circumference of 200m/220yd. There is a distant view of Kinko Bay and Lake Miike to the east from the top.

Takachiho

The 1700m/5577ft Karakuni can be climbed from Onamiike-Tozan-guchi (on the Kirishima main road) via a 3.5km/2.2mi route (around 3½ hours). Around halfway to the top the Onami crater lake is surrounded by fields of azaleas. There is a wonderful view of the area from the moss-covered crater.

Karakuni

The northern part of the national park is made up of the approx. 1200m/3900ft Ebino Plateau (bus from Kobayashi and Kirishima-on-sen to Ebino, 55 and 25 minutes respectively), Kyushu's highest spa region. The plateau extends between the mountains of Karakuni, Koshiki and Kurino and is rich in lakes and hot springs. There are extensive broad-leaved woodlands and stone pine groves to the south. The **azalea blossom** (Kirishima-tsutsuji) in May is particularly attractive; trips to Lake Byakushi and Lake Rokukannon in the northeast are also recommended.

Ebino
Plateau

Kirishima-jingu is in the south of the park together with the shrine of the same name (bus, 15 minutes), which is dedicated to Ninigi-no-mikoto, the legendary first ancestor of the Japanese imperial family. The shrine surrounded by a dense cedar forest is said to have been founded in the 6th century and was subsequently renewed in 1715.

The island of **Yakushima** (503 sq km/194 sq mi), around 70km/

Waterfall at Kirishima shrine

▶ VISITING KIRISHIMA-YAKU NATIONAL PARK

GETTING THERE

By rail: from Fukuoka (Hakata) JR Kagoshima main line to Yatsushiro (2 hours), then Hisatsu line to Kirishima-Nishiguchi.
By bus: several regional lines in the national park.
By boat: ferry connection from Kagoshima to Miyanoura (Yakushima Island; 3½ hours).

ACCESS TO THE PARK

Excellent roads make this park accessible via Yatsushiro and Hitoyoshi from the north, via Kagoshima and Karato from the west as well as via Miyazaki and Kobayashi from the east. Those travelling by train should use the Kirishima-Nishiguchi (Hisatsu line), Kirishimajingu (Nippo main line) and Takaharu (Kittu line) stations as their starting points.

45mi off the southern tip of Kyushu, is a UNESCO World Heritage Site and can be reached by ferry (daily service, 3½ hours) from the port town of ► Kagoshima. The 32 extinct volcanoes that make up the island and have a height of well over 1000m/3300ft are the reason why the island is also called the **Japanese maritime alps**. Three-quarters of the island are covered in dense forest. The magnificent ancient cedars (yaku-sugi) are famous far and wide. Yakushima is a ramblers' paradise. One of the most strenuous routes leads to the highest peak, Miyanoura (1935m/6348ft); those with less stamina will find shorter and more comfortable walks in the Yaku-sugi nature park.

Kitakyushu

F 8 • c 4

Main island: Kyushu   **Prefecture:** Fukuoka
Population: 1,017,000

北九州

Already a gateway to the Asian mainland from early on, the town is now one of Japan's largest centres for industry and international trade. For a long time Kitakyushu had the image of a dirty industrial town, but has become one of the most progressive Japanese cities in matters of environmental protection and recycling.

Centre of trade and transport

The city of Kitakyushu is situated on the Kammon Strait, which separates the main islands of Honshu and Kyushu. The city has a total area of 473 sq km/183 sq mi, making it the largest city on Kyushu by area. It was formed in 1963 by merging the previously independent cities of Moji, Kokura, Tobata, Yahata and Wakamatsu.
Industrialization began in this area in the late 19th and early 20th century. The city's economic foundations were the coal deposits to the south and close trading contacts to the Asian mainland. A signifi-

cant event was the merger of two smelting works to become the Nippon Steel Corporation, which opened a factory here that is now an international industry leader.

What to See in Kitakyushu

The district of Moji, only 680m/750yd from Shimonoseki on Honshu, is located in the northeast of the settlement area. The Hayatomo-no-Seto Strait is now spanned by the 1068m/1168yd Kammon Bridge, a suspension bridge which ends in Dannoura (a district of ▶Shimonoseki). The Taira suffered their decisive defeat in their fight against the Minamoto in the Kammon Straits in 1185.

★
Kammon Bridge

The Shin-Kammon railway tunnel is another connection between the two main island. With a total length of 18.67km/11.6mi it is one of the longest railway tunnels in the world.

◀ Kammon Tunnel

There is an impressive view of the bridge and the surrounding area from the Mekari Park 2.5km/1.5mi north of Mojiko station (bus, 10 minutes). The Mekari shrine is at the tip of Cape Mekari, which according to tradition was founded in 269 by Empress Jingu after returning from a trip to Korea. During the shrine's annual festival (January) three priests gather seaweed early in the morning, which they then sacrifice to the shrine deity. In the east of the park is the 30m/100ft **peace pagoda** donated by the Burmese government in 1958; it is a cenotaph for the victims of World War II.

Mekari Park

The district of Kokura can be found to the southwest of the park. 500m/550yd from its station visitors will find Kokura Castle, once the seat of the Hosokawa clan; it was built in 1602. Nothing remains of the 18m/60ft wall, the 48 gates and the 148 towers; it was not until 1959 that parts of the castle destroyed in 1866 were rebuilt (main tower, Tsukiki Wall and Tsukimi Tower).

Kokura Castle

 VISITING KITAKYUSHU

GETTING THERE

By air: from Osaka (1½ hours).
By rail: from Tokyo (central station) JR Sanyo shinkansen line to Kokura (5½ hours); from Fukuoka (Hakata; 20 minutes).
By boat: ferry connection from Osaka to the district of Moji (14 hours); Regular boat service from Kobe (Higashi-Kobe) to the district of Kokura (14 hours).

EVENTS

Mekari-shinji (1 January), during low tide at the Mekari shrine; Minato-matsuri (folk festival; beginning of May), in the Moji district; Numagaku (historical folk festival; beginning of May), in the Kokura-minami district; Gion-taiko (festival procession, drumming competition; mid-July), at the Yasaka shrine; Tobata Gion and Kurozaki Gion (lantern festivals; mid/end of July respectively).

Hobashira

The Hobashira nature reserve close to the town (bus from Yahata, 20 minutes) has a diverse landscape; a cableway goes up Mount Hobashira, from where there is a broad view of the town and Dokai Bay.

Sembutsu Cave

The green plain of the **Hiraodai Plateau**, which is covered in limestone rocks, can be found to the south of the town. The Sembutsu limestone cave at the plateau's eastern edge is particularly attractive.

Kobe

H 7 • h 3

Main island: Honshu   **Prefecture:** Hyogo
Population: 1.5 million

神戸

Kobe is considered a preferred centre of commerce and a popular place for Europeans to live and work. This cosmopolitan city has a population of 45,000 foreigners, together with their Western shops, restaurants and consulates.

Japan's most significant commercial port

The city of Kobe, located in southwestern Honshu on Osaka Bay, is an important industrial location as well as the capital of Hyogo Prefecture. While factories and port facilities extend far into the bay on artificially raised land in the south of the city, the residential areas nestle at the foothills of the Rokko Mountains bordering the city in the north. These mountains are part of the Inland Sea National Park (►Inland Sea). These mountains shelter Kobe, giving it a mild climate.

Around a quarter of all of Japan's imports and exports pass through Kobe. Raw materials are the most important import; exports include iron and steel, textiles, synthetic fibre products and electronic goods. The Hanshin industrial zone between Kobe and Osaka contains heavy industry, wharfs, engineering and more. Since 1997 Honshu has been directly connected to Shikoku via the Akashi-Kaikyo Bridge to Awaji and the Naruto Bridge from Awaji to Naruto. In January 1995 greater Hanshin was severely damaged by a major earthquake that killed more than 5000 persons, but today all traces of it have long been eliminated.

What to See in Kobe

Ikuta shrine

The Ikuta shrine lies in the Ikuta-ku district 400m/440yd northwest of Sannomiya station; it is consecrated to Kobe's patron goddess Wakahirume-no-mikoto. According to legend it was founded by Empress Jingu after her return from a military campaign to Korea. The name is said to derive from the Japanese word for serfs (kambe), whom the imperial court gave to the shrine. The current buildings are reconstructions. The 160m/525ft-high Suwayama is to the west; there is a nice view of the city from the top.

Further north is the district of Kitano-cho, the foreigners' quarter, which is extremely popular with Japanese tourists. It has a number of Western-style buildings from the Meiji period, which now house cafés, boutiques or historical museums.

Kitano-cho

On the way to the harbour, south of Motomachi station, is the Nankin-machi quarter, Kobe's Chinatown.

Chinatown

Kobe Map

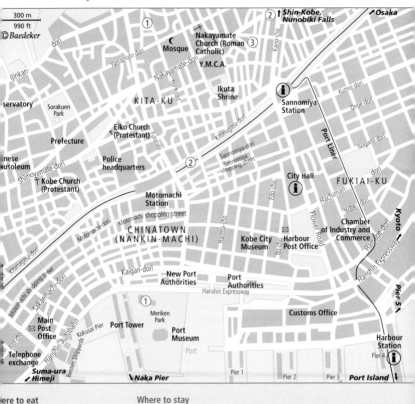

View of the brightly lit up Mosaic entertainment pier from Port Tower

Harbour The revolving observation deck of the 108m/354ft Port Tower provides a good view of the harbour, including the Mosaic amusement **Maritime** pier opposite to the west. A conspicuous structure next to the tower **Museum ▶** is the filigree roof construction of the Maritime Museum in the shape of a sailing boat; in addition to various ship models it also has ⏲ a 360° diorama and a holographic historical display of Kobe (open Tue–Sun 9am–5pm, ¥ 200). Ships docking at the Naka pier travel across the Inland Sea, while ships providing tours of the harbour (approx. 50 minutes) and small boat tours depart from the Meriken-Hatoba pier. A piece of the destroyed pier left as a memorial next to the Maritime Museum commemorates the Great Hanshin Earthquake of 1995.

Harbour islands ▶ The huge artificial island known as **Port Island** is off the coast of the harbour. To get to it take the fully automatic, unmanned »Port Liner« urban railway from JR Sannomiya station. This island has an aviary, a science museum with a planetarium, a coffee museum and a pearl museum (Tasaki Pearl Plaza). Kobe's new airport was opened at the island's southern end in 2006. A second artificial island further to the east called **Rokko Island**, which has a fashion museum and a silk carpet museum amongst other things, can be reached by monorail.

Kobe City The Kobe City Museum (Kobe Shiritsu Hakubutsukan) north of the **Museum** harbour displays exhibits relating to the city's history and archaeology; the **Namban art collection** is also part of the museum; it con- ⏲ tains paintings by Japanese masters influenced by Western styles (open Tue–Sun 10am–5pm).

The lower terminus of the 1.5km/1mi aerial cable car known as Yumefusen (»dream balloon«), which was opened in 1992, can be found in the north of the city, near the Shin-Kobe station and the Shin-Kobe Oriental Hotel. It goes up **Mount Yotsugie**. There is a small pharmacy museum at the upper terminus. Descend the mountain on foot through the 72ha/178-acre Nunobiki Herb Garden.

Yumefusen

The Nunobiki Falls are to the west, beyond the shinkansen train line (Shin-Kobe station). The Odaki waterfall is 45m/148ft high, the Medaki waterfall 19m/62ft; this forested area is a popular place for excursions.

Nunobiki Falls

These eastern city districts have some interesting museums. 10 minutes' walk from the south entrance of Nada station (JR Hanshin line) is the prefecture's leading art museum, the **Hyogo Prefectural Museum of Modern Art**, and right next door the **Earthquake Museum** (Hanshin-Awaji Earthquake Memorial) with films, dioramas and all the latest museum technology. It tells of the extent and consequences of the 1995 earthquake (both museums daily 10am–6pm). To the north of the JR Sumiyoshi station at the foot of the 932m/3058ft Mount Rokko is the **Hakutsuru Art Museum**, a recent building in the style of the Momoyama period, which exhibits Chinese and Japanese antiques (bronze, ceramics, lacquerwares; open March–May and Sept–Nov Tue–Sun 10am–4.30pm). To the south of the same station is the **Hakutsuru Sake Museum**, where free samples are available (Thu–Sun 9.30am–4.30pm). There are a number of old sake breweries in this district along the railway line.

Naga and Higashinada districts

Taisanji temple (bus from the station, 30 minutes), which belongs to the Tendai sect, can be found to the west outside of the actual urban

Taisanji temple

 VISITING KOBE

INFORMATION

Tourist information
At Sannomiya station
Tel. 0 78/3 22 02 20
Daily 9am–7pm
In Shin-Kobe station
Tel. 0 78/2 41 95 50
Daily 9am–6pm
www.city.kobe.jp
www.feel-kobe.jp/english
www.hyogo-tourism.jp/english
(about the prefecture)

TRANSPORT

By air: from Tokyo (Haneda Airport) to Osaka (1 hour), then bus (40 minutes).
By rail: from Tokyo (central station) JR Tokaido and Sanyo shinkansen line to Shin-Kobe station (2¾ hours); from Kyoto JR Tokaido main line to Sannomiya station (1 hour); also local public transport (urban railway).
By ferry: regular ferry connections from Beppu (Kyushu), Takamatsu, Imabari and Matsuyama (Shikoku);

there are also ferry connections to the islands of Shodo and Awaji.

EVENTS

Tsuinashiki (ghost dance; beginning of Feb.), in the Nagata shrine, Shinkosai (spring festival; mid-April), in the Ikuta shrine; Nanko-matsuri (procession in old suits of armour in remembrance of the people's hero Kusunoki Masashige; end of May), at the Minatogawa shrine; harbour festival (3rd weekend in May).

SHOPPING & GOING OUT

The shopping and entertainment district extends southeast of the old foreign quarter towards the *Sannomiya* district. Santica Town's underground shopping facilities or the indoor Gai shopping centre (above ground) are worth a visit. A second shopping and entertainment district with a picturesque »Chinatown« (Nankin-machi) can be found in *Motomachi* west of Tor Road. The city's largest entertainment quarter is in *Shinkaichi*.

WHERE TO EAT

▶ Expensive

① *Totenkaku*
Chuo-ku, Yamamoto-dori 3-14-18
Tel. 0 78/2 31 13 51
www.totenkaku.com
Daily 11am–2pm and 5pm–9pm,
Sat 11am–9pm
Fine Chinese restaurant in the city's oldest *ijinkan*, built in 1894. This restaurant has a grand interior and serves Beijing cuisine. Not cheap!

▶ Moderate

② *Omoni*
Chuo-ku, Kitanagasa-dori 3 chome 31, Kokashita 73
Tel. 0 78/3 91 35 05
Daily 11am–10pm

Korean cuisine, friendly atmosphere. Speciality: chige-nabe, a spicy hotpot with vegetables and fish.

WHERE TO STAY

▶ Luxury

① *Hotel Okura Kobe*
2-1 Hatoba-cho, Chuo-ku,
Kobe 650-8560
Tel. 0 78/3 33 01 11, fax 3 33 66 73
www.kobe.okura.com
10 minutes' walk from Sannomiya station in the Meriken Park opposite the Port Tower. All 489 rooms have views of the bay and there are two specially for the physically disabled. A large gym, tennis court, child care and everything else guests could expect from a hotel of this price category.

Baedeker recommendation

② *Goshobo*
858 Arima-cho, Kita-ku,
Kobe, Hyogo-ken, 651-1401
Tel. 0 78/9 04 05 51, fax 9 04 36 01
www.goshobo.co.jp/goshobo
20 Japanese-style rooms in a traditional ryokan in Arima Onsen. It is said that this ryokan has been taking guests since 1191, including such high-standing people as the warlord Toyotomi Hideyoshi, Japan's first prime minister Ito Hirobumi and the author Yoshikawa Eiji. The spring water contains salt and iron and is said to help against all sorts of ailments. No single rooms.

▶ Mid-range

③ *Kitagami Hotel Annex*
4-8-19 Kanocho, Chuo-ku,
Kobe, Hyogo-ken, 650-0001
Tel. 0 78/3 91 87 81, fax 3 91 87 85
www.kitagami.jp
Not far from Sannomiya station. Good business hotel with 55 Japanese-style rooms.

area, 10km/6mi north of Akashi station (JR Sanyo main line). The temple was founded by one of Kamatari's grandsons, Fujiwara Uma-kai, in 716; the Hondo main hall (1304), the Nio-mon gate from the Muromachi period and the sitting statue of Amida in the Amida Hall are particularly worth seeing. Other **temple treasures** include 31 volumes of the Hokekyo-Sutra, old weapons and some paintings. The interior is only accessible on one day in June, however (lunar calendar, movable date).

Around Kobe

Bordering the city in the north are the Rokko Mountains, most of which are part of the Inland Sea National Park. They are a scenically attractive and easily accessible destination. Mount Rokko (932m/3058ft; bus from Rokko station, 10 minutes) is the highest mountain. Take a cableway to the peak from Arima-onsen. There is a lovely view of the sea and Awaji Island from the top as well as an impressive night view of Kobe. The area around the peak, an extensive recreational area, has golf courses, a botanical garden and several hotels. The Rokko mountains around Tajima and Tanba are home to the famous dwarf **Kobe-Wagyu cattle**. Some stockbreeders are said to give their animals beer and to massage them, but the result, a fat, marbled beef which is regarded as a delicacy (albeit a very expensive one), is doubtless due to the breeding skills and the quality of the feed. The top breeders sell their animals exclusively to Japanese restaurants, where they are consumed in equally rarefied circles.

Rokko Mountains

! Baedeker TIP

Kobe beef just once
You almost have to try it once: Kobe beef. It's just about affordable in Wakkoku (in the Avenue Shopping Centre by the Crowne Plaza Hotel, Shin-Kobe underground station).

There is a daily bus service (35 minutes) between the Rokkosan Hotel and the hot-spring town of Arima-onsen to the north, as well as direct bus and train connections from Kobe and Osaka. The town has an idyllic setting at an elevation of 363m/1191ft; it is particularly attractive at the time of the spring blossom and in the autumn when the leaves change their colours. It is much visited by the inhabitants of the nearby cities because of its mild climate.

Arima-onsen

The region's second-highest mountain is the 699m/2293 Mount Maya (bus from Kobe, Sannomiya station, to Mount Takao, cableway from there); it too has leisure and accommodation facilities at the top. A stone stairway with 400 steps leads from the cableway's mountain station to the Toritenjoji temple, which belongs to the Shingon sect. It is said to have been founded by the priest Hodo in 646. There is a statue of the eleven-headed Kannon inside.

Maya

Futatabi

✱

Dairyuji temple ▶

Mount Futatabi (468m/1535ft), southwest of Mount Maya can be reached from Kobe's city centre (Suwayama Park) via a picturesque mountain road. TheDairyuji temple below the peak, which belongs to the Shingon sect, was founded by Wake-no-Kiyomaro in 678. It contains an impressive statue of Nyoirin-Kannon, presumably from the Nara period. The mountain's name (»mountain visited twice«) refers to the sect's founder Kobo-daishi, who stayed here on two occasions. The entire region of the densely forested mountain is part of the Futatabisan Park; Lake Shohogahara can be found on its northern slope.

Kochi

G 8 • f 4

Main island: Shikoku   **Prefecture:** Kochi
Population: 324,000

高知

This city at the centre of the Kochi Prefecture prides itself on having produced the famous and tragic hero Sakamoto Ryoma (1835–67) who at the end of the Edo period campaigned against the rigid class barriers and in favour of the restoration of the imperial rule.

Old castle town

Kochi is situated north of Urado Bay, a continuation of the wide Tosa Bay which extends inland as a narrow arm of the sea on the southern coast of the Japanese main island of Shikoku. The city is surrounded by mountains to the north and east and is located in the area of influence of the warm Kuroshio current, which gives it a particularly mild climate. The city's main economic activities are fishing, forestry and agriculture; coral jewellery, Japanese paper and Odo-yaki ceramics are also significant.

What to See in Kochi

✱

Castle

Kochi's landmark, its castle, is located on Otakasakayama Hill 1km/0.6mi southwest of the station. The five-storey main tower, which was renewed in 1753, now houses an archaeological museum; there is a distant view of the city and the sea from the top.

✱

Museum of the Yamanouchi shrine

In the south of the castle is the museum of the Yamanouchi shrine (Yamanouchi-Jinja homotsu shiryokan) with items from the possessions of the Yamanouchi family (including old weapons and a valuable collection of No masks from the Momoyama period) on display.

Anrakuji temple

1km/0.6mi west of the station is the Anrakuji temple with an impressive statue of the seated Amida-nyorai Buddha.

4km/2.5mi southeast of the Harimayabashi Bridge (bus, 20 minutes) visitors will find Godaisan Park on a 145m/476ft hill. There is a wonderful view of Urado Bay and the Pacific from the top; the **cherry and azalea blossom** in the springtime is particularly attractive. The park consists of a garden from the Edo period and the Chikurinji temple, which belongs to the Shingon sect; it was built by priest Gyoki in 724, making it the Prefecture's oldest temple and the 31st of the 88 temples of pilgrimage on Shikoku. The Monjudo main hall and the collection of Buddhist sculptures are both of interest.

Godaisan Park

✳

◄ Chikurinji temple

At the foot of the stone stairway leading up to the temple is the 2.34 ha /5.6-acre botanical garden (Shokubutsuen), which was created in memory of the botanist Makino Tomitaro (1862–1957); it contains ponds with huge water lilies, a large number of tropical plants and a small museum exhibiting a collection of fossils (open Tue–Sun 9am–5pm, ¥ 500).

◄ Botanical garden

🕐

5km/3mi northeast of the station (bus, 10 minutes) in an old cedar forest is the Tosa shrine; some of its buildings date back to the 16th century.

✳
Tosa shrine

Around Kochi

Take a bus southbound from the station to the harbour town of Urado at the entrance of Urado Bay, which is spanned by the 1480m/1620yd Urado-Ohashi bridge. The ruins of the old castle, built in 1591, are worth a visit.

Urado

Tosa shrine is a much visited destination of pilgrimage

▶ VISITING KOCHI

INFORMATION

Tourist information
In the station
Tel. 0 88/8 82 77 77
Daily 9am–5pm
www.city.kochi.kochi.jp/info/english

! *Baedeker* TIP

Market day
Every Sunday a market, the Nichiyo-ichi, which has a 300-year-old tradition, is held east of the castle. On these days 600 stalls block two lanes of the four-lane Otesuji-dori from the castle gate, selling everything from food to flowers and knick-knacks to household goods – in short, everything the heart desires.

TRANSPORT

By air: from Tokyo (Haneda Airport; 1½ hours); from Osaka (1 hour).
By rail: from Takamatsu JR Dosan line (via Tadotsu; 2½ hours); from Tokushima (via Awa Ikeda; 3½ hours).
By ferry: ferry connection from Osaka (9½ hours), from Tokyo (21 hours).

EVENTS

Castle festival (end of March/beginning of April); Doronko festival (early April), in the Wakamiya-Hachimangu shrine; Yosakoi festival (with processions, the city's largest festival, beginning of August); Shinane-matsuri (end of August), in the Tosa shrine; Tachi-odori (sword dance; autumn), in the Niida shrine, Sagawa; Ryoma-matsuri (early Oct), at Katsurahama beach.

Katsurahama The entire coastal region is popular for water sports. The seaside town of Katsurahama with stone-pine groves, bizarre rock formations and a white sandy beach can be found 8km/5mi south of Kochi (bus from the Harimayabashi Bridge, 40 minutes). The town has an aquarium and the Tosa Token Center, a stadium for dog fights; there is a pavilion on a slope that has a particularly nice view of the surrounding area during autumnal moonlit nights.

Nankoku The town of Nankoku (population 45,000) is located 10km/6mi east of Kochi (JR Otochi bus route, 30 minutes). The district of Oshino is known for breeding Onaga-dori, cockerels with black tail feathers reaching lengths of 4–7m (13–23ft).

✳ Kokubunji temple The Kokubunji temple, which belongs to the Shingon sect, is 4km/2.5mi northwest of Gomen, the railway station for Nankoku. The temple was built by the priest Gyoki in 739 and is the 29th of the 88 temples of pilgrimage on Shikoku; the main hall and two wooden statues of Yakushi-nyorai are particularly interesting.

Ryugado Cave The Ryugado dripstone cave can be found east of Gomen (bus from Kochi, 1 hour). It was discovered in 1931. 1.5km/1mi of the 4km/2.5mi cave are accessible to the public; it has attractive stalactites and sinter formations.

Cape Muroto, the southernmost point of the Muroto-Anan Coastal Quasi-National Park, extends into the Pacific (bus from Kochi, 2 hours) at the eastern end of Tosa Bay. The picturesque, rugged coastal landscape transforms into a zone of lavish, subtropical vegetation further inland; at the farthest point of the cape there is a **lighthouse** and a meteorological station. As a result of the many typhoons occurring here during the autumn months the cape has been given the nickname »Typhoon-Ginaz«. The entire strip of coastline of the Quasi-National Park, which extends around 90km/55mi northwards, is also known as »Awa-Matsushima« because of the many islands dotted in the bay, as it is reminiscent of the coastal landscape of ►Matsushima.

✷ Cape Muroto

The Hotsu-Misaki temple is not far from the cape. It was founded by Kobo-daishi in 807 and contains three Buddha statues from the Nara and Heian periods. This temple is also one of the island's 88 temples of pilgrimage. There is a particularly nice view from the Muroto coastal road.

✷ ◄ Hotsu-Misaki temple

The JR Dosan main lines departs Kochi northbound to Osugi (39km/24mi); the Yasaka shrine is 1km/0.6mi west of the station. The two magnificent cedars in its grounds have an estimated age of 2000 years. The larger of the two trees has a height of 68m/223ft and a girth of 30m/33yd.

Osugi

8km/5mi further north (Otaguchi station) is the Burakuji temple, whose main hall (Yakushido) built in 1151 is a significant example of Heian-period architecture.

✷ Burakuji temple

✷ ✷ Koya-san

Main island: Honshu   **Prefecture:** Wakayama
Population: 7000

The mountainous area known as Koya-san, at an elevation of almost 900m/3000ft, is around 70km/45mi south of►Osaka on the Kii Peninsula. It is still a very isolated area. 125 temple buildings set in a densely forested area bear witness to the heyday of Japanese Buddhism in the 9th century.

高野山

✷ ✷ Monastery settlement

The region extends 2.2km/1.5mi north-south and 5.5km/3.5mi east-west along the eastern flank of the Takamine Mountains. The temple and monastery settlement here is one of the most significant centres for the study of Buddhism and as the cradle of the Shingon sect the destination of more than a million pilgrims every year.

Nyonindo

Leaving Gokurakubashi station a cableway makes its way through some picturesque landscape, past waterfalls up to the plateau; the upper terminus is the starting point of buses to the region's most important sights. The first stop is the nyonindo (women's hall). Until 1873 women were only allowed to access the Koya-san up to this point.

✷✷
Kongobuji
temple
Opening hours:
Daily
8.30am–4.30pm,
¥ 500

After around 800m/0.5mi the access route to the Kongobuji temple branches off from the main road to the right. This main temple of the Koya-san-Shingon sect was founded in 816; the current complex was rebuilt in 1863.

The temple's founder was Kobo-daishi, who was called Kukai in his lifetime. He was born on the 15 June 774 on Shikoku and at the age of 24 wrote the *Sanogshiki*, a comparative study of Buddhism, Confucianism and Taoism. He became a monk at 25. In 804 he accompanied an imperial mission to China where he gained crucial impulses. He studied in Ch'an-an for two years and was instructed in the secret teachings of the Mi-tsung by Huikuo, a master of the Chinese Tantra school.

After his return from China in 806 he became abbot of the Todaiji temple in Nara. While searching for a place where he could spread his teachings of esoteric Buddhism he was given permission in 816 to build a monastery on Koya-san. His versatile talents also brought him great fame as a poet, calligrapher and sculptor; the authenticity of his works is not, however, always satisfactorily proven. After his death (835) Kukai was posthumously awarded the honorary title of Kobo-daishi.

The rooms of the Kongobuji have nice paintings on sliding doors, some of which are attributed to Kano Tanyu. The temple also boasts **Japan's largest rock garden**. There are several schools of the Shingon sect as well as the Buddhist university in the vicinity of the Kongobuji temple.

Further southwest the **Mieido founder's hall** lies in the middle of an old cedar and umbrella-pine grove. The hall contains a portrait of Kobo-daishi as well as a painting

Praying monk in Kongobuji temple

from 1086 that depicts Buddha's entry into nirvana. Behind the founder's hall is the Kompon-daito main pagoda (destroyed by fire several times, the current building dates to 1937), which houses five sculptures of the sitting Buddha. The kondo main hall is also one of the newer buildings (1932).

The oldest surviving building of the monastery complex is the Fudo-do (1197) east of the main hall; it is considered a national treasure. It was built during the Heian Period (8th–10th century) in the Shinden-zukuri style. The god Fudo banishes everything evil.

✷ ✷
Fudo-do

The Reiho-kan, the monastery's museum and treasury, was built south of the main hall in 1920. A number of artworks from the history of the Koya-san are on display in its rooms, including sculptures, picture scrolls and documents from several centuries (open daily 8.30am–4.30pm, ¥ 600).

✷
Reiho-kan

⊙

 VISITING KOYA-SAN

INFORMATION
Tourist information at the upper end of the cableway station
Information online: www.shukubo.jp

TRANSPORT
By rail: from Osaka (Namba station) Nankai-Dentetsu Express to Gokura-kubashi (1½ hours); from Osaka (Tennoji station) JR Hanwa and Wakayama line to Hashimoto (change in Wakayama; 2½ hours); from Osaka on the Loop Line to Shin-Imamiya, there change to the Nankai line.
By cableway: from Gokurakubashi up Koya-san (5 minutes).

ALL-IN TICKET
Inquire about the »Koyasan Free Service« package at Nankai station: it includes the outbound and return journey, any bus trips in Koya-san, reduced admission charges and discounts in some souvenir shops.

MEDITATIVE VISIT
Many temples these days are in danger of falling into disrepair and depend on

the money made from accommodation they provide for visitors. Guests are expected to participate in the Buddhist ceremonies starting at 6am.

► Food
All dishes (including those for visitors) are entirely vegetarian, such as vegetable soup, tofu, lotus roots, rice and green tea.

► Accommodation
53 temples provide accommodation here (starting at ¥ 9500 per person including two meals). The accommodation consists of tatami rooms with communal bathrooms. It is best to choose temple accommodation where some English is spoken, such as Rengejoin (2nd stop from the cableway station); the tourist information centre will make reservations. A *directory of monasteries providing accommodation* is available from Japanese tourist offices in other countries (►Information).

The great Daimon gate (1705) is located west of the main hall; it has two guard figures by the sculptor Uncho. There is a distant view to the west from here over the Kii Channel and Awaji Island.

★★
Necropolis

The main road leads eastwards to the Kukai mausoleum. First visitors reach the Ichinohashi bridge, beyond which is the necropolis with its 200,000 or so graves. It is situated in a mystic forest of ancient cedars and crossed by a 2km/1mi road.

★
Oku-no-in

The Gokusho sacrificial hall and the Torodo hall of lamps, which contains several thousand lanterns (some of them very old) donated by believers, are passed before reaching the mausoleum. The mausoleum of Kobo-daishi, the temple's founder, is called Oku-no-in and is located behind an enclosure of golden lotus leaves.

Kumamoto

F8 • c5

Main island: Kyushu   **Prefecture:** Kumamoto
Population: 644,000

熊本

Kumamoto is located in central Kyushu near Shimabara Bay, which extends inland from the west and is the connection between Lake Ariake and the open sea. The city is famous for its castle and its landscape garden Suizenji.

»City of Forests«

Kumamoto is the capital of the prefecture of the same name and the third-largest city on Kyushu. Once of historic significance, it has become one of the region's important commercial and educational centres.

The city is the trans-shipment centre for the agricultural products of the surrounding area; well-known craft products include metal-inlay works (higo-zogan; artistic swords in the past), bamboo goods, ceramics (shodai-yaki) and wooden toys. Amakusa cultivated pearls are also popular.

What to See in Kumamoto

Castle
🕐
Opening hours:
Daily
8.30am–5.30pm,
Nov–March until
4.30pm, ¥ 500

The castle can be found on Chausuyama Hill 2km/1mi northeast of the station. It was built between 1601 and 1607 for Kato Kiyomasa, the lord of Kumamoto, and was severely damaged in 1877. The complex originally contained three main buildings, 49 towers, 29 castle gates and 18 two-storey gates. Today all that remains are the castle wall, some gates and guard towers, including one that was brought here in 1600 from Uto Castle south of the city (northwestern corner tower). The castle walls are a typical example of the **technique used for building strongholds** known as »mushagaeshi«: the wall is still slightly slanted at the base, but becomes increasingly steep as it rises until it forms an overhang at the top, which was meant to make it harder for enemies to enter. The reconstructed main tower houses a historical museum. Not far from the main tower is the ginkgo tree allegedly planted by Kato; it is this tree that has earned the castle the sobriquet »Ginkgo Castle«. Information about the castle is also available in English as an audio-guide.

The Kato shrine not far north of the castle houses the lord's helmet and sword. An old stone bridge is also part of the shrine complex, which is said to be a trophy of Kato's military campaign to Korea. The prefectural **art museum** and the **crafts museum** are also north of the castle.

Kato shrine

3km/2mi north of Kumamoto station or 1km/0.6mi west of Kami-Kumamoto station visitors will find the Hommyoji temple, the main temple of the Nichiren sect on Kyushu founded by Kato in 1574. An avenue lined by cherry trees and then a stairway flanked by stone lanterns lead to the temple. Kato's tomb is further north.

Hommyoji temple

Kitaoka Park is 1km/0.6mi northwest of Kumamoto station; it contains the Bussharito pagoda built on the 133m/436ft Hanaokayama

Kitaoka Park

Kumamoto Castle is a great example of Japanese stronghold architecture

Hill in 1954 in memory of the victims of World War II. On the occasion of its completion Nehru, then prime minister of India, had some of Buddha's ashes brought here.

Fujisaki-Hachimangu shrine

The Fujisaki-Hachimangu shrine can be found 4km/2.5mi northeast of Kumamoto station (bus) or 1km/0.6mi northwest of Suizenji station; the city's protective shrine is dedicated to Emperor Ojin and holds an interesting annual festival on 15 September. The Yoshida-Tsukasake House, which contains a sumo museum, is not far away.

✳ Suizenji Park

🕐 Opening hours:
Daily 7.30am–6pm,
Dec–Feb
8.30am–5pm, ¥ 400

Take the tram or bus (20 minutes from the Kotsu Center) to get to the Suizenji Park, 5km/3mi east of the station. The park, formerly called Joju-en (65ha/160 acres), was set up in 1632 as a landscape garden for the summer residence of the Hosokawa and is **one of the country's most famous gardens**. It has miniature versions of some of the 53 landscapes on the Tokaido Road as depicted on Hiroshige's series of woodblock prints, such as Mount Fuji and Lake Biwa. Standing in the park close to a lake fed by springs are the Izumi shrine, dedicated to the ancestors of the Hosokawa family, and a tea house.

Around Kumamoto

Tatsuda Park

Tatsuda Park (in the park) northeast of the city (bus, 20 minutes, and 20 minutes on foot) is home to the Taishoji temple, a temple of the Hosokawa clan, as well as to the Koshoken tea house built by Hosokawa Tadaoki (1563–1645). The Gyobu residence is the home of the family of Hosokawa Morihiro, who was Japan's prime minister from 1993 to 1994.

 VISITING KUMAMOTO

INFORMATION
Tourist information
In the station
Tel. 0 96/3 52 37 43
Daily 8.30am–7pm

In the airport
Tel. 0 96/2 32 28 10
Daily 6.30am–9.30pm
www.manyou-kumamoto.jp

TRANSPORT
By air: from Tokyo (Haneda Airport; 1¾ hours); from Osaka (1 hour).

By rail: from Tokyo (central station) JR Sanyo shinkansen line to Fukuoka (Hakata; 5¼ hours), then JR Kagoshima main line (1¼ hours); from Beppu JR Hohi main line via Oita (3½ hours).
By bus: from Beppu via the Trans-Kyushu Expressway (4¼ hours).
Take a tram to get to the city centre.

SHOPPING
The main streets, Ginza and Shimo-dori, are lined by shopping arcades with a southern atmosphere.

Around 25km/16mi north of Kumamoto the valley of the Kikuchi River, which flows into the Ariake Sea, is an attractive recreational area with numerous spas.

Kikuchi Valley

The Kumamoto Electric Railway, a private line, runs to Kikuchi-onsen around 25km/16mi away. From the 11th to 16th centuries the castle of Kikuchi-onsen was the home of the aristocratic Kikuchi family; there are lovely walks in the pretty wooded area along the river.

Kikuchi-onsen

The JR Kagoshima main line goes to Yatsushiro (population 108,000), the largest industrial town in Kumamoto Prefecture (cement and paper factories), which is also where Koda-yaki ceramics are made. The harbour on Yatsushiro Bay is known for the **glowing sea** called »shiranui«, a phenomenon that appears in late summer.

Yatsushiro

The Hisotsu train line departs Yatsushiro and makes its way inland to Hitoyoshi (population 43,000) approx. 52km/32mi to the southeast. This town is also called the »Kyoto of Kyushu«. The former castle town on the Kumakamu River, which flows through the Hitoyoshi Basin, is now a valued spa. The Aoi-Aso shrine is 500m/550yd from the station. The main hall and a tower have survived from the time the shrine was founded (17th century).

Hitoyoshi

> ! **Baedeker TIP**
>
> **Take a boat through the rapids**
> Why not go on an exciting boat trip through the Kuma rapids? They are some of the best-known rapids in the country. The boats depart opposite the former site of the castle (1.5km/1mi southeast of Hitoyoshi station) and arrive in Osakama 18km/11mi to the west after around 2½ hours.

✶✶ Kurashiki

Main island: Honshu   **Prefecture:** Okayama
Population: 474,000

Old homes and warehouses, and canals lined by willow trees and crossed by stone bridges, make Kurashiki a worthwhile destination with a number of interesting museums; it also has plenty of cultural activities.

倉敷

Kurashiki is in the west of the Japanese main island of Honshu near the Inland Sea. Even though the city is part of the significant industrial area around Mizushima, the old town has largely held on to its character of days gone by.

Old trading town

What to See in Kurashiki

Ohashi House

Make a detour to the Ohashi House on the way to the old town. This house, built in 1796, belonged to an influential merchant family (open Tue–Sun 9am–5pm, ¥ 500).

Museums

★

Ohara Museum of Art ▸

The Ohara Museum of Art (Ohara-bijutsukan), 1km/0.6mi southeast of the station, was built by Ohara Magosaburo in 1930 in classically-inspired forms on the model of Greek temples. It exhibits **European art** (El Greco, Renoir, Monet, Gauguin, Picasso, Rodin) and works from of Japanese modernism, Middle Eastern and Far Eastern art, woodblock prints and ceramics (open Tue–Sun 9am–5pm, ¥ 1000). The **Museum of Folkcraft** (Kurashiki-mingei-kan) was set up in four former rice silos on the Kurashiki River to the east. It has ceramics, textiles, bamboo goods and more on display. The **Toy Museum** (Nihon Kyodo Gangenkan), not far away, displays around 5000 items

 VISITING KURASHIKI

INFORMATION

Tourist information
In the station, tel. 0 86/4 24 12 20
Daily 9am–7pm
In the old canal quarter near the
Museum of Folkcraft
Tel. 0 86/4 22 05 42
April–Oct 9am–6pm,
Nov–March until 5.15pm
www.kurashiki.or.jp

TRANSPORT

By air: from Tokyo (Haneda Airport) to Okayama (1¼ hours).

! *Baedeker* TIP

Ivy Square

Walk southeast from the canal to get to the Ivy Square complex. The ivy-covered brick building houses the Ivy Studio, which allows its visitors to become creative themselves: why not participate in an introduction to the various dyeing techniques, ceramic-production or paper-making (open daily except Wed 9am–5.30pm, tel. 0 86/4 22 00 11)?

By rail: from Tokyo (central station) JR Sanyo shinkansen line via Osaka and Okayama (4¼ hours).

WHERE TO STAY

▸ Luxury
Ryokan Kurashiki
Honcho 4-1, Kurashiki-shi,
Okayama-ken
Tel. 0 86/4 22 07 30
Luxury the Japanese way: sophisticated ryokan in the middle of the Bikan old town by the canal. Five individually furnished rooms with a lot of wood in an old warehouse protected as a heritage site. Everything is top class, which is reflected in the prices.

▸ Mid-range
Kurashiki Ivy Square
7-2, Honmachi, Kurashiki-shi,
Okayama-ken 710-0054
Tel. 0 86/4 22-00 11, fax 4 24-05 15
Romantic atmosphere in a former factory building used to make textiles in the Meiji period, which also houses several cultural institutions.

collected from all over Japan. On the other side of the river is the **archaeological museum** (Koko-kan), which opened in 1950. It displays artefacts from the Kibi district (modern-day Okayama Prefecture), China and South America. The **Historical Museum** (Kurashiki-rekishi-kan) is not far to the northeast. It has extensive collections from the Kamakura period (weapons, Buddhist liturgical apparatus, household items).

Kurashiki's old town is characterized by picturesque canals

Around Kurashiki

The Entsuji-en garden, home to the Entsuji temple, in which the monk Ryokan (1758–1831), a well-known calligrapher, lived for a few years, can be found approx. 3km/2mi southwest of Shin-Kurashiki station. There is a fine view of the Inland Sea from the hill on which the temple stands. **Entsuji-en**

The Kojima Peninsula extends into the Inland Sea to the south of Kurashiki (bus to Washuzan, then on foot to the mountain of the same name). There is a great panoramic view of the sea and the main island of Shikoku (ferry connection from Shimotsui harbour) from the top of the 133m/436ft Washuzan Hill. The 9.4km/6mi Seto-Ohashi bridge (six individual bridges) also connects the islands of Honshu and Shikoku. **Kojima Peninsula** ✳ ◄ Washuzan

The JR Hakubi line, which runs north from Kurashiki, goes by the town of Soja (population 51,000), the birthplace of the famous priest and painter Sesshu (1420–1506), who spent his novice years in the Hofukuji temple 1.5km/1mi north of the station. **Soja**

The next stop along the line, Gokei, is the starting place for a lovely excursion (especially during the autumn) to the attractive Gokei-kyo gorge (bus, 25 minutes), through which the Makitani River flows. **Gokei-kyo**

The Hakubi line then makes its way to Takahashi (population 26,000) on the Takahashi River with its rich fish stocks. Mount Gagyuzan (foot path, 10 minutes) rises up over its eastern riverbank with Matsuyama Castle at the top; the three-storey main tower and an exterior tower are still extant. This castle is one of the few 17th-century strongholds that was not built on the lowlands but rather in the mountains. There is a particularly lovely view of the town and the surrounding area from the Komatsu peak. At the foot of the mountain is the Gagyuzan wildlife park, which is home to troops of wild monkeys. **Takahashi** ✳ ◄ Matsuyama Castle

Kushiro

Main island: Hokkaido　　　　**Prefecture:** Hokkaido
Population: 186,000

釧路　The town of Kushiro located on Hokkaido's southeast coast is a cultural, economic and political centre of the eastern part of Japan's northernmost main island.

Japan's coldest city　Just a hundred years ago the area was still populated by the Ainu, Hokkaido's aboriginal inhabitants. Despite the severe climate and the low summertime temperatures, Kushiro is the island's only ice-free harbour besides Wakkanai further north.

What to See in and around Kushiro

Tsurugatai Park　Tsurugatai Park, which is home to the municipal museum and its exhibition of Ainu culture can be found 1.5km/1mi southeast of the station. There is a hidden Ainu settlement on the northern shore of Lake Harutori (bus from the station, 20 minutes).

Kushiro National Park　There is a bus connection (1 hour) from the station to the Kushiro National Park 20km/12mi to the northwest. The reserve, set up in a marsh area, is the last habitat of rare red-crowned cranes (tancho). There are around 600 of them and they can be watched from the wooden walkways starting at the observation centre; the best time to do this is winter. From April to September JR trains with viewing windows go through the park.

 KUSHIRO

TRANSPORT

By air: from Tokyo (Haneda Airport; 1 hours); from Sapporo (40 minutes).
By rail: from Sapporo JR Nemuro line (3½ hours).
By ferry: from Tokyo (30 hours).

EVENTS

Harbour festival (with a firework display; beginning of August), on the Kushiro River; snow festival (with numerous snow sculptures; beginning of December), in the Yone-machi Park.

Around 50km/30mi east of Kushiro the **Akkeshi Peninsula** protrudes into the bay of the same name (JR Nemuro main line, 50 minutes). The town of Akkeshi is divided by a lagoon into a northern (Shinryu) and southern (Honcho) part. The Akkeshi lagoon (32 sq km/12 sq mi) is an important oyster-farming area, and the bay is the only place in Japan where herring can be fished. The **Kokutaiji temple** can be found on the peninsula's southern coast. It was founded in 1802 and belongs to the Nanzenji school, which is part of the Rinzai sect. In 1804 it became one of Hokkaido's three mission temples.

Manshuin Garden in Kyoto in autumnal colours

✦✦ Kyoto

Main island: Honshu
Population: 1.47 million

Prefecture: Kyoto

京都

The old imperial city is one of the most significant, if not the most important, destination in Japan. Every year millions and millions of tourists both from within Japan and from overseas come to see the city. Nevertheless Kyoto has managed to maintain much of the old atmosphere, which also has something to do with the fact that it was the only Japanese city with more than a million inhabitants that remained undamaged in World War II.

The city of Kyoto, surrounded by hills, is located in the central part of the Japanese main island of Honshu, near the southwestern end of Lake Biwa; situated between the Katsura River (to the west) and the Kamo River (to the east) in a basin which is open to the south, it covers an area of more than 600 sq km/230 sq mi and is the country's seventh-largest city as well as one of its most significant industrial centres. Kyoto is also the capital of Kyoto Prefecture and the educational centre of western Japan with several colleges and universities.

Kyoto was the **imperial residence** for almost 1100 years, from 794 to 1868, making it the country's most significant cultural centre, where architecture, sculpture, painting and many other arts flourished. Buddhism had an impact on the city's arts, so that a large number of

Japan's cultural centre

the surviving works can be found in the old temples. Kyoto still has a dominant role in Japan's religious life; 30 of the city's temples are centres of the various Buddhist sects. In addition there are around 200 Shinto shrines in the city.

History In 794, ten years after the seat of government had been moved from Nara to Nagaoka, Emperor Kammu had the country's new capital built on the site of the village of Uda, to the northeast of where Kyoto is today; initially it was called Heiankyo (»capital of peace«), then Miyako (»imperial residence«) and since the Meiji period Kyoto (»capital«).

The model of China ▶ The city was built on a rectangular grid-pattern layout, modelled on the Chinese urban pattern used in Xian. It was surrounded by walls and a double ditch. It extended 5.2km/3.2mi in a north-south direction and 4.4km/2.7mi in an east-west direction. To the south of the Daidairi imperial palace the 83m/91yd wide Suzaku-oji road marks the dividing line between the eastern part of the city (Sakyo) and the western part (Ukyo). There are 18 gates from which to access the city. The city is already said to have had 400,000 inhabitants in the year it was founded. Parts were destroyed on numerous occasions by earthquakes or fire. The imperial palace was the centre and the nine main east-west roads are still numbered nos. 1, 2, 3, etc. from north to south. In the years 960, 1177 and 1227 the imperial palace burned down and was not rebuilt after the last fire.

Highlights *Kyoto*

Nishiki Market
Every Japanese ingredient the heart desires to cook with or to serve as it is can be found here
▶ page 344

Nishi-Honganji temple
A most beautiful example of Buddhist architecture with wonderful paintings.
▶ page 348

Sanjusangen-do
1001 golden Kannon statues stand in a line here.
▶ page 349

Kiyomizu temple
There is a far-reaching view from the veranda of this wooden temple perched on a steep cliff.
▶ page 350

Nijo-jo
Once the residence of the powerful shogun, now visitors wander across the nightingale floor.
▶ page 356

Fushimi-Inari shrine
An avenue of red torii leads to the shrine of the goddess of rice cultivation.
▶ page 362

Ryoan-ji
A stone garden belonging to the temple invites visitors to do some quiet contemplation.
▶ page 366

Kinkakuji
This consummate pavilion radiates in a golden shimmer, reflected in the temple garden.
▶ page 367

In the early 9th century the imperial family, which was increasingly committed to non-political matters, already stood in the shadow of the **Fujiwara family**, which took possession of all key political positions. Later the empire came under increasing pressure from the militant monasteries of the surrounding area. Unrest led to the Taira coming to power, who in turn were decisively defeated at the Battle of Dannoura by the Minamoto clan in 1185. Minamoto Yoritomo (1147–99), proclaimed shogun by the emperor, moved the seat of government to Kamakura and the disempowered imperial family limited itself to promoting culture and the arts; life at court reached the highest degree of sophistication.

◄ Loss of power of the imperial family

Emperor Godaigo (1288–1339), who ascended the throne in 1318, decided to offer resistance to the Kamakura shogunate; his commander, Ashikaga Takauji, who had fought successfully against the shogunate, invaded Kyoto himself in 1336, drove away Godaigo and enthroned Komyo (d. 1380) as a rival emperor. In 1392 the southern court, which Godaigo had set up in Yoshino while in exile, waived its claim to power so that Kyoto remained the unchallenged seat of government. In 1467 new fighting erupted over the disputed succession of the Ashikaga. At the end of these **Onin Wars** (1477) Kyoto was reduced to rubble. At the emperor's request Oda Nobunaga went to Kyoto in 1568 and began reconstruction of the old imperial palace and the city. After his death Toyotomi Hideyoshi continued his work. The peace he managed to bring to the whole country allowed a new golden age and Kyoto became the centre of the Japanese renaissance.

◄ Fighting for Kyoto

Nevertheless, governing power remained in the hands of the shoguns, and the city's political significance came to an end when Tokugawa Ieyasu (1542–1616) moved the seat of government to Edo, modern-day Tokyo. Yet again disastrous fires destroyed parts of the city in 1708 and 1788. Kyoto sustained the most severe damage in the earthquake of 1830. The decision of the shogunate in Edo to open up Japan to the outside world after centuries of isolation strengthened the position of the imperial family, which had been opposed to the isolation policy; with the subsequent abolition of the shogunate in 1867 the imperial family came to power again. However, since Emperor Meiji also moved his seat of government to Edo in 1869, Kyoto continued to remain politically insignificant. By imperial decree, however, Kyoto did remain the city where the Japanese rulers are enthroned.

◄ Loss of the positions of power

✳ Around the Station

Visitors are greeted with a surprise upon arrival in Kyoto: a highly modern station in the old imperial city which seems to be the epitome of Japanese tradition. Indeed, not all of Kyoto's inhabitants find this new building by the architect Hara Hiroshi, which was opened in 1997, suitable, but it is definitely impressive. There is a good view of the surrounding area from the skywalk.

Kyoto station

Kyoto – Nozomi Express arrives at the station

Kyoto Tower Building

Only a few steps north of the central station in the Shimogyo-ku district is the nine-storey Kyoto Tower Building, which together with the Kyoto Tower on the roof of the building has a height of 131m/ 430ft.

Higashi-Honganji temple

Not far to the north (Karasuma-Shichijo) is the Higashi-Honganji, a temple founded in 1602 by the Jodo-Shinshu sect; it was destroyed several times and last renewed in 1859.

The Jodo-shinshu sect was **founded** in 1224 and goes back to Shin-ran-shonin (alias Keishin-daishi, 1173–1262). He had spent several years on the monastic Mount Hiei northeast of Kyoto, after which he became a pupil of the founder of the Jodo sect, Ho-nen, who inspired him to found the Jodo-shinshu. At the core of this new teaching was the belief in Amida-Buddha, who would bring complete salvation, and the rejection of celibacy. This sect's increasing influence also moved Ieyasu to divide the Honganji temple in 1602; he founded the Otani school in the Higashi-Honganji temple. The original Honganji subsequently became the Nishi-Honganji. Only the founder's hall and the main hall are freely accessible; the latter is however being renovated until 2011.

Kyoto Map

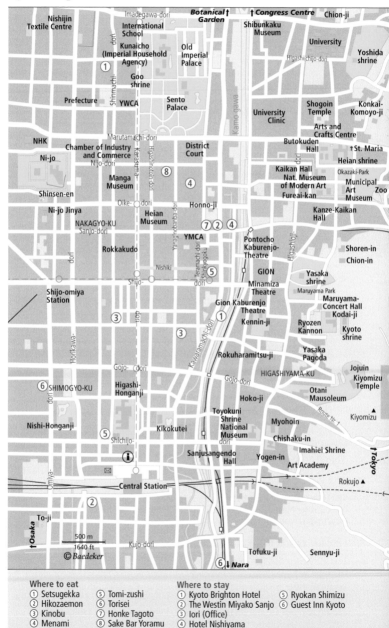

Where to eat
① Setsugekka   ⑤ Tomi-zushi
② Hikozaemon   ⑥ Torisei
③ Kinobu   ⑦ Honke Tagoto
④ Menami   ⑧ Sake Bar Yoramu

Where to stay
① Kyoto Brighton Hotel   ⑤ Ryokan Shimizu
② The Westin Miyako Sanjo   ⑥ Guest Inn Kyoto
③ Iori (Office)
④ Hotel Nishiyama

⏵ VISITING KYOTO

INFORMATION

Tourist information

Kyoto International Center,
in the station building, 9th floor
(the information centre on the 2nd
floor is for Japanese tourists),
accessible via a lift in the Isetan
department store
Tel. 0 75/3 44 33 00
Daily except for the 2nd and 4th Tue
of the month 10am–6pm
www.pref.kyoto.jp/visitkyoto/en
www.city.kyoto.lg.jp
http://raku.city.kyoto.jp

TRANSPORT

By rail: Kyoto is the junction of the
JR Tokaido shinkansen line, the JR
Tokaido main line, the JR San-in line
and the Nara lines. From Tokyo
(central station) JR
Tokaido shinkansen line (Hikari 3
hours, Kodama 4 hours); from Nagoya JR Tokaido shinkansen line
(Hikari 50 minutes, Kodama 1 hours);
from Osaka JR Tokaido shinkansen or
main line (20 minutes or 45 minutes
respectively); from
Nara Kinki-Nippon private train line
(40 minutes) and JR Nara line (1
hour).
By bus: from Osaka (airport; 1½
hours).
Airport transfer: an express train
departs the central station for Kansai
International Airport (KIX, 75 minutes) and there is also a bus (1¾
hours, reservations necessary, tel.
0 75/6 82 44 00).

LOCAL TRANSPORT

It is easier for foreign tourists to *find
the way* in Kyoto than it is in other
Japanese cities because the streets are
laid out in a grid pattern: the major
east-west roads are numbered or have
names; the main road is Shijo-dori
(4th street), and the north-south
roads also have names. Kyoto is a
great city to *explore on foot* for those
with the necessary stamina. Many
pretty corners are waiting to be
discovered on walks through the city.
Maps and brochures, available from
the tourist information centres, make
suggestions for this.

Buses: buses depart from the station
to all of the city's attractions. It is best
to acquire the English version of the
Raku Bus Map, which contains all the
important information about taking
the bus in Kyoto. The lines most
important for tourists are 100, 101
and 102. They all go past the most
important sights. A simple trip in the
centre costs ¥ 220 (pay the driver
before exiting), a day pass just for
Kyoto city buses ¥ 500.
There are also two *underground lines*:
the Karasuma line connects north and
south Kyoto, and the Tozai line goes
back and forth between southeast and
west Kyoto. The lines cross at Kar-
asuma-Oike station. A trip costs a
minimum of ¥ 200. A day pass for city
buses, suburban buses and the
underground lines costs ¥ 1200 (2
days cost ¥ 2000). The underground
runs from 5.30am to 11pm.
Some destinations, such as Arashiyama in the west of the city, can be
reached faster on the *private lines*
(Hankyu, Keifuku or Eizan).
Those who are not in possession of a
JR Rail Pass and would like to travel
around the whole region should
inquire about the *Surutto Kansai
Thru Pass* in the station; it allows the
use of the underground, private train
lines and buses in Osaka, Kobe and
Kyoto for two (¥ 3800) or three

(¥ 5000) days; it also gives discounts to various attractions (more information at www.surutto.com/conts/ticket).

ADVANCE BOOKINGS FOR ATTRACTIONS

Visits to the following sights (guided tours in English) have to be booked in advance with the *Imperial Household Agency;* a passport must be shown:

Kyoto Gosho (old imperial palace, guided tours Mon–Fri at 10am and 2pm, reservations possible up to 20 minutes beforehand).
Katsura Rikyu (imperial villa, guided tours Mon–Fri at 9am, 10am, 11am, 1.30pm, 2pm, 3pm).
Shugaku-in Rikyu (guided tour Mon–Fri at 9am, 10am, 11am, 1.30pm and 3pm).
Sento Gosho (guided tour Mon–Fri 11am and 1.30pm, as well as every 3rd Sat of the month and every Sat in April, May, Oct and Nov).

With the exception of the Kyoto Gosho visitors must be over the age of 18 (or be accompanied by someone over 18). While it is theoretically possible to queue up 20 minutes before the time of the tour, to be sure of a place should book the desired tour by internet in good time (three months in advance).

Imperial Household Agency, Kunaicho
In the imperial park near the Kyoto Gosho, 3 Kyotogyoen, Kamigyo-ku
Tel. 0 75/2 11 12 15
Mon–Fri 8.45am–noon
and 1pm–4pm
http://sankan.kunaicho.go.jp/english

EVENTS

January: first shrine visit (believers take a flame of the holy fire with which they prepare the first meal of the new year; beginning of Jan), at the Yasaka shrine. Hadaka-odori (dance of the naked men; mid-Jan), in the Hokaiji temple; Toshiya (traditional archery; mid-Jan), at the Sanjusangen-do.
February: Baika-sai (plum blossom festival with an outdoor tea ceremony, end of Feb), at the Kitano shrine.
March: Hina-matsuri (puppet festival; beginning of March), in the Hokyoji temple; Nehan-e (Nirvana ceremony on the anniversary of Buddha's death; mid-March), in several temples, such as in the Tofukuji and Seiryoji temples.
April: Miyako-odori (cherry blossom dances; April/May), in the Gion-

Gion-matsuri in July is one of the most important religious festivals

Kaburenjo Theatre; Hana-matsuri (Buddha's birthday; beginning of April), in all of the temples; Taiko-no-Hanami Gyoretsu (cherry blossom procession; 2nd Sun), at the Daigoji temple; Matsunoo-matsuri (procession with portable shrines; 4th Sun), at the Matsunoo shrine.

May: Kamogawa-odori (Geisha dances; early to mid-May), in the Pontocho-Kaburenjo Theatre; Aoi-matsuri (procession with historic costumes, shrine ceremony; mid-May), in the Kamigamo and the Shimogamo shrine; Mifune-matsuri (boat festival on the Oi River; 3rd Sun), at the Kurumazaki shrine.

June: Takigi-no (night-time performance of No dramas; beginning of June), at the Heian shrine.

July: Cormorant fishing (night-time fishing with trained birds; July–Aug), in Arashiyama; Gion-matsuri (procession with 29 large floats, going back to the year 876; mid-July), starting at the Yasaka shrine; O-taue-matsuri (rice planting festival; end of July), at the Matsunoo shrine.

August: Daimonji-gozan-okuribi (lighting of fires making written characters on the mountain slopes; mid-Aug); Toronagashi (lantern festival; mid-Aug), in Arashiyama Park; Matsuage (fire festival on the riverbank; end of Aug), in Hanase; Jizo-bon (festival for the patron god of children; end of Aug), in several temples.

September: Hassaku-sai (harvest festival; 1st Sun), in the Matsuo shrine; Karasu-sumo (child wrestling; beginning of Sept), in the Kamigamo shrine.

October: Zuiki-matsuri (procession with floats; beginning of Oct), at the Kitano-Temmangu shrine; Kamogawa-odori (Geisha dances; Oct–Nov), in the Pontocho-Kaburenjo Theatre; Ushi-matsuri (play in traditional costumes; mid-Oct), in the Koryuji tem-

ple; Jidai-matsuri (festival commemorating the city's founding in 794, large procession in historical costumes; end of Oct), leaving the Heian shrine.

November: Momiji-matsuri (boat trips in the style of the 10th century; 2nd Sun), in Arashiyama Park.

December: Kaomise (Kabuki performances), in the Minamiza Theatre; Shimai-Kobo (commemorative ceremony for Kobo-daishi; end of Dec), in the Toji temple.

The highly recommendable *Kyoto Visitor's Guide*, which appears every month in English, lists events as well as restaurants, accommodation and shops. Available from the tourist information centres, various museums and other public institutions. Online: www.kyotoguide.com.

SHOPPING

Kyoto is a shopping paradise and known for its high-quality arts and crafts such as fans, lacquerware, ceramics and silk.

A large range of *craft goods* can be found in the Kyoto Handicraft Center, Marutamachi, north of the Heinan shrine (tel. 0 75/7 61 80 01, daily 10am–6pm, www.khc-kyoto.jp) and in the souvenir shop of the Museum of Traditional Crafts, Fureai-kan, somewhat south of the Heian shrine.

The best places to buy *ceramic goods* are to be found on the way to the Kiyomizudera, at the Kiyomizuzaka, Sannenzaka and Ninenzaka.

Popular *shopping districts* are the area around the crossing of Shijo-dori and Kawaramachi-dori, where visitors will also find the large department stores; the Teramachi and Shinkyogoku shopping streets as well as the impressive *Nishiki Market*, which sells food, are not far away. Teramachi Street (coming from the Takashimaya department store, to the left not far from the entrance) has an old, very atmospheric *tea shop* called Horaido (www.kyoto-teramachi.or.jp/horaido). Also in Teramachi on the left side somewhat further up the street a shop called Daishodo sells old woodblock prints (daily except Wed 11am–8pm). The famous *Japanese kitchen knives* and other kitchen equipment can be found in Aritsugu, in Nishiki Street not far from the Teramachi shopping street (www.aritsugu.com, 9am–5.30pm). The Shinkyogoku shopping street is home to a shop called Iwai, which has a large selection of *souvenirs*; its website will give a good impression of the kind of items it sells (www.kyoto-iwai.co.jp); although it is in Japanese, a click on the headings will open pictures. Traditional Japanese *sweets* can be bought in the well-established Kagizen Yoshifusa shop in Gion on the north side of the Shijio-dori, west of the Hanami-koji (Tue–Sun 9am–6pm, until 7pm at weekends). The *central station* is also a lively shopping area, with its many restaurants, cafés, shops and the Isetan department store

Anyone who has the chance should definitely visit one of Kyoto's *flea markets*. The most famous one is »Kobo-san« near the Toji temple (every 21st of the month). It sells many antiques, old kimonos, ceramics and a lot of knick-knacks. On the 25th of every month a similar market is held at the Kitano Tenmangu shrine, which is known as the »Tenjin-san«. There are other markets; to find out when they take place contact the tourist information centres.

WHERE TO EAT
▶ Expensive
① *Setsugekka*
Shimogyo-ku, Kiyamachi-dori, Bukkoji-sagaru, Higashigawa
Tel. 0 75/3 42 17 77
www.kyoto-hanatsubaki.co.jp
11am–3pm and 5.30pm–11pm
One of the most romantic restaurants on the Kamogawa with places to sit outside on a kind of wooden terrace over the river (May–Sept). Serves Kaiseki cuisine amongst other things. Lunch is significantly cheaper.

② *Hikozaemon*
Nakagyo-ku, Sanjo-dori, Teramachi, Higashi-iru, Ishibashi-cho 19
Tel. 0 75/2 29 69 29
Mon–Fri 11am–2pm
and 5pm–11pm,
Sat and Sun 11am–11pm
Stylish restaurant in an old ryokan with separate tatami dining rooms. Specializes in beef. Serves shabu-shabu amongst other things. English menu.

③ *Kinobu*
Shimogyo-ku, Shinmachi-dori, Bukkoji-sagaru, 416 Iwatoyamacho
Tel. 0 753 52 00 01
Daily 11am–2.30pm and 5pm–9.30pm
This elegant restaurant decorated in the country's typical style serves traditional Kyoto cuisine (only Japanese).

▶ Moderate
④ *Menami*
Nakagyo-ku, Kiyamachi
Sanjo-agaru
Tel. 0 75/2 31 10 95
Mon–Sat 5pm–11pm
This restaurant is popular with the locals and the right place to try traditional Kyoto cuisine (Obanzai): although there is no English menu, the food can be found in large bowls on the counter. Just point to the desired

dish. Since there are no actual main dishes, it is best to order several things at once.

⑤ **Tomi-zushi**
Nakagyo-ku, Shinkyogoku-dori, Shijo-agaru, Higashi-iru, Nakanomachi 578-5
Tel. 0 75/2 31 36 28
Daily except Thu 5pm–midnight
Popular sushi restaurant centrally located next to Shinkyogoku shopping street. It can be recognized by the large red lantern above its entrance.

⑥ **Torisei**
Fushimi-ku, 186 Kamiaburakake-cho
Tel. 075/6 22 55 33
Tue–Sun 11am–10pm
The bar belongs to a sake brewery and occupies the storage cellar. Chicken dishes are the house speciality (only Japanese).

▶ **Inexpensive**
⑦ **Honke Tagoto**
Nakagyo-ku, 12 Sanjo-dori, Teramachi Higashi-iru
Tel. 0 75/2 21 30 30
Daily 11am–9pm
Comfortable soba restaurant with a long tradition (established in 1868). During the summer it is possible to enjoy *zaru-soba* (cold noodles) here.

GOING OUT

The city's traditional *entertainment districts* are Gion and Pontocho, which is not just where all the restaurants, bars and hostess clubs are to be found, but also where the city's *geishas* are at home. Their dancing skills (Kyomai, »Kyoto dance«) can be admired several times a year (April–May and Oct–Nov) in the Pontocho Kaburenjo theatre amongst others. In addition there are regular short pro-

Delicious – Japanese soba noodles

grammes in the context of performances of different Japanese traditional
arts for tourists (and correspondingly
commercial) at Gion Corner, Yasaka
Hall (Gion, Hanamikoji Shijo-sagaru,
tel. 0 75/5 61 11 19).

The best place to go for an evening
stroll in Ponotocho is the river,
particularly during the summer when
many restaurants have outside seating.
The local geisha houses are generally
closed to foreigners. This kind of
entertainment is hardly affordable for
mere mortals anyway.

A visit to one of the *beer gardens* that
open on the roofs of several hotels
during the summer are however quite
affordable; one of them is the New
Miyako Hotel opposite the station
(south side), exit Hachijo Central.
Fans of *sake* should give the
⑧ *Yoramu sake bar* in Nakagyo-ku
a try; it serves all sorts of varieties
(including a taster set consisting of
three varieties) in a cosy atmosphere.
The Israeli innkeeper is a sake connoisseur and likes to share what he
knows (daily except Mon and 1st Sun
of the month, 6pm–midnight, south
side of the Nijo-dori, near its intersection with the Higashi-no-toin-dori,
tel. 2 13 15 12).

WHERE TO STAY
► **Luxury**
① *Kyoto Brighton Hotel*
Nakadachiura, Shinmachi-dori,
Kamigyo-ku, 602-8071 Kyoto
Tel. 075/4 41-44 11
Fax 4 31-23 60
www.brightonhotels.co.jp/kyoto-e
This hotel, only around ten minutes'
walk away from the imperial palace, is
a member of the Leading Hotels of the
World; it offers a traditional atmosphere, comfortably furnished rooms as
well as excellent cuisine in each of its
various restaurants (including French

cuisine in Vis-à-Vis; Chinese cuisine in
Kakan). The open-air swimming pool
is on the second floor.

② *The Westin Miyako Sanjo*
Keage, Higashiyama-ku,
605-0052 Kyoto
Tel. 075/7 71-71 11
Fax 7 51-24 90
www.westinmiyako-kyoto.com
This hotel is around 75 minutes away
from the International Kansai Airport;
it is situated on a hillside, giving its
rooms excellent views. This hotel is
also one of the Leading Hotels of the
World; the deluxe Western-style rooms
and the traditional Japanese rooms in
an elegant neighbouring guesthouse
with a garden have provided accommodation for many high-ranking and
famous people. In addition to a heated
indoor pool, an outdoor swimming
pool and a beauty salon the hotel also
has banquet and convention facilities
as well as a tennis court.

Baedeker recommendation

③ *Iori*
Shimogyo-ku, Tominokoji-dori,
Takatsuji-agaru, Sujiya-cho 144-6,
600-8061 Kyoto
Tel. 0 75/3 52 02 11
www.kyoto-machiya.com
Six old Kyoto town houses (machiya) have
been lovingly restored and tastefully decorated. They are available to tourists for both
short-term and long-term stays. Visitors
always have to book the entire house. Upon
arrival guests should go to the address listed
above, from where they will then be taken to
the house. For groups of four the Ebisuya-
cho is not too expensive at ¥ 40,000;
otherwise visitors have to pay a relatively
high price for privacy and such stylish
surroundings.

▶ Mid-range

④ *Hotel Nishiyama*

Gokomachi St, Nijo-sagaru,
Nakagyo-ku,
604-0933 Kyoto
Tel. 075 / 2 22 11 66
www.ryokan-kyoto.com
25 Japanese-style rooms, most of them
with their own bathrooms, but there is
also a communal bath with a view of
the Japanese garden. Inviting entrance
with a Noren curtain and lantern.
Curfew at midnight.

⑤ *Ryokan Shimizu*

644 Kagiyacho, Wakamiya,
Agaru Shichijo, Shimogyo-ku,
600-8317 Kyoto
Tel. 075/3 71 55 38
www.kyoto-shimizu.net

A modern hotel opened in 2002, but
built in the traditional style. Close to
the station. Clean and friendly. 12
rooms with bathrooms, also a communal bath. Good Japanese breakfast.
Bicycle rental.

▶ Budget

⑥ *Guest Inn Kyoto*

174-5 Hanaya-cho, Kushige,
Nishiiru, Yakuencho, Shimogyo-ku
Tel. 0 75/3 41 13 44
www.guest-inn-kyoto.jp
Friendly Japanese-style guesthouse
close to the station. Rooms with
bathrooms starting at ¥ 3500 per
person. Bicycle rental. Bus 206 to the
Shimabara-guchi stop, then westwards
through the Shimabara shopping
street.

A walk through the Higashi-Honganji ▶ Pass through the large two-storey Daishi-do-mon gate to get to the **Daishi-do**, the founder's hall, which is supported by massive wooden columns. It houses a statue of Shinran that was allegedly carved by the sect's founder himself. Towards the south the hall is connected via a gallery to the **Hondo**, the main hall, where there is an Amida statue sculpted by the artist Kaikei. The smaller, locked north gate, the Chokushi-mon (gate for imperial delegates), is of interest. In addition to Amida statues by Shotoku-taishi the temple also possesses the original of the sect's teachings (Kyogyoshinsho) as written by Shinran. Another interesting sight is a rope made of women's hair (rezuna). The hair was »donated« when ropes were needed to get the wood needed to build the temple to the construction site. The 17th-century **Shosei-en** garden is quite impressive; it was created by Ishikawa Jozan and Kobori Enshu.

★ ★
Nishi-Honganji temple Go westwards from the temple to the Horikawa-dori (Nishi-Rokujo) to get to the Nishi-Honganji, the main temple of the original Jodoshinshu sect. It is the most beautiful example of Buddhist architecture and also a **World Heritage Site**. The main hall, Amida-do, was rebuilt in 1760; it contains highly ornamented rooms with paintings on gold ground by unknown masters of the Kano school and an Amida statue by a master of the Kasuga school. The side rooms house statues of Shotoku-taishi (573–621) and the priest Ho-nen (1133–1212). The Goei-do founder's hall from 1636 holds one of the sect's **special treasures**: a statue of Shinran seated, presumably a

self-representation dating from 1244. After Shinran's death it was given a coat of lacquer into which his ashes had been mixed.

South of the Nishi-Honganji, on the other side of the train tracks in the Minami-ku district is the Toji temple (also Kyoo-gokokuji; World Heritage Site), which was founded in 796. In 823 the temple was given to the founder of the Shingon sect, Kobo-daishi. After the destruction caused by the civil war of the 15th century the temple was rebuilt; the main hall, built by Toyotomi Hideyoshi in 1603, is one of the largest Buddhist buildings still extant from the Momoyama period. The construction of **Japan's highest pagoda** (56m/ 184ft) goes back to Tokugawa Iemitsu. Also worth seeing are the founder's hall (1380), the Rengemon gate (1191) and the lecture hall of 1598. The **Temple Museum**, built in 1197 using the azekura-zukuri (▶Nara, p.421) technique, houses some significant works of art.

✳
Toji temple

The five-storey pagoda of Toji temple

Higashiyama-ku

The district of Higashiyama-ku can be found to the east of the central station. This »eastern mountain« district protects Kyoto from the evil spirits coming from this direction; for that reason a particularly large number of temples and shrines are to be found on the slopes of these mountains.

The first temple on the other side of the Kamo River is the Sanjusan-gen-do (also Rengyoin temple, founded in 1164), whose buildings were renewed in 1266 after a fire (bus 206, 208, 100 from the station). The temple's name (»Sanju-San« means »33«) comes from the 33 spaces between the supporting pillars. Its most significant artwork is the wooden statue of the seated thousand-handed Kannon; 1000 small Kannon statues stand to its left and right. The **»thousand-handed Kannon«** only needs 40 hands by the way, because she can save 25 worlds with each of them. The 21st pair are folded in prayer. The statues of her 28 disciples as well as those of the god of wind and the god of thunder stand in front of her. All of the sculptures were made by Unkei, Tankei and their pupils (open April–Nov 8am–5pm, Dec–March 9am–4pm, ¥ 600).

✳ ✳
Sanjusangen-do

National Museum

Opposite to the north is the National Museum of 1897 with exhibits from the country's history, arts and crafts from the Heian to the Edo period, an overview of the east Asian cultures and a multimedia exhibition centre (open Tue–Sun 9.30am–5pm, ¥ 420, 2nd and 4th Sat of the month free admission, www.kyokaku.go.jp).

Chishaku-in-temple

To the east, beyond the Higashi-Oji-dori road, is the Chishaku-in temple, the main temple of the Chizan school, which is part of the Shingon sect. The temple was originally built in Kii province (modern-day Wakayama Prefecture); in 1598 Tokugawa Ieyasu ordered it to be moved to its current location. The garden was made by Sen-no Rikyu (1522–91).

Myohoin temple

A bit further north is the Myohoin temple, which belongs to the Tendai sect. It was brought here from Mount Hiei. The great hall contains pictures by Kano Eitoku (1543–90) and Kano Shoei (1519–92); the temple also possesses art that once belonged to Toyotomi Hideyoshi. More than 500 steps lead up to the Hokokubyo (Hideyoshi's tomb) with a five-storey pagoda and a funerary shrine restored in 1897.

Kiyomizu temple

🕐 Opening hours: Daily 6am–6.30pm, in the winter until 6pm, ¥ 300

Kiyomizu Hill rises up further to the northeast, on which the temple of the same name stands (bus 100 or 206 to the Gojo-zaka bus stop). The road to the temple goes past numerous pottery shops. The temple consecrated to the eleven-headed Kannon was founded in 798 and is reminiscent of the unification of Buddhism with Shinto.

The temple complex, which is listed as a World Heritage Site, is accessed through the two-storey Seimon gate (western gate), whose side niches contain guard figures (Kongo-Rikishi). The bell-tower and the three-storey pagoda are not far away. The scripture hall (Kyodo), the founder's hall (Tamurado) and the Asakura Hall (Asakurado) built by Asakura Sadagake (1473–1512) are next. Behind them is the Hondo, the main hall, with a wooden veranda erected over the bluff. It has a lovely view of Kyoto and the surrounding Hills. Here Buddhist pilgrims clad in white are given the temple seal in their letter of pilgrimage. The Japanese call a daredevil act »jumping from the veranda of the Kiyomizu temple«.

Love stones ►

To the left behind the main hall a few steps lead up to the »love stones«, which are easily overlooked. Many young girls dare to tackle this test: if they are able to walk blindfold from the large starting stone to the end stone 20m/22yd away without making a mistake, their secret wish for a steady partner will come true: occasion enough for spontaneous joy and laughter.

Eastern complex ►

The Shakado and Amidado halls can be found in the eastern part of the temple complex and below them the Otowa waterfall, where the Fudo-Myo-o deity, which punishes evil people, is worshipped. Pilgrims drink from the water, which is said to have a **healing effect**. Numerous restaurants line the path leading down the Hill. It is best

Only the foolhardy dare jump off the veranda of Kiyomizu temple

to take the left-hand path from the temple complex down to the city. It goes through a huge Buddhist cemetery.

At the Hill's western foot is the 39m/128ft five-storey Yasaka Pagoda (14th–15th century, renewed in 1618); not far to the northeast is the Kodaiji temple built by Toyotomi Hideyoshi's widow in 1606. The temple's founder's hall (Kaisando) is decorated inside with pictures from the Kano school; the nearby funerary shrine (1606) contains nice lacquer works (tata-makie). The two small pavilions, which stand on a knoll, used to belong to Fushimi Castle. The landscape garden by Kobori Enshu is worth a visit.

Yasaka Pagoda
Kodaiji temple

✷ Gionmachi

Take a bus (100, 206) or the underground to Shijo-dori with a short walk to Kawaramachi to get from the central station to the Gionma-chi district further to the northeast. It is home to several entertainment establishments; however Kyoto's nightlife is quite pricey. Of

Entertainment
district

Woman in a traditional kimono in Gionmachi

note are the Minamiza Theatre, one of Japan's oldest (built at the beginning of the 17th century), and Gion Corner, where performances of traditional arts such as the tea ceremony, puppet shows, music, dancing and flower arranging are held. There are many restaurants in the narrow streets.

The **Yasaka shrine** (also known as the Gion shrine) is at the Gion bus stop; it is consecrated to the deity Susanoo-no-mikoto and his wife Inadahime, as well as their sons. The buildings from 1854 are replicas of the original architecture. The main shrine is covered in shingles made of cypress wood; south of it is a 9.5m/31ft stone torii. The shrine's art treasures include the wooden koma-inu (lion-like animal figures), attributed to the sculptor Unkei. Gion-matsuri, celebrated in July, is one of the country's largest festivals.

Maruyama Park forms the shrine complex's eastern extension. It can be found at the foot of Higashiyama Hill and is particularly lovely during the **cherry blossom** (it is lit up at night).

Chion-in temple Follow the road separating the Yasaka shrine from Maruyama Park northwards to get to the Chion-in, one of the country's most extensive temple complexes. It was founded by the priest Genchi as the centre of the Jodo sect in 1234. The main hall and the priests' homes date back to the 17th century. The 24m/80ft main gate, the sammon, is **Japan's largest temple gate**. The main hall and the assembly hall are connected by a corridor, whose floor is constructed in such a way to produce a squeaking sound at every step. This prevents anyone from coming up unnoticed. Behind the assembly hall (also called the »hall of a thousand mats«, although it only has 360 mats) are the priests' homes, whose folding screens are decorated with works by the Kano school. The adjoining garden is attributed to Kobori Enshu, but was probably only created at a later date. There is a **belfry** southeast of the temple; its bell was cast in 1633 and is allegedly the largest in Japan. It is rung in remembrance of the sect's founder around 19 April and at New Year. The sutra library, Kyozo, from 1616, contains sutras from the time of the Sung dynasty; the Kara-mon gate from the same year and Honen's tomb are also worth seeing.

The Shoren-in temple (also known as the Awata Palace) is to the north; it is the residence of the abbots from the Enryakuji temple (Mount Hiei). The main hall (renewed in 1895) contains folding screens with works by Kano Mitsunobu, Kano Motonobu and Sumiyoshi Gukei; also notable is the neat landscape garden created by Soami and Kobori Enshu.

Shoren-in temple

Sakyo-ku

The Heian shrine can be reached from the Kumano-jinja-mae bus stop in the district of Sakyo-ku. It was built in 1895 to commemorate the 1100th anniversary of the city's founding and is dedicated to the founder, Emperor Kammu, as well as to the last emperor to reside here, Emperor Komei. The complex is a smaller **copy of the first imperial palace of 794**. Go through the large entrance gate and the red Ote-mon gate to get to the great state hall (Daigokuden), the eastern and western main halls (honden) as well as the pagodas to the side. The back part of the complex has an attractive landscape garden with pink-blossoming sakura cherry trees and numerous artificial lakes covered in water lilies, which can be crossed on stepping stones.

Heian shrine

Okazaki Park is just a stone's throw to the southeast of the Heian shrine; it is bordered by a waterway connecting Lake Biwa with the Kamo River. The 8.7ha/21.5-acre complex is home to the National Museum of Modern Art, the Municipal Museum of Art, the city hall, a library and a zoo.

Cherry blossom at Heian shrine

! Baedeker TIP

A rewarding walk
Strolling along the Philosophers' Walk (Tetsugaku-no-michi) is particularly enjoyable during the cherry blossom in the spring and when the leaves turn red in the autumn. It is a good idea to come here on a weekday, when it is less crowded. On the way visit the Eidando temple, which contains an unusual statue of an Amida Buddha looking back over his shoulder.

Nanzenji temple

The Nanzenji temple, which belongs to the Rinzai sect, can be found to the east, close to Okazaki Park in the middle of a spruce grove. It was founded in 1293. The current buildings are reconstructions from the time of Tokogawa Ieyasu. The main gate (sammon) of 1628 contains ceiling paintings by the Kano school. The main hall was rebuilt after a fire in 1895. The Daihojo, the priests' home, a former residence hall of the imperial palace, which was given to the temple in 1611, also contains works by the Kano school. A famous painting by Kano Tan'yu (1602–74), *Tiger in Bamboo Grove*, is in the smaller room, Shohojo, which used to be part of the Fushimi Castle. The veranda overlooks the **famous early 17th-century Zen garden**. The temple grounds have twelve smaller temples, including the Nanzen-in, temporarily the home of Emperor Kameyama (1249–1305), which also has a garden from the 14th century. Konchi-in's garden was created in the 17th century. The tombs of Daimei-kokushi, the founder of the Nanzenji, and Hosokawa Yusai, a scholar and poet (1534–1610), can be found near the Tenjuan temple.

★★
Ginkakuji temple

The »**Philosophers' Walk**« (30 minutes) runs along the hillside next to the Biwakosui stream up to a causeway full of cherry trees (blossom in April) and further northwards to the Ginkakuji temple, also called the Silver Pavilion or Jishoji (Ginkakuji-mae bus stop). The complex was built in 1482, originally as Ashikaga Yoshimasa's country residence; after his death it was transformed into a temple. The silver paintwork, from which the temple gets its sobriquet, was never carried out, however. The buildings frame a Zen garden of white sand created by Soami. The two-storey pavilion contains a gilded Kannon statue (not accessible); the Butsuden Buddha hall houses a standing Buddha statue and the Jogudo statue further east a statue of Yoshimasa. The small tea room in the northeastern part of the hall is thought to be the country's oldest.

The Ginkakuji-michi bus stop is just to the west of the temple; take bus no. 5 northbound to the Shugakuin-rikyu station. From there it is around 1km/0.6mi to the former imperial summer villa, Shuga-kuin-rikyu, at the southwestern foot of Mount Hiei. Guided tours of the villa and the garden only with advance booking (►p.343).

★ ★
Shugakuin-rikyu's garden

The villa complex and the garden, which is on three levels, was com-missioned by Emperor Go-Mizunoo, who became a monk under the name of Enjo after abdicating in 1629. He found a suitable location in 1655 and by 1659 the upper and lower garden complex was al-ready completed. The central garden with the villa belonging to Ake, the emperor's daughter, was added later, and when she entered a convent it became the Rinkyuji temple. In 1855 the terrain was in-corporated into the overall complex as the Middle Garden.

◄ History

The visitors' entrance to the lower garden (Shimo-no-chaya) is a small gate on its north side, from where visitors also reach to the sec-ond gate (chumon). There is a roofed veranda to the left of the path, and to the right a path leads to the emperor's house, originally built in 1659 and renewed in the early 19th century (not open to the pub-lic).

◄ Lower garden

The path goes through the eastern gate, between rice plants and along an avenue lined with pines to the Middle Garden (Naka-no-chaya), which is home to the Rinkyuji temple with a pond garden and waterfall. The villa with the Kyaku-den reception hall and the smaller Rakushi-ken (1668) building are at the centre of the garden. The reception hall has some lovely paintings, including motifs of the Gion festival and depictions of carp covered by a net on wooden slid-ing doors. It is said the net was painted on by Maruyama Okyo in the 18th century because the fish always escaped to the garden pond at night time.

◄ Middle Garden

The upper garden (Kami-no-chaya) is the largest part of the complex and has been designed according to the »borrowed landscape« (shak-kei-zukuri) principle, which incorporates the surroundings into the overall composition. To the left of the entrance, behind a hedge and through a covered earth mound is the elevated Rinun-tei pavilion (renewed in 1824), from where there is a nice view of the garden and its lake.

◄ Upper garden

The Kyusui-tei summer house is situated on an island below the Ri-nun-tei; it was rebuilt in 1824 according to its original design (open 15 March to Nov daily 8.30am–5pm, Dec until 14 March 9am–4.30pm, ¥ 500).

◄ Kyusui-tei summer house
🕓

The Shisendo temple is located around 1.5km/1mi to the south of the villa. It was originally the residence of the poet and soldier Ishi-kawa Jozan (1583–1672). It houses paintings by Kano Tan'yu; for ex-ample in the study (shisen) there are 36 portraits of Chinese poets. There is a sand garden from the Edo period in front of the shisen. The temple complex is located in tranquil woods and is also famous for its collection of Japanese azaleas.

Shisendo temple

<table>
<tr><td>

✳
Shimogamo shrine

</td><td>

Further west is the Shimogamo shrine, a World Heritage Site (bus no. 4 or 205 from central station). The majority of the buildings date back to 1628, the main hall to 1863. The shrine is known for its Aoi-matsuri temple festival in mid-May.

</td></tr>
</table>

Botanical garden

Take bus no. 205 further northwest to the botanical garden, which was created in 1923 to commemorate the enthronement of Emperor Taisho.

Nakagyo-ku

International Manga Museum

From Kyoto main railway station take the green (Karasuma) line to Karasuma Oike station in the Nakagyo-ku district. The entrance to the manga readers' paradise lies to the north of the station on the Karasuma dori: the new International Manga Museum (daily except Wed 10am–8pm).

✳ ✳
Nijo-jo

Take bus no. 9 or 101 from Kyoto central station to the district of Nakagyo-ku. Immediately west of the bus stop is the Nijo-jo-mae, the castle of Nijo-jo, which is also a World Heritage Site. It was built by Tokugawa Ieyasu in 1603 as an expression of the shogun's power; it already received extensive renovations in 1626. At the beginning of the Meiji period it was also temporarily the seat of government; from here the shogun announced the restoration of the emperor's sovereignty (open 9am–4pm, in July, Aug, Dec and Jan closed on Tue, ¥ 300). The castle is surrounded by moats and stone walls with corner towers. The area is entered through the Higashi Otemon, the eastern gate, and the **Karamon, the black gate**. The latter is decorated with artistic carvings by Hidari Jingoro as well as with beautiful metalwork. It was originally part of Fushimi Castle.

◷

Ninomaru Castle ►

Ninomaru Castle is situated on the other side of the Mikuruma-yose, the inner gate, which is also decorated with works by Hidari Jingoro. It consists of five buildings, connected by corridors. The rooms were decorated with paintings by Kano Tan'yu and his students. The first part of the building includes the rooms in which visitors were registered, the Tozamurai-no-ma »waiting room« and the room in which the shogun received the emperor's emissaries (Chokushi-no-ma). The walls have pictures of tigers, which did not exist in Japan; lacquer intarsia, gilded items and the magnificent paintings on the sliding doors of the simple rooms transform the complex into a fairytale palace. The connective corridors (like those of the Chion-in) have floors which produce a sound at every step, thus announcing approaching guests. This type of floor is called a **»nightingale floor«**.

Remaining parts of the building ►

Walk through the second section with rooms where the shogun's ministers received daimyo, to get to the third section, the great audience hall, which is surrounded by a gallery. The sliding doors have large pictures of spruces on a gold background; the neighbouring rooms have artistic carvings by Hidari Jingoro. The fourth section,

A perfect example of a Zen garden – the stone garden in Daisen-in

once the residence of Ikkyu (1394–1481), who is one of the most enigmatic figures in Zen history, an exceptionally gifted poet and one of the creators of the tea ceremony. The wall paintings are works by Soga Dasoku (d. 1483). The Sarugaku dancer Kan'ami (1333–84) and his son Zeami (1363–1443), who gained a high reputation as a master of the No theatre, are also buried here.

West of the Shinju-an is the Daisen-in, a garden presumably created in 1513 to designs by its founder Kogaku Soko (1465–1548); it is considered to be an **outstanding example of a Zen garden**. The garden design has precursors in Chinese ink and wash paintings. The complex is divided into four areas; a mountain landscape with a waterfall is created with a sparse use of plants, mainly of stones and sand; its artistic arrangement produces the impression of spatial depth. The sliding doors in the inside of the building have paintings by Kano Motonobu, Soami and Kano Yukinobu (the scenes depicting peasant life, shikikosaku-zu, are particularly interesting). ◀ Daisen-in

The tomb of Sen-no-Rikyu is in the Shoku-in, west of the abbot's residence; to the west of it in the Soken-in are the tombs of Oda Nobunaga and his sons as well as Hideyoshi's widow. In the far west of the complex Kobori Enshu created the **famous Zen garden** Koho-an, where he and his family are also buried. ◀ Shuko-in

Around 2km/1mi north (bus no. 9 to the Kamigamo-jinja-mae stop) is the Kamigamo shrine, which was built in the city's founding days and is listed as a World Heritage Site. A traditional horserace and the famous Aoi-matsuri take place here in May. ★ **Kamigamo shrine**

An artisan painting a torii at Fushimi-Inari shrine

Fushimi-ku

Take the JR Nara line southbound from the central station to Tofukuji station. The **Tofukuji temple**, which belongs to the Rinzai sect, is nearby. The sammon gate built in the 13th century contains sculptures attributed to Jocho (d. 1057). The ceiling paintings are probably works by Mincho (1352–1431) and his pupil Kandensu. The spacious garden grounds contains the founder's hall (with a likeness of the temple founder) as well as the main hall, which burned down in 1882, but was rebuilt in 1932. One of the temple's art treasures is a 12 x 8 m (40 x 26ft) picture scroll by **Mincho**, which depicts Buddha's entrance into Nirvana (it can only be seen on 15 March).

★★
Fushimi-Inari shrine

Immediately to the east of Inari station on the train line already mentioned is the Fushimi-Inari shrine, founded in 711 and one of Japan's most important. The shrine is consecrated to the goddess of rice cultivation, Ukanomitama-no-mikoto. The main building (1499) displays the style typical of the Momoyama period. The 4km/2.5mi avenue of red torii is remarkable; it was donated by believers. There are numerous fox sculptures in the grounds: the fox is considered to be a messenger from the gods.

Momoyama

Momoyama Hill is south of Momoyama station; it is covered in a large number of peach trees. It was once the location of Fushimi Castle.

A flight of more than 230 steps leads up to the mausoleum of Emperor Meiji and his consort Shoken. The tomb surrounded by three walls was made of granite blocks, hewn on the island of Shodo. The access path to the Nogi shrine branches off to the right from the path leading up to the mausoleum. The Nogi shrine is dedicated to General Nogi Maresuke, who had his headquarters here during the Russo-Japanese War (1904–05). At the age of 64 the general, who was extremely loyal to the emperor and had become a national hero for his services to his country, committed suicide together with his wife in the year of Emperor Meiji's death.

Nishikyo-ku

Take the Hankyu train westbound to get to the district of Nishikyo-ku, the starting point for a visit to the Katsura- Rikyu imperial villa (admission only with advance booking, ►p.343) on the western bank of the Katsura River.

The villa was originally built for Prince Hachijo Toshihito (1579–1629), Emperor Goyozei's brother. Large parts of the complex were completed in 1624, the rest was still under construction until 1658. The designer of the landscape garden is said to have been Kobori Enshu, but it can only be said for certain that the design originated within his circle. It is also believed that Prince Toshihito, a great art connoisseur, participated in the design work. It is reported that Kobori accepted the commission only on **three conditions**: firstly, there should be no financial limits; secondly, there should be no deadline; and thirdly, none of those commissioning this garden should be allowed to visit the site before the garden was finished. He thereby wanted to rule out subsequent changes to the designs.

The entire complex is designed in such a way that the beholder only seems to have views from the front. Small gardens are grouped around the pond; the peaks of the Arashiyama and Kameyama hills can be seen in the distance. The three unaligned parts of the building in the Shoin-zukuri style have influenced modern Japanese architecture and even that of other countries.

The Miyuki-mon gate (1658) is the visitors' entrance. The garden paths, some of which are made of river pebbles, others of quarried stones, are lined by moss and shrubbery. The inner part of the garden is accessed through two further gates. It is divided into three parts: Furu-shoin, Naka-shoin and Miyuki-den. The veranda of the **Furu-shoin** was designed for moon-watching. The three rooms of the **Naka-shoin** contain valuable paintings by Kano Tan'yu (first room; a famous picture of a crow and other works), Kano Naonobu (second room) and Kano Yasunobu (third room). The hall for imperial visits, **Miyuki-den**, also contains a picture by Tan'yu; the decorative metal fittings (Kugi-kakushi) are also worth seeing; they were used to cover up the build-

★ ★
Katsura Rikyu

◄ Imperial villa

◄ Complex

Imperial Villa Map

50 m
165 ft

1
2
Visitor Centre
4
3
5
Shoin
Shokin-tei
7   6
Shoiken
©Baedeker

1 Onari-mon (gate)
2 Miyuki-mon (gate)
3 Gepparo
4 Machiai
5 Manji-tei
6 Shoka-ti
7 Enrindo

ing's nail heads. The fittings have the shape of flowers and are attributed to the goldsmith Kacho.

Adjoining buildings ► The simple **Gepparo** can be found to the east of the main building complex on a hill; the **Shokin-tei**, which contains several rooms, is on the other side of the pond. Every corner of its tea room is lit up through the use of cleverly directed lighting. A pebble-covered promontory extends into the pond, which is a highly stylized representation of the coastal landscape of Ama-no-hashidate. The **Shoiken** building, which consists of ten rooms, is in the southwest of the garden.

Saihoji temple

Garden ► Take the Arashiyama section of the Hankyu train line northbound from Katsura station to reach the Saihoji temple, a World Heritage Site which is not far from Kamikatsura station. It belongs to the Rinzai sect and was probably founded in the 12th century and then renewed in 1339 by the priest Muso-kokushi, who was also a significant landscape gardener. The lower part of the Zen garden surrounding the temple contains a lake with many bays as well as a tea house, probably dating from the Momoyama period. When visitor numbers got out of control measures were put in place to limit the grounds to 200 visitors per day (written reservations at least two weeks in advance with a reply card to: Saihoji temple, 56, Jingatani-cho, Matsuo, Nishikyo-ku, Kyoto, tel. 6 15 82 86). The temple demands a »donation« of ¥ 3000 from every visitor. Before the actual tour of the complex visitors participate in a Zen meditation.

Matsuo shrine The next station is Matsuo-jinja-mae, from where it is only a few minutes' walk westward to the Matsuo shrine, which is known for a rice-planting ceremony (Otaue-matsuri) that takes place between the 12th June and mid-July, during the rainy season. The shrine's deity is mainly worshipped by sake brewers – hence the many sake barrels which were donated by thankful breweries.

Horinji temple Not far from the line's terminus, Arashiyama, is the Horinji temple, probably founded in 713, which is famous for the Jusan-mairi festival held in April.

Katsura-gawa At Arashiyama station a bridge crosses the Katsura River, which is also called the Hozu or Oi here. Its riparian landscape is particularly attractive (direct access from Shijo-Omiya station, near Hankyu-Omiya station, with the Keifuku private train line on the Arashiyama route). Arashiyama Hill rises up over the river; it is covered with cherry trees and thick maple woods. This hill is famous for its cherry blossom and autumn colours of the trees. The retired emperor Kameyama (1248–1304) had cherry trees brought from Yoshino (►Yoshino-Kumano National Park) and planted here.

Cross the Togetsukyo Bridge at Arashiyama station up the hill to a small pond and further on a smaller path to the Daihikaku temple, which contains a representation of the thousand-handed Kannon and a wooden statue of **Suminokura Ryoi** (1554–1614), who made large sections of the river navigable.

Daihikaku temple

Arashiyama Park (also Kameyama Park) extends along the river; further downstream is the departure quay of the spectator boats which accompany the fishing boats during the cormorant fishing events (beginning of July–mid-August). Buses no. 28 and 93 go directly from the city centre to Arashiyama (1½ hours).

Arashiyama Park

To the north, close to the bridge over the Katsura River, is Tenryuji temple, founded in 1339 by Ashikaga Takauji, the first Ashikaga shogun, in memory of Emperor Godaigo; it is the headquarters of the Tenryuji school, which is part of the Rinzai sect. Muso-Kokushi, the temple's first abbot, created a garden extending behind the priests' residences. The current temple buildings date back to around 1900 (open daily 8.30am–5.30pm, Nov–March until 5pm, ¥ 500).

Tenryuji temple

🕐

One bus goes further north to the Seiryoji temple (also Shaka-do). There is a very remarkable 1.6m/5ft **Shakyamuni statue** made of sandalwood in the temple's main hall. It was allegedly carved in 987 by the Indian master Bishu Katsua and brought from China to Japan by the priest Cho-nen. The statue can only be seen on 8 April (Buddha's birthday) and 19 April (cleansing ceremony).

✳
Seiryoji temple

A few steps north of Seiryoji temple is Daikakuji temple, once the residence of Emperor Saga; it was transformed into a temple in 876. The main hall contains statues by Kobo-daishi (Godai Myo-o); the reception hall Kyaku-den was originally the throne room. The temple's paintings are works of Kano Motonobu, Kano Tan'yu, Kano Sanraku and Watanabe Shiko.

✳ ✳
Daikakuji temple

Take the Keifuku private train line from Arashiyama terminus to Katabiranotsuji station not far to the east. Koryji temple (also Uzumasa-dera) is close to the station (from the city centre Keifuku train line to Uzumasa station). The temple was founded by Hata Kawakatsu in 622, but the current buildings were constructed later. The lecture hall of 1165 is Kyoto's second-oldest building and houses **three old statues**: the central statue is a sitting Buddha; the other two are a thousand-handed Kannon and a Fukujenjaku-Kannon, one on each side. In the hall to the back, the Taishi-do (1720), there is a wooden statue of Shotoku-taishi (most likely a self-portrait; 606).

✳ ✳
Koryuji temple

Keigu-in The northwestern part of the temple grounds is home to the octagonal Keigu-in hall (also Hakkaku-do; 1251), which contains a statue of the 16-year-old Shotoku-taishi as well as sculptures of the Nyoirin-Kannon (a gift of a Korean ruler) and of Amida. Further interesting sculptures can be seen in the **Reiho-kan temple museum**, including wooden sculptures of Yakushi-nyorai (864) and Miroku-bosatsu, the oldest surviving sculpture in Kyoto (6th–7th century; supposedly by Shotoku).

Myoshinji temple Take the Kitano branch line of the Keifuku private line northbound from Katabiranotsuji station to Omuro station. A few steps to the south of this station is Myoshinji temple, the main temple of the Myoshinji school, which is part of the Rinzai sect. Several other temples are subordinate to it.

The temple was built in 1337 where Emperor Hanazono's residence once stood. West of the Buddha Hall is a bell-tower with a bell cast in 698; the Butsuden Buddha Hall contains a Shakyamuni statue. The ceiling paintings in the Hatto lecture hall were made by Kano Tan'yu. To the east, in the Gyokuho-in hall, there is a likeness of Hanazono. There are some smaller temples to the west of the priest's residence, of which the **Reiun-in** is notable for its numerous paintings by Kano Motonobu. The Tenkyu-in temple contains works by Kano Sanraku.

✱
Ninnaji temple The Ninnaji temple (World Heritage Site) can be found to the north of Omuro station; it was originally known as the Omuro palace, started in 886. After abdicating, Emperor Uda (9th century) was the temple's first abbot. The buildings visible today date from the first half of the 17th century. To the right of the central gate is a 33m/108ft five-storey pagoda, in the main hall a wooden Amida statue. The temple complex with its many cherry trees is particularly attractive when they blossom in April.

Ryoanji temple
✱ ✱
Garden ► Not far north of the Ninnaji temple is the Ryoanji temple famous for its Zen garden, a dry garden and a World Heritage Site. The highly stylized composition consists of 15 boulders as islands of life and raked white sand as oceans of life. There is no angle from which all 15 boulders can be seen at once. The tomb of the founder Hosokawa Katsumoto is located in the grounds. The pool with the Zen inscription »All I need for contentment is knowledge« is very well
🕐 known (open March–Nov 8am–5pm, Dec–Feb 8.30am–4.30pm, ¥ 500).

Toji-in temple Further southeast near Toji-in station (Keifuku private line) is the Toji-in temple, which was founded in 1341 by Takauji, the first Ashikaga shogun. The last time the building was renewed was in 1818. The main hall contains the statues of all Ashikaga shoguns (with the exception of the fifth and the tenth) as well as **ink and wash paintings**

Around Kyoto (Southeast)

Daigoji temple, which belongs to the Shingon sect, can be found on the southeastern outskirts of the city (JR Nara line); it was founded in 874 as one of two centres of the ascetic Shugendo teaching by the priest Shobo. The five-storey pagoda is particularly remarkable. It was built in 951 and is one of Kyoto's oldest structures.

✱ **Daigoji temple**

Next door is Sambo-in, the main temple of the Daigo school, which is also part of the Shingon sect. The structures, built in the time of Toyotomi Hideyoshi, house a collection of paintings and calligraphy, as well as wall paintings by Kano Sanraku. The 16th-century garden is particularly beautiful during the cherry blossom.

✱ ✱ **Sambo-in temple**

Take the JR Nara line further to Obaku station. A little north of it is Mampukuji temple, the main temple of the Obaku sect founded by the Chinese priest Ingen in 1661. The main hall (Daiyu-hoden) is made of Thai teak; lecture hall behind it (Hatto) houses the 60,000 wooden printing blocks with which the entire edition of the Obaku sutras was made in the 17th century.

✱ **Mampukuji temple**

18km/11mi south of Kyoto along the JR Nara line is the town of Uji (population 165,000), where green tea and sake are produced. Extensive tea plantations make this an attractive place to get out and take a tour of various picturesque farms.

Uji

The island of **Tonoshima** in the Uji River is home to a pagoda built by the priest Eison in the 13th century; in the summer the evening cormorant fishing takes place near the island. South of the old bridge is Hojo-in temple

? DID YOU KNOW ...?

■ ... that the Phoenix Hall of Uji is depicted on the 10-yen coin?

(also Hashi-dera, bridge temple), which belongs to the Shingon-Ritsu sect; it contains a stone with an inscription regarding the first bridge that was built here in 646.

Not far south from here is the Uji shrine, which is said to have been founded in 313 on the site of the former residence of Prince Uji-no-Wakiiratsuko (d. 312). The shrine is dedicated to this prince and his father, Emperor Ojin, and his brother, Emperor Nintoku. The complex, a World Heritage Site, consists of two parts, of which the upper shrine (10th century) is the older. In contrast to most other shrines the buildings were not demolished from time to time, so that they are now considered the country's **oldest shrine buildings still in their original state**. One of the Uji's seven springs is in the forecourt. They are known for their clear water. The lower shrine dates back to the Kamakura period.

✱ ◄ Uji shrine

Not far away is the idyllically situated Koshoji temple, the first founded by Dogen's Soto sect, and renewed in 1646. The trees on the grounds represent the most popular ones in Japan.

◄ Koshoji temple

Phoenix Hall at Byodoin temple

★ ★
Byodoin
temple ▶

Byodoin temple is located to the southeast of the station. As a characteristic example of Heian-period temple architecture it is also listed as a World Heritage Site. It came from a country estate inhabited by Minamoto Toru, Fujiwara no Michinaga and Yorimichi. In 1052 Yorimichi provided the land for the building of the temple, whose main hall, the Hoo-do (after the floor plan also the Phoenix Hall) was built the following year. On either side of roof is a **bronze phoenix**; the interior from the Heian period, which has been seriously damaged or restored in some places, contains works of the master Takuma Tamenari, who was active during the 11th century. The gilded Amida statue made by Jocho in the 11th century dominates the hall's interior. The altar and ceilings contain inlay works of bronze and mother-of-pearl; there is not much left of the ceiling paintings of the 25 Bosatsu. The Amida statue itself has recently been restored.

The next hall is the Kannon-do, also named Tsuri-dono (Fishing Hall) after its location directly above the river. Next to it a monument to Minamoto Yorimasa (1104–80), who took his own life after his defeat by the Taira (his tomb is in the Saisho-in behind the Byodo-in). Opposite the Phoenix Hall is a bell-tower with a copy of the country's most famous bell. The original can be seen in the Homotsu-den's temple museum. The building complex together with the garden forms a compositional unit symbolizing the paradise of the »Pure Land«, as heralded by the Jodo sect (open 8.30am–5.30pm, museum 9am–5pm, ¥ 600, Phoenix Hall 9.30am–4.10pm, admission every 20 minutes, ¥ 300 extra).

MIHO Museum

I. M. Pei built the MIHO Museum in the middle of the mountains and forests of ▶Lake Biwa, making its site and architecture almost more impressive than its collection of classical art from Japan (some from the Momoyama and Kamakura periods), Asia and Egypt as well as ancient Greece and Rome (no regular opening hours, tel. 07 48/ 82 34 11, www.miho.or.jp, take the Biwako line from Kyoto to Ishiyama, 15 minutes, then a bus).

Around Kyoto (Northeast)

Mount Hiei (848m/2782ft) northeast of Kyoto can be reached by bus in one hour from the city centre; there is also a train connection (Keihan line to Demachi-yanagi, then Keifuku-Eizan private line) to Yase-yuen, the location of the valley terminus, which makes its way up to the top in two stages. There is a **viewpoint** near the Shimeigatake mountain terminus with a revolving tower (good view of Kyoto and ►Lake Biwa). The mountain is also accessible from the lake by taking a train to Sakamoto, then a cableway.

★
Hiei

Mount Hiei is also the location of Enryakuji temple, previously one of the country's most powerful. Today it is the main temple of the Esoteric Buddhist school. It too has been given World Heritage status. The Buddhist priest Saicho (767–822), who came from a family of Chinese origin, founded the temple after returning from a trip to China at the request of Emperor Kammu in 788; its site in the northeast of the city was chosen because the temple could then dispel the evil spirits coming from that direction. The ever-growing number of monks gained more and more political influence and soon were a threat to Kyoto, so that Oda Nobunaga felt forced to destroy the temple in 1571. Despite being rebuilt by Toyotomi Hideyoshi and extended on the orders of Tokugawa Iemitsu, the temple never again achieved any real secular power.

★ ★
◄ Enryakuji
temple

The eastern area (Toto) contains the ordination hall Kaidan-in, the Amida Hall of 1937 and the lecture hall Daiko-do (1956), a belfry, the hall of the black god Daikoku-do, the gate Monju-ro as well as the central hall Konpon-chudo, which houses a wooden statue of Yakushi-nyorai made by Saicho as well as some other carvings. The western area (Saito), the Shaka-do hall and the 10m/33ft Sorinto Pagoda are of note.

Those who need to recover from all these temples might like to visit the enchanting Hiei Garden Museum, which has designed its gardens on the model of French Impressionist paintings, reproductions of which are on hand to compare.

Hiei Garden
Museum

Take the Kyoto bus no. 16, 17 or 18 to get to the suburb of Ohara in the northeast (from the central station approx. 50 minutes). Sanzenin temple, which belongs to the Tendai sect, can be found here. It was renewed in 860 by the priest Joun. The main hall Ojo-gokuraku-in (»paradise of reincarnation«) is a work by the priest Enshin (942–1017). The hall's ceiling, shaped like a boat's keel, is decorated

Ohara
◄ Sanzen-in
temple

with 25 Bodhisatva representations; there are Mandara pictures by Enshin on the walls; the gilded Amida statue was made in 1148. Other buildings in the temple grounds were built in the early 17th century from pieces of the hall of ceremony of the Shishinden imperial palace.

Around Kyoto (West)

Kameoka

The town of Kameoka, 22km/14mi west of Kyoto, has a population of 76,000 (JR San-in line, 30 minutes, or bus, 1 hour). The castle town located in the Kameoka Basin on the banks of the Hozu River is the starting point for a 16km/10mi boat trip to Arashiyama (western outskirts of Kyoto) through the rapids. Rice and wood were transported in this manner in the past.

A boat trip through the rapids ►

The trips through the rapids in traditional boats that run from March to November (heated in the winter, tel. 07 71/22 58 46) last around 2 hours. The rapids begin at around Miyanoshita; then the river winds its way through the hills of Atagoyama (to the left) and Arashiyama (to the right). This section of the river was made navigable in 1606 by Suminokura Ryoi. The places along the river passed during the trip are Kanagisone, Koayu-no-taki, Takase, Shishigakuchi (»lion's mouth«), Nagase and Gakugase.

★ ★ Matsue

G 7 • f 2

Main island: Honshu	**Prefecture:** Shimane
Population: 147,000	

松江

Matsue's most famous inhabitant was the author Lafcadio Hearn (alias Koizumi Yakumo), who lived here towards the end of the 19th century and who, with his books, contributed greatly to making Japan and its culture known in the Western world.

Matsue, the capital of Shimane Prefecture and the largest city in the historical San-in region, is situated close to Honshu's northwest coast on the Ohashi River, which forms the connection between Lake Shinji in the west and the Naka-no-umi lagoon in the east.

What to See in Matsue

Castle

1.8km/1mi northwest of the station, on Kamedayama Hill, is the castle built in 1607–11. Its three-storey main tower, a reconstruction from 1642, contains old suits of armour as well as exhibits on the town's history; from the top floor there is a nice view of the town, the mountains to the north and Lake Shinji in the west (open April–Sept 7am–7.30pm, Oct–March 8.30am–5pm, castle

Shiroyama Park ►

¥ 550, castle grounds free). The castle is surrounded by Shiroyama

Main tower of Matsue Castle

Park, known for its cherry and azalea blossom. The **Cultural Museum** (Matsue-Kyodokan), built in the style of the Meiji period, is nearby.

A nice walk (15 minutes) leads past the castle moat in a northbound direction to the samurai houses (Bukeyashiki); the house of the vassal Shiomi with its rich furnishings is particularly worth seeing. In the same road are the former home of Lafcadio Hearn and the memorial hall Yakumo-kinenkan with memorabilia of his stay in Matsue.

Samurai houses

Further to the east on a hill is the Meimei-an tea house from 1779 with an atmospheric tea garden; it was built at the request of Matsudaira Harusato, a supporter of the tea ceremony (open daily 9am–5pm, ¥ 300).

Meimei-an

The Gesshoji temple, built by Matsudair Naomas (1601–66), a grandson of Tokugawa Ieyasu, with the tombs of the Matsudaira dynasty (1st–9th generation) can be found in the west of the town south of Mount Asahi (342m/1122ft) The treasury has the possessions of Matsudaira Harusato (swords, etc.) on display.

Gesshoji temple

Around Matsue

The Adachi Art Museum outside the town (free shuttle bus from the JR Yasugi station, east of Matsue) has an extensive collection of Japanese paintings from the end of the 19th century. Also part of the museum is an impressive landscape garden (open April–Sept 9am–5.30pm, Oct–March until 5pm, ¥ 2200, www.adachi-museum.or.jp/e)

Adachi Art Museum

The village of Fudoki-no-oka, which is of archaeological interest, can be found in the south of town. It shows the traditional chequerboard subdivision, burial mounds (Futago-zuka), reconstruction of old

Fudoki-no-oka

▶ VISITING MATSUE

INFORMATION

Tourist information
665 Asahi-machi, by the station
Tel. 08 52/21 40 34
Daily 9am–6pm
www.city.matsue.shimane.jp

TRANSPORT

By air: from Tokyo (Haneda Airport) to Izumo (1½ hours); from Osaka to Izumo (1 hour).
By rail: from Osaka (Shin-Osaka station) JR shinkansen line to Okayama (1 hour), then JR Hakubi and San-in line (2¾ hours); from Izumo JR San-in line (30 minutes).

EVENTS

Oshiro-matsuri (castle festival, beginning of April); Matsue-odori (summer festival with fireworks; end of July); shrine festival (end of July), in the Temmangu shrine; Toro-nagashi (end of the Bon festival, when paper lanterns are released on the lake; mid-Aug); shrine festival (end of August), in the Takeuchi shrine; Taiko-gyoretsu (procession with large drums; beginning of November); shrine festival (beginning of November), in the Matsue shrine.

homes from the Kofun period (3rd–7th centuries, remains of an old provincial temple (Koku-bunji; 741) and the museum (Shiryo-kan) at the centre of the village.

✳ **Kamosu shrine**

The Kamosu shrine is located west of Fudoki-no-oka; its main hall (honden) from 1364 is the oldest extant structure in the Taisha-zukuri style. To the north of the Kamosu shrine, 7km/4.5mi south of the station (15 minutes by bus), is the Yaegaki shrine. It is consecrated to the god of marriage, who plays a major role in the country's legend and poetry. Young women like to go to the shrine to find out how soon they will get married: they float a coin on a piece of wax paper on the pond behind the shrine: the sooner it sinks, the better.

✳ **Lake Shinji**

Shimane Kenritsu Bijutsukan ▶

Lake Shinji, west of the town, is Japan's sixth-largest lake, with an area of 80 sq km/30 sq mi and a circumference of 50km/30mi. The art museum of Shimane Prefecture (www2.pref.shimane.jp/sam) can be found on its eastern shore (15 minutes on foot from Matsue station). In addition to displaying Japanese and Western paintings, it also exhibits photographs, sculptures, prints and crafts (open March–Sept from 10am to 30 minutes after sunset, Oct–Feb 10am–6.30pm, Jan until 11 April daily except Mon, then daily except Tue, ¥ 300). Matsue-onsenin the east has a nice view of the lake. The popular spa of Tamatsukuri-onsenwith hot springs (50–70°C/122–158°F) is on the lake's southern shore, 8km/5mi west of Matsue (30 minutes by bus). There is a surprise on the northern shore: the **Louis C. Tiffany Garden Museum** (Ichibata private line station of the same name).

The Naka-no-umi lagoon extends east of Matsue. With an area of 99 sq km/38 sq mi it has a circumference of 83.5km/52mi; in the east it is separated by a wide strait from Miho Bay, with which it is connected in the north. The 6 sq km/2.3 sq mi island of **Daikon** at the centre of the lagoon has unusual lava formations in the southeast near Osoe.

Naka-no-umi Lagoon

Matsumoto

K 6 • k 1

Main island: Honshu
Population: 197,000

Prefecture: Nagano

松本

The university town of Matsumoto in central Honshu, situated in the Matsumoto Basin, is the starting point for excursions to the ►Chubu-Sangaku National Park and to the Utsukushigahara Plateau east of the town. The landmark of the town, whose streets and alleyways are filled with many mountaineers, is the castle.

What to See in Matsumoto

1km/0.6mi northeast of the station is Matsumoto Castle, dating from 1504. It is also called »Crow Castle« (Karasu-jo) because of its black exterior. The complex is a classic example of a Hirashiro-style stronghold. The castle towers above a wide plain and is surrounded by moats with red bridges and low walls. The six-storey main tower is connected via corridors to the northern barbican. There is a lovely view of the surrounding area from the top floor. It is worth visiting the **Tsukimi Veranda** for moonwatching (open daily 8.30am–5pm, ¥ 500 incl. the Folk Museum).

★ ★
Castle

The **Folk Museum** (Nihon Minzoku Shiryokan; also a bus from the station, 15 minutes) is immediately outside the castle walls. It displays exhibits about the region's archaeology, history and folklore (the collection of Tanabata dolls is notable); there is also an extensive clock collection.

An artistically assembled bridge leads to the castle

Ukiyo-e Museum
Law Court
Museum

To the southwest outside of the town centre is the modern building of the Ukiyo-e Museum (Nihon Ukiyoe Hakubutsukan) with more than 100,000 woodblock prints, printing blocks, books and paintings (open Tue–Sun 10am–4.30pm, ¥ 1000). The Nihon Shiho Hakubutsukan, the Law Courts Museum, is very close by in the country's oldest wooden courthouse, which was built in 1908.

Alps Park

A nice attraction north of the town is the Alps Park (Alps Koen), which has a zoo of small animals and a summer toboggan run as well as a view of the town and the Japanese Alps.

Archaeological
Museum

The Archaeological Museum (Matsumoto-shiritsu Koko Hakubutsu-kan; bus connection) southeast of the centre houses finds from the local area.

Gofukuji temple

Even further to the southeast, at the foot of the 1929m/6329ft Mount Hachibuse, lies the Gofukuji temple of the Shingon sect, known for its many statues.

Around Matsumoto

Utsukushigahara

The Utsukushigahara Plateau extends to the east of the town. Having an altitude of sometimes more than 2000m/6500ft, it offers lovely views of the Hida mountains. There is a bus connection from Matsumoto station; after 20 minutes the bus reaches the spa of Asama-on-sen (hot springs, numerous Ryokan). Further south in this region there are also the **hot spring spas** of Oboke, Yamabe, Fujii, Iriyamabe and Tobira, which are collectively called the Utsukushigahara-onsen spa region.

▶ VISITING MATSUMOTO

INFORMATION
Tourist information
In the station, tel. 02 63/32 28 14
April–Oct 9.30am–6.15pm,
Nov–March 9am–5.45pm

TRANSPORT
By air: from Osaka (1¼ hours).
By rail: from Tokyo (Shinjuku station) JR Chuo main line (2½ hours); from Osaka JR Chuo main line via Nagoya (4 hours); from Nagano JR Shinonoi line (1 hour)

By bus: from Matsumoto airport to the town centre (30 minutes); regional lines to the Utsukushigahara Plateau as well as to Kamikochi (April–Oct).

EVENTS
Saito Kinen Festival Matsumoto (classical concert series, mid-Aug to mid-Sept)

SHOPPING
There are a lot of shops offering all kinds of local arts and crafts.

The open-air museum (Utsukushigahara Kogen Bijutsukan; open from the end of April to mid-Nov 9am–5pm, ¥ 1000) in the vicinity of Matsumoto is also well worth seeing. The bus departs from Matsumoto station and after 40 minutes along steep hairpin bends reaches the terminal station on the plateau. There are two roads leading to the open-air museum, which displays large sculptures; one is closed to vehicles, another shorter mountain road leads to the NHK TV station and then along a 2km/1mi road past mountain pastures with black-and-white cattle. Make sure not to miss the last bus down from the plateau; it departs at 3.35pm (mid-July to Aug 5.30pm).

Open-air museum

The bus then makes its way from Asama to the Misuzu Dam (circumference: 3km/2 mi); it is a popular campsite during the summer (boat trips, fishing), in the winter people come here to go ice skating. There is a lift between the shore and a hill with an observation tower (nice all-round view).

Misuzu Dam

Hotaka is the home of the Rokuzan Bijutsukan Art Museum. It mainly contains works by the sculptor Ogiwara Rokuzan, whose style earned him the sobriquet »**Rodin of the Orient**«. It is a 45-minute walk from Hotaka station, where bicycles can be rented, to the large Japanese horseradish farm Gohoden Wasabi-en, situated in an idyllic valley.

Hotaka

★★ Matsushima

L 5

Main island: Honshu
Population: 17,000

Prefecture: Miyagi

The name Matsushima means »Pine Island«; it gets its name from the more than 260 pine-covered rocky islands in the bay. The landscape here is very diverse as a result of the many rock formations and strange growth of the trees on the bare ground, and has always been much valued in Japan.

松島

Matsushima Bay forms the inner part of Sendai Bay, which extends to the south of the Ojika Peninsula on Honshu's east coast. Some of its islands consist of volcanic tuff, others, like the majority of the coast's rock formations, of white sandstone. Some of the larger islands are inhabited, while the smallest are mere rocky islets with an area of just a few square metres. The impact of the waves has greatly hollowed out the rock, creating grottos, tunnels, towers and arches; the windswept pines manage to hold on to even the steepest cliffs.
This region is a **traditional holiday destination of the Japanese**, as can be deduced from the fact that there are more than 40 ryokan (traditional Japanese guesthouses) along the 12km/7.5mi bay (north-south). Nevertheless **timely reservations are essential**; around the

Famous coastline

JAPAN'S »THREE MOST FAMOUS LANDSCAPES«

Many Japanese people enjoy the harmony between land and sea, and every Japanese person knows the sankei: the three famous landscapes: Ama-no-hashidate near Miyazu, Matsushima Island near Sendai and Itsukushima, the shrine island with torii in the water near Hiroshima.

Heaven's Bridge

The beautiful landscape of Ama-no-hashidate is shrouded in legend: when two gods Izanami and Izanagi plunged the holy spear into the floods aeons ago, Japan's first island was created from the falling droplets. According to the **myth**, the two gods descended to the Japanese island world via Heaven's Bridge. The numerous Japanese tourists surrender to this famous view by turning their backs on it and then bending down to look at it through their legs, which causes the pines on the headland to look like mystical pillars that lead directly to heaven, thus connecting heaven with the sea. A swing bridge with the only access to the spit goes over an island in front of Heaven's Bridge.

Bathers have taken possession of the wide sandy strip on the spit's seaward side; children search for shells and snorkellers observe the colourful world of fish. A hiking trail almost 4 km/2.5mi long makes its way through this beautifully scenic landscape, un-

*The pine islands of Matsushima
float offshore like ships*

der thousands of pines, past quiet shrines and with views of the rocky coast of Wakasa Bay. A faded votive tablet lies under an old tree, comparing the beauty of Ama-no-hashidate with a one-sided love.

The Pine Islands

The wide bay near Sendai is home to more than 260 tiny islands made of black tuff or white sandstone. They rise vertically up from the calm Pacific Ocean, forming arches, towers and grottoes. Bizarre formations bring to mind images of a whale coming to the surface or of a giant tortoise whose back is covered in windswept pine trees. Many of these islands can be accessed by **red arched bridges** and in the middle of all of these green islands is a temple inviting passers-by to meditate. **Basho**, the country's most famous haiku poet, captured his impressions in just the 17 syllables used in a haiku: »O Matsushima, Matsushima, o Matsushima wo mita« (»Oh, I have seen Matsushima«).

The Sacred Island

Itsukushima shrine on Miyajima Island off the coast of Hiroshima is the largest attraction in the city's vicinity. The red **Shinto torii**, 16m/52 ft tall and 23m/75ft wide is the largest of its kind; it emerges out of the waters of the Inland Sea, except at low tide; beyond it, far out to sea is the red shrine's bugaku stage, framed by steep green mountains. Seemingly endless corridors make up the country's oldest **No open-air stage** (16th century).

Powerful stone lions prevent evil spirits from accessing the sacred island. Until the Meiji period nobody was allowed to die or be born here, no tree was allowed to be felled and no animal could be killed. Even today the island does not have a cemetery; the dead are buried on the mainland.

time of the »star festival« (Tanabata-matsuri, beginning of August), which takes place in nearby Sendai, it is necessary to book around six months in advance. Besides ▶ Ama-no-hashidate on Honshu's west coast northwest of Kyoto and ▶ Miyajima (Itsukushima) in the bay of Hiroshima, Matsushima is one of Japan's three famous strips of coastline (Sankei) (▶ Baedeker Special p.380).

◀ Matsushima shi-daikan ▶

The appearance of the bay and its many islands constantly changes with the changing seasons and times of day. Watching this phenomenon is a fascinating pastime from many places along the coast. The strongly formalizing approach of the Japanese people, which has been influenced by their ink-and-wash painting style, has led them to pick out **four viewpoints** considered to be particularly attractive; they are called the »Matsushima shi-daikan« (»the four excellent views of Matsushima«):

Otakamori, a 106m/348ft hill on the island of Miyato in the eastern part of the bay; one hour by boat from Matsushima railway station or by land across a causeway.

Ogidani in the bay's central part, a mountain south of Matsushima station; it can be reached in 25 minutes on foot.

Tamonzan , an elevation on Cape Yogasaki in the southwest of the bay, 30 minutes by boat from Shiogama harbour.

Tomiyama , a mountain 20 minutes' walk north of Rikuzen-Tomiyama station (JR Senseki line, 10 minutes from Matsushima station). It is also the location of the 17th-century Daigyoji temple.

 VISITING MATSUSHIMA

INFORMATION

Matsushima Information Center
7-1 Hamiuchihama, close to the station
Tel. 0 22/3 54 22 63
Daily 9.30am–4.30pm
www.town.matsushima.miyagi.jp

TRANSPORT

By air: from Osaka to Sendai (1¼ hours).
By rail: from Tokyo (Ueno station) JR Tohoku shinkansen line (2 hours); also JR Tohoku line to Sendai (4¼ hours), then JR Senseki line to Matsushima-Kaigan (35 minutes).
By bus: from Sendai Airport to Sendai station (10 minutes); from Sendai to Matsushima-Kaigan (1 hour).
By ferry: round trips between Matsushima-Kaigan and Shiogama (1 hour).

EVENTS

Matsushima Toro-Nagashi (»floating lantern festival«, fireworks; mid-August).

WHERE TO STAY

▶ **Mid-range**
Hotel Taikanso
10-76 Inuta, tel. 0 22/3 54 21 61
www.taikanso.co.jp/eg
Affordable resort hotel on a hill with a view of the coast. With an outdoor swimming pool (for the summer months), rotemburo and a herb bath. Anyone wanting to have some Japanese-style entertainment should visit the karaoke lounge.

What to See in and around Matsushima

Not far from Matsushima-Kaigan station at the centre of the bay is the Marinepia Matsushima Aquarium. Take the main road in a northeasterly direction to get to the sea view pavilion (Kanran-tei), situated on a cliff by the pier; it is a simple tea house from the end of the 16th century, once part of Fushimi Castle and a gift from Toyotomi Hideyoshi for his vassal Date Masamune (1567–1636). The sliding doors on the inside were painted by Kano Sanraku (1559–1635), a significant artist of the Momoyama style. As its name states, the pavilion has a nice view of the bay; the garden contains a small museum with memorabilia from the Date aristocratic family, which was the most powerful line of princes in northeast Japan for a period during the Middle Ages (open daily 8.30am–5pm, Nov–March until 4.30pm, ¥ 200).

Aquarium
◀ Sea view pavilion

A little bit further north two bridges lead to a pine-covered island, which is the location of the Godaido temple, built on the orders of Date Masamune. It contains five Buddha statues.
1km/0.6mi south of the Godaido temple a red wooden bridge (Togetsukyo) leads to the picturesque **island of Oshima**; the waves have hollowed grottoes into its cliffs. Buddhist images in these caves prove they once served as hermitages.
Another red wooden bridge northeast of the Godaido temple leads to the **island of Fukuura**, known for its diverse flora.

✱
Godaido temple

Further west (inland), a five-minute walk from Matsushima-Kaigan station an avenue lined by Sugi trees leads to the Zuiganji temple, founded in 828, which later became a centre of the Zen Rinzai sect (Myoshinji school). There are **caves** on both sides of the avenue, which the monks used as places to practice their meditation; there is a larger one to the left behind the temple entrance in which Abbot Hosshin, who studied the new teaching in China in the 13th century, is said to have meditated. The current structures were built in 1609 on the orders of Date Masamune. Some of the buildings that stand out are the central gate (Naka-mon), the imperial gate (Onari-mon), the residential area (Kuri), the gallery (Kairo) and the main hall (Hondo), whose sliding doors were painted by masters of the Kano school. The interesting **»peacock room«** has a wooden sculpture of Date Masamune, who was also called the »one-eyed shogun« (Dokuganryu Shogun), in full armour. The grounds also contain a museum, Seiryuden, with historical evidence of the Date, including portraits, tea bowls and statues.

✱ ✱
Zuiganji temple

🕐
Opening hours:
Daily 8am–5pm, Oct and March until 4.30pm, Feb and Nov until 4pm, Dec/Jan until 3.30pm, ¥ 700

To the northeast, beyond the island of Miyato, which borders the bay in this direction, is the harbour town of Ishinomaki (population 122,000) on the mouth of the Kitami River; it takes 50 minutes to get here on the JR Senseki line from Matsushima-Kaigan.

Ishinomaki

✴ Ishinomaki is the starting point of the ferries (approx. 2 hours) de-
Kinkazan parting for Kinkazan Island (no automobile and bus traffic), which
is 4km/2.5mi southeast of the Ojika Peninsula. The island's name
means »golden flower« and stems from the shiny pigments in the
rock that sparkle when the sun hits them. The entire island, which
extends 4km/2.5mi from east to west and 5km/3mi from north to
south, is covered in lavish vegetation, interspersed by rugged rocks
protruding out from the island's green carpet. The fauna, which is
unusually rich by Japanese standards, consists of red deer, monkeys
and many different bird species.

Koganeyama The Koganeyama shrine is not far from the pier; it is consecrated to
shrine the two Shinto deities of wealth and luck. A 2km/1mi path begins
behind the shrine, which leads up Mount Kinkazan (445m/1460ft);
the picturesque walk is crowned by a sweeping view from the peak:
in the east the wide expanse of the Pacific and in the west Matsushima Bay in front of a backdrop of forested mountains.

Senjojiki A three-hour walk from the pier leads to the east coast where there
are some unusual formations: cube-shaped rocks standing parallel
next to each other, called Senjojiki.

Onagawa 17km/11mi northeast of Ishinomaki (train, 30 minutes) is the town
of Onagawa, situated on Onagawa Bay. Its harbour is a centre of
deep-sea fishing, particularly of whaling (marine laboratory of the
Tohoku University). There is also a ferry connection from here to
Kinkazan Island (1¼ hours). The Oshika Cobalt toll road starts
south of the harbour and runs across the peninsula, dividing it in
two. It ends in the small town of Oshika, at the southern tip of the
peninsula, where a museum (Oshika Whale Land) displays exhibits
on the history of whaling.

Matsuyama

G 8 • e 4

Main island: Shikoku   **Prefecture:** Ehime
Population: 467,000

松山 **In addition to one of the few Japanese castles still extant in their
original state, Matsuyama also has one of the most traditional
onsen.**

Shikoku's Matsuyama, the largest city on Shikoku Island, is situated on the
largest city northwest coast and is the capital of Ehime Prefecture (formerly
Iyo). Matsuyama is the trans-shipment centre for agricultural products, particularly for oranges from the local farms, making it the region's economic centre.

▶ VISITING MATSUYAMA

INFORMATION

Tourist information
In the station, tel. 0 89/9 31 39 14
Daily 8.30am–8.30pm
Ehime Prefectural International
Center, 1-1 Dogoichiman
Tel. 0 89/9 17 56 78
Mon–Sat 8.30am–5pm,
Tue, Thu until 7pm

www.city.matsuyama.ehime.jp
www.pref.ehime.jp (about Ehime Prefecture)

TRANSPORT

By air: from Tokyo (Haneda Airport;
1½ hours); from Osaka (50 minutes);
from Fukuoka (1 hour).
By rail: from Takamatsu JR Yosan
main line (3 hours); from Okayama
(2¾ hours).
By bus: from Matsuyama Airport to
the city centre (20 minutes).
By ferry: regular ferry connections
from Hiroshima (also hovercraft; 2¾
hours or 1¼ hours respectively).

EVENTS

Tsubaki-matsuri (Japanese camellia
festival; beginning of January); Dogo-
onsen-matsuri (mid-March), in Dogo-
onsen; castle festival (beginning of
April); Matsuyama festival (summer
festival; mid-August); Funa-odori
(»ship dance« with pantomimes on
barques; mid-October), on Gogoshi-
ma Island.

WHERE TO STAY

▶ **Mid-range**
Hotel Patio Dogo
Dogo Onsen Honkanmae,
Matsuyama-shi,
Ehime-ken 790-0842
Tel. 0 89/9 41 41 28, fax 9 41 41 29
www.patio-dogo.co.jp
Tram no. 5 from Matsuyama.
This hotel's Western-style décor and
exterior are nothing to write home
about, but the location is fantastic: it is
directly opposite the famous bath-
house of Dogo-onsen. Very clean and
friendly.

What to See in Matsuyama

500m/550yd east of the station in the city centre the densely forested
hill Katsuyama (also Shiroyama) is crowned by the castle. The
stronghold built between 1602 and 1627 has four gates with barbi-
cans; the three-storey main tower is a museum containing objects
from the possessions of the daimyo of Matsudaira, swords and suits
of armour in particular. The area around the castle has been transformed into a park (a cableway runs up the hill on its east side),
which is most beautiful during the cherry blossom (open daily
9am–5pm, ¥ 350).

✳ **Castle**

⊕

The long-famous spa Dogo-onsen can be found 4km/2.5mi northeast of the station (tram, 20 minutes), set on a hillside. These hot
springs (alkaline, 46°C/115°F) were already mentioned in the Manyoshu anthology in the 8th century; to this day they have remained a

✳ **Dogo-onsen**

popular destination amongst the Japanese. Some of the buildings, particularly the three-storey Shinrokaku bath-house, a wooden building in the Momoyama style, still have a lot of the traditional atmosphere.

Ishiteji temple ✴

The Ishiteji temple is not located very far east of Dogo. It is one of the 88 stops on the traditional path of pilgrimage on the island of Shikoku. It was founded in 728 by Prince Ochi Tamazumi, then rebuilt in 1318 after being destroyed by fire. It is thus an example of the buildings of the Kamakura period with the typical mix of Japanese and Chinese stylistic elements. The Niomon gate with the temple guards from the 12th century is a listed national treasure of Japan, the main hall (hondo), the Gomado Hall, a three-storey pagoda and the bell-tower are the most interesting structures.

! **Baedeker TIP**

Cycling on Shikoku

Shikoku is wonderfully suited for bike-rides, a great way to see some of the 88 temples of pilgrimage on the island. Another option is to cycle the Shimanami Kaido, which crosses the Inland Sea via ten bridges all the way to Honshu. Imabari is the starting point (information at www.kancycling.com).

Shiki Museum

The Shiki-kinen museum can be found to the south, directly next to the Dogo-onsen. Shiki Masaoka (1867–1902) is the most famous **haiku poet** after Basho and Issa. Haiku poems are just 17 syllables long, making them the shortest poetic form in the world. Thoughts and experiences of daily life, as well as seasonal sentiments, are the theme of this art form. Even the emperor hosts annual haiku competitions in his palace. One example by Shiki: »Snow is falling now / no sound but the mew of a / white cat on the roof«.

Around Matsuyama

Takahama

The town has two harbour sites on the west coast: Takahama, also called Matsuyama Kanko, where the ferries from Honshu and Kyushu dock; somewhat further south near the airport is Mitsuhama. The local colours unfold on the **morning market** Asa-ichi, where seafood is sold.

Ishizuchi Quasi-National Park

The Ishizuchi Quasi-National Park, which contains 107 sq km/41 sq mi of mountainous land begins around 40km/25mi further inland in a southeasterly direction.

Omogokei Gorge ▶

The park's main attraction is the ruggedly picturesque Omogokei Gorge, through which the Omogo River flows for 11km/7mi. There are numerous meanders in the river. Cliffs, waterfalls and narrows together with the lavish green or lively autumn colours make this landscape very diverse. The best starting point for trips to the gorge is Kammon station (bus from Matsuyama station; 2¾ hours); next along the road are Kamehara (waterfalls), the Kanayama Bridge and Goraiko (waterfalls).

The highest point of the park and Shikoku Island is Mount Ishizuchi (1982m/6503ft). It is best reached from the industrial town of Saijo (population 56,000), around 50km/30mi northeast of Matsuyama. Buses depart Iyo-Saiyo station and drive half-way up the mountain (32km/20 mi, 1¼ hours), where visitors will find the lower terminus of a cableway and a shrine. The start of the season for pilgrims and mountain climbers is celebrated here at the beginning of July (mountaineering season until November).   ◄ Ishizuchi Saijo

5km/3mi east of Matsuyama, at the tip of the Takahawa Peninsula, is Chikamiyama Hill (244m/801ft), from where there is a nice view of the rapids which form in the Kurushima Strait as a result of the different tidal ranges of the Hiuchi-Nada Sea (to the east) and the Aki-Nada Sea (to the west).   ★ Chikamiyama

Mito

Main island: Honshu   **Prefecture:** Ibaraki
Population: 245,000

The main reason for visiting Mito is the Kairaku-en, one of Japan's three famous gardens. This landscape park is particularly attractive in February, when the plum trees are in full bloom. 水戸

Mito, not far away from Honshu Island's east coast and around 100km/60mi northeast of Tokyo, is the capital of Ibaraki Prefecture and an important traffic junction. The town centre was once dominated by a powerful castle, which was, however, almost completely destroyed during the domestic turmoil of the Meiji Restoration in 1865.

What to See in Mito

In the town centre, where the castle once stood, there is now a park named **Kodokan Park**, after the Kodokan school founded by Nariaki (1800–60), the ninth lord of Mito, in

 VISITING MITO

INFORMATION
www.city.mito.ibaraki.jp/english

TRANSPORT
By rail: from Tokyo (Ueno station) JR Joban line (1½ hours).

the year 1842. There are two shrines behind the school building, dating from the same period; reflecting the main direction of education at the time, they are dedicated to the commander Kashima-Myojin and the philosopher Confucius.

✱
Kairaku-en

3km/2mi west of the station is the Kairaku-en garden (also Tokiwa Park), originally created by Nariaki; it was later transformed into a public park and is more famous for the natural beauty of the 3000 plum trees (in bloom: Feb–March) than for the art of the landscape gardener. The trees are not purely ornamental varieties: their fruit is preserved and plays an important role on Japanese menus as »ume-boshi«; in Mito they are used **to make pastries**. The park contains a replica of the Kobun-tei tea house from the time of Nariaki; there is a fine view of the town and the surrounding area from the third floor (open April to 15 Sept daily 6am–7pm, 16 Sept to March 7am–6pm, free admission).

Around Mito

Oarai

12km/7.5mi southeast of the station is the seaside resort of Oarai. The Joyo-Meiji Commemoration Mansion on the top of a pine-covered hill near the Oarai-Isozaki shrine is dedicated to the memory of Emperor Meiji (1852–1912).

Kasama

Kasama (population 31,000), around 25km/15mi west of Mito (JR Mito line), was once the ancestral seat of the Makino family. Today it is the destination of more than one million pilgrims a year, who come to visit the **Kasama-Inari shrine** (1.5km/1mi north of the station), where a well-known chrysanthemum festival takes in late October or early November.

Kobun-tei tea house surrounded by flowering azalea bushes and cedars

The **Sainenji temple** is located in the suburb of Inada to the south-west. It was once the hermitage of the monk Shinran (1173–1262), who founded the Jodo-shinshu sect and wrote down its doctrines in the work Kyogyo-shinsho.

> ! **Baedeker** TIP

> **Market and workshop**
> Many of the more than 150 workshops which produce the pottery known as Mashiko-yaki are open to the public; some even give hobby-potters the opportunity to try their own hand. It is worthwhile visiting during the Golden Week at the end of April or in early May and for the pottery market held at the beginning of November.

Around 40km/25mi northwest of Mito is the small town of Mashiko in the prefecture of Tochigi. It is the best-known centre of folk pottery in the area around Tokyo. The development of the local **ceramic manufactures** began with the establishment of the first kiln by Otsu-ka Keizaburo (1853); one of its sponsors was the art potter Hamada Shoji (1894–1977), who, together with the Englishman Bernard Leach, made the local products world-famous.

Mashiko

✱ Miyajima (Itsukushima)

G 7 • e 3

Main island: Honshu
Population: 3600

Prefecture: Hiroshima

The island of Miyajima is also called Itsukushima after its famous shrine and, together with the Bay of ►Matsushima and the Strait of►Ama-no-hashidate, is amongst Japan's most beautiful stretches of coastline.

宮島

Miyajima (Shrine Island) is an island with an area of around 30 sq km/10 sq mi in the bay of Hiroshima, which forms a part of the Inland Sea. It has been sacred ground since ancient times; until the Meiji Restoration births and deaths were not allowed to occur here and no dogs were permitted to be kept. The last prohibition is still in place, but now probably has more to do with the large number of fallow deer; the island still does not have a cemetery so that burials take place in Ono on the mainland. Even then the family members still have to subject themselves to certain cleansing rituals before they step on the »holy« Miyajima.

Holy Island

✱ ✱ Itsukushima Shrine

A path decorated with stone lanterns (5 minutes) leads from the ferry jetty to the spacious Itsukushima shrine. It is dedicated to the daughters of the Shinto wind deity Susanoo, the princesses Ichikishi-ma-hime, Tagori-hime and Tagitsu-hime. The first mention of this

🕐
Opening hours:
Daily 6.30am–6pm,
¥ 300

Itsukushima Shrine

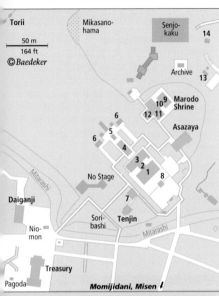

Torii | Mikasano-hama | Senjo-kaku 14
50 m
164 ft
©Baedeker
Archive 13
Marodo Shrine 10 9
12 11
6
Asazaya
6 5
4
3 2
No Stage 1 8
Mitarashi
7
Daiganji
Sori-bashi | Tenjin
Nio-mon
Mitarashi
Treasury
Pagoda | Momijidani, Misen

1 Honden (Main Hall)
2 Heiden (Sacrificial Hall)
3 Haiden (Prayer Hall)
4 Haraiden
(Hall for cleansing
ceremonies)
5 Takabutai (stage)
6 Music pavilions
7 Okuni Shrine

8 Fumyo-mon (gate)
9 Honden (Main Hall)
10 Heiden (Sacrificial Hall)
11 Haiden (Prayer Hall)
12 Haraiden
(Hall for cleansing
ceremonies)
13 Araebisu Shrine
14 Five-storey Pagoda

early Shinto shrine occurred in the year 811. Newly built under Taira Kiyomori (1118–81), the shrine had to be restored several times after that. The buildings have been constructed in **stilt-house style** above the water in a small bay; during high tide they appear to float and make for a very picturesque view with their red beams and white walls. Time a visit according to the tides. The primary and secondary complexes are connected via covered walkways.

To the northeast of the main shrine is a small bay. It contains the former hall of the morning prayer (Asazaya), which is now the office of the shrine administration (exhibition of masks and costumes, weapons, pictures). A covered walkway leads to the **Marodo shrine**, which resembles the main shrine in its configuration and sequence.

The **main shrine** consists of several halls, as Shinto ritual demands: from the shore the first hall is the main hall (honden), behind it the sacrificial hall (heiden), which goes out into the bay, the prayer hall (haiden) and the hall for cleansing ceremonies (haraiden), finally at the far end the stage (takabutai) for cult dances (bugaku, kagura), flanked by two music pavilions. Exactly along the extension of the main shrine's axis to the northwest is a red wooden torii 200m/220yd before the stage at the mouth of the bay. It is the largest torii in Japan (pillars 16.2m/53ft, cross beams 23.3m/76ft). It was built in 1875 in the Ryobu style and has an inscription by Prince Arisugawa (1835–95).

Okuni shrine
Tenjin shrine

There are two further buildings on stilts to the southwest of the main shrine: the Okuni shrine and the Tenjin shrine, dedicated respectively

Fireworks over Itsukushima shrine

to the Okuninushi deity and Sugawara Michizane (845–903), who was deified as Tenjin. This group of buildings is connected to the shore via a walkway and the boldly curved red wooden bridge (Sori-bashi).

Further northwest, at the edge of bay on a platform is **Japan's oldest No stage**, originally built in 1568, but then restored during the Edo period.

No theatre

To the southwest on the mainland is the modern fire and earth-quake-proof treasury. Of the more than 4000 valuable objects kept here, such as masks, suits of armour and cult objects, 130 are classed as **»national treasures«**; the picture scrolls and written scrolls with a chronicle of the Taira dynasty (Heike-monogatari) in a richly orna-mented chest are quite fantastic.

Treasury

The **Daiganji temple** north of the treasury belongs to the Buddhist Koyasan-Shingon sect and is dedicated to Benzaiten, the goddess of luck, whose statue Itsukushima-Benten adorns the temple along with statues of Buddha and his students.

There is another walkway from the Marodo shrine to the shore, which is the path used to get to the Hall of a Thousand Mats (Senjo-kaku) on a hill further north. The name is meant to highlight the size of this much-admired building; in truth it only contains around 450 tatami: rice-straw mats with a size of 90 x 180cm (35 x 70in). The hall was donated by Toyotomi Hideyoshi in 1587. For this rea-son it has been dedicated to his memory as the Hokoku shrine since 1872; according to legend it was made from a single camphor tree.

✱
Hall of a thousand mats
🕐
Opening hours:
Daily
8.30am–4.30pm,
¥ 100

▶ VISITING MIYAJIMA

INFORMATION

Tourist information
At the ferry pier, tel. 08 29/44 20 11
Daily 9am–5pm
www.miyajima.or.jp

TRANSPORT

By rail: from Hiroshima JR Senyo main line towards Iwakuni to Miyajimaguchi (25 minutes) or Hiroshima Electric Railway (from Hiroshima station) to Hiroden-Miyajima (1 hour).
By ferry: from Hiroshima (Ujina harbour) to Miyajima (25 minutes); ferry connections between Miyajimaguchi and Miyajima (10 minutes).

BOAT TRIPS

Ferries go to all of the islands of the ►Inland Sea. The route runs via Hiroshima and Miyaura (Omishima Island) to Setoda (Ikuchi Island) and from there back to the mainland (Mihara, Onomichi).

EVENTS

Toshikoshi (New Year's festival; beginning of January); Kangen-sai (night-time procession on the water with portable shrines and music; mid-June); Tamatori-matsuri (swimming competition around a holy ball; mid-July).

Momijidani   South of the main shrine a pleasant walk leads through the Momijidani (maple valley; several tea houses) to the lower terminus of a cableway (1.7km/1mi, 50 minutes), which runs up **Mount Misen**, at 530m/1739ft, the island's highest mountain. The Gumonji-do temple founded in the early 9th century by Kobo-daishi can be found close to the peak; the Japanese pilgrims circle the island and give sacrifices at the »Nanaura«, the seven beaches.

Miyazaki

Main island: Kyushu
Population: 306,000

Prefecture: Miyazaki

Miyazaki, the capital of Miyazaki Prefecture on Kyushu's southeast coast, advertises the fact that it is one of Japan's most sunny places. The appearance of the town, through which the Oyodo River flows, is shaped by its wide streets. Most attractions are outside the town.

What to See in and around Miyazaki

Miyazaki shrine   The Miyazaki shrine, dedicated to Emperor Jimmu, is 3km/2mi north of the station (bus). The grounds house a prefectural museum with finds from the Kofun period (haniwa figures amongst other things).

Heiwadai Park with the peace tower erected in 1940 is next to the shrine. The Haniwa-en garden can be found in a corner of the park; it owes its name to the replicas of haniwa terracotta figures here; there is a further exhibition in the affiliated Haniwa Museum.

Heiwadai Park

Nichinan-kaigan Quasi-National Park

The 48 sq km/19 sq mi Nichinan-kaigan Quasi-National Park begins around 10km/6mi south of the town; it extends around 50km/30mi along the Pacific coast. In the north of the park the small uninhabited island of Aoshima can be accessed via a bridge (bus from Miyazaki, 20 minutes); it is covered in lavish tropical and subtropical vegetation. The beach's sediment rocks have been eroded into the form of a huge washboard by the impact of the waves. There is a large **cactus garden** on the mainland coast opposite the island.

✳
Aoshima

Further south the no. 220 road makes its way over the Horikiri Pass after which it reaches the Udo shrine (bus from Miyazaki, 1½ hours), whose main buildings stand in a cave made by the waves at Cape Udo. The red colour of the torii creates an impressive contrast to the blue of the sea and the grey-brown of the rocks.

✳
Udo shrine

The southernmost part of the Quasi-National park is the plateau 300m/1000ft above sea level, which extends into the Pacific as Cape Toi. The plateau is home to wild horses. There is a large **lighthouse** at the cape with a far view over the ocean.

Cape Toi
✳
◄ View

27km/17mi north of Miyazaki is **Saitobaru** (Tsuma train line to Tsuma, then bus), famous for the approx. 380 burial mounds from the Kofun period. The most important archaeological finds are exhibited in the local museum.

Sobo-Katamuki Quasi-National Park

It takes two hours (JR Takachiho line) from Nobeoka to get to the town of Takachiho at the southwest fringe of the Sobo-Katamuki Quasi-National Park. The region, covered in jungle-like vegetation, reaches elevations of 1602m/5256ft in Mount Katamuki and 1758m/5768ft in Mount Sobo and is home to **rare animal species** such as the Japanese serow and the Japanese marten. The park's main attraction is the 7km/4.5mi Takachiho Gorge, which the Gokase River cut to a depth of up to 80m/260ft into the igneous rocks

In Takachiho Gorge

▶ VISITING MIYAZAKI

INFORMATION

Tourist information
In the station
Tel. 09 85/22 64 69
March–Nov daily 9am–7pm,
Dec–Feb until 6.30pm

TRANSPORT

By air: from Tokyo (Haneda Airport,
1¾ hours); from Fukuoka (1 hour).
By rail: from Fukuoka (Hakata) JR
Nippo main line (5 hours, via Beppu);
from Kagoshima (Nishi-Kagoshima
station) JR Nippo main line (2¼
hours).
By bus: from Miyazaki Airport to the
town centre (25 minutes).

✳ **Takachiho Gorge** thrown out by the volcano Mount Aso. Many Japanese myths are connected to this gorge; it is said, for example, that a goddess danced the first dance in the world here in order to entice the sun goddess out of a cave.

Takachiho shrine ► Go west of Takachiho station to get to Takachiho shrine, where four representative Yokagura dances are performed every evening (8–9pm, ¥ 500). It is not far from the shrine to the hiking trail, which runs along the gorge for approx. 1km/0.5mi (rowing boat rental).

Morioka

L 5

Main island: Honshu
Population: 281,000

Prefecture: Iwate

盛岡 **Morioka, the capital of Iwate Prefecture, is in the far north of the Japanese main island of Honshu. Mount Iwate rises up in the northwest; it is the town's landmark.**

What to See in Morioka

Iwate Park At the centre of town is Iwate Park, 1.7km/1mi southeast of the station (bus, 5 minutes); it contains a monument of the poet Ishikawa Takuboku (1886–1912), who spent his youth in Morioka. The site of the park was once occupied by the castle.

Not far from here **Kaminohashi Bridge** crosses the Nakatsu River. It dates back to the time the castle was being built and has rich bronze decorations (giboshi) from the 17th century.

Ho-onji temple Ho-onji temple, probably built in 1732, is not far away (ten minutes' walk); the main hall contains the small sculptures of the 500 Rakan (ascetics), including depictions of Marco Polo and Kublai Khan.

Hashimoto Museum northeast of the station (bus, 20 minutes, half way up Mount Iwayama) has works by the painter Hashimoto Yaoji as well as ceramics and metalware on display. A wonderful view of the town and Mount Iwate is to be had from the peak of Mount Iwayama.

> **!** *Baedeker* TIP
>
> **Kettles and kokeshi**
> Morioka's best-known product is ironware, particularly »nambu-tetsubin«, cast-iron tea kettles. The carved wooden dolls (kokeshi) are also popular, as are the ceramics from Kuji (Kuji-yaki) further north. These and other local crafts can be admired in the Morioka Tezukuri Mura (bus from the station, 25 minutes).

Around Morioka

The romantic small mountain town of **Amihari-onsen** (JR Taza-wako line to Shizukuishi, then bus, 50 minutes) and »Koiwai Farm« (bus from Morioka station, 35 minutes) with a restaurant, hotel and more are located along the southern foothills of the volcano Mount Iwate (► Towada-Hachimantai National Park).

Further west (JR Tazawako line) is the beautiful Lake Tazawa (425m/ 1394ft deep, 2570ha/6350 acres), which is surrounded by densely forested hills all around (40-minute boat trips from mid-April to mid-Nov). The best view of the lake is from the top of the 1637m/ 5371ft Mount Komagatake (► Towada-Hachimantai National Park). On the lake's eastern shore there is a 35m/115ft Kannon statue, the largest in Japan.

★
Lake Tazawa

South of the town (JR Tohoku line, 30 minutes) lies the agricultural centre of Hanamaki (population 69,000). The Hanamaki-matsuri festival is celebrated here every year from 5 to 7 September; the festival's climax is the »dance of the stags« (Shika-odori).

Hanamaki

 VISITING MORIOKA

INFORMATION

Tourist information
In the centre, Plaza Odette,
1-1-10, Nakanohashi-dori
Tel. 0 19/6 04 33 05
Daily 9am–8pm,
except 2nd Tue of the month
www.city.morioka.iwate.jp
For northern Tohoku:
On the 2nd floor of the JR station,
Tel. 0 19/6 25 20 90
Daily 9am–5.30pm

TRANSPORT

By air: from Osaka (1½ hours).
By rail: from Tokyo (Ueno station) JR Tohoku shinkansen line (2½ hours); also JR Tohoku main line via Sendai (6¼ hours).
By bus: from Hanamaki Airport to the town centre (1 hour).

EVENTS

Chagu-chagu Umakko (horse festival with festively dressed children; mid-June), at Komagata shrine.

Northwest of Hanamaki (bus connections) is the extensive Hanama-ki-onsenkyo spa region. There is a **sports and leisure area** (winter sports too) near Hanamaki-onsen; the cherry trees on the banks of the Dai are very attractive, as is the large rose garden created by Miyazawa Kenji.

Ryusendo Cave

Northeast of Morioka (JR Yamada line to Moichi, then JR Iwaizumi line, four hours) is Iwaizumi; further north the large Ryusendo drip-stone cave has impressive sinter formations, lakes and waterfalls; the cave museum (Ryusenshindo-kagakukan) can be found at the cave's entrance (open daily 8.30am–6pm, Oct–April until 5pm, ¥ 1000).

★ Nagano

K 6 • I 1

Main island: Honshu	**Prefecture:** Nagano
Population: 359,000	

長野

The tranquil town of Nagano became internationally famous in 1998 when it was chosen as the site for the Olympic Winter Games. The 60m/197ft ski-jumping hill in Hakuba is their symbol. The town has been famous for a long time within Japan for its Zenkoji temple.

Olympic town

Prior to being made the capital of a prefecture in the centre of Honshu, the town of Nagano was called Zenkoji after the famous temple of the same name. In addition to breeding silk worms, another important activity is the sale of the fruit cultivated in the surrounding area, particularly apples.

Pilgrims have hung up tablets with their wishes at Zenkoji temple

What to See in Nagano

The M-Wave, a large sporting arena in Nagano with an Olympic Museum (bus from the station, 15 minutes) recalls the 18th Olympic Winter Games.

M-Wave

2km/1mi from the station (bus) is Zenkoji temple, founded by Zenko (alternative reading: Yoshimitsu) in 624; the temple is visited by large numbers of Buddhist pilgrims (open daily 5.30am–4.30pm, Oct–March 6.30am–4pm, free admission). The main hall was built in 1707; the bronze statues of the gods Amida-nyorai, Kannon and Seishi, which presumably came to Japan as early as 552 as a gift from a Korean ruler, are said to have been thrown into a canal near Osaka by an opponent of Buddhism, found again in 602 and brought to Nagano in 1598. The central figure can only be seen every six years (2009, 2015).

**✶ ✶
Zenkoji
temple**

Joshin-etsu-kogen National Park

North and east of the town are the two non-contiguous areas that make up the Joshin-etsu-kogen National Park. In the north are the mountains around Mount Myoko (2466m/8091ft), Mount Kurohime (2053m/6736ft), Mount Togakushi (1911m/6270ft) and Mount Iizuna (1917m/6289ft); in the east is the area around the 1963m/6440ft Mount Tanigawa and the two active volcanoes Shirane (2162m/7093ft) and Asama (2542m/8340ft; last eruption September 2004). The **large ski areas** of Suga-daira and Shiga-kogen (numerous lifts) are located on Mount Asama. During the summer months the plateau with its clear lakes and airy birch woods is a popular destination (boat rental, golf courses, several hotels).

Landscape

Around 20km/12.5mi from Nagano (Nagano Dentetsu line, 20–30 minutes) is the pretty artist town of Obuse in front of the Shirane Mountains. The famous painter Hokusai and the calligrapher Kozan worked here together. The internationally famous *Great Wave of Kanagawa* was painted here. The Hokusai Museum (10 minutes on foot to the southeast of the station) exhibits less well-known works by the master: in addition to woodblock prints there are also some watercolours and floats decorated by Hokusai (open daily 9am–5pm, April–Sept until 6pm, ¥ 500).

Obuse

⊕

This part of the national park is traversed by the Shiga-Kusatsu-kogen mountain road, which connects the towns of Yudanaka (to the north) and Karuizawa (to the south); it climbs to a height of around 2000m/6600ft. It takes 40 minutes for the Limited Express Train to travel from Nagano to the town of **Yudanaka**. Take a taxi or bus to **Jigokudani Park**, where 270 wild monkeys enjoy bathing in the hot springs, something that is particularly interesting in winter (open 8.30am–5pm, Nov–March 9am–4pm, ¥ 500).

Mountain road

⊕

⏵ VISITING NAGANO

INFORMATION

Tourist information
In the station, tel. 0 26/2 26 56 26
Daily 9am–6pm
www.city.nagano.nagano.jp/english

TRANSPORT

By rail: from Tokyo Nagano shin-kansen (1½ hours); from Nagoya JR Chuo and Shinonoi line (3 hours).

WHERE TO STAY

▶ Mid-range
Saihokukan Hotel
Agata-machi 528-1, Nagano-shi,
Nagano-ken 380-0838
Tel. 0 26/2 35 33 33, fax 2 35 33 65
www.saihokukan.com
Standard hotel with 89 rooms, established in 1890. Pleasant terrace and popular bakery/pâtisserie. Good location between station and Zenkoji temple.

▶ Budget
Uotoshi Ryokan
In Yudanaka Onsen
2563 Sano, Yamanouchi-machi,
Shimo Takai-gun,
Nagano-ken 381-0402
Tel. 02 69/33 12 15
Fax 33 00 74
www.avis.ne.jp/~miyasaka
From Nagano station with the Naga-no-Dentetsu line.
Pleasant minshuku with 19 rooms and an old bath made of cypress wood at the foot of Shiga Heights, where the 1998 Olympic Winter Games were held. Near a natural hot spring. On request the friendly owner, who speaks English, will give an introduction to Japanese archery (kyudo). Not far from here is the park, where Japanese macaques enjoy bathing in the hot spring water.

Kusatsu Leaving Yudanaka, take the Shiga Plateau and Kustatsu Pass to the small mountain resort of Kusatsu, idyllically situated on a precipice over Agatsuma River. The hot springs of Yubatake and Sainokawara (60–67°C/140–153°F) contain sulphur, iron, alum and arsenic. The German physician **Erwin Bälz** made this spa famous far beyond Japan's borders. There is a Bälz Museum in the town. In addition to the steaming Sai no Kawara Park the hot natural bath can be used free of charge. From 1 to 3 August the town festival, Onsen-matsuri, takes place.

Shirane A cableway leads up Mount Shirane (volcano, also known as Kusatsu-Shirane) starting in the town of Sesshogawara, which is located in the winter sports region of Kusatsu; the three craters can be reached in 30 minutes from the mountain station.

Takada Around 70km/45mi north of Nagano is the town of Takada (JR Shin-etsu main line), where an Austrian major named von Lerch first introduced skiing to Japan in 1910. The most important ski area of this snowy region is Mount Kanaya to the southwest.

Nagasaki

E8 • b5

Main island: Kyushu
Population: 449,000

Prefecture: Nagasaki

長崎

The city, which has spread into the forested heights around the harbour, is considered to be one of the most beautifully located in Japan. A further attraction is the mix of Eastern and Western culture and the city's cosmopolitan flair, which is rarely found in Japan.

Nagasaki, the capital of Nagasaki Prefecture, is situated on Kyushu's northwest coast, nestled in a fjord-like bay, which, protected by the offshore islands, makes for an excellent natural harbour; it was the only port open to European ships between the 16th and 19th centuries. This significant industrial city is a centre of Japanese ship-building; the shipyards extend over several kilometres along the west coast of Nagasaki Bay; their huge docks have room for super tankers and giant container ships.

Prosperous port city

At the end of the 12th century the area of the fishing village then called Fukae-no-ura or Tama-no-ura came into the hands of the feudal lord Nagasaki Kotaro, whose family name the city still bears today. In 1571 the port was opened to European merchants. The Portuguese, Dutch and Spaniards opened trading posts. Since the Japanese did not build ships suitable for the high seas, they let the European seafarers, and the Portuguese in particular, trade with China, the Philippines, Macao, Goa and from there to Europe. Soon the first Christian missionary work began. However, since the Japanese ruling class feared that the Jesuits in Nagasaki wanted to influence the political system, and since they had had enough of the Portuguese

History

! Baedeker TIP

Further reading

In his novel *Silence* (Chinmoku, 1966) Endo Shusak (1923–96) addressed Christian persecution on Kyushu: a Portuguese priest comes to Nagasaki to find out what happened to his brother. He has to hide, but is ultimately discovered and tortured. Will he, like so many before him, renounce his faith?

trade monopoly and incipient Westernization, Toyotomi Hideyoshi decreed an **edict against the missionaries** in 1587. In 1597, 26 Christians were crucified.

The trading activities continued, but now exclusively with the Dutch and the Chinese. The Dutch merchants and seafarers were not initially allowed to leave the area of **Dejima** (then an island, now attached to the mainland). These regulations were only relaxed somewhat later, permitting delegations to the court of Edo.

Japan's opening to the West during the Meiji period caused Nagasaki's significance to be greatly reduced, since the monopoly on im-

Nagasaki Map

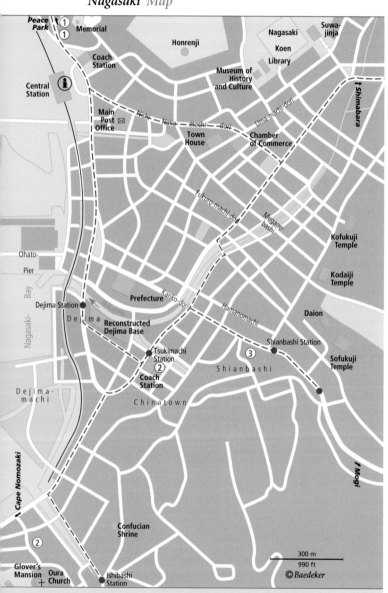

Where to eat
① Ichihana
② Chukasaikan Fukuju

Where to stay
① Europe
② Hotel Majestic
③ Ryokan Nishikiso Bekkan

porting European goods and ideas was broken. The port was temporarily still the destination of large numbers of Japanese who were hungry to learn the Western sciences and techniques finally accessible to them.

On **9 August 1945** the second atomic bomb exploded above Nagasaki. It was dropped by the United States, which was hoping to break Japanese resistance, already greatly weakened (► Hiroshima); the explosion caused terrible destruction and according to conservative estimates killed between 25,000 and 75,000 civilians.

What to See in Nagasaki

Not far from the station is the memorial for the 26 Christians (20 of them Japanese, six foreigners) who were crucified here on 5 February 1597 following an edict targeting Catholicism, and the Jesuits in particular. The site was initially made into a park in 1949 on the occasion of the 400th anniversary of Francisco de Javier's arrival in Japan; in 1962, 100 years after the martyrs were canonized, a commemorative hall was built, containing reliefs of the 26 saints.

Memorial for the 26 martyrs of Japan

North of the station in the district of Urakami (tram to Matsuyama-cho, 10 minutes) is Peace Park with the almost 10m/33ft-high peace statue by Kitamura Seibo, one of the city's landmarks. Further east is Urakami Church (1914, rebuilt 1959). South of Peace Park, surrounding ground zero, is another park, and close by the moving **Atomic Bomb Museum** (Nagasaki Gembaku Shiryokan) with remains of clothes, film footage, a clock that stopped at the moment of the explosion, eye-witness reports and other harrowing evidence of the disaster (open daily 8.30am–5.30pm, ¥ 200).

Peace Park

Not far east of the station is the park Nagasaki Koen (formerly Suwa Park) on the slopes of Nishizaka Hill. The prefectural library can be found on its southwest side, as can be the Museum of History and Culture, which addresses the historical contacts to Europe, China and Korea, amongst other things. The park contains Buddhist terrace cemeteries as well as a memorial stone for Carl Peter Thunberg, who worked as a surgeon in Nagasaki in 1775–76 and penned the first work on Japanese flora.

Nagasaki Koen

Adjoining the park in the northeast is Suwa-jinja shrine, founded in the mid-16th century and modelled on the shrines of the same name in central Japan. 73 steps lead up to it; there is a nice panorama of the town and port from the top. The Okunchi festival is held here every year (►Events, p.404).

Suwa-jinja

The reflections of the round arches helped give Spectacles Bridge its name

»Spectacles Bridge« South of Nagasaki Park several bridges cross Nakajima River, including the Chinese-style »Spectacles Bridge«, Meganebashi, commissioned by Abbot Nyojo in 1634; its two round arches are reflected in the water. In front of the bridge crossing visitors can see a porcelain frieze with the historical complex of Dejima.

Kofukuji temple East of Spectacles Bridge is the temple known as Chinese temple (1620); for a long time it was the temple of the Chinese business magnates. As Kofukuji temple is belongs to the Obaku sect, which practises Zen Buddhism.

Kodaiji temple Not far south of Kofukuji temple is Kodaiji temple, whose monks are members of the Zen Buddhist Soto school. It contains two interesting sights: a 7m/23ft Buddha statue and the tomb of Takashima Shuhan (1798–1866), who introduced Western weapons technology to Japan.

★★
Sofukuji temple Yet further south is Sofukuji temple (Obaku sect), which was founded by a Chinese Zen master in 1629. Hence the buildings are good examples of the late Ming style, particularly the **gate tower**, whose decorations represent the mythological paradise on the bottom of the sea known as Ryugu. The original second gate and the main hall are also worth seeing (open daily 8am–5pm, ¥ 300).

Dejima extends south of the mouth of Nakajima River, where the Dutch had a strongly guarded base from 1641 to 1854. There are plans to reconstruct it completely. Currently two warehouses (nos. 1 and 2), the captain's quarters, the kitchen and the house of the deputy director as well as a museum (in the former Protestant seminary) with an annexe can be seen. In another old warehouse a film is shown (open daily 9am–5pm, admission just to the museum, annexe and warehouse no. 2 ¥ 300). There is a model showing what the base once looked like.

East of Dejima is Nagasaki's **Chinatown**, Shinchi-machi, with numerous Chinese restaurants.

Dejima

In the southwest of the city is Glover Garden, a park with a number of old Western homes, including Glover's Mansion, the former residence of a Scottish merchant, which the Japanese like to present as the scene of **Puccini's Madame Butterfly** to tourists. Giacomo Puccini used Pierre Loti's *Madame Chrysantheme* as the model for his opera, using the Nagasaki of 1900 as his setting. The emotional attraction and separation of the Eastern and Western world, between the »butterfly« Cho Cho San and the naval lieutenant Pinkerton, is portrayed here in a tragic manner. The life-sized bronze statue of the singer Miura Tamaki as Cho Cho San, who points her child to the harbour bay, is the moving testimony of a failed approach between two cultures. There is a nice view of the harbour from the garden (open daily 8am–6pm, ¥ 600).

★
Glover's Mansion

 VISITING NAGASAKI

INFORMATION

Tourist information
In the station, tel. 0 95/8 23 36 31
Daily 8am–8pm
www.at-nagasaki.jp
www1.city.nagasaki.nagasaki.jp

Prefectural information office
Opposite the station in the bus station building,
2nd Floor, Nagasaki Ken'ei Bus Terminal, 3-1 Daikoku-machi
Tel. 0 95/8 26 94 07
Daily 9am–5.30pm
www.pref.nagasaki.jp/naisnet/en

TRANSPORT

By air: from Tokyo (Haneda Airport, 1¾ hours).

By rail: from Tokyo (central station) JR Tokaido shinkansen line to Hakata (5¼ hours), then JR Nagasaki and Sasebo main line (2 hours).
By bus: from the airport to the city centre (1 hour).

LOCAL TRANSPORT

The four *tram lines* in Nagasaki go to all of the city's attractions. Lines 1 and 3 (there is no no. 2) go from the station to Urakami to Peace Park and the Atomic Bomb Museum. In the other direction line no. 1 goes southwards to Dejima. Visitors wanting to go to the Glover Garden should take this line one stop further to Tsukimachi, then transfer into line no. 5. A one-way ticket costs ¥ 100, a day pass ¥ 500.

EVENTS

Hata-age (kite festival on the surrounding mountains; April/May); Peiron (rowing regatta; beginning of June), in the harbour; Bon festival (soul festival; mid-Aug); Okunchi festival (procession with floats and dragon dance; beginning of Oct), at Suwa shrine.

SHOPPING

Nagasaki is known for glass, pearls and Koga dolls, amongst other things. The *Amu Plaza Nagasaki* close to the station is a complex of shops, cinemas, restaurants and such like. The main shopping centre is Hamanomachi, a shopping street on the other side of the Nakajima River. From here it is just a short walk to one of Nagasaki's institutions, *Fukusaya Honten*, which has been manufacturing the local cake speciality Castella since 1624; it derives from a Portuguese recipe (3-1 Funadaiku-machi, daily 8.30am–8pm).

GOING OUT

The city's entertainment district is Shianbashi, situated between Chinatown and Hamanomachi, on the southern shore of Nakashimagawa River.

WHERE TO EAT

► **Expensive**
① *Ichihana*
In the Seiyokan
13-1 Kawaguchi-machi
Tel. 0 95/8 43 40 00
Daily 11am–2.30pm and 5pm–10.30pm, Sat, Sun from 4pm
Tram to Hamaguchi-machi
Anyone feeling a little peckish after a visit to Peace Park can enjoy some Japanese cuisine here, including shabu shabu.

► **Inexpensive**
② *Chukasaikan Fukuju*
Shinchimachi 2-5
Tel. 0 95/8 21 30 32
Daily 11am–2.30pm and 5–8.30pm
2 minutes from Tsukimachi tram station, near the main bus station. Here, in Chinatown, Nagasaki's famous noodle dish is served: champon.

WHERE TO STAY

► **Luxury**
① *Europe*
7-7 Huis ten Bosch, Sasebo-shi, 859-3293 Nagasaki
Tel. 0 95/6 58 11 11, fax 6 27 05 20
www.nagasaki.okura.com
This hotel, one of the Leading Hotels of the World, is situated near Sasebo in Omura Bay in the Dutch Huis ten Bosch theme park; it can be reached directly from the water via canal boats. It is fitted with European furniture and modern comforts. Restaurants serving French/European cuisine, amongst other things. Scheherazade cocktail lounge with a pianist, 18-hole golf course and tennis courts.

Baedeker recommendation

► **Mid-range**
② *Hotel Majestic*
2-28 Minami Yamate-machi
Tel. 0 95/8 27 77 77, fax 8 27 61 12
Nice Western-style hotel with 23 inviting rooms (all of them with a balcony) and pleasant terrace. Near Glover Garden.

► **Budget**
③ *Ryokan Nishikiso Bekkan*
1-2-7 Nishikoshima
Tel. 0 95/8 26 63 71, fax 8 28 07 82.
Tram line no. 1 to Shianbashi. Cosy Japanese-style accommodation. With a coin launderette.

The Catholic **Oura Church** can be found close to the park; it is Japan's oldest surviving church and has beautiful stained-glass windows.

Go northwest from Ishibashi tram station to get to the Confucian shrine (Koshibyo), built in the Chinese style in 1893. An adjoining museum displays Chinese works of art.

Koshibyo

On the bay's western side is Inasayama Hill (332m/1089; nature park); its summit can be reached in five minutes by cableway. There is a particularly nice view of the city from up here, especially when it is dark.

Inasayama

Around Nagasaki

11km/7mi southeast (50 minutes by bus) on the wide Chijiwa Bay the picturesque fishing port of Mogi lies among mandarin and orange groves. Among the crops grown here are loquats (Chinese »luh kwat«): orange, pear-shaped fruit, with a sweet-sour flesh.

Mogi

Around 20km/12mi south of Nagasaki (bus, 90 minutes) at Cape Nomozaki there is a fine view far into the East China Sea.

Cape Nomozaki

Regular ferry services exist between Nagasaki and the Goto archipelago (►Saikai National Park) in the west as well as to the port of Sasebo (population 251,000; naval base) further north on the mainland.

Sasebo

Nagoya

J 7 • j2

Main island: Honshu   **Prefecture:** Aichi
Population: 2.2 million

Even though Nagoya has more than a million inhabitants it does not attract many tourists. There are no outstanding attractions here. On the other hand, with its wide post-war roads and interesting industrial heritage, it is a pleasantly relaxing city.

名古屋

Nagoya, the capital of Aichi Prefecture, is situated in the middle of the Japanese main island of Honshu. Its location on the wide Ise Bay, which opens up to the Pacific, has favoured the development of the port, now the country's third-largest after Yokohama and Kobe. Nagoya is also of great significance as an industrial centre: the Toyota factory is just outside the city.

Japan's fourth-largest city

Nagoya developed around the fort built by the Imagawa and Oda families in the 16th century. Another fact giving the city even greater

History

significance was that Tokugawa Ieyasu had the large castle built for his son here in 1612 and made him the ruler of Owari Province. In this way he also created a stronghold against the ruling Toyotomi family. After Ieyasu beat his opponents in battle in 1614–15, the Owari Tokugawa resided in Nagoya until 1868, but then had to give up their power to the central government in Tokyo. The industrialization process began a short while later and laid the foundation for Nagoya's modern companies. The aerial attacks of 1945 caused severe damage to the city. During these bombings the castle was largely destroyed.

What to See in Nagoya

Castle Take the underground (Higashiyama line to Shiyakusho station) from the central station to the castle, whose 48m/157ft main tower was reconstructed in 1959. Its gables are decorated by a pair of gilded dolphins (shachi); inside there is a **museum** displaying artworks from

The television tower rises over the Oasis 21 complex, opened in 2002

Nagoya Map

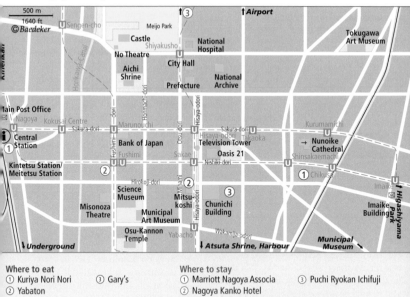

Where to eat
① Kuriya Nori Nori   ③ Gary's
② Yabaton

Where to stay
① Marriott Nagoya Associa   ③ Puchi Ryokan Ichifuji
② Nagoya Kanko Hotel

the palace destroyed in World War II. It contains painted folding screens and sliding doors as well as ceiling paintings, primarily from the Kano school. There is a panoramic view of the city and Nobi Plateau from the tower's fifth floor. Three corner towers, the second gate and some of the walls have survived from the original castle structures. East of the main tower is Ninomaru Garden with a tea house of the same name.

Opening hours:
Daily 9am–4.30pm,
¥ 500

To the south (Marunouchi, district of Naka-ku) two shrines lie close together: Toshogu shrine, dedicated to Tokugawa Ieyasu, was founded in 1619 and reconstructed in 1952; Nagono shrine, founded by Emperor Daigo in 911, was moved here from its original location in the castle grounds in 1876.

**Toshogu shrine
Nagono shrine**

The 180m/590ft television tower, whose observation platform provides an excellent panorama, is located on the wide Hisaya-odori road, which runs in a north-south direction to the east of the two shrines. A few steps south of the tower is Sakae underground station.

Television tower

Not far from the television tower, on the other side of the road, is the futuristic Oasis 21 complex: a park, shopping centre and a bus stop for the city buses all in one. The complex, which opened in 2002, is thematically modelled on a space ship.

Oasis 21

Shirakawa Park   Further southwest, quite a way away from the television tower, is Shirakawa Park with the science museum (physics, chemistry, engineering; planetarium) and the city's art museum.

★ ★
Tokugawa Art Museum   Go 3km/2mi east from the castle to get to Tokugawa Art Museum (Tokugawa bijutsukan; Tokugawaen Shin-Deki bus stop; open Tue–Sun 10am–5pm, ¥ 1200, www.tokugawa-art-museum.jp) with exhibits from the possessions of the Tokugawa resident in Nagoya, including paintings, porcelain, weapons and documents, particularly 43 parts of the **picture scroll** *Genji-monogatari-emaki* by Fujiwara Takayoshi (the originals are however usually under lock and key) as well as the *Saigyo-monogatari-emaki* picture scroll (depictions from the life of the priest Saigyo, 1118–90).

! *Baedeker* TIP

»Moving Forward«
Anyone wanting to visit the Toyota factory in the town of Toyota should make sure to book in time (take the Tsurumai line from Nagoya to Toyota-shi, then the bus to Toyota Honsha Mae). To do this call between three months and two weeks in advance (tel. 00 81-5 65/23 39 22, English) and then fax or mail the necessary details. The two-hour guided tours start at 11am in the Toyota Kaikan, which can also be visited without advance bookings (car models). More information at www.toyota.co.jp/en/about_toyota/facility/toyota_kaikan.

To the east, outside the city centre (Higashiyama underground line) is **Nittaiji temple**, built on Kakuozan Hill in 1904; it contains a gilded Buddha statue (a gift from the king of Siam in 1900).

Higashiyama Park (Higashiyama-koen; the underground station has the same name, 15 minutes from the station) is an 82ha/203-acre recreational area containing a zoo, a botanical garden, observatory and more, as well as a 10m/3ft wooden Kannon statue. To its north is the extensive **Heiwakoen** complex (»Peace Park«), a cemetery with the tomb of Oda Nobunaga (1534–1582).

★
Osu-Kannon temple   Take the underground (Higashiyama line to Fushimi station, then Tsurumai line to Osu-Kannon station) from the central station southeast-bound to Osu-Kannon temple (also Hoshoin), built anew at the site of a temple founded in 1612. It has a significant library, which contains the oldest surviving copy of the historical work *Kojiki* (712). A lively shopping quarter begins at the temple (▶p.410).

Toyota Commemorative Museum of Industry and Technology   Those who cannot make it to the Toyota factory should visit the Toyota Commemorative Museum of Industry and Technology (Sangyo Gijutsu Kinenkan, www.tcmit.org) north of the station (Meitetsu line to Sako or Higashiyama underground to Kameyama, then bus to Sangyo Gijutus Kinenkan). The museum is housed in an old factory building from the beginning of the 20th century and addresses the city's industrial history. In addition to looms (Nagoya is an old centre of the textile industry) the museum exhibits robots used in automobile production (open Tue–Sun 9.30am–5pm, ¥ 500).

In the south of the city (Meitetsu train line, Jingu-mae station) is the Atsuta shrine, second only to Ise (►Ise-Shima National Park) as Japan's most significant Shinto shrine. It once housed **one of Japan's three imperial regalia**, the »grass-mowing sword« (Kusanagi-no-tsurugi), which is now kept in Ise shrine.

Atsuta shrine

According to legend the sword originally came from the storm god Susanoo. When the legendary hero Yamato-takeru set off to conquer the eastern provinces he was given the fantastic weapon by the high priestess of Ise shrine, Yamato-hime. When his enemies set fire to the tall, dry grass in order to kill him, he saved himself by mowing it

▶ VISITING NAGOYA

INFORMATION

Tourist information centres
In the **station**, tel. 0 52/5 41 43 01
Daily 9am–7pm
Near the **television tower** in Sakae, in Oasis 21 (basement)
Tel. 0 52/9 63 52 52
Daily 10am–8pm
District **Naka-ku**, north exit of the underground station Kanayama
Tel. 0 52/3 23 01 61
Daily 9am–8pm
At the **harbour**, next to Nagoya-ko underground station, Minato-ku
Tel. 0 52/6 54 70 00
Tue–Sun 9am–5pm (21 July to 31 Aug until 8pm)
Nagoya International Center Building, 3rd Floor, 1-47-1 Nagono, Nakamura-ku, in the Sakura-dori, one stop east of the station
Tel. 0 52/5 81 01 00
Tue–Sat 9am–8.30pm
Sun until 5pm (closed 2nd Sun in Feb and Aug)
Internet: www.ncvb.or.jp/kankou_e
www.city.nagoya.jp/global/en
www.aichi-kanko.jp/english
(information on Aichi Prefecture)
http://ckp.ivcreation.com
(information on the Chubu region)

TRANSPORT

By air: from Tokyo (Narita Airport; 1 hour); also connections to Hokkaido, Tohoku, western Japan, Kyushu and Okinawa; international flights to Asia, Europe, the United States and Oceania.
Central Japan International Airport: Meitetsu trains (½ hour) and buses from Sakae Bus Terminal (50 minutes) go to the new international airport south of the city (Centrair, www.centrair.jp, tel. 05 69/38 11 95, flights to Frankfurt and Paris).
JAL flies to various Japanese cities in the north and south of the country from the old **Nagoya Kuko Airport**, northeast of the city (bus from the railway station 30 minutes).

! Baedeker TIP

A bath before flying

Anone who wants to relax before catching his flight should try the Miya-no-Yu bath (the sign says »General relaxation«, open daily 8am–10pm) on the 4th floor (Skytown) of the airport and enjoy a great view.

By rail: from Tokyo (central station) JR Tokaido shinkansen line (2 hours); from Osaka JR Tokaido shinkansen line (1 hour); Nagoya is also the stop for the JR Tokaido, Chuo and Kansai main lines.

By bus: from Tokyo JR and Nihon-Kyuko bus route via the Tomei Expressway (6 hours); from Kyoto and Osaka via the Meishin Expressway (2¾ hours and 3½ hours respectively).

LOCAL TRANSPORT

Nagoya has an efficient underground network. The Higashiyama line and the Sakura-dori line are useful for tourists; they depart the station and go via the city centre to the east and southeast of the city respectively; another good line is the Meiji ring line, which forms a circle around the centre and stops at the castle and Atsuta shrine; in Kanayama the Meiko line branches off to the harbour. Take the Tsurumai line to Osu-Kannon south of the centre. A ticket costs ¥ 200 and up, a day pass for bus and train costs ¥ 850.

A useful *bus* is the Key Route Bus, which goes from the station via the castle to Tokugawa Museum (¥ 200). The *trains* of the Kintetsu line run towards Mie (including to Ise shrine) and Kansai, those of the Meitetsu line (private trains) head to Gifu (including Inuyama) and Aichi. Their main railway stations are next to the JR station.

More information at www.kotsu.city.nagoya.jp.

EVENTS

Archery (collection of lucky arrows; mid-Jan), at Atsuta shrine; fertility festival (procession with phallus symbols; mid-March), at Tagata shrine; shrine festival (procession with floats and old puppets; mid-April), at Toshogu shrine; Atsuta-matsuri (with martial arts competitions, No performances and fireworks; beginning of June), at Atsuta shrine; Minato-matsuri (harbour festival with processions and fireworks; mid-July); Nagoya-matsuri (procession with medieval costumes, fireworks and more; mid-Oct).

Good tips about matsuri, restaurants and more can be found in the quarterly magazine *Avenues* (www.avenuesmagazine.com).

SHOPPING

The main shopping district is *Sakae.* All major department stores and bookshops with English-language sections are also located here, e.g. Maruzen. The Oasis 21 complex is relatively new; it also houses shops, including a Pokemon shop for those visitors still in search of a souvenir for their little ones …

There is an underground labyrinth of *shopping streets* between the station and the city centre. Almost anything the heart desires can be purchased here: cosmetics, clothes, photography equipment, tea, bread and so on. The station itself houses the two department stores Takashimaya and Tokyu Hands.

A shopping area that is a little bit different is the *quarter around Osu-Kannon temple.* Visitors will not find any fancy shops here, but rather shops selling everything from second-hand kimonos to rice cakes. On the 18th and 28th of every month an antique market takes place here.

WHERE TO EAT

▶ **Moderate**

① *Kuriya Nori Nori*
Naka-ku, Aoi 2-13-22

KD Place, 1st floor
Tel. 0 52/9 35 59 88
Mon–Sat 11am–2pm
and 5pm–3am
The winning décor emanates simple elegance, the cuisine is creative new Japanese. The restaurant also serves Guinness and has changing ikebana flower arrangements.

► Inexpensive
② *Yabaton*
3-6-1 Naka-ku, in La Chic (Mitsukoshi), 7th floor
Tel. 0 52/2 69 70 70
Daily 11am–11pm
Serves one of Nagoya's specialities: misokatsu, pork schnitzel in red miso (which makes the meat taste less greasy). The restaurant's logo is a pig with a sumo loincloth. It also adorns plates, glasses and suchlike, which can be purchased as souvenirs. Expect queues. Food can also be ordered to go (however, Japanese people do not eat on the street, let alone while walking).

GOING OUT
Nagoya's nightlife mainly takes places in *Sakae*. A time-tested address is
③ *Gary's*
(basement of the Koasa Building 4-2-10 Sakae, tel. 0 52/2 63 47 10, Mon–Sat 6pm–4am, Sun until 2am), where a foreign band provides the musical entertainment with Motown, Soul and R'n'B (dancing).

WHERE TO STAY
► Luxury
① *Marriott Nagoya Associa*
1-1-4 Meieki, Nakamura-ku
Tel. 0 52/5 84 11 11
www.associa.com/english/nma
One of the city's top hotels, if not the best. In one of the two Central Towers of the JR station, the city's new landmark. The rooms have the usual comforts as well as a great view of the city (all the way to the castle). Good restaurants with Western and Japanese-style cuisine, including the recommendable ka-un. Front desk on the 15th floor.

Baedeker recommendation

► Mid-range
② *Nagoya Kanko Hotel*
1-19-30 Nishiki, Naka-ku
Tel. 0 52/2 31 77 11
www.nagoyakankohotel.co.jp
Pleasant hotel with rooms that are relatively spacious for Japan. Relaxed atmosphere, friendly, helpful staff. It is not far from here to the old Nayabashi Bridge, reconstructed in 1981, which crosses the Horikawa River, a romantic spot in this city of two million inhabitants.

► Budget
③ *Puchi (Petit) Ryokan Ichifuji*
Kita-ku, Saikobashi-dori 1-7
Tel. 0 52/9 14 28 67
Fax 9 81 68 36
www.jin.ne.jp/ichifuji
Heian-dori underground station (Meijo line)
5 minutes' walk from exit 2.
Cosy Japanese-style accommodation, run by a young woman. The neighbouring restaurant serves Chinese dim sum in addition to Japanese cuisine. Somewhat out of the way in the north of the city, but good public transport links.

with the sword. When he hung the weapon from a mulberry tree Princess Miyazu-hime took it away. The blade's bright sheen set fire to a cedar. Popular etymology derives the town's name (»Atsuta« means »burning field«) from this event. In the northern part of the forested shrine complex are the **main shrine Hongu**, which is surrounded by a wall and is thus inaccessible. The **treasury** can be found in the east; it contains numerous remarkable art treasures, including old and modern paintings, ceramics, jewellery, theatre masks and much more (open daily except the last Wed of the month 9am–4.30pm, ¥ 300).

Shiratori-no-misasagi Around 500m/550yd northwest of the shrine is the Shiratori-no-misasagi burial mound (»grave of the white bird«), allegedly the tomb of Yamato-takeru, who is said to have turned into a white bird after his death.

Harbour The harbour area extends south of the city (terminal of the Meiko underground line; 30 minutes from Nagoya station); it has a water surface of around 25,000ha/62,000 acres. The Maritime Museum's observation platform has a view far out to sea. The 63m/207ft Port Building was opened in 1984; the **research ship *Fuji*** is nearby; it contains exhibits relating to Antarctic research. Take Port Bridge to get to the city's aquarium.

Around Nagoya

Gifu Take the Meitetsu private line to get to Gifu (population 404,000), 30km/19mi to the north. It is the capital of Gifu Prefecture and lies in the shadow of Mount Inaba. The paper parasols, lanterns, fans etc. produced here are famous. Gifu Park, set up in 1888, extends along the bank of the Nagara River; it also contains an aquarium.

Inaba ▶ Take a cableway up Mount Inaba; its peak is crowned by the reconstructed castle (museum). There is an interesting view of the bare mountain sides: large amounts of rock are removed from here for the land reclamation project along the coast (»yamakiri« means »mountain cutting«).

Cormorant fishing ▶ A special attraction is cormorant fishing (ukai) on the Nagara River. Every night between 1 June and 30 September (except during full moon and after heavy rainfall) fishing and spectator boats set sail. The light of the fire baskets attached to the boats' prows attracts ayu or sweetfish. The master (usho) directs the trained cormorants with the help of a leash, who are prevented from swallowing their catch by a ring around their neck. Every bird is able to catch up to 50 fish. This fishing method is ancient and was probably adopted from China. Grilled ayu can be sampled on the boats.

Inuyama East of Gifu, via the castle town of Inuyama, is the **open-air museum Meiji-mura** (Meitetsu bus route from Nagoya, 1 hour) with original

Fishing with trained cormorants is a popular spectacle

buildings from around 40 parts of the country from the Meiji period, an old train and more (open Jan, Feb and Dec Tue–Sun 9.30am–5pm, Nov–Feb until 4pm, ¥ 1600).

Inuyama's Nihon Monkey Park is worth a visit; it contains a botanical garden, a zoo, a collection of folkcraft and a monkey research station (open daily 10am–5pm, 20 July until end of Aug 9.30am–6pm, Dec–Feb 10am–4.30pm, 12–27 Feb only Sun, ¥ 1500).

◄ Nihon Monkey Park

The Meitetsu private train goes on to Imawatari, the starting point for riding the rapids on the Kiso River, which is particularly attractive along this stretch (trip duration to Inuyama approx. 1 hour; Meitetsu-Hiromi train line from Shin-Nagoya station to Imawatari, 1 hour).

Imawatari

A delightful trip leads to Kiso Valley, to the former Tsumago and Magome post stations on the Nakasendo, an old trade route through the mountains from Kyoto to Edo (Tokyo). The picturesque small towns have been successfully restored to their former condition: the ugly power lines, which usually run above ground, were hidden, motorized traffic was banned and the old houses were lovingly restored. After visiting Magome, walk along the old trade route through forests, past waterfalls to Tsumago (8km/5mi). Take the Chuo line from Nagoya to Nakatsugawa (50 minutes), from there the bus to Magome (30 minutes).

✹ ✹
Tsumago and Magome

East of Nagoya is the old pottery town of Seto (population 124,000; Meitetsu private train line from Nagoya, 30 minutes). The first, still unglazed, ware was produced here as early as 1200. The old pottery

Seto

called Ko-Seto by the 13th-century master Kato Toshiro is still highly valued today. Fukagawa shrine contains two Koma-inu representations (mythological dog-lion creatures) allegedly made by Toshiro; Kama shrine in the north in the town is dedicated to Kato Tamaki-chi, who introduced porcelain production in Seto based on the Arita method in 1807. Suehiko shrine was set up for Toshiro, whose porcelain monument stands in Seto Park.

Mikawa Bay Southeast of Nagoya is Mikawa Bay, which is part of Mikawa Quasi-National Park. A favourable starting point is Gamagori (Meitetsu private train line from Nagoya, 1½ hours), a pretty seaside town. The train lines carries on via Toyohashi to Atsumi Peninsula, the park's southernmost point, with its attractive coastal landscape. Take the bus from Toyohashi via Mikawa-Tahara to Cape Irako to see the Irako shrine and a grotto. There is a ferry connection to Toba (►Ise-Shima National Park).

★ ★ Nara

H 7 • h 3

Main island: Honshu	**Prefecture:** Nara
Population: 363,000	

奈良 **This famous city radiates a peaceful, tranquil atmosphere, despite its hordes of tourists. In addition to the Great Buddha it contains a large number of worthwhile temples and shrines. Those who do not have a lot of time should select two or three highlights instead of rushing from temple to temple.**

Cradle of Japanese culture The famous city of Nara is located in the central part of the main island of Honshu, south of Lake Biwa. The modern-day capital of Nara Prefecture is surrounded by hills, forests and wide fields; the Nara Basin extends to the south. Its exceptional wealth of cultural attractions means the city is visited by more than a million tourists every year. Nara's old buildings are situated in picturesque landscape, which can be seen particularly well from the top of **Mikasayama Hill**.

! *Baedeker* TIP

Souvenirs from Nara

The most important craft products are carved wooden dolls (Nara-ningyo), lacquerware (Nara-shikki), fans (Nara-uchiwa) and ceramics (Aka-hada-yaki).

From the time of the legendary founding of the empire by Emperor Jimmu in the Yamato Basin (Nara Basin) the capital was always moved after the death of a ruler. In 710, under the rule of **Empress Gemmyo** (661–721), the first permanent capital was founded: Heijo-kyo, modern-day Nara. Based on the town planning pattern of the

History

Nara *Map*

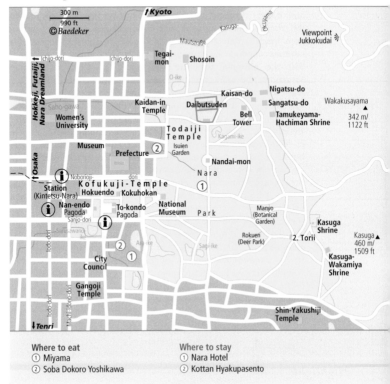

300 m
990 ft
© Baedeker

↑ Kyoto

Kasuga-

Ōkuyama

Mautstraße

Viewpoint
Jukkokudai

Ichijo-dori

Ichijo-dori

Hokkeji, Futaiji
Nara Dreamland

Tegai-
mon

Shosoin

O-ike

Kaisan-do

Nigatsu-do

Kaidan-in
Temple

Daibutsuden

Saho-gawa

Women's
University

Bell
Tower

Todaiji
Temple

Sangatsu-do

Wakakusayama

▲
342 m/
1122 ft

Tamukeyama-
Hachiman Shrine

Kagami-ike

Museum

Prefecture ②

Isuien
Garden

Nandai-mon

Nara

Osaka

ℹ Noborioji-   dori

Station
(Kintetsu-Nara)

Kofukuji-Temple

①

Hokuendo   Kokuhokan

Manyo
(Botanical
Garden)

Kasuga
Shrine

Kasuga ▲
460 m/
1509 ft

ℹ Nan-endo
Pagoda

To-kondo
Pagoda

National
Museum

Park

Sanjo-dori

Sanso-wani-
ike

ℹ

Ate-ike

Rokuen
(Deer Park)

Sagi-ike

2. Torii

Kasuga-
Wakamiya
Shrine

Todo-dori

② ①

City
Council

Gangoji
Temple

Todo-dori

Machinado-dori

Shin-Yakushiji
Temple

↓ Tenri

Where to eat
① Miyama
② Soba Dokoro Yoshikawa

Where to stay
① Nara Hotel
② Kottan Hyakupasento

Chinese T'ang Dynasty the city was built on a chequerboard plan to the west of its current centre. The Chinese city of Ch'ang-an was used as the model. The city extending south of the imperial palace was divided into an eastern and a western part. It measured 4.8km/ 3mi from north to south and 4.3km/2.5mi from east to west. The significance of Nara, which quickly developed into the country's political and cultural centre, was also reflected in its population: even in those days Nara already had 200,000 inhabitants. Nara remained the seat of government for 74 years and for that reason the era is called the Nara period. The adoption of Buddhism as well as a strong imitation of the art of the T'ang Dynasty took place under state leadership. Official emissaries travelled to China and from there monks came to Japan to teach, for example **Ganjin** (►Famous People), who was invited by Emperor Shomu in 753. As a result Buddhist sects became more influential and Confucianism was also adopted, though to a lesser extent.

Literature ▶ Under Empress Gemmyo works of literature were written that are still of great significance today, particularly for historians. In 712 **Ko-jiki**, the first surviving work with historical contents (albeit infused with legend), was written; in 713 *Fudoki*, Japan's first topography, commissioned by the empress and written in Chinese characters; in 720 **the national chronicle Nihonshoki**, modelled on Chinese historiography. *Monyoshu*, the oldest still extant anthology (4173 poems) was also compiled around that time.

Temple buildings ▶ The Nara period reached its peak under the rule of **Emperor Shomu** (701–756), who commissioned the Daibutsu, a 16m/52ft bronze Buddha statue. The spread of Buddhism was promoted by an imperial edict envisioning the construction of provincial temples (Kokubunji). An office subordinate to the government (Shakyoshi) was set up to make copies of Buddhist manuscripts. China's influence led to the construction of large temple complexes; sculpture and painting largely followed the stylistic forms and techniques from China, which in turn took elements from the Indian cultural sphere. While the sculptures from the Suiko period (552–645) were still highly rigid, the new sculptures began displaying softer forms. Especially the Tempyo period of the late Nara period shows such influences.

In 784 **Emperor Kammu** (737–806) had his residence moved from Nara to Nagaoka in order to remove politics from the great influence of the Buddhist priests. Nara lost its political significance, but has remained Japan's most significant cultural site to this day. Over time the city's area has shifted eastwards so that the historic city is now on the outskirts.

Highlights *Nara*

Nara Park
Take a stroll among tame sika deer under ancient trees in a peaceful atmosphere.
▶ page 418

Kofukuji temple
The protective temple of the Fujiwara is decorated with a five-storey pagoda, a remarkable example of Nara architecture.
▶ page 418

Kasuga shrine
Thousands of stone lanterns line the path to the shrine, which has been ornamented with attractive carvings.
▶ page 420

Todaiji temple
This temple houses the impressive Great Buddha made of bronze, Japan's largest ancient Buddha statue.
▶ page 422

Toshodaiji temple
It is the most significant example of Tempyo architecture.
▶ page 427

Yakushiji temple
It houses a famous Yakushi Trinity.
▶ page 428

Horyuji temple
The oldest still extant wooden buildings in the world contain significant artworks.
▶ page 429

VISITING NARA

INFORMATION

Tourist information centres
In *Kintetsu station*, 1st floor
tel. 07 42/24 48 58
Daily 9am–5pm
In the *JR station*
tel. 07 42/22 98 21
Daily 9am–5pm
In the *city centre*, Sanjo-dori,
23-4 Kami-sanjo-cho
Tel. 07 42/22 39 00
Daily 9am–9pm
By the Sarusawa pond not far from
Kofukuji temple
tel. 07 42/26 19 91
Daily 9am–5pm
Online:
www.narashikanko.jp/english
www.pref.nara.jp/nara_e

TRANSPORT

By rail: from Kyoto Kintetsu private
train line (40 minutes) or JR Nara
line (45 minutes); from Osaka JR
Kansai line (45 minutes, from Tennoji
30 minutes) or Kintetsu line from
Namba (30 minutes).

Local transport: from the central
station there are numerous buses
going to the most important attractions in the city and the surrounding
area.

EVENTS

Wakakusa-yama-yaki (grass fire festival; mid-Jan), on Wakakusa Hill;
Setsubun (with a lantern festival;
beginning of Feb), at Kasuga shrine;
Onioi-shiki (expulsion of the demons;
beginning of Feb), at Kofukuji temple;
Omizu-tori (with torch lighting and
scooping holy water; beginning of
March), at Todaiji temple; Kasuga
festival (bugaku; mid-March), at Kasuga shrine; Hanae-shiki (flower sacrifices in honour of Buddha's birthday;
beginning of April), at Yakushiji temple; Shomu-ten-no-sai (procession;
beginning of May), at Todaiji temple;
Takigi-no (night-time No performances; mid-May), on the No stage of
Kofukuji temple; lantern festival (mid-
Aug), at Kasuga shrine; On-matsuri
(procession with historical costumes;
mid-Dec), at Kasuga shrine.

WHERE TO EAT

► **Moderate**
① *Miyama*
Nara Koen Daibutsu-mae,
Kosaten-kado
Tel. 07 42/23 02 18
Daily except Thu 10.30am–5pm
Anyone wanting to take a break after
visiting an attraction in Nara Park
should stop by this restaurant with its
favourable location in the Noborioji-
dori. It serves tasty teishoku of the
more upscale kind (tip: kurigozen,
with sweet chestnuts).

Baedeker recommendation

► **Inexpensive**
② *Soba Dokoro Yoshikawa*
Suimon-cho 50, Nara-shi
Tel. 07 42/22 04 48
Wed–Sun approx. 11am–2pm
(until all the soba are gone)
Known for its home-made soba noodles.
Even the plates were made by the owners of
this characterful restaurant. Lunch only.

WHERE TO STAY

► **Luxury**
① *Nara Hotel*
1096 Takahata-cho,
Nara-shi, Nara-ken, 630-8301
Tel. 07 42/26 33 00

The deer in Nara Park are famous

Fax 23 52 52
yoyaku@narahotel.co.jp
Old-style hotel founded in 1909. Its

► Nara

132 rooms are divided between the main building (Honkan) and the new building (Shinkan). Located at the southeast border of Nara Park near the pretty Sarazuwa pond. Nice views of the five-storey pagoda and the Wakagusayama.

► **Mid-range**
② *Kottan Hyakupasento guesthouse*
Takabatake-cho 1122-21,
Nara-shi, Nara-ken
Tel. 07 42/22 71 17
Small, cosy guesthouse with 14 rooms in a favourable location near Nara Park.

✴ ✴ Nara Park

Leave Kintetsu-Nara station (here is a worthwhile exhibition with objects from the Jomon period to the Nara period on the 3rd and 4th floors) along the Noborioji-dori shopping street, which runs parallel along Sanjo-dori to the south, to Nara Park; at 525ha/1297 acres it is the largest of its kind in Japan. The area is covered in huge old trees and contains a large number of historic structures; the many tame deer living here are a further attraction. To the right of the entrance is Sarasuwa pond (circumference: 360m/390yd), in which the reflection of the five-storey pagoda of Kofukuji temple can be seen. Uneme shrine is on its northern shore.

✴ ✴
Kofukuji temple

A path leads from the pond's eastern shore northwards to Kofukuji temple (Kencho-mae bus stop, 10 minutes from the station), one of Nara's seven great temples and a **World Heritage Site**. The temple founded by Kagami-no-Himehiko, Fujiwara-no-Kamatari's wife, in 669 was this family's protective temple and the main temple of the Hosso sect. Originally built in Kyoto under the name Yamashina-de-ra, the temple was moved to Umasaka (south of Nara) in 678 and with the founding of the capital by Fubito, Kamatari's son, in 710 it was moved to its current location and renamed »Kofukuji«. The temple's significance grew along with the power of the Fujiwara. In its heyday it possessed 175 buildings. Most of them, however, were destroyed during the fighting between the Minamoto and the Taira during the 12th century.

Nan-endo ► The surviving buildings can be seen from the former location of the great southern gate. One of them is the octagonal Nan-endo Hall, built by Fujiwara Fuyutsugu in 813 and renewed in 1741. Its most significant art treasure is the statue of Fukukenjaku-Kannon made by Kokei, Unkei's father, in 1188; also of note are the statues of the four heavenly guards as well as those of the patriarchs of the Hosso sect. There is a bronze lantern from the 9th century in front of the hall; it is said Kobo-daishi (► Koya-san, p.328) made its inscription. Southwest of here is the three-storey pagoda, a graceful building from the Fujiwara period.

North of the Nan-endo is the northern hall Hoku-endo, also with an octagonal floor plan. It was originally built on the orders of Empress Gensho in 721 in remembrance of Fubito, the founder of the Kofu-kuji; it was renewed in 1208. The wooden statue of Miroku-bosatsu was probably made by Unkei in 1212.

◄ Hoku-endo

To the east is Chu-kondo, which was built in 710 and rebuilt in 1819; it houses a wooden Shakyamuni statue. The eastern main hall To-kondo, reconstructed true to its original in 1415 after being destroyed several times, contains a 15th-century statue of Yakushi-nyorai, surrounded by statues of Nikko-bosatsu and Gakko-bosatsu (presumably 8th century) and other sculptures.

◄ Chu-kondo,
To-kondo

Opposite to the south is the five-storey pagoda, built by Komyo, Emperor Shomu's wife, in 730. It burned down five times and was then rebuilt in the old style in 1426. At a height of 50m/164ft it is the **second-tallest pagoda in Japan** and a remarkable witness to Nara architecture. It houses statues of Amida-nyorai, Shakyamuni, Yakushi-nyorai and Miroku-bosatsu.

◄ Pagoda

Northeast of To-kondo Hall in Kokoho-kan Treasury of 1959 some of the temple's most significant art treasures have been brought together, including a 7th-century bronze Buddha head, a wooden group of figures of the Juni-shinsho (»twelve divine generals«, Heian period), two Nio sculptures (Kongo, Misshaku), an Ashura statue in dry lacquer technique (early Nara period) as well as the two guard figures Kongo-rikishi (open daily 9am–5pm, ¥ 500).

◄ Kokuho-kan
treasury

The eastbound path from Kofukuji leads to the National Museum. It exhibits significant artworks, particularly from the Nara period. A changing selection of all of the objects stored here is displayed (www.narahaku.go.jp, open Tue–Sun 9.30am–5pm, ¥ 420).

★
National
Museum

Southeast of the museum (turn right off Noborioji-dori, then left, Kasuga-taisha-Omote-sando bus stop) is a path lined by cypresses and cedars past Manyo Garden (to the left) and the deer park Rokuen (to the right) to Kasuga shrine. Manyo Garden has a small stage for gagaku and bugaku performances. All the plants occurring in this garden are mentioned in Manyoshu's poetry collection, hence its name. The animals living in the deer park are considered messengers of the gods, because according to legend the Fujiwara, the builders of the shrine, invited to Nara the deity Takemikazuchi-no-mitoko, who entered the city on the back of a deer.

**Manyo Garden
Rokuen Deer
Park**

★★
Kasuga shrine

The way to Kasuga shrine leads through the seconKasuga shrinned torii (Ni-no torii) and continues between two rows of a total of 3000 stone lanterns that are lit twice a year during the Mandoro festival. Next along the way is the south gate, a one-storey structure from 1179; artistic lanterns hang in its corridors; beyond it is the heiden cult hall (1650) and to the left in front of it the festival hall naorai-den, built at the same time. A stone stairway leads up to the middle gate (chumon); the roofed corridors going out to either side from this gate contain the main buildings of Kasuga shrine.

Japan's second-highest pagoda stands in Nara Park

Kasuga shrine, also a World Heritage Site, was founded by Fujiwara Nagate (714–771). It consists of four individual buildings and is consecrated to the deities Takemikazuchi and Futsunushi as well as the ancestor deities of the Fujiwara, Amenokoyane and his wife Himeokami. The buildings are a typical example of the **Kasuga-zukuri building style** and can be distinguished from older, wooden buildings left in their natural state by the red paint on the beams and white plasterwork as well as by the curved roof line. Until 1863 the buildings were demolished and re-built in their old form every 20 years (like Ise shrine; ▶ Ise-Shima National Park); since then this renewal has been limited to the roofs. On the left is the processional hall Utsushi-dono, where the images of the deities are brought during the renewal works on the shrine buildings. The covered path from here to the main shrine Nejiri-ro-ka, a work by the famous Hidari Jingoro (probably 1594–1634), is ornamented with fantastic carvings. North of the processional hall is the **Yadorigi tree**; it has six other species grafted on to its stem. The paper streamers attached to the branches by shrine visitors contain prayers asking for luck.

★
Kasuga-Wakamiya shrine

Another path makes its way between stone lanterns from Kasuga shrine southwards to Kasuga Wakamiya shrine, consecrated to the god Ameno-oshikumo, son of Amenokoyane; it was most likely founded in 1135. The current buildings were built in 1863, also in

room are the statues of Shakyamuni and Taho-nyorai, in the corners the standing sculptures of the four heavenly guards in full armour. »Kaidan« was originally the term used for the terrace where priests were ordained; the earth used to build the temple was brought by the Chinese priest Ganjin. He is said to have ordained 500 monks as priests here.

★
Belfry

East of the Buddha Hall is an old bell-tower whose bell was cast in 749 and then severely damaged in 989 during a typhoon (it was recast in 1239). At a height of 3.9m/13ft and a diameter of 2.8m/9ft it is Japan's second-largest bell.

Hall of the Second Month

Even further east on an elevation is the Hall of the Second Month (Nigatsu-do), built by the priest Jitchu, a student of Roben (689–773, first abbot of Todaiji temple), in 752 and then rebuilt in 1669 after a fire. It owes its name to the water drawing ceremony »Omizu-tori«, which, in the past, fell on the second month of the lunar calendar (today between 1 and 14 March).

★ ★
Hall of the Third Month

The next hall to the south is the Hall of the Third Month (Sangatsu-do), built by Roben in 733. It is the oldest extant building in the temple complex (admission ¥ 500). The Raido prayer hall was added around 1200 (Kamakura period); the two structures can be distinguished by their roof constructions. The hall's name comes from readings of the Hokke-sutra (kept here) held here during the third lunar month. In the middle of the building's interior is the 3.6m/12ft Fukukensaku-Kannon, a dry-lacquer statue attributed to abbot Roben, whose crown is adorned with 20,000 pearls and gemstones. It is flanked by the terra cotta figures of Nikko-bosatsu and Gakko-bosatsu (Nara period). To the side are the standing statues of Bonten and Taishakuten, also made in the dry-lacquer technique. In front of the Bonten statue is the wooden statue of Fudomyoo, in front of Taishakuten the statue of Jizo-bosatsu. Each of the room's four corners contains a statue of one of the four heavenly guards (dry lacquer). Behind Fukukensaku-Kannon behind a locked door is the »secret likeness« of Shukongo-jin, which can only be seen on 16 December.

Isuien Garden
🕐
Opening hours:
Daily except Tue
9.30am–4.30pm,
¥ 650

West of the south gate to the Todaiji temple complex is Isuien Garden; to the left of the entrance is the small **Neiraku Museum** opened in 1969; it exhibits ancient Chinese and Korean arts and crafts. Isuien Garden is a landscape garden in the Shakkei style (»borrowed landscape«: the surrounding area is incorporated into the overall appearance). At the front are the Seishuan and Sanshutei tea houses as well as the Teishuken waiting room. The back of the garden, created in 1899, has the southern gate of the Todaiji temple and Mount Wakakusa as its backdrop. the small pond's island contains a foundation stone of the Buddha Hall; the stepping stones are old mill stones used in the production of dyes.

Around Nara (northwest)

Heijo-kyuden Imperial Palace

Northwest of the city is Heijo-kyuden Imperial Palace (bus from Nara central station, 15 minutes, or from Yamato-Saidaiji station, 5 minutes), which was uncovered during archaeological excavations. Built on an area of 107ha/264 acres it formed the political and cultural centre of the old capital Heijokyo. When the seat of government was moved to Nagaoka in 784 the complex became derelict, meaning that all there is to be seen today are its foundations. The outline of the hall of ceremonies Daigokuden can still be made out. There were twelve further buildings to the south, including the Choshuden assembly hall; the entire complex was surrounded by a gallery with several gates. During the **excavation works** ditches, wells and paving were uncovered; the finds are exhibited in the hall known as the Material Hall (Shiryokan).

Hokkeiji temple
✳

Around 800m/875yd east of the palace is Hokkeji temple founded by Empress Komyo in the 8th century; its main hall was renewed in 1601. The wooden statue of the eleven-headed Kannon, allegedly made by an Indian artist, is worth visiting.

Kairyuoji temple

Not far away is Kairyuoji temple, founded by the same empress. All that survives are its western main hall, the sutra library (both partially rebuilt in the 12th century) and the five-storey pagoda.

Akishino temple
✳
🕐
Opening hours:
Daily
9.30am–4.30pm,
¥ 500

Northwest of Yamato-Saidaiji station is Akishino temple, founded around 780 and largely destroyed by fire in 1135. All that survived is the recital hall (Kodo), which was later made the main hall (hondo). It is a good architectural example of the Nara period. The dry-lacquer statue of Gigeiten, goddess of music and dance, was made in part during that period and in part is attributed to the sculptor Unkei.

Saidaiji temple
✳ ✳

Only a few steps west of the station is another of Nara's Seven Great Temples: Saidaiji temple (»Great West Temple«) built in 765 on the orders of Empress Shotoku (called Empress Koken during her first incumbency from 749–758). It is the main temple of the Shingon-Ritsu sect. The buildings mostly date from recent times. The main hall north of the ruins of the east pagoda dates from 1752. It contains a wooden statue of Shakyamuni, a work by **the priest Eizon** (1201–90), as well as a statue of Monju-bosatsu of 1302. Southwest of the main hall is Aizendo Hall with sitting statues of Aisen-myoo (1247) and of Priest Eizon (Kamakura period).

Near the East Gate is Shiodo Hall with a number of statues from the late Nara period (Tempyo culture), including the four heavenly guards (the one of Tamonten made of wood, the others of bronze); the demon figures at the feet of the statues were made at the same time the temple was founded. The wooden statue of the eleven-headed Kannon was made in the 12th century.

To the east of the Main Hall are the temple treasury Shuhokan with sculptures, paintings and calligraphy. The temple also owns twelve picture scrolls with depictions of the guards (Juni-shinsho) on silk (open daily 8.30am–4.30pm, admission Hondo ¥ 400, Aizendo ¥ 300, Shiodo ¥ 300). Northeast of the temple is the tomb of Emperor Seimu, a typical burial mound of the Kofun period.

West of Saidaiji temple (Gakuen-mae station) is Yamato-bunka-kan Museum, set in a hilly landscape with many forests and lakes. It contains art treasures of the Asian region (sculptures, paintings, ceramics, lacquerware, etc.).

Yamato-bunka-kan Museum

Around Nara (southwest)

The area southwest of Nara is now a quiet agricultural region. In the 8th century it was one of the region's spiritual centres, a fact to which a few temples can attest; Toshodaiji and Yakushiji are part of the Nara World Heritage Site. They are an attractive contrast to the green paddy fields and farmsteads. To get to them take the Nara line of the Kintetsu private trains from Nara (Kintetsu-Nara station) to Yamato-Saidaiji, then the Kashihara line to Nishinokyo. Not far from Amagatsuji station (one stop before Nishinokyo) is the tomb of Emperor Suinin in a lake, a burial mound built on a key-hole outline. This tomb also dates back to the Kofun period.

World Heritage Site in green paddy fields

600m/660yd south of Amagatsuji station (or north of Nishinokyo station) is the Toshodaiji temple, founded by Ganjin in 759. It is the highest of the Ritsu sect's approx. 30 temples. Only the main hall and the recital hall are still extant from the temple's founding days; the other buildings are newer.

★ ★
Toshodaiji temple
Opening hours:
Daily 8.30am–5pm,
¥ 600

The Great South Gate (nandaimon, reconstruction from 1960) is the access to the main hall kondo, which has an area of 15 x 29m (16 x 32yd), making it the largest and most significant example of Tempyo architecture (it is being restored until 2010; until then the statues can be seen in the Kodo). The **columned gallery** has classical beauty. The hall contains a 3.3m/11ft sitting statue of Rushana-butsu (dry-lacquer technique), designed by the Chinese students of Ganjin, T'an Ching and Szu T'o. Its magnificent halo was originally decorated with 1000 small Buddha figures, of which 864 are still extant. To the left of it is a thousand-handed Kannon (dry lacquer, 5.5m/18ft), to the right a statue of Yakushi-nyorai, also made in the dry-lacquer technique and attributed to Ganjin's students Szu T'o and Ju Pao. Furthermore there are two

? DID YOU KNOW ...?

■ The temple's name comes from the word »shodai«, which means something like »temple for a guest priest«. It refers to the fact that Ganjin, at the time the greatest Buddhist authority, was invited to Japan to teach.

1.7m/5.5ft wooden statues (Bonten and Taishakuten) made by the master Chun Fa-li as well a wooden sitting statue of Dainichi-nyorai (3.7m/12ft) from the early Heian period.

◀ Kodo lecture hall

The Kodo lecture hall is located behind the main hall. It was originally the assembly hall of Keijo-kyuden Imperial Palace, but was brought here when the temple was founded. Renewal works by Chun Fa-li (759) and later repairs caused the original style to be adulterated. The hall's most significant sculpture is the 2.4m/8ft Miroku-bosatsu by Chun Fa-li; also worth seeing are the statues of Jikokuten and Zochoten, carved from a block of cypress wood.

Priests' residences ▶

To the right of the lecture hall an elongated building houses the priests' residences Higashimuro (to the north) and the liturgical Raido room (to the south). In front of it is a drum tower (Koro or Shariden) where the **Uchiwa-maki festival** takes place on the 19 May. During this festival heart-shaped fans are handed out, which are meant to provide protection against bad luck.

Library and treasury ▶

East of the priests' residences are two buildings in the Azekura-zukuri technique: the sutra library Kyozo (to the south) and the treasury Hozo (to the north). The new treasury Shin-hozo (1970) contains paintings and fragments of sculptures.

★★
Yakushiji temple
⏱
Opening hours:
Daily 8am–5pm,
¥ 500

Yakushiji temple, founded in 680 by Emperor Temmu, which today (along with Kofukuji temple) is the main temple of the Hosso sect, can be reached from the train station to the south (Nishinokyo station) or on foot from Toshodaiji temple (750m/800yd).

During its construction, which dragged on until 698, Emperor Temmu died. His wife ascended the throne in 687. After the seat of government was transferred to Nara, the temple was moved from Asuka to its current location in 718. It was damaged several times, particularly severely in the civil war of 1528. All that is left of this temple's original complex, which is one of the Seven Great Temples of Nara, is the eastern pagoda; all of the other buildings date back to the Kamakura period.

Kondo main hall ▶

The kondo main hall, renewed in 1600, and in 1976 rebuilt on its old foundations, contains the famous **Yakushi Trinity**. Its central figure is the 2.6m/8.5ft Yakushi-nyorai (ruler of the eastern paradise); to the sides are the statues of Nikko-bosatsu and Gakko-busatsu. The statues, which were originally gilded, were blackened by the fire of 1528; only the haloes are still gilded. The central statue's large bronze pedestal displays Chinese and Indian influences. All of the three statues date from the year 697, as does the Yakushi Trinity of the lecture hall (Kodo), located behind the main hall. Diagonally opposite is the three-storey **East Pagoda** (37.9m/124ft, probably built in 698). Small intermediate roofs were added making it

? DID YOU KNOW …?

■ The temple was planned by Emperor Temmu in 680, in order to pray for the healing of his very sick wife Jito. The actual building was then built after his death under the direction of the empress.

appear as if the pagoda had six storeys. The metal roof ornaments (sorin) are also highly artistic.

Behind the pagoda is the East Hall (Toin-do, 1285). It contains the 1.9m/6ft bronze Sho-Kannon (also Kudara-Kannon, around 600), a gift from the king of Paekche (Korea). On the other side of the pagoda is Bussokudo hall, which contains a stone that is said to have **Buddha's footprint** (Bussoku-seki) on it.

Southern Nara Basin

The Nara Basin extending south of the city is also called Yamato Basin, because the Yamato River's tributaries flow through it. The Yamato itself leaves the basin to the west and flows into the sea south of Osaka. This region contains yet more of the significant temple complexes dating back to Japan's early days.

Take the train from Nara (Kintetsu-Nara station) via the stations of Yamato-Saidaiji and Amagatsuji (see above) to Kintetsu-Koriyama (15 minutes); from there take the bus (20 minutes) to Hokkiji temple. Its founding in 638 goes back to the priest Fukuryo, who was thereby fulfilling Shotoku-taishi's (574–622) last wish. It is also called Okamoto temple, after the location of his palace, where the temple was originally built. The three-storey pagoda of 685 displays the style of the early Nara period.

Hokkiji temple

It is a 15-minute walk to Horinji temple to the southwest; it was built by one of Shotoku-taishi's sons in 821. The dominant figure in the main hall (kondo) is the wooden sitting statue of Yakushi-nyorai, in the Tori-busshi style oriented on Chinese and Korean models. Next to it are the sculptures of Kichijo-ten, Sho-Kannon and Bishamonten from the late Heian period.

Horinji temple

Around 1km/0.6mi further southwest is Japan's oldest completely preserved temple complex, the Horyuji temple, a magnificent structure of the Asuka period (552–645), with masterly artworks from all of Japan's cultural periods. Horyuji temple is also part of the Nara World Heritage Site. Yomei, Japan's first Buddhist emperor, was stricken with a severe illness in 586. He commissioned a statue of the healing Buddha (Yakushi-nyorai), but died before it was completed. In order to fulfil his wish Shotoku-taishi, the emperor's son, had Horyuji temple built in 607, which, as one of the Seven Great Temples of Nara, became the centre of Buddhism in Japan, from where the new teaching was brought to the rest of the country. At that time there was a road connection from the imperial court to the coast that ran past here.

** **
Horyuji temple
⏱
Opening hours:
22 Feb to 3 Nov
8am–5pm, otherwise until 4.30pm,
¥ 1000

The entire complex of this main temple of the Shotoku sect contains 45 buildings, built between the Asuka and the Momoyama periods. 17 of them are classified as »**significant national treasures**«. The temple is divided into the To-in complex (also Higashi-no-in, eastern part) with 14 buildings and the Sai-in complex (also Nishi-no-in, western part) with 31 buildings.

Central gate ▶ The main entrance to the Sai-in and the entire temple complex is the great south gate (nandaimon), a structure renewed several times (the last time was during the Muromachi period, 1438). Continue onwards from here past the temple office to the central gate (chu-mon), which dates back to the founding year. The gate, from which roofed corridors (kairo) lead away to either side, is distinguished from other gate structures in that its design has it supported on columns. On either side of the entrance supported by columns are guard figures (nio). The right one is red as a symbol of light, the left one is black as a symbol of darkness. Both were made in 711 and were fully restored in 1964.

Inner temple courtyard ▶ The corridors emanating from the central gate go around the inner temple courtyard. It contains the main hall (kondo) on the right, a two-storey wooden building that is 9.1 x 7.3m (10 x 8yd) and has a height of 17.8m/58ft. It dates back to the Asuka period and is allegedly the oldest extant wooden building in the world. The interior walls were adorned with **famous frescoes**, which in their style and execution were comparable to those in the caves of Ajanta (India); they were however destroyed by fire in 1949. Photographs of the frescoes can be seen in the Great Treasury. The hall contains several statues of the 7th century; the best-known is the **bronze Shaka Trinity**, which was cast in 623 by Tori-busshi. The main figure, Shakyamuni, is flanked by Yakuo-bosatsu and Yakujo-bosatsu. To the right of the trinity is a statue of Yakushi-nyorai, commissioned by Emperor Yomei and cast in bronze in 607. To the left of the trinity is a bronze statue of Amida-nyorai (1232) as well as the wooden statues of the goddess Kichijo-ten and the god of war Bishamonten, both from 1078. The wooden statues of the four heavenly guards date from the later Asuka period. They are the oldest surviving representations of this kind.

Pagoda ▶ The five-storey pagoda on the left side of the temple courtyard dates back to the temple's founding year and is 32m/105ft tall. The roofs' corners contain lucky charms meant to protect them from fire. There is an intermediate roof lower down (mokoshi). On the ground floor are four scenes form Buddha's life worked into clay: on the east side »conversation between Yumia and Monju«, on the south side »the paradise of Miroku«, on the west side »Buddha's cremation« and on the north side »Buddha's entrance into Nirvana«.

Daikodo: great lecture hall ▶ In the north of the temple courtyard is the great lecture hall (daikodo), whose original building was destroyed by lightning in 925. It was subsequently rebuilt in 990. It houses a gilded wooden Yakushi Trinity (flanking the central figure are Nikko-bosatsu and Sakko-bosatsu) as well as the sculptures of the four heavenly guards.

Sutra hall Kyozo ▶ West of the Lecture Hall is the sutra hall (kyozo) from the Tempyo period. It contains a wooden statue of the Korean priest Kanroku,

Horyuji temple *Plan*

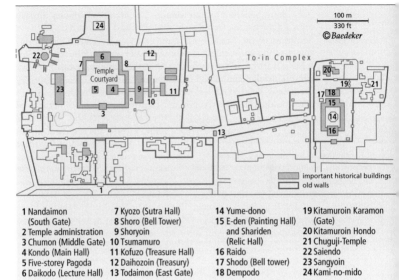

1 Nandaimon (South Gate)	7 Kyozo (Sutra Hall)	14 Yume-dono
2 Temple administration	8 Shoro (Bell Tower)	15 E-den (Painting Hall) and Shariden (Relic Hall)
3 Chumon (Middle Gate)	9 Shoryoin	16 Raido
4 Kondo (Main Hall)	10 Tsumamuro	17 Shodo (Bell tower)
5 Five-storey Pagoda	11 Kofuzo (Treasure Hall)	18 Dempodo
6 Daikodo (Lecture Hall)	12 Daihozoin (Treasury)	19 Kitamuroin Karamon (Gate)
	13 Todaimon (East Gate)	20 Kitamuroin Hondo
		21 Chuguji-Temple
		22 Saiendo
		23 Sangyoin
		24 Kami-no-mido

important historical buildings
old walls

who came to Nara in 607. The **belfry (shoro)** was newly built during the Heian period; the bell is said to date back to the 8th century.

In front of the gallery bounding the courtyard in the east is Shoryoin ◄ Shoryoin hall, dedicated to Shotoku-taishi's soul. Renewed in 1121, it was once the priest's residence. It houses a statue of Shotoku-taishi, which displays the 25-year-old regent in the festive robes of the T'ang dynasty. It is flanked by sculptures of dignitaries, including the priest Eji.

Beyond the adjoining building, Tsumamuro, is the small treasury ◄ Treasury (Kofuzo), which houses some Buddhist sculptures. Walk between Tsumamuro and Kofuzo to get to Daihozoin, the gallery of temple treasures, built in the old style in 1998. It displays excellent works of art from several stylistic periods. Of particular note are the **Kudara-Kannon from Korea** (in the Kudara-Kannon-do Hall built especially for it), whose soft lines form a stark contrast to the rigid Japanese sculptures of the time; a **nine-headed Kannon** made of wood and Yumetagai-Kannon, which transforms bad dreams into good ones (both sculptures are from the Hakuho period). The southern building contains some items from the main hall, including the 2.4m/8ft **Tamamushi-no-zushi miniature shrine of Empress Suiko**. It owes its name to an insect species (Chrysochroa elegans) called »tamamushi« because parts of the shrine used to be covered in its multi-coloured wings (today this is only visible on a tiny part of the building). The shrine, adorned with pierced bronze mounts, has paintings on a black background on all sides depicting Buddhist content (on the front doors are the heavenly guards, the side doors contain Bosatsu representations, the far side pagodas, stars and a phoenix).

To-in complex ▶ Southeast of the treasury the great east gate (todaimon) is the entrance to the To-in complex, whose location was the site of Shotoku-taishi's Ikaruga Palace until 622. After the regent's death the palace became derelict and in 739 the emperor ordered it to be replaced by the East Temple, which was dedicated to Shotoku's family.

After passing through the corridor (Kairo) visitors get to the Hall of Dreams (Yume-dono), which has some artistic bronze roof ornaments. It is the oldest Japanese building with an octagonal floor plan. The hall's most significant artwork is a **gilded wooden Kuse-Kannon** (also Nyoirin-Kannon), which resembles Shotoku and was allegedly made by him (all that can be said without any doubt is that it came from the school of Tori-bus-shi). The statue can only be seen

from 11 April to 5 May and 22 October to 3 November. A statue of the priest Gyoshin Sozu (dry lacquer; Tempyo period) and a terra cotta figure of the priest Dosen (Heian period) are also worth seeing.

Hall of Paintings ▶ On the north-side of the enclosure is the Hall of Paintings (E-den) with paintings from the life of Shotoku; to the right is Shariden Hall (»Hall of Buddha's Ash«). This hall and the belfry visible on the left both date from the Kamakura period.

Prayer hall ▶ To the north, beyond the Hall of Paintings, is the prayer hall (dempodo), which used to be the residence of the empress's mother Tachibana, but was then given to the temple in 739. The sculptures to be found in the hall date back to the late Nara period; at its centre is an Amida Trinity made in the dry-lacquer technique. There are further wooden Amida groups on either side as well as wooden sculptures from the Heian period.

Chuguji temple ▶ The northeastern part of the To-in complex is made up of Chuguji temple, a nunnery originally reserved to members of the imperial family. It contains a 1.8m/6ft expressive wooden Nyoirin-Kannon, apparently by Shotoku, which is worth seeing. It also houses the 7th-century Tenjukoku-Mandara, a fragment of Japan's oldest-known piece of embroidery, originally 4.8m/16ft long, which was made by Shotoku's widow and her court ladies. It displays scenes from life during the Asuka period.

Tenri 10km/6mi south of Nara is the town of Tenri (population 69,000), the centre of the Tenri-kyo sect, founded in 1838, and the location of a folkcraft museum. 1.5km/1mi east of the station is Isonokami shrine with a two-storey gate and a lovely **cult hall**. According to legend a sword that is housed here was a gift from the deity Takemi-kazuchi-no-mitoko to the first emperor Jimmu.

Further south along the train line is Miwa (train from Miwa, 40 minutes), the starting point for a visit to the Omiya shrine (alias Miwa Myojin), situated at the foot of the 467m/1532ft Mount Miwa. The shrine is consecrated to the deity Omonoushi and is considered to be one of the oldest in the country, with an alleged founding date sometime in the first century BC. It is connected to Isonokami shrine further north via an old road leading past early burial mounds and old settlements.

Miwa Omiya shrine

The next train station is Sakurai, from where a bus (25 minutes) goes to Hase-dera temple to the east.
The temple founded in 686 is the centre of the Buzan school, which is part of the Shingon sect. There is an 8m/26ft wooden statue of the eleven-headed Kannon in the main hall founded by Emperor Shomu and renewed in 1650. In front of the temple are a **No stage** and the temple treasure museum. The temple area is a popular destination, particularly during the cherry blossom (April–May) and when the peonies are in bloom (early April to early May).

Hase-dera temple

Departing Sakurai the Osaka line of the Kintetsu private line goes eastwards to Muro-guchi-Ono station; around 8km/5mi to south of this station is Muroji temple, which belongs to the Shingon sect. It was built in 681 and renewed in 824 by Kobo-daishi. The pretty complex has a 16.2m/53ft pagoda. The temple is said to have been built especially for women, since for a long time they were not permitted to access the holy mountain Koya-san. For that reason Muroji also became known as »women's Koya-san«. The main hall (kondo) contains a wooden Juichimen-Kannon as well as sitting statues of Nyoirin-Kannon and Shaka-nyorai, all three from the early Heian period.

★ ★
Muroji temple
⏲
Opening hours:
Daily 8am–5pm,
winter
8.30am–4pm, ¥ 500

Sakurai is also the starting point of a bus connection to the southern part of Nara Basin. It takes 30 minutes to get to Tanzan shrine at the foot of Mount Tonomine. Founded in 701 by the priest Joe, Fujiwara no Kamatari's eldest son, it was subsequently renewed several times, on the last occasion in 850. Until the Meiji period, when a policy of separating Buddhism and Shinto was pursued, a temple and a shrine existed here side by side. Near the entrance to the shrine there is thus a 13-storey pagoda, probably the only one of its kind in Japan. The shrine itself (also called »Nikko shrine of Kansai«) is emphatically plain inside.

Tanzan shrine

West of Sakurai is the town of Kashihara (population 112,000; Sakurai train line to Unebi station) at the foot of the 199m/653ft Mount **Unebi**, where the legendary Emperor Jimmu is said to have built his

Kashihara

palace and his tomb can also be found. Not far away is also Kashi-hara shrine dedicated to him and his wife Himetatara-Isuzu-hime; it was built in 1889 using wood from the imperial palace in Kyoto. Behind it is the empress's tomb.

Asuka Historical Park ▶
To the northeast near the shrine is the Archaeological Museum (Yamato-rekishikan) with finds from Nara Basin from the late Stone Age amongst other things. Here, in Asuka Historical Park, a World Heritage Site, visitors can admire the huge imperial stone tombs and foundations of palaces, reminiscent of the founding days of the hereditary Japanese empire in the 4th century.

A steep staircase leads up to Muroji temple

Take the bus (20 minutes) from Kashihara-jingu station (Yoshino line of the Kintetsu private line) not far south of the historical park to get to the Tachibana temple, which belongs to the Tendai sect. It was built at the probable birthplace of Shotoku-taishi; all that remains of the once large complex is the main hall (kondo), renewed in 1864. It contains a wooden sculpture of Shotoku from the Muromachi period.

◄ Tachibana temple

Not far north (also 15 minutes by bus from Sakurai) is the Asuka temple or Gangoji temple. It was built in 588 as Japan's first Buddhist temple. It was given the name of Hokoji Monastery, which was moved to Heijokyo, and was later renamed Gangoji. Asuka or Gangoji temple is considered the **founding cell of Japanese Buddhism** and the centre of the Asuka culture, newly introduced from China. The temple also houses a bronze statue of Shakyamuni, created by Tori-busshi in 606. Gangoji temple has been a World Heritage Site since 1998.

◄ Asuka temple

There is another bus connection from Kashihara-jingu to Okadera temple (old name Ryugaiji). It was originally the palace of Emperor Tenchi, but was then given to the Hosso sect in 663. Inside there is a Heian-period terra cotta statue of Nyoirin-Kannon as well as a wooden sitting statue of the priest Gien (d. 728) from the Nara period.

Okadera temple

South of Okadera temple two burial mounds were uncovered during archaeological excavations (bus from Kashihara-jingu, 15 minutes). Ishibutai Tomb, probably the grave of Soga-no-Umako, was made in the 7th century; to the southwest is the tomb of Takamatsuzuka (7th century), in which burial goods with Chinese and Korean influences were found. Their replicas are exhibited in the nearby Asuka-shiryo-kan Museum. Take the Kintetsu private line from Asuka station to return to Nara (30km/20 mi).

Burial mounds

Niigata

K 6

Main island: Honshu   **Prefecture:** Niigata
Population: 780,000

Niigata, the capital of Niigita Prefecture, is the most significant port on Honshu's west coast and the stepping stone to Sado Island as well as to the Asian mainland.

新潟

The Shinano River flows through the city and then into the Sea of Japan. The city, traversed by canals, is protected from the sea by sandy hills. After Japan opened up to other countries Niigata became a significant port for trade with Siberia.

Port on the Sea of Japan

⏵ VISITING NIIGATA

INFORMATION
Tourist information
In the station
Tel. 0 25/2 41 79 14
Daily 9am–6pm
www.city.niigata.niigata.jp
www.pref.niigata.jp
(about the prefecture)

TRANSPORT
By air: from Tokyo (Haneda Airport;
50 minutes); from Osaka (1 hour).

By rail: from Tokyo (Ueno station)
JR Joetsu shinkansen line (1¾ hours);
from Osaka JR Tokaido line to
Tokyo, then Joetsu shinkansen (4¾
hours).

EVENTS
Niigata Festival (city festival with a big
firework display; end of August).

What to See in Niigata

Aquarium Northwest of the station, close to the coast, the aquarium (Marinepia Nihonkai) has fauna from the Sea of Japan and an entertaining dolphin show.

Hakusan Park On the left bank of the Shinano is Hakusan Park with Hakusan shrine (bus from the station, 15 minutes).

Niigata-yuen Niigata-yuen, a flower garden (near Terao station on the JR Echigo line, also a bus from Niigata station, 25 minutes), is particularly beautiful in the springtime (April–May). It also has a lovely view of the Sea of Japan. A further worthwhile viewpoint is the hill Hiyoriyama.

Lake Toyano Lake Toyano south of the station (bus connection, 25 minutes) is a popular local recreation area. The **Science Museum** (Niigata Kenritsu Shizen Kagakukan) on its northwest shore with exhibits about space flight and energy technology as well as a planetarium is worth a visit.

Cultural centre Southwest outside of the city (bus connection, 30 minutes) the culture and event centre Niigata Furosato Mura has a permanent exhibition (with audio-visual media) about the prefecture's culture and history; the region's traditional products can also be bought here.

Shirone The town of Shirone (population 35,000; private line from Niigata) is mainly visited for its **kite festival »Takoage«**, which takes place every year at the beginning of June. It is an exciting competition with huge paper kites (up to 7m/23ft across) where the two parties on either side of the river try to cause the opponent's kite to crash.

★ ★ Nikko

K 6 • m 1

Main island: Honshu   **Prefecture:** Tochigi
Population: 21,000

The town of Nikko, situated in eastern Honshu at the edge of Nikko National Park is known for its magnificent mausoleums. There is
a Japanese proverb that says: »Never say ›kekko‹ (magnificent),
before you've seen Nikko.«

日光

At the end of the 8th century the Buddhist monk Shodo Shonin   **History**
founded the first temple on Nikko-zan. Nikko subsequently developed into a holy place of Buddhism and Shinto. Shogun **Tokugawa
Ieyasu** commanded a shrine to be built for him here after his death.
Thus the Toshogu shrine was constructed. Iyeasu's grandson Tokugawa Jemitsu rebuilt after it just 20 years with much greater magnificence that the original.

Edo Wonderland is an attempt to bring the Edo period to life
through a theme park. There is a reconstructed village of the period,
where classical theatrical pieces are performed and demonstrations
of martial arts and acrobatics are held, while visitors find themselves
sharing the site with geishas, samurai and ninjas (free shuttle bus
from JR Nikko station).

The famous monkey trinity in Toshogu shrine in Nikko

▶ VISITING NIKKO

INFORMATION

Tourist information
In Tobu station
Tel. 02 88/53 45 11
Daily 8.30am–5pm
In the Kyodo Center, 591 Goko-machi, main road towards the shrine district
Tel. 02 88/53 37 95
Daily 9am–5pm
www.nikko-jp.org/english
www.city.nikko.lg.jp/kankou

TRANSPORT

By rail: from Tokyo (Ueno station) JR Tohoku shinkansen line to Utsunomiya (45 minutes), then JR Nikko line (45 minutes); from Tokyo (Asakusa station) Tobu private line to Tobu-Nikko (with a possible change in Shimo-Imaichi; 1¾ hours).
By bus: several buses go to Nikko National Park.

EVENTS

Yayoi-matsuri (the portable shrines are brought to the Takino-o and Hongu shrines; mid-April), starting at the Futarasan shrine; Ennen-no-mai (cultish dance from the Kamakura period; mid-May), in the Rinnoji temple; spring festival (with portable shrines, parade in old suits of armour and archery; mid-May), at the Toshogu shrine; Tohai-matsuri (nocturnal pilgrimage to Futarasan's inner shrine on Mount Nantai; beginning of August), starting at Lake Chuzenji.

ALL-IN TICKET

There is an all-in ticket (¥ 1000) for most of the Toshogu, Rinnoji and Futarasan shrines. It is definitely cheaper than buying single tickets. Some areas however cost extra (such as the sleeping cat of Toshogu shrine).

WHERE TO STAY

▶ Mid-range

Nikko Kanaya Hotel
1300 Kami-Hatsuishi-machi, Nikko, Tochigi-ken, 321-1401
Tel. 02 88/54 00 01
www.kanayahotel.co.jp
Historic hotel, consisting of four buildings, the oldest dating back to the Meiji period, the most recent to the 1950s. On a hill west of the main road from the station to the shrine complex. Prices depending on the type of room and season, starting at ¥ 12,000 to more than ¥ 40,000 for a double room.

Mokuba Guesthouse
95-1 Kujira-machi, Nikko-shi, Tochigi-ken 321-1436
Tel. 02 88/54 02 71
Fax 54 02 73
www.osk.3web.ne.jp/~mokuba
From Tobu Nikko station by bus towards Lake Chuzenji to Arasawa bus stop (10 minutes).
Pretty house with a garden, sauna, barbecue place and a small piano bar. Western-style rooms.

Temple and Shrine Complex

✳
Shinkyo Bridge
The Daiya River separates the eastern old town from the new town (Nishi-machi or Iri-machi) on the western bank, where all the famous sites are located.

It is a 15-minute walk from the stations of the JR and the Tobu lines, located closely together, to the Shinkyo (Sacred Bridge, also Mihashi), the sacred bridge painted in red lacquer that crosses the River Daiya and leads to the temple and shrine complex, where the sacred buildings stand amidst cedars. The **avenues** along the road leading to the shrine complex were planted between 1625 and 1651 by Matsudaira Masatsuna, who, less affluent than other Daimyo contributing to the shrine's construction, thereby made his contribution to building the mausoleum of Tokugawa Ieyasu, the founder of the shogunate. Around 13,000 of these trees can still be seen. The 28m/92ft-long and 7.2m/24ft-wide sacred bridge, a reconstruction of the original built in 1636 and destroyed by a flood in 1902, marks the place where, according to legend, the priest Shodo (735–817) crossed the river on the backs of two giant snakes. Once reserved for the shogun and his retinue, the elaborately restored bridge can now be crossed for ¥ 500.

Take the neighbouring bridge to get to Hongu shrine (also Futarasan-Hongo) founded by Shodo in 784. It is one of Nikko's oldest shrines. However, the buildings standing on the site today were rebuilt in the late 17th century. Likewise the temple Shihonryuji behind the shrine, whose main hall contains a statue of the thousand-handed Kannon as well as standing sculptures of Godaison, the Five Great Kings of Wisdom and of Shodo, the temple's founder (the latter apparently a self-representation).

Hongu shrine

◄ Shihonryuji temple

Nikko Map

Rinnoji temple ✳

Take the path leading left from the bridge to the pilgrim street Omotesando, which in turn goes to Toshogu shrine. First along Omotesando Road is Rinnoji temple, which belongs to the Tendai sect. It

was probably built by the priest Ennin (794–864, posthumously Jikaku-daishi) in 848 on the model of a temple on the sacred mountain Hiei. The main hall (Sambutsu-do, Hall of the Three Buddhas; 1648) houses the 8m/26ft gilded statues of Amida-nyorai, the thousand-handed Kannon and Bato-Kannon (the latter with a horse's head on the forehead, the symbol of the patron goddess of animals), as well as the portraits of the temple abbots Tenkai (1536–1643, posthumously Jigendaishi) and Ryogen (912–985, posthumously Gansan-daishi). The temple also has a treasury (homotsuden) and a garden (shoyoen) from the Edo period (open daily 8am–5pm, Nov–March until 4pm, admission: Sanbutsudo ¥ 400, treasury and garden ¥ 300).

Mean-looking guard figures protect the temples

The pilgrim road then continues onwards to **Nikko's most significant shrine**, Toshogu. The complex's 22 buildings date back to a time when architecture and arts and crafts were at their peak. A total of around 15,000 artisans participated in building Toshogu shrine, most of them from Kyoto and Nara. The result was a building complex lavishly adorned and decorated, which once more combined all of the magnificence of the previous Momoyama period. The process of renewing shrine buildings every 20 years led to almost non-stop work.

Toshogu shrine ✳✳

Opening hours:
April–Oct daily
8am–5pm, otherwise until 4pm,
¥ 1,300

Visitors first get to the Stairway of a Thousand (Sennin-ishidan) the outermost point on the way to the shrine that was formerly accessible to the people. Beyond it visitors then pass through a 8.4m/28ft granite torii with a tablet by Emperor Go-Mizunoo (1596–1680). Go left to the five-storey pagoda of 1818; at the top of the stairs is the main gate (Nio-mon, also Omote-mon), the entrance to the courtyard with the three sacred stores and the stable for the sacred horses. The topmost of the three storage buildings is decorated with a polychrome, carved relief on its gable side, showing two elephants; it is said to have been designed by Kano Tan'yu (1602–74) using a literary description as a model (elephants were unknown in Japan at the time).

Group of monkeys ✳✳ ▶

The stable contains carved depictions of monkeys, including the famous triad (»see no evil, hear no evil, speak no evil«). The courtyard

The halls built in 848 modelled on a building on Mount Hiei house numerous Buddhist statues from the Toshogu shrine, which were removed from there during the course of the Shinto renaissance during the Meiji period. South of here, at Daikoku Hill, is Jingen-do Hall, also part of Rinno-ji. It is consecrated to Tenkai (1536–1643), Ieyasu's confidant and high priest of Nikko. On the way there visitors pass the Amida hall (to the left) and sutra hall (to the right) as well as a bell-tower; behind the cult hall enclosed by a wall is Tenkai's tomb.

Not far to the west is Taiyuin, the mausoleum of Iemitsu, the third Tokugawa shogun. Even though this mausoleum was built only 16 years after the Toshogu shrine, it already shows signs of the move towards the simpler style of the Edo period. The colouring is limited to black and gold.

★★
Taiyuin

Walk through the first gate Nio-mon to get to the second gate Nitem-mon, a two-storey structure with statues of the Buddhist gods Komokuten and Jikokuten (exterior niches) as well as of the wind god and the god of thunder (interior niches).

In the central courtyard is a belfry and a drum tower. The path then leads through the third gate Yasha-mon (also Botam-mon, Peony Gate) with depictions of four Buddhist deities and the fourth gate Kara-mon (Chinese Gate) to the inner courtyard. Here visitors will find the cult hall connected to the main hall (honden) via the Ai-no-ma corridor. The main hall contains a sitting statue of Iemitsu. At the entrance to the innermost courtyard is the Koka-mon gate, built in the style of the Ming Dynasty, followed by the Inuki-mon gate, behind which visitors will find the inner cult hall and, somewhat elevated, the bronze tomb of Iemitsu (open April–Oct daily 8am–5pm, otherwise until 4pm, ¥ 550).

The shrines' treasury is to the southeast of the mausoleum. It contains numerous artworks from the individual sacred buildings (hours as Taiyuin, ¥ 500).

◄ Treasury

The road leading west from Futarasan goes past the Takino-o shrine with the tomb of the priest Shodo; the waterfall Shiraito-no-taki can be found close to the entrance.

★
Takino-o

✳ Nikko National Park

The Nikko National Park extends west of the town over an area of 1407 sq km/874 sq mi. With its magnificent mountains, ancient forests, wide-open moorland, lakes and waterfalls it is one of the most beautiful and most visited regions in the country. A former imperial villa houses the **Nikko Museum** (bus from Nikko station, 15 minutes), which exhibits items about the national park's flora and fauna as well as regional arts and crafts.

A number of waterfalls can be found to the north and northwest of Nikko. It takes 1½ hours to walk to Kirifuri-no-taki (there is also a bus in summer); there is a lovely view from the lookout point. Further north, the slopes of Mount Maruyama are a winter sports area with several lifts.

Lake Chuzenji ✳ A bus goes to the more western part of the national park. Go via Umagaeshi to get to Lake Chuzenji. The **Kegon Falls** plummet 100m/330ft to the ground (boat trips) on its eastern shore near Chuzenji-onzen (from Nikko station 50 minutes). The lake, over which the 2484m/8150ft Mount Nantai towers (lift to the viewing platform) is a popular holiday destination; when the leaves change colours in the autumn the southern shore with the towns of Teragasaki and Matsugasaki are particularly attractive. Chuzenji temple (also Tachiki-Kannon) can be found on the eastern shore; it houses a thousand-handed Kannon by the priest Shodo.

Anyone wanting to climb the extinct volcano **Mount Nantai** (early May to mid-October) should start at the central shrine (Chugushi), which is part of Futarasan shrine and whose cult hall (haiden) and main hall (honden) are worth visiting. The crater region (diameter approx. 400m/450yd) can be reached in around four hours; a small fee is charged for climbing the mountain. the innermost shrine (Okumiya) is close to the peak.

Kegon Falls in Nikko National Park is one of Japan's great natural attractions

The bus leaves Chuzenji-onsen following the lake's northern shore to **Jigokuchaya**; the Ryuzu Falls are nearby.

Go via Senjogahara Plateau with its rich alpine flora to get to Nikko-Yumoto-onsen by **Lake Yunoko**, which is a much visited summer holiday and winter sports area.

Ozegahara Cross the Konsei Pass (2024m/6640ft) to get to the moor Ozegahara with Lake Ozenuma in the far west of the national park.

At the foot of the Nasu volcanoes is the **spa region of Nasu-onsen-kyo** with the spas of Nasu-Yumoto, Kita, Benten, Omaru, Sandogoya, Takao and Itamuro. The Nasu Plateau Toll Road leads into the volcano region; the starting point of the relatively easy ascent route (cableway to Tenguhana) up Mount Chausu (also Nasu; 1917m/6289ft) is Kakkodaira. From Mount Chausu's peak there is a route to the 1903m/6243ft Mount Asahi.

Nasu volcanoes

Noto Peninsula

J 6

Main island: Honshu   **Prefecture:** Ishikawa

能登 半島

The appeal of the Noto Peninsula lies in its ruggedly picturesque coast and untouched condition. Visitors will still be able to discover traces of traditional Japan here. Large parts of the coastal landscape have been made into the Noto Peninsula Quasi-National Park.

Noto Peninsula extends far into the Sea of Japan on the northern coast of central Honshu. Its western part consists of green mountainous land with a rugged coastline and a rough climate, while its eastern part with its large number of bays is more sheltered.

What to See on Noto

In the southeast of the peninsula near Toyama Bay is the town of **Takaoka** (population 175,000). Opposite the station is Sakurababa Park. A 200-year-old avenue lined by cherry trees leads from this park to Takaoka Park with the sparse remains of the old castle.

The town of **Hakui** (population 29,000), a traffic junction at the train line coming from Kanazawa and production site of highly sought after silk fabrics, is situated on the strip of coastline known as Chirihama in the west of the peninsula. North of the town close to the sea is Keta shrine with a nice main hall; not far away is Myojoji temple, which belongs to the Nichiren sect. The founder's hall

 VISITING NOTO

TRANSPORT

By rail: from Nagoya JR Hokuriku main line to Takaoka (4 hours), from there JR Himi line to Himi; from Osaka (central station) JR Hokuriku main line to Kanazawa (3 hours), then JR Nanao line via Nanao to Wakura (35 minutes), from there Noto private line to Anamizu, further by bus to Wajima (30 minutes)

By bus: from Kanazawa to Wajima (2 hours) and Sosogi (2¾ hours).

❓ DID YOU KNOW ...?

■ ... that Hakui on Noto reports the most UFO sightings in Japan?

Bizarre rock formations along the coast of Noto Peninsula

(kaisando), the cult hall (kigando) and the five-storey pagoda are particularly lovely. Both places can be reached by bus from Hakui station (approx. 20 minutes).

Noto-Kongo The 8km/5mi white sandy beach known as Chirihama (Chirihama Beach Driveway) gives way in the north to the 15km/9mi Noto-Kongo coastal landscape with its picturesque rock formations (bus from Hakui).

Nanao The JR Nanao line connects Hakui with the lively port of Nanao (population 50,000). An important shipyard developed from the navy base of the Edo period.

Wakura-onsen 5km/3mi northwest of Nanao, where Cape Benten extends out into the bay, is the well-known spa Wakura-onsen (springs up to 90°C/194°F); there are some worthwhile excursions to the surrounding area with its many bays.

Wajima The town of Wajima (population 31,000) on the north coast (bus from Kanazawa or Anamizu), an old centre of lacquerware production, is the starting point for boat trips to Hekurajima Island. The morning market and the lacquerware centre Wajima Shikki Kaikan with an exhibition and shop are both worth visiting.

Hekurajima ▶ The island of Hekurajima, approx. 50km/30mi off the coast (ferry connection, 2 hours) is visited by many fisherfolk from Wajima during the summer months, who come here to collect shells and seaweed. This activity is often performed by female divers (ama).

Bus connections exist from Wajima to Sosogi Coast (also Oku-Noto-Kongo, which extends to the northeast. It has picturesque rock formations. On the way there visitors can see tiny rice terraces on the hillsides. Because machines cannot be used here, everything is still done by hand. With its area of 624 sq m/746 sq yd the Tokikunike Estate here is **one of Japan's largest farmsteads**, divided into two parts: Kamin and Shimo Tokikunike. It was built in the early Edo period by the descendants of Taira Tokikuni, who had been banished here by Minamoto Yoritomo.

✱ Sosogi Coast

◄ Tokikunike Estate

✱ Oga Peninsula

K 5

Main island: Honshu   **Prefecture:** Akita

The steep cliffs of the Oga Peninsula, which has been much eroded by the often very stormy seas, has rugged ledges and cliffs, grottoes, arches and other picturesque rock formations. Many places along the coast sell seafood; the rock spurs make for good places to go fishing.

男鹿　半島

The peninsula on Honshu's northwest coast, around 40km/25mi northwest of Akita, was once the mountainous southern end of a spit that extended towards the northeast almost to Noshiro. Hachirogata Lagoon, which used to lie behind it, was drained in a land reclama-

Rocky peninsula

 VISITING OGA

INFORMATION

Tourist information
In Oga, 1-1 Shinhama-cho, Funakawaminato
Tel. 01 85/24 47 00
Daily 8.30am–5pm

TRANSPORT

By rail: from Tokyo (Ueno station) JR Akita shinkansen and JR Oga lines (5¾ hours).
By bus: (currently only in summer): from Oga to Oga-onsen (1 hour).
By ferry: excursion boats from Oga (aquarium) to Monzen (50 minutes; only May–Oct).

EVENTS

An interesting popular custom on Oga that takes place on 31 December is called *Namahage*, where »hage« stands for removing and »nama« for a blotch said to form on the relevant body part after squatting behind the oven for too long. Young men in shaggy straw cloaks and demon masks knock on every door. The master of the house welcomes them in traditional public holiday dress; after they have bowed in front of the domestic altar they start to murmur and hum in a threatening manner: »are there any lazy people in the house?« Only once they have been pacified with rice cakes and sake do they move on.

tion project and is now a pleasant-looking area with canals making their way through green paddy fields. The narrowest point of the almost triangular peninsula, not far west of Kampu Hill (335m/ 1165ft) measures around 10km/6mi; the steep west coast of the northern Cape Nyudo to the southern Cape Shioze measures more than 25km/15mi. The highest peaks are Mount Honzan (716m/ 2349ft), Mount Kenashi (673m/2208ft) and Mount Shinzan (571m/ 1873ft).

A beautiful panoramic road winds its way along Oga-nishi-kaigan **cliff road**; a good way to explore it is from the seaward side in rented boats.

What to See on the Oga Peninsula

Oga

When coming from Akita, the first town on the peninsula's south coast is Oga (population 37,000). Not far away is the fishing village of Funakawa, situated in a pretty bay (boat rental).

Monzen

Monzen is located on the picturesque west coast. During the season (May–October) it is the starting point for boat trips to Toga near the northern Cape Nyudo (1¼ hours; also round trips). It takes half an hour to walk from Monzen to the Akagami-Goshado shrine, an undertaking for which 999 steps have to be climbed. According to **legend** the steps were made by demons who would have had power over the town's pretty girls if they had managed to build a stairway with 1000 steps by dawn. However, the evil spirits were not able to complete the final step.

Toga Bay

Monzen is the starting point for bus trip along the northbound panoramic road. Oga Suizokukan in the pretty Toga Bay with its aquarium is a worthwhile place for a stopover. A favourable base in the north is the spa Oga-onsen. A lighthouse stands at Cape Nyudo.

✱ Okayama

Main island: Honshu	**Prefecture:** Okayama
Population: 614,000	

The city's largest attraction is Koraku-en, one of Japan's three most famous landscape gardens alongside Kanazawa and Mito.

Commercial and industrial centre

The city of Okayama is situated in the west of Honshu on both sides of the Asahi River, which flows into the Inland Sea at Kojima Bay. Bounded in the north by the foothills of the Chugoku Mountains, it is the starting point for excursions into the picturesque surrounding area. In addition to machine construction and a textile and chemical industry, traditional ceramic manufacturing (bizen-yaki) also plays a significant role.

What to See in Okayama

Around 1.5km/1mi east of the station (bus connection) is Koraku-en Park. Commissioned by Ikeda Tsunamasa, the city's castellan, in 1687 and completed in 1700, it is a typical **example of a promenade garden from the school of Kobori Enshu** (1579–1647). The 11.5ha/28-acre terrain contains tea pavilions, ponds, waterfalls, as well as pines, maple trees, cherry trees and plum trees (open April–Sept daily 7.30am–6pm, Oct–March 8am–5pm, ¥ 350).

★ ★
Koraku-en

🕐

The garden's backdrop is the castle on the other side of the river across Tsukimi Bridge. It is also called U-jo (crow castle) because of its black exterior. Of the structures built in the 16th century only two outer towers survive. The rest was reconstructed after being destroyed in World War II.

Castle

Higashiyama Park (also Kairaku-en), 3.5km/2.2mi southeast of the station, has a lovely view of the city and Kojima Bay to the southwest.

Around Okayama

Take the JR Kibi line to the town of **Kibitsu** 8.5km/5.3mi further west. It was most likely founded in the 4th century and is home to a shrine consecrated to the legendary Prince Kibitsuhiko. The current buildings date back to 1425 and display the Kibitsu-zukuri building style typical of the Kibi region.

A bus goes from Okayama southbound over a 1550m/1700yd dike, which shelters the mouth of Kojima Bay against the sea, to **Uno**, the harbour of Tamano, a town not far west of here. There are ferry connections from Uno to Takamatsu on Shikoku Island (with picturesque views of small forested islands in the Inland Sea) as well as

Koraku-en Map

© Baedeker

50 m
164 ft

Plum Trees

Kakonoike

Asahi

Castle

Chishio-no-Mori

Iris

Tea   Paddy Field   Cycads

▲ Yuishin   Renchiken

Tea-house   Hyotanike

Sawanoike   Tsukimi Bridge

Jigendo

Koshikakejaye

Kayonoike

Kankitei   En-yotei

Kakumeikan

Gate

Park Administration

Okayama Station

P

Tsurumi Bridge

to Shodoshima Island. Since 1988 Seto-Ohashi (»Great Inland Sea Bridge«), a suspension bridge, has been the road and rail connection between Tamano (Honshu) and Sakaide (Shikoku).

Shibukawa 8km/5mi west of Uno is the white sandy beach Shibukawa (bus, 25 minutes), one of the loveliest beaches of the Inland Sea. In addition to several leisure facilities there is a marine museum with an aquarium here.

Washuzan ►Kurashiki, around

Saidaiji The town of Saidaiji, 14km/9mi east of Okayama (JR Ako line, 20 minutes) is known for the Shingon sect's Saidaiji temple founded in 777, where the **Hadaka-matsuri festival (also Eyo, »festival of the naked«)** takes place in February. Young men dressed only in loincloths subject themselves to a night-time ritual cleansing in Yoshi-i River; after this they attempt to capture one the pieces of wood thrown into the darkness by priests, which are said to bring luck.

Bizen ceramics centre Around Imbe station (JR Ako line, 35 minutes) there are countless ceramic workshops producing the traditional, unglazed Bizen pottery (► Arts and Culture, p.73). A museum close to the station has old and new pieces on display.

 VISITING OKAYAMA

INFORMATION
Tourist information
In the station, tel. 0 86/2 22 29 12
Daily 9am–6pm

In the Okayama International Center, 2-2-1 Hokan-cho, near the station's west exit
Tel. 0 86/2 56 29 14
Mon–Sat 9am–5pm
www.city.okayama.okayama.jp
www.pref.okayama.jp (about the prefecture)

TRANSPORT
By air: from Tokyo (Haneda Airport; 1¼ hours).
By rail: from Tokyo (central station) JR shinkansen line via Osaka (Shin-Osaka station; 4 hours); from Takamatsu (Shikoku) JR Marine-Liner (1 hour).
By bus: from Takamatsu (1½ hours).

One of Japan's three famous landscape gardens – Koraku-en

✴ ✴ Okinawa

Main island: Okinawa   **Prefecture:** Okinawa
Area: 2267 sq km/875 sq mi (total)

Okinawa is Japan's southernmost prefecture. Subtropical vegetation, coral reefs and its unique culture make Okinawa's islands an exotic destination, not just for Europeans, but for Japanese holidaymakers too.

沖縄

Okinawa is located around 500km/300mi south of the main island of Kyushu in an island arc separating the Pacific Ocean from the East China Sea. Okinawa Prefecture is made up of Okinawa Island, the largest island of the group, as well as around 100 smaller islands (less than half of them inhabited), with a total area of 2267 sq km/875 sq mi. In addition to the Okinawa island group there are the Daito Islands far to the east as well as the Miyako and Yaeyama Islands to the south. The name **Ryukyu**, which dates back to the T'ang Dynasty, is used to label the island groups of Okinawa, Miyako and Yaeyama. Most of the islands in this chain are of volcanic origin and surrounded by coral reefs that make the sea appear in different colours depending on their size and composition. They are rich in tropical fish and ideal diving areas. In various parts of this island world nature reserves and national parks have been set up; numerous leisure and sports facilities attract tourists from the Japanese main islands.

Three large island groups

> **? DID YOU KNOW ...?**
>
> ■ ... that the residents of Okinawa have the highest life expectancy in the world? The reasons include their healthy traditional cooking and their relaxed outlook on life.

The main economic activities are fishing, agriculture, petrochemicals and tourism; the arts and crafts industry produces traditional goods, such as bingata, a dyed fabric, bashofu, a fabric made of plant fibres and used to make kimonos and coral jewellery.

There are differing theories about the origin of the islands' inhabitants. Much speaks in favour of the hypothesis that immigrants from the Southeast Asian or Pacific area were the first to settle on the islands; ceramic discoveries suggest a connection to the Japanese mainland during the Jomon period. There are also certain linguistic similarities. In the first half of the 20th century many of Okinawa's inhabitants emigrated because of the bad economic situation, particularly to Hawaii, Brazil, Peru, Argentina and the Philippines. To this day Okinawa is one of Japan's poorest prefectures.

History

In the last months of World War II American troops conquered the islands after heavy fighting. They subsequently set up large military bases. Despite the return of the islands to Japan in May 1972, Ameri-

! *Baedeker* TIP

Underwater paradise

Okinawa is an attractive destination for divers and snorkellers. In addition to the main island the nearby Kerama Islands are particularly recommendable: an American destroyer from World War II lies at the bottom of the sea in front of them; Ishigaki Island is considered one of Japan's best diving areas. Apart from the many corals the other main attraction is manta rays. The tourist information centres have details of diving schools with English-speaking staff.

can troops are still stationed here. However, there are plans to greatly reduce the number of military personnel here by 2014.

Okinawa

The main island of Okinawa, situated between latitude 26° 10' and 26° 50' north and longitude 127° 10' and 128° 20' east is the largest of the Ryukyu group, with a total area of 1185 sq km/458 sq mi. Mountain ranges shape the landscape in the north (Yonahadake, 498m/1634ft) while settlements are concentrated in the flatter south. Around 80% of the Okinawa group's inhabitants live in the catchment areas of Naha and Okinawa.

Naha

Naha, the prefectural capital (population 300,000), is situated in the southwest of Okinawa at the mouth of the Kokuba River. Completely destroyed in World War II, the city was rebuilt with modern architecture.

The 1.6km/1mi Kokusai-dori road, with its many shops, department stores, the Daiichi Makishi Public Market and restaurants is the city's main transport axis.

Naminoue shrine ▶

The Naminoue shrine can be found between the harbours of Naha and Tomari, next to Naha's only bathing beach. It is dedicated to the three ancestral gods of the Japanese imperial family and has a view of the coast and the Kerama Islands.

Gokokuji ▶

Not far from here to the southeast is Gokokuji temple, which belongs to the Shingon sect. It has a monument to the Protestant missionary Bernard Jean Bettelheim, who was born in Bratislava and came to Nara in 1846. He stayed for several years, during which time he translated the New Testament into Japanese.

Shintoshin ▶

The district of Shintoshin is home to the **Okinawa Prefectural Museum**, which has exhibits relating to the island's history art and culture.

Tsuboya ▶

The Tsuboya district southeast of Kokusai-dori is home to Naha's old ceramic workshops still in operation today. There is also a pottery museum. To get there take the Heiwa-dori.

★
Shuri fortress and palace

To the east, around 6km/3.5mi outside of the city, is Shuri, the seat of the ruling Ryukyu dynasty from 1429 to 1879. At the centre of the complex is **Shuri Castle**, a reconstruction from the 1990s after war destruction and since 2000 a World Heritage Site. First stop after the information centre with a shop and café is Shurei-no-mon, originally built in the 16th century and reconstructed in 1958. Prior to the castle's reconstruction it was **Naha's landmark**. Before reaching the palace visitors pass Sonohyan-utaki, a stone gate in front of which the local inhabitants pray before big events, as well as a number of other gates. From the forecourt to the red-painted Kofukumon tower (admission charge payable from here) there is a path leading an observation tower called Iri-no-Azana, from where the entire city can be seen. Back in the forecourt the Hoshinmon gate forms the entrance to the palace square Una. This gate is opened in a small ceremony by costumed guards every morning. The middle entrance was reserved for the king and his high officials. There are buildings to the left and right of the palace square, which were used for government business and functions. Straight ahead is the actual palace, Seiden, a wooden building with original stylistic features such as the dragon columns (monorail station Shuri-eki; open daily from 9am, closing between 6pm and 8pm depending on season. Seiden opens half an hour later and closes half an hour earlier. Admission to the inner palace area from Kofukumon ¥ 800. www.shurijo.com). ⏲

Diving in the crystal-clear water of Okinawa allows everyone to experience the bio-diversity of tropical fish

▶ VISITING OKINAWA

INFORMATION

Tourist information
Naha Airport
Tel. 0 98/8 57 68 84
Daily 9am–9pm
www.japanupdate.com
www.city.naha.okinawa.jp/
kanko/nahatabi
www.naha-navi.or.jp
www.pref.okinawa.jp/english
(about the prefecture)

GETTING THERE

By air: from Tokyo (Haneda Airport:
2½ hours), from Kagoshima (1¼
hours), from Osaka (2 hours); from
Fukuoka (1½ hours) to Naha, from
there connection flights.

Welcome to Okinawa

ISLAND TRANSPORT

All of Okinawa Island's former train
lines were destroyed in World War II
and not rebuilt. For that reason
travellers have to use buses or hire a
car in Nara Airport or the town
centre. Naha has a monorail called
Yuri-Rail, which runs from the airport via the town centre to Shuri
(tickets starting at ¥ 200).

EVENTS

Juri-uma (processions with dances;
mid-January), in Naha-Tsuji; Haryusen (boat race, asking for good
catches of fish; beginning of May), in
the harbours of Tomari, Naha and
Itoman; Eisa (men's dance festival,
August), in Okinawa; tug of war (with
a 500m/550yd rope; mid-August), in
Itoman.

WHERE TO EAT

Okinawa's cuisine differs from that of
the rest of Japan. Pork is a staple food
and every part of the pig gets used,
from the feet to the ears. Popular
ingredients include tofu in its fer-
mented form, known as tofu-yo,
seaweed and the bitter goya melon.

WHERE TO STAY

▶ Luxury
JAL Private Resort
Okuma Okinawa
913 Aza-okuma, Kunigami-son,
Okinawa 905
Tel. 09 80/41 22 22
Fax 41 22 34
www.jalokuma.co.jp
Nice holiday complex in the north of
the main island (approx. 100km/60mi
from Naha). Differently designed
»villas« and »cottages« in large
grounds, private white sandy beach.
Several restaurants, including a grill
restaurant by the sea and a cocktail
and karaoke bar.

▶ Budget
Okinawa Sora House
2-24-15 Kumoji, Okinawa 900-0015
Tel. 0 98/8 61 99 39
sora39@mco.ne.jp
Hostel in Naha's town centre, opened
in 2005. Has a pleasant roof terrace.
The dorms (max. eight beds) are very
small, but there are also private
rooms. Close to Miebashi monorail
station.

There are a few other historic buildings in the area surrounding the palace complex, including Tama-udon, the burial site of the Sho dynasty, Bezaitendo temple, founded in 1502 and rebuilt in 1968, and parts of Enkakuji temple of 1492.

◄ Tama-udon

Go south from Shureimon along an old cobbled street to the picturesque Kinjo-cho quarter, which still has the atmosphere of old Ryukyu.

◄ Kinjo-cho

12km/47.5mi south of Naha is **Itoman Harbour**, a centre of deep sea fishing and the place where the Haryusen boat race is held.
Further south and southeast is the 30.8 sq km/12 sq mi Okinawa Old Battlefield Quasi-National Park, with numerous cenotaphs for war victims, including Himeyuri Tower, which was built in memory of 200 schoolgirls who committed suicide here at the end of World War II, and the trenches of the former navy headquarters. Mabuni Hill south of Itoman has a lovely sea view.
Around 8km/5mi east of Itoman is the approx. 5km/3mi-long **Gyukusen-do** dripstone cave, of which about 850m/950yd are open to the public. There is also the theme park Okinawa World.
Around 7km/4.5mi northeast of Naha is a mountain with pretty views and the ruins of Urasoe Castle. 10km/6mi further to the northeast, near the Pacific coast, are the ruins of Nakagusuku Castle with a largely extant wall from the 15th century; the surrounding park has a lovely view of the Pacific Ocean and the East China Sea. It is a ten-minute walk northwards to **Nakamura House**, a 200-year-old wooden farmhouse which was constructed without nails.

Further surroundings of Naha

◄ Urasoe

★
◄ Nakagusuku

The central and northern parts of the west coast between Nagahama Beach and Nago Bay as well as between Nakijin and Cape Hedo, the island's northern tip, make up the 67 sq km/26 sq mi Okinawa Coastal Quasi-National Park with many different **water sports opportunities** (glass floor boats; snorkelling and more). Some of the protected area is taken up by Okinawa Marine Park (Okinawa Kaichu Koen); there is an underwater observatory at Cape Fusena, where visitors can watch coral fish in their natural habitat.

★
Okinawa Marine Park

The town of Nago (population 49,000; bus from Naha, 2½ hours) by Nago Bay is the starting point for trips to the northern part of Okinawa as well as to Motobu Peninsula in the west. Not far from the town centre is the castle ruin, surrounded by cherry trees (blossom January–February). there is a lovely view of the Kunigami Mountains (to the northeast) and the peninsula from here.

Nago

Motobu Peninsula extends around 8km/5mi into the East China Sea. From July 1975 to January 1976 the international marine exhibition Expo '75 took place here; what is now the **Ocean Expo Park** houses the Churaumi Aquarium, one of the largest in the world, in which even whale-sharks can be seen (open daily from 8.30am).

Motobu

Coastal landscape at Miyako Archipelago

✳ **Nakijin** Near the north coast is the ruin of Nakijin Castle (take the bus from Nago to Oyadomari, then 15 minutes on foot), the residence of King Hokuzan in the 14th century. The ramparts and lower walls have survived. The view of the East China Sea and offshore islands makes the short climb to the top worthwhile.

Miyako Islands

Miyako The largest island of the eight-island archipelago is Miyako (area: 176 sq km/68 sq mi; population 45,000; flight connections from Naha 45 minutes, boat connections 13½ hours), surrounded by coral reefs and covered in sugar-cane fields.

Hirara The island's economic and administrative centre Hirara (population 33,000) is situated on the west coast. 150m/164ft south of the harbour is a monument donated by Kaiser Wilhelm I as a thank you for the rescue of German castaways in 1873. As a result of this connection there is also a **German theme park** here. Hirara was the location for the G8 summit meeting in the year 2000.

The island's highest elevation is Nobaru Hill (109m/358ft); there is a botanical garden on its western slope. Nearby is also the tax stone (Nintozeiseki); from the 17th to the 19th century it served as a measure of taxation for the island's inhabitants: anyone at least as tall as the stone (1.40m/4ft 6in) was liable for taxation. Miyako's nicest swimming beach, Yonahamae, is in the south of the island.

Yonahamae ▶

Yaeyama Islands

This group includes the islands of Ishigaki, Iriomote, Taketomi and Yonaguni, as well as 15 smaller islands.

Ishigaki Island (flight connection from Naha, 55 minutes; boat connection 14–19 hours) has white sandy beaches and lavish vegetation (palm trees, sugar cane). The island's main town is Ishigaki (population 41,000); the samurai residence **Miyara-donchi** from 1819 and its landscape garden are worth seeing. Mount Omoto, further north from here, is the highest in Okinawa Prefecture at 525m/1722ft. ◄ Kabira Bay
Kabira Bay with its little islands and idyllic sandy beaches is particularly attractive. The sought-after black pearls are cultivated here.

Ishigaki

Iriomote Island, 289 sq km/112 sq mi in size, is situated to the southwest opposite Ishigaki (40 minutes by speedboat). Around a third of the island, together with the smaller islands of Kohama, Taketomi, Kurojima, Aragusuku and the Nakanokami group, make up Iriomote National Park. The region is characterized by long coral reefs with a **diverse marine fauna** and by impassable jungle with many wild animals (including the Iriomote wildcat). Haimita, situated at Cape Haimita in the south of the island is the best beach.

★ ★
Iriomote

A footpath (20 minutes) leads southwards from the port of Funaura on the north coast to Nipa palm forest and further to the Maiudo Falls and Kampira Falls, formed by the Urauchi River (river round trip from Funaura, 2½ hours).

Funaura

The island of Taketomi (hovercraft from Iriomote, 20 minutes) is known for its »star sand«, which is made up of the shells of tiny crustaceans. Taketomi can be explored from a cart drawn by buffalo.

Taketomi

Osaka

Main island: Honshu   **Prefecture:** Osaka
Population: 2.6 million

Osaka is an old merchant town, whose inhabitants seem more active and down-to-earth than those of other places. Instead of boasting large numbers of outstanding sights, Osaka is good for down-to-earth entertainment: shopping and going out.

大阪

Osaka, the capital of Osaka Prefecture, is situated in the west of central Honshu, where the Yodo River flows into the wide Osaka Bay on the Pacific Ocean. The bay is bounded in the southeast by the Kii Peninsula and is separated from the Inland Sea in the west by Awaji

Japan's third-largest city

Island. The city is western Japan's commercial and administrative centre and is an important part of the Hanshin industrial area, which extends all the way to Kobe.

The city is located in the Yodo delta, whose branching waterways criss-cross through it in a whole network of canals. This fact has earned the city with its more than 1000 bridges the sobriquet **»Venice of the East«** and also created favourable conditions for developing trade. Even though Osaka was outperformed by Tokyo commercially after World War II, it still plays a major role, in international terms too. The following maxim is still true today: Osaka earns the yen and Tokyo makes politico-economic decisions in order to spend them again with class in Kyoto.

History

Osaka's roots go back to the mythological early days of the Japanese empire. The legendary Emperor Jimmu is said to have landed at the mouth of Yodo River and called the place Naniwa (»fast waves«) after his mythical odyssey from Kyushu through the Inland Sea. What is certain is that people settled here from very early on because of the favourable location; in the 4th century Emperor Nintoku may have had a fortified residence in the area. Rulers also resided here from the 7th and 8th centuries and via Naniwa harbour maintained political and economic relations with Korea, which at the time was experiencing the heyday of its early kingdom.

In the 16th century **Toyotomi Hideyoshi** gave the castle new, strong fortifications and forced merchants from Kyoto and Sakai, a trading centre south of Osaka, to take up residence in the area under his dominion. During the bloody feuds about the shogunate the castle was held by Toyotomi Hideyoshi in the summer of 1615. The siege of Osaka by the troops of his rival **Tokugawa Ieyasu,** commanded by his son Hidetada, is a famous episode in the battle for mastery of medieval Japan.

The Tokugawa shoguns had their residence in Edo, but administered Osaka through a governor known

? DID YOU KNOW ...?

■ ... that instant noodle soups were invented in Osaka? Momofuku Ando (see p.106) had the idea and later also thought of cup noodles.

as the Jodai, protecting and supporting the class of ever more powerful merchants, who in turn acted as patrons of many famous artists. These artists created many excellent works in the port during that time, often showing criticism at the decay of the traditional customs and values which was caused by the decline of the impoverished samurai. Still, trade and industry continued to flourish; Osaka became the largest trading and port city in Japan and was called »Japan's kitchen«. During the Meiji period Osaka had almost half a million inhabitants and at the beginning of the World War II the port's population had grown to around 3.25 million. In 1970 the **EXPO '70 world fair** took place in Osaka and the complex created at the time has now been converted into a park.

Osaka Map

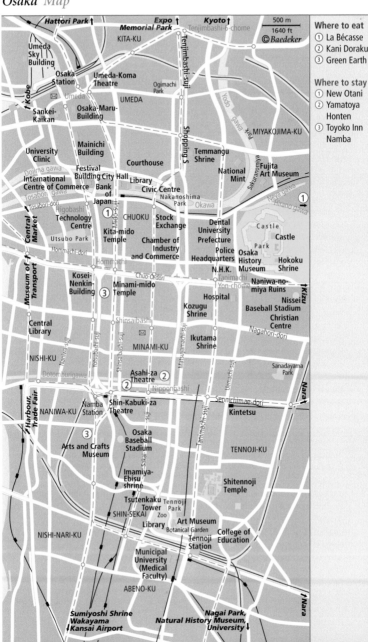

Where to eat
1. La Bécasse
2. Kani Doraku
3. Green Earth

Where to stay
1. New Otani
2. Yamatoya Honten
3. Toyoko Inn Namba

▶ VISITING OSAKA

INFORMATION

Tourist information

JR station Osaka in Umeda,
Midosuji exit/south side
Tel. 06/63 45 21 89
JR Shin-Osaka station, 3rd floor
Tel. 06/63 05 33 11
JR Namba station
Tel. 06/66 43 21 25
JR Tennoji station
Tel. 06/67 74 30 77
All daily 8am–8pm

It is a good idea to get the bilingual
(English/Japanese) *Osaka Tourist
Guide* here. It contains all the important
information needed when
visiting Osaka, as well as a detailed
map, the *Osaka City Map*.

Online: www.octb.jp
www.city.osaka.jp/english
www.kanko-osaka.or.jp/eng
www.kippo.or.jp (about the entire
Kansai region)

GETTING THERE

By air: from Tokyo (Narita International
Airport and Haneda Airport; 1
hour); from Fukuoka (1 hour); from
Sapporo (1¾ hours); from Kagoshima
(1 hour); from Naha (Okinawa; 2
hours); as well as scheduled flights
from overseas.
Osaka has two airports: *Osaka Airport*
(Itami) in the northwest and the
newer, larger *Kansai International
Airport* (www.kansai-airport.or.jp/
english), located in the south of the
city on an artificial island. Osaka
Airport can be reached by bus from
Osaka station or Shin-Osaka station
(approx. 25 minutes); Kansai International
Airport is best reached via
the Nankai train from Namba (35–45
minutes); with the JR Haruka Express

from Shin-Osaka or Tennoji (45 and
30 minutes respectively)
By rail: from Tokyo (central station)
JR Tokaido shinkansen line via Nagoya
and Kyoto to Shin-Osaka (3½
hours); from Fukuoka (Hakata)
JR San'yo shinkansen line via Hiroshima
and Okayama (3 hours).
The JR Tokaido main line and the JR
San'yo main line (much longer travel
times) run parallel to each other.
Take the Midosuji Subway to get to
Shin-Osaka city centre.

By ferry: across the Inland Sea via
Kobe, Sakaide, Takamatsu, Imabari
and Matsuyama to Beppu (Kansai
Steamship Co.; 15 hours); hovercraft
via Kobe and Sakaide to Takamatsu
(3¼ hours); also from Osaka-Minami
harbour to Hiroshima, Tokushima,
Kochi (Shikoku) and Hyuga
(Kyushu).

LOCAL TRANSPORT

Osaka has an extensive *underground
network* consisting of seven lines as
well as the useful JR*Loop Line* (free
for JR pass holders). In addition there
are private regional trains, such as the
Nankai line, the Hankyu line (incl. to
Takarazuka), the Hanshin line (incl.
to Kobe), the Keihan line (incl. to
Kyoto) and the Kintetsu line (incl. to
Nagoya, Nara, Ise).
The underground trains run from
approx. 5am to midnight. A day pass
for the underground, city buses and
tram line costs ¥ 850 and has
discounts to several attractions in
Osaka. More information at
www.surutto.com/conts/ticket.

EVENTS

Toka-Ebisu (first shrine visit and
procession with women carried in

The wide Midosuji-dori boulevard leads over the river channel and into the district of Chuo-ku. To the east of this road is the castle surrounded by a park (15 minutes' walk from Tanimachi-Yon-chome underground station). The original building was completed in 1596 by Toyotomi Hideyoshi after a three-year construction period and at the time it was the country's largest castle complex. The current buildings are a reinforced concrete reconstruction dating from 1931. It was elaborately restored in 1997.

Castle
⊙
Opening hours:
Daily 9am–5pm,
600

The five-storey main tower is 42m/ 138ft tall and stands on a 14m/46ft stone pedestal. It houses exhibitions on the history of the castle and city; there is a splendid panorama from the top floor.

> **! Baedeker TIP**
>
> **Brand-new electronics**
> Between Ebisucho station and Nippon-bashi station is the 2 km/1mi Denden Town, a shopping street with 300 electronic-appliance and camera shops as well as tax-free shops.

Take the Chuo underground line westbound to the district of **Minato-ku**. Near Bentencho station (also Osaka Loop Line) is the **Transport Museum** (land, air, and maritime traffic, automobile and aeroplane models).

The underground Chuo line ends at the harbour (Osaka-ko station) at the trade fair grounds. Originally the port facilities were located at the mouth of the Ajikawa river channel, which bounds the district to the north. As a result of increasing silting it was moved and now extends to the more southern districts of Taisho-ku and Suminoe-ku. To the northwest of the underground station a large aquarium was opened in 1990 (www.kaiyukan.com). Its main basin is 9m/30ft deep and it also has 13 smaller pools. The thematic focal point is the marine life of the Pacific (open daily 10am–8pm, ¥ 2000). The cruise liner *Santa Maria* departs from here. Not far away are the Suntory Museum with an IMAX theatre and the Tempozan complex with a huge number of shops and restaurants. The **artificial offshore island of Sakishima** (OTS line from Osakako) is the site of the World Trade Center. The 256m/840ft Cosmo Tower has a panorama of Osaka Bay from the 55th floor. Opposite is the architecturally interesting **ATC** (Asia & Pacific Trade Center) with shops and restaurants. Nearby the marine museum with a replica of a 17th-century merchant vessel.

Harbour

★
◄ Aquarium

◄ Cosmo Tower

Neighbouring Chuo-ku in the south is the district of Minami-ku, which is known for its entertainment venues. In the southernmost section of the Shinsaibashi-suji is Osaka's most lively business centre; the southbound Ebisubashi-suji road is lined by a large number of smaller shops and restaurants.

Minami-ku

The area around Namba station has managed to hold on to an air of old Osaka, particularly in Hozenji Yokocho, the alleyway in the old theatre district, which is home to the small Hozenji temple and a moss-covered Fudo statue. Believers come here to pour water over it,

◄ Hozenji Yokocho

thereby asking for good fortune. Both sides of this short, narrow alleyway are lined with bars, pubs and smaller snack bars.

◄ Kozugu shrine ►

Not far east of Tanimachi-suji road is Kozugu shrine, dedicated to Emperor Nintoku, who lived in Osaka. The original buildings were destroyed in World War II; the hall is a new building from 1961. The surrounding park has a historical stone lantern and a fine view of the city. 200m/220yd away is the tomb of the famous playwright Chikamatsu Monzaemon (1653–1724).

Tennoji Park

South of Minami-ku district is Tennoji-ku with Tennoji Park (Shitennoji-mae underground station; Tanimachi line). It is home to the municipal art museum, a large zoo, a botanical garden and several sports facilities. Chausuyama Hill, a prehistoric burial mound, was the location of Tokugawa Ieyasu's camp during the siege of Osaka.

✳
Shitennoji

Further northeast is the Shitennoji (also Tennoji) temple. It was founded in 593 by Prince Shotoku Taishi, the author of the first Confucian code of law and promoter of Buddhism in Japan, making it older than Horyuji temple in ►Nara. Enter the reconstructed temple square through the western Saijumon Gate. It contains a five-storey pagoda, the main hall (kondo) and the lecture hall (Kodo). To the east is the treasury with Sotoku-taishi's sword and a copy of the Hokkekyu sutra from the late Heian period. A stone torii of 1294 is at the west entrance; it is the oldest of its kind in Japan (open April–Sept daily 8.30am–4.30pm, otherwise until 4pm, ¥ 300). Travellers in need of some peace and quiet can visit the temple garden (admission ¥ 300).

Brightly lit – the shopping quarter around Namba station

Large parts of Shitennoji were rebuilt using the old plans

On the other side of the express way bordering Tennoji Park in the west, is the 103m/338ft **Tsutenkaku look-out tower** (»the tower that leads up to the sky«) in the district of Naniwa-ku. It is surrounded by the Shin-Sekai district, a somewhat sleazy area with amusement arcades, cheap taverns and bars.

Take the JR Nainkai main line southbound from Daikoku-cho station to the district of Sumiyoshi-ku (Sumiyoshi-koen station), which used to be part of the harbour. The stone lighthouse pedestal on the east bank of Jsuangenbori Canal is evidence of this. Silting has caused the coastline to push further westwards.

East of the station is Sumiyoshi Park, one of the city's most popular parks with magnificent pines and camphor trees. Further east is **Sumiyoshi shrine** (Nankai line, Sumiyoshi-Taisha station), which was founded in Kobe in 202 and later moved to its current location. It is consecrated to the four patron deities of seafarers; the entrance is flanked by numerous stone lanterns that were donated by believers. The buildings, painted in red and white and covered in cypress bark, were renewed in 1810. They display the purely Shinto Sumiyoshi style with a projecting pitched roof and crossed bargeboards.

To reach the only Universal Studios theme park outside the USA take the JR Osaka Loop or the JR Yumesaki Line from Umeda station (about ten minutes) and feel as if you're in Orlando, because most attractions have been copied from there.

Around Osaka

Around 10km/6mi south of the city centre is the town of Saikai (train connections from Namba to Mikunigaoka station; Koya line).

Naniwa-ku

Sumiyoshi-ku

Sumiyoshi Park

Universal Studios Japan

Saikai

Lively all-female opera

The famous Takarazuka Revue (25km/16mi north of Osaka), a three-hour performance with lively action, dancing and music is highly recommendable. The special thing about this theatre and music school founded in 1914 is that all of the roles are played by women. More information at http://kageki.hankyu.co.jp/english. Tickets cost ¥ 3500–10,000; telephone reservations should best be made by the hotel.

It is the site of the 21ha/52-acre area containing Emperor Nintoku's (»Daisen-ryo«) grave, a **typical Kofun burial mound** with the keyhole-shaped outline (3rd–7th century). The actual burial mound is the circular back section; the densely forested burial mound is surrounded by a moat on all sides. There is a good view of the burial complex from the roof of the town hall.

Senri

Expo Memorial Park ▶

The satellite town of Senri north of Osaka can be reached by underground (Midosuji line, Senri-chuo station). A bus goes from the station to Expo Memorial Park (264ha/652 acres), where the world fair of 1970 was held. It contains an ethnological national museum (Japanese folkcraft etc.), a Japanese garden, the amusement park Expo Land and much more.

Toyonaka

Take the Hankyu-Takarazuka line northbound from Osaka to get to the city of Toyonaka (population 413,000) further inland (20 minutes). Hattori-Ryokuchi Park contains the Hattori-minka-shuraku open air museum with old farmhouses from central Japan (open Tue–Sun 9.30am–5pm, ¥ 500).

✱ Iwashimizu-Hachiman shrine

32km/20mi north of the city (Keikan line from Yodoyabashi station to Yawatacho) is Iwashimizu-Hachiman shrine on the top of Otokoyama Hill (cableway from the station). The magnificent main hall (honden) is dedicated to Emperor Ojin, worshipped as the god of war Hachiman; costumes of the Heian period are worn for the shrine festival in mid-September.

Otaru

`L 3`

Main island: Hokkaido	**Prefecture:** Hokkaido
Population: 185,000	

小樽

Even though this town was only founded in the mid-19th century, it is one of the oldest settlements on Hokkaido. As a result of its favourable location it was already an important port for trade with Russia and for herring fishing before World War II.

Nice location

Otaru is situated in the west of Hokkaido on Ishikari Bay, which opens towards the north onto the Sea of Japan. The rambling coastal landscape and the hills in the south give the city attractive surroundings. The town's name goes back to an Ainu term: »Ota oru« means »river at the sandy beach«.

What to See in Otaru

Northwest of the station (bus connection) is Otaru Museum, a brick building from 1906 based on English architecture. It houses exhibits on the town's history and the visual arts. It is situated near a romantic canal lined by gas lanterns.

Otaru Museum

Around 5km/3mi further is Shukuzu Marine Park (bus from the station, 25 minutes; shows) with Hokkaido's largest aquarium and a museum in an old fishing hut.

Marine park

Close to the coast, 2km/1mi northeast of the city is Temiya Park, with Temiya Grotto, which is of archaeological interest: it contains a rock inscription 2m/6.5ft tall and 4.5m/15ft wide that has so far not been deciphered (there is a copy at the entrance to the cave).

Temiya Park

Around Otaru

West of the city Ishikari Bay is bounded by the Shakotan Peninsula, whose coastal area forms Niseko-Shakotan-Otaru-kaigan Quasi-National Park. There are lovely views of the Sea of Japan from Cape Kamui and Cape Shakotan in the far north. The steep cliffs, eroded by the waves, drop 250m/820ft down to the sea at **Cape Nomanai**.

Shakotan

Ranshima beach is particularly beautiful; 1.5km/1mi southeast of the station is the stone circle of Oshoro (diameter: 28m/31yd), a prehistoric site whose purpose is as yet unknown.

◄ Ranshima

West of the station, in Yoichimachi, is Fugoppe Cave, discovered in 1950, whose walls contain a pictorial inscription estimated to be 1500 years old.

◄ Fugoppe Cave

▶ VISITING OTARU

GETTING THERE
By rail: from Sapporo (40 minutes) or Hakodate (4 hours) JR Hakodate main line.

EVENTS
Skiing competitions (end of February), at Tenguyama-Ski complex; Ushio-matsuri (processions with folk dances; around the end of July), in Otaru Park.

SHOPPING
Otaru is known for its glassware. One of the best-known studios is *Kitaichi Glass* dating from 1901, with a wonderful café (southeast of the canal district, 10 minutes from the station Minami-Otaru, open daily 9am–6pm).

Rikuchu-kaigan National Park

L 5

Main island: Honshu
Area: 123 sq km/47 sq mi

Prefectures: Iwate and Miyagi

陸中海岸国立公園 The stretch of coastline in Rikuchu-kaigan National Park on the east coast of northern Honshu is more than 180km/110mi long and has diverse coastal landscapes with cliffs, rock terraces and small bays. There are many petrels and seagulls here; the vegetation largely consists of rhododendrons.

What to See in Rikuchu-kaigan National Park

Miyako
The town of Miyako is a useful starting point for trips to the park, from where **bus tours** to the most beautiful sites are organized.

Jodogahama
Not far north of the town is Jodogahama beach, with dark pine trees and white sand. It is one of the nicest areas. Further attractive beaches can be found to the north near Taro, Omoto and Kurosaki. Near Kitayamazaki the steep cliffs reach a height of 300m/985ft (boat trips).

Wild coastal landscape in the national park

▶ VISITING RIKUCHU-KAIGAN NATIONAL PARK

GETTING THERE

By rail: from Tokyo JR Tohoku shinkansen line to Ichinoseki (2½ hours) or Morioka (3¼ hours); from Ichinoseki JR Ofunato line to Kesennuma (1½ hours), from Morioka JR Yamada line to Miyako (1½ hours).

By bus: several bus connections within the national park.

By ferry: round trips from Miyako.

The coasts along the southern part of the park are flatter and lined by dunes covered in pine trees. The scenic highlight along this stretch of the national park is Goishi-kaigan's pebble beach.

Goishi-kaigan

Karakuwa Peninsula protrudes into the Pacific near Kesennuma. At its tip is the **Tsunami Museum**, which demonstrates the power of these seaquakes by means of films, a shaking floor and wind simulations.

Karakuwa

Off the shore of Karakuwa Peninsula is the small island of Oshima, which has some nice bathing beaches. The waters surrounding it have been made into a marine park; why not take a trip in one of the **glass-bottomed boats**?

Oshima

Rishiri-Rebun-Sarobetsu National Park

L 2

Main island: Hokkaido   **Prefecture:** Hokkaido
Area: 340 sq km/131 sq mi

利尻礼文国立公園

Japan's northernmost national park protects an area rich in alpine flora and different bird species. It includes the Sarobetsu Plateau at the northern tip of Hokkaido as well as the offshore islands of Rishiri and Rebun.

What to See in Rishiri-Rebun-Sarobetsu N.P.

The area of the national park can be reached from Wakkanai. The port (population 46,000) at Soya Bay is free of ice all year round thanks to the warm Tsushima ocean current. From an observation tower in Wakkanai Park there is a panorama over the sea with Rishiri Island and Rebun Island all the way to the Russian Sakhalin Peninsula.

Wakkanai

⏵ VISITING

GETTING THERE

By air: from Sapporo to Wakkanai
(1 hour)
By rail: from Asahikawa JR Soya main
line via Toyotomi to Wakkanai
(4 hours).

By bus: from Toyotomi and Wakkanai
to Sarobetsu Plateau; round trip on
Rishiri
By ferry: from Wakkanai to Rishiri
and Rebun (each approx. 1¾ hours).

Toyotomi Further south are Toyotomi and the small spa town Toyotomi-onsen. Take the bus from Toyotomi station to the wide, fertile Sarobetsu Plain, which is home to the remarkable **Sarobetsu Gensei Kaen** garden, a wetland with a sub-arctic wild flora (azaleas, iris, etc.). June and July are the best times to visit.

Rishiri Opposite Sarobetsu Plain is the almost circular island of Rishiri (183 sq km/71 sq mi), dominated by the 1721m/5646ft volcano of the same name. Between the forest belt surrounding the volcano and the coast is a road connecting the island's four towns of Oshidomari, Oniwaki, Senboshi and Kutsugata. A **round trip by bus** (approx. 2 hours) or on a hired bicycle is worthwhile. Lake Himenuma is good for fishing; there are some lovely walks to Misaki Park and Kutsugata-Misaki Park. Climbing Mount Rishiri takes 9–11 hours there and back, depending on the route.

Rebun 10km/6mi to the northwest is Rebun Island (82 sq km/32 sq mi), also called »flower island« because between June and August more than 300 different plant species come into bloom here. From the island there is a good view of the Rishiri volcano. Motochi-kaigan beach with its steep, 50m/165ft Jizo cliff and the cliffs of Nishito-mari-kaigan are two attractive spots on the island.

Sado

K 5–6

Main island: Honshu **Prefecture:** Niigata
Area: 857 sq km/331 sq mi

佐渡 **For a long time Sado had no contacts to the mainland worth mentioning. To this day the names of the landscapes, the customs and the culture are all testament to this self-sufficiency, which lasted into the 13th century.**

The island of Sado, which lies off the coast of eastern central Honshu in the Sea of Japan, is the largest Japanese island after the four main islands and Okinawa with an area of 857sq km/331 sq mi. The Kuninaka Plain at the centre is enclosed by two ranges of mountains that run parallel to the east and west coast respectively. Today most of the island is part of the Sado-Yahiko Quasi-National Park.

The warm Tsushima ocean current gives Sado its attractive climate. The inhabitants live mainly from agriculture and fishing. The flora of the south of Sado consists to a large extent of camellias and bamboo groves.

What to See on Sado

The island's capital and port for ships from Honshu is Ryotsu (population 21,000), from where buses depart to all areas of the island. In the town's vicinity there are a couple of recreation areas, namely Sumiyoshi-onsen (bus, 15 minutes) and Shiizaki-onsen (bus, 10 minutes), both lovely places for a relaxing stay. Kamo Lagoon not far to the south is connected to the sea and overshadowed by Mount Kimpoku (1173m/3848ft) in the north and west.

Ryotsu

Kuninaka Plain with its paddy fields has a number of cultural attractions waiting to be discovered. One of them is Izumi 10km/6mi southwest of Ryotsu, which is home to the Kuroki-gosho, the former residence of Emperor Juntoku.

Izumi

Not far away is the village of **Niibo**; its Komponji temple was the first domicile of **Nichiren** while he was in exile. These days the members of the sect go on pilgrimages to Myosho-ji temple, situated on a hill to the southwest: it was the place of his second residence.

The town of Aikawa (population 10,000; bus from Ryotsu, 1¼ hours) on the west coast became very significant in the 17th century with the discovery of abundant **gold deposits**; at times it had close

Aikawa

> ! **Baedeker TIP**
>
> ### Drum roll
>
> Sado is the home of the internationally famous taiko drumming troupe Kodo. Every year in August they hold a three-day music festival on Sado called Earth Celebration, with drum concerts, workshops and a colourful market. A performance by these strong drummers is definitely something nobody visiting Japan should miss! (More information at www.kodo.or.jp/ec/en.)

▶ VISITING

GETTING THERE

By air: from Niigata to Ryotsu (25 minutes).
By ferry: from Niigata (1–2½ hours); from Naoetsu (3 hours).

WHEN TO GO

The best time to visit Sado is between April and October because during the colder half of the year storms can make the crossing quite uncomfortable.

to 200,000 inhabitants. The red clay from the pits is used for the typical pottery (Mumyoi-yaki).

Old gold mines ▶ From Chomyoji temple in the town a path leads to the former gold mines. They house an interesting museum of gold mining and processing (open April–Oct daily 8am–5pm, otherwise 8.30am–4.30pm, ¥ 700). The nearby Aikawa Folk Museum (Aikawa Kyodo Hakubutsukan) has exhibits on the region's history, the woodblock-print museum (Sado Hangamura Bijutsukan) has changing exhibitions presenting contemporary woodblock prints.

A steep, picturesque cliff extends all the way to Cape Hajikizaki at Sado's northern tip. The island's nicest stretch of coastline is Senkaku Bay north of Aikawa.

Ogi The harbour town of Ogi in the island's far south is quite pretty. It is home to Rengebuji temple, probably founded in 808 by the priest Kukai. In May (female) collectors go out in barrel-shaped wooden boats to collect seaweed, which is then dried on the beach. Tourists can also take a tour of the harbour in one of these **tub boats** (tarai-bune) with the women. The maritime museum (Kaiun Shiryokan) displays regional nautical equipment. A lovely boat trip goes from the rocky coast of Nansenkyo to Cape Sawazaki.

★ Saikai National Park

E 8 • b 4–5

Main island: Kyushu **Prefecture:** Nagasaki
Area: 243 sq km/94 sq mi

西海国立公園 **Scenic beauty and historical attraction make this national park on Kyushu an attractive destination. The flora is subtropical; the rugged coastline is interspersed by pretty beaches. Pearls are cultivated in parts of the sea.**

Location Saikai National Park is situated in the far northwest of Kyushu. In addition to a small strip of Kyushu's coastline it contains parts of Hirado Island, the Kujukushima Islands (literally »Ninety-nine Islands«) and several small islands of the Goto Archipelago (literally »Five Islands«).

What to See in Saikai National Park

Kujukushima Islands Immediately off Kyushu's northwest coast is the crowded Kujukushima island group, situated in the inlet separating the main island from Hirado. Boat trips leave from Sasebo. These approx. 170 islands are covered in subtropical vegetation.

Hirado ▶ The hilly island of Hirado, which is only 600m/660yd from Kyushu's coast and has an area of 171 sq km/66 sq mi, is connected to the main island via a road bridge. It played a significant role during the

16th century when Japan opened up to foreign trade for the first time. When persecution of Christians started towards the end of that century, many of them looked for refuge here and built churches that looked like temples from the outside.

The island capital of Hirado (population 28,000) in the far northeast was once **the first Japanese harbour to trade with overseas countries**. The Dutch and the English built factories. However, the development of the port of ► Nagasaki with its more favourable location meant that Hirado lost its commercial significance. The town can comfortably be explored on foot. There is a path northeast from the ships' landing stage to the historical museum (Kanko-shiryokan); some memorials are located on the hill beyond the museum, including one for the English pilot William Adams, who ran ashore in Japan in April 1600, built ships for the Japanese fleet at the behest of Tokugawa Ieyasu and acted as the middleman between the government and the foreign factories in Hirado. Approx. 200m/220yd from here are the remains of Oranda-Shokan-Ato, a Dutch settlement. West of the landing stage the Matsuura Museum (Matsuura-shiryo-hakubutsu-kan) displays possessions of this aristocratic family. To the southwest on a hill is the neo-Gothic church of Saint Francis Xavier (built in 1931). The castle (originally built in the 18th century, modern reconstruction) is located on Kameoka Hill in the southeast and has a view of the sea and the bridge to the mainland. The Kokusai cultural centre, a modern building in the shape of a ship, is nearby.

◄ Hirado

 DID YOU KNOW ...?

■ Hirado is the birth place of Coxinga (Zheng Chenggong, 1624–64), a legendary pirate commander who is revered as a hero in Japan, China and Taiwan.

The western part of the national park is made up of the Goto Islands, around 50km/30mi off the coast of Kyushu (ferry connections from Sasebo and Nagasaki). The group consists of five large islands: Fukue, Naru, Wakamatsu, Nakadori and Uku as well as around 150 smaller islands.

Goto Islands

The 327 sq km/126 sq mi island of Fukue is an important area for livestock, agriculture and fishing. Its coast has pretty beaches; Cape Osezaki in the southwest has impressive cliffs. The island also has a castle ruin and old Samurai houses.

◄ Fukue

 VISITING

GETTING THERE

By rail: from Sasebo private Matsuura line to Tabira Hiradoguchi (1¼ hours), then bus to Hirado Sanbashi, Hirado's ferry quay (15 minutes).

By ferry: from Sasebo to Hirado (1½ hours); ferry from Hiradoguchi to Hirado (15 minutes).

Sakata

K 5

Main island: Honshu
Population: 101,000

Prefecture: Yamagata

The town of Sakata on the west coast of northern Honshu at the mouth of the Mogami River has one of the most significant ports on the Sea of Japan.

Economy Sakata was already a trans-shipment centre for rice cultivated on Shonai Plain during the Edo period, which is why the country's first large rice silo was built here in 1672. Industrialization brought a great economic upswing to the town; today it is dominated by the chemical industry. The cultivation of benibana, golden-yellow flowers used to dye silk, also plays an important role.

The merchant families **Honma** and Abumiya became incredibly wealthy both in money and in land through trading rice. A folk song says it is impossible to become as rich as a Honma: all anyone could dream of is to become as rich as a daimyo.

> ## ! Baedeker TIP
>
> ### Inspiring
>
> When the great poet Matsuo Basho (1644–94) saw the coast of Sakata he wrote: »Mogami River / washes the glowing sun-globe / down to the sea's waves.« He wrote down his experiences of his 150-day hike through northern Japan in the wonderful volume *A Narrow Road to the Interior*, which also contains much commentary (Shambhala, Boston 2007).

What to See in Sakata

Art museum 500m/550yd west of the station (footpath, 5 minutes) in a house that once belonged to the Honma merchant family, the Honma Art Museum exhibits swords, pictures, sculptures and porcelain from the family possessions. The artistically landscaped Tsurumai-en garden is also part of the museum (open daily 9am–5pm, Nov–March until 4.30pm, Dec–Feb closed Mon, ¥ 700).

▶ VISITING SAKATA

GETTING THERE

By rail: from Tokyo JR Joetsu shinkansen to Niigata (1¾ hours), then JR Uetsu line to Sakata (2¼ hours); from Yamagata JR Yamagata shinkansen to Shinjo (¾ hours), then Rikuu-sai line (1 hour).

In the west near the harbour is **Hiyoriyama Park**, situated on a small hill. An old wooden lighthouse stands at the top of it; from here there is a broad view of the mouth of the Mogami River and the Sea of Japan.

Close by is **Kaikoji temple**, which houses the mummies of the monks Chukai-shonin and Emmyokai-shonin.

The significance of rice cultivation for the region is illustrated by the **Shonai May Rekishi Shiryokan**, housed in one of the old rice silos of 1893 that are still in use today.

Around Sakata

North of the town is **Chokai Quasi-National Park** (take the JR Uetsu main line from Sakata to Fukura, 30 minutes). In its eastern part the 2230m/7316ft Mount Chokai (it gets its name from the old provincial name, also Dewa-Fuji), the main peak of the Chokai volcano range, which runs parallel to the coast. There is a bus from Fukuoka (45 minutes) to the foot of the

Rice planting with view of Mount Chokai

mountain; climbing it will take around seven hours. A second ascent route (approx. five hours) starts in Kisakata (north of Fukura along the JR Uetsu main line). There is a panoramic view from the peak.

South of Sakata (JR Uetsu main line, 30 minutes) is the old castle town of Tsuruoka (population 100,000), once the seat of the Sakai ruling family and to this day an important trading place for rice. The castle's remains and Shonai shrine, dedicated to the Sakai, can be seen 2km/1mi southwest of the station (bus, 10 minutes) in Tsuruoka Park (cherry blossom in April). The nearby **Chido Open-Air Museum** contains some of the town's historic buildings, including the former Sakai residence. Tsuruoka-Temmangu shrine 2km/1mi **Tsuruoka**

> ## ! *Baedeker* TIP
>
> ### Trip on Mogami River
> Leave Sakata eastbound upstream of Mogami River to a town called Furukuchi, from where visitors can go on enjoyable one-hour boat trips down Mogami River. Along the way the coxswain will sing a famous song.

from the station is the location of the annual Bakemono festival in May, a jolly procession in which men and women cross-dress.

Northwest of Tsuruoka (bus, 30 minutes) the extensive building complex of Zempoji temple, largely built in the Heian period, extends along the side of Mount Takadate. **Zempoji temple**

The popular little spa Yunohama-onsen is situated along the coast (private train line from Tsuruoka, 30 minutes; bus, 40 minutes); a further small spa, **Atsumi-onsen**, is south of the town (bus hour); the morning market held near Kumano shrine is picturesque. **Yunohama-onsen**

Sapporo

L 3

Main island: Hokkaido
Population: 1.82 million

Prefecture: Hokkaido

Sapporo, the capital of the northernmost Japanese main island of Hokkaido, is a young city designed on the drawing board, which is why historical attractions are few and far between. Sapporo is known for its beer, its spectacular snow-sculpture festival and relaxing green spaces.

Home of the Ainu

Sapporo's urban area extends across the basin of the Toyohira River, which forms the southern part of Ishikari Plain. Even though Sapporo is located somewhat further south than Florence, the winters are cold and snowy. Until the 19th century the area was exclusively inhabited by the indigenous Ainu and it is from their language that the city gets its name: »Sato poro petsu« means »long dry riverbed«.

Around the mid-19th century Japanese settlers came to the island of Hokkaido and in 1871 the Meiji government decided to move the office responsible for colonization (Kaitakushi), which until then had been located in Hakodate, to Sapporo and promote the city's development by using the United States town planning model. In 1886 Sapporo was made the prefectural capital and in 1970 the population reached the one-million mark. The 11th Olympic Winter Games were held in Sapporo in 1972.

What to See in Sapporo

University

Northwest of the central station is the large complex of the University of Hokkaido (12 faculties), which emerged from the agricultural college moved here from Tokyo in 1875. The campus of the agricultural science faculty has a portrait bust of the American William Smith Clark (1826–86), who founded the agricultural college and bid farewell to his students with the words »Boys, be ambitious!«.

Botanical garden

The grounds of the botanical garden southwest of the station (open 29 April to Sept 9am–4pm, Oct to 3 Nov until 3.30pm, ¥ 400) also contain the **Ainu Museum** (Batchelor Museum), a building constructed in 1891 on the English model. The museum has exhibits addressing all the areas of the indigenous Ainu culture. In addition the university museum displays its archaeological, ethnological and zoological collections.

Sapporo Map

Where to eat
① Sapporo beer garden
② Ramen Yokocho

Where to stay
① Nakamuraya
② Pension Setsurin

Close to the entrance of the botanical garden is the brick building of the former prefecture (1888). 500m/550yd to the east is the **city's landmark**, a tower built in 1878; it is the only surviving Russian-style building in Sapporo. Today it is a library and an exhibition room on Hokkaido's colonization history.

Tower

▶ VISITING SAPPORO

INFORMATION

Tourist information
Chitose Airport,
International Arrival Lobby
Tel. 01 23/23 01 11
Daily 6.30am–11pm
Sapporo International Communica-
tion Plaza, Sapporo MN Building, 3rd
Floor, North 1, West 3, Chuo-ku
Tel. 0 11/2 11 36 78
Mon–Sat 9am–5.30pm,
Sapporo Steller Place Center,
1st Floor, North 5, West 3, Chuo-ku
Tel. 0 11/2 09 50 30
Daily 9am–5.30pm

Sapporo Tourist Association
runs the »Cuckoo's Window«
in the city hall, 2nd Floor, North 1,
West 2, Chuo-ku
Tel. 0 11/2 51 21 41
Mon–Fri 8.45am–5.15pm

Online
www.city.sapporo.jp/city/english
www.welcome.city.sapporo.jp/english

GETTING THERE

By air: from Tokyo (Haneda Airport;
1½ hours); from Osaka (1¾ hours);
from Nagoya (1½ hours).
By rail: from Tokyo JR Tohoku
shinkansen line to Hachinohe (3
hours), then JR Tohoku line through
the 36km/22mi Seikan Tunnel 240m/
800ft under the sea to Hakodate (3
hours) and JR Hakodate line (3½
hours).

LOCAL TRANSPORT

Sapporo has three *underground lines*:
Namboku, Tozai and Toho – all three
of them meet at Odori station in the
city centre south of the JR station.
The tickets cost from ¥ 200 for the
shortest trip to ¥ 800 for a day pass.

To the southwest of here there is also
a *tram* (shiden) – ticket price ¥ 170.
Another means of transport useful to
tourists is the *City Bus* Kan 88/
Factory Bus, which goes past Sapporo
Factory Shopping Mall to the beer
museum (¥ 200).

EVENTS

Yuki-matsuri (snow festival, with
numerous snow sculptures; beginning
of February); Hokkaido shrine festival
(procession with portable shrines and
floats; mid-June); summer festival
(carnival-like festival with Bon dances
and fireworks; 21 July to 20 Aug).

SHOPPING

One of Sapporo's well-known shopping areas is the covered *Tanukikoji*
(between South 2 and 3 / West 1 and
7), which has many specialist stores
and clothes shops. Beyond its eastern
end is the *Nijo fish market*. Further
shopping centres can be found
around Sapporo station, some of
them underground.

GOING OUT

The city's nightlife district is *Susukino*, southeast of O-dori street.

WHERE TO EAT
▶ Moderate
① *Sapporo beer garden*
North 7, East 9
Higashi-ku
Tel. 0 11/7 42 15 31
Daily 11.30am–9pm
This place naturally serves the beer
from the Sapporo brewery in a lively
atmosphere. The city's speciality can
also be enjoyed here: Genghis Khan
(Jingisukan), grilled lamb.

► Inexpensive

② *Ramen Yokocho*

South 5, West 3, Chuo-ku
Sixteen noodle restaurants in »Ramen
Street«, all serving the same thing:
Sapporo ramen in every possible
variety!

WHERE TO STAY

► Mid-range

① *Nakamuraya*

Kita 3, Nishi 7, Chuo-ku,
Sapporo, Hokkaido 060-0003
Tel. 0 11/2 41 21 11
fax 2 41 21 18
www.nakamura-ya.com
Modern ryokan hotel in a favourable
location near the university's botanical garden. Immaculate service, quiet,
good food. Rooms with bathrooms, as
well as a public bath for all the guests.

► Budget

② *Setsurin Guesthouse*

Misono 7-3, Toyohira-ku,
Sapporo, Hokkaido 062-0008
Tel. 0 11/8 22 71 23
Fax 8 22 66 35
www.tabi-hokkaido.co.jp/
p.setsurin/english
Take the Toho line 10 minutes from
the station to Toyohira-koen station
(exit 3).
Friendly, cosy and clean guesthouse
with tatami rooms and communal
baths.

500m/550yd south of the central station the city is crossed in an
east-west direction by O-dori Street, a boulevard decorated with
many flowers on which the famous**snow festival** takes place in early
February. The 147m/482ft television tower stands at its eastern end.
Its platform at 90m/295ft has a lovely view of Ishikari Plain.

O-dori

500m/550yd to the south the Tanuki-koji shopping street, also called
»Sapporo Ginza«, runs parallel to O-dori. A large number of bars,
restaurants and more can be found in the neighbouring entertainment district of Susukino to the southeast.

Tanuki-koji

Southeast of the station is the former Sapporo brewery, established
in 1876, which has been transformed into Sapporo Factory Shopping
Mall. The Factory Bus (City Bus Kan 88) departs from here to another old brewery, which is home to a beer museum and a beer garden.

**Sapporo
Factory**

Take the Namboku underground line from the station via Susukino
to Nakajima Park, which is bounded in the east by the Toyohira River. It is home to a landscape garden, a tea house (Hasso-an), which
was created by Kobori Enshu as part of Kohoan temple (Shiga Prefecture) and brought here in 1918, and a concert hall.

Nakajima Park

Maruyama Park, at the foot of the hills rising up west of the city
(bus from the station, 20 minutes), has sporting venues and a zoological garden. Hokkaido shrine, founded in 1869 (current buildings
1964), can be found in the north of the park. It is particularly attrac-

★
**Maruyama
Park**

To experience what can be made out of ice and snow, visit the Snow Festival

Winter Sports Museum ▶ tive during the cherry blossom (beginning of May). West of the park, on Mount Okurayama, is the Olympic ski jump and a winter sports museum with a ski jump simulator and memorabilia from the Olympic Games. The protected primeval Maruyama Forest, which contains many different tree species, extends along the 226m/741ft Maruyama Hill.

Moiwa Mount Moiwa (530m/1739ft) rises in the far southwest of the city (bus from the station, 25 minutes). A cableway and chair lift go up to peak from where there are great views. A panoramic toll road runs from the peak via the southern slope down to the valley.

Around Sapporo

Jozankei-onsen Jozankei-onsen lies in the mountains southwest of the city (bus, 1 hour). Besides Noboribetsu it is Hokkaido's best-known spa. The Nakayama-Toge mountain road goes from Sapporo to Jozankei-on-zen and further to Lake Toya in ▶Shikotsu-Toya National Park.

Teine Olympic zone 15km/9mi west of Sapporo is an excellent winter sports area with fa-cilities from the Olympic Winter Games of 1972 (bus, 45 minutes). The Teine Olympic zone at the foot of the 1024m/3360ft Mount Teine has 13 lifts, a golf course and a swimming pool.

11km/7mi northeast of Sapporo (bus, 50 minutes) is the 20km/12mi Nopporo-Shinrin Park. The attractions here are the 100m/328ft Hyakunen Kinen-to memorial tower built in 1971 on the occasion of the 100th anniversary of Hokkaido's colonization, the History Museum (Hokkaido Kaitaku Kinenkan) and a village with reconstructions of historical buildings from 100 years of island history (open Tue–Sun 9.30am–4.30pm, ¥ 830).

Nopporo-Shinrin Park

Satsunan Islands

D–F 9–11

Main island: Kyushu   **Prefecture:** Kagoshima

The Satsunan group forms the northern part of the Nansei arc of islands, which extends from the southern tip of the Japanese main island of Kyushu to Taiwan. It includes Tanegashima, Yakushima, the Tokara Islands and the Amami archipelago. The beautiful subtropical landscape with romantic coastlines and a deep blue sea attracts large numbers of visitors.

薩南諸島

What to See on the Satsunan Islands

Tanegashima (448 sq km/173 sq mi, population 25,000), the northernmost of the Satsunan Islands, is separated from Kyushu by Osumi Strait. In 1543 Portuguese seafarers landed here, bringing the first firearms to Japan. The island lord Tanega Tokitaka copied this weapon, which was named »Tanega-bo« after the island. Tanegashima is home to the **Japan Aerospace Exploration Agency**, from where the first Japanese space rocket was launched in February 1981, putting an ETS-4 satellite into an elliptical orbit.

Tanegashima

The ferries from Kagoshima dock in the harbour of Nishi-no-Omote (population 23,000) on the island's northwest coast. Take the bus through the interior of the relatively flat island to Cape Kadokura in the far south (1 hour). Misaki shrine with a memorial for the Portuguese seafarers is located here. The rocky coast of Kumano, eroded by the heavy waves, is quite an impressive sight.

Nishi-no-Omote

►Kirishima-Yaku National Park

Yakushima

Around 500km/310mi south of Kyushu are the Amami Islands with a total area of 1237 sq km/478 sq mi and a population of 162,000 people.
The largest and northernmost of the Amami Islands is Amami-Oshima (709 sq km/274 sq mi), the island's transport hub. The harbour of Naze (population 49,000) is located on its north coast. The rich, subtropical flora alternates with sugar cane, banana and pineapple

Amami Islands

◄ Amami-Oshima

SATSUNAN ISLANDS

GETTING THERE

By air: from Kagoshima to Tanega-shima (35 minutes), Amami-Oshima (1¼ hours) and Yoron-to (1¾ hours).
By ferry: from Kagoshima to Nishi-no-Omote (Tanegashima; 3 hours), Miyanoura (Yakushima; 3½ hours), Naze (Amami-Oshima; 11 hours) and Yoron-to (21 hours); from Naha (Okinawa) to Yoron-to (4 hours).

plantations. Coral reefs can be found off the coast of the white sandy beaches. The production of the Oshima-tsumugi silk fabrics has a big tradition here. It is possible to take a ship from Naze to Tokunosh-ima and Okinoerabushima.

The much visited bull fights are one of **Tokunoshima's** tourist attrac-tions; the jolly dance festival Hachi-gatsu-odori is also celebrated on the neighbouring island of Okinoera-bushima to the south. Both islands have **more than 100 dripstone caves**; Shoryu-do Cave on Okinoer-abushima is one of the largest of its kind in Asia. Other worthwhile sights are the cliffs of Inno-jo-buta and the beach of Sumiyoshi.

Yoron-to ▶ Yoron-to, the southernmost Satsunan Island, is surrounded by coral reefs and a diverse marine fauna, which offers good diving opportu-nities. The island's inhabitants live almost exclusively from tourism. The most suitable means of transport is the bicycle (rentals avail-able). There is a road from Tachibana Bay on the north coast to Yu-nyu botanical garden in the island's interior; there is a lovely round view from the Kotobira shrine, which has a somewhat elevated loca-tion. Further southeast is the 40m/130ft Yuukino-misaki cliff. The road going further east goes past Mingu-kan, an old settlement with huts made of straw and clay as well as a small local history exhibi-tion. The coastal road reaches the beach of Yurinohama, where visi-tors can go on boat trips in glass-bottomed boats (approx. 1 hour). There are several offshore »star sand« banks, which are made of the skeletons of maritime crustaceans.

★ Sendai

L 5

Main island: Honshu	**Prefecture:** Miyagi
Population: 1 million	

仙台 **The former castle town of Sendai is situated in the north of the Japanese main island of Honshu, 10km/6mi from the Pacific coast, between forested hills.**

»Forest City« As the capital of Miyagi Prefecture and the political, cultural and economic centre of the district of Tohoku, Sendai is of great signifi-cance. Its most important economic sectors are the food industry, wood products, electronics and metal processing. Traditional goods are lacquerware and wooden dolls.

► VISITING SENDAI

INFORMATION

Tourist information
In the JR station, 2nd floor
Tel. 0 22/2 22 40 69
Daily 8.30am–8pm

International Center, Aobayama,
Aoba-ku, west of the station, towards
Tohoku University and the castle,
across Ohashi Bridge
Tel. 0 22/2 65 24 71
Daily 9am–8pm
www.city.sendai.jp

GETTING THERE

By air: from Osaka (1¼ hours).
By rail: from Tokyo JR Tohoku
shinkansen line (2 hours).
By bus: from Sendai Airport to the city
centre (40 minutes).

EVENTS

Dondo-matsuri (burning of the New
Year's decorations; mid-Jan), in Osaki-
Hachimangu shrine; shrine festival
(procession with medieval suits of
armour; end of May), at Aoba shrine;
Tanabata (star festival, has a 700-year
tradition; beginning of Aug).

What to See in Sendai

Aoba Hill is located west of the station (bus, 10 minutes); visitors can still see the last remains of the ramparts, castle, a reconstructed tower and an equestrian statue of the powerful feudal lord Date Masamune. Objects from the possessions of the Date clan are exhibited in the museum north of the castle ruins.

Aoba Hill

◄ Sendai Shi Hakubutsukan

Go southwards, past a bronze statue of Masamune, to get to the Gokoku shrine, which has a broad view of the city and the sea.

Gokoku shrine

Southwest of the city centre is Date Masamune's mausoleum, situated on a river bend (Zuihoden; modern-day reconstruction in the style of the Momoyama Period; open daily 9am–4.30pm, Dec–Jan until 4pm, ¥ 550).

Zuihoden

4km/2.5mi northwest of the station (bus, 15 minutes) is the Osaki-Hachimangu shrine (1607). It is covered in black lacquer and is a fine example of Momoyama architecture. The richly adorned main hall resembles those of Zuiganji temple in Matsushima.

Osaki-Hachimangu shrine

Rinnoji temple (bus from the station, 15 minutes), dedicated to the Date clan, has a three-storey pagoda. It dates back to the Meiji period and is known for its lily garden (open daily 8am–5pm, ¥ 300).

Rinnoji temple

1.5km/1mi east of the central station is Tsutsujigaoka Park, which gets many visitors when the old cherry trees are in bloom.

Tsutsujigaoka Park

Around Sendai

Shiogama

The northbound JR Senseki train line goes to Shiogama (population 61,000; there are also boats from Matsushima), a lively fishing port in the southwest part of Matsushima Bay. Shiogama shrine, consecrated to the patron god of seafarers and mothers-to-be, can be found about 700m/750yd northwest of Hon-Shiogama station on a forested hill. One of its treasures is an iron lantern donated by Izumi Saburo in 1187.

! **Baedeker TIP**

Samurai on horseback

The Yabusame festival is held in Shiogama in mid-July: there are equestrian displays dating back to the 13th century with archery and a big fair. The lively harbour festival takes place in mid-August.

Take the Rikuu-Tosen train line (1½ hours) from Sendai northeastbound to the spa of Naruko-onsen (hot springs, 60–100°C/140–212°F). Every year at the beginning of September the Kokeshi Festival is celebrated here; Kokeshi are wooden dolls also on display in the local Kokeshi Museum (Nihon kokeshi-kan).

Naruko-onsen

Akiu-onsen

West of Sendai are two popular resorts, both reachable by bus. Akiu-onsen (50 minutes) has hot springs of 55°C/131°F. A nice excursion from here is to the 55m/180ft Akiu-Otaki Falls (bus from Akiu-onsen, 30 minutes) 14km/9mi upstream along Natori River; the romantic Rairaikyu Gorge can also be found nearby.

Matsushima

▶Matsushima

★ Shikotsu-Toya National Park

L 3

Main island: Hokkaido
Area: 993 sq km/383 sq mi

Prefecture: Hokkaido

支笏洞爺国立公園 **Shikotsu-Toya National Park in western Hokkaido protects an extremely attractive volcanic landscape with crater lakes and hot springs in its three spatially distinct areas. The most suitable starting places are ▶Sapporo and Tomakomai.**

What to See in Shikotsu-Toya National Park

Jozankei-onsen

The largest part of the national park by area begins just outside of Sapporo. First stop by bus (1 hour) is the spa of Jozankei-onsen (salt springs) at Toyohira River; after the road connection from Sapporo was opened in 1871 it quickly became a lively spa town. The main attractions of the surrounding area are the Shiraito-no-taki Falls, Nishikibashi Bridge and the rock Futami-Iwa.

West of Jozankei-onsen in the national park's northwest section is the 1893m/6211ft extinct **volcano Yotei** and at its northern foot the town of Kutchan (from Sapporo JR Hakodate line, 2 hours). There is a bus connection from here to Lake Hangetsu, the starting point for a four-hour hike to the peak (alternative route from Hirafu, the next bus stop). Yotei's three peak craters are called »Father Caldera«, »Mother Caldera« and »Little Caldera«; the loop path around the main crater is 2km/1 mi.

Kutchan

South of Jonzankei-onsen the road crosses the 836m/2743ft Nakayama Pass (with a great view) and makes its way to the crystal-clear Lake Toya (bus, 1½ hours), which is surrounded by mountains all sides. At the centre of the almost circular 183m/600ft lake, which does not freeze over even in severe winters, is the densely forested island of Nakanoshima (also Oshima), surrounded by the far smaller islands of Kannon, Manju and Benten. Located on the lake's southern shore is the popular spa **Toyako-onsen** (springs of up to 60°C/140°F; bus from Sapporo, 2¾ hours), from where boats set off to Nakanoshima (20 minutes).

★
Lake Toya

Mount Usu and Mount Showa-Shinzan rise to the south. The best base from which to climb them is Sobetsu on Lake Toya's southern shore.
It takes five minutes by bus to reach the foot of the active Showa-Shinzan volcano (408m/1339ft), which only formed in 1944–45 and formed its last new peak in 1977. A documentary exhibition at the bus stop informs visitors about all of the details of the volcano's development (ascent to the peak 1 hour).

Showa-Shinzan

From the same bus stop a 1365m/1493yd cableway goes to the eastern foot of Mount Usu, also an active volcano. In the great eruption of 1910 it formed Meiji-Shinzan (»new mountain of the Meiji era«) on its northern slope, and in 1944–45 Showa-Shinzan (»new mountain of the Showa era«) to the east. The 725m/793ft Great Usu (to the east) and Little Usu (to the west) rise up around the peak, which, together with the Byobuyama mountain range, surround Lake Ginnuma.

Usu

The eastbound JR Muroran main line goes to Noboribetsu; not far north from here are the hot springs of Noboribetsu-onsen (»Eleven Springs«). The spa can also be reached by bus from Sapporo (at least 1¾ hours) and Chitose Airport (at least 1 hour). Noboribetsu-onsen, surrounded by wonderful forests, is Hokkaido's largest spa. The Daiichi-Takimoto-kan is a public bath (the town's oldest) whose 40 pools are fed by around ten different springs (45–93°C/113–199°F).

Noboribetsu

► VISITING

GETTING THERE

By rail: from Sapporo JR Chitose line and Muroran line to Toya station (1¾ hours), then bus.

By bus: several buses go to the national park, also from Sapporo and Chitose Airport to Shikotsu-Kohan (1½ or 1 hours) and to Lake Toya (a good hour more); there are also buses from Noboribetsu and Muroran.

Jigokudani The hot springs rise up in Jigokudani (»Hell Valley«) with its volcanic rock formations 400m/450yd from the actual town. There is a short climb from here to the simmering Lake Oyunuma, located in an old crater basin. Next to it the 366m/1201ft Mount Hiyoriyama has a column of sulphur vapours towering above it.

Kuma Bokujo Mount Kuma (549m/1801ft; cableway) rises up east of Noboribetsu-onsen. There is a field called Bear Field, which is home to around 140 brown bears; however it is presented in a circus-like manner (admission: ¥ 2520!) At the mountain's eastern foot is Lake Kuttara (in the summer bus from Noboribetsu-onsen, 25 minutes) in a picturesque setting. There is also a bus to Karurusu-onsen (springs 38–56°C/100–133°F), situated in the valley of Mount Chitose.

Shiraoi   The JR Muroran main line then reaches the coastal village of Shiraoi near Lake Porotoko. 700m/770yd to the southwest is an **Ainu settlement**, Poroto Kotan, which was set up in 1965 in order to preserve this people's ancient traditions. Though marketed for tourism, the settlement is worth visiting. An insight into the Ainu people's former way of life is provided by the associated museum.

Tomakomai Lake Shikotsu There is a road (bus, 50 minutes) from Tomakomai (JR Muroran main line) to the picturesque Lake Shikotsu further inland, situated in the part of the national park that is also home to the region of Jozankei-onsen (see above). The 363m/1191ft-deep lake, which never freezes over, is bordered in the south and north by the two active volcanoes Mount Tarumae (1024m/3360ft) and Mount Eniwa (1320m/4331ft) respectively.

Tarumae ► Mount Tarumae has erupted several times since the late 17th century. A particularly violent eruption took place in 1909. Climbing Mount Tarumae from Morappu at the lake's southern shore, to the peak's crater takes around 45 minutes (bus to the 7th mountain station, only in summer).

Eniwa ► Mount Eniwa can be climbed from Shikotsu-Kohan via Poropinai in three hours; the view from the top reaches all the way to Sapporo. In 1972 the mountain's slopes were part of the Olympic complex.

Shimonoseki

`F 8 • c 4`

Main island: Honshu **Prefecture:** Yamaguchi
Population: 300,000

The important deep-sea fishing port of Shimonoseki is situated at the far western tip of the Japanese main island of Honshu. At its narrowest point the city is only separated from the island of Kyushu by the approx. 700m/750yd Kammon Strait.

下関

The Battle of Dannoura (1185), fought in coastal waters between the Taira (or Heike), who lost, and the Minamoto (also Genji), who won, is of great historic significance. Before the beginning of the Meiji era, Shimonoseki was the main base of the Choshu, who were against the shogunate's policy of opening Japan to other countries. Their motto was »honour the emperor, drive out the barbarians«, and thus they shot at the foreign ships anchoring offshore in 1863. American, French, British and Dutch naval units subsequently attacked the city in 1864 and occupied it within three days. In 1895 the peace treaty between Japan and China was signed in Shimonoseki.

History

 SHIMONOSEKI

INFORMATION
www.city.shimonoseki.yamaguchi.jp

GETTING THERE
By air: from Tokyo (Haneda Airport) to Kitakyushu (1½ hours).
By rail: from Tokyo (central station) JR Sanyo shinkansen line via Osaka (Shin-Osaka station) and Hiroshima (5 hours); from Fukuoka (Hakata) via Kitakyushu (Kokura station; 45 minutes).

EVENTS
Large firework display on Kammon Road (13 August).

What to See in Shimonoseki

A hill around 2.5km/1.5mi east of Shin-Shimonoseki station (bus, 10 minutes) is the site of the Kameyama-Hachimangu shrine. It is consecrated to the legendary Emperors Chuai, Ojin and Nintoku as well as to Empress Jingu, who is said to have moved from here to Korea in the 3rd century. There is a nice view of the strait from the shrine grounds; behind the shrine is the house in which the Treaty of Shimonoseki was signed by Japan and China in 1895.

Kameyama-Hachimangu shrine

500m/550yd to the northeast on Mount Benishiyama, stands Akama-jingu shrine, dedicated to the child emperor Antoku (1178–85). It houses the tombs of Antoku, who drowned in the naval battle of Dannoura, and of seven members of the Taira family, one of the leading aristocratic families of the Heike dynasty.

Akama-jingu shrine

Dannoura Dannoura's approx. 1km/0.6mi-long strip of coastline is even further to the east (bus connection). The memory of the naval battle of 1185 is kept alive in many stories; the popular belief that the Heike killed in the battle were transformed into marine animals is reflected in the terms »koheike« for a species of fish living here and »heike-gani« for small crabs.

Kammon Tunnel Dannoura station is the starting point for Kammon Tunnel and Kammon Bridge, which both connect Honshu with Kyushu; it is also the location of the cableway that goes up Mount Hinoyama. From the top there is a good view of the strait and the town of Kitakyushu across from it.

Chofu Around 5km/3mi east of the city centre is Chofu, once inhabited by Samurai. Some of the old streets are still extant. **Kozanji temple**, founded in the 14th century and with a main hall of 1325, is worth visiting; the other buildings are newer.

Sotoura It takes seven minutes by bus from the station to the coast of Sotoura, which boasts an extensive recreational area and the large Shimonoseki Aquarium.

★ Shiretoko National Park

N 2

Main island: Hokkaido   **Prefecture:** Hokkaido
Area: 386 sq km/149 sq mi

知床国立公園 **This national park, declared a UNESCO World Heritage Site in July 2005, is considered Japan's last wilderness. The Ainu gave this place a fitting name: Shiretoko, »land's end«.**

Volcanic peninsula Shiretoko Peninsula, the majority of which is part of Shiretoko National Park, protrudes as a narrow wedge of around 65km/40mi from Hokkaido's east coast into the Sea of Okhotsk. The primordial landscape is shaped by the extinct volcanoes Rausu (1661m/5449ft), Shiretoko (1254m/4114ft) and Io (1563m/5128ft). The peninsula's southern part is accessible via good roads; the most suitable starting point is the seaside resort of Utoro on the northwest coast.

What to See in Shiretoko National Park

Utoro Shiretoko-goko Take a bus from Shari station (JR Semmo main line) along the coast to Utoro (50 minutes) and onwards to the five lakes Shiretoko-goko, where there are many hiking trails. Further north from here are the impressive Kamuiwakka Falls. A main road connects Utoro and Rau-

▶ VISITING SHIRETOKO NATIONAL PARK

GETTING THERE

By rail: from Kushiro or Abashiri JR Semmo main line to Shari (2¼ or ¾ hours).

By bus: from Shari via Utoro to Shiretoko-goko and Rausu.

By ferry: ferry connection from Tokyo to Kushiro (30 hours); boat connection from Utoro to Rausu (4½ hours; only in summer).

WHEN TO GO

This park can only be visited from May to October.

su along the peninsula's southeast coast. Along the way, after Shireto-ko-toge Pass, a path branches off to Lake Rausu (circumference: 6km/3.5 mi); it is about 1½ hours' walk to the lake.   ◀ Lake Rausu

Boat trips depart from Utoro to the tip of the peninsula at Cape   Rausu
Shiretoko (June–Sept approx. 3 hours). The coast largely consists of steep cliffs of up to 200m/655ft. The national park is home to brown bears, foxes, seals, whales and white-tailed eagles in addition to around 250 other bird species.

Shizuoka

Main island: Honshu   **Prefecture:** Shizuoka
Population: 472,000

The prefectural capital Shizuoka is situated on the south coast of the Japanese main island of Honshu, around halfway between To-kyo and Nagoya. It is the country's most important trans-shipment centre for green tea (around 60% of the total production).   静岡

What to See in Shizuoka

The northern part of town contains the grounds of the castle, which   **Castle complex**
was completely destroyed in 1945. All that is left are moats, some re-   **Sumpu Park**
maining walls, the reconstructed south tower and the east tower. The grounds have now been made into a park. It contains a statue of To-kugawa Ieyasu.

On the city's northern edge, 2km/1mi from the station, is Mount   **Sengen shrine**
Shizuhata-yama, a hill known for its cherry blossom (beginning of April); at its southern foot is the 17th-century Sengen shrine (the current buildings are from the 19th century). The ceiling paintings are by the masters of the Kano school. At the back of the shrine is a stairway to the park, from where visitors have a lovely view.

Rinzai-ji temple   Near Sengen shrine, situated in a pretty garden, is the Rinzai-ji temple of the Rinzai sect. It was founded in the early 16th century as a protective temple for the Imagawa clan that ruled the province of Suruga at the time. Among the temple treasures are an Amida statue from the Kasuga school and drawings by Kano Tan'yu (1602–74). One of Tokugawa Ieyasu's studies, kept in its original style, is also worth seeing.

Toro   The excavation site of Toro is situated 2.5km/1.5mi south of the station (bus, 15 minutes). After the first discoveries were made by chance in 1943, a **settlement of the late Yayoi period** (approx. 2nd–3rd century) was uncovered on an area of 16.5ha/41 acres. The largest of the twelve originally thatched houses built on an oval floor plan is 12m/13yd long and 11m/12yd wide. Outhouses built on stilts presumably served as storehouses; the fields indicate rice was cultivated here. The household effects and jewellery from that time are exhibited in the museum.

Around Shizuoka

Kunozan   10km/6mi to the south is Mount Kunozan (bus to Kunozanshita, 35 minutes), which drops off steeply to Suruga Bay; this area has a particularly mild climate. The mountain was Tokugawa Ieyasu's last resting place until his mortal remains were brought to Nikko. His

60% of all green tea in Japan comes from the Shizuoka region

▶ VISITING SHIZUOKA

INFORMATION

Tourist information
In the JR station
Tel. 0 54/2 52 42 47
Daily 8.30am–6pm

www.city.shizuoka.jp/english
www.shizuoka-guide.com (about the prefecture)

GETTING THERE

By rail: from Tokyo (central station) JR Tokaido shinkansen line (1½ hours); from Nagoya JR Tokaido shinkansen line (1¼ hours).

EVENTS

Shizuoka-matsuri (procession with historical costumes; beginning of April), at Sengen shrine.

---

son Hidetada founded Toshogu shrine on the mountain's peak in 1617; it was built in the Gongen-zukuri style. The shrine houses objects from Ieyasu's possessions, including suits of armour and swords.

✷
◀ Toshogu shrine

A little below the shrine is a cableway station to the Nihon-daira Plateau, where there are extensive tea plantations. Suruga Bay, Mount Fuji (northeast), Mount Kunozan and the Pacific coast can all be seen from up here. The **pine grove** Miho-no-matsubara, which extends east along a long sandy beach, has been immortalized in poems and paintings. The plateau can also be reached directly by bus from Shizuoka.

✷
Nihon-daira

Shodoshima

Prefecture: Kagawa
Island area: 155 sq km/60 sq mi

Population: 44,000

小豆島

Shodoshima is the Inland Sea's second-largest island after Awajish-ima. The southern part is used to cultivate olives; the gorges of the north have long been used as a source for building blocks, which were used amongst other things to build the castle in Osaka (1586).

What to See on Shodoshima

The ships departing from Okayama (Honshu) and Takamatsu (Shi-koku) anchor in the port of Tonosho (population 23,000), which is also the starting point for bus trips around the island (4 or 7 hours). To the east of the port basin on a hill is the peacock garden, from where there are some lovely views.

Tonosho

Kankakei Kankakei Gorge (»cold foggy valley«; bus from Tonosho) at the heart of the island is worth a visit. The 8km/5mi long and 2km/1mi wide valley is flanked by hills with bizarrely eroded rocks; the slopes are covered in dense forests of maples, pines and azaleas, which display glowing autumn colours in November. There is a cableway from the bottom of the valley to **Shibocho viewpoint**, from where visitors can see a part of the Inland Sea considered particularly attractive.

VISITING SHODOSHIMA

GETTING THERE
By ferry: from Okayama to Tonosho (1¼ hours; hydrofoil 40 minutes); from Osaka via Kobe (2–3 hours) to Sakate and Tonosho-Higashi; from Takamatsu to Tonosho (30–60 minutes).

An organized **tour of the island** (guide speaks Japanese) includes Futagoura Bay, Myonan Beach, Silver Beach, the quarry that provided the stone for Osaka Castle, Choshikei Monkey Park, Kankakei Gorge, Peace Park and the very scenic Kankakei Road.

★ Takamatsu

H 7 • g 3

Main island: Shikoku   **Prefecture:** Kagawa
Population: 334,000

高松

Takamatsu, Shikoku's second-largest city and the capital of Kagawa Prefecture, has a wonderful landscape garden. Large areas of the surrounding coast are part of the ►Inland Sea National Park.

What to See in Takamatsu

Tamamo Park The port basin and the central station (JR Yosan main line) are both in the north of the city. 300m/330yd to the east is Tamamo Park with the remains of a castle (Takamatsu-jo) built by Ikoma Chikamasa in 1587. It is one of Japan's very few moated castles. The park also contains the 1917 Hiunkaku Pavilion and Chinretsukan Museum with treasures of the Matsudaira family. It also has an attractive view of the Inland Sea.

★★
Ritsurin Park A bus leaving from the central station goes to Ritsurin Park (10 minutes), which used to belong to the Matsudaira clan's summer villa. The 75ha/185-acre landscape garden follows the »borrowed landscape« principle and incorporates the nearby Mount Shiun into the overall picture, which is otherwise characterized by ponds, hills, tea pavilions, groups of rocks and bizarre trees. The park is also home to a zoo and the folkcraft museum Sanuki Mingeikan (open park: daily at least 7am–5pm, longer in summer, ¥ 400).

Around Takamatsu

Megishima Island (also Onigashima), situated around 4km/2.5mi offshore, can be reached by ferry. There are some lovely views of the Inland Sea from the island's mountain tops.

6km/3.5mi east of Takamatsu (bus and tram connections) is the former **island of Yashima**, which is now connected to Shikoku via a headland. Yashimaji temple is located in the south of the plateau on Mount Nanrei (cableway, 5 minutes). It houses a lot of objects from the time the Minamoto and Taira families were feuding.
Shikoku-mura **open-air museum** (10 minutes on foot from Yahsima station), situated at the foothills of Mount Nanrei, has a collections of old buildings from all over Shikoku, including a kabuki stage (open April–Oct daily 8.30am–6pm, Nov–March until 5.30pm, ¥ 800).

Further east is the **Shingon** sect's Shidoji temple (from Takamatsu Kotoku train line, 25 minutes), which was founded in the late 7th century and is one of Shikoku's 88 temples of pilgrimage. It contains a wooden statue and an image of the eleven-headed Kannon as well as the Shidodera-engi-zue, a series of coloured drawings about the temple's history.

Ritsurin Park Map

Next is the town of Sanuki-Tsuda; a pretty trail runs along the 4km/2.5mi white beach (Tsuda-no-Matsubara). 3km/2mi northwest of the station of Chofukuji temple of 524, with a 14m/46ft wooden statue of Yakushi-nyorai from the early Fujiwara period. **Sanuki-Tsuda**

West of Takamatsu, at the top of the 357m/1171ft Mount Shirame, is the mausoleum of Emperor Sutoku (1119–64). **Shiramine**

The JR Yosan main line, which follows the coastline here, goes on to Sakaide (population 66,000). **Seto-Ohashi Bridge**, opened in 1988 crosses the Inland Sea here. Further westwards is Marugame (popu- **Marugame** lation 74,000). 1km/0.6mi to the south are the remains of the castle (three-storey main tower and two gates) built in 1597. The town is known for its production of round fans. Several ferries cross the Inland Sea to Honshu.

Zentsuji South of Marugame the JR Dosan main line turns southeast towards Zentsuji (40 minutes), the birth place of Kobo-daishi (also called Kukai, 774–835), who founded the Buddhist Shingon sect. He was also responsible for the erection of Zentsuji temple 1.2km/0.75mi further west. It is the main temple of the Shingon sect, and many of the current buildings date back to the 17th century. There is a Buddha likeness in Jogyodo Hall; there are a five-storey pagoda in the west of the temple grounds, which has a height of 45.6m/150ft (renewed in 1882), and a 14th century main hall (kondo) with a wooden statue of Yakushi-nyorai.

Kotohira
★ ★
Kompira shrine ► Further south is Kotohira (Takamatsu JR Dosan line, Kotohira private train line and bus, 1 hour). 2km/1mi west of the station half way up the 521m/1709ft Mount Zozusan, is Kompira shrine (also Kotohiragu), one of the most significant destinations of pilgrimage for seafarers and travellers in Japan. A **stairway of 1300 steps**, starting at the Great Gate O-mon leads up to this shrine consecrated to the deity Omononushi-no-mitoko. The first stop is the former abbot's residence (shoin), whose doors and walls are decorated with works by the landscape painter Maruyama Okyo (1733–95). Next to the left is the tea hall (chadokoro), then the Hall of the Morning Sun Asahi-no-yashiro with carvings from the early 19th century. A further stairway (785 steps) goes up to the main shrine (hondo) with

Ritsurin Park is the green oasis of Takamatsu

▶ VISITING TAKAMATSU

INFORMATION

Tourist information
Next to the station
Tel. 0 87/8 51 20 09
Daily 9am–6pm

www.city.takamatsu.kagawa.jp/english
www.town.kotohira.kagawa.jp/english
(about Kotohira)

GETTING THERE

By air: from Tokyo (Haneda Airport; 1¼ hours); from Osaka (40 minutes).
By rail: from Tokyo (central station) JR Tokaido shinkansen line via Okayama (4¾ hours); from Okayama JR Marine Liner (1 hour).
By ferry: from Uno (1 hour); from Osaka Inland Sea line (5½ hours).

EVENTS

Okaya-matsuri (beginning of May), in Tamura shrine; large shrine festival (beginning of August; every two years), in Sumiyoshi shrine; Takamatsu-matsuri (summer festival; mid-August).

the music hall (for cult dances), which was rebuilt in the Taisha-zukuri style in 1878 after parts of the old syncretist shrine complex had been removed during the Meiji Reform. Not far from the main shrine is the votive hall (ema-do; numerous sacrificial images). A third staircase (583 steps) connects the main shrine with the inner shrine (okusha) in the midst of a cedar and camphor grove. There is a **fantastic view** of the surrounding area from the inner shrine. The rock wall in front of the building depicts Tengu, the long-nosed mountain spirit. The shrine's annual festivals take place at the beginning of January and from 9 to 11 October. During these festivals kemari, an approx. 1400-year-old Chinese ball game, is played. A small ball has to be thrown from one player to another; the goal is to keep it in the air for as long as possible.

Kotohira-koen Park is home to Kanamaruza Theatre. It was built in 1836, making it the country's oldest kabuki stage.

The town of Kan-onji further to the west can be reached with the JR **Kan-onji** Seisan bus line from Takamatsu via Marugame (around 60km/35mi). At the coast, 1.5km/1mi north of the station lies Kotohiki Park with its large number of cedars. At the foot of Mount Kotohiki stands Kan-onji temple, a place of pilgrimage with a Buddha statue and significant picture scrolls. From the top of Mount Kotohiki there is a good view of a ditch system created at the coast in the 17th century, depicting the image of a coin with a rectangular central hole and four characters.

5km/3mi south of Takamatsu centre (private train line, 20 minutes) **Ichinomiya** is Ichinomiya temple, built between 701 and 703; Honenji, the family **temple** **Honenjio temple**

temple of the Matsudaira) is nearby. It has a 4m/13ft sculpture of a lying Buddha.

Awa-Ikeda

The traffic junction of Awa-Ikeda southwest of Takamatsu (JR Dosan main line, 1 hour, or bus, 1½ hours) is a suitable starting point for a trip to Tsurugi Quasi-National Park.

Tsurugi Quasi National Park
★
Iyadani Gorge ►

A 50km/3mi road starting in Ori follows Iya, a tributary of Yoshino River, through Iyadani Gorge upwards to Sugeoi. The landscape, which is particularly attractive during the autumn, is said to have provided refuge for the Taira, who were being persecuted by the Minamoto in the 12th century. In the past the gorge was crossed by several **rope bridges made of plant fibres**; one of the few extant examples is Iya-no-Kazurabashi Bridge (45m/50yd long, 14m/46ft high/ 1.4m/4.5ft wide) near Zentoku.

★
Oboke Gorge, Koboke Gorge ►

The starting point for the connection road to Oboke Gorge (bus from Awa-Ikeda, 40 minutes) and Koboke Gorge is nearby. They make up the largest gorge system on Shikoku. The ruggedly picturesque terrain can be explored from Oboke by boat (30 minutes). The gorge is also criss-crossed by hiking trails.

★★ Takayama

J 6 • k 1

Main island: Honshu
Population: 65,000

Prefecture: Gifu

The attractive small town of Takayama is not just a good base from which to explore the Japanese Alps, it is also a worthwhile destination in itself: antique shops, old warehouses (which tower far back in the backyards because of the former street-front tax), folkcraft museums and craft shops are all reminiscent of old Japan.

Old trading town

Takayama is in the heart of the Japanese main island of Honshu, west of the Hida Mountains, which are part of ►Chubu-Sangaku National Park. Many of the old houses display the craftsmanship of the local carpenters, who were considered the masters of their craft in the Middle Ages. Ceramic goods (shibukusa-yaki) and lacquerware (shunkei-nuri) from Takayama also have a rich tradition.

What to See in Takayama

★
Kokubunji temple

Not far east of the station is Kokubunji temple, the town's oldest. Its main hall built in 1615 contains a sitting statue of the healing Buddha (Yakushi-nyorai) and a Kannon statue; there is also a three-storey pagoda in the forecourt (1807).

Further to the northeast is the **Lacquer Museum** (Shunkei Kaikan), which has more than 1000 examples of local lacquer art from the 17th century to the present on display.

Further east, on the other side of the Miyagawa River, stands Kusakabe-mingeikan, a house built in the traditional style for a rich merchant family around 1880 (open March–Nov daily 8.30am–5pm, Dec–Feb until 4.30pm, longer in summer, ¥ 500).

★ **Kusakabe-min-geikan**

At the northeastern end of town is the modern Yatai-Kaikan hall, where the artistic floats of the Takayama-matsuri festival are on display during the year.

Yatai-Kaikan

The lion dance is a firm part of many regional festivals. The lion dance hall (shishi kaikan), not far to the south, has around 800 lion masks on display; supplemented with videos.

Lion dance hall

In the old town's centre, San-machi-suji, old wooden houses, sake breweries and shops line three small parallel streets.

★ **San-machi-suji**

> ! **Baedeker** TIP
>
> **Feast in the Alps**
> A sukiyaki meal with original Hida beef or a San-sai dish with vegetables from the Japanese Alps as well as grilled ayu fish from the mountains waters are all a real pleasure.

 VISITING TAKAYAMA

INFORMATION

Tourist information
In front of the JR station
Tel. 05 77/32 53 28
Daily 8.30am–6.30pm,
Nov–March until 5pm
www.hida.jp

GETTING THERE

By rail: from Nagoya JR Takayama line via Gifu (3 hours); from Toyama JR Takayama line (1½ hours).

EVENT

Takayama-matsuri (also Sanno-matsuri, procession with traditional and sometimes historical floats and night-time puppet shows; mid-April), at Hie shrine. A similar festival takes place in October at Hachiman shrine.

WHERE TO STAY

► **Mid-range**
Rickshaw Inn
54 Suehiro-cho
Takayama-shi
Gifu-ken 506-0016
Tel. 05 77/32 28 90
Fax 32 24 69
www.rickshawinn.com/e
Small, cosy rooms. Also family rooms with bathrooms and kitchenettes. Inviting lounge. Coin launderette (washing machines and dryers). Breakfast by request, otherwise no meals, but there is a kitchen for self-caterers. The staff speak English. In walking distance to the station and to the attractions.

Folkcraft Museum	This part of town is also home to the Folkcraft Museum (Hirata Kinen-kan), housed in a grand former merchant home; it has a collection of household items.
Wild Bird Museum	On the other side of Yasukawa-dori is the Wild Bird Museum (Oita Yacho-kan) with exhibits from the surrounding area and the Japanese Alps.
Shorenji temple	Further south Mount Shiroyama rises in Shiroyama Park; this is where the castle once stood. Shorenji temple with its main hall (1504) is worth a visit.
Takayama Jin'ya	On the other side of the Miyagawa River, near the old Takayama Jin'ya, which was once the residence of the princely Kanamori family and later the seat of the district administration, a **traditional market** takes place every morning (7am–noon).
Open-air museum	Southwest of the station is the Hida-no-sato open-air museum (bus, 10 minutes), where old farm houses are on display. Traditional handicrafts are also demonstrated here (open daily 8.30am–5pm, ¥ 700).

The old village of Shirakawago nestles in idyllic surroundings

Around Takayama

Further northwest is the village of Shirakawago (Nohi bus line to Makido, 1½ hours, then JR bus to Ogimachi, 1 hour). Its more than 100 steep-roofed farm houses are listed as a **World Heritage Site**. The Gassho-Zukuri-style roofs were built this way to cope with the large amount of snow that falls during the winter. An open-air museum lets visitors explore some restored Gassho-Zukuri houses in more depth. A viewpoint (Ogimachi-Joshi) has a good view of the picturesque village.

✱ ✱
Shirakawago

Tokushima

H 7 • g 3

Main island: Shikoku   **Prefecture:** Tokushima
Population: 265,000

Tokushima, the capital of Tokushima Prefecture, is situated on the east coast of the Japanese main island of Shikoku. The local cotton fabrics and wood products are well-known, as is the jolly Awa-odori dance festival.

徳島

Tokushima is the administrative, economic and educational centre of eastern Shikoku. The Yoshino River flows into Kii Strait north of the city.

Centre of eastern Shikoku

What to See in Tokushima

In the city centre, around 400m/450yd east of the station, is the largely forested Mount Shiroyama; most of its area is part of Tokushima Park. The park grounds contains remains of a castle built in 1586, consisting of walls, an old bridge and the restored Wahsi-no-mon gate); the castle's garden with boulders and ponds is characteristic of the landscaping of the Momoyama Period and has an attractive view of the city. The **Castle Museum** displays suits of armour and a model of the castle, amongst other things. The park is affiliated to a zoo.

Tokushima Park

600m/650yd southwest of the station, on the eastern slope of Mount Otaki (Bizan), is Bizan Park with the prefectural museum, the peace pagoda set up in 1958 in commemoration of the victims of World War II, and the former residence of the Portuguese navy officer Wenceslao de Moraes (1854–1929), who settled here in 1893 and wrote a 16-volume work about Japan (his tomb can be found in Cho-onji temple). A cableway goes up the 279m/915ft hill, from where is a lovely all-round view of the Yoshino delta, the Inland Sea and the mountains.

Bizan Park

Around Tokushima

Jorokuji temple
There are many old temples southwest of the town. Around 9km/5.5mi from the station (bus, 30 minutes) is Jorokuji temple (Soto sect), which was founded in the 8th century. Kannondo Hall contains a wooden Sho-Kannon, probably created by the priest Gyoki (670–749).

✳ **Nyorinji temple**
6km/3.5mi further south (bus from Tokushima, 30 minutes, then footpath, 30 minutes), on the slope of the 730m/2395ft Nakatsumine is the Nyoirinji, the main temple of the Hoju-Shingon sect. It has a wooden statue of Nyoirin-Kannon. The temple is surrounded by a wood with several waterfalls.

Tatsueji temple
Tatsueji temple (Mugi train line to Tatsue), one of Shikoku's 88 temples of pilgrimage, contains a fine Buddha painting.

✳ **Kakurinji temple**
13km/8mi southwest of Tatsue is another place of pilgrimage, the Kakurinji temple, in the midst of an old cedar grove. It houses a wooden statue of Jizo-Bosatsu.

Anan
The JR Mugi line departing Tokushima southbound towards the coast reaches the fishing port of Anan after 25km/16mi (30 minutes, also bus, 1 hour), which is romantically situated on Tachibana Bay.

Yahoko shrine
To the west of the station (4.5km/2.8 mi; bus, 10 minutes) is the Yahoko shrine with two wooden statues of Shinto deities, probably from the Fujiwara period.

✳ **Cape Muroto**
Muroto-Anan Coastal Quasi-National Park (►Kochi, around) extends between Anan to Cape Muroto, approx. 90km/55mi to the south.

 VISITING TOKUSHIMA

INFORMATION

TOPIA
At the station
6th Floor Clement Plaza,
1-61 Terashima-honcho-nishi
Tel. 0 88/6 56 33 03
Daily 10am–6pm
www.city.tokushima.tokushima.jp
www.tokushima-kankou.or.jp

GETTING THERE

By air: from Tokyo (Haneda Airport; 1¼ hours).
By rail: from Takamatsu JR Kotoku main line (1½ hours).
By bus: from Tokushima Airport to the city centre (25 minutes); from Osaka Awa-Express Bus (2¾ hours)
By ferry: Nanka ferry from Wakayama (2 hours)

EVENTS

Tokushima festival (beginning of April); Awa-ningyo-joruri (puppet theatre; beginning of June and mid-Aug); Awa-odori (historical dance festival; 12–15 Aug).

The JR Tokushima main line, departing Tokushima westbound upstream of the Yoshino River, goes to Anabuki (40 minutes); to the northeast there are numerous earth pyramids, 12–18m/40–60ft high, which were formed by erosion (bus, 15 minutes).

Anabuki

Anabuki is the base for excursion to the eastern part of Tsurugi Quasi-National Park (►Takamatsu, around). A bus route (2½ hours) follows Anabuki River upstream, which rises at Mount Tsurugi, along the romantic Tsurugikyo Gorge (particularly lovely in the autumn) to Misogibashi, the starting point for climbing the 1,955m/6,414ft Mount Tsurugi.

Tsurugi Quasi National Park

Around 2km/1mi above the town is the **Ryukoji temple**; not far away is the **Tsurugisan shrine** with prayer halls (overnight accommodation) and Lake Fujinoike. The shrine's annual festival is held in mid-July.

It is another 4km/2.5mi on foot to the peak of Mount Tsurugi where visitors are rewarded with a wonderful panorama view. One possible descent is via Minokoshi and Lake Meotoike to Tsurugibashi, from where there is a bus connection (1¼ hours) to Sadamitsu at the JR Tokushima main line. Between Minokoshi and this route's 9th mountain station there is a cableway, which makes an ascent from this direction a lot shorter.

✷
◄ Tsurugi

✷ ✷ Tokyo

Main island: Honshu
Prefecture: Tokyo

Population: 8.13 million (city);
12.37 million (prefecture)

Tokyo is certainly not a pretty city with its wild development, no green spaces, the crowds and the noise, but it is undoubtedly Japan's political, economic and cultural centre. This is a great place to study new social phenomena and to observe Japan's fashion trends of tomorrow. If it exists, it exists in Tokyo, and there's a lot that doesn't exist anywhere else.

東京

The rivers Sumida, Arakawa and Tama all flow through Tokyo, Japan's capital city, and meet the Pacific Ocean at Tokyo Bay. Tokyo and the two cities of Kawasaki and Yokohama to the south make up the industrial conurbation of Keihin. Alongside Mexico City and Shanghai, Tokyo is one of the world's largest cities, both in area and population. Greater Tokyo includes the prefectures Chiba, Kanagawa and Saitama and is home to more than 34 million people.

Japan's capital

The city centre is home to shopping centres and office districts, while the residential areas are more concentrated around the periphery. Tokyo's industry (particularly electrical goods, the electronics and optics industry, precision engineering, textiles, printing) is

Tokyo Tower rises above the capital's sea of light

largely located in the coastal area. Greater Tokyo is made up of 23 districts, 26 towns, 5 municipalities and 8 villages; some of the latter are situated on Izu and Ogasawara Island, which fall under Tokyo's administrative jurisdiction.

History The first pieces of evidence of human settlement are 5000-year-old omori (shell heaps), which were discovered in the southwest of the modern city area (Shinagawa-ku). Agriculture began in the 3rd century BC and the first evidence of village settlements on the lower course of the Tama dates back to the 8th century AD. The **old city name of Edo** originally denoted a fishing village, first appearing in the light of history in 1457 when Ota Dokan built a castle where the imperial palace now stands. Temporarily owned by the Uesugi, Edo became the seat of the Odawara-Hojo in 1534 and in 1590 fell into the hands of Tokugawa Ieyasu as part of the Kanto fief. Edo then became the administrative centre of this fief until it became the country's political centre when Ieyasu was proclaimed shogun in 1603. In order to guarantee the compliance of the daimyo (feudal lords), the shogun decreed that their families had to live in Edo and the daimyo

Highlights Tokyo

Shopping
Hip or elegant, department store or flea market, Tokyo is a place to shop till you drop!
▶ page 514

Mori Tower
Get a first overview of the city from Mori Tower in Roppongi.
▶ page 527

Meiji shrine
Relax under trees and bushes around the Meiji shrine.
▶ page 529

Omote Sando
Stroll along »Tokyo's Champs Élysées« in Harajuku, do some people-watching and go shopping for some fashion.
▶ page 529

Rikugien Garden
Another oasis of calm in the hustle and bustle of the city is the idyllic Rikugien Garden.
▶ page 531

Tokyo Metropolitan Government Office
There is a magnificent panorama view to be had from the city's modern landmark in the district of Shinjuku.
▶ page 532

Ginza
Ginza is pedestrianized on Sundays, inviting visitors to do some window-shopping.
▶ page 534

Tsukiji fish market
The best time to take in Tsukiji fish market is early in the mornings during the tuna auction.
▶ page 534

Ueno Park
Ueno Park awaits with not just one, but several museums.
▶ page 536

Asakusa-Kannon temple
The area around Asakusa-Kannon temple has still managed to hold on to an air of the old Edo.
▶ page 540

themselves had to take turns coming here and living here for a while. Even though 60% of the city was destroyed in a major fire in 1657, it was considered the biggest city in the world in the 18th century, when it had approx. 1.2 million inhabitants.

The 15th Tokugawa shogun, Yoshinobu, had to hand power to Emperor Meiji, who in 1868 moved his residence from Kyoto to Edo, which was renamed Tokyo (eastern capital). Severe damage was caused by the 1923 earthquake, and bombing during World War II destroyed around 800,000 houses; but reconstruction began soon after and with it came Tokyo's development as a global city. The tectonically unstable region is currently registering frequent tremors, and the city fearfully awaits the next big earthquake. Earthquake-proof skyscrapers were built and in 1964 the first Olympic Games in Asia were held in Tokyo. Despite the recession since the end of the 1980s, ambitious building projects have been implemented and highly modern districts have been created on reclaimed land in Tokyo Bay.

◄ Edo becomes Tokyo

Tokyo Overview

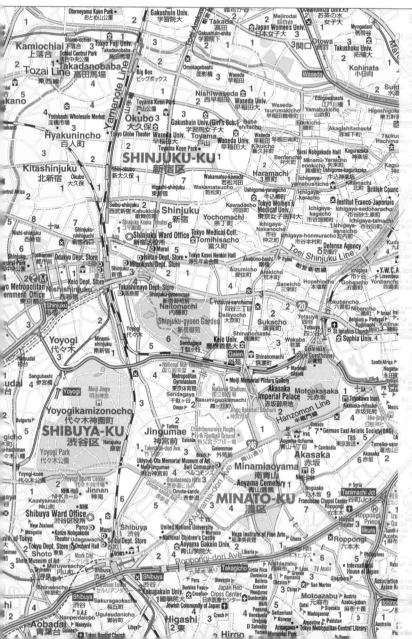

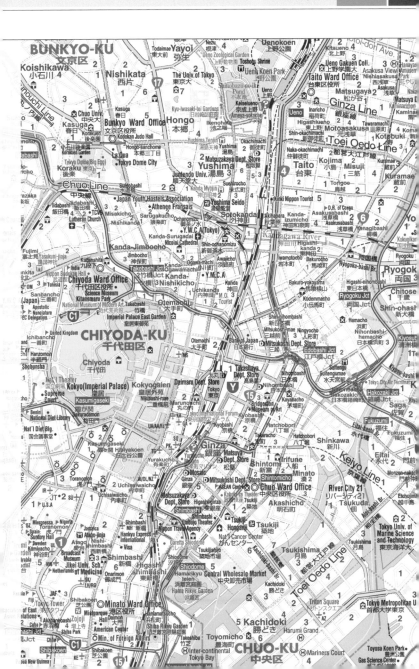

Subway and Railway in Tōkyō

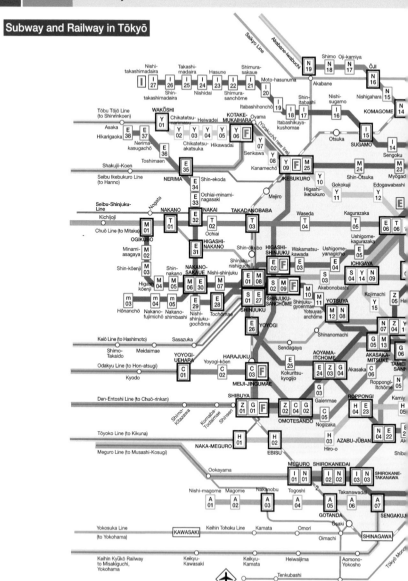

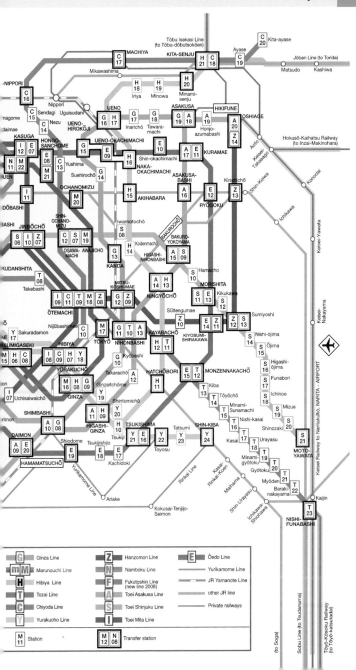

▶ VISITING TOKYO

INFORMATION

Information of the JNTO
In the district of Chiyoda-ku,
2-10-1 Yurakucho, Tokyo Kotsu
Kaikan Building, 10th Floor
(near JR Yurakucho station)
Tel. 03/32 01 33 31
Daily 9am–5pm

Tourist information centres
Tokyo Metropolitan Government
Building Nr. 1
Ground Floor,
2-8-1 Nishi-Shinjuku, Shinjuku-ku
Tel. 03/53 21 30 77
Daily 9.30am–6.30pm

In Keisei-Ueno station,
1-60 Uenokoen, Taito-ku
Tel. 03/38 36 34 71
Daily 9.30am–6.30pm

At **Haneda Airport**,
Big Bird Terminal
Ground Floor
Tel. 03/57 57 93 45
Daily 9am–10pm

At **Narita Airport**
information hall,
Terminal 1 Tel. 04 76/30 33 83
Terminal 2 Tel. 04 76/34 58 77
Both daily 8am–8pm
This is a good place to get a free map
of Tokyo.

Online
www.tourism.metro.tokyo.jp (Tokyo
city's official tourism homepage)
www.tcvb.or.jp (Tokyo Convention
and Visitors Bureau)
www.tokyoessentials.com

GETTING THERE

By plane: international airlines fly to
Narita International Airport (around
60km/35mi to the northeast); domestic Japanese flights as well as
flights from Taiwan and Hawaii fly to
Haneda Airport (in the south of the
city).
By rail: Tokyo Central Station is the
main junction of the shinkansen lines;
train lines from northern Japan go via
Ueno station, trains from the west via
Shinjuku station. It is best to avoid
these stations during rush hour,
because it is definitely possible to
become disoriented in the large
crowds.
By ferry: most passenger ships dock in
Yokohama Harbour (30km/20mi to
the south).
Expressways connect Tokyo with
Nagoya (Tomei-Expressway), Lake
Yamanaka (Chuo-Expressway), Aomori (Tohoku Expressway) and with
Niigata (Kan'etsu Expressway).

LOCAL TRANSPORT

Tokyo's public local transport network is very extensive and correspondingly confusing, especially since
it is in the hands of different companies. It is not necessary for tourists to
use the city buses. The trams and
underground run from approx. 5am
to midnight.
Underground
The twelve underground lines (eight
are operated by Tokyo Metro, four by
Toei) are colour-coded and marked
with a letter (e.g. A for Asakusa line,
G for Ginza line). A fare depends on
the distance travelled and can be
determined from the maps and ticket
machines. Anyone who is unsure
should just buy the cheapest ticket
and pay the difference at the counter
at the destination.
The **JR Yamanote loop line**, which
goes in a big circle around the city

centre is very useful. It stops at all of the important junctions. It is best to avoid the underground during rush hour. Tokyo's only remaining tram, the Toei-Arakawa line (from Waseda) operates in the north of the city.

It is a good idea to buy a *day pass* for the underground trains of Toei and Tokyo Metro; it costs ¥ 1000 (Tokyo Metro-Toei-kyotsu-ichinichi-joshaken; available from the ticket machines; a day pass for just one of the two companies ¥ 700 or ¥ 710). JR passholders can use all of the city's JR urban railways for free (just show the Rail Pass). Anyone not in possession of a JR pass can purchase a *Tokyo Free Ticket*, valid for both underground networks, buses and JR lines within the city (Tokyo furii kippu, ¥ 1580). Information counters for Tokyo's underground can be found in Ginza, Shinjuku, Otemachi and Nihombashi station. Online at www.tokyometro.jp/e (Tokyo Metro), www.kotsu.metro.tokyo.jp/english (Toei).

Airport transfer

The fastest way to get to *Narita International Airport* (tel. 04 76/34 50 00, www.narita-airport.jp) east of the city is by taking the JR Narita Express (NEX) via Tokyo station (55 minutes); there are also trains from Shinjuku (1¼ hours). The private Keisei line has a connection via Nippori from/to Ueno (Keisei Skyliner, 1 hour). Both companies also have slower and thus cheaper connections. In addition there are buses operated by the major hotels, but they are at risk of getting caught in traffic jams.

To get to the smaller *Haneda Airport* (tel. 03/5 75 78 11 11, www.tokyo-airport-bldg.co.jp/english) in the southwest of the city (almost exclusively domestic flights) take the private

Keikyu line from Shinagawa (15 minutes). There are bus and train connections between the two airports (approx. 1¼ hours).

EVENTS

January: Dezome-shiki (fire brigade parade with acrobatic performances; beginning of Jan), Odaiba.

February: Setsubun (spring festival; beginning of Feb), in Asakusa-Kannon temple, Zojoji temple and Gokokuji temple, amongst other places; »Tokyo Big Marathon« from the city hall Shinjuku to Odaiba Big Sight (www.tokyo42195.org).

April: spring festival (with old dances, No performances and archery; April–May), in Meiji shrine.

May: Kanda-sai (procession with two large portable shrines; mid-May, in uneven years), at Kanda-Myojin shrine; Sanja-matsuri (procession with a large number of portable shrines, Geisha-procession; mid-May), at Asakusa shrine; Sumo competitions (Jan, May and Sept), in Ryogoku-Kokugi-kan-Sumo hall.

June: Sanno-matsuri (procession with portable shrines, children's procession; mid-June), at Hie shrine and at Asakusa-Kannon temple.

July: Hanabi Taikai (large firework display at Sumidagawa, since 1773, end of July).

September: Kakunori (loggers' festival with balancing acts on floating wood; Sept–Oct), at the Sumida River.

October: Tokyo Festival (city festival with processions and various events; beginning of Oct); autumn festival (Oct–Nov), at Meiji shrine.

November: Shichi-go-san (shrine visit of the 7-year-old, 5-year-old and 3-year-old children, mid-Nov), in Meiji shrine, Hie shrine and Kanda-Myojin shrine amongst others.

December: Gishi-sai (commemorative

festival for the 47 Ronin; mid-Dec), in Sengakuji temple; Hegoita-ichi (stalls sell Hagoita, traditional Japanese badminton rackets; 17–19 Dec), at Asakusa-Kannon temple.

An excellent source of information for concerts, exhibitions, festivals and other events is the English-language magazine *Metropolis*, which also contains interesting articles about current affairs, restaurant critiques and a classifieds section. It comes out every Friday and is available from tourist information centres, book shops and a large number of bars (http://metropolis.japantoday.com).
Tickets for concerts and other events are available through *Ticket Pia*, which has offices in the department stores Isetan and Keio in Shinjuku, in 109 Building in Shibuya and in the Sony Building in Ginza, amongst other things.

SHOPPING

Shopping centres

Tokyo's largest shopping centres are the sophisticated *Ginza* (Chuo-ku district), the hip *Omotesando* (Harajuku) and the shopping streets around *Shinjuku station*. There are many small boutiques around Daikanyama station (northwest of Ebisu), some of which are hidden away in homes in side streets. Akihabara spe-

Window shopping in Ginza

cializes in electronics (►Baedeker Tipp p.536), Kappabashi in household goods (►Baedeker Tipp p.539) and Jimbocho in second-hand book shops. The *Ameyoko shopping street* in Ueno is an inexpensive place where the locals do their daily shopping. A huge selection of food/drink can be found in every large department store (usually in the basement).

Flea markets
Antique markets take place at Togo shrine (near Harajuku station; 1st and 4th Sun, also 5th Sun of the month, if applicable; not if it is raining).
Antique market at Nogi shrine (near Nogizaka station, 2nd Sun; not if it is raining).
A market with a more than 400-year-old tradition is Setagaya Boro-ichi (5 minutes on foot from Setagaya station (Tokyu-Setagaya line); 15th–16th Dec as well as 15th–16th Jan).
Five times a year (3rd–5th May, 30th July, 1st and 2nd July, 15th–17th Sept, 22nd–24th Dec) Heiwajima Komingu Kotto-sai takes place in a huge hall in the Tokyo-Tyutsu Centre, Heiwajima (15 minutes, monorail to Tokyu Ryutsu).
The International Forum flea market every 2nd Sun 10am–4pm, antique market every 1st and 3rd Sun 8am–4.30pm (Yurakucho underground station).
More information available from Tokyo's recycling company, tel. 03/32 26-68 00.

Kurofune Antiques
7-4, Roppongi 7-chome, Minato-ku
Tel. 03/34 79-15 52
www.kurofuneantiques.com
Daily except Sun 10am–6pm
High-quality antiques worth their price.

Ohya-Shobo
1-1, Kanda-Jinbocho
Chiyoda-ku
Tel. 03/32 91-00 62
www.ukiyoe.or.jp/ohya
Mon–Sat 10am–6pm
Large selection of old illustrated Japanese books and cards, art prints, Japanese drawings and photographs.

Kinokuniya
17-7, Shinjuku 3-chome
Shinjuku-ku
Tel. 03/33 54-01 31
www.kinokuniya.co.jp/english
Daily 10am–9pm
Bookshop with foreign-language books.

Maruzen
1F-4F Oazu
6-4 Marunouchi,
1-chome, Chiyoda-ku
Tel. 03/52 88-88 81
www.maruzen.co.jp/home-eng
Bookshop with foreign-language books.

Tower Books
1-22-14 Jinnan
Shibuya-ku
Tel. 03/34 96 36 61
Daily 10am–11pm
On the 7th floor of the Tower Records building. Foreign-language books and magazines.

Laox
2-9, Sotokanda 1-chome
Chiyoda-ku
Tel. 03/ 32 53-71 11
www.laox.co.jp/english
Daily 10am–9pm
A large selection of electronic goods from kitchen appliances to iPods and digital cameras, spread out over seven floors. In Akihabara.

Bic Camera
1-24-12 Shibuya, Shibuya-ku,
Tel. 03/54 66 11 11
Daily 10am–8pm
This place sells not just cameras, but
also other inexpensive goods, from
computers to DVD players.

Yodobashi Camera
11-1, Nishi Shinjuku 1-chome,
Shinjuku-ku
Tel. 03/33 46-10 10
Daily 9.30am–10pm
Overwhelming selection of all kinds of
cameras, including inexpensive ones,
electronic goods. Branch in Akihabara.

Fine Arts Fuji
1st Floor, Azabudai Houei Bldg., 3-20,
Azabudai 2-chome, Minato-ku 106
Kamiyacho station in Akasaka
Tel. 03/35 82 18 70
Daily except Tue 10.30am–7pm
The shop opposite the American Club
sells kimonos, lacquerware and porcelain lamps as well as antique chests
of drawers, small furniture, bronze
works and small souvenirs.

Oriental Bazaar
9-13, Jingumae 5-chome, Shibuya-ku
Tel. 03/34 00-39 33
Daily except Thu 10am–7pm
This shop (several floors), which also
has a great branch at Narita International Airport (Terminal 1, 4th floor),
sells a large selection of art and
antiques, modern and traditional
clothes, porcelain, ceramics, lacquerwares, folding screens, lamps, household objects and gifts.

Takumi Craft Shop
4-2, Ginza 8-chome, Chuo-ku
Tel. 03/35 71 20 17
Sells Japanese toys, kitchen utensils
and fabrics as well as small furniture
amongst other things.

Muji Yurakucho
3-8-3 Marunouchi, Chiyoda-ku
Tel. 03/52 08 82 41
Daily 10am–9pm
Shop of the famous Muji chain
(▶Shopping, p.145).

Itoya
2-7-15 Ginza, Chuo-ku
Tel. 03/35 61 83 11
Mon–Sat 10am–7pm,
Sun 10.30am–7pm
Famous stationery shop with high-
quality Japanese paper, writing imple-
ments and much more.

Hakuhinkan
8-8-11 Ginza, Chuo-ku
Shimbashi underground station
Tel. 03/35 71 80 08
Daily 11am–8pm
Toys on nine floors: everything that
little (and big) hearts desire!

K. Mikimoto
5-5 Ginza, 4-chome, Chuo-ku
Tel. 03/35 35 46 11
Daily except Wed 11am–7pm
Mikimoto, the founder of this upmarket pearl shop, was the inventor of
the cultivated pearl (▶Ise-Shima National Park). Further shops, also in
various hotels, including Imperial
Hotel.

WHERE TO EAT
▶ Expensive
① Apicius
Sanshi Kaikan, basement,
1-9-4, Yuraku-cho, Chiyoda-ku
Tel. 03/32 14-13 61/62
www.apicius.co.jp
Daily except Sun 11.30am–2pm,
5.30pm–9pm (last order)
This stylishly decorated restaurant
with three rooms situated in the
Marunouchi shopping centre is one of
the »Grandes Tables du Monde«;

French specialities, including fish and seafood.

② *Tableaux*
B1F Sunrose Daikanyama Building,
Sarugakucho 11-6, Shibuya-ku
Daikanyama underground station
Tel. 03/54 89 22 01
Daily 5pm–1am
Californian cuisine in an elegant set-
ting, prices set accordingly. After a
meal guests can smoke a cigar in the
bar and listen to live music.

③ *Kappo Toyoda*
1-12-3 Nihonbashi-muromachi
Chuo-ku
Mitsukoshi-mae underground station
Tel. 03/32 41-10 25
Mon–Fri 11.30am–2.30pm,
5pm–10.30pm, Sat 5pm–10pm
(only Japanese)
The tradition of this restaurant goes
back to the Edo period. So of course it
serves traditional Japanese cuisine. The
chef gets the ingredients directly from
Tsukiji wholesale market.

④ *Ninja*
Akasaka Tokyu Plaza,
2-14-3 Nagata-cho, Chiyoda-ku
Tel. 03/51 57 39 36
www.ninja.tv
Mon–Sat daily 5.30pm–2am,
Sun and public holidays until 11pm
Original theme restaurant: diners are
led by a ninja through black hallways
and trap-doors to one of the booths.
These booths are visited by ninjas
performing magic tricks (tips of approx. ¥ 1000 are expected). Modern
Japanese cuisine. Reservations necessary. Downside: maximum stay is
limited to two hours.

⑤ *Kyubei*
7-6 Ginza 8-chome, Chuo-ku
Tel. 03/35 71 65 23

Mon–Sat 11.30am–2pm
and 5pm–10pm
Very elegant (and correspondingly
expensive) Sushi restaurant in Ginza
with a 70-year tradition.

! *Baedeker* TIP

Dining on the water

A pleasure with a centuries-long tradition,
which still has not lost any of its appeal, is
dining in a yakatabune, a narrow, roofed
boat for 20–100 people, while it floats in
leisurely fashion over the water. There are
various operators, some accept couples as
well as groups (inquire about noriai yakatabune), e.g. Funasei (www.funasei.com/
fsei_english, tel. 03/54 79 27 31 – only
Japanese, it is best to ask the front desk to
make reservations), and Harumiya (tel.
03/36 44 13 44). Both ask approx. ¥ 10,000
for a 2½-hour trip in the bay of Tokyo.

---

⑥ *Kakiden*
(map p.530)
Yasuyo Building, 8th Floor,
3-37-11 Shinjuku
Shinjuku-ku
Tel. 03/33 52-51 21
Daily 11am–9pm
In the context of a tea ceremony this
restaurant, which is part of the Relais
et Châteaux chain, serves culinary
dishes from Kaseki cuisine (►Food
and Drink, p.121), sublimely presented.

⑦ *Shinjuku Tsunahachi Honten*
(map p.530)
3-31-8 Shinjuku, Shinjuku-ku
Tel. 03/33 52 10 12
Daily 11.15am–10pm
Main restaurant of a very successful
restaurant chain, specializing in tempura.

► Moderate

⑧ *Moti*

6-2-35 Roppongi, 3rd Floor, Roppongi
Hama Building, Minato-ku
Tel. 03/34 79-19 39
Mon–Sat 11.30am–11pm,
Sun noon–11pm
A Tokyo institution for simple Indian
dishes with many branches in the city.

⑨ *Winds*

1-7-4 Kanda Suruga-dai,
Chiyoda-ku
Tel. 03/32 19-06 33
Daily 11.30am–2.30pm,
5.30pm–10pm
This Californian-style spacious res-
taurant and its terrace have a pleasant
atmosphere; serves fish.

⑩ *Tsukiji Edogin Honten*

5-1 Tsukiji 4-chome, Chuo-ku
Tel. 03/35 43 44 01
Mon–Sat 11am–9.30pm
The gigantic portions of fresh sushi
attract plenty of diners. Those lucky
enough to find a seat at the bar can
even watch the sushi masters work
their magic.

Bowls with goodies

⑪ *Cicada*

5-2-40 Minami-Azabu, Minato-ku
Hiroo underground station, exit 3
Tel. 03/54 47 55 22
www.cicada.co.jp
Tue–Sat noon–3pm
and 6pm–2am,
Sun and Mon 6pm–10.30pm
Spanish cuisine with a Moroccan
touch. Large windows with a view of
the road. International audience.

⑫ *Gonpachi*

1-13-11 Nishi-Azabu, Minato-ku
Tel. 03/57 71 01 70
Daily 11.30am–5am
Traditional Japanese cuisine (incl. soba, yakitori and sushi). Excellent and
fresh. Equally popular amongst foreigners and the Japanese. President
Bush and Prime Minister Koizumi
have also dined here.

► Inexpensive

Baedeker recommendation

Crayon House (map p.528)

3-8-15 Kita-Aoyama, Minato-ku,
Omotesando underground station (at the
Hanae-Mori shop to the left)
Tel. 03/34 06 64 09
Daily 11am–9pm
One of the city's best vegetarian restaurants,
with dishes made from organic ingredients.
Superb! Also sells organic food.

Tonkatsu Maisen (map p.528)

4-8-5 Jingumae, Shibuya-ku
Tel. 03/34 70 00 71
Daily 11am–10pm
Near Omotesando underground sta-
tion.
Well-known and popular Tonkatsu
restaurant. Simple décor, mixed
audience.

Il Castello (map p.530)
1-34-14 Takadano-baba,
Shinjuku-ku
Tel. 03/32 08-04 32
Daily except Sun noon–2pm,
5.30pm–10.30pm (last order)
This restaurant is one of the most
popular meeting place amongst students and young working adults,
because of its inexpensive Italian
dishes.

Yakitori stalls
Under the rail tracks south of Yurakucho (or Hibiya underground station,
exit A1) are a number of small,
atmospheric Yakitori restaurants,
some of them are nothing more than
stalls with chairs outside, where many
Japanese people like to have a snack.

GOING OUT

The most popular entertainment districts are *Roppongi*, which is particularly popular amongst the city's
foreign inhabitants (visitors are positively thrown into the nightlife) and
Kabuki-cho, in the district of Shinjuku, which is a little bit rougher. This is
also where visitors can find »*Golden
Gai*« (golden alley), which is lined by
small pubs and bars. Classical Japanese
entertainment can be found in the
Kabuki Theatre (▶p.534). The best
place to enjoy operas, ballets, western
plays and modern dance is the *New
National Theatre* (Honcho 1-1-1,
Shibuya-ku, tel. 03/53 51 30 11,
www.nntt.jac.go.jp, Hatsudai underground station, Keio New Line). One
of the stages here also performs
experimental theatre and Butoh dance.
The theatre is part of the Opera City
complex, which also has a concert hall
(www.operacity.jp/en). *Classical concerts* can also be enjoyed in Tokyo
Bunka Kaikan in Ueno Park (Uenokoen 5-45, tel. 03/38 28 21 11) and in

Suntory Hall (Akasaka 1-13-1,
tel. 03/35 84 99 99, www.suntory.com/
culture-sports/suntoryhall).
There is also a large number of other
venues, the current schedules are listed
in the English-language magazine
Metropolis (▶event tips, p.516).

Blues Alley Japan
Hotel Wing International Meguro,
Basement B1, 1-3-14, Meguro-ku
tel. 03/54 96-43 81
JR Meguro underground station
Sophisticated restaurant bar, serves
Mediterranean cuisine, live jazz events.

Blue Note Tokyo
6-3-16 Raika Building,
Minami-Aoyama, Minato-ku
Tel. 03/54 85 00 88
Daily 5.30pm–1am (live acts at 7pm
and 9.30pm)
The most important stage for live jazz,
an institution in the city.

Maduro
6-10-3 Roppongi, Minato-ku
In Grand Hyatt Hotel (4th floor) in
Roppongi Hills complex
Tel. 03/43 33 88 88
www.grandhyatttokyo.com
Daily 5pm–2am, Fri/Sat until 3am
Elegant, high-class bar with comfortable leather couches and dimmed
lighting. From 9pm (Sun from
8.30pm) Cover charge of ¥ 1575.

What the Dickens
Roob 6 Building, 4th Floor,
1-13-3 Ebisu-Nishi, Shibuya-ku
Ebisu underground station
Tel. 03/37 80 20 99
Tue–Wed 5pm–11pm, Thu–Sat
5pm–2am, Sun 3pm–midnight
Comfortable English-style pub with a
lot of wood. Popular with foreigners
living in Tokyo. Often has live music
(incl. rock, pop, folk).

Azabu Juban Onsen
1-5-22 Azabu Juban, Minato-ku
Roppongi underground station
Tel. 03/34 04 26 10
Daily except Tue 11am–9pm
Admission ¥ 1260
An onsen in Tokyo? There is such a thing and this is not the only one! After a bath in the brownish spring water, which has a pleasantly cool temperature of 26°C/79°F, visitors can enjoy a beer here on Sundays after 3pm and listen to some Japanese pop music (enka).

▶ Karaoke
When visiting Japan it really is a must to try karaoke, this typically Japanese pastime. There are always English songs to choose from. For the most part people book a private karaoke room: that way no-one need feel embarrassed! Here are some examples:

Pasela
5-16-3 Roppongi
Roppongi station (exit 3)
Tel. (mobile): 01 20/91 10 86
Mon–Fri 5pm–8am,
Sat and Sun 2pm–10am
Twenty karaoke rooms (four with MD players for live recordings) on the 4th–10th floors. 10,000 foreign titles to choose from. 30 minutes Mon–Fri ¥ 500, Sat–Sun ¥ 600.

WHERE TO STAY
▶ Luxury
① **Dai-ichi Hotel Tokyo (map p.530)**
1-2-6 Shimbashi, Minato-ku,
Tokyo 105-8621
Tel. 03/35 01-44 11, fax 35 95-26 34
www.daiichihotel-tokyo.com/english
15 minutes from Tokyo's City Air Terminal, in the heart of the government and finance district, not far from Ginza shopping district. This hotel, a member of the Leading Hotels of the World, combines the Japanese tradition of sincere hospitality with European elegance. The hotel has twelve excellent restaurants, serving Japanese, French/European and Chinese cuisine. Also a gym with a pool. Direct access to the underground.

② **Four Seasons Hotel Chinzan-So**
10-8 Sekiguchi 2-chome, Bunkyo-ku, Tokyo 112-8667
Tel. 03/39 43-22 22, Fax 39 43-23 00
www.fourseasons.com/tokyo
The Four Seasons, located in Chinzan-so Gardens, is also a member of the Leading Hotels of the World. It provides a perfect synthesis between classical European and Far Eastern comforts. All of the rooms are spacious and are fitted with marble bathtubs. The *gourmet restaurants* are famous; they include Bice, serving excellent Italian cuisine; Yang Yuan Zhai, Chinese specialities; the Miyuki serves traditionally Japanese Kaiseki dishes; there is also a sushi bar, the Seasons Café, as well as the Le Jardin for snacks and afternoon tea. Other noteworthy features of this hotel are an amphitheatre, several shops as well as a health club with an indoor pool, fitness room, beauty salon and traditional baths; this hotel also offers activity programmes for children.

③ **Imperial**
1-1, Uchisaiwai-cho 1-chome,
Chiyoda-ku 100, Tokyo 100-8558
Tel. 03/35 04-11 11, fax 35 81-91 46
www.imperialhotel.co.jp
This is the preferred hotel of heads of state, members of the world's royal families and managers. It is close to all the city's important locations. The cuisine of its 13 restaurants (including the world-famous *Les Saisons*) with French, Japanese and Chinese specialities, has won several awards. The

Teppan-yaki restaurant Kamon pre-
pares steaks and seafood directly at the
table. The Old Imperial Bar, decorated
with memorabilia of the hotel's architect Frank Lloyd Wright, is a popular
meeting place in the evenings. Further
facilities including a heated swimming
pool on the top floor, the Executive
Service Centre as well as a Japanese
tea-house, where guests can participate
in tea ceremonies.

④ *Shinagawa Prince Hotel*
4-10-30 Takanawa, Minato-ku,
Tokyo 108-8611
Tel. 03/34 40 11 11
Fax 54 21 78 88
www.princehotelsjapan.com/
shinagawaprincehotel
A total of 3680 rooms in a modern
hotel complex. The nicest ones are the
type D double rooms, painted in red,
in the 32-storey Executive Tower,
which also houses an IMAX cinema
and a bowling alley. There are also less
expensive rooms.

⑤ *Park Hyatt Hotel*
3-7-1-2 Nishi Shinjuku, Shinjuku-ku
Tel. 03/53 22 12 34
Fax 53 22 12 88
www.tokyo.park.hyatt.com
In Shinjuku Park Tower. The hotel
starts on the 41st floor. Nice bamboo
garden in the lobby. The New York Bar
on the 52nd floor is known from the
award-winning film *Lost in Translation*; since then many a movie buff
has come here to see the bar in person.
Popular amongst VIPs. Everything is
top quality of course!

► **Mid-range**
⑥ *Shibuya Tobu Hotel*
3-1 Utagawamachi, Shibuya-ku,
Tokyo 150-0042
Tel. 03/34 76 01 11, fax 34 76 09 03
www.tobuhotel.co.jp/shibuya/rsv.html

7 minutes on foot from Shibuya
station. Cheaper if booked online. The
twin rooms are the nicest. With a sushi
and tempura restaurant.

⑦ *Ryokan Asakusa Shigetsu*
(map p.540)
1-31-11 Asakusa, Taito-ku,
Tokyo 110-0032
Tel. 03/38 43 23 45, fax 38 43 23 48
www.shigetsu.com/e
Comfortable ryokan in the middle of
Asakusa, from the Japanese baths
made of cypress wood on the 6th floor
there is a view of the Sensoji temple
pagoda. Japanese and Western rooms,
the latter are smaller and not so nice,
but cheaper. Japanese restaurant.

Baedeker recommendation

⑧ *Suigetsu Hotel Ohgaisou (map p.538)*
3-3-21 Ikenohata, Taito-ku,
Tokyo 110-0008
Tel. 03/38 22 46 11
Fax 38 23 43 40
Tel. within Japan (toll-free)
01 20/26 62 66
www.ohgai.co.jp
Directly beside Ueno Park. Japanese-style
hotel with a lot of character, both Japanese
and Western rooms (the latter are more
expensive). Has a nice old house, which was
once the home of the great author Mori
Ogai, and a Japanese garden. Public marble
bath for men, cypress wood bath for women.

► **Budget**
⑨ *Sawanoya Ryokan (map p.538)*
2-3-11 Yanaka, Taito-ku,
Tokyo 110-0001
Tel. 03/38 22 22 51
Fax 38 22 22 52
www.tctv.ne.jp/members/sawanoya
10 rooms without bathrooms (but
with wash-basins), 2 with bathrooms.

Two communal baths. Comfortable ryokan run by a family in the area around Ueno Park. Clean and cheap. With coin washers and dryers. Tea, coffee and internet free. Lion-dance performance and tea ceremony. Popular with foreign tourists, timely reservations necessary.

⑩ *Sakura Hotel*
2-21-4 Kanda-Jimbocho, Chiyoda-ku, Tokyo 101-0051
Tel. 03/32 61 39 39
Fax 32 64 27 77
www.sakura-hotel.co.jp
Simple, but clean and in a favourable location: Jimbocho underground station, exit A6. Small single and double rooms, twin rooms (with bunk beds)

and communal rooms with bunk beds (also suitable for families). The staff speak English. Internet café. Also lets furnished rooms for longer stays (in Shinjuku).

⑪ *Ours Inn Hankyu*
1-50-5 Ooi, Shinagawa-ku, Tokyo 140-0014
Tel. 03/37 75 61 21
Fax 37 78 38 61
www.hankyu-hotel.com/en/oursinn
Ooimachi station.
Only single rooms (830). Small, but completely adequate rooms. One storey is reserved for women. The hotel's best feature is the public bath on the top floor with a view all the way to Mount Fuji.

Chiyoda: Around the Imperial Palace

The district of Chiyoda-ku is home to the imperial palace and the most important public and private administrative centres, as well as to the central station, from where the trains of the Tokaido shinkansen lines depart.

Tokyo International Forum

The Marunouchi quarter extending west of the central station contains several banks, department stores, the main post office and more. South of the station is Tokyo International Forum, an architecturally interesting conference and exhibition centre with a number of cafés and restaurants. It was designed by Rafael Vinoly and opened in 1997. Not far to the west is the imperial theatre (Teikoku Theatre). On the 9th floor of the theatre building the Idemitsu Art Museum exhibits Chinese and Japanese ceramics, amongst other things.

Imperial Palace

Near the Chamber of Industry and Commerce, visitors can cross a moat to the forecourt (Kokyo Gaien) in front of the Imperial Palace. Here visitors can see the Nijubashi »double bridge« leading to the inner area of the palace complex, which is surrounded by strong walls. The palace is **not generally accessible** to the public. The palace garden can only be accessed on the 2 January and 23 December (the emperor's birthday); otherwise the permission of the Imperial Household Agency is necessary (bookings either online, http://sankan.kunaicho.go.jp/english, up to four days in advance, or by phone up to one day in advance, tel. 03/32 13 11 11; the permit has to be picked up from the Tour Office of the Imperial Household Agency: 1-1 Chiyoda-ku, Tokyo 100-8111. Guided tours: Mon–Fri 10am and 1.30pm, 21 July to 31 Aug only at 10am).

After being destroyed in World War II, the Imperial Palace was rebuilt in its old form, but this time reinforced concrete was used. The east part of the garden, Higashi-Gyo-en, is freely accessible. It contains a few old buildings (Nov–Feb Tue–Sun 9am–3.30pm, March–Oct until 4pm). In the north, on the other side of the road that goes through the grounds, is Kitanomaru Park. It is particularly attractive during the cherry blossom. The National Museum of Modern Art is on this road; it features exhibits from the Meiji era and later. Somewhat further north is the Science Museum (technology and natural sciences; nuclear energy, space flight). Its active, hands-on educational approach make it worth a visit.

◄ Higashi-Gyo-en

◄ Kitanomaru Park

To the northwest, outside of the park and across from the moat surrounding it, is the Yasukuni shrine (1869) on Mount Kudan. It is dedicated to the Japanese victims of war, including some war criminals, which is why visits to this shrine by Japanese prime ministers regularly cause protests in other Asian countries. On the way there is the bronze standing statue of Omura Masujiro (1825–69), a statesman of the early Meiji era. Two koma-inu (mythological animal creatures) and a stone torii approx. 12m/39ft high stand close to the south gate.

Yasukuni shrine

Spot the imperial palace behind the »double bridge«

Tokyo *Chiyoda-ku*

② ↑ TOSHIMA-KU, BUNKYO-KU, KITA-KU ↑ *Kitanomaru Park, Korakuen*

↑ SHINJUKU-KU

Hanzo moat

CHIYODA-KU

Hanzomon

Imperial Household Agency

Sakashitamon

National Theatre

Imperial Palace

④

Meiji shrine

Biological Laboratory

Kokyo Gaien

Supreme Court

↑ Aoyama dori

Sakurada moat

Nijubashi

National Library

Sakuradamon

Constitution Hall

Gaisen moat

KASUMIGASEKI

Police

Hibiya moat

Akasaka Palace

Parliament

Transport Ministry

Building Ministry

Ministry of Justice

Sakurada-dori

Ministry of the Interior

6

Hibiya Park

Ministry of Foreign Affairs

⑪
⑧
⑫
②
⑥

Ministry of Health

7

Hibiya-dori

Prime Minister's Office

4

Ministry of Finance

8

11

12   15

1

9

10

Library

13   14

↑ Expressway no. 3

Patent Office

3

Ministry of Education

5

Hibiya Hall

③

2

Nippon Press Center

Imperial Hotel

↓ MEGURO-KU, MINATO-KU, SHIBUYA-KU

Konpira shrine

Sotobori-dori

Uchi-Sawai-cho

Okura Shukokan Museum

Sakurada-dori

Seinenkan

①

New Shimbashi Building

Shimbashi Station

④ ⑪ ↗ *Yokohama*

Sotobori-dori

Hibiya-dori

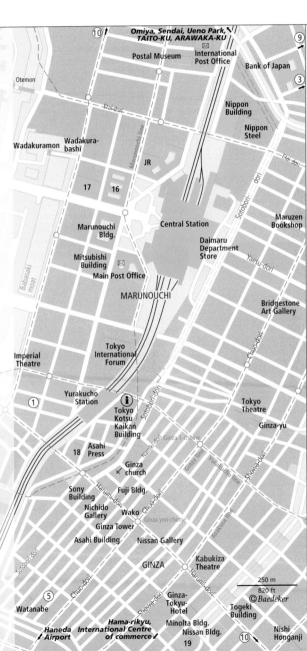

Omiya, Sendai, Ueno Park,
TAITO-KU, ARAWAKA-KU

Postal Museum

International
Post Office

Bank of Japan

Otemon

Etai-dori

Nippon
Building

Nippon
Steel

Wadakuramon

Wadakura-
bashi

JR

Etai-dori

Marunouchi-line

Sotobori-dori

Wadakuramon

17   16

Maruzen
Bookshop

Marunouchi
Bldg.

Central Station

Daimaru
Department
Store

Yaesu-dori

Mitsubishi
Building

Main Post Office

MARUNOUCHI

Babasaki moat

Bridgestone
Art Gallery

Chuo-dori

Tokyo
International
Forum

Imperial
Theatre

Yurakucho
Station

Tokyo
Theatre

Ginza-yu

Tokyo
Kotsu
Kaikan
Building

Sotobori-dori

Yurakucho line

Asahi
Press

18

Ginza 1-chome

Ginza
church

Namiki-dori

Ginza line

Sony
Building

Harumi-dori

Fuji Bldg.

Chuo-dori

Showa-dori

Nichido
Gallery

Wako

Ginza yon-chome

Ginza Tower

Asahi Building

Nissan Gallery

Asakusa line

GINZA

Kabukiza
Theatre

250 m

820 ft

© Baedeker

Watanabe

⑤

Chuo-dori

Sotobori-dori

Showa-dori

Ginza-
Tokyu-
Hotel

Harumi-dori

Togeki
Building

Haneda
Airport

Hama-rikyu,
International Centre
of commerce

Minolta Bldg.
Nissan Bldg.

19

⑩

Nishi
Honganji

Hibiya Park   South of the Imperial Palace is Hibiya Park. It was opened in 1903 and was the first Western-style park in Japan. It is home to the Hibiya-kokaido Hall, built in 1929 with Gothic-inspired forms, and the Hibiya Library. East of the large fountain is the Imperial Hotel. Cross underneath the main train line to get into the district of Ginza (►p.534).

Government quarter   To west of here is Kasumigaseki, the government quarter, with a large number of ministries. Kokkai-gijido, the parliament building of 1936, is also located here. It is a granite structure with a 65m/213ft tower.

Akasaka and Roppongi

Hie shrine   Southwest of the government quarter is the upscale Asakasa district with a number of luxury hotels, many embassies and fancy restaurants. The Hie shrine (also Sanno-sama), originally built in the early Edo period and consecrated to the deity Oyamakui-no-kami, can also be found here. The shrine festival in mid-June is one of the city's best known.

West of Nagatacho station is **Suntory Art Museum** (old Japanese arts and crafts) and past the well-known New Otani Hotel the **Asakasa Palace** (Geihinkan), situated in a park. To this day it houses the state's guesthouse. The building was constructed from 1899 to 1909, using earthquake-proof engineering. The site was previously the location of the Kii-Tokugawa residence, in which the emperor lived while the Imperial Palace was being built. Asakasa Palace displays designs akin to those used in France in the late 18th century. It is not accessible to the public.

Bordering Asakasa in the east is **Roppongi quarter**, home to large numbers of foreigners and the seat of many diplomatic representations as well as entertainment quarters (bars, restaurants, nightclubs, etc.).

Tokyo Tower is one of the highest self-supporting steel towers in the world

At the corner of Roppongi-dori and TV Asahi-dori, southwest of Roppongi station, is **Roppongi Hills**, a complex opened in 2003. There is a magnificent panoramic view of Tokyo from the 52nd floor of its round Mori Tower. Attractions here are the Mori Art Museum and the elegant Grand Hyatt Hotel as well as a number of restaurants and shops, several green spaces, including a roof garden and a garden with a colourful sculpture by the artist Murakami Takeshi. English-language tours through the complex are also available (tel. 03/64 06 66 77, www.roppongihills.com).

The Toei-Oedo eastbound underground line goes from Roppongi past Shiba-Koen (also Toei-Mita line from the city centre). To the north of the shady green space is **Zojoji temple**, to which the park once belonged. Here visitors can see

Memorial place for the »water children« in Shiba Park

Shiba Park

long rows of Jinzo gods, who are consecrated to the »water children« (aborted children). The temple was founded in 1393 and is the centre of the Jodo sect in Kanto District. Noteworthy are the red main gate (sanmon), the large bell and the likeness of the black Buddha. The temple is also in possession of an illustrated biography of the sect's founder Honen.

Tokyo Tower

Not far from here Tokyo Tower, a 333m/1093ft steel frame built in 1958 that resembles the Eiffel Tower in Paris, offers some great views of Tokyo, the bay as well as Boso and Izu Peninsula from its two viewing platforms at 150m/492ft and 250m/820ft. At the foot of this broadcasting tower is a **museum** with exhibitions about the development of electronics as well as a **Waxworks Museum** (open daily 9am–10pm, admission to the viewing platforms ¥ 820).

Shibuya and Harajuku

Take the Yamanote line to the western district of Shibuya. In front of the station is a monument to the loyal dog Hachiko. He accompanied his master every morning to the underground station and greeted him there again in the evening. When his owner died Hachiko came here every day for eleven years until he himself passed away. This is a popular meeting place for young people.

Meiji Shrine Map

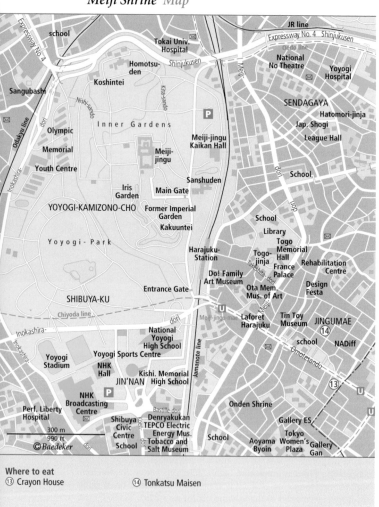

Where to eat
⑬ Crayon House
⑭ Tonkatsu Maisen

Meiji shrine
Inner Garden ▶

One stop further north is Meiji shrine's inner garden (72.4ha/179 acres; Harajuku station). The trees and bushes were largely donations from all around the country. The most noteworthy of the festivals and events held here are Emperor Meiji's birthday (beginning of November) and performances of courtly dances and music (May and November). A pond and the **iris garden** can be found in the south of the park.

The Meiji shrine is at the centre of the park. It is consecrated to Emperor Meiji and his wife (www.meijijingu.or.jp/english). It is **one of the most significant places of pilgrimage in Japan** and its construction began soon after the monarch's death in 1912, with completion in 1920. The simple buildings were largely destroyed in 1945, but in 1958 rebuilt in their original style. The torii at the entrances were made from cypress wood sourced from Mount Ari in Taiwan. The shrine's treasury is close to the north pond; it contains objects from the emperor's possessions.

★
◄ Meiji shrine

Take the Odakyu line to Sangubashi or the Keio line to Hatsudai to get to the Japanese Sword Museum (Token Hakubutsukan), a collection of 120 blades, three of which are classed as national treasures.

Japanese Sword Museum

Adjoining the inner garden to the south is Yoyogi Sports Centre, which was set up as the Olympic Village for the Summer Games in 1964. Here visitors can see a bronze bust of the aviation pioneer Tokugawa Yoshitoshi (1884–1963); the biplane he used can be found in the Transport Museum (between Ochanomizu station and Akihabara station).

Yoyogi Sports Centre

The best place to watch the Japanese youth scene is at the Tokyo Metro station Meiji-jingu-mae. A large number of exclusive fashion shops such as Chanel and Vuitton, as well as bizarre happenings, enliven Omotesando Boulevard, somewhat grandiosely called the »Champs Élysées of Tokyo«. The Prada building's glass façade and the new complex **Omote Sando Hills** are particularly impressive. North of Omotesando Boulevard, starting at Yoyogi Park, the narrow Takeshita-dori runs parallel to the boulevard for a bit; this is where Tokyo's younger inhabitants go to buy their clothes.

Harajuku

Not far east of Harajuku station is Ota-Ukiyoe Museum, which boasts an extensive collection of colourful woodblock prints (www.u-kiyoe-ota-muse.jp, open Tue–Sun 10.30am–5.30pm, closed from 27th to the end of the month, changing admission prices).

Ota-Ukiyoe Museum

Shinjuku

North of Harajuku (northwest of the city centre) lies the urban secondary centre (»Shintoshin«) Shinjuku. During the Edo period a post station was located here on the historic Koshu Road.

Shinjuku station is one of the most heavily used in the world. 3.3 million people enter it daily to travel by one of the twelve rail lines on five subterranean levels. On its eastern side are several department stores and shopping arcades; to the northeast is the **Kabuki-cho entertainment district** without a doubt the largest and most extravagant of its kind in Japan.

Shinjuku station

Shinjuku Map

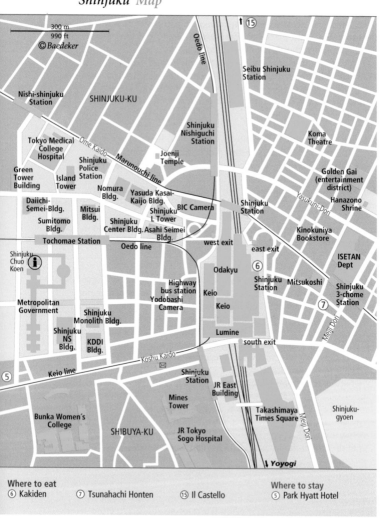

300 m
990 ft
©Baedeker

Oedo line

⑮

Seibu Shinjuku
Station

Nishi-shinjuku
Station

SHINJUKU-KU

Koma
Theatre

Shinjuku
Nishiguchi
Station

Tokyo Medical
College
Hospital

Ome Kaido

Joenji
Temple

Golden Gai
(entertainment
district)

Shinjuku
Police
Station

Marunouchi line

Yasukuni-Dori

Hanazono
Shrine

Green
Tower
Building

Island
Tower

Nomura
Bldg.

Yasuda Kasai-
Kaijo Bldg.

Shinjuku
Station

Kinokuniya
Bookstore

Daiichi-
Semei-Bldg.

Mitsui
Bldg.

BIC Camera

Sumitomo
Bldg.

Shinjuku
Center Bldg.

Shinjuku
L Tower

Asahi Seimei
Bldg.

ISETAN
Dept

Tochomae Station

Oedo line

west exit

east exit

Shinjuku
Chuo
Koen
ℹ

⑥

Odakyu

Shinjuku
Station

Mitsukoshi

Shinjuku
3-chome
Station

Metropolitan
Government

Highway
bus station

Keio

Yodobashi
Camera

Keio

⑦

Shinjuku
Monolith Bldg.

Shinjuku
NS
Bldg.

KDDI
Bldg.

Lumine

south exit

Koshu Kaido

✉

Keio line

⑤

Shinjuku
Station

JR East
Building

Mines
Tower

Takashimaya
Times Square

Shinjuku-
gyoen

Meiji Dori

Bunka Women's
College

SHIBUYA-KU

JR Tokyo
Sogo Hospital

↓ Yoyogi

Where to eat
⑥ Kakiden   ⑦ Tsunahachi Honten   ⑮ Il Castello

Where to stay
⑤ Park Hyatt Hotel

Skyscraper
architecture ►

The view of this part of the city is shaped by a number of modern skyscrapers to the west of the station, such as the Shinjuku Mitsui Building (212m/696ft), the Shinjuku Sumitomo Building (200m/656ft) with a viewing platform on the 51st floor, the Shinjuku Center Building, the Shinjuku Nomura Building, the KDD Building (164m/479ft), the Shinjuku NS Building (134m/440ft) and the Shinjuku Dai-ichi Seimei Building (114m/374ft).

However, Tokyo's outstanding, most modern landmark is the **new city hall** of 1991 with its 246m/807ft double towers designed by Tange Kenzo. There is no need to worry: the freely accessible **Sky Lobby** on the 45th floor safely swings up to 6m/20ft from side to side in the event of an earthquake (free tours in English start at the information centre, bookings Mon–Fri 10am–2.30pm).

★ ★
Tokyo Metropolitan Government Building
▶ 3 D p.532–533

Not far south of Shinjuku station is Shinjuku Gyoen Park. It was once in possession of the imperial family but was given to the state after World War II. The area covers 58.5ha/145 acres and is divided into one part that is in the classical Japanese pattern (cherry blossom in April, chrysanthemum show in November) and another part based on French/English models; a conservatory has many tropical plants on display (www.shinjukugyoen.go.jp).

★
Shinjuku Gyoen

🕐
Opening hours:
Tue–Sun 9am–4pm,
¥ 200

North Tokyo

Gokokuji temple is located along the underground Yurakucho line (Gokokuji stop) in the district of Bunkyo-ku. It is the centre of the Buzan school, which is part of the Shingon sect. It is one of the city's largest temples.
The hill behind the temple has been the **imperial family's burial place** since 1873; the stone lanterns in the temple grounds are copies of the best pieces from Kyoto and Nara. The temple houses a Kannon statue made of amber, presumably from India. The temple treasure includes a Mandala depiction form the Kamakura period. The author Lafcadio Hearn (1850–1904) is buried to the east of the temple building.

Gokokuji temple

Around 800m/875yd south of Gokokuji temple is the Roman Catholic St Mary's Cathedral, designed by the famous Japanese architect Tange Kenzo. The bells in the 62m/203ft bell-tower were a donation from Germany.

St Mary's
Cathedral

A good 1km/0.6mi northwest of Gokokuji temple, in the Ikebukuro quarter, is the new building complex Sunshine City, with its 240m/787ft Sunshine City 60 Building, one of Tokyo's highest skyscrapers; it only takes 35 seconds to get to the top in the express lift.

Sunshine City

In the northern part of the district of Bunkyo-ku, near Komagome station (JR Yamanote lien) is Rikugien Garden, a typical landscape garden of Japan's feudal period (open daily 9am–5pm, ¥ 300).

★
Rikugien
Garden

The JR Keihin-Tohoku line runs from Ueno station to Oji in the district of Kita-ku. Close to the station is the interesting Paper Museum (paper manufacture and products, www.papermuseum.jp/english.htm, open Tue–Sun 10am–5pm, ¥ 300). The museum covers both Western and Japanese paper-making and also offers workshops.

★
Paper Museum

TOKYO METROPOLITAN GOVERNMENT BUILDING

✳ ✳ 13,000 employees pour into the towers of Tokyo's city hall every single weekday. It is located in West Shinjuku, where, over the course of the city hall's construction towards the end of the 1980s, Japan's largest concentration of skyscrapers was created. When designing this building, architect Tange Kenzo is said to have been inspired by Notre Dame Cathedral in Paris. Some may like this building, others may not, but everyone will agree on one thing: the view from the 45th floor wows everybody, not just fans of modern skyscraper architecture.

🕐 Open:
viewing platform north: daily except 2nd and 4th Mon 9.30am–11pm; viewing platform south: daily except 1st and 3rd Tue 9.30am–5.30pm, Sat, Sun, public holidays 9.30am–7.30pm (when north platform is closed until 11pm).
Free admission. Last admission half an hour before closing. From Monday to Friday volunteers give guided tours in English through the complex, starting at the reception of the tourist information on the ground floor of main building no. 1, tel. 03/53 20-78 90, www.metro.tokyo.jp/ENGLISH/TMG

Some facts
Built between 1988 and 1991 to Tange Kenzo's designs, with a floor space of 27,500 sq m/296,000 sq ft. The costs are said to have been so high that some people mockingly called it »Tax Tower«. The location of the new city hall was carefully chosen: the metropolitan government wanted to separate itself from the county government in the district of Marunouchi, while in the same stroke enhancing the underdeveloped district of West Shinjuku, a plan that was successful.

The architect
»The idea of becoming an architect was one I had for the first time when I saw designs by Le Corbusier in a Japanese magazine in the 1930s.« Tange Kenzo (1913–2005) said about himself. Japan's best-known architect and internationally sought-after teacher started combining avant-garde tendencies with his country's traditional architecture from an early stage. He saw his work as a fusion of technology and humanity. The Tokyo Metropolitan Government Building, like all of his buildings, was characterized by clear structural order. The geometric granite pattern was apparently inspired by windows in traditional Japanese houses, while the façade is said to be reminiscent of a computer chip.

① **Main Building No. 1**
This building contains the offices of Tokyo's mayor
Height: 243m/797ft
Floors: 48 as well as three basement floors
Starting on the 33rd floor, the building splits into two towers. On the 45th floor, or at a height of 202m/663ft, are two viewing platforms, north and south, from where it is possible to see all the way to Mount Fuji on clear days. A lift can go all the way to the top in just 55 seconds.

② **Main Building No. 2**
The stepped, asymmetrical building with more offices is connected to Main Building No. 1 via Fureai Mall.
Height: 163m/535ft
Floors: 34 and three basement floors.

③ **Assembly Building**
This building houses the 127 members of the metropolitan government, who are elected for four years; it also accommodates their staff.
Height: 41m/135ft
Floors: seven as well as one basement floor

④ **Tomin Hiroba (Citizen's Plaza)**
Size: 5000 sq m/54,000 sq ft
It is said St Peter's Square in Rome was the inspiration for this plaza. It has a symmetrical arrangement, is surrounded by multi-storey porticoes and is set deeper than the surrounding buildings. The open space is used for events and has room for up to 6000 people.

⑤ **Safety**
Seismographs, antennae, wind gauges and a helipad are just a few of the safety features the building has at its disposal in the event of an emergency.

On Sundays pedestrians rule the roost on Ginza's intersections

North of Ginza District on Chuo-dori Road Western art and Japanese contemporary painting can be viewed in the Bridgestone Art Museum. Follow the road to get to Nihonbashi Bridge, built in 1603 and most recently renewed in 1911. It was once considered to be the heart of the city and reference point for all of the country's distance calculations. Today it is overbuilt by an urban expressway consisting of several lanes. On the other side of the bridge is the **traditional Mitsukoshi department store**, which started as a draper's shop in the 17th century.

Chuo-dori
◄ Bridgestone
Art Museum

Ochanomizu

Take the train or underground from the central station to Ochanomizu station in the northeast of the city.

North of the canal is Yushima Seido Hall, originally built in 1690 and consecrated to the Chinese philosopher Confucius. It was rebuilt several times after falling victim to fires. The current buildings date back to 1935. The hall contains a bronze statue of Confucius; the school previously affiliated to the shrine gave many a statesman a Confucian education. Further west is the Tokyo Medical University.

Yushima Seido

North of the hall is the Kanda-Myojin shrine (current buildings from 1934), where the lively Kanda-matsuri festival is held in mid-May.

Kanda-Myojin
shrine

Kanda
book district

The Surugadai district is located south of the canal on the hill of the same name. The orthodox St Nikolai Cathedral stands at its eastern end (1884; restored in 1929). Diagonally opposite is the famous Meiji University. 500m/550yd further south is the Yasukuni-dori intersection and 300m/330yd to the east near Jimbocho station is the Kanda book district, with countless secondhand book shops.

✳
Koishikawa
Korakuen

One stop further north (Suidobashi) is Koishikawa Korakuen Garden, which was created by Tokugawa Yorifusa in 1626. It is one of the city's most significant landscape gardens and also displays some Chinese influences in its design. There is a small temple on the pond island, which is consecrated to the goddess of luck, Benten. The bridge is also called »**full moon bridge**« because of its reflection, which completes its arch into a full circle.

Ueno

Take the train or underground northbound from the central city district of Chiyoda-ku to the district of Taito-ku (Ueno station and stop). Ueno station is the starting point for all the trains going to the northern part of Honshu.

! | *Baedeker* TIP

Multimedia in the evening
West of Akihabara station the huge electronics district lures buyers in with the newest entertainment electronics and camera products. The best time to visit is after sunset because of the bright, colourful neon advertisements. Everything about the local duty-free shops, opening times and how to get here can be found on the website www.akiba.or.jp/english.

Immediately to the west is the large Ueno Park (84ha/208 acres). The area originally belonged to a daimyo, but it was taken over by the shogunate in the 17th century and in 1878 it was opened up to the public.

The main entrance is located at the southeastern end of the park, near the station of the Keisei private line (towards Narita). A broad staircase

✳
Ueno Park

leads up to the cherry tree hill (Sakuragaoka), where a statue of Saigo Takamori (1827–77) and a monument to the Shogitai (supporters of the shogunate who fell in the restoration war) stand. The park's southern part is made up of the Shinobazu pond (circumference: 2km/1mi; boat rental); Benten temple stands on a headland protruding into it. The pond is known for its lotus blossom in August. Neighbouring the pond in the northwest is the aquarium (also amphibians and reptiles), from where a monorail goes to Japan's oldest

Toshogu shrine ▶

zoo. East of the stop is the Toshogu shrine, built in 1627 in memory of Tokugawa Ieyasu. The richly decorated buildings were renewed in 1651. The access route is lined by more than 250 stone lanterns that were donated by the daimyo. The Gongen-zukuri-style main shrine can be accessed via the Kara-mon gate; behind it is a five-storey pagoda and a bell-tower.

The **Shitamachi Museum** is located next to Shinobazu Pond in the southeast. It displays exhibition on life in the pre-war era. North of the zoo is the **city art museum** with changing exhibitions. Further along is the Horyuji treasury (Horyuji Homotsukan), which contains weapons, furniture and more; behind it is a pretty garden with three old pavilions. To the west, beyond the park's borders, is the Tokyo National University of Fine Arts and Music.

◄ Museums

The imposing building in the north of the park houses the national museum, the country's largest museum. It emerged from the imperial museum and displays changing exhibitions in 25 rooms, addressing the history and art history of the Far East (www.tnm.go.jp/en, open Tue–Sun 9.30am–5pm, April–Sept Sat and Sun until 6pm, ¥ 420)

✳
◄ National Museum

Turn southeast to get to the gallery for far-eastern art (Toyokan; cultural monuments from China and Korea) and further to the notable National Science Museum, which contains exhibits from the fields of

✳
◄ National Science Museum

A feast for the eyes – cherry blossom in Ueno Park

Ueno Park *Map*

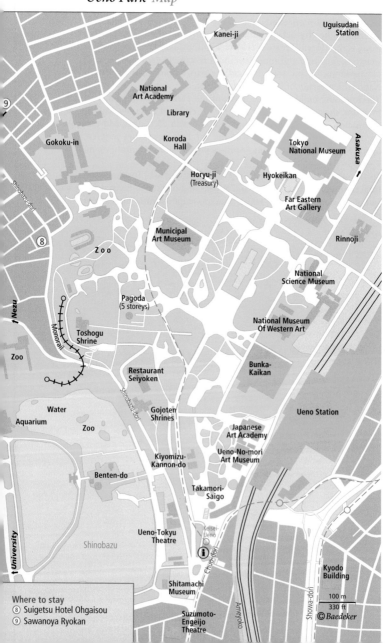

Kanei-ji

Uguisudani
Station

⑨

National
Art Academy

Library

Koroda
Hall

Gokoku-in

Tokyo
National Museum

Shinobazu-dori

Horyu-ji
(Treasury)

Hyokeikan

Asakusa

Far Eastern
Art Gallery

Municipal
Art Museum

Rinnoji

⑧

Z o o

National
Science Museum

Nezu

Pagoda
(5 storeys)

Monorail

Toshogu
Shrine

National Museum
Of Western Art

Zoo

Restaurant
Seiyoken

Shinobazu-dori

Bunka-
Kaikan

Water
Aquarium

Zoo

Gojoten
Shrines

Ueno Station

Japanese
Art Academy

Kiyomizu-
Kannon-do

Ueno-No-mori
Art Museum

Benten-do

Takamori-
Saigo

University

Shinobazu

Ueno-Tokyu
Theatre

Keisei-
Ueno

ℹ

Chuo-dori

Kyodo
Building

100 m

330 ft

Shitamachi
Museum

Ameyoko

Showa-dori

ⓒ *Baedeker*

Suzumoto-
Engeijo
Theatre

Where to stay
⑧ Suigetsu Hotel Ohgaisou
⑨ Sawanoya Ryokan

zoology, botany, geography, chemistry, astronomy, meteorology and oceanography (www.kahaku.go.jp, open Tue–Sun 9am–4.30pm, ¥ 420). In front of the museum is a statue of the Japanese bacteriologist Noguchi Hideyo (1876–1928).

The National Museum of Western Art (reinforced concrete building, designs by Le Corbusier, 1959) houses the collection of Western sculpture and painting created by the industrialist Matsukata Kojiro

> ! **Baedeker** TIP

Plastic fried eggs

Go east of Ueno station, 1km/1100yd along Asakusa-dori, to get to the street of household goods »Kappabashi« in Nishi-Asakusa. Among the popular souvenirs on sale here are deceptively real-looking fried eggs, sushi or tasty ice cream, all made of plastic of course. They are used as advertisements in restaurants (Tawaramachi underground station, Ginza line, exit no. 3).

as well as works by Cézanne, Degas, Monet, Rodin and others (www.nmwa.go.jp, open Tue–Sun 9.30am–5pm, Fri until 8pm, admission ¥ 420, 2nd and 4th Sat of the month free).

✳ ◄ National Museum of Western Art

Opposite to the south is the city's Bunka Kaikan hall (1961), where concerts and plays are put on and conferences are held. It is next to the Tokyo National Museum of Fine Arts and Music.

Past Kiyomizu temple the path leads back to the main entrance and to the south through Ameyoko, the shopping and entertainment district, which was the site of a black market after the war, to Yushima-Tenjin shrine, founded in the 14th century. It is surrounded by a small park with plum trees which blossom in February. Many students come here before the university's entry exam in February and March, to ask Tenjin, the god of scholarship, for success on votive tablets.

Yushima-Tenjin shrine

Continue further northwards (to the left is the campus of the famous University of Tokyo) to the **Nezu shrine** (also an underground from Yushima station), which is consecrated to four Shinto deities and the deified scholar Sugawara Michizane (845–903). It was allegedly founded around the time of Christ's birth; the current buildings date back to 1706. Several thousand azalea bushes come into bloom in the shrine grounds towards the end of April.

Votive tablets at Yushima-Tenjin shrine

Asakusa Map

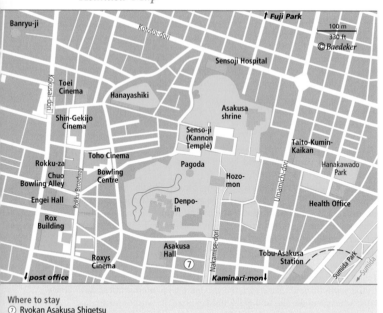

↑ Fuji Park

Banryu-ji

Kototoi-dori

100 m
330 ft
© Baedeker

Sensoji Hospital

Kokusai-dori

Toei
Cinema

Hanayashiki

Shin-Gekijo
Cinema

Asakusa
shrine

Senso-ji
(Kannon
Temple)

Taito-Kumin-
Kaikan

Toho Cinema

Pagoda

Rokku-za

Chuo
Bowling Alley

Bowling
Centre

Rokku Broadway

Hozo-
mon

Hanakawado
Park

Umamichi-dori

Engei Hall

Denpo-
in

Health Office

Rox
Building

Asakusa
Hall

Roxys
Cinema

⑦

Nakamise-dori

Tobu-Asakusa
Station

Sumida Park

Sumida

↓ post office

Kaminari-mon ↓

Where to stay
⑦ Ryokan Asakusa Shigetsu

Asakusa

East of Ueno is Asakusa, a centre of the Edokko, the natives of Tokyo. It is a much-visited entertainment district, as it has many cinemas, theatres and restaurants. 100 years ago the notorious Yoshiwara
red light district was here. The main attraction for tourists is Asakusa-Kannon temple. At the shore of Sumida River is the landing stage
of the boats going to Hama-rikyu Garden.

✹ ✹
Asakusa-
Kannon temple

East of Ueno station (underground to Asakusa station) is Asakusa-
Kannon temple (Sensoji temple) the centre of the Buddhist Sho-
Kannon sect. Nakamise Road lined by souvenir shops leads from the
Kaminari-mon gate with its red lanterns to the temple grounds. The
temple was allegedly founded by three fishermen, who found a Kannon statuette in their net. The large Kannon Hall of 1651 was rebuilt
in 1958 after suffering damage in the war; although now made of reinforced concrete it has been kept in the old style. The temple treasures are housed in Hozomon gate, which has also been restored. Behind the temple is Asakusa shrine, founded in the 17th century.

On the other side of Azumabashi Bridge the golden flame can be
seen over the **Asahi Brewery**, a building by Philippe Starck with a

restaurant serving Japanese and Western food as well as of course Asahi beer. This place is a welcome break on a tour of the city!

The underground (Toei-Asakusa line) leaves Asakusa station southbound. East of Asakusabashi station or north of Ryogoku station is **Kokugikan-Sumo Hall**, an important centre of Sumo wrestling (13,000 seats; martial arts events in January, May and September); a small Sumo Museum is attached. The multimedia shows and dioramas on the history of old Tokyo made the nearby **Edo Tokyo Museum** well worth a visit (open Tue–Sun 9.30am–5.30pm, Thu and Fri until 8pm, ¥ 600).

> ! **Baedeker** TIP
>
> **Cruise on Sumidagawa River**
>
> Why not enjoy a boat trip from Asakusa to Odaiba? The boats depart from Azumabashi Bridge (near Asakusa station) and dock at Hamarikyu Garden (approx. 30-minute trip). Those who feel like it can stay on to Hinode Pier and transfer there into a boat to Odaiba. This latter section has a good view of Rainbow Bridge. Reservations are not necessary. More information at www.suijobus.co.jp/english.

Meguro

Southwest of the centre is the quiet, friendly Meguro district. Near Meguro station is the National Park for Nature Study (Kokuritsu Shizen Kyoiku-en, 20ha/49 acres), boasting some impressive vegetation. **National park**

Southeast of the park (underground, Toei-Asakusa line) is Sengakuji temple (Sengakuji station). It is largely famous for being the place where the **47 Ronin**, who are still today revered as the epitome of extreme loyalty, were buried (►Famous People). The temple museum contains memorabilia and wooden likenesses of the Ronin. **Sengakuji temple**

South of the park (entrance in Meguro-dori), Teien Art Museum, housed in a building from 1933 with art deco elements, has changing exhibitions (www.teien-art-museum.ne.jp, open daily except 2nd and 4th Wed of the month, 10am–6pm, admission price depends on the exhibition). **Teien Art Museum**

Between the National Park and Ebisu station further to the north is the Ebisu Garden Place complex with inviting cafés and the interesting Tokyo Metropolitan Museum of Photography (Tokyo-to Shashin Bijutsu-kan, open Tue–Sun 10am–6pm, Thu, Fri until 8pm, admission price depends on the exhibition). **Tokyo Metropolitan Museum of Photography**

Southwest of the national park, on the other side of the canal, is Meguro-Fudo temple (Ryusenji), which belongs to the Tendai sect. After destruction in World War II the temple was rebuilt and is consecrated to the god of fire Fudo; the main hall's ceiling has a painting **Meguro-Fudo**

The tomb stones of the 47 Ronin in the courtyard of Sengakuji temple

of a dragon by Kawabata Ryushi (1885–1966). The **Fudo Falls** are located in the temple grounds. In the wintertime ascetic believers come here to bathe.

Odaiba

The district of Odaiba, opened in 1996, is located on an artificial island. To get to this part of Tokyo, take the automatically controlled Yurikamome train from Shimbashi, which makes its way on quiet rubber wheels over the boldly shaped **Rainbow Bridge** to Odaiba-Kaihinkoen station. The 2km/1mi bridge can also be crossed on foot by anyone willing to put up with the inevitable traffic noise. It is, however, definitely a worthwhile undertaking for photographers. A visit is also possible in an excursion boat from Asakusa or by ferry from Hinode station.

This new district has modern shopping facilities in Palette Town as well as an international exhibition centre (Tokyo Big Site), several theme parks and Joyopolis (a game centre) to offer.

Museum of Maritime Science

A 2km/1mi walk along the coast, past the beach and through Odaiba Park or the train to Fune-no-Kagakukan station both lead to the Museum of Maritime Science, built in the shape of a ship. The adjacent former ferry between Honshu and Hokkaido has been made into a sea pavilion and contains interesting subject matters from the sea in lifelike scenes all about Tsugaru Strait in the 1950s (open daily 10am–5pm, Sat, Sun and in summer until 6pm, ¥ 700).

Around Tokyo

Anyone who likes animated films should pay a visit to the new Ghibli Museum in Inokashira Park in the west of the city (JR Chuo line from Shinjuku to Mitaka). Visitors playfully learn about the film productions of this famous studio founded by Miyazaki Hayao, which produced the award-winning film *Spirited Away*. Reservations are necessary, as this museum is extremely popular (tel. 04 22/ 40 22 77, www.ghibli-museum.jp).

Ghibli Museum

Opening hours:
Daily except Tue
10am–6pm, ¥ 1000

Around 10km/6mi east of Tokyo (bus from the central station, Ueno station and Narita Airport) the huge Tokyo Disneyland amusement park, the first of its kind outside the United States, was opened in 1983 (www.tokyodisneyresort.co.jp). The park followed the time-tested pattern of a main road (World Bazaar, in the style of the late 19th century), from where visitors can access the various theme areas Adventureland (motifs from Africa, South America and Asia, steam engine and boat trips, pirate adventures), Fantasyland (Disney characters, dolls in costume, haunted house; alpine cableway with a good view of Tomorrowland), Westernland (paddle-steamer and native American canoes, Tom Sawyer island, Wild West show) and Tomorrowland (technology and science fiction, flight simulations; history of Japan).

Tokyo Disneyland

Foreign tourists usually only know about Narita as the site of Tokyo's international airport; a lesser known fact is that every year more than seven million believers go on a pilgrimage to Narita's Shinshoji temple. From the JR station go northbound through the lively Omotesando shopping quarter to Naritasan-Shinshoji temple, approx. 1km/0.6mi away. It was founded in 940. The 20ha/49-acre temple complex contains Niomon gate, the Hall of the Three Saints, Buddha Hall and main hall (hondo), which was built in 1963–1968 in the traditional style, as well as a belfry and a three-storey pagoda. The temple gets many visitors at New Year and for the Setsubun festival in early February.

Narita

◄ Shinshoji temple

The 16.5ha/41-acre Naritasan Park can be found next to the temple grounds; it is particularly attractive during the cherry and plum blossoms. The park is home to a historical museum with exhibits from the temple possessions and archaeological discoveries from the Boso Peninsula.

◄ Naritasan Park

Buses go from the JR station (20 minutes) to Sogo-Reido, the memorial for **Kiuchi Sogo** (also Sakura Sogo, 1612–53). Disregarding the prohibition against turning directly to the shogun, Sogo gave Tokugawa Ietsuan a petition from the farmers who were suffering from bad harvests and high taxes. Even though his mission was successful, he and his family of five were sentenced to death and executed. Scenes from Sogo's life are depicted in the Sogo Goichidai-Kinenkan Memorial Hall.

◄ Sogo-Reido

Makuhari Techno Garden in Chiba

South of the airport is **Shibayama**, an ancient place. A few old tombs have been uncovered here; the haniwa (terra cotta figures) found in them are now exhibited in the local museum.

Historical National Museum ▶ In Sakura, located to the southwest of Narita (train 15 minutes, then bus, 15 minutes) the Historical National Museum (Kokuritsu Rekishi Minzoku Hakubutsukan) built on the site that was once the location of Sakura Castle is well worth a visit.

Boso Peninsula The Boso Peninsula extends into the Pacific to the south of Narita, where it forms the eastern boundary of Tokyo Bay. As a result of the peninsula's extensive agricultural production it is also called **»Tokyo's Kitchen«**. The coasts in the southern part of the peninsula make up Minami-Boso Quasi-National Park.

Chiba ▶ A favourable starting point for a trip along the coast is Chiba, the prefectural capital, situated in the west of the peninsula on Tokyo Bay (from Narita JR Narita main line or Kashima main line, 30 minutes), from where the southbound JR Uchibo line follows the coast. Chiba has a castle built that was newly built some decades ago on old foundations (it houses the town's folkcraft museum). The Kasori Kaizuka museum with discoveries from the nearby prehistoric settlement site (bus connection from the station, 20 minutes) is also worth visiting.

Otsubo ▶ The 120m/394ft Otsubo Hill (near Sanukimachi station) has a 56m/184ft hollow Kannon statue that can be seen from within and a nice view of Tokyo Bay. There is also a bus connection from the station

Kano ▶ (30 minutes) to Mount Kano (352m/1155ft) with a 42m/138ft observation tower that has a lovely view of the bay, the Fuji-Hakone region and the mountains of Nikko; the Jin-yaji temple not far away, allegedly founded by Shotoku-taishi, was renewed in the 16th–18th centuries.

The lower terminus of a cableway up the 329m/1079ft **Mount Noko-giri** is located in Kanaya (also a ferry connection from Yokosuka, Miura Peninsula); there is an old temple close to the peak, as well as some rock caves and around 1300 Buddhist stone sculptures.

◄ Kanaya

Near Tateyama the Uchibo line reaches its southernmost point. There is a bus from the station (45 minutes) to Shirahama at the peninsula's southern tip; the nearby Cape Nojima commands an attractive view of the coastline.

◄ Tateyama

Take the JR Sotobo line to Awa-Amatsu to reach the 383m/1257ft **Mount Kiyosumi** (bus, 25 minutes) and the temple of the same name, which was presumably founded in 771. It was here that the sect founder Nichiren spent his novitiate. The main hall dates back to the late Edo period. The wonderful sea landscape Ubara Risokyo extends along the coast. The Katsu-ura Marine Park underwater observatory can also be found here. The Sotobo line goes on in a northeasterly direction and back to Chiba (1¼ hours).

◄ Awa-Amatsu

◄ Ubara Risokyo

Around 60km/35mi northeast of the Japanese capital at the foot of Mount Tsukuba (876m/2874ft) is Tsukuba Science City (Tsukuba Express from Akihabara, 45 minutes), the most modern and one of the largest science centres in the world.

Tsukuba Science City

The complex extends over approx. 2700ha/6700 acres. Since the 1970s a test-tube city with futuristic skyscrapers, a central axis area and spacious pedestrian zones designed by architect Maki Fumihiko has been developing on a green-field site. Today already around 40% of all national Japanese research institutes and two universities can be found here; residential areas, shopping centres, schools, leisure facilities and entertainment venues are also available. Part of the technological and scientific outfit of this »think tank« are extremely modern laboratories as well as a seven-storey reinforced concrete building with an earthquake simulator, a more than 6km/3.5mi-long road traffic test track as well as a 380m/416yd tunnel for experiments on noise reduction, ventilation and lighting and other environmental aspects.

It is 15 minutes by bus from Tsukuba station to Mount Tsukuba. Both the main peak, Nyotai (»female mountain«) and the secondary peak, Nantai (»male peak«, 870m/951ft) are home to shrines; Nantai also has a weather station and a rotating viewing platform (view over Kanto Plain and of Mount Fuji). **Cableways** go up to both peaks; climbing down on foot is somewhat laborious but worthwhile because of the mountain's bizarre rock formations.

◄ Tsukuba

North of Tsukuba station is Makabe on the Kanto line with Den-shoji temple founded in 1268 by the Makabe-born Zen master Hosshin after his return from China. Now the temple belongs to the Soto sect and contains statues of the famous 47 Ronin by Ako (► Famous People). The cherry blossom in the temple garden lasts until mid-April.

Makabe

Tottori

H 7 • g 2

Main island: Honshu   **Prefecture:** Tottori
Population: 200,000

Tottori, the capital of Tottori Prefecture, is situated on the coast of western Honshu. This provincial town is a good starting point for tourists visiting the nearby Coastal National Park.

What to See in Tottori

Kyushu Park   Remains of an 18th-century castle can be found in Kyushu Park, which is situated on an elevation 1.7km/1mi northeast of the station. Jimpukaku Villa, built in 1907, is nearby.

Kannon-in   A bit further in this direction are Kannon-in garden and Kannon-in temple as well as the neighbouring Ouchidani shrine built in 1650, which is dedicated to Tokugawa Ieyasu. Yamabiko Museum (addresses the town's history and culture) is of interest, as is the cemetery of the former Ideka ruling family (southwest of the station).

San-in-kaigan National Park

Extensive dune landscape   The Sendai River flows into the Sea of Japan north of the town. Its estuary is well-known for its extensive dune landscape (bus, 20 minutes, Sakyu Kaikan stop) on both sides of the river. Its eastern part belongs to Sai-in-kaigan National Park, which extends almost 80km/50mi to the east. Visitors can even hire camels here to ride through the dunes or simply take a picture with them. Some of the diverse landscape's main attractions are the Kasumi coast, Uradome beach and the seaside town of Kinosaki. The JR San-in main line departs from Tottori and makes its way along this protected stretch of coastline.

Bathing beaches   Some excellent bathing beaches can be found at Uradome, Tajiri and Ajiro; there are cliffs and islands with grottoes in front of the small bays.

Hamasaka-onsen   The spa Hamasaka-onsen is situated somewhat further inland, surrounded by mountains (bus from Hamasaka station, 25 minutes). During the summer the area is lovely for hiking; in the winter it is an excellent ski region.

Kasumi   The area around Kasumi is considered particularly attractive. 1.5km/1mi south of the station is Daijoji temple, which belongs to the Shin-gon sect (probably founded in the 8th century); it contains numerous works by the painter Maruyama Okyo (1753–95). Why not go on one of the lovely boat trips (March–November) that explore the coastline?

▶ VISITING TOTTORI

INFORMATION	GETTING THERE
Tourist information	*By air:* from Tokyo (Haneda Airport;
In the station	1¼ hours); from Osaka (45 minutes).
(only has material in Japanese)	*By rail:* from Okayama JR Imbi line
www.city.tottori.tottori.jp	(1¾ hours).
www.pref.tottori.jp/english (about the	
prefecture)	

Kinosaki-onsen, situated amidst hills, has a nice view of the park. **Kinosaki-onsen**
There is a cableway up Mount Daishi (excellent view of Maruyama
estuary), which departs near Onsenji temple.

★★ Towada-Hachimantai National Park

`L 5`

Main island: Honshu   **Prefecture:** Akita, Aomori and Iwate
Area: 854 sq km/330 sq mi

The landscape in the national
park in the far north of Honshu, 十和田八幡平国立公園
one of Japan's main islands, is still largely unspoilt; the landscape
is shaped by wonderful forests, clear lakes and volcanic cones.

Towada-Hachimantai National Park is divided into two distinct **Dimensions**
areas. The northern section includes the region surrounding Lake
Towada, the southern part Hachimantai Plateau with Mounts Iwate,
Nyuto and Koma-gatake.

What to See in Towada-Hachimantai National Park

The Hakkoda Mountains are situated to the south of the coastal **Hakkoda**
town of ▶Aomori. A bus route makes its way through this landscape **Mountains**
(3½ hours) to Sukayu-onsen and Tsuta-onsen.
The Hakkoda Mountains can be reached on foot from Sukayu-on- **★**
sen. They consist of eight extinct volcanoes, the highest being Mount **◀ Odake**
Odake (also Sukayu; 1585m/1733ft). The autumn colours of the
dense forests give the area a particular appeal. The view from the top
reaches all the way to the Sea of Japan and the Pacific. The mountains are also developing a good reputation among snowboarders
and skiers.

Oirase Valley   The bus route then continues through the picturesque Oirase Valley, which flows between rocks covered in vegetation. The 14km/9mi section between Yakeyama and the town of Nenokushi on the eastern shore of Lake Towada is particularly attractive.

★ ★
Lake Towada   The 334m/1096ft-deep Towada-ko crater lake (area: 59 sq km/23 sq mi), situated in the middle of old forests, is surrounded by a road that goes all the way around it. Two **peninsulas** extend into the lake on its southern side, which separate the three basins Higashi-no-umi (»eastern lake«), Naka-no-umi (»middle lake«) and Nishi-no-umi (»western lake«).

Lake Towada *Map*

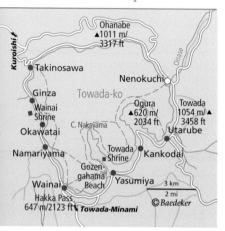

The Oirase River flows into the sea near Nenokuchi. It takes 20 minutes by bus to get to the 1054m/3458ft **Mount Towada** for a magnificent view of the lake; the descent route goes to Utarube at the Higashi-no-umi. A detour to the headland and Mount Ogura (620m/2034ft; view) is worthwhile.

The coastal road then makes its way to the lake district's main town, **Yasumiya** (there is also a boat from Nenokuchi, 1½ hours). Here visitors can find a bronze sculpture by the sculptor Takamura Kotaro (1883–1958); the **Towada Museum** (Towada Kagaku Hakubutsukan), displaying geological information about the lake, is also worth visiting. The town has a **bicycle rental**. Set aside 6–8 hours for a bicycle tour around the lake. Past Gozengahama beach to the northwest is Towada shrine, situated on the peninsula.

Wainai   The lake road then goes along Nishi-no-umi to the small town of Wainai (also called Oide), which is known for its farmed trout. Here the road branches off to Hakka Pass (647m/2123ft) to the south, which has some lovely views.

Southern area   The national park's southern area is accessible via Hachimantai or Morioka. Its volcanic mountains and the far-flung recreational towns are very popular amongst mountaineers and winter sports enthusiasts. The many hot springs have favoured the development of onsen.

Hachimantai Plateau   A road (the central section is the toll road Hachimantai-Aspite; bus) goes from Hachimantai (JR Hanawa line) through Hachimantain

Plateau, which makes up the region's northern section, to Koma, on the JR Tohoku main line. Near the line are the spas of Tamagawa-on-sen (hot springs, 98°C/208°F), Goshogake-onsen (steam baths) and Fukenoyu-onsen, the 1366m/4482ft Yakeyama volcano towering above them.

Take the JR Tohoku main line from Morioka, to the east outside of the park, to Takizawa and from here the bus (40 minutes) to Yanagi-sawa at the eastern foot of the dormant Iwate volcano (2038m/6686ft). It is well worthwhile climbing this mountain range, which is divided into the Higashi-Iwate (eastern section) and Nish-Iwate (western section), to see the diverse mountain flora and the good view from the peak. One descent route goes via the southwest side to Amihari-onsen. **Iwate**

 ## VISITING TOWADA-HACHIMANTAI N.P.

INFORMATION

Lake Towada
Visitor Center in Yasumiya
Tel. 01 76/75 29 24
Daily 8.30am–5pm,
Dec–March 9am–4pm

Hachimantai
Tourist information centres in Kazuno
Kazuno Kanko Furusatokan Antler
Tel. 01 86/22 05 55
Daily 9am–5.30pm,
Dec–March until 3.30pm

GETTING THERE

By rail: to Lake Towada: from Tokyo JR Tohoku shinkansen to Hachinohe (3 hours), then onwards by bus (2¼ hours).
To Lake Tazawa and to Hachimantai: Akita shinkansen to Tazawako (3 hours), then bus. Hachimantai: Akita shinkansen to Tazawako.
By bus: several lines, including from Aomori, Towada-Minami, Hachi-mantai, Misawa and Odate into the national park's two areas.
By ferry: boat connection between

Yasumiya and Nenokuchi (1 hour). Cruises from Yasumiya.

WHERE TO STAY

► **Mid-range**
Towada Hotel
Towadako Nishikohan, Kosaka-cho, 018-5511 Akita-ken
Tel. 01 76/75 11 22, fax 75 13 13
Nice hotel from the 1930s with a view of the lake. Japanese and Western-style rooms.

Landscape in Oirase Valley

Koma

The JR Tazawako line and the Akita shinkansen line departing Morioka westbound go past the nearby Lake Tazawa. There is a bus from Tazawako station (July–October) to the 8th station of the ascent route up the 1637m/5371ft) Komagatake volcano. From here the peak can be reached in an hour. From the top there is a lovely view

✴
Lake Tazawa ▶

of Lake Tazawa, situated outside the national park; it is one of the country's deepest lakes (▶Morioka, around).

Tsuruga

J 7 • j 2

Main island: Honshu   **Prefecture:** Fukui
Population: 65,000

敦賀

The port of Tsuruga in the west of central Honshu, north of Lake Biwa, is situated by Tsuruga Bay, which penetrates deep inland. This favourable situation made it an important gateway to Korea from a very early date.

What to See in Tsuruga

Kanagasakigu shrine

Not far north of the station, between several thousand cherry trees, is Kanagasakigu shrine, dedicated to two sons of Emperor Godaigo.

Kehi shrine

1.5km/1mi further north is the Kehi shrine. The wood used to make the torii's columns was allegedly washed here from Sado Island in the 17th century

Jogu shrine

Jogu shrine, 9km/6mi northwest of the station, has an old bell, said to have been brought back by Hideyoshi from his military campaign to Korea. The Omi-ishi stone is known for the fact that it produces sounds when touched.

Matsubara Park

Along the coastline of Tsuruga Bay, 6km/3.5mi to the west, is Matsubara Park with its pine tree grove. It contains the burial site of Takeda Kounsai (1803–65), who was executed here together with his supporters because of his resistance to the Tokugawa family's policy towards opening Japan up to other countries.

Wakasawan Quasi-National Park

Mikata

To the west of the town, beyond a headland at the end of Tsuruga Bay, is Wakasawan Quasi-National Park. The JR Obama line goes into this area and then arrives at the town of Mitkata after 25km/16mi. Between the town and the coast are the five Mikata Lakes (Mikata-goko), connected with each other via waterfalls. An attractive road

► VISITING TSURUGA

GETTING THERE

By rail: from Tokyo (central station) JR Tokaido shinkansen line to Maibara (2½ hours), then JR Hokuriku main line (30 minutes); from Osaka JR Kosei and Hokuriku line (1¾ hours).

EVENTS

Ebisu-daikoku Tsunahiki (fair; mid-January); Sounomairi (procession; mid-July), at Kehi shrine; Kehi-no-Nagamatsuri (procession; beginning of September), at Kehi shrine.

goes up the 395m/1296ft Mount Baijo (bus, 35 minutes); the Uwase shrine with a good view of the lakes stands on its peak.

The main town at Wakasa Bay is Obama (population 34,000), where the famous Wakasa-nuri lacquerwares are produced. There are several temples worth visiting, including Jingu-ji, Myotsu-ji with its three-storey pagoda, Minatoku-ji with a nice garden, Myoraku-ji, which has a statue of the thousand-handed Kannon, and Renge-ji, with a bronze standing statue of Yakushi-nyorai.   **Obama**

Excursion boats run to the picturesque Sotomo coast with its rocks, grottoes and waterfalls. At the western end of Wakasa Bay is the scenically impressive coastal landscape of ►Ama-no-hashidate.   ◄ Sotomo Coast

Tsuwano

F 7 • d 3

Main island: Honshu   **Prefecture:** Shimane
Population: 8000

In western Honshu, around 60km/35mi northeast of Yamaguchi, is the idyllic former castle town of Tsuwano. A fair number of old buildings, including samurai houses, are still extant.   津和野

What to See in Tsuwano

The old samurai houses bordered by canals can be found in the centre (Tonomachi).   **Samurai houses**

Behind the station the Maria Memorial Church stands on Otome-toge Pass surrounded by cherry trees. It was built in memory of the 153 martyrs who were banished from Nagasaki to Tsuwano, where some of them were tortured and killed. Every year the establishment of the church and the martyrdom of the Christians is celebrated on May 3 with a procession and a mass.   **Maria Memorial Church**

▶ **TSUWANO**

GETTING THERE
By rail: from Yamaguchi
JR Yamaguchi line (1¼ hours).

Yomeiji temple near the station contains the tomb of the novelist and physician Mori Ogai (▶ Famous People) and the mausoleum of the Kamei family.

South of the station the **History Museum** (Yoro-kan), housed in the building of the former princely college, has a collection of weapons, amongst other things. Next door is the **Folk Art Museum** (Kyodo-kan) with exhibits relating to local history and objects which belonged to aristocratic families. Opposite the station in the **Tsuwano Industrial Museum** traditional paper production and brewing techniques are explained.

Inari shrine

West of town is Mount Shiroyama, crowned by the majestic Inari shrine; there are some good views from the top of the hill. A cableway goes up to the ruins of a castle located in a park.

Unzen-Amakusa National Park

F 8 • c 5

Main island: Kyushu
Area: 282 sq km/109 sq mi

Prefectures: Nagasaki, Kumamoto and Kagoshima

雲仙天草国立公園

The main attraction of the national park in the far west of Kyushu are the Unzen Mountains, where visitors can go for a walk between foul-smelling »hells«. This area is particularly popular with tourists in the springtime during the azalea blossom and in the autumn, when the leaves change colours.

Unzen-Amakusa National Park covers the centre of Shimabara Peninsula and the Amakusa Island group off the coast of Kumamoto. The area is framed by Ariake Sea, Chijiwa Bay and Yatsushiro Bay.

What to See in Unzen-Amakusa National Park

Unzen Mountains

The Unzen Mountains form the centre of Shimabara Peninsula. The volcanic origin of the massif can still be seen in the geysers, fumaroles and bubbling mud pits.

Unzen-onsen

There is a road from Obama on the peninsula's west coast to the Unzen Mountains and further to Shimabara. The much-frequented spa Unzen-onsen (altitude: 727m/2385ft; hot springs up to 95°C/203°F)

The five bridges of Amakusa from the bird's eye view ➔

is situated at the southern foot of Mount Myoken. Near the town visitors can see the Unzen-jigoku fumaroles; 1km/0.6mi to the northeast is Japan's oldest golf course.

✳
Myoken
✳
Fugen ►

A bus (30 minutes) goes to the 1100m/3609ft Nita Pass, where a cableway ascends the 1334m/4377ft Mount Myoken. A footpath (1 hour) connects Mount Myoken to the 1360m/4462ft Mount Fugen, site of the Fugen shrine. 43 people died when this volcano erupted in 1991. There are some wonderful views of Ariaka Sea (north), Mount Aso (east), the Kirishima Mountains (southeast) and the Amakusa Islands (south) from the two summits.

Shimabara

The old castle town of Shimabara (population 46,000) is situated at the centre of the east coast. The castle of 1615, 400m/450yd west of the station, was reconstructed in 1964 and houses a museum on the history of Christianity in Japan. Behind the castle is Seibo Museum, exhibiting works by the artist Kitamura Seibo, whose works also include the statue in Nagasaki's Peace Park. Further west is an old street lined by **samurai houses**. A little way offshore are the Tsukumojima Islands that were formed in 1792 when the volcano Mount Mayuyama (west of the town) erupted.

Harajo

The southbound Shimabara private rail line continues along the coast and reaches Harajo station after 28km/17mi. 500m/550yd to the east are the ruins of Hara Castle, where the Christians made their last stand against the troops of the Tokugawa shogunate in 1637. The siege ended in the death of almost 20,000 Christians.

Amakusa Islands

Shimoshima ►

Hondo ►

The Amakusa Islands are located south of Shimabara Peninsula, on the other side of Hayasaki Strait. A lovely route goes from Misumi (Kyuhsu) across the five bridges Amakusa Gokyo, which form a road connection from the eastern island of Oyanoshima via Kamishima to the western island of Shimoshima. About 120 smaller islands are dotted around the sea in this area.

The town of Hondo on Shimoshima's east coast is the administrative centre of the Amakusa Islands. Where the castle once stood there is now Sennin-Zuka Park (Christian Memorial Park) with a cenotaph for the victims of the uprising of 1637 and a museum. The statue of

 VISITING UNZEN-AMAKUSA NATIONAL PARK

GETTING THERE

By rail: from Nagasaki JR Nagasaki main line to Isahaya (25 minutes), then Shimabara private train line via Shimabara and at the peninsula's east coast to Kazusa (2¼ hours).

By bus: from Isahaya via Obama to Unzen; from Kumamoto to Hondo (Amakusa; 2½ hours).
By ferry: from Misumi (Uto Peninsula) to Shimabara (1 hour).

Kannon with the baby Jesus (the Kannon, generally depicted as female, was worshipped in place of the Madonna) is quite well-known. Further attractions in the area are Meitokuji temple, Gionbashi Bridge and the aquarium.

There is a road connection from Hondo via Oniike harbour in the northeast of the island to Tomioka, situated close to some picturesque stretches of coastline, and further to the seaside resort of Shimoda (several hot springs).

◄ Tomioka
Shimoda

Uwajima

G 8 • e 4

Main island: Shikoku　　　　**Prefecture:** Ehime
Population: 75,000

The port of Uwajima on Shikoku's west coast is situated along an exceptionally attractive, diverse coastal landscape. The mild climate promotes the growth of citrus fruits and other demanding crops. The sea provides rich fish stocks and good conditions for cultivating pearls.

宇和島

What to See in Uwajima

700m/765yd southwest of the station (bus, 5 minutes) visitors will find the main tower of the former castle, situated on an 80m/262ft hill. The town is known for its Taga Jinja, which houses a huge wooden phallus.

Castle

The pretty landscape garden Tensha-en 2km/1mi southwest of the station was created for the summer residence of the Date family in the 19th century. The **Date Museum** (Date-hakubutsukan) can be found in the nearby Gotenmachi; it has weapons, picture scrolls and more on display from the possessions of the Date family.

Tensha-en

Around 2km/1mi southeast of the station is Uwatsushiko shrine (annual festival takes place at the end of October); beyond it, on a hill, **Atago Park** has a view of the town and the surrounding area.

Around Uwajima

Around 30km/20mi to the north (bus, 1 hour) is the harbour town of **Yawatahama** (population 41,000), from where ferries depart

> **!** *Baedeker* TIP
>
> **Bull Sumo**
>
> The bull-fighting stadium 1km/0.6mi north of the Uwajima station stages the bull-fights known as »Togyu« (animal against animal) four times a year; the rules are similar to those of Sumo wrestling. This tradition goes back to the second half of the 17th century. At the time Uwajima was given two bulls as a present in return for saving a Dutch vessel.

▶ UWAJIMA

GETTING THERE

By rail: from Matsuyama JR Yosan line (1¾ hours).

EVENTS

Uwajima Festival (with a firework display and a procession; 23/24 July), at Warei shrine; Yatsushida-dori (procession with large animal figures; end of October), at Uwatsushiko shrine; bull fighting (January, April, July, August, October, November).

to Kyushu's east coast (Beppu and Usuki harbour). The cultivation of **mandarin oranges** on the terraced fields is a typical feature of the surrounding area.

6km/3.5mi further north the 820m/2690ft **Kinzan** rises; Kinzan-Shussekiji temple is to be found near the peak (great views).

Further west the 52km/32mi narrow Sadamisaki Peninsula extends into the sea, thus separating the Inland Sea from Bungo Canal. Between Cape Sada (ferry connection from Yawatahama, 1½ hours) and Cape Jizo (opposite) (Kyushu) is Hoyo Strait just 15km/9mi wide. The peninsula's coast, which is dotted with many bays, has lovely views of the Inland Sea and its many islands.

Ozu   15km/9mi northeast of Yawatahama is the old castle town of Ozu (population 39,000); the remains of the castle can be found 1.5km/1mi southwest of the station. Why not take a look at the evening fishing expeditions with the trained cormorants on Hiji River (June–September).

Wakayama

H 7 • h 3

Main island: Honshu	**Prefecture:** Wakayama
Population: 375,000	

和歌山   **The old castle town on Kii Peninsula's west coast, opposite Shikoku, was a gateway to the country's interior from very early on. The nearby coastal area of Wakanoura is a popular travel destination.**

What to See in and around Wakayama

Castle   At the centre of town is the castle built by Toyotomi Hideyoshi in 1585. It is surrounded by a park. The three-storey main tower was rebuilt after having been destroyed in the war. On its northern side is the **Momiji-dani Teien garden**, one of the few dating from the Edo period still extant. The **Bandokoro Teien garden** on Cape Saikazaki to the south has a splendid view over the sea.

Not far to the south is the well-known seaside resort of Wakanoura (bus, 25 minutes) with its attractive coastal landscape and good view of Awaji Island. Not far away is Kimiidera temple, founded by the Chinese priest Iko in 770. It is the centre of the Guse-Kannon sect and one of the temples of pilgrimage in the western provinces. The main gate is particularly worth seeing, as are the bell-tower, the pagoda, a wooden statue of the eleven-headed Kannon and further sculptures.

★
Wakanoura

◄ Kimiidera
temple

There are some more noteworthy temples to the north/northeast of Wakayama. They can be reached on the JR Hanwa line. 8km/5mi east of Kii station is Negoroji temple, which belongs to the Shingi-Shingon sect (founded 1126). The reliquary casket (tahoto) was renewed in 1515; the hall (daishido, built in 1391) houses a portrait of the temple's founder Kakuban (also Kokyo-daishi). Attractive cherry blossom (beginning of April).

Negoroji temple

WAKAYAMA

INFORMATION
www.city.wakayama.wakayama.jp/english (about the town)
www.pref.wakayama.lg.jp/english (about the prefecture)

GETTING THERE
By rail: from Osaka (Tennoji station) JR Hanwa line (45 minutes); from Namba station Nankai private line to Wakayama-shi (1 hour).

The next stop along the train line is Izumi-Hashimoto. Not far away are **Mizuma-Kannon temple** of the Tendai sect (4km/2.5mi) and **Ko-onji temple** (also Kozumi-Kannon; 4.8km/3mi), in whose hall there are numerous Buddhist sculptures.

14km/9mi to the south is Mount **Ushitaki**, covered in maple forests that are particularly attractive in the autumn when the leaves change colour; here are also numerous waterfalls.

Yaba-Hita-Hikosan Quasi National Park

F 8 • c–d 4

Main island: Kyushu
Area: 852 sq km/329 sq mi

Prefectures: Fukuoka and Oita

Yaba-Hita-Hikosan Quasi-National Park is situated in the northeast of the Japanese main island of Kyushu. High mountain ranges, waterfalls, deep gorges and dense forests characterize the landscape.

耶馬日田彦山国定公園

What to See in Yaba-Hita-Hikosan National Park

Hikosan shrine
At the border between the prefectures of Fukuoka and Oita is the 1200m/3937ft Mount Hikosan (bus from Hikosan station, 20 minutes). Hikosan shrine stands at the top of one of the five peaks; the bus goes all the way to the torii at the edge of the large complex. The shrine, situated in a thick cedar forest, was founded by the priest Enno-Ozuno in the 7th century. It was the first Shinto centre on Kyushu and grew to become greatly significant as the base of the ascetic Shugendo sect, when Buddhism and Shinto were consolidated. In the late 16th century several thousand monks are said to have lived here; the abbots quite often came from the imperial family. The renaissance of pure Shinto in the Meiji era caused the shrine to lose its influence, but it is still a classic example of the mountain shrines of the Shugendo sect.

> ## ! *Baedeker* TIP
>
> **Trip to Onda**
> There is a bus (1 hour) from Hita to the pottery town of Onda, situated in a romantic landscape near the prefectural border. The town mainly produces rough household pottery (pottery market beginning of October). Visitors wanting to visit the pottery museum (Togei-kan) should sign up in one of the pottery workshops.

Hita
On the southwest border of the national park, in the Hita Basin, is the town of Hita (population 85,000), a popular summer holiday destination, home to many wood processing companies. Using trained cormorants, the town's inhabitants fish on the Mikuma River, which flows through the town, from May to October.

Koishiwara
Koishiwara is located 25km/16mi from Onda (also a bus from Fukuoka, 2½ hours; change in Haki), which also has numerous pottery workshops (market in April–May and the beginning of October).

Tsuetate-onsen
The spa Tsuetate-onsen is located south of Hita (bus, 1 hour) is situated in the picturesque valley of Tsuetate River. It has several hot springs of up to 98°C/208°F. There is a road from here to Uchinomaki in ►Aso National Park.

Yamakuni
Go northeast from Hita through a particularly attractive part of the national park (bus). At Yamakuni the road meets the Yamakuni River and follows its course downstream. The Yamautsuri River (from the southeast) flows into the Yamakuni River at Kakizaka.

 VISITING YABA-HITA-HIKOSAN QUASI-N.P.

GETTING THERE

By rail: from Kitakyushu (Kokura station) Hita-Hikosan line to Hikosan station (1½ hours); from Fukuoka (Hakata station) JR Kyudai main line to Hita (1¼ hours).
By bus: from Nakatsu to Shin-Yabakei (1¼ hours).

Yamautsuri River flows through Shin-Yabakei Gorge, into which a road branches off here. The gorge's most attractive part begins at Fumonjibashi (8km/5mi). Hitome-Hakkei has a particularly impressive viewpoint; 3km/2mi further the road reaches Utsukushidani, which is particularly attractive in the autumn when the leaves change colours.

Shin-Yabakei Gorge

Leaving Kakizaka the main road follows Yabakei-kyo Gorge in a northeasterly direction, passing impressive steep cliffs, side gorges and lavish vegetation. The road goes through Ao-no-Domon Tunnel, said to have been completed by the priest Zenkai in 1764 after **having worked on it for 30 years**.

✷ Yabakei-kyo

Yamagata

L 5

Main island: Honshu

Prefecture: Yamagata

Population: 252,000

Yamagata, the capital of Yamagata Prefecture, is situated in north-eastern Honshu and is one of Japan's best-known winter sports regions. The most important ski area is to the southwest on Mount Zao.

山形

What to See in Yamagata

Kajo Park (north of the station, 10 minutes on foot) contains the remains of the castle built by Shiba Kaneyori in the 14th century as well as the prefectural museum (Yamagata-kenritsu hakubutsukan).

Kajo Park

A bus (10 minutes) goes to Senshoji temple of the Jodo sect; the tomb of Komahime, one of Toyotomi Hidetsugu's concubines, can be found here. She was sentenced to death for high treason.

Senshoji temple

One of Tohoku region's most beautiful gardens is the one near Kozenji temple.

Kozenji temple

2km/1mi northeast of the station is Chitose Park; it is home to Yakushido temple (8th century). There is a nice view of the town and Yamagata Plain from the top of the densely forested Chitose Hill (4km/2.5mi east of the station). At its foot stands Banshoji temple, which presumably dates back to the 7th or 8th century.

✷ Chitose Park

Zao Quasi-National Park

To the east outside the town the Zao Quasi-National Park covers an area of 400 sq km/154 sq mi. The volcanic Zao mountain range has the following peaks: Kumano (1841m/6040ft), Goshiki (1674m/5492ft) and Katta (1759m/5771ft); it is the region's most significant winter sports resort (buses from Yamagata, approx. 1 hour). The heavily snowed-in trees are known as the »snow monsters of Zao«.

Zao-Echo line (closed Nov–April) ▶ The 26km/16mi »Zao-Echo line« toll road crosses the region from Kaminoyama (south of Yamagata; train connection) over Mount Kattadake to Togatta-onsen in Miyagi Prefecture (between Katta and Togatta there is a bus connection). There is a cableway from Katta-dake bus stop up to the top of the mountain. There is a nice walk from the peak to the cobalt-blue Okama crater lake.

Zao-onsen The largest recreational area in the Zao mountains is Zao-onsen (bus from Yamagata, 45 minutes), a place also valued for its hot springs. There are several cableways and many ski lifts nearby.

Jizosan The peak of the 1735m/5692ft Mount Jizosan can be reached by cableway (Zao Ropeway from Zao Onsen) and a short walk. Between Mount Jizosan and the 1703m/5587ft Mount Sanpokojinyama is the

 VISITING YAMAGATA

INFORMATION

Tourist information
In Kajo Central Complex, near the station's west exit
Tel. 0 23/6 47 23 33
Daily 10am–6pm
At the airport (Higashine)
Tel. 02 37/47 31 11
Daily 8.30am–7pm
www.yamagatakanko.com/english

GETTING THERE

By air: from Tokyo (Haneda Airport; 1 hour); from Osaka (Itami Airport, 1¼ hours).
By rail: from Tokyo JR Yamagata shinkansen (2½ hours); from Sendai JR Senzan line (1¼ hours).

EVENT

Hanagasa-matsuri (dance through the streets; beginning of August).

SHOPPING

The region's main products are items made of cast iron (such as teapots) and wooden dolls (kokeshi).

WHERE TO STAY

▶ Luxury
Meigetsuso
5-50 Hayama, Kaminoyama, Yamagata-ken 999-3242
Tel. 0 23/6 72 03 30, fax 6 72 69 05
www.meigetsuso.co.jp
15 minutes by train from Yamagata to Kaminoyama Onsen.
Interesting ryokan, a mixture of Japanese and Western stylistic elements. The best time to stay here is during a full moon (Japanese *meigetsu*, hence the name) in order to experience the »moonshine concert«. Has a wine and sake cellar.

▶ Mid-range
Uta-no-Yado Wakamatsuya
In Zao Onsen
951-1 Zao Onsen, Yamagata-shi, Yamagata-ken 990-2301
Tel. 0 23/6 94 95 25, fax 6 94 95 16
27 large Japanese-style rooms. Pleasant communal baths (also rotemburo). 5 minutes to the ski lift.

landscape garden Zao Shinzen Shokubutsen-en (bloom June–Sept); also a statue of Jizo (patron god of travellers), set up in 1775 to **protect mountain climbers**.

Kaminoyama-onsen, one of the three nicest spas in Tohoku District can be reached from Yamagata on the southbound JR Ou main line (20 minutes). The **Kaisendo Museum** near the station exhibits weapons and lacquerware and is worth a visit. Tsukioka Park, home to a castle ruin, is known for its cherry blossom.

Kaminoyama-onsen

The JR Ou main line goes on to Yonezawa (population 93,000), a town known for its textile production. There is a bus from the station to Matsugasaki Park, where the castle of the powerful Uesugi clan was once located. Today visitors can admire Uesugi shrine here, which was founded by Uesugi Harunori (1756–1822), who established the town's **silk manufacture**. The tomb of the Uesugi can also be reached by bus (15 minutes).

Yonezawa

North of Yamagata (train, 25 minutes; bus, 40 minutes) is Yamadera, home to Yamadera temple (also Risshakuji temple), the largest temple of the Tendai sect in northern Japan. The temple, presumably founded by the priest Ennin in 860, is scattered over a mountainside. A stairway with 1000 steps leads up to Okunoin, the main temple at the summit. There are many grottoes in the mountain's tuff stone and it is said the temple's founder died in one of them.

Yamadera

14km/9mi north of Yamagata is the town of Tendo (population 55,000; JR Ou main line, 25 minutes), once the castle town of the Tendo family and later the residence of Oda Nobunaga's descendants. Maizuru Park contains the castle ruins and Kenkun shrine, dedicated to Oda Nobunaga. Tendo is known for producing the Japanese board game shogi. The nearby Tendo-onsen with a folk art museum (Tendo-mingeikan) is worth a visit.

Tendo

Yamaguchi

F 7 • d 3

Main island: Honshu   **Prefecture:** Yamaguchi
Population: 135,000

Only a few buildings still attest to the former splendour of Yamaguchi, the capital of Honshu's westernmost prefecture. However, this one-time »Kyoto of the west« has one of the country's most beautiful pagodas.

From the 14th century this town, under the patronage of the Ouchi family, produced a wealth of artworks, a development that was fur-

Kyoto of the West

ther favoured during the Onin War (1467–77) when many artists moved here, including the painter Sesshu (1420–1506).

What to See in Yamaguchi

Kameyama Park is situated on a hill 1.5km/1mi northwest of the station. It has plenty of lovely views and is itself particularly attractive when the azalea bushes and cherry trees are in bloom and when the leaves take on their autumn colours. The park contains bronze statues of members of the Mori family, who rendered outstanding services to the Meiji reforms.

YAMAGUCHI

INFORMATION
Tourist information
In Shin-Yamaguchi station
Tel. 0 83/9 72 63 73
April–Nov daily 9am–6pm,
Dec–March 8.30am–5.30pm

GETTING THERE
By air: from Tokyo (Haneda Airport) to Ube (1½ hours).
By rail: from Tokyo (central station) JR Sanyo shinkansen line to Shin-Yamaguchi (4¾ hours), then JR Yamaguchi line (30 minutes) to Yamaguchi station.

Daidoji temple is situated 2.5km/1.5mi northeast of the station. It was once the place Francisco de Javier (Francis Xavier) performed his missionary work and houses a 6m/20ft granite cross as well a bust of the missionary (1926). Xavier Memorial Church (1.5km/1mi northwest of the station) also commemorates his stay in Yamaguchi in 1551. The church was rebuilt in 1991 after the original building burned down in 1952.

Daidoji temple

3km/2mi north of the station is Rurikoji temple with its famous five-storey pagoda of 1442. Even further north is the Zen Joeiji temple, with a garden landscaped by the artist Sesshu.

★★
Rurikoji temple

Around Yamaguchi

South of the town (bus, 12 minutes) is the well-known spa of Yuda-on-sen (hot springs, 30–70°C/86–158°F), situated in a picturesque setting.

Yuda-onsen

Kumano Park, located in the north of the town, is particularly worth a visit during the springtime cherry blossom and in the autumn when the leaves change colours; the town festival takes place at the beginning of April.

Kumano Park

North of Yamaguchi the Abu River flows through Chomonkyo Gorge (around 20km/12mi from the town). Between Chomonkyo station and the town of Uzugahara waterfalls, grottoes and thick woods create a romantic scenery.

Chomonkyo Gorge

← *Rurikoji temple is hidden amongst a lot of green*

Yokohama

横浜

Main island: Honshu   **Prefecture:** Kanagawa
Population: 3.59 million

Yokohama is not just Japan's second-largest city, it is the country's most important port. Since this city was one of the first to open up to the West at the end of the Meiji era, many foreigners naturally settled here, hence its international atmosphere.

Important commercial and industrial city

Yokohama is situated in eastern central Honshu, not far south of Tokyo, together with which it makes up the industrial conurbation of Keihin (Tokyo-Kawasaki-Yokohama). Yokohama is the capital of Kanagawa Prefecture and the most important gateway into Japan for those travelling by ship. The city's main industry includes shipyards, machine and automobile construction, petrochemicals and more. Yokohama is still relatively young. When Commodore Perry's Black

The old harbour district was transformed into the »Minato Mirai 21« skyscraper and entertainment mile

Ships entered Tokyo Bay and he managed to force through Japan's opening to the West in the Convention of Kanagawa (1854), the small fishing village developed in next to no time into a lively port and centre of commerce. In 1859 the first foreigners settled here, including the first United States consul-general in Japan, Townsend Harris. By 1889 Yokohama's population had grown to more than 120,000. Large parts of the city were destroyed in the disastrous earthquake of 1923 and during World War II.

What to See in Yokohama

Southeast of the central station, close to the city centre, is Sakuragi-cho station, from where all of the city's most important attractions can be reached. It was from here that Japan's first train line ran for 29km/18mi to Shimbashi in Tokyo.

To the northwest of Sakuragicho station (10 minutes on foot) is the **Iseyama shrine** Iseyama shrine (1870), which belongs to the group of Ise shrines and is consecrated to the patron god of the city. It has a 10m/33ft torii made of cypress wood. Just north of the shrine is **Kamon-yama Park** known for its cherry blossom (mid-April).

Southwest of Iseyama shrine (approx. 7 minutes on foot) is Nogeya-ma Park with a zoo and a swimming pool. It is situated on a hillside. **Nogeyama Park**

To the southeast is Isezaki-cho shopping street, which leads into the centre of Naka-ku.

From Sakuragicho station's east exit a pedestrian conveyor belt takes visitors to Landmark Tower, currently Japan's highest skyscraper at 296m/971ft. A ride to the 69th floor takes only 40 seconds in the fastest lift in the world. Once at the top (273m/896ft) visitors are rewarded with a breathtaking view across **Landmark Tower** Tokyo Bay all the way to Fuji-san (open Sky Garden: daily 10am–9pm, Sat and July–Aug until 10pm, ¥ 1000).

> ! **Baedeker** TIP
>
> **Red lanterns ...**
> From Sakuragicho station an old road leads west through the historic Noge quarter. Red lanterns invite passers-by to enjoy some noodles or yakitori shish kebabs.

The tower is located in the newly built area of Minato Mirai 21, built **Minato Mirai 21** on reclaimed land. It is a futuristic complex of skyscrapers that house hotels, apartments, offices and entertainment venues. Two museums ◄ Museums complete the attractions: **Yokohama Art Museum** with art of the 20th century and **Mitsubishi Minato Mirai Industrial Museum**, which is devoted exclusively to technological achievements, including a helicopter flight simulator. To the east of the tower is Nippon-maru Memorial Park, which has a retired sailing ship used as a training vessel, the »Nippon-maru«, and a **Maritime Museum**.

Akarenga ▶ There is a promenade from here to an island. At its eastern end are two old warehouses made of red brick (Akarenga). They contain a successful mix of shops (furniture, accessories, fashion) and cosy restaurants.

Port Leave Yokohama Park (Kannai station) in a northward direction to get to the port (round trips several times a day). Osambashi Pier is home to the nine-storey Silk Center, which houses the Yokohama International Tourist Association, the Silk Hotel and the Silk Museum (www.silkmuseum.or.jp). Yamashita Park extends along the port basin to the right (ship connection from the landing stage east of Yokohama station, 15 minutes, view of the harbour); the former ocean

Yokohama Map

liner *Hikawa Maru* is moored in the harbour; today it serves as a museum and also contains aquariums with tropical fish.

To the southwest is the 108m/354ft Marine Tower, built in 1961 for the 100th anniversary of the port's opening; the view over the city is particularly attractive in the evening (open daily 9.30am–9pm, in winter until 7pm, ¥ 700).

◀ Marine Tower

🕐

500m/550yd further west is the Chinese Quarter (Chuka-gai) with many restaurants, shops and entertainment venues.

Chinese Quarter

To the south, on the other side of Nakamura River, is the Motomachi shopping street; the foreigners' quarter, also known as Bluff, begins

Yamate-machi

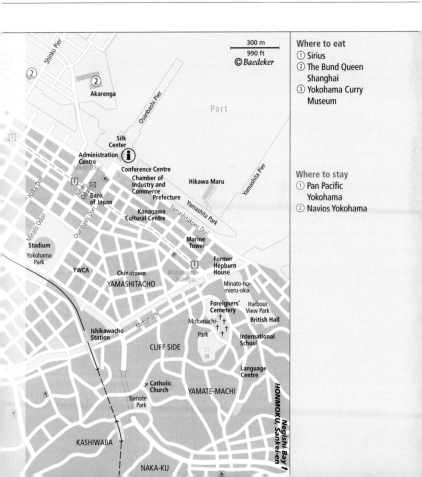

Where to eat
① Sirius
② The Bund Queen Shanghai
③ Yokohama Curry Museum

Where to stay
① Pan Pacific Yokohama
② Navios Yokohama

▶ VISITING YOKOHAMA

INFORMATION

Tourist information

In Yokohama station
Tel. 0 45/4 41 73 00
Daily 9am–7pm
In Shin-Yokohama station
Tel. 0 45/4 73 28 95
Daily 10am–6pm
Near Yakuragicho station (on the side towards Minato Mirai)
Tel. 0 45/2 11 01 11
Daily 9am–7pm
In the Sangyo Boeki Center Building near Yamashita Park,
2 Yamashita-cho, Naka-ku
Tel. 0 45/6 41 47 59
Mon–Fri 9am–5pm

About Kanagawa Prefecture:
in the Silk Center, tel. 0 45/6 81 00 07
Tue–Sun 10am–6pm

Online
www.city.yokohama.jp/en

GETTING THERE

By rail: from Tokyo (central station) JR Yokosuka line (30 minutes); also from Yurakucho station JR Keihin-Tohoku line (40 minutes), from Shimbashi station via Shinawa station JR Yokosuka line (30 minutes), from Shibuya station Toyoko private train line (40 minutes).
By bus: from Narita (Tokyo International Airport; 1½ hours).

EVENTS

First shrine visit (beginning of January), amongst others Iseyama shrine, Nishi-ku; port festival (with processions, early May); annual festival (mid-June), in Iseyama shrine; anniversary of the port's opening (2 June); large firework display (mid-July), in Yamashita Park, Naka-ku.

WHERE TO EAT

▶ Expensive

① *Sirius*
70th Floor, Landmark Tower
2-2-1-3 Minato Mirai, Nishi-ku
Tel. 045-2211155
7am–10am (breakfast), 11.30am–2.30pm (lunch), 5pm–9pm (dinner), after that cocktail bar until 1am.
Regardless of the time of day, the food and service here are always outstanding! And the fantastic view is an added bonus. The lunch buffet has a huge selection of dishes and is highly recommendable for everyone. In the evening this restaurant also often has live jazz.

▶ Moderate

② *The Bund Queen Shanghai*
3F Yokohama Akarenga,
1-1-2 Shinko, Naka-ku
Tel. 0 45/6 50 87 72
Daily 11am–11pm
Tastefully decorated Chinese restaurant serving Shanghai cuisine (Yokohama is twinned with Shanghai) and German beer.

▶ Inexpensive

③ *Yokohama Curry Museum*
1-2-3 Isezaki-cho, Naka-ku
Tel. 0 45/2 50 08 33
Daily 11am–10pm
Kannai underground station.
Restaurants serve different variations of curry (Japanese: karee) dishes over several storeys in a »museum« (more like a theme park), where everything is about curry. It can be recognized by the tacky »Indian« elephant in yellow and pink above the entrance.

GOING OUT

The Akarenga has a well-known jazz club, *Motion Blue Yokohama*, with a

separate lounge bar (tel. 0 45/
2 26 19 19,
daily 5pm–11.30pm, live music
6.30pm and 9.30pm, earlier on Sundays and public holidays).

WHERE TO STAY
► Luxury
① *Pan Pacific Yokohama*
2-3-7 Minatomirai, Nishi-ku,
Yokohama, Kanagawa, 220-8543
Tel. 0 45/6 82 22 22, fax 6 82 22 23
www.yokohama.panpacific.com
Modern luxury hotel with 480 rooms
and every possible creature comfort,
including saunas, a pool, a spa and a
beauty salon. Chapel for weddings.
Cosy bar. Great view of the bay.

► Mid-range
② *Navios Yokohama,*
International Seamen's Club & Inn
Shinko 2 chome 1-1, Naka-ku,
Yokohama-shi,
Kanagawa-ken, 231-0001
Tel. 0 45/6 33 60 00
Fax 6 33 60 01
www.navios-yokohama.com
Modern, red brick building in Minato
Mirai. Inexpensive rooms (also Japanese-style rooms for up to six people)
in a city that tends to be more on the
expensive side and it's not just for
seamen. Has rooms that are wheel-
chair accessible. Large bar and karaoke. Coin-operated washing
machines.

here; it also contains the foreigners' cemetery. To the east is Minato-
no-mieru-oka-koen Park (Harbour View Park), which has a lovely
view of the harbour.

Situated on the city's southeastern periphery is the pleasant garden
Sankei-en (bus from the station's east exit 35 minutes, then 10 minutes on foot). Several historic buildings can be found here; they
were brought here from other parts of the country; they include the
500-year-old three-storey pagoda of Tomyoji temple in Kamo (Kyoto), Rinshun-kaku (former villa of the Tokugawa resident on Kii
Peninsula; 1649), Tokugawa Iemitsu's Choshu-kaku tea pavilion, Ya-
nohara-ke farm (18th century) Tenzuiji Juto Sayado temple (from
Daitoku-ji in Kyoto; 1592), and more.

✱
Sankei-en

In the south of the park the Hasseiden building houses the statues of
(from a Japanese point of view): **the world's eight wise people** Shakyamuni, Confucius, Socrates, Christ, Shotoku-taishi, Kobo-daishi,
Shinran and Nichiren (open daily 9am–5pm, ¥ 500).

◄ Hasseiden

🕐

An 860m/940ft architecturally artistic bridge over Yokohama Bay towards Tokyo has been attracting many visitors since 1989. A 320m/
350yd pedestrian bridge (Sky Walk) leads from Daikoku Pier across
a canal to an observation tower, from where there is a good view of
the bold construction and the sea.

**Yokohama
Bay Bridge**

Take the Keihin-Kyuko private train line or the underground from
the central station in a southwest direction to Gumyo-ji temple. It
belongs to the Shingon sect and is the city's oldest temple. It contains
a 9th-century wooden statue of the eleven-headed Kannon.

Gumyo-ji temple

Sojiji temple	Take the northeast-bound JR Tohoku line from the central station to Tsurumi station to get to Sojiji temple, which belongs to the Soto sect. It was built in Ishikawa Prefecture in 1321 and rebuilt at its current location after a fire in 1898. It is one of Japan's most significant Zen temples and the centre of around 15,000 branch temples.

★★ Yoshino-Kumano National Park

h–j 3–4

Main island: Honshu   **Prefectures:** Nara, Mie and Wakayama
Area: 597 sq km/231 sq mi

吉野熊野国立公園 **Yoshino-Kumano National Park is located on Kii Peninsula, which extends into the Pacific in the west of central Honshu. The landscape is shaped by the mountains of the Yoshino region as well as the deep gorges of the Kumano region. Many temples that were once the goal of large numbers of pilgrims can still be seen.**

What to See in Yoshino-Kumano National Park

Yoshino Mountains	The national park's isolated northwestern section is made of the Yoshino Mountains (Hana-eshiki), which rise up over the town of the same name. The mountains are quite well known for the cherry blossom; there are around **100,000 cherry trees** growing in four extensive groves; depending on their altitude they flower sometime between the beginning and the end of April. Closest to the cableway mountain station is the wood Shimo-no-Sembon (»Lower Thousand Trees«), then comes Naka-no-Sembon (»Middle Thousand Trees«), Kami-no-Sembon (»Upper Thousand Trees«) and Oku-no-Sembon (»Inner Thousand Trees«). The Hanao-eshiki cherry blossom festival is celebrated in mid-April. It is said that the priest En-no-Ozunu planted the trees in the 7th century, consecrating them to the mountain deity Zao-Gongen.
✦ Kimpusenji temple	There is a path from the lower cherry tree grove upwards to Kimpusenji temple, whose original buildings were destroyed in a fire in 1348 (rebuilt in the 15th century). The main hall (Zaodo) is 34m/112ft high, making it one of Japan's tallest wooden buildings. The two Deva statues at the entrance are attributed to the artists Unkei and Tankei (12th–13th century). Next the path goes in a southward direction to the nearby Yoshimizu shrine as well as to Katte shrine.
✦ Chikurin-in temple	Further to the south is Chikurin-in temple, whose garden was created by the tea master Sen-no-Rikyu (1522–91). Cross Tenno-bashi Bridge to get to Saruhikizaka viewpoint, which has a great view of Mount Yoshino's eastern slope with its upper cherry tree grove.

INDEX

LIST OF MAPS AND ILLUSTRATIONS

PHOTO CREDITS

PUBLISHER'S INFORMATION

Illustrations etc: 226 illustrations, 51 maps and diagrams, one large map
Text: Dr. Walter Giesen, Prof. Dr. Wolfgang Hassenpflug, Karin Khan, Peter M. Nahm, Winfried Schneider, Jessika Zollickhofer
Editing: Baedeker editorial team (John Sykes)
Translation: Michael Scuffil
Cartography: Franz Huber, München; MAIRDUMONT / Falk Verlag, Ostfildern (map)
3D illustrations: jangled nerves, Stuttgart
Design: independent Medien-Design, Munich; Kathrin Schemel

Editor-in-chief: Rainer Eisenschmid, Baedeker Ostfildern

1st edition 2009
Based on Baedeker Allianz Reiseführer »Japan«, 10. Auflage 2008

Copyright: Karl Baedeker Verlag, Ostfildern
Publication rights: MAIRDUMONT GmbH & Co; Ostfildern

Printed in China

BAEDEKER GUIDE BOOKS AT A GLANCE
Guiding the World since 1827

- Andalusia
- Austria
- Bali
- Barcelona
- Berlin
- Brazil
- Budapest
- Cologne
- Dresden
- Dubai
- Egypt
- Florence
- Florida
- France
- Greece
- Iceland
- Ireland
- Italy
- Japan
- London
- Mexico
- New York
- Norway
- Paris
- Portugal
- Prague
- Rome
- South Africa
- Spain
- Thailand
- Tuscany
- Venice
- Vienna

DEAR READER,

We would like to thank you for choosing this Baedeker travel guide. It will be a reliable companion on your travels and will not disappoint you.
This book describes the major sights, of course, but it also recommends the most atmospheric onsen, as well as hotels in the luxury and budget categories, and includes tips about where to eat or go shopping and much more, helping to make your trip an enjoyable experience. Our author Jessika Zollickhofer ensures the quality of this information by making regular journeys to Japan and putting all her know-how into this book.

Nevertheless, experience shows us that it is impossible to rule out errors and changes made after the book goes to press, for which Baedeker accepts no liability. Please send us your criticisms, corrections and suggestions for improvement: we appreciate your contribution. Contact us by post or e-mail, or phone us:

► **Verlag Karl Baedeker GmbH**
Editorial department
Postfach 3162
73751 Ostfildern
Germany
Tel. 49-711-4502-262, fax -343
www.baedeker.com
www.baedeker.co.uk
E-Mail: baedeker@mairdumont.com